Application Environment Specification (AES) User Environment Volume

Revision C

Open Software Foundation

P T R Prentice Hall, Englewood Cliffs, New Jersey 07632

Cover design
  and cover illustration: **BETH FAGAN**

This book was formatted with troff

 Published by P T R Prentice-Hall, Inc.
A Simon & Schuster Company
Englewood Cliffs, New Jersey 07632

Printed in the United States of America
10 9 8 7 6 5 4 3 2 1

ISBN 0-13-043621-6

Prentice-Hall International (UK) Limited, *London*
Prentice-Hall of Australia Pty. Limited, *Sydney*
Prentice-Hall Canada Inc., *Toronto*
Prentice-Hall Hispanoamericana, S.A., *Mexico*
Prentice-Hall of India Private Limited, *New Delhi*
Prentice-Hall of Japan, Inc., *Tokyo*
Simon & Schuster Asia Pte. Ltd., *Singapore*
Editora Prentice-Hall do Brasil, Ltda., *Rio de Janeiro*

Contents

List of Tables

Preface

Part of the charter of the Open Software Foundation™ (OSF™) is to foster the development of portable software that will run on a variety of hardware platforms. The Application Environment Specification (AES) specifies the interfaces that support such software.

Specifically, this document, the *Application Environment Specification — User Environment Volume*, Revision C, specifies interfaces for the user environment portion of OSF's applications environment.

Chapter 1 describes the purpose of the Application Environment Specification, incorporating a document originally published by itself as "The AES Definition." It provides a detailed description of the relationship of the AES to

- Formal (de jure) standards and specifications

- Implementations; for example, operating systems like OSF's operating system component (OSC)

- Portable applications software

Audience

This document is written for

- Software engineers developing AES-compliant applications to run on AES-compliant implementations.

- Software engineers developing AES-compliant implementations on which AES-compliant applications can run.

- Organizations (for example, standards-setting bodies) for whom the AES (or some part of it) is an appropriate part of the formal, de jure process.

Document Usage

This document is organized into two chapters.

- Chapter 1 introduces the AES, providing the general AES definition, and the general rationale for inclusion and specification of interfaces in the AES. This chapter includes the AES Service Outline.

- Chapter 2 contains reference pages for all of the AES/UE interfaces. They are ordered alphabetically within commands and functions.

Related Documents

For additional information about OSF/Motif, refer to the following documents:

- The *OSF/Motif Style Guide* explains the principles of user interface design for application developers.

- The *OSF/Motif Programmer's Guide* explains how to write applications using the OSF/Motif widget set.

- The *OSF/Motif Programmer's Reference* provides detailed reference information for programmers writing Motif applications.

- The *OSF/Motif User's Guide* explains how users can interact with OSF/Motif based applications.

Typographic and Keying Conventions

This document uses the following typographic conventions:

Bold
: **Bold** words or characters represent system elements that you must use literally, such as commands, flags, and pathnames.

Italic
: *Italic* words or characters represent variable values that you must supply.

`Constant width`
: Examples and information that the system displays appear in the `constant width` typeface.

[ ]
: Brackets enclose optional items in format and syntax descriptions.

{ }
: Braces enclose a list from which you must choose an item in format and syntax descriptions.

|
: A vertical bar separates items in a list of choices.

< >
: Angle brackets enclose the name of a key on the keyboard.

...
: Horizontal ellipsis points indicate that you can repeat the preceding item one or more times. Vertical ellipsis points indicate that you can repeat the preceding item one or more times.

Interface Definition Reference Page Format

The reference pages for interface definitions in this volume use the following format:

Purpose
: This section gives a short description of the interface.

AES Support Level
: This section indicates whether the interfaces' AES support status is full, trial, or temporary use.

Compatibility

This section lists the standards and industry specifications in which the interface exists.

Synopsis

This section describes the appropriate syntax for using the interface.

Description

This section describes the behavior of the interface. On widget reference pages there are tables of resource values in the descriptions. Those tables have the following headers:

Name Contains the name of the resource. Each new resource is described following the new resources table.

Class Contains the class of the resource.

Type Contains the type of the resource.

Default Contains the default value of the resource.

Access Contains the access permissions for the resource. A **C** in this column means the resource can be set at widget creation time. An **S** means the resource can be set at any time. A **G** means the resource's value can retrieved.

Return Value

This section lists the values returned by function interfaces.

Errors

This section describes the error conditions associated with using this interface.

Related Information

This section provides cross references to related interfaces and header files described within this document.

Problem Reporting

If you have any problems with the software or documentation, please contact your software vendor's customer service department.

Chapter 1

Introduction

This chapter introduces the user environment volume of the AES. Section 1.1 defines the AES. Section 1.2 is the AES/UE service outline. Section 1.3 is a table of AES support levels ordered by functional area.

1.1 The Application Environment Specification Definition

This section provides a detailed description of the Application Environment Specification (AES).

1.1.1 Introduction to the AES Definition

Part of the charter of the Open Software Foundation (OSF) is to foster the development of portable software applications that will run on a wide variety of hardware platforms. The software required to support such applications is an **application environment** provided by systems or software vendors. An application environment is a set of programming and user interfaces and their associated semantics, available to applications and users.

The AES is a specification for a consistent application environment across different hardware platforms. This definition uses the term **implementation** to describe the application environment that vendors supply to application developers, because such software is an implementation of the AES.

The AES specifies the following:

- Application-level interfaces that an implementation must provide in order to support portable applications

- Semantics or protocols associated with each of these interfaces

This definition describes the purpose, contents, and organization of the AES. It also discusses the meaning of AES compliance for applications and implementations, the relationship of the AES to other industry documents (standards and specifications) and to implementations. Finally, the document describes the AES development process and the support levels used to characterize interfaces within the AES.

1.1.2 Purpose of the AES

The primary purpose of the AES is to provide a common definition of application interfaces that both systems providers and systems users can rely on in the development of portable applications. The composite AES defines the stable, reliable, application-level interfaces in several functional areas. Systems sellers who comply with the AES know exactly what interfaces they must provide, and how each element of those interfaces must behave. Systems buyers who look for AES conformance know unequivocally the interfaces they can rely on.

A secondary purpose of the AES is to take advantage of OSF's organizational charter to expedite the specification of application environments. Unlike specifications and standards bodies, OSF also provides vendor-neutral, hardware-independent implementations. The task of providing these implementations gives practical experience and feedback that enables the AES to expand faster than standards documents can. Also, OSF's technical staff is chartered to provide an expeditious resolution of the conflicts that can delay the decision process in other types of organizations.

By integrating functionality that is already standardized with newer functionality that is suitable for eventual standardization, the AES provides material that contributes to future standards. Because of OSF's timely, vendor-neutral decision process, this newer functionality can be added relatively quickly.

1.1.3 Contents of the AES

As previously stated, the AES is a set of specifications for programming and user interfaces and their associated semantics. The library routines, user commands, and data objects specified in the AES have the following characteristics:

- They provide valuable services to portable applications.

- They can be implemented on a wide variety of hardware platforms and support hardware-independent applications.

- They are stable (they are not likely to need to change).

- They are reliable (because they are tightly specified, applications writers can rely on consistent behavior across applications platforms).

We call AES-specified program and user interfaces **portability interfaces**, because they provide support for portable (hardware-independent) applications.

In order to be useful for applications development within these criteria, the AES must provide the richest possible function set. Development of the AES requires a balance between expansion to provide richer functionality, and conservatism to guarantee the stability of included interfaces.

Internal interfaces are interfaces that are not visible to applications. Internal interfaces are not part of the AES. The AES specifies only application-level portability interfaces (as previously defined).

1.1.4 Organization of the AES

The AES is an evolving set of **area specifications**. Each area specification describes portability interfaces for one **functional area** of the application environment. OSF has identified the following functional areas:

- Operating System Programming Interfaces

- Operating System Commands and Utilities

- Network Services

- User Environment Services

- Graphics Services

- Database Management Services

- Programming Languages (BASIC, Fortran, Pascal, C, COBOL, Ada, and Lisp)

In certain functional areas, OSF publishes its own area specifications, which add to or extend existing standards and specifications. This definition focuses on the development process for the specifications that OSF publishes. In other areas, the AES just points to widely known existing standards and specifications.

The initial AES area specifications for OSF publication are in three functional areas:

- The *AES/Operating System* area specification describes the programming interfaces that an AES-conforming operating system must provide.

- The *AES/Network Services* area specification describes protocol-independent and protocol-specific interfaces to network services.

- The *AES/User Environment* area specification describes the programming interfaces that an AES-compliant user interface must provide.

An area specification can consist of one or more volumes, and the term **AES Volume** describes the document that contains all or part of an area specification.

OSF's goal is to promote usability and coherence of the AES documents themselves; therefore, document titles are as descriptive as possible. Also, OSF uses revisions, rather than supplements, to add functions to existing AES volumes.

Each revision of an AES Volume includes, for reference, the complete list of standards and specifications that make up the Application Environment. (This list first appeared as "AES Level 0" in May, 1988.) Because, unless otherwise stated, the standards and specifications that comprise the Application Environment are independent of one another, this list is provided only for user reference. Any direct dependencies that an area AES has on specifications in another area are listed within the AES Volume for the first area.

1.1.5 The Meaning of AES Conformance

This section provides a brief, general discussion of AES conformance for implementations and applications. This document does not discuss the specific means of measuring or proving conformance or such issues as validation, compliance, branding, and waivers.

Implementations and applications that conform to the AES do so on the basis of area functionality. An implementation or application that conforms to one AES area is considered to be AES-conforming for that area.

Implementations and applications conform to the AES differently, since implementations provide services and applications use interfaces specified in the AES to access these services. A conforming implementation provides at least the interfaces defined in the AES. A conforming application uses only the interfaces defined in the AES and those defined in any standards or specifications that the AES depends on. Such dependencies are called out explicitly in AES area specifications.

1.1.5.1 AES Conformance for Implementations

For an implementation to be AES conforming in a functional area, it must implement each interface element as specified by the AES volume for that functional area.

AES area-conforming implementations may offer additional interfaces not specified in the AES, or extensions to AES interfaces, provided they do not affect the conformance of any element of the AES-specified interfaces.

Unless specifically called out within the area specification, an implementation that conforms to one functional area need not provide services from other functional areas, or conform to other functional areas.

1.1.5.2 Conformance Document

Vendors of AES-conforming implementations should make available to their customers a conformance document that describes

- The AES area and revision the implementation conforms to

- The values of all implementation-defined variables and limits that the implementation supports

- The actual behavior of all features described in the AES as implementation defined

If the implementation supports any nonstandard extensions that change the behavior of interfaces specified in the AES, the conformance document must specify how to create an environment that provides the AES-specified behavior. If conformance information exists in other documents provided with the implementation, the AES conformance document can provide a reference to that information rather than repeat it.

1.1.5.3 AES Conformance for Applications

For an application to be AES conforming in a functional area, it must use only the interfaces in the relevant AES area specification or those in other standards and specifications the area specification depends on. Standards or specifications included by reference are considered to be part of the AES for conforming applications.

The application must depend only on AES-specified behavior for AES interfaces. An application should not depend on any behavior that the AES describes as unspecified, undefined, or implementation defined.

1.1.5.4 AES Support Levels and Conformance

Each AES interface element has a support level, which specifies the commitment OSF makes to its definition. The higher the support level, the longer the warning period required before OSF can delete the element, or make an incompatible change in the element's definition. (An incompatible change is one that might require conforming applications to be rewritten.)

Conforming implementations will provide all AES interfaces for the relevant area at all support levels. Developers of conforming applications can choose to use or not use elements at any support level. Support levels serve as advisories for application developers because they indicate the length of time that an interface specification is guaranteed to remain stable.

During the AES development process, OSF staff members propose support levels for interface elements, based on criteria defined later in this document. OSF members review and comment on these support levels along with the rest of the document.

Section 1.1.9 provides detailed information about AES support levels.

1.1.6 Relationship of the AES to Standards and Other Specifications

The AES incorporates relevant industry standards and selected industry specifications. When an AES area specification incorporates an industry standard or specification, the area specification either points to that standard or specification, or includes the text. (Document revision schedules, source availability, and document usability influence the decision to use pointers or text.)

The AES may extend or further specify interface elements derived from an included standard or specification, and when such extensions occur, they are clearly marked as such within the appropriate AES Volume.

An AES-conforming implementation of an interface should also conform to all included standards and specifications that contain the interface. If this is not possible, because of conflicts between definitions in included standards, the AES resolves conflicts based on a defined precedence order of standards. AES Volumes define, in an introductory chapter, the order of precedence of any included standards and specifications.

Inclusion of whole standards and specifications in the AES sometimes results in inclusion of interfaces or interface elements that might not have been selected for inclusion on their own merit. In such cases, OSF still includes the element because it is in the standard and the standard takes precedence. However, the AES interface definition notes any problems and discourages applications' use of the problematic interface. OSF also works within the standards or specification bodies to remove or modify such interfaces.

1.1.7 Relationship of the AES to Implementations

The AES is a specification to which vendors can build implementations. OSF itself provides implementations for some of the AES functional areas. These OSF implementations include the portability interfaces defined in the AES, and may also include interfaces not specified in the AES, or extensions to AES-specified interfaces. These extensions may be obsolete interfaces provided for support of existing applications, or they may be experimental, new interfaces. Only those interfaces that are recommended for use by new portable applications will be included in the AES. Some of the interfaces that are not in the AES may be candidates for inclusion in a subsequent AES revision.

1.1.8 The AES Development Process

This section describes the processes for development of the AES, for document revision control, and for membership review cycles.

For each functional area, OSF produces one or more AES area specification drafts for its membership to review (see Section 1.1.8.3). After incorporating review comments, OSF produces a final AES area specification. A final AES area specification for a particular revision includes the interface definitions for a stable set of portability interfaces in one functional area of the OSF-supported Application Environment.

1.1.8.1 Document Control and the AES

OSF labels the AES for each functional area with a revision letter. As the collection of revisions grows, OSF may group the existing revisions into an AES Level. For example, an AES Level might include AES/UE revision B, AES/OS revision A, and so on.

1.1.8.2 The Service Outline

A Service Outline is a document that lists all the elements in each AES interface for a functional area and indicates the support level for each element without giving detailed descriptions. OSF makes two uses of Service Outlines.

- In some functional areas, a Service Outline may be a draft document that precedes a full AES volume. (A full AES volume provides complete interface definitions or pointers to other information or conceptual descriptions.)

A draft Service Outline proposes the interfaces to be included in a full AES volume. In this case, the full AES volume draft, when complete, supersedes the Service Outline draft.

- In other functional areas, a Service Outline may become a permanent document. If all the interfaces for a functional area are completely specified, with no conflicts, in industry standards or other specification documents, the AES area specification for that functional area may remain as a Service Outline and never evolve into a full AES volume.

When appropriate, a Service Outline also contains a table that shows each element and lists relevant industry standards, specifications, and implementations that include the element.

Complete AES documents (not Service Outlines) provide complete interface definitions and pointers to other information or conceptual descriptions.

1.1.8.3 The Membership Review

In general, membership review proceeds as follows:

1. OSF prepares a draft Service Outline and/or AES Volume for a functional area, and circulates it to OSF members. This review period may last from one to several months.

2. Members submit comments using a prescribed comment template.

3. OSF responds to members' comments in the next version of the document, or in a discussion that takes place in an electronic news group or at a meeting.

OSF considers all review comments during the development of AES documents and brings important or controversial issues up for further discussion. However, the review process is not a voting process, and OSF does not wait for consensus among the membership before adding new interfaces to the AES or making other technical decisions.

1.1.9 AES Support Levels

This section defines the support levels assigned to each AES interface element. As previously mentioned, support levels define OSF's commitment to interface definitions by indicating the warning period required to make an incompatible modification or deletion of the definition.

New AES revisions may introduce upwardly compatible changes at any time, regardless of the support level. Any such changes will be noted in the associated **Specification Context** section.

The support levels are

- Full use

- Trial use

- Temporary use

Typically, elements in the AES have full-use or trial-use support levels. Conforming implementations must provide them, and application developers can use them freely (with the knowledge that trial-use elements are subject to more rapid change than full-use elements). The temporary-use support level appears only rarely in area specifications; it is for special cases, as described in section 1.1.9.3. Implementations must provide temporary-use elements too, when they appear.

The following sections explain each support level. Section 1.1.9.4 describes how elements move from proposed status (in draft specifications) to final status (in published specifications).

1.1.9.1 Full Use

A full-use element has the highest support level, so it is the most protected from incompatible modification or deletion from the AES.

OSF assigns a support level of full use to elements for reasons such as the following:

- The element already exists in an approved de-jure standard. (A de-jure standard is one that is set by an official standards body.)

- The element as specified in the AES is considered stable and already in widespread use in applications.

- The element has been upgraded to full-use status after a period of trial-use status in an earlier AES revision.

There should rarely be a need to remove a full-use element, or make incompatible modifications to it. However, if this ever becomes necessary, a full-use element keeps its full-use status, but a warning describing the proposed future change must be published in at least two successive revisions of the AES area volume before the change can be made. This provides time for applications to be altered to deal with a different behavior, and for implementations to prepare for the change.

For example, suppose it becomes necessary to modify a full-use element that appeared in revision A of an AES Volume. The draft for revision B shows the element as "proposed-for-modification/removal." Assuming the review concludes that this change is appropriate, the element in revision B still has full-use status, but is accompanied by a warning. The warning states that the element is scheduled for modification after revision C, and describes the modified behavior. Application developers can now allow for either the original or the modified behavior. Revision C contains the same warning. Revision D provides the modified definition only. The **Specification Context** section of the interface element definition documents the history of such changes.

1.1.9.2 Trial Use

A trial-use element is easier to modify or delete than a full-use element. There are several reasons that OSF classifies elements as trial use instead of full use. An element may be under consideration for inclusion in a de-jure standard and so may possibly change as a result of the standards process.

Or, OSF may perceive that the element is new compared to other included elements and, therefore, the implementation and use of the element may suggest revisions in its definition.

If it becomes necessary to modify or delete a trial-use element, it keeps its trial-use status, with warnings about its removal or incompatible change, for one full revision of the AES. Using the example in the previous section, if the element to be modified were a trial-use element, revision B would include the unmodified definition with a warning and description of the change, and revision C would include the modified definition only.

1.1.9.3 Temporary Use

A temporary-use element is a special case. Because it is limited in use, not sufficiently general, or faulty in some other way, it is likely to be changed. As such, it does not meet the criteria for inclusion in the AES with a full-use or trial-use support level, but it provides necessary functionality not available through other full-use or trial-use interface elements. Conforming applications may use these elements as necessary; an application containing a temporary-use element should be labeled as such. The AES replaces temporary-use interface elements when appropriate full-use or trial-use elements become available.

Giving an element temporary-use status makes it clear from the outset that OSF intends to replace it. In the meantime, the element provides necessary and clearly specified functionality. Compliant implementations must provide services classified as temporary use, and applications can use them, although it is clear that the element will eventually be replaced. Once a replacement exists, the AES includes a warning in the temporary-use element's definition and lists the removal date. As in the case of a trial-use element, the warning exists for one revision only.

For example, certain network interfaces provide a general service using a protocol-specific algorithm. These might be candidates for temporary-use status, because as time passes, interfaces based on protocol-independent algorithms will become available to replace them.

1.1.9.4 Proposed Usage Levels

Draft versions of specifications give newly added or changed elements a proposed-for-*level* status, where *level* is one of those defined previously. In final versions, these elements move from proposed-for-*level* status to level status.

In the review draft of the first revision of an AES area specification, all elements are at proposed-for-*level* status. In review drafts of subsequent revisions, the elements may have one of several statuses. Most existing elements retain their support level from the existing revision. A few may carry a proposed-for-*change* status. New elements carry a proposed-for-*level* status.

The following list describes the AES proposed-for-inclusion and proposed for-change levels.

Proposed-for-*level*-use
> A review level leading to *level*-use inclusion on acceptance, and no change in status otherwise. This status may be used to propose a new element for *level*-use, or to move an existing element to a higher status.

Proposed-for-modification/removal
> A review level for existing elements that OSF proposes to make an incompatible modification in or remove from the AES. If this proposal is accepted during the review process, a full-use element remains as is, with a warning, for two revisions; a trial-use or temporary-use element remains as is with a warning, for one revision. If the proposal is rejected, the element remains as is.

Proposed-for-correction

A review level for elements of any support level in which OSF wishes to correct a specification error. OSF will propose correcting an element if a definition was obviously wrong (and implementations and applications could never follow the specification as it is written), if clarification of an unclear section is required, or if an error makes a definition clearly internally inconsistent or inappropriate. Elements proposed for correction return to their original status, in corrected form, on acceptance of the correction. They return to their original status in uncorrected form on rejection of the correction. (Proposal for correction is not required for OSF to fix a typographical error.)

Proposed-for-enhancement

A review level for elements in which OSF wants to make an upwardly compatible change in definition. If accepted, the definition change is effective in the published revision after the draft in which the proposal for enhancement occurred.

1.2 Service Outline

This Service Outline lists all the services included in the AES/UE.

- The first column is the name of the service. The table is organized alphabetically by this column. All services that are new in this revision are marked by an asterisk (*).

- The second column is the type of the service. The type is widget, function, command, data type, or file format.

- The third column is the proposed AES support level.

Table 1–1. Service Outline

Service Name	Service Type	AES Level
ApplicationShell	widget	full-use
Composite	widget	full-use
Constraint	widget	full-use
Core	widget	full-use
MrmCloseHierarchy	function	full-use
MrmFetchColorLiteral	function	full-use
MrmFetchIconLiteral	function	full-use
MrmFetchLiteral	function	full-use
MrmFetchSetValues	function	full-use
MrmFetchWidget	function	full-use
MrmFetchWidgetOverride	function	full-use
MrmInitialize	function	full-use
MrmOpenHierarchy	function	trial-use
MrmOpenHierarchyPerDisplay*	function	trial-use
MrmRegisterClass	function	trial-use
MrmRegisterNames	function	trial-use
MrmRegisterNamesInHierarchy	function	trial-use
Object	widget	full-use
OverrideShell	widget	full-use
RectObj	widget	full-use
Shell	widget	full-use
TopLevelShell	widget	full-use
TransientShell	widget	full-use
Uil	function	full-use
VendorShell	widget	full-use
WMShell	widget	full-use
XmActivateProtocol	function	trial-use
XmActivateWMProtocol	function	trial-use

Service Name	Service Type	AES Level
XmAddProtocolCallback	function	trial-use
XmAddProtocols	function	trial-use
XmAddTabGroup	function	full-use
XmAddWMProtocolCallback	function	trial-use
XmAddWMProtocols	function	trial-use
XmArrowButton	widget	full-use
XmArrowButtonGadget	widget	full-use
XmBulletinBoard	widget	full-use
XmCascadeButton	widget	full-use
XmCascadeButtonGadget	widget	full-use
XmCascadeButtonGadgetHighlight	function	trial-use
XmCascadeButtonHighlight	function	full-use
XmClipboardCancelCopy	function	full-use
XmClipboardCopy	function	full-use
XmClipboardCopyByName	function	full-use
XmClipboardEndCopy	function	full-use
XmClipboardEndRetrieve	function	full-use
XmClipboardInquireCount	function	full-use
XmClipboardInquireFormat	function	full-use
XmClipboardInquireLength	function	full-use
XmClipboardInquirePendingItems	function	full-use
XmClipboardLock	function	full-use
XmClipboardRegisterFormat	function	full-use
XmClipboardRetrieve	function	full-use
XmClipboardStartCopy	function	full-use
XmClipboardStartRetrieve	function	full-use
XmClipboardUndoCopy	function	full-use
XmClipboardUnlock	function	full-use
XmClipboardWithdrawFormat	function	full-use
XmCommand	widget	full-use

Service Name	Service Type	AES Level
XmCommandAppendValue	function	full-use
XmCommandError	function	full-use
XmCommandGetChild	function	full-use
XmCommandSetValue	function	full-use
XmConvertUnits	function	trial-use
XmCreateArrowButton	function	full-use
XmCreateArrowButtonGadget	function	full-use
XmCreateBulletinBoard	function	full-use
XmCreateBulletinBoardDialog	function	full-use
XmCreateCascadeButton	function	full-use
XmCreateCascadeButtonGadget	function	full-use
XmCreateCommand	function	full-use
XmCreateDialogShell	function	full-use
XmCreateDrawingArea	function	full-use
XmCreateDrawnButton	function	full-use
XmCreateErrorDialog	function	full-use
XmCreateFileSelectionBox	function	full-use
XmCreateFileSelectionDialog	function	full-use
XmCreateForm	function	full-use
XmCreateFormDialog	function	full-use
XmCreateFrame	function	full-use
XmCreateInformationDialog	function	full-use
XmCreateLabel	function	full-use
XmCreateLabelGadget	function	full-use
XmCreateList	function	full-use
XmCreateMainWindow	function	full-use
XmCreateMenuBar	function	full-use
XmCreateMenuShell	function	full-use
XmCreateMessageBox	function	full-use
XmCreateMessageDialog	function	full-use

Service Name	Service Type	AES Level
XmCreateOptionMenu	function	full-use
XmCreatePanedWindow	function	full-use
XmCreatePopupMenu	function	full-use
XmCreatePromptDialog	function	full-use
XmCreatePulldownMenu	function	full-use
XmCreatePushButton	function	full-use
XmCreatePushButtonGadget	function	full-use
XmCreateQuestionDialog	function	full-use
XmCreateRadioBox	function	full-use
XmCreateRowColumn	function	full-use
XmCreateScale	function	full-use
XmCreateScrollBar	function	full-use
XmCreateScrolledList	function	full-use
XmCreateScrolledText	function	full-use
XmCreateScrolledWindow	function	full-use
XmCreateSelectionBox	function	full-use
XmCreateSelectionDialog	function	full-use
XmCreateSeparator	function	full-use
XmCreateSeparatorGadget	function	full-use
XmCreateText	function	full-use
XmCreateTextField*	function	trial-use
XmCreateToggleButton	function	full-use
XmCreateToggleButtonGadget	function	full-use
XmCreateWarningDialog	function	full-use
XmCreateWorkArea	function	trial-use
XmCreateWorkingDialog	function	full-use
XmCvtCTToXmString	function	trial-use
XmCvtXmStringToCT	function	trial-use
XmDeactivateProtocol	function	trial-use
XmDeactivateWMProtocol	function	trial-use

Service Name	Service Type	AES Level
XmDestroyPixmap	function	full-use
XmDialogShell	widget	full-use
XmDrawingArea	widget	full-use
XmDrawnButton	widget	full-use
XmFileSelectionBox	widget	full-use
XmFileSelectionBoxGetChild	function	full-use
XmFileSelectionDoSearch	function	full-use
XmFontList	data type	full-use
XmFontListAdd	function	trial-use
XmFontListAppendEntry*	function	trial-use
XmFontListCopy*	function	trial-use
XmFontListCreate	function	trial-use
XmFontListEntryCreate*	function	trial-use
XmFontListEntryFree*	function	trial-use
XmFontListEntryGetFont*	function	trial-use
XmFontListEntryGetTag*	function	trial-use
XmFontListEntryLoad*	function	trial-use
XmFontListFree	function	full-use
XmFontListFreeFontContext*	function	trial-use
XmFontListInitFontContext*	function	trial-use
XmFontListNextEntry*	function	trial-use
XmFontListRemoveEntry*	function	trial-use
XmForm	widget	full-use
XmFrame	widget	full-use
XmGadget	widget	full-use
XmGetAtomName	function	full-use
XmGetColors	function	trial-use
XmGetMenuCursor	function	full-use
XmGetPixmap	function	full-use
XmGetPostedFromWidget	function	trial-use

Service Name	Service Type	AES Level
XmInstallImage	function	full-use
XmInternAtom	function	full-use
XmIsMotifWMRunning	function	full-use
XmLabel	widget	full-use
XmLabelGadget	widget	full-use
XmList	widget	full-use
XmListAddItem	function	full-use
XmListAddItemUnselected	function	full-use
XmListAddItems	function	full-use
XmListDeleteAllItems	function	full-use
XmListDeleteItem	function	full-use
XmListDeleteItems	function	full-use
XmListDeleteItemsPos	function	full-use
XmListDeletePos	function	full-use
XmListDeselectAllItems	function	full-use
XmListDeselectItem	function	full-use
XmListDeselectPos	function	full-use
XmListGetMatchPos	function	full-use
XmListGetSelectedPos	function	full-use
XmListItemExists	function	full-use
XmListItemPos	function	trial-use
XmListReplaceItems	function	full-use
XmListReplaceItemsPos	function	full-use
XmListSelectItem	function	full-use
XmListSelectPos	function	full-use
XmListSetAddMode	function	trial-use
XmListSetBottomItem	function	full-use
XmListSetBottomPos	function	full-use
XmListSetHorizPos	function	full-use
XmListSetItem	function	full-use

Service Name	Service Type	AES Level
XmListSetPos	function	full-use
XmMainWindow	widget	full-use
XmMainWindowSep1	function	full-use
XmMainWindowSep2	function	full-use
XmMainWindowSep3	function	full-use
XmMainWindowSetAreas	function	full-use
XmManager	widget	full-use
XmMenuPosition	function	full-use
XmMenuShell	widget	full-use
XmMessageBox	widget	full-use
XmMessageBoxGetChild	function	full-use
XmOptionButtonGadget	function	full-use
XmOptionLabelGadget	function	full-use
XmPanedWindow	widget	full-use
XmPrimitive	widget	full-use
XmProcessTraversal	function	full-use
XmPushButton	widget	full-use
XmPushButtonGadget	widget	full-use
XmRemoveProtocolCallback	function	trial-use
XmRemoveProtocols	function	trial-use
XmRemoveTabGroup	function	full-use
XmRemoveWMProtocolCallback	function	trial-use
XmRemoveWMProtocols	function	trial-use
XmResolvePartOffsets	function	full-use
XmRowColumn	widget	full-use
XmScale	widget	full-use
XmScaleGetValue	function	full-use
XmScaleSetValue	function	full-use
XmScrollBar	widget	full-use
XmScrollBarGetValues	function	full-use

Service Name	Service Type	AES Level
XmScrollBarSetValues	function	full-use
XmScrolledWindow	widget	full-use
XmScrolledWindowSetAreas	function	full-use
XmSelectionBox	widget	full-use
XmSelectionBoxGetChild	function	full-use
XmSeparator	widget	full-use
XmSeparatorGadget	widget	full-use
XmSetMenuCursor	function	full-use
XmSetProtocolHooks	function	trial-use
XmSetWMProtocolHooks	function	trial-use
XmString	data type	full-use
XmStringBaseline	function	trial-use
XmStringByteCompare	function	trial-use
XmStringCompare	function	trial-use
XmStringConcat	function	trial-use
XmStringCopy	function	trial-use
XmStringCreate*	function	trial-use
XmStringCreateLocalized*	function	temporary-use
XmStringCreateSimple	function	trial-use
XmStringDirection	data type	full-use
XmStringDraw	function	trial-use
XmStringDrawImage	function	trial-use
XmStringDrawUnderline	function	trial-use
XmStringEmpty	function	trial-use
XmStringExtent	function	trial-use
XmStringFree	function	trial-use
XmStringFreeContext	function	trial-use
XmStringGetNextSegment	function	trial-use
XmStringHasSubstring	function	trial-use
XmStringHeight	function	trial-use

Service Name	Service Type	AES Level
XmStringInitContext	function	trial-use
XmStringLength	function	trial-use
XmStringLineCount	function	trial-use
XmStringNConcat	function	trial-use
XmStringNCopy	function	trial-use
XmStringSegmentCreate	function	trial-use
XmStringSeparatorCreate	function	trial-use
XmStringTable	data type	full-use
XmStringWidth	function	trial-use
XmText	widget	full-use
XmTextClearSelection	function	full-use
XmTextCopy	function	full-use
XmTextCut	function	full-use
XmTextField*	widget	trial-use
XmTextFieldClearSelection*	function	trial-use
XmTextFieldCopy*	function	trial-use
XmTextFieldCut*	function	trial-use
XmTextFieldGetBaseline*	function	trial-use
XmTextFieldGetEditable*	function	trial-use
XmTextFieldGetInsertionPosition*	function	trial-use
XmTextFieldGetLastPosition*	function	trial-use
XmTextFieldGetMaxLength*	function	trial-use
XmTextFieldGetSelection*	function	trial-use
XmTextFieldGetSelectionPosition*	function	trial-use
XmTextFieldGetString*	function	trial-use
XmTextFieldInsert*	function	trial-use
XmTextFieldPaste*	function	trial-use
XmTextFieldPosToXY*	function	trial-use
XmTextFieldRemove*	function	trial-use
XmTextFieldReplace*	function	trial-use

Service Name	Service Type	AES Level
XmTextFieldSetAddMode*	function	trial-use
XmTextFieldSetEditable*	function	trial-use
XmTextFieldSetHighlight*	function	trial-use
XmTextFieldSetInsertionPosition*	function	trial-use
XmTextFieldSetMaxLength*	function	trial-use
XmTextFieldSetSelection*	function	trial-use
XmTextFieldSetString*	function	trial-use
XmTextFieldShowPosition*	function	trial-use
XmTextFieldXYToPos*	function	trial-use
XmTextGetBaseline	function	full-use
XmTextGetEditable	function	full-use
XmTextGetInsertionPosition	function	full-use
XmTextGetLastPosition	function	full-use
XmTextGetMaxLength	function	full-use
XmTextGetSelection	function	full-use
XmTextGetSelectionPosition	function	full-use
XmTextGetSource	function	trial-use
XmTextGetString	function	full-use
XmTextGetTopCharacter	function	full-use
XmTextInsert	function	full-use
XmTextPaste	function	full-use
XmTextPosToXY	function	full-use
XmTextPosition	data type	full-use
XmTextRemove	function	full-use
XmTextReplace	function	full-use
XmTextScroll	function	full-use
XmTextSetAddMode	function	trial-use
XmTextSetEditable	function	full-use
XmTextSetHighlight	function	full-use
XmTextSetInsertionPosition	function	full-use

Service Name	Service Type	AES Level
XmTextSetMaxLength	function	full-use
XmTextSetSelection	function	full-use
XmTextSetSource	function	trial-use
XmTextSetString	function	full-use
XmTextSetTopCharacter	function	full-use
XmTextShowPosition	function	full-use
XmTextXYToPos	function	full-use
XmToggleButton	widget	full-use
XmToggleButtonGadget	widget	full-use
XmToggleButtonGadgetGetState	function	full-use
XmToggleButtonGadgetSetState	function	full-use
XmToggleButtonGetState	function	full-use
XmToggleButtonSetState	function	full-use
XmTrackingLocate	function	trial-use
XmUninstallImage	function	full-use
XmUpdateDisplay	function	full-use
mwm	command	full-use

1.3 Overview of Services by Type and Function

All the services are broken into four types in the tables below.

- Window manager
- Widgets and widget functions
- Toolkit functions
- User interface language

Within each table, components are organized by function.

1.3.1 Window manager

Table 1–2. Window Manager Services

Service Name	Service Type	AES Level
mwm	command	full-use

1.3.2 Widgets and Widget Functions

The following table organizes widgets by hierarchy. Position in the hierarchy is shown by the indentation of the service name. The functions for each widget immediately follow the widget.

Table 1–3. Widget Services

Service Name	Service Type	AES Level
Core	widget	full-use
Object	widget	full-use
RectObj	widget	full-use
XmPrimitive	widget	full-use
XmArrowButton	widget	full-use
XmCreateArrowButton	function	full-use
XmLabel	widget	full-use
XmCreateLabel	function	full-use
XmCascadeButton	widget	full-use
XmCreateCascadeButton	function	full-use
XmCascadeButtonHighlight	function	full-use
XmDrawnButton	widget	full-use
XmCreateDrawnButton	function	full-use
XmPushButton	widget	full-use
XmCreatePushButton	function	full-use
XmToggleButton	widget	full-use
XmCreateToggleButton	function	full-use
XmToggleButtonGetState	function	full-use
XmToggleButtonSetState	function	full-use
XmList	widget	full-use
XmCreateList	function	full-use
XmListAddItem	function	full-use
XmListAddItemUnselected	function	full-use

Service Name	Service Type	AES Level
XmListAddItems	function	full-use
XmListDeleteAllItems	function	full-use
XmListDeleteItem	function	full-use
XmListDeleteItems	function	full-use
XmListDeleteItemsPos	function	full-use
XmListDeletePos	function	full-use
XmListDeselectAllItems	function	full-use
XmListDeselectItem	function	full-use
XmListDeselectPos	function	full-use
XmListGetMatchPos	function	full-use
XmListGetSelectedPos	function	full-use
XmListItemExists	function	full-use
XmListItemPos	function	trial-use
XmListReplaceItems	function	full-use
XmListReplaceItemsPos	function	full-use
XmListSelectItem	function	full-use
XmListSelectPos	function	full-use
XmListSetAddMode	function	trial-use
XmListSetBottomItem	function	full-use
XmListSetBottomPos	function	full-use
XmListSetHorizPos	function	full-use
XmListSetItem	function	full-use
XmListSetPos	function	full-use
XmScrollBar	widget	full-use
XmCreateScrollBar	function	full-use
XmScrollBarGetValues	function	full-use
XmScrollBarSetValues	function	full-use
XmSeparator	widget	full-use
XmCreateSeparator	function	full-use
XmText	widget	full-use

Service Name	Service Type	AES Level
XmCreateText	function	full-use
XmTextClearSelection	function	full-use
XmTextCopy	function	full-use
XmTextCut	function	full-use
XmTextField*	widget	trial-use
XmCreateTextField*	function	trial-use
XmTextFieldClearSelection*	function	trial-use
XmTextFieldCopy*	function	trial-use
XmTextFieldCut*	function	trial-use
XmTextFieldGetBaseline*	function	trial-use
XmTextFieldGetEditable*	function	trial-use
XmTextFieldGetInsertionPosition*	function	trial-use
XmTextFieldGetLastPosition*	function	trial-use
XmTextFieldGetMaxLength*	function	trial-use
XmTextFieldGetSelection*	function	trial-use
XmTextFieldGetSelectionPosition*	function	trial-use
XmTextFieldGetString*	function	trial-use
XmTextFieldInsert*	function	trial-use
XmTextFieldPaste*	function	trial-use
XmTextFieldPosToXY*	function	trial-use
XmTextFieldRemove*	function	trial-use
XmTextFieldReplace*	function	trial-use
XmTextFieldSetAddMode*	function	trial-use
XmTextFieldSetEditable*	function	trial-use
XmTextFieldSetHighlight*	function	trial-use
XmTextFieldSetInsertionPosition*	function	trial-use
XmTextFieldSetMaxLength*	function	trial-use
XmTextFieldSetSelection*	function	trial-use
XmTextFieldSetString*	function	trial-use
XmTextFieldShowPosition*	function	trial-use

Service Name	Service Type	AES Level
XmTextFieldXYToPos*	function	trial-use
XmTextGetBaseline	function	full-use
XmTextGetEditable	function	full-use
XmTextGetInsertionPosition	function	full-use
XmTextGetLastPosition	function	full-use
XmTextGetMaxLength	function	full-use
XmTextGetSelection	function	full-use
XmTextGetSelectionPosition	function	full-use
XmTextGetSource	function	trial-use
XmTextGetString	function	full-use
XmTextGetTopCharacter	function	full-use
XmTextInsert	function	full-use
XmTextPaste	function	full-use
XmTextPosToXY	function	full-use
XmTextRemove	function	full-use
XmTextReplace	function	full-use
XmTextScroll	function	full-use
XmTextSetAddMode	function	trial-use
XmTextSetEditable	function	full-use
XmTextSetHighlight	function	full-use
XmTextSetInsertionPosition	function	full-use
XmTextSetMaxLength	function	full-use
XmTextSetSelection	function	full-use
XmTextSetSource	function	trial-use
XmTextSetString	function	full-use
XmTextSetTopCharacter	function	full-use
XmTextShowPosition	function	full-use
XmTextXYToPos	function	full-use
Composite	widget	full-use
Shell	widget	full-use

Service Name	Service Type	AES Level
OverrideShell	widget	full-use
XmMenuShell	widget	full-use
XmCreateMenuShell	function	full-use
WMShell	widget	full-use
VendorShell	widget	full-use
XmGetAtomName	function	full-use
XmInternAtom	function	full-use
TopLevelShell	widget	full-use
ApplicationShell	widget	full-use
TransientShell	widget	full-use
XmDialogShell	widget	full-usE
XmCreateDialogShell	function	full-use
Constraint	widget	full-use
XmManager	widget	full-use
XmBulletinBoard	widget	full-use
XmCreateBulletinBoard	function	full-use
XmCreateBulletinBoardDialog	function	full-use
XmForm	widget	full-use
XmCreateForm	function	full-use
XmCreateFormDialog	function	full-use
XmMessageBox	widget	full-use
XmCreateMessageBox	function	full-use
XmCreateErrorDialog	function	full-use
XmCreateInformationDialog	function	full-use
XmCreateMessageDialog	function	full-use
XmCreateQuestionDialog	function	full-use
XmCreateWarningDialog	function	full-use
XmCreateWorkingDialog	function	full-use
XmMessageBoxGetChild	function	full-use
XmSelectionBox	widget	full-use

Service Name	Service Type	AES Level
XmCreateSelectionBox	function	full-use
XmCreatePromptDialog	function	full-use
XmCreateSelectionDialog	function	full-use
XmSelectionBoxGetChild	function	full-use
XmCommand	widget	full-use
XmCreateCommand	function	full-use
XmCommandAppendValue	function	full-use
XmCommandError	function	full-use
XmCommandGetChild	function	full-use
XmCommandSetValue	function	full-use
XmFileSelectionBox	widget	full-use
XmCreateFileSelectionBox	function	full-use
XmCreateFileSelectionDialog	function	full-use
XmFileSelectionBoxGetChild	function	full-use
XmFileSelectionDoSearch	function	full-use
XmDrawingArea	widget	full-use
XmCreateDrawingArea	function	full-use
XmFrame	widget	full-use
XmCreateFrame	function	full-use
XmPanedWindow	widget	full-use
XmCreatePanedWindow	function	full-use
XmRowColumn	widget	full-use
XmCreateRowColumn	function	full-use
XmCreateMenuBar	function	full-use
XmCreateOptionMenu	function	full-use
XmCreatePopupMenu	function	full-use
XmCreatePulldownMenu	function	full-use
XmCreateRadioBox	function	full-use
XmCreateWorkArea	function	trial-use
XmGetMenuCursor	function	full-use

Service Name	Service Type	AES Level
XmGetPostedFromWidget	function	trial-use
XmMenuPosition	function	full-use
XmOptionButtonGadget	function	full-use
XmOptionLabelGadget	function	full-use
XmSetMenuCursor	function	full-use
XmScale	widget	full-use
XmCreateScale	function	full-use
XmScaleGetValue	function	full-use
XmScaleSetValue	function	full-use
XmScrolledWindow	widget	full-use
XmCreateScrolledWindow	function	full-use
XmCreateScrolledList	function	full-use
XmCreateScrolledText	function	full-use
XmScrolledWindowSetAreas	function	full-use
XmMainWindow	widget	full-use
XmCreateMainWindow	function	full-use
XmMainWindowSep1	function	full-use
XmMainWindowSep2	function	full-use
XmMainWindowSep3	function	full-use
XmMainWindowSetAreas	function	full-use
XmGadget	widget	full-use
XmArrowButtonGadget	widget	full-use
XmCreateArrowButtonGadget	function	full-use
XmLabelGadget	widget	full-use
XmCreateLabelGadget	function	full-use
XmCascadeButtonGadget	widget	full-use
XmCascadeButtonGadgetHighlight	function	trial-use
XmCreateCascadeButtonGadget	function	full-use
XmPushButtonGadget	widget	full-use
XmCreatePushButtonGadget	function	full-use

Service Name	Service Type	AES Level
XmToggleButtonGadget	widget	full-use
XmCreateToggleButtonGadget	function	full-use
XmToggleButtonGadgetGetState	function	full-use
XmToggleButtonGadgetSetState	function	full-use
XmSeparatorGadget	widget	full-use
XmCreateSeparatorGadget	function	full-use

1.3.3 Toolkit Functions and Data Types

Table 1–4. Toolkit Services

Service Name	Service Type	AES Level
XmActivateProtocol	function	trial-use
XmActivateWMProtocol	function	trial-use
XmAddProtocolCallback	function	trial-use
XmAddProtocols	function	trial-use
XmAddTabGroup	function	full-use
XmAddWMProtocolCallback	function	trial-use
XmAddWMProtocols	function	trial-use
XmClipboardCancelCopy	function	full-use
XmClipboardCopy	function	full-use
XmClipboardCopyByName	function	full-use
XmClipboardEndCopy	function	full-use
XmClipboardEndRetrieve	function	full-use
XmClipboardInquireCount	function	full-use
XmClipboardInquireFormat	function	full-use
XmClipboardInquireLength	function	full-use
XmClipboardInquirePendingItems	function	full-use
XmClipboardLock	function	full-use
XmClipboardRegisterFormat	function	full-use
XmClipboardRetrieve	function	full-use
XmClipboardStartCopy	function	full-use
XmClipboardStartRetrieve	function	full-use
XmClipboardUndoCopy	function	full-use
XmClipboardUnlock	function	full-use
XmClipboardWithdrawFormat	function	full-use
XmConvertUnits	function	trial-use
XmCvtCTToXmString	function	trial-use

Service Name	Service Type	AES Level
XmCvtXmStringToCT	function	trial-use
XmDeactivateProtocol	function	trial-use
XmDeactivateWMProtocol	function	trial-use
XmDestroyPixmap	function	full-use
XmFontList	data type	full-use
XmFontListAdd	function	trial-use
XmFontListAppendEntry*	function	trial-use
XmFontListCopy*	function	trial-use
XmFontListCreate	function	trial-use
XmFontListEntryCreate*	function	trial-use
XmFontListEntryFree*	function	trial-use
XmFontListEntryGetFont*	function	trial-use
XmFontListEntryGetTag*	function	trial-use
XmFontListEntryLoad*	function	trial-use
XmFontListFree	function	full-use
XmFontListFreeFontContext*	function	trial-use
XmFontListInitFontContext*	function	trial-use
XmFontListNextEntry*	function	trial-use
XmFontListRemoveEntry*	function	trial-use
XmGetColors	function	trial-use
XmGetPixmap	function	full-use
XmInstallImage	function	full-use
XmIsMotifWMRunning	function	full-use
XmProcessTraversal	function	full-use
XmRemoveProtocolCallback	function	trial-use
XmRemoveProtocols	function	trial-use
XmRemoveTabGroup	function	full-use
XmRemoveWMProtocolCallback	function	trial-use
XmRemoveWMProtocols	function	trial-use
XmResolvePartOffsets	function	full-use

Service Name	Service Type	AES Level
XmSetProtocolHooks	function	trial-use
XmSetWMProtocolHooks	function	trial-use
XmString	data type	full-use
XmStringBaseline	function	trial-use
XmStringByteCompare	function	trial-use
XmStringCompare	function	trial-use
XmStringConcat	function	trial-use
XmStringCopy	function	trial-use
XmStringCreate*	function	trial-use
XmStringCreateLocalized*	function	temporary-use
XmStringCreateSimple	function	trial-use
XmStringDirection	data type	full-use
XmStringDraw	function	trial-use
XmStringDrawImage	function	trial-use
XmStringDrawUnderline	function	trial-use
XmStringEmpty	function	trial-use
XmStringExtent	function	trial-use
XmStringFree	function	trial-use
XmStringFreeContext	function	trial-use
XmStringGetNextSegment	function	trial-use
XmStringHasSubstring	function	trial-use
XmStringHeight	function	trial-use
XmStringInitContext	function	trial-use
XmStringLength	function	trial-use
XmStringLineCount	function	trial-use
XmStringNConcat	function	trial-use
XmStringNCopy	function	trial-use
XmStringSegmentCreate	function	trial-use
XmStringSeparatorCreate	function	trial-use
XmStringTable	data type	full-use

Service Name	Service Type	AES Level
XmStringWidth	function	trial-use
XmTextPosition	data type	full-use
XmTrackingLocate	function	trial-use
XmUninstallImage	function	full-use
XmUpdateDisplay	function	full-use

1.3.4 User Interface Language

Table 1–5. User Interface Language Services

Service Name	Service Type	AES Level
MrmCloseHierarchy	function	full-use
MrmFetchColorLiteral	function	full-use
MrmFetchIconLiteral	function	full-use
MrmFetchLiteral	function	full-use
MrmFetchSetValues	function	full-use
MrmFetchWidget	function	full-use
MrmFetchWidgetOverride	function	full-use
MrmInitialize	function	full-use
MrmOpenHierarchy	function	trial-use
MrmOpenHierarchyPerDisplay*	function	trial-use
MrmRegisterClass	function	trial-use
MrmRegisterNames	function	trial-use
MrmRegisterNamesInHierarchy	function	trial-use
Uil	function	full-use

Chapter 2

Reference Pages

This chapter contains the reference pages for the Application Environment Specification User Environment Volume. Each supported service is described on a separate reference page.

mwm—The Motif Window Manager

AES Support Level

Full-use

History/Direction

The **f.restore** function, which restores a window to its previous state, has been added (for trial-use).

Synopsis

mwm [*options*]

Description

mwm is an X Window System client that provides window management functionality and some session management functionality. It provides functions that facilitate control (by the user and the programmer) of elements of window state such as placement, size, icon/normal display, and input-focus ownership. It also provides session management functions such as stopping a client.

Options

-display *display*

This option specifies the display to use; see **X(1)**.

-xrm *resourcestring*

This option specifies a resource string to use.

-multiscreen

This option causes **mwm** to manage all screens on the display. The default is to manage only a single screen.

-name *name*

This option causes **mwm** to retrieve its resources using the specified name, as in *name*resource*.

-screens *name [name [...]]*

This option specifies the resource names to use for the screens managed by **mwm**. If **mwm** is managing a single screen, only the first name in the list is used. If **mwm** is managing multiple screens, the names are assigned to the screens in order, starting with screen 0. Screen 0 gets the first name, screen 1 the second name, and so on.

Appearance

The following sections describe the basic default behaviors of windows, icons, the icon box, input focus, and window stacking. The appearance and behavior of the window manager can be altered by changing the configuration of specific resources. Resources are defined under the heading **X Defaults**.

Screens

By default, **mwm** manages only the single screen specified by the **-display** option or the DISPLAY environment variable (by default, screen 0). If the **-multiscreen** option is specified or if the **multiScreen** resource is True, **mwm** tries to manage all the screens on the display.

When **mwm** is managing multiple screens, the **-screens** option can be used to give each screen a unique resource name. The names are separated by blanks, for example, **-screens mwm0 mwm1**. If there are more screens than names, resources for the remaining screens will be retrieved using the first name.

Windows

Default **mwm** window frames have distinct components with associated functions:

Title Area

In addition to displaying the client's title, the title area is used to move the window. To move the window, place the pointer over the title area, pressing button 1 and dragging the window to a new location. A wire frame is moved during the drag to indicate the new location. When the button is released, the window is moved to the new location.

Title Bar The title bar includes the title area, the minimize button, the maximize button, and the window menu button.

Minimize Button

To turn the window into an icon, click button 1 on the minimize button (the frame box with a *small* square in it).

Maximize Button

To make the window fill the screen (or enlarge to the largest size allowed by the configuration files), click button 1 on the maximize button (the frame box with a *large* square in it).

Window Menu Button

The window menu button is the frame box with a horizontal bar in it. To pull down the window menu, press button 1. While pressing, drag the pointer on the menu to your selection, then release the button when your selection is highlighted.

Alternately, you can click button 1 to pull down the menu and keep it posted; then position the pointer and select. You can also post the window menu by pressing **<Shift> <Esc>** or **<Alt> <Space>**. Double-clicking button 1 with the pointer on the window menu button closes the window. The following table lists the contents of the window menu.

Default Window Menu		
Selection	**Accelerator**	**Description**
Restore	**<Alt> <F5>**	Restores the window to its size before minimizing or maximizing
Move	**<Alt> <F7>**	Allows the window to be moved with keys or mouse
Size	**<Alt> <F8>**	Allows the window to be resized
Minimize	**<Alt> <F9>**	Turns the window into an icon
Maximize	**<Alt> <F10>**	Makes the window fill the screen
Lower	**<Alt> <F3>**	Moves window to bottom of window stack
Close	**<Alt> <F4>**	Causes client to terminate

Resize Border Handles

To change the size of a window, move the pointer over a resize border handle (the cursor changes), press button 1, and drag the window to a new size. When the button is released, the window is resized. While dragging is being done, a rubber-band outline is displayed to indicate the new window size.

Matte   An optional matte decoration can be added between the client area and the window frame. A matte is not actually part of the window frame. There is no functionality associated with a matte.

Icons

Icons are small graphic representations of windows. A window can be minimized (iconified) with the minimize button on the window frame. Icons provide a way to reduce clutter on the screen.

Pressing mouse button 1 when the pointer is over an icon causes the icon's window menu to pop up. Releasing the button (pressing and releasing a button without moving the mouse equals a click) causes the menu to stay posted. The menu contains the selections described in the following table.

Icon Window Menu		
Selection	**Accelerator**	**Description**
Restore	**<Alt> <F5>**	Opens the associated window
Move	**<Alt> <F7>**	Allows the icon to be moved with keys
Size	**<Alt> <F8>**	Inactive (not an option for icons)
Minimize	**<Alt> <F9>**	Inactive (not an option for icons)
Maximize	**<Alt> <F10>**	Opens the associated window and makes it fill the screen
Lower	**<Alt> <F3>**	Moves icon to bottom of icon stack
Close	**<Alt> <F4>**	Removes client from **mwm** management

Note that pressing button 3 over an icon also causes the icon's window menu to pop up. To make a menu selection, drag the pointer over the menu and release button 3 when the desired item is highlighted.

Double-clicking button 1 on an icon invokes the **f.restore** function and restores the icon's associated window to its previous state. Double-clicking button 1 on the icon box's icon opens the icon box and allows access to the contained icons.

Icon Box

When icons begin to clutter the screen, they can be packed into an icon box. (To use an icon box, **mwm** must be started with the icon box configuration already set.) The icon box is an **mwm** window that holds client icons. It includes one or more scroll bars when there are more window icons than the icon box can show at the same time. Double-clicking button 1 on the icon box's icon opens the icon box and allows access to the contained icons.

Icons in the icon box can be manipulated with the mouse. The following table summarizes the behavior of this interface. Button actions apply whenever the pointer is on any part of the icon. Note that invoking the **f.raise** function on an icon in the icon box raises an already open window to the top of the stack.

Button Action	Description
Button 1 click	Selects the icon
Button 1 double-click	Restores (opens) the associated window or raises an already open window to the top of the stack
Button 1 drag	Moves the icon
Button 3 press	Causes the menu for that icon to pop up
Button 3 drag	Highlights items as the pointer moves across the menu

Icon Menu for the Icon Box		
Selection	**Accelerator**	**Description**
Restore	<Alt> <F5>	Opens the associated window (if not already open)
Move	<Alt> <F7>	Allows the icon to be moved with keys
Size	<Alt> <F8>	Inactive
Minimize	<Alt> <F9>	Inactive
Maximize	<Alt> <F10>	Opens the associated window (if not already open) and maximizes its size
Lower	<Alt> <F3>	Inactive
Close	<Alt> <F4>	Removes client from **mwm** management

To pull down the window menu for the icon box itself, press button 1 with the pointer over the menu button for the icon box. The window menu of the icon box differs from the window menu of a client window: The "Close" selection is replaced with the "PackIcons" **<Shift> <Alt> <F7>** selection. When selected, PackIcons packs the icons in the box to achieve neat rows with no empty slots.

You can also post the window menu by pressing **<Shift> <Esc>** or **<Alt> <Space>**. Pressing **<Menu>** (the pop-up menu key) causes the icon window menu of the currently selected icon to pop up.

Input Focus

mwm supports (by default) a keyboard input focus policy of explicit selection. This means when a window is selected to get keyboard input, it continues to get keyboard input until the window is withdrawn from window management, another window is explicitly selected to get keyboard input, or the window is iconified. Several resources control the input focus. The client window with the keyboard input focus has the active window appearance with a visually distinct window frame.

The following tables summarize the keyboard input focus selection behavior.

Button Action	Object	Function Description
Button 1 press	Window / window frame	Keyboard focus selection
Button 1 press	Icon	Keyboard focus selection

Key Action	Function Description
<Alt> <Tab>	Move input focus to next window in window stack
<Alt> <Shift> <Tab>	Move input focus to previous window in window stack

X Defaults

mwm is configured from its resource database. This database is built from the following sources. They are listed in order of precedence, low to high:

- **/usr/lib/X11/app-defaults/Mwm**

- **$HOME/Mwm**

- RESOURCE_MANAGER root window property or **$HOME/.Xdefaults**

- XENVIRONMENT variable or **$HOME/.Xdefaults-**_host_

- **mwm** command line options

The filenames **/usr/lib/X11/app-defaults/Mwm** and **$HOME/Mwm** represent customary locations for these files. The actual location of the system-wide class resource file may depend on the XFILESEARCHPATH environment variable and the current language environment. The actual location of the user-specific class resource file may depend on the XUSERFILESEARCHPATH and XAPPLRESDIR environment variables and the current language environment.

Entries in the resource database may refer to other resource files for specific types of resources. These include files that contain bitmaps, fonts, and **mwm** specific resources, such as menus and behavior specifications (for example, button and key bindings).

Mwm is the resource class name of **mwm**, and **mwm** is the resource name used by **mwm** to look up resources. The **-screens** command line option specifies resource names, such as **mwm_b+w** and **mwm_color**. In the following discussion of resource specification, **Mwm** and **mwm** (and the aliased **mwm** resource names) can be used interchangeably, but **mwm** takes precedence over **Mwm.**

mwm uses the following types of resources:

Component Appearance Resources

These resources specify appearance attributes of window manager user interface components. They can be applied to the appearance of window manager menus, feedback windows (for example, the window reconfiguration feedback window), client window frames, and icons.

General Appearance and Behavior Resources

These resources specify **mwm** appearance and behavior (for example, window management policies). They are not set separately for different **mwm** user interface components.

Client Specific Resources

These **mwm** resources can be set for a particular client window or class of client window. They specify client-specific icon and client window frame appearance and behavior.

Resource identifiers can be either a resource name (for example, foreground) or a resource class (for example, Foreground). If the value of a resource is a filename and if the filename is prefixed by ~/ (tilde, slash), then it is relative to the path contained in the HOME environment variable (generally the user's home directory).

Component Appearance Resources

The syntax for specifying component appearance resources that apply to window manager icons, menus, and client window frames is

Mwm**resource_id*

For example, **Mwm*foreground** is used to specify the foreground color for **mwm** menus, icons, client window frames, and feedback dialogs.

The syntax for specifying component appearance resources that apply to a particular **mwm** component is

Mwm*[menu|icon|client|feedback]**resource_id*

If **menu** is specified, the resource is applied only to **mwm** menus; if **icon** is specified, the resource is applied to icons; and if **client** is specified, the resource is applied to client window frames. For example, **Mwm*icon*foreground** is used to specify the foreground color for **mwm** icons, **Mwm*menu*foreground** specifies the foreground color for **mwm** menus, and **Mwm*client*foreground** is used to specify the foreground color for **mwm** client window frames.

The appearance of the title area of a client window frame (including window management buttons) can be separately configured. The syntax for configuring the title area of a client window frame is

Mwm*client*title*_resource_id_

For example, **Mwm*client*title*foreground** specifies the foreground color for the title area. Defaults for title area resources are based on the values of the corresponding client window frame resources.

The appearance of menus can be configured based on the name of the menu. The syntax for specifying menu appearance by name is

Mwm*menu*_menu_name_*****_resource_id_

For example, **Mwm*menu*my_menu*foreground** specifies the foreground color for the menu named **my_menu**.

The following component appearance resources that apply to all window manager parts can be specified.

Component Appearance Resources—All Window Manager Parts			
Name	Class	Value Type	Default
background	Background	color	varies[1]
backgroundPixmap	BackgroundPixmap	string[2]	varies[1]
bottomShadowColor	Foreground	color	varies[1]
bottomShadowPixmap	BottomShadowPixmap	string[2]	varies[1]
fontList	FontList	string[3]	"fixed"
foreground	Foreground	color	varies[1]
saveUnder	SaveUnder	T/F	F
topShadowColor	Background	color	varies[1]
topShadowPixmap	TopShadowPixmap	string[2]	varies[1]

[1]The default is chosen based on the visual type of the screen.
[2]Image name. See **XmInstallImage(3X)**.
[3]X11 R4 Font description.

background (class **Background**)
> This resource specifies the background color. Any legal X color may be specified. The default value is chosen based on the visual type of the screen.

backgroundPixmap (class **BackgroundPixmap**)
> This resource specifies the background pixmap of the **mwm** decoration when the window is inactive (does not have the keyboard focus). The default value is chosen based on the visual type of the screen.

bottomShadowColor (class **Foreground**)

This resource specifies the bottom shadow color. This color is used for the lower and right bevels of the window manager decoration. Any legal X color may be specified. The default value is chosen based on the visual type of the screen.

bottomShadowPixmap (class **BottomShadowPixmap**)

This resource specifies the bottom shadow pixmap. This pixmap is used for the lower and right bevels of the window manager decoration. The default is chosen based on the visual type of the screen.

fontList (class **FontList**)

This resource specifies the font used in the window manager decoration. The character encoding of the font should match the character encoding of the strings that are used. The default is "fixed."

foreground (class **Foreground**)

This resource specifies the foreground color. The default is chosen based on the visual type of the screen.

saveUnder (class **SaveUnder**)

This resource is used to indicate whether "save unders" are used for **mwm** components. For this to have any effect, save unders must be implemented by the X server. If save unders are implemented, the X server saves the contents of windows obscured by windows that have the save under attribute set. If the **saveUnder** resource is True, **mwm** will set the save under attribute on the window manager frame of any client that has it set. If **saveUnder** is False, save unders will not be used on any window manager frames. The default value is False.

topShadowColor (class **Background**)

This resource specifies the top shadow color. This color is used for the upper and left bevels of the window manager decoration. The default is chosen based on the visual type of the screen.

topShadowPixmap (class **TopShadowPixmap**)

This resource specifies the top shadow pixmap. This pixmap is used for the upper and left bevels of the window manager decoration. The default is chosen based on the visual type of the screen.

The following component appearance resources that apply to frame and icons can be specified.

Frame and Icon Components			
Name	**Class**	**Value Type**	**Default**
activeBackground	Background	color	varies[1]
activeBackgroundPixmap	BackgroundPixmap	string[2]	varies[1]
activeBottomShadowColor	Foreground	color	varies[1]
activeBottomShadowPixmap	BottomShadowPixmap	string[2]	varies[1]
activeForeground	Foreground	color	varies[1]
activeTopShadowColor	Background	color	varies[1]
activeTopShadowPixmap	TopShadowPixmap	string[2]	varies[1]

[1]The default is chosen based on the visual type of the screen.
[2]See **XmInstallImage(3X)**.

activeBackground (class **Background**)

    This resource specifies the background color of the **mwm** decoration when the window is active (has the keyboard focus). The default is chosen based on the visual type of the screen.

activeBackgroundPixmap (class **ActiveBackgroundPixmap**)

    This resource specifies the background pixmap of the **mwm** decoration when the window is active (has the keyboard focus). The default is chosen based on the visual type of the screen.

activeBottomShadowColor (class **Foreground**)

    This resource specifies the bottom shadow color of the **mwm** decoration when the window is active (has the keyboard focus). The default is chosen based on the visual type of the screen.

activeBottomShadowPixmap (class **BottomShadowPixmap**)

    This resource specifies the bottom shadow pixmap of the **mwm** decoration when the window is active (has the keyboard focus). The default is chosen based on the visual type of the screen.

activeForeground (class **Foreground**)

    This resource specifies the foreground color of the **mwm** decoration when the window is active (has the keyboard focus). The default is chosen based on the visual type of the screen.

activeTopShadowColor (class **Background**)

    This resource specifies the top shadow color of the **mwm** decoration when the window is active (has the keyboard focus). The default is chosen based on the visual type of the screen.

        activeTopShadowPixmap (class **TopShadowPixmap**)
            This resource specifies the top shadow pixmap of the **mwm** decoration when the window is active (has the keyboard focus). The default is chosen based on the visual type of the screen.

General Appearance and Behavior Resources
    The syntax for specifying general appearance and behavior resources is

Mwm*_resource_id_

For example, **Mwm*****keyboardFocusPolicy** specifies the window manager policy for setting the keyboard focus to a particular client window.

The following general appearance and behavior resources can be specified.

<table>
<tr><td colspan="4" align="center">**General Appearance and Behavior Resources**</td></tr>
<tr><td>**Name**</td><td>**Class**</td><td>**Value Type**</td><td>**Default**</td></tr>
<tr><td>autoKeyFocus</td><td>AutoKeyFocus</td><td>T/F</td><td>T</td></tr>
<tr><td>autoRaiseDelay</td><td>AutoRaiseDelay</td><td>millisec</td><td>500</td></tr>
<tr><td>bitmapDirectory</td><td>BitmapDirectory</td><td>directory</td><td>**/usr/include/\
X11/bitmaps**</td></tr>
<tr><td>buttonBindings</td><td>ButtonBindings</td><td>string</td><td>**DefaultBut\
tonBindings**</td></tr>
<tr><td>cleanText</td><td>CleanText</td><td>T/F</td><td>T</td></tr>
<tr><td>clientAutoPlace</td><td>ClientAutoPlace</td><td>T/F</td><td>T</td></tr>
<tr><td>colormapFocusPolicy</td><td>ColormapFocusPolicy</td><td>string</td><td>keyboard</td></tr>
<tr><td>configFile</td><td>ConfigFile</td><td>file</td><td>**.mwmrc**</td></tr>
<tr><td>deiconifyKeyFocus</td><td>DeiconifyKeyFocus</td><td>T/F</td><td>T</td></tr>
<tr><td>doubleClickTime</td><td>DoubleClickTime</td><td>millisec.</td><td>multiclick
time</td></tr>
<tr><td>enableWarp</td><td>enableWarp</td><td>T/F</td><td>T</td></tr>
<tr><td>enforceKeyFocus</td><td>EnforceKeyFocus</td><td>T/F</td><td>T</td></tr>
<tr><td>fadeNormalIcon</td><td>FadeNormalIcon</td><td>T/F</td><td>F</td></tr>
<tr><td>frameBorderWidth</td><td>FrameBorderWidth</td><td>pixels</td><td>5</td></tr>
<tr><td>iconAutoPlace</td><td>IconAutoPlace</td><td>T/F</td><td>T</td></tr>
<tr><td>iconBoxGeometry</td><td>IconBoxGeometry</td><td>string</td><td>6x1+0-0</td></tr>
<tr><td>iconBoxName</td><td>IconBoxName</td><td>string</td><td>iconbox</td></tr>
<tr><td>iconBoxSBDisplayPolicy</td><td>IconBoxSBDisplayPolicy</td><td>string</td><td>all</td></tr>
<tr><td>iconBoxTitle</td><td>IconBoxTitle</td><td>XmString</td><td>Icons</td></tr>
<tr><td>iconClick</td><td>IconClick</td><td>T/F</td><td>T</td></tr>
<tr><td>iconDecoration</td><td>IconDecoration</td><td>string</td><td>varies</td></tr>
<tr><td>iconImageMaximum</td><td>IconImageMaximum</td><td>wxh</td><td>50x50</td></tr>
<tr><td>iconImageMinimum</td><td>IconImageMinimum</td><td>wxh</td><td>16x16</td></tr>
<tr><td>iconPlacement</td><td>IconPlacement</td><td>string</td><td>left bottom</td></tr>
<tr><td>iconPlacementMargin</td><td>IconPlacementMargin</td><td>pixels</td><td>varies</td></tr>
<tr><td>interactivePlacement</td><td>InteractivePlacement</td><td>T/F</td><td>F</td></tr>
<tr><td>keyBindings</td><td>KeyBindings</td><td>string</td><td>**DefaultKey\
Bindings**</td></tr>
</table>

Name	Class	Value Type	Default
keyboardFocusPolicy	KeyboardFocusPolicy	string	explicit
limitResize	LimitResize	T/F	T
lowerOnIconify	LowerOnIconify	T/F	T
maximumMaximumSize	MaximumMaximumSize	wxh (pixels)	2X screen w and h
moveThreshold	MoveThreshold	pixels	4
multiScreen	MultiScreen	T/F	F
passButtons	PassButtons	T/F	F
passSelectButton	PassSelectButton	T/F	T
positionIsFrame	PositionIsFrame	T/F	T
positionOnScreen	PositionOnScreen	T/F	T
quitTimeout	QuitTimeout	millisec.	1000
raiseKeyFocus	RaiseKeyFocus	T/F	F
resizeBorderWidth	ResizeBorderWidth	pixels	10
resizeCursors	ResizeCursors	T/F	T
screens	Screens	string	varies
showFeedback	ShowFeedback	string	all
startupKeyFocus	StartupKeyFocus	T/F	T
transientDecoration	TransientDecoration	string	menu title
transientFunctions	TransientFunctions	string	-minimize -maximize
useIconBox	UseIconBox	T/F	F
wMenuButtonClick	WMenuButtonClick	T/F	T
wMenuButtonClick2	WMenuButtonClick2	T/F	T

autoKeyFocus (class **AutoKeyFocus**)

> This resource is available only when the keyboard input focus policy is explicit. If **autoKeyFocus** is given a value of True, then when a window with the keyboard input focus is withdrawn from window management or is iconified, the focus is set to the previous window that had the focus. If the value given is False, there is no automatic setting of the keyboard input focus. The default value is True.

autoRaiseDelay (class **AutoRaiseDelay**)

> This resource is available only when the **focusAutoRaise** resource is True and the keyboard focus policy is pointer. The **autoRaiseDelay**

resource specifies the amount of time (in milliseconds) that **mwm** will wait before raising a window after it gets the keyboard focus. The default value of this resource is 500 (ms).

bitmapDirectory (class **BitmapDirectory**)
This resource identifies a directory to be searched for bitmaps referenced by **mwm** resources. This directory is searched if a bitmap is specified without an absolute pathname. The default value for this resource is **/usr/include/X11/bitmaps**. The directory **/usr/include/X11/bitmaps** represents the customary locations for this directory. The actual location of this directory may vary on some systems.

buttonBindings (class **ButtonBindings**)
This resource identifies the set of button bindings for window management functions. The named set of button bindings is specified in the **mwm** resource description file. These button bindings are *merged* with the built-in default bindings. The default value for this resource is **DefaultButtonBindings**.

cleanText (class **CleanText**)
This resource controls the display of window manager text in the client title and feedback windows. If the default value of True is used, the text is drawn with a clear (no stipple) background. This makes text easier to read on monochrome systems where a background pixmap is specified. Only the stippling in the area immediately around the text is cleared. If False, the text is drawn directly on top of the existing background.

clientAutoPlace (class **ClientAutoPlace**)
This resource determines the position of a window when the window has not been given a user-specified position. With a value of True, windows are positioned with the top left corners of the frames offset horizontally and vertically. A value of False causes the currently configured position of the window to be used. In either case, **mwm** will attempt to place the windows totally on-screen. The default value is True.

colormapFocusPolicy (class **ColormapFocusPolicy**)
This resource indicates the colormap focus policy that is to be used. If the resource value is explicit, a colormap selection action is done on a client window to set the colormap focus to that window. If the value is pointer, the client window containing the pointer has the colormap focus. If the value is keyboard, the client window that has the keyboard input focus has the colormap focus. The default value for this resource is keyboard.

configFile (class **ConfigFile**)

The resource value is the pathname for an **mwm** resource description file.

If the pathname begins with ˜/ (tilde, slash), **mwm** considers it to be relative to the user's home directory (as specified by the HOME environment variable). If the LANG environment variable is set, **mwm** looks for **$HOME/$LANG/***configFile*. If that file does not exist or if LANG is not set, **mwm** looks for **$HOME/***configFile*.

If the **configFile** pathname does not begin with ˜/, **mwm** considers it to be relative to the current working directory.

If the **configFile** resource is not specified or if that file does not exist, **mwm** uses several default paths to find a configuration file. If the LANG environment variable is set, **mwm** first looks for the configuration file in **$HOME/$LANG/.mwmrc.** If that file does not exist or if LANG is not set, **mwm** looks for **$HOME/.mwmrc**. If that file does not exist and if LANG is set, **mwm** next looks for the file **system.mwmrc** in the $LANG subdirectory of an implementation-dependent directory. If that file does not exist or if LANG is not set, **mwm** looks for the file **system.mwmrc** in the same implementation-dependent directory.

deiconifyKeyFocus (class **DeiconifyKeyFocus**)

This resource applies only when the keyboard input focus policy is explicit. If a value of True is used, a window receives the keyboard input focus when it is normalized (deiconified). True is the default value.

doubleClickTime (class **DoubleClickTime**)

This resource is used to set the maximum time (in ms) between the clicks (button presses) that make up a double-click. The default value of this resource is the display's multiclick time.

enableWarp (class **EnableWarp**)

The default value of this resource, True, causes **mwm** to warp the pointer to the center of the selected window during keyboard-controlled resize and move operations. Setting the value to False causes **mwm** to leave the pointer at its original place on the screen, unless the user explicitly moves it with the cursor keys or pointing device.

enforceKeyFocus (class **EnforceKeyFocus**)

If this resource is given a value of True, the keyboard input focus is always explicitly set to selected windows even if there is an indication that they are "globally active" input windows. (An example of a globally active window is a scroll bar that can be operated without setting the focus to that client.) If the resource is False, the keyboard input focus is not explicitly set to globally active windows. The default value is True.

fadeNormalIcon (class **FadeNormalIcon**)
If this resource is given a value of True, an icon is grayed out whenever it has been normalized (its window has been opened). The default value is False.

frameBorderWidth (class **FrameBorderWidth**)
This resource specifies the width (in pixels) of a client window frame border without resize handles. The border width includes the 3-D shadows. The default value is 5 pixels.

iconAutoPlace (class **IconAutoPlace**)
This resource indicates whether the window manager arranges icons in a particular area of the screen or places each icon where the window was when it was iconified. The value True indicates that icons are arranged in a particular area of the screen, determined by the iconPlacement resource. The value False indicates that an icon is placed at the location of the window when it is iconified. The default is True.

iconBoxGeometry (class **IconBoxGeometry**)
This resource indicates the initial position and size of the icon box. The value of the resource is a standard window geometry string with the following syntax:

$[=][width\mathbf{x}height][\{+-\}xoffset\{+-\}yoffset]$

If the offsets are not provided, the iconPlacement policy is used to determine the initial placement. The units for width and height are columns and rows.

The actual screen size of the icon box window depends on the **iconImageMaximum** (size) and **iconDecoration** resources. The default value for size is (6 * **iconWidth** + padding) wide by (1 * **iconHeight** + padding) high. The default value of the location is +0 -0.

iconBoxName (class **IconBoxName**)
This resource specifies the name that is used to look up icon box resources. The default name is **iconbox**.

iconBoxSBDisplayPolicy (class **IconBoxSBDisplayPolicy**)
This resource specifies the scroll bar display policy of the window manager in the icon box. The resource has three possible values: **all**, **vertical**, and **horizontal**. The default value, **all**, causes both vertical

and horizontal scroll bars always to appear. The value **vertical** causes a single vertical scroll bar to appear in the icon box and sets the orientation of the icon box to horizontal (regardless of the **iconBoxGeometry** specification). The value **horizontal** causes a single horizontal scroll bar to appear in the icon box and sets the orientation of the icon box to vertical (regardless of the **iconBoxGeometry** specification).

iconBoxTitle (class **IconBoxTitle**)

This resource specifies the name that is used in the title area of the icon box frame. The default value is **Icons**.

iconClick (class **IconClick**)

When this resource is given the value of True, the system menu is posted and left posted when an icon is clicked. The default value is True.

iconDecoration (class **IconDecoration**)

This resource specifies the general icon decoration. The resource value is label (only the label part is displayed) or image (only the image part is displayed) or label image (both the label and image parts are displayed). A value of activelabel can also be specified to get a label (not truncated to the width of the icon) when the icon is selected. The default icon decoration for icon box icons is that each icon has a label part and an image part (label image). The default icon decoration for standalone icons is that each icon has an active label part, a label part, and an image part (activelabel label image).

iconImageMaximum (class **IconImageMaximum**)

This resource specifies the maximum size of the icon *image*. The resource value is *width*x*height* (for example, 64x64). The maximum supported size is 128x128. The default value of this resource is 50x50.

iconImageMinimum (class **IconImageMinimum**)

This resource specifies the minimum size of the icon *image*. The resource value is *width*x*height* (for example, 32x50). The minimum supported size is 16x16. The default value of this resource is 16x16.

iconPlacement (class **IconPlacement**)

This resource specifies the icon placement scheme to be used. The resource value has the following syntax:

primary_layout secondary_layout

The layout values are described in the following table.

Value	Description
top	Lay the icons out top to bottom.
bottom	Lay the icons out bottom to top.
left	Lay the icons out left to right.
right	Lay the icons out right to left.

A horizontal (vertical) layout value should not be used for both the *primary_layout* and the *secondary_layout* (for example, do not use top for the *primary_layout* and bottom for the *secondary_layout*). The *primary_layout* indicates whether, when an icon placement is done, the icon is placed in a row or a column and the direction of placement. The *secondary_layout* indicates where to place new rows or columns. For example, top right indicates that icons should be placed top to bottom on the screen and that columns should be added from right to left on the screen. The default placement is left bottom (icons are placed left to right on the screen, with the first row on the bottom of the screen, and new rows added from the bottom of the screen to the top of the screen).

iconPlacementMargin (class **IconPlacementMargin**)
This resource sets the distance between the edge of the screen and the icons that are placed along the edge of the screen. The value should be greater than or equal to 0 (zero). A default value is used if the value specified is invalid. The default value for this resource is equal to the space between icons as they are placed on the screen (this space is based on maximizing the number of icons in each row and column).

interactivePlacement (class **InteractivePlacement**)
This resource controls the initial placement of new windows on the screen. If the value is True, the pointer shape changes before a new window is placed on the screen to indicate to the user that a position should be selected for the upper left corner of the window. If the value is False, windows are placed according to the initial window configuration attributes. The default value of this resource is False.

keyBindings (class **KeyBindings**)
This resource identifies the set of key bindings for window management functions. If specified, these key bindings *replace* the built-in default bindings. The named set of key bindings is specified in the **mwm** resource description file. The default value for this resource is **DefaultKeyBindings**.

keyboardFocusPolicy (class **KeyboardFocusPolicy**)
If this resource is set to pointer, the keyboard focus policy is to have the keyboard focus set to the client window that contains the pointer (the

pointer could also be in the client window decoration that **mwm** adds). If this resource is set to explicit, the policy is to have the keyboard focus set to a client window when the user presses button 1 with the pointer on the client window or any part of the associated **mwm** decoration. The default value for this resource is explicit.

limitResize (class **LimitResize**)

If this resource is True, the user is not allowed to resize a window to greater than the maximum size. The default value for this resource is True.

lowerOnIconify (class **LowerOnIconify**)

If this resource is given the default value of True, a window's icon appears on the bottom of the window stack when the window is minimized (iconified). A value of False places the icon in the stacking order at the same place as its associated window. The default value of this resource is True.

maximumMaximumSize (class **MaximumMaximumSize**)

This resource is used to limit the maximum size of a client window as set by the user or client. The resource value is *widthxheight* (for example, 1024x1024) where the width and height are in pixels. The default value of this resource is twice the screen width and height.

moveThreshold (class **MoveThreshold**)

This resource is used to control the sensitivity of dragging operations that move windows and icons. The value of this resource is the number of pixels that the locator is moved with a button down before the move operation is initiated. This is used to prevent window/icon movement when you click or double-click and there is unintentional pointer movement with the button down. The default value of this resource is 4 (pixels).

multiScreen (class **MultiScreen**)

This resource, if True, causes **mwm** to manage all the screens on the display. If this resource is False, **mwm** manages only a single screen. The default value is False.

passButtons (class **PassButtons**)

This resource indicates whether or not button press events are passed to clients after they are used to do a window manager function in the client context. If the resource value is False, the button press is not passed to the client. If the value is True, the button press is passed to the client window. The window manager function is done in either case. The default value for this resource is False.

passSelectButton (class **PassSelectButton**)

This resource indicates whether or not to pass the select button press events to clients after they are used to do a window manager function in the client context. If the resource value is False, then the button press will not be passed to the client. If the value is True, the button press is passed to the client window. The window manager function is done in either case. The default value for this resource is True.

positionIsFrame (class **PositionIsFrame**)

This resource indicates how client window position information (from the WM_NORMAL_HINTS property and from configuration requests) is to be interpreted. If the resource value is True, the information is interpreted as the position of the MWM client window frame. If the value is False, it is interpreted as being the position of the client area of the window. The default value of this resource is True.

positionOnScreen (class **PositionOnScreen**)

This resource is used to indicate that windows should initially be placed (if possible) so that they are not clipped by the edge of the screen (if the resource value is True). If a window is larger than the size of the screen, at least the upper left corner of the window is on-screen. If the resource value is False, windows are placed in the requested position even if totally off-screen. The default value of this resource is True.

quitTimeout (class **QuitTimeout**)

This resource specifies the amount of time (in milliseconds) that **mwm** will wait for a client to update the WM_COMMAND property after **mwm** has sent the WM_SAVE_YOURSELF message. The default value of this resource is 1000 (ms). (Refer to the **f.kill** function description for additional information.)

raiseKeyFocus (class **RaiseKeyFocus**)

This resource is available only when the keyboard input focus policy is explicit. When set to True, this resource specifies that a window raised by means of the **f.normalize_and_raise** function also receives the input focus. The default value of this resource is False.

resizeBorderWidth (class **ResizeBorderWidth**)

This resource specifies the width (in pixels) of a client window frame border with resize handles. The specified border width includes the 3-D shadows. The default is 10 (pixels).

resizeCursors (class **ResizeCursors**)

This resource is used to indicate whether the resize cursors are always displayed when the pointer is in the window size border. If True, the cursors are shown, otherwise the window manager cursor is shown. The default value is True.

screens (class **Screens**)

This resource specifies the resource names to use for the screens managed by **mwm**. If **mwm** is managing a single screen, only the first name in the list is used. If **mwm** is managing multiple screens, the names are assigned to the screens in order, starting with screen 0 (zero). Screen 0 gets the first name, screen 1 the second name, and so on. The default screen names are 0, 1, and so on.

showFeedback (class **ShowFeedback**)

This resource controls when feedback information is displayed. It controls both window position and size feedback during move or resize operations and initial client placement. It also controls window manager message and dialog boxes.

The value for this resource is a list of names of the feedback options to be enabled or disabled; the names must be separated by a space. If an option is preceded by a minus sign, that option is excluded from the list. The *sign* of the first item in the list determines the initial set of options. If the sign of the first option is minus, **mwm** assumes all options are present and starts subtracting from that set. If the sign of the first decoration is plus (or not specified), **mwm** starts with no options and builds up a list from the resource.

The names of the feedback options are shown in the following table.

Name	Description
all	Show all feedback (Default value)
behavior	Confirm behavior switch
kill	Confirm on receipt of KILL signal
move	Show position during move
none	Show no feedback
placement	Show position and size during initial placement
quit	Confirm quitting **mwm**
resize	Show size during resize
restart	Confirm **mwm** restart

The following sample command line illustrates the syntax for showFeedback:

Mwm*showFeedback: placement resize behavior restart

This resource specification provides feedback for initial client placement and resize, and enables the dialog boxes to confirm the restart and set behavior functions. It disables feedback for the move function. The default value for this resource is all.

startupKeyFocus (class **StartupKeyFocus**)

This resource is available only when the keyboard input focus policy is explicit. When given the default value of True, a window gets the keyboard input focus when the window is mapped (that is, initially managed by the window manager).

transientDecoration (class **TransientDecoration**)

This resource controls the amount of decoration that **mwm** puts on transient windows. The decoration specification is exactly the same as for the **clientDecoration** (client specific) resource. Transient windows are identified by the WM_TRANSIENT_FOR property, which is added by the client to indicate a relatively temporary window. The default value for this resource is menu title (that is, transient windows have frame borders and a titlebar with a window menu button).

An application can also specify which decorations **mwm** should apply to its windows. If it does so, **mwm** applies only those decorations indicated by both the application and the **transientDecoration** resource. Otherwise, **mwm** applies the decorations indicated by the **transientDecoration** resource. For more information, see the description of **XmNmwmDecorations** on the **VendorShell(3X)** reference page.

transientFunctions (class **TransientFunctions**)

This resource is used to indicate which window management functions are applicable (or not applicable) to transient windows. The function specification is exactly the same as for the **clientFunctions** (client specific) resource. The default value is **-minimize -maximize**.

An application can also specify which functions **mwm** should apply to its windows. If it does so, **mwm** applies only those functions indicated by both the application and the **transientFunctions** resource. Otherwise, **mwm** applies the functions indicated by the **transientFunctions** resource. For more information, see the description of **XmNmwmFunctions** on the **VendorShell(3X)** reference page.

useIconBox (class **UseIconBox**)

If this resource is given a value of True, icons are placed in an icon box. When an icon box is not used, the icons are placed on the root window (default value).

> **wMenuButtonClick** (class **WMenuButtonClick**)
> > This resource indicates whether a click of the mouse when the pointer is over the window menu button posts and leaves posted the window menu. If the value given this resource is True, the menu remains posted. True is the default value for this resource.
>
> **wMenuButtonClick2** (class **WMenuButtonClick2**)
> > When this resource is given the default value of True, a double-click action on the window menu button does an **f.kill** function.

Client Specific Resources
> The syntax for specifying client specific resources is
>
> **Mwm***client_name_or_class*resource_id
>
> For example, **Mwm*****mterm*****windowMenu** is used to specify the window menu to be used with mterm clients. The syntax for specifying client specific resources for all classes of clients is
>
> **Mwm***resource_id
>
> Specific client specifications take precedence over the specifications for all clients. For example, **Mwm*****windowMenu** is used to specify the window menu to be used for all classes of clients that do not have a window menu specified.
>
> The syntax for specifying resource values for windows that have an unknown name and class (that is, windows that do not have a WM_CLASS property associated with them) is
>
> **Mwm*****defaults***resource_id
>
> For example, **Mwm*****defaults*****iconImage** is used to specify the icon image to be used for windows that have an unknown name and class.
>
> The client specific resources in the following table can be specified.

Client Specific Resources			
Name	**Class**	**Value Type**	**Default**
clientDecoration	ClientDecoration	string	all
clientFunctions	ClientFunctions	string	all
focusAutoRaise	FocusAutoRaise	T/F	varies
iconImage	IconImage	pathname	(image)
iconImageBackground	Background	color	icon background
iconImageBottomShadowColor	Foreground	color	icon bottom shadow
iconImageBottomShadowPixmap	BottomShadow-Pixmap	color	icon bottom shadow pixmap
iconImageForeground	Foreground	color	varies
iconImageTopShadowColor	Background	color	icon top shadow color
iconImageTopShadowPixmap	TopShadow-Pixmap	color	icon top shadow pixmap
matteBackground	Background	color	background
matteBottomShadowColor	Foreground	color	bottom shadow color
matteBottomShadowPixmap	BottomShadow-Pixmap	color	bottom shadow pixmap
matteForeground	Foreground	color	foreground
matteTopShadowColor	Background	color	top shadow color
matteTopShadowPixmap	TopShadow-Pixmap	color	top shadow pixmap
matteWidth	MatteWidth	pixels	0
maximumClientSize	MaximumClientSize	wxh	fill the screen

Name	Class	Value Type	Default
UseClientIcon	UseClientIcon	T/F	F
windowMenu	WindowMenu	string	**Default-Window-Menu**

clientDecoration (class **ClientDecoration**)

This resource controls the amount of window frame decoration. The resource is specified as a list of decorations to specify their inclusion in the frame. If a decoration is preceded by a minus sign, that decoration is excluded from the frame. The *sign* of the first item in the list determines the initial amount of decoration. If the sign of the first decoration is minus, **mwm** assumes all decorations are present and starts subtracting from that set. If the sign of the first decoration is plus (or not specified), then **mwm** starts with no decoration and builds up a list from the resource.

An application can also specify which decorations **mwm** should apply to its windows. If it does so, **mwm** applies only those decorations indicated by both the application and the **clientDecoration** resource. Otherwise, **mwm** applies the decorations indicated by the **clientDecoration** resource. For more information, see the description of **XmNmwmDecorations** on the **VendorShell(3X)** reference page.

Name	Description
all	Include all decorations (default value)
border	Window border
maximize	Maximize button (includes title bar)
minimize	Minimize button (includes title bar)
none	No decorations
resizeh	Border resize handles (includes border)
menu	Window menu button (includes title bar)
title	Title bar (includes border)

clientFunctions (class **ClientFunctions**)

This resource is used to indicate which **mwm** functions are applicable (or not applicable) to the client window. The value for the resource is a list of functions. If the first function in the list has a minus sign in front of it, then **mwm** starts with all functions and subtracts from that set. If the first function in the list has a plus sign in front of it, then **mwm** starts with no functions and builds up a list. Each function in the list must be preceded by the appropriate plus or minus sign and separated from the next function by a space.

An application can also specify which functions **mwm** should apply to its windows. If it does so, **mwm** applies only those functions indicated by both the application and the **clientFunctions** resource. Otherwise, **mwm** applies the functions indicated by the **clientFunctions** resource. For more information, see the description of **XmNmwmFunctions** on the **VendorShell(3X)** reference page.

The following table lists the functions available for this resource.

Name	Description
all	Include all functions (default value)
none	No functions
resize	f.resize
move	f.move
minimize	f.minimize
maximize	f.maximize
close	f.kill

focusAutoRaise (class **FocusAutoRaise**)
> When the value of this resource is True, clients are raised when they get the keyboard input focus. If the value is False, the stacking of windows on the display is not changed when a window gets the keyboard input focus. The default value is True when the **keyboardFocusPolicy** is explicit and False when the **keyboardFocusPolicy** is pointer.

iconImage (class **IconImage**)
> This resource can be used to specify an icon image for a client (for example, **Mwm*myclock*iconImage**). The resource value is a pathname for a bitmap file. The value of the (client specific) **useClientIcon** resource is used to determine whether or not user supplied icon images are used instead of client supplied icon images. The default value is to display a built-in window manager icon image.

iconImageBackground (class **Background**)
> This resource specifies the background color of the icon image that is displayed in the image part of an icon. The default value of this resource is the icon background color (whcih is specified by **Mwm*background** or **Mwm*icon*background**).

iconImageBottomShadowColor (class **Foreground**)
> This resource specifies the bottom shadow color of the icon image that is displayed in the image part of an icon. The default value of this

resource is the icon bottom shadow color (which is specified by **Mwm*icon*bottomShadowColor**).

iconImageBottomShadowPixmap (class **BottomShadowPixmap**)
This resource specifies the bottom shadow pixmap of the icon image that is displayed in the image part of an icon. The default value of this resource is the icon bottom shadow pixmap (which is specified by **Mwm*icon*bottomShadowPixmap**).

iconImageForeground (class **Foreground**)
This resource specifies the foreground color of the icon image that is displayed in the image part of an icon. The default value of this resource varies depending on the icon background.

iconImageTopShadowColor (class **Background**)
This resource specifies the top shadow color of the icon image that is displayed in the image part of an icon. The default value of this resource is the icon top shadow color (which is specified by **Mwm*icon*topShadowColor**).

iconImageTopShadowPixmap (class **TopShadowPixmap**)
This resource specifies the top shadow pixmap of the icon image that is displayed in the image part of an icon. The default value of this resource is the icon top shadow pixmap (which is specified by **Mwm*icon*topShadowPixmap**).

matteBackground (class **Background**)
This resource specifies the background color of the matte when **matteWidth** is positive. The default value of this resource is the client background color (which is specified by **Mwm*background** or **Mwm*client*background**).

matteBottomShadowColor (class **Foreground**)
This resource specifies the bottom shadow color of the matte, when **matteWidth** is positive. The default value of this resource is the client bottom shadow color (which is specified by **Mwm*bottomShadowColor** or **Mwm*client*bottomShadowColor**).

matteBottomShadowPixmap (class **BottomShadowPixmap**)
This resource specifies the bottom shadow pixmap of the matte, when **matteWidth** is positive. The default value is the client bottom shadow pixmap (which is specified by **Mwm*bottomShadowPixmap** or **Mwm*client*bottomShadowPixmap**).

matteForeground (class **Foreground**)
This resource specifies the foreground color of the matte, when **matteWidth** is positive. The default value of this resource is the client

foreground color (which is specified by **Mwm*foreground** or **Mwm*client*foreground**).

matteTopShadowColor (class **Background**)
This resource specifies the top shadow color of the matte, when **matteWidth** is positive. The default value of this resource is the client top shadow color (which is specified by **Mwm*topShadowColor** or **Mwm*client*topShadowColor**).

matteTopShadowPixmap (class **TopShadowPixmap**)
This resource specifies the top shadow pixmap of the matte, when **matteWidth** is positive. The default value of this resource is the client top shadow pixmap (which is specified by **Mwm*topShadowPixmap** or **Mwm*client*topShadowPixmap**).

matteWidth (class **MatteWidth**)
This resource specifies the width of the optional matte. The default value is 0 (zero), which effectively disables the matte.

maximumClientSize (class **MaximumClientSize**)
This is a size specification that indicates the client size to be used when an application is maximized. The resource value is specified as *width*x**height**. The width and height are interpreted in the units that the client uses (for example, for terminal emulators this is generally characters). If this resource is not specified, the maximum size from the WM_NORMAL_HINTS property is used if set. Otherwise the default value is the size where the client window with window management borders fills the screen. When the maximum client size is not determined by the **maximumClientSize** resource, the **maximumMaximumSize** resource value is used as a constraint on the maximum size.

useClientIcon (class **UseClientIcon**)
If the value given for this resource is True, a client-supplied icon image takes precedence over a user-supplied icon image. The default value is False, giving the user-supplied icon image higher precedence than the client-supplied icon image.

windowMenu (class **WindowMenu**)
This resource indicates the name of the menu pane that is posted when the window menu is popped up (usually by pressing button 1 on the window menu button on the client window frame). Menu panes are specified in the MWM resource description file. Window menus can be customized on a client class basis by specifying resources of the form

> **Mwm****client_name_or_class*****windowMenu** (see **Mwm Resource Description File Syntax**). The default value of this resource is **DefaultWindowMenu**.

Resource Description File

The MWM resource description file is a supplementary resource file that contains resource descriptions that are referred to by entries in the defaults files (**.Xdefaults, app-defaults/Mwm**). It contains descriptions of resources that are to be used by **mwm**, and that cannot be easily encoded in the defaults files (a bitmap file is an analogous type of resource description file). A particular **mwm** resource description file can be selected using the **configFile** resource.

The following types of resources can be described in the **mwm** resource description file:

Buttons   Window manager functions can be bound (associated) with button events.

Keys   Window manager functions can be bound (associated) with key press events.

Menus   Menu panes can be used for the window menu and other menus posted with key bindings and button bindings.

mwm Resource Description File Syntax

The **mwm** resource description file is a standard text file that contains items of information separated by blanks, tabs, and newline characters. Blank lines are ignored. Items or characters can be quoted to avoid special interpretation (for example, the comment character can be quoted to prevent it from being interpreted as the comment character). A quoted item can be contained in double quotes ("). Single characters can be quoted by preceding them with the \ (backslash). All text from an unquoted # (pound sign) to the end of the line is regarded as a comment and is not interpreted as part of a resource description. If ! (exclamation point) is the first character in a line, the line is regarded as a comment.

Window manager functions can be accessed with button and key bindings and with window manager menus. Functions are indicated as part of the specifications for button and key binding sets and menu panes. The function specification has the following syntax:

function = function_name [function_args]
function_name = window manager function
function_args = {quoted_item | unquoted_item}

The following functions are supported. If a function is specified that is not one of the supported functions, then it is interpreted by **mwm** as **f.nop**.

f.beep   This function causes a beep.

f.circle_down [**icon** | **window**]

This function causes the window or icon that is on the top of the window stack to be put on the bottom of the window stack (so that it no longer obscures any other window or icon). This function affects only those windows and icons that obscure other windows and icons, or that are obscured by other windows and icons. Secondary windows (that is, transient windows) are restacked with their associated primary window. Secondary windows always stay on top of the associated primary window and there can be no other primary windows between the secondary windows and their primary window. If an **icon** function argument is specified, the function applies only to icons. If a **window** function argument is specified, the function applies only to windows.

f.circle_up [**icon** | **window**]

This function raises the window or icon on the bottom of the window stack (so that it is not obscured by any other windows). This function affects only those windows and icons that obscure other windows and icons, or that are obscured by other windows and icons. Secondary windows (that is, transient windows) are restacked with their associated primary window. If an **icon** function argument is specified, the function applies only to icons. If a **window** function argument is specified, the function applies only to windows.

f.exec or **!**

This function causes *command* to be executed (using the value of the MWMSHELL environment variable if it is set, otherwise, the value of the SHELL environment variable if it is set, otherwise **/bin/sh**). The **!** notation can be used in place of the **f.exec** function name.

f.focus_color

This function sets the colormap focus to a client window. If this function is done in a root context, the default colormap (set up by the X Window System for the screen where MWM is running) is installed and there is no specific client window colormap focus. This function is treated as **f.nop** if **colormapFocusPolicy** is not explicit.

f.focus_key

This function sets the keyboard input focus to a client window or icon. This function is treated as **f.nop** if **keyboardFocusPolicy** is not explicit or the function is executed in a root context.

f.kill   This function is used to terminate a client. If the **WM_DELETE_WINDOW** protocol is set up, the client is sent a client message event, indicating that the client window should be deleted. If the **WM_SAVE_YOURSELF** protocol is set up, the client is sent a client message event, indicating that the client needs to prepare to be terminated. If the client does not have the **WM_DELETE_WINDOW** or **WM_SAVE_YOURSELF** protocol set up, this function causes a client's X connection to be terminated (usually resulting in termination of the client). Refer to the description of the **quitTimeout** resource and the **WM_PROTOCOLS** property.

f.lower [-*client*]

This function lowers a client window to the bottom of the window stack (where it obscures no other window). Secondary windows (that is, transient windows) are restacked with their associated primary windows. The *client* argument indicates the name or class of a client to lower. If the *client* argument is not specified, the context that the function was invoked in indicates the window or icon to lower.

f.maximize

This function causes a client window to be displayed with its maximum size.

f.menu   This function associates a cascading (pull-right) menu with a menu pane entry or a menu with a button or key binding. The *menu_name* function argument identifies the menu to be used.

f.minimize

This function causes a client window to be minimized (iconified). When a window is minimized when no icon box is used, its icon is placed on the bottom of the window stack (so that it obscures no other window). If an icon box is used, the client's icon changes to its iconified form inside the icon box. Secondary windows (that is, transient windows) are minimized with their associated primary windows. There is only one icon for a primary window and all its secondary windows.

f.move   This function causes a client window to be interactively moved.

f.next_cmap

This function installs the next colormap in the list of colormaps for the window with the colormap focus.

f.next_key [**icon** | **window** | **transient**]

This function sets the keyboard input focus to the next window/icon in the set of windows/icons managed by the window manager (the ordering of this set is based on the stacking of windows on the screen). This function is treated as **f.nop** if **keyboardFocusPolicy** is not explicit. The keyboard input focus is moved only to windows that do not have an associated secondary window that is application modal. If the **transient** argument is specified, transient (secondary) windows are traversed (otherwise, if only **window** is specified, traversal is done only to the window that last had focus in a transient group). If an **icon** function argument is specified, the function applies only to icons. If a **window** function argument is specified, the function applies only to windows.

f.nop This function does nothing.

f.normalize

This function causes a client window to be displayed with its normal size. Secondary windows (that is, transient windows) are placed in their normal state along with their associated primary window.

f.normalize_and_raise

This function causes the corresponding client window to be displayed with its normal size and raised to the top of the window stack. Secondary windows (that is, transient windows) are placed in their normal state along with their associated primary windows.

f.pack_icons

This function is used to re-layout icons (based on the layout policy being used) on the root window or in the icon box. In general this causes icons to be "packed" into the icon grid.

f.pass_keys

This function is used to enable/disable (toggle) processing of key bindings for window manager functions. When it disables key binding processing, all keys are passed on to the window with the keyboard input focus and no window manager functions are invoked. If the **f.pass_keys** function is invoked with a key binding to disable key-binding processing, the same key binding can be used to enable key-binding processing.

f.post_wmenu

This function is used to post the window menu. If a key is used to post the window menu and a window menu button is present, the window menu is automatically placed with its top-left corner at the bottom-left corner of the window menu button for the client window. If no window menu button is present, the window menu is placed at the top-left corner of the client window.

f.prev_cmap

This function installs the previous colormap in the list of colormaps for the window with the colormap focus.

f.prev_key [**icon** I **window** I **transient**]

> This function sets the keyboard input focus to the previous window/icon in the set of windows/icons managed by the window manager (the ordering of this set is based on the stacking of windows on the screen). This function is treated as **f.nop** if **keyboardFocusPolicy** is not explicit. The keyboard input focus is moved only to windows that do not have an associated secondary window that is application modal. If the **transient** argument is specified, transient (secondary) windows are traversed (otherwise, if only **window** is specified, traversal is done only to the last focused window in a transient group). If an **icon** function argument is specified, the function applies only to icons. If a **window** function argument is specified, the function applies only to windows.

f.quit_mwm

> This function terminates **mwm** (but *not* the X window system).

f.raise [*-client*]

> This function raises a client window to the top of the window stack (where it is obscured by no other window). Secondary windows (that is, transient windows) are restacked with their associated primary window. The *client* argument indicates the name or class of a client to raise. If the *client* argument is not specified, the context that the function was invoked in indicates the window or icon to raise.

f.raise_lower

> This function raises a client window to the top of the window stack if it is partially obscured by another window, otherwise it lowers the window to the bottom of the window stack. Secondary windows (that is, transient windows) are restacked with their associated primary window.

f.refresh   This function causes all windows to be redrawn.

f.refresh_win

> This function causes a client window to be redrawn.

f.resize   This function causes a client window to be interactively resized.

f.restore   This function restores the previous state of an icon's associated window. If a maximized window is iconified, then **f.restore** restores it to its maximized state. If a normal window is iconified, then **f.restore** restores it to its normalized state.

f.restart   This function causes **mwm** to be restarted (effectively terminated and re-executed).

f.send_msg *message_number*

This function sends a client message of the type **_MOTIF_WM_MESSAGES** with the *message_type* indicated by the *message_number* function argument. The client message is sent only if *message_number* is included in the client's **_MOTIF_WM_MESSAGES** property. A menu item label is grayed out if the menu item is used to do an **f.send_msg** of a message that is not included in the client's **_MOTIF_WM_MESSAGES** property.

f.separator

This function causes a menu separator to be put in the menu pane at the specified location (the label is ignored).

f.set_behavior

This function causes the window manager to restart with the default behavior (if a custom behavior is configured) or revert to the custom behavior. By default this is bound to **<Shift> <Ctrl> <Meta>** *<Key>***!**.

f.title   This function inserts a title in the menu pane at the specified location.

Each function may be constrained as to which resource types can specify the function (for example, menu pane) and also what context the function can be used in (for example, the function is done to the selected client window). Function contexts are

root   No client window or icon has been selected as an object for the function.

window   A client window has been selected as an object for the function. This includes the window's title bar and frame. Some functions are applied only when the window is in its normalized state (for example, **f.maximize**) or its maximized state (for example, **f.normalize**).

icon   An icon has been selected as an object for the function.

If a function's context has been specified as **icon|window** and the function is invoked in an icon box, the function applies to the icon box, not to the icons inside.

If a function is specified in a type of resource where it is not supported or is invoked in a context that does not apply, the function is treated as **f.nop**. The following table indicates the resource types and function contexts in which window manager functions apply.

Function	Contexts	Resources
f.beep	root, icon, window	button, key, menu
f.circle_down	root, icon, window	button, key, menu
f.circle_up	root, icon, window	button, key, menu
f.exec	root, icon, window	button, key, menu
f.focus_color	root, icon, window	button, key, menu
f.focus_key	root, icon, window	button, key, menu
f.kill	icon, window	button, key, menu
f.lower	icon, window	button, key, menu
f.maximize	icon, window(normal)	button, key, menu
f.menu	root, icon, window	button, key, menu
f.minimize	window	button, key, menu
f.move	icon, window	button, key, menu
f.next_cmap	root, icon, window	button, key, menu
f.next_key	root, icon, window	button, key, menu
f.nop	root, icon, window	button, key, menu
f.normalize	icon, window(maximized)	button, key, menu
f.normalize_and_raise	icon, window	button, key, menu
f.pack_icons	root, icon, window	button, key, menu
f.pass_keys	root, icon, window	button, key, menu
f.post_wmenu	root, icon, window	button, key
f.prev_cmap	root, icon, window	button, key, menu
f.prev_key	root, icon, window	button, key, menu
f.quit_mwm	root, icon, window	button, key, menu (root only)
f.raise	icon, window	button, key, menu
f.raise_lower	icon, window	button, key, menu
f.refresh	root, icon, window	button, key, menu
f.refresh_win	window	button, key, menu
f.resize	window	button, key, menu
f.restore	icon, window	button, key, menu
f.restart	root, icon, window	button, key, menu (root only)
f.send_msg	icon, window	button, key, menu

Function	Contexts	Resources
f.separator	root, icon, window	menu
f.set_behavior	root, icon, window	button, key, menu
f.title	root, icon, window	menu

Window Manager Event Specification

Events are indicated as part of the specifications for button and key-binding sets, and menu panes.

Button events have the following syntax:

button = [modifier_list]<button_event_name>
modifier_list = modifier_name {modifier_name}

All modifiers specified are interpreted as being exclusive (this means that only the specified modifiers can be present when the button event occurs). The following table indicates the values that can be used for *modifier_name*. The **<Alt>** key is frequently labeled **<Extend>** or **<Meta>**. **<Alt>** and **<Meta>** can be used interchangeably in event specification.

Modifier	Description
<Ctrl>	Control Key
<Shift>	Shift Key
<Alt>	Alt/Meta Key
<Meta>	Meta/Alt Key
<Lock>	Lock Key
<Mod1>	Modifier1
<Mod2>	Modifier2

Modifier	Description
Mod3	Modifier3
Mod4	Modifier4
Mod5	Modifier5

The following table indicates the values that can be used for *button_event_name*.

Button	Description
Btn1Down	Button 1 Press
Btn1Up	Button 1 Release
Btn1Click	Button 1 Press and Release
Btn1Click2	Button 1 Double-Click
Btn2Down	Button 2 Press
Btn2Up	Button 2 Release
Btn2Click	Button 2 Press and Release
Btn2Click2	Button 2 Double-Click
Btn3Down	Button 3 Press
Btn3Up	Button 3 Release
Btn3Click	Button 3 Press and Release
Btn3Click2	Button 3 Double-Click
Btn4Down	Button 4 Press
Btn4Up	Button 4 Release
Btn4Click	Button 4 Press and Release
Btn4Click2	Button 4 Double-Click
Btn5Down	Button 5 Press
Btn5Up	Button 5 Release
Btn5Click	Button 5 Press and Release
Btn5Click2	Button 5 Double-Click

Key events that are used by the window manager for menu mnemonics and for binding to window manager functions are single key presses; key releases are ignored. Key events have the following syntax:

key = [modifier_list]<key>key_name
modifier_list = modifier_name {modifier_name}

All modifiers specified are interpreted as being exclusive (this means that only the specified modifiers can be present when the key event occurs). Modifiers for keys are the same as those that apply to buttons. The *key_name* is an X11 keysym name. Keysym names can be found in the **keysymdef.h** file (remove the **XK_** prefix).

Button Bindings

The **buttonBindings** resource value is the name of a set of button bindings that are used to configure window manager behavior. A window manager function can be executed when a button press occurs with the pointer over a framed client window, an icon, or the root window. The context for indicating where the button press applies is also the context for invoking the window manager function when the button press is done (this is significant for functions that are context sensitive).

The button binding syntax is

Buttons *bindings_set_name*
{
  button   context   function
  button   context   function

         .

         .

   button   context   function
}

The syntax for the *context* specification is

context = *object*[| *context*]
object = **root** | **icon** | **window** | **title** | **frame** | **border** | **app**

The context specification indicates where the pointer must be for the button binding to be effective. For example, a context of **window** indicates that the pointer must be over a client window or window management frame for the button binding to be effective. The **frame** context is for the window management frame around a client window (including the border and titlebar), the **border** context is for the border part of the window management frame (not including the titlebar), the **title** context is for the title area of the window management frame, and the **app** context is for the application window (not including the window management frame).

If an **f.nop** function is specified for a button binding, the button binding is not done.

Key Bindings

The **keyBindings** resource value is the name of a set of key bindings that are used to configure window manager behavior. A window manager function can be executed when a particular key is pressed. The context in which the key binding applies is indicated in the key binding specification. The valid contexts are the same as those that apply to button bindings.

The key binding syntax is

Keys *bindings_set_name*
{
  key   context   function
  key   context   function

         .

         .

  key   context   function
}

If an **f.nop** function is specified for a key binding, the key binding is not done. If an **f.post_wmenu** or **f.menu** function is bound to a key, **mwm** will automatically use the same key for removing the menu from the screen after it has been popped up.

The *context* specification syntax is the same as for button bindings. For key bindings, the **frame**, **title**, **border**, and **app** contexts are equivalent to the **window** context. The context for a key event is the window or icon that has the keyboard input focus (**root** if no window or icon has the keyboard input focus).

Menu Panes

Menus can be popped up using the **f.post_wmenu** and **f.menu** window manager functions. The context for window manager functions that are done from a menu is **root**, **icon** or **window** depending on how the menu was popped up. In the case of the **window** menu or menus popped up with a key binding, the location of the keyboard input focus indicates the context. For menus popped up using a button binding, the context of the button binding is the context of the menu.

The menu pane specification syntax is

Menu *menu_name*
{
   label [*mnemonic*] [*accelerator*] *function*
   label [*mnemonic*] [*accelerator*] *function*

    .

    .

   label [*mnemonic*] [*accelerator*] *function*
}

Each line in the **Menu** specification identifies the label for a menu item and the function to be done if the menu item is selected. Optionally a menu button mnemonic and a menu button keyboard accelerator may be specified. Mnemonics are functional only when the menu is posted and keyboard traversal applies.

The *label* may be a string or a bitmap file. The label specification has the following syntax:

label = text | *bitmap_file*
bitmap_file = @file_name
text = quoted_item | *unquoted_item*

The string encoding for labels must be compatible with the menu font that is used. Labels are greyed out for menu items that do the **f.nop** function, an invalid function, or a function that does not apply in the current context.

A **mnemonic** specification has the following syntax

mnemonic = _character

The first matching *character* in the label is underlined. If there is no matching *character* in the label, no mnemonic is registered with the window manager for that label. Although the *character* must exactly match a character in the label, the mnemonic does not execute if any modifier (such as Shift) is pressed with the character key.

The **accelerator** specification is a key event specification with the same syntax as is used for key bindings to window manager functions.

Environment

        mwm uses the environment variable HOME for specifying the user's home directory.

        mwm uses the environment variable LANG for specifying the user's choice of language for the **mwm** message catalog and the **mwm** resource description file.

        mwm uses the environment variables XFILESEARCHPATH, XUSERFILESEARCHPATH, XAPPLRESDIR, XENVIRONMENT, LANG, and HOME in determining search paths for resource defaults files.

        mwm reads the **$HOME/.motifbind** file if it exists to install a virtual key bindings property on the root window.

        mwm uses the environment variable MWMSHELL (or SHELL, if MWMSHELL is not set), for specifying the shell to use when executing commands with the **f.exec** function.

Files   **$HOME/Mwm**
                    $HOME/.Xdefaults
                    $HOME/$LANG/.mwmrc
                    $HOME/.mwmrc
                    $HOME/.motifbind

Related Information
        VendorShell(3X), **X(1)**, and **XmInstallImage(3X)**.

ApplicationShell—The ApplicationShell widget class

AES Support Level

Full-use

Synopsis

#include <Xm/Xm.h>
#include <X11/Shell.h>

Description

ApplicationShell is used as the main top-level window for an application. An application should have more than one ApplicationShell only if it implements multiple logical applications.

Classes

ApplicationShell inherits behavior and resources from **Core**, **Composite**, **Shell**, **WMShell**, **VendorShell**, and **TopLevelShell**.

The class pointer is **applicationShellWidgetClass**.

The class name is **ApplicationShell**.

New Resources

The following table defines a set of widget resources used by the programmer to specify data. The programmer can also set the resource values for the inherited classes to set attributes for this widget. To reference a resource by name or by class in a **.Xdefaults** file, remove the **XmN** or **XmC** prefix and use the remaining letters. To specify one of the defined values for a resource in a **.Xdefaults** file, remove the **Xm** prefix and use the remaining letters (in either lowercase or uppercase, but include any underscores between words). The codes in the access column indicate if the given resource can be set at creation time (C), set by using **XtSetValues** (S), retrieved by using **XtGetValues** (G), or is not applicable (N/A).

ApplicationShell Resource Set		
Name	**Default**	**Access**
Class	**Type**	
XmNargc	0	CSG
XmCArgc	int	
XmNargv	NULL	CSG
XmCArgv	String *	

XmNargc Specifies the number of arguments given in the **XmNargv** resource. The function **XtInitialize** sets this resource on the shell widget instance it creates by using its parameters as the values.

XmNargv Specifies the argument list required by a session manager to restart the application if it is killed. This list should be updated at appropriate points by the application if a new state has been reached that can be directly restarted. The function **XtInitialize** sets this resource on the shell widget instance it creates by using its parameters as the values.

Inherited Resources

ApplicationShell inherits behavior and resources from the following superclasses. For a complete description of each resource, refer to the reference page for that superclass.

TopLevelShell Resource Set		
Name	**Default**	**Access**
Class	**Type**	
XmNiconic	False	CSG
XmCIconic	Boolean	
XmNiconName	NULL	CSG
XmCIconName	String	
XmNiconNameEncoding	dynamic	CSG
XmCIconNameEncoding	Atom	

VendorShell Resource Set		
Name **Class**	**Default** **Type**	**Access**
XmNbuttonFontList XmCButtonFontList	dynamic XmFontList	CSG
XmNdefaultFontList XmCDefaultFontList	dynamic XmFontList	CG
XmNdeleteResponse XmCDeleteResponse	XmDESTROY unsigned char	CSG
XmNkeyboardFocusPolicy XmCKeyboardFocusPolicy	XmEXPLICIT unsigned char	CSG
XmNlabelFontList XmCLabelFontList	dynamic XmFontList	CSG
XmNmwmDecorations XmCMwmDecorations	-1 int	CSG
XmNmwmFunctions XmCMwmFunctions	-1 int	CSG
XmNmwmInputMode XmCMwmInputMode	-1 int	CSG
XmNmwmMenu XmCMwmMenu	NULL String	CSG
XmNtextFontList XmCTextFontList	dynamic XmFontList	CSG

WMShell Resource Set		
Name	**Default**	**Access**
Class	**Type**	
XmNbaseHeight	XtUnspecifiedShellInt	CSG
XmCBaseHeight	int	
XmNbaseWidth	XtUnspecifiedShellInt	CSG
XmCBaseWidth	int	
XmNheightInc	XtUnspecifiedShellInt	CSG
XmCHeightInc	int	
XmNiconMask	NULL	CSG
XmCIconMask	Pixmap	
XmNiconPixmap	NULL	CSG
XmCIconPixmap	Pixmap	
XmNiconWindow	NULL	CSG
XmCIconWindow	Window	
XmNiconX	-1	CSG
XmCIconX	int	
XmNiconY	-1	CSG
XmCIconY	int	
XmNinitialState	NormalState	CSG
XmCInitialState	int	
XmNinput	True	CSG
XmCInput	Boolean	
XmNmaxAspectX	XtUnspecifiedShellInt	CSG
XmCMaxAspectX	int	
XmNmaxAspectY	XtUnspecifiedShellInt	CSG
XmCMaxAspectY	int	
XmNmaxHeight	XtUnspecifiedShellInt	CSG
XmCMaxHeight	int	
XmNmaxWidth	XtUnspecifiedShellInt	CSG
XmCMaxWidth	int	
XmNminAspectX	XtUnspecifiedShellInt	CSG
XmCMinAspectX	int	

Name
    Class
	Default
	    Type
		Access

XmNminAspectY
    XmCMinAspectY
	XtUnspecifiedShellInt
	    int
		CSG

XmNminHeight
    XmCMinHeight
	XtUnspecifiedShellInt
	    int
		CSG

XmNminWidth
    XmCMinWidth
	XtUnspecifiedShellInt
	    int
		CSG

XmNtitle
    XmCTitle
	dynamic
	    String
		CSG

XmNtitleEncoding
    XmCTitleEncoding
	dynamic
	    Atom
		CSG

XmNtransient
    XmCTransient
	False
	    Boolean
		CSG

XmNwaitForWm
    XmCWaitForWm
	True
	    Boolean
		CSG

XmNwidthInc
    XmCWidthInc
	XtUnspecifiedShellInt
	    int
		CSG

XmNwindowGroup
    XmCWindowGroup
	dynamic
	    Window
		CSG

XmNwinGravity
    XmCWinGravity
	dynamic
	    int
		CSG

XmNwmTimeout
    XmCWmTimeout
	5000 ms
	    int
		CSG

Shell Resource Set

Name	Default	Access
Class	Type	
XmNallowShellResize	False	CG
XmCAllowShellResize	Boolean	
XmNcreatePopupChildProc	NULL	CSG
XmCCreatePopupChildProc	XtCreatePopupChildProc	
XmNgeometry	NULL	CSG
XmCGeometry	String	
XmNoverrideRedirect	False	CSG
XmCOverrideRedirect	Boolean	
XmNpopdownCallback	NULL	C
XmCCallback	XtCallbackList	
XmNpopupCallback	NULL	C
XmCCallback	XtCallbackList	
XmNsaveUnder	False	CSG
XmCSaveUnder	Boolean	
XmNvisual	CopyFromParent	CSG
XmCVisual	Visual *	

Composite Resource Set

Name	Default	Access
Class	Type	
XmNchildren	NULL	G
XmCReadOnly	WidgetList	
XmNinsertPosition	NULL	CSG
XmCInsertPosition	XtOrderProc	
XmNnumChildren	0	G
XmCReadOnly	Cardinal	

Core Resource Set		
Name	**Default**	**Access**
Class	**Type**	
XmNaccelerators	dynamic	CSG
XmCAccelerators	XtAccelerators	
XmNancestorSensitive	dynamic	G
XmCSensitive	Boolean	
XmNbackground	dynamic	CSG
XmCBackground	Pixel	
XmNbackgroundPixmap	XmUNSPECIFIED_PIXMAP	CSG
XmCPixmap	Pixmap	
XmNborderColor	XtDefaultForeground	CSG
XmCBorderColor	Pixel	
XmNborderPixmap	XmUNSPECIFIED_PIXMAP	CSG
XmCPixmap	Pixmap	
XmNborderWidth	0	CSG
XmCBorderWidth	Dimension	
XmNcolormap	dynamic	CG
XmCColormap	Colormap	
XmNdepth	dynamic	CG
XmCDepth	int	
XmNdestroyCallback	NULL	C
XmCCallback	XtCallbackList	
XmNheight	dynamic	CSG
XmCHeight	Dimension	
XmNinitialResourcesPersistent	True	C
XmCInitialResourcesPersistent	Boolean	
XmNmappedWhenManaged	True	CSG
XmCMappedWhenManaged	Boolean	
XmNscreen	dynamic	CG
XmCScreen	Screen *	
XmNsensitive	True	CSG
XmCSensitive	Boolean	

Name	Default	Access
Class	Type	
XmNtranslations	dynamic	CSG
XmCTranslations	XtTranslations	
XmNwidth	dynamic	CSG
XmCWidth	Dimension	
XmNx	0	CSG
XmCPosition	Position	
XmNy	0	CSG
XmCPosition	Position	

Related Information

Composite(3X), **Core(3X)**, **Shell(3X)**, **WMShell(3X)**, **VendorShell(3X)**, and **TopLevelShell(3X)**.

Composite—The Composite widget class

AES Support Level

Full-use

Synopsis   #include <Xm/Xm.h>

Description

Composite widgets are intended to be containers for other widgets and can have an arbitrary number of children. Their responsibilities (implemented either directly by the widget class or indirectly by Intrinsics functions) include:

- Overall management of children from creation to destruction.

- Destruction of descendants when the composite widget is destroyed.

- Physical arrangement (geometry management) of a displayable subset of managed children.

- Mapping and unmapping of a subset of the managed children. Instances of composite widgets need to specify the order in which their children are kept. For example, an application may want a set of command buttons in some logical order grouped by function, and it may want buttons that represent filenames to be kept in alphabetical order.

Classes

Composite inherits behavior and resources from **Core**.

The class pointer is **compositeWidgetClass**.

The class name is **Composite**.

New Resources

The following table defines a set of widget resources used by the programmer to specify data. The programmer can also set the resource values for the inherited classes to set attributes for this widget. To reference a resource by name or by class in a **.Xdefaults** file, remove the **XmN** or **XmC** prefix and use the remaining letters. To specify one of the defined values for a resource in a .Xdefaults file, remove the **Xm** prefix and use the remaining letters (in either lowercase or uppercase, but include any underscores between words). The codes in the access column indicate if the given resource can be set at creation time (C), set by using **XtSetValues** (S), retrieved by using **XtGetValues** (G), or is not applicable (N/A).

Composite Resource Set		
Name	**Default**	**Access**
Class	**Type**	
XmNchildren	NULL	G
XmCReadOnly	WidgetList	
XmNinsertPosition	NULL	CSG
XmCInsertPosition	XtOrderProc	
XmNnumChildren	0	G
XmCReadOnly	Cardinal	

XmNchildren
>A read-only list of the children of the widget.

XmNinsertPosition
>Points to the **XtOrderProc** function described below.

XmNnumChildren
>A read-only resource specifying the length of the list of children in **XmNchildren**.

The following procedure pointer in a composite widget instance is of type **XtOrderProc**:

Cardinal (* XtOrderProc) (*widget*)
>**Widget**   *w*;

w   Specifies the widget.

Composite widgets that allow clients to order their children (usually homogeneous boxes) can call their widget instance's **insert_position** procedure from the class's **insert_child** procedure to determine where a new child should go in its children array. Thus, a client of a composite class can apply different sorting criteria to widget instances of the class, passing in a different **insert_position** procedure when it creates each composite widget instance.

The return value of the **insert_position** procedure indicates how many children should go before the widget. A value of 0 (zero) indicates that the widget should go before all other children; returning **num_children** indicates that it should go after all other children. The default **insert_position** function returns **num_children** and can be overridden by a specific composite widget's resource list or by the argument list provided when the composite widget is created.

Inherited Resources

Composite inherits behavior and resources from the superclass described in the following table. For a complete description of each resource, refer to the reference page for that superclass.

Core Resource Set		

Name
   Class
	Default
	       Type
		Access

XmNaccelerators
   XmCAccelerators
	dynamic
	       XtAccelerators
		CSG

XmNancestorSensitive
   XmCSensitive
	dynamic
	       Boolean
		G

XmNbackground
   XmCBackground
	dynamic
	       Pixel
		CSG

XmNbackgroundPixmap
   XmCPixmap
	XmUNSPECIFIED_PIXMAP
	       Pixmap
		CSG

XmNborderColor
   XmCBorderColor
	XtDefaultForeground
	       Pixel
		CSG

XmNborderPixmap
   XmCPixmap
	XmUNSPECIFIED_PIXMAP
	       Pixmap
		CSG

XmNborderWidth
   XmCBorderWidth
	1
	       Dimension
		CSG

XmNcolormap
   XmCColormap
	dynamic
	       Colormap
		CG

XmNdepth
   XmCDepth
	dynamic
	       int
		CG

XmNdestroyCallback
   XmCCallback
	NULL
	       XtCallbackList
		C

XmNheight
   XmCHeight
	dynamic
	       Dimension
		CSG

XmNinitialResourcesPersistent
   XmCInitialResourcesPersistent
	True
	       Boolean
		C

XmNmappedWhenManaged
   XmCMappedWhenManaged
	True
	       Boolean
		CSG

XmNscreen
   XmCScreen
	dynamic
	       Screen *
		CG

XmNsensitive
   XmCSensitive
	True
	       Boolean
		CSG

Composite(3X)

Name	Default	Access
Class	Type	
XmNtranslations	dynamic	CSG
XmCTranslations	XtTranslations	
XmNwidth	dynamic	CSG
XmCWidth	Dimension	
XmNx	0	CSG
XmCPosition	Position	
XmNy	0	CSG
XmCPosition	Position	

Related Information

Core(3X).

Constraint—The Constraint widget class

AES Support Level

Full-use

Synopsis

#include <Xm/Xm.h>

Description

Constraint widgets maintain additional state data for each child. For example, client-defined constraints on the child's geometry may be specified.

When a constrained composite widget defines constraint resources, all of that widget's children inherit all of those resources as their own. These constraint resources are set and read just the same as any other resources defined for the child. This resource inheritance extends exactly one generation down, which means only the first-generation children of a constrained composite widget inherit the parent widget's constraint resources.

Because constraint resources are defined by the parent widgets and not the children, the child widgets never directly use the constraint resource data. Instead, the parents use constraint resource data to attach child-specific data to children.

Classes

Constraint inherits behavior and resources from **Composite** and **Core**.

The class pointer is **constraintWidgetClass**.

The class name is **Constraint**.

New Resources

Constraint defines no new resources.

Inherited Resources

Constraint inherits behavior and resources from **Composite** and **Core**. The following table defines a set of widget resources used by the programmer to specify data. The programmer can also set the resource values for the inherited classes to set attributes for this widget. To reference a resource by name or by class in a **.Xdefaults** file, remove the **XmN** or **XmC** prefix and use the remaining letters. To specify one of the defined values for a resource in a **.Xdefaults** file, remove the **Xm** prefix and use the remaining letters (in either lowercase or uppercase, but include any underscores between words). The codes in the access column indicate if the given resource can be set at creation time (C), set by using **XtSetValues** (S), retrieved by using **XtGetValues** (G), or is not applicable (N/A).

Core Resource Set		
Name	**Default**	**Access**
Class	**Type**	
XmNaccelerators	dynamic	CSG
XmCAccelerators	XtAccelerators	
XmNancestorSensitive	dynamic	G
XmCSensitive	Boolean	
XmNbackground	dynamic	CSG
XmCBackground	Pixel	
XmNbackgroundPixmap	XmUNSPECIFIED_PIXMAP	CSG
XmCPixmap	Pixmap	
XmNborderColor	XtDefaultForeground	CSG
XmCBorderColor	Pixel	
XmNborderPixmap	XmUNSPECIFIED_PIXMAP	CSG
XmCPixmap	Pixmap	
XmNborderWidth	1	CSG
XmCBorderWidth	Dimension	
XmNcolormap	dynamic	CG
XmCColormap	Colormap	
XmNdepth	dynamic	CG
XmCDepth	int	
XmNdestroyCallback	NULL	C
XmCCallback	XtCallbackList	
XmNheight	dynamic	CSG
XmCHeight	Dimension	
XmNinitialResourcesPersistent	True	C
XmCInitialResourcesPersistent	Boolean	
XmNmappedWhenManaged	True	CSG
XmCMappedWhenManaged	Boolean	
XmNscreen	dynamic	CG
XmCScreen	Screen *	
XmNsensitive	True	CSG
XmCSensitive	Boolean	

Name	Default	Access
Class	Type	
XmNtranslations	dynamic	CSG
XmCTranslations	XtTranslations	
XmNwidth	dynamic	CSG
XmCWidth	Dimension	
XmNx	0	CSG
XmCPosition	Position	
XmNy	0	CSG
XmCPosition	Position	

Related Information

Composite(3X) and **Core(3X)**.

Core—The Core widget class

AES Support Level

Full-use

Synopsis

#include <Xm/Xm.h>

Description

Core is the Xt Intrinsic base class for windowed widgets. The **Object** and **RectObj** classes provide support for windowless widgets.

Classes

All widgets are built from **Core**.

The class pointer is **widgetClass**.

The class name is **Core**.

New Resources

The following table defines a set of widget resources used by the programmer to specify data. The programmer can also set the resource values for the inherited classes to set attributes for this widget. To reference a resource by name or by class in a **.Xdefaults** file, remove the **XmN** or **XmC** prefix and use the remaining letters. To specify one of the defined values for a resource in a **.Xdefaults** file, remove the **Xm** prefix and use the remaining letters (in either lowercase or uppercase, but include any underscores between words). The codes in the access column indicate if the given resource can be set at creation time (C), set by using **XtSetValues** (S), retrieved by using **XtGetValues** (G), or is not applicable (N/A).

Core Resource Set		
Name	**Default**	**Access**
Class	**Type**	
XmNaccelerators	dynamic	CSG
XmCAccelerators	XtAccelerators	
XmNancestorSensitive	dynamic	G
XmCSensitive	Boolean	
XmNbackground	dynamic	CSG
XmCBackground	Pixel	
XmNbackgroundPixmap	XmUNSPECIFIED_PIXMAP	CSG
XmCPixmap	Pixmap	
XmNborderColor	XtDefaultForeground	CSG
XmCBorderColor	Pixel	
XmNborderPixmap	XmUNSPECIFIED_PIXMAP	CSG
XmCPixmap	Pixmap	
XmNborderWidth	1	CSG
XmCBorderWidth	Dimension	
XmNcolormap	dynamic	CG
XmCColormap	Colormap	
XmNdepth	dynamic	CG
XmCDepth	int	
XmNdestroyCallback	NULL	C
XmCCallback	XtCallbackList	
XmNheight	dynamic	CSG
XmCHeight	Dimension	
XmNinitialResourcesPersistent	True	C
XmCInitialResourcesPersistent	Boolean	
XmNmappedWhenManaged	True	CSG
XmCMappedWhenManaged	Boolean	
XmNscreen	dynamic	CG
XmCScreen	Screen *	
XmNsensitive	True	CSG
XmCSensitive	Boolean	

Name	Default	Access
Class	Type	
XmNtranslations	dynamic	CSG
XmCTranslations	XtTranslations	
XmNwidth	dynamic	CSG
XmCWidth	Dimension	
XmNx	0	CSG
XmCPosition	Position	
XmNy	0	CSG
XmCPosition	Position	

XmNaccelerators

Specifies a translation table that is bound with its actions in the context of a particular widget. The accelerator table can then be installed on some destination widget.

XmNancestorSensitive

Specifies whether the immediate parent of the widget receives input events. Use the function **XtSetSensitive** to change the argument to preserve data integrity (see **XmNsensitive**). For shells, the default is copied from the parent's **XmNancestorSensitive** resource if there is a parent; otherwise, it is True. For other widgets, the default is the bitwise AND of the parent's **XmNsensitive** and **XmNancestorSensitive** resources.

XmNbackground

Specifies the background color for the widget.

XmNbackgroundPixmap

Specifies a pixmap for tiling the background. The first tile is placed at the upper left corner of the widget's window.

XmNborderColor

Specifies the color of the border in a pixel value.

XmNborderPixmap

Specifies a pixmap to be used for tiling the border. The first tile is placed at the upper left corner of the border.

XmNborderWidth

Specifies the width of the border that surrounds the widget's window on all four sides. The width is specified in pixels. A width of 0 (zero) means that no border shows.

XmNcolormap
> Specifies the colormap that is used for conversions to the type **Pixel** for this widget instance. When this resource is changed, previously generated pixel values are not affected, but newly generated values are in the new colormap. For shells without parents, the default is the default colormap of the widget's screen. Otherwise, the default is copied from the parent.

XmNdepth
> Specifies the number of bits that can be used for each pixel in the widget's window. Applications should not change or set the value of this resource as it is set by the Xt Intrinsics when the widget is created. For shells without parents, the default is the default depth of the widget's screen. Otherwise, the default is copied from the parent.

XmNdestroyCallback
> Specifies a list of callbacks that is called when the widget is destroyed.

XmNheight
> Specifies the inside height (excluding the border) of the widget's window.

XmNinitialResourcesPersistent
> Specifies whether or not resources are reference counted. If the value is True when the widget is created, the resources referenced by the widget are not reference counted, regardless of how the resource type converter is registered. An application that expects to destroy the widget and wants to have resources deallocated should specify a value of False. The default is True, implying an assumption that the widget will not be destroyed during the life of the application.

XmNmappedWhenManaged
> If this resource is set to True, it maps the widget (makes it visible) as soon as it is both realized and managed. If this resource is set to False, the client is responsible for mapping and unmapping the widget. If the value is changed from True to False after the widget has been realized and managed, the widget is unmapped.

XmNscreen
> Specifies the screen on which a widget instance resides. It is read only. When the Toolkit is initialized, the top-level widget obtains its default value from the default screen of the display. Otherwise, the default is copied from the parent.

XmNsensitive
> Determines whether a widget receives input events. If a widget is sensitive, the Xt Intrinsics' Event Manager dispatches to the widget all keyboard, mouse button, motion, window enter/leave, and focus events. Insensitive widgets do not receive these events. Use the function **XtSetSensitive** to change the sensitivity argument. Using **XtSetSensitive** ensures that if a parent widget has **XmNsensitive** set to False, the ancestor-sensitive flag of all its children is appropriately set.

XmNtranslations
> Points to a translations list. A translations list is a list of events and actions that are to be performed when the events occur.

XmNwidth
> Specifies the inside width (excluding the border) of the widget's window.

XmNx
> Specifies the x-coordinate of the upper left outside corner of the widget's window. The value is relative to the upper left inside corner of the parent window.

XmNy
> Specifies the y-coordinate of the upper left outside corner of the widget's window. The value is relative to the upper left inside corner of the parent window.

Related Information

Object(3X) and **RectObj(3X)**.

MrmCloseHierarchy—Closes a UID hierarchy

AES Support Level

Full-use

Synopsis

#include <Mrm/MrmPublic.h>

Cardinal MrmCloseHierarchy(*hierarchy_id***)**
MrmHierarchy*hierarchy_id***;**

Description

The **MrmCloseHierarchy** function closes a UID hierarchy previously opened by **MrmOpenHierarchyPerDisplay**. All files associated with the hierarchy are closed by the Motif Resource Manager (MRM) and all associated memory is returned.

hierarchy_id Specifies the ID of a previously opened UID hierarchy. The *hierarchy_id* was returned in a previous call to **MrmOpenHierarchyPerDisplay**.

Return Value

This function returns one of the following status return constants:

MrmSUCCESS
The function executed successfully.

MrmBAD_HIERARCHY
The hierarchy ID was invalid.

MrmFAILURE
The function failed.

Related Information

MrmOpenHierarchyPerDisplay(3X).

MrmFetchColorLiteral—Fetches a named color literal from a UID file

AES Support Level

Full-use

Synopsis

#include <Mrm/MrmPublic.h>

int MrmFetchColorLiteral(*hierarchy_id, index, display, colormap_id, pixel*)
    MrmHierarchy *hierarchy_id*;
    String   *index*;
    Display   **pixmap* *display*;
    Colormap   *colormap_id*;
    Pixel   **pixel*;

Description

The **MrmFetchColorLiteral** function fetches a named color literal from a UID file, and converts the color literal to a pixel color value.

hierarchy_id   Specifies the ID of the UID hierarchy that contains the specified literal. The value of *hierarchy_id* was returned in a previous call to **MrmOpenHierarchyPerDisplay**.

index   Specifies the UIL name of the color literal to fetch. You must define this name in UIL as an exported value.

display   Specifies the display used for the pixmap. The *display* argument specifies the connection to the X server. For more information on the **Display** structure, see the Xlib function **XOpenDisplay**.

colormap_id   Specifies the ID of the color map. If *colormap_id* is NULL, the default color map is used.

pixel   Returns the ID of the color literal.

Return Value

This function returns one of the following status return constants:

MrmSUCCESS
    The function executed successfully.

MrmBAD_HIERARCHY
    The hierarchy ID was invalid.

MrmNOT_FOUND
> The color literal was not found in the UIL file.

MrmWRONG_TYPE
> The caller tried to fetch a literal of a type not supported by this function.

MrmFAILURE
> The function failed.

Related Information

MrmOpenHierarchyPerDisplay(3X), **MrmFetchIconLiteral(3X)**, **MrmFetchLiteral(3X)**, and **XOpenDisplay(3X)**.

MrmFetchIconLiteral—Fetches an icon literal from a hierarchy

AES Support Level

Full-use

Synopsis

#include <Mrm/MrmPublic.h>

int MrmFetchIconLiteral(*hierarchy_id, index, screen, display, fgpix, bgpix, pixmap*)

MrmHierarchy	*hierarchy_id*;
String	*index*;
Screen	**screen*;
Display	**display*;
Pixel	*fgpix*;
Pixel	*bgpix*;
Pixmap	**pixmap*;

Description

The **MrmFetchIconLiteral** function fetches an icon literal from an MRM hierarchy and converts the icon literal to an X pixmap.

hierarchy_id Specifies the ID of the UID hierarchy that contains the specified icon literal. The *hierarchy_id* was returned in a previous call to **MrmOpenHierarchyPerDisplay**.

index Specifies the UIL name of the icon literal to fetch.

screen Specifies the screen used for the pixmap. The *screen* argument specifies a pointer to the Xlib structure **Screen**, which contains the information about that screen and is linked to the **Display** structure. For more information on the **Display** and **Screen** structures, see the Xlib function **XOpenDisplay** and the associated screen information macros.

display Specifies the display used for the pixmap. The *display* argument specifies the connection to the X server. For more information on the **Display** structure, see the Xlib function **XOpenDisplay**.

fgpix Specifies the foreground color for the pixmap.

bgpix Specifies the background color for the pixmap.

pixmap Returns the resulting X pixmap value.

Return Value

2–67

This function returns one of the following status return constants:

MrmSUCCESS

> The function executed successfully.

MrmBAD_HIERARCHY

> The hierarchy ID was invalid.

MrmNOT_FOUND

> The icon literal was not found in the hierarchy.

MrmWRONG_TYPE

> The caller tried to fetch a literal of a type not supported by this function.

MrmFAILURE

> The function failed.

Related Information

MrmOpenHierarchyPerDisplay(3X), **MrmFetchLiteral(3X)**, **MrmFetchColorLiteral(3X)**, and **XOpenDisplay(3X)**.

MrmFetchLiteral—Fetches a literal from a UID file

AES Support Level

Full-use

Synopsis

#include <Mrm/MrmPublic.h>

int **MrmFetchLiteral**(*hierarchy_id, index, display, value, type*)
    MrmHierarchy *hierarchy_id*;
    String   *index*;
    Display   **display*;
    XtPointer   **value*;
    MrmCode   **type*;

Description

The **MrmFetchLiteral** function reads and returns the value and type of a literal (named value) that is stored as a public resource in a single UID file. This function returns a pointer to the value of the literal. For example, an integer is always returned as a pointer to an integer, and a string is always returned as a pointer to a string.

Applications should not use **MrmFetchLiteral** for fetching icon or color literals. If this is attempted, **MrmFetchLiteral** returns an error.

hierarchy_id   Specifies the ID of the UID hierarchy that contains the specified literal. The value of *hierarchy_id* was returned in a previous call to **MrmOpenHierarchyPerDisplay**.

index   Specifies the UIL name of the literal (pixmap) to fetch. You must define this name in UIL as an exported value.

display   Specifies the display used for the pixmap. The *display* argument specifies the connection to the X server. For more information on the **Display** structure, see the Xlib function **XOpenDisplay**.

value   Returns the ID of the named literal's value.

type   Returns the named literal's data type. Types are defined in the include file **Mrm/MrmPublic.h**.

Return Value

This function returns one of the following status return constants:

MrmSUCCESS

> The function executed successfully.

MrmBAD_HIERARCHY

> The hierarchy ID was invalid.

MrmNOT_FOUND

> The literal was not found in the UIL file.

MrmWRONG_TYPE

> The caller tried to fetch a literal of a type not supported by this function.

MrmFAILURE

> The function failed.

Related Information

MrmOpenHierarchyPerDisplay(3X), **MrmFetchIconLiteral(3X)**, **MrmFetchColorLiteral(3X)**, and **XOpenDisplay(3X)**.

MrmFetchSetValues(3X)

MrmFetchSetValues—Fetches the values to be set from literals stored in UID files

AES Support Level

Full-use

Synopsis

#include <Mrm/MrmPublic.h>

Cardinal MrmFetchSetValues(*hierarchy_id, widget, args, num_args*)
    MrmHierarchy *hierarchy_id*;
    Widget   *widget*;
    ArgList   *args*;
    Cardinal   *num_args*;

Description

The **MrmFetchSetValues** function is similar to **XtSetValues**, except that the values to be set are defined by the UIL named values that are stored in the UID hierarchy. **MrmFetchSetValues** fetches the values to be set from literals stored in UID files.

hierarchy_id   Specifies the ID of the UID hierarchy that contains the specified literal. The value of *hierarchy_id* was returned in a previous call to **MrmOpenHierarchyPerDisplay**.

widget   Specifies the widget that is modified.

args   Specifies an argument list that identifies the widget arguments to be modified as well as the index (UIL name) of the literal that defines the value for that argument. The name part of each argument (*args[n].name*) must begin with the string **XmN** followed by the name that uniquely identifies this attribute tag. For example, **XmNwidth** is the attribute name associated with the core argument *width*. The value part (*args[n].value*) must be a string that gives the index (UIL name) of the literal. You must define all literals in UIL as exported values.

num_args   Specifies the number of entries in *args*.

This function sets the values on a widget, evaluating the values as public literal resource references resolvable from a UID hierarchy. Each literal is fetched from the hierarchy, and its value is modified and converted as required. This value is then placed in the argument list and used as the actual value for an **XtSetValues** call. **MrmFetchSetValues** allows a widget to be modified after creation using UID file values the same way creation values are used in **MrmFetchWidget**.

As in **MrmFetchWidget**, each argument whose value can be evaluated from the UID hierarchy is set in the widget. Values that are not found or values in which conversion errors occur are not modified.

Each entry in the argument list identifies an argument to be modified in the widget. The name part identifies the tag, which begins with **XmN**. The value part must be a string whose value is the index of the literal. Thus, the following code would modify the label resource of the widget to have the value of the literal accessed by the index **OK_button_label** in the hierarchy:

```
args[n].name = XmNlabel;
args[n].value = "OK_button_label";
```

Return Value

This function returns one of the following status return constants:

MrmSUCCESS
> The function executed successfully.

MrmPARTIAL_SUCCESS
> At least one literal was successfully fetched.

MrmBAD_HIERARCHY
> The hierarchy ID was invalid.

MrmFAILURE
> The function failed.

Related Information

MrmOpenHierarchyPerDisplay(3X), XtSetValues(3X).

MrmFetchWidget—Fetches and creates an indexed (UIL named) application widgets and its children

AES Support Level

Full-use

Synopsis

#include <Mrm/MrmPublic.h>

Cardinal MrmFetchWidget(*hierarchy_id, index, parent_widget, widget, class***)**
    MrmHierarchy *hierarchy_id*;
    String   *index*;
    Widget   *parent_widget*;
    Widget   **widget*;
    MrmType   **class*;

Description

The **MrmFetchWidget** function fetches and creates an indexed application widget and its children. The indexed application widget is any widget that is named in UIL. In fetch operations, the fetched widget's subtree is also fetched and created. This widget must not appear as the child of a widget within its own subtree. **MrmFetchWidget** does not execute **XtManageChild** for the newly created widget.

hierarchy_id   Specifies the ID of the **UID** hierarchy that contains the interface definition. The value of *hierarchy_id* was returned in a previous call to **MrmOpenHierarchyPerDisplay**.

index   Specifies the UIL name of the widget to fetch.

parent_widget
           Specifies the parent widget ID.

widget   Returns the widget ID of the created widget.

class   Returns the class code identifying MRM's widget class. The widget class code for the main window widget, for example, is **MRMwcMainWindow**. Literals identifying MRM widget class codes are defined in **Mrm.h**.

An application can fetch any named widget in the **UID** hierarchy using **MrmFetchWidget**. **MrmFetchWidget** can be called at any time to fetch a widget that was not fetched at application startup. **MrmFetchWidget** can be used to defer fetching pop-up widgets until they are first referenced (presumably in a callback), and then used to fetch them once.

MrmFetchWidget can also create multiple instances of a widget (and its subtree). In this case, the **UID** definition functions as a template; a widget definition can be fetched any number of times. An application can use this template to make multiple instances of a widget, for example, in a dialog box box or menu.

The index (UIL name) that identifies the widget must be known to the application.

Return Value

This function returns one of the following status return constants:

MrmSUCCESS
> The function executed successfully.

MrmBAD_HIERARCHY
> The hierarchy ID was invalid.

MrmNOT_FOUND
> The widget was not found in UID hierarchy.

MrmFAILURE
> The function failed.

Related Information

MrmOpenHierarchyPerDisplay(3X), MrmFetchWidgetOverride(3X).

MrmFetchWidgetOverride—Fetches any indexed (UIL named) application widget. It overrides the arguments specified for this application widget in UIL

AES Support Level

Full-use

Synopsis

#include <Mrm/MrmPublic.h>

Cardinal MrmFetchWidgetOverride(*hierarchy_id, index, parent_widget, override_name, override_args, override_num_args, widget, class*)

MrmHierarchy	*hierarchy_id*;
String	*index*;
Widget	*parent_widget*;
String	*override_name*;
ArgList	*override_args*;
Cardinal	*override_num_args*;
Widget	**widget*;
MrmType	**class*;

Description

The **MrmFetchWidgetOverride** function is the extended version of **MrmFetchWidget**. It is identical to **MrmFetchWidget**, except that it allows the caller to override the widget's name and any arguments that **MrmFetchWidget** would otherwise retrieve from the UID file or one of the defaulting mechanisms. That is, the override argument list is not limited to those arguments in the UID file.

The override arguments apply only to the widget fetched and returned by this function. Its children (subtree) do not receive any override parameters.

hierarchy_id   Specifies the ID of the UID hierarchy that contains the interface definition. The value of *hierarchy_id* was returned in a previous call to **MrmOpenHierarchyPerDisplay**.

index   Specifies the UIL name of the widget to fetch.

parent_widget

Specifies the parent widget ID.

override_name

Specifies the name to override the widget name. Use a NULL value if you do not want to override the widget name.

override_args Specifies the override argument list, exactly as given to **XtCreateWidget** (conversion complete and so forth). Use a NULL value if you do not want to override the argument list.

override_num_args
>Specifies the number of arguments in *override_args*.

widget   Returns the widget ID of the created widget.

class   Returns the class code identifying MRM's widget class. Literals identifying MRM widget class codes are defined in the include file **Mrm/MrmPublic.h**.

Return Value

This function returns one of the following status return constants:

MrmSUCCESS
>The function executed successfully.

MrmBAD_HIERARCHY
>The hierarchy ID was invalid.

MrmNOT_FOUND
>The widget was not found in UID hierarchy.

MrmFAILURE
>The function failed.

Related Information

MrmOpenHierarchyPerDisplay(3X), **MrmFetchWidget(3X)**.

MrmInitialize—Prepares an application to use MRM widget-fetching facilities

AES Support Level

Trial-use

Synopsis

void MrmInitialize()

Description

The **MrmInitialize** function must be called to prepare an application to use MRM widget-fetching facilities. You must call this function prior to fetching a widget. However, it is good programming practice to call **MrmInitialize** prior to performing any MRM operations.

MrmInitialize initializes the internal data structures that MRM needs to successfully perform type conversion on arguments and to successfully access widget creation facilities. An application must call **MrmInitialize** before it uses other MRM functions.

MrmOpenHierarchy—Allocates a hierarchy ID and opens all the UID files in the hierarchy

AES Support Level

Trial-use

History/Direction

The **MrmOpenHierarchy** function is scheduled for removal in revision D.

Synopsis

#include <Mrm/MrmPublic.h>

Cardinal MrmOpenHierarchy(*num_files, file_names_list, ancillary_structures_list, hierarchy_id***)**

MrmCount	*num_files*;
String	*file_names_list*[];
MrmOsOpenParamPtr	**ancillary_structures_list*;
MrmHierarchy	**hierarchy_id*;

Description

This routine is obsolete and exists for compatibility with previous releases. It is replaced by **MrmOpenHierarchyPerDisplay**. **MrmOpenHierarchy** is identical to **MrmOpenHierarchyPerDisplay** except that **MrmOpenHierarchy** does not take a *display* argument.

num_files   Specifies the number of files in the name list.

file_names_list
     Specifies an array of character strings that identify the UID files.

ancillary_structures_list
     A list of operating-system-dependent ancillary structures corresponding to items such as filenames, clobber flags, and so forth. This argument should be NULL for most operations. If you need to reference this structure, see the definition of **MrmOsOpenParamPtr** in the **MrmPublic.h** header file for more information.

hierarchy_id   Returns the search hierarchy ID. The search hierarchy ID identifies the list of UID files that MRM searches (in order) when performing subsequent fetch calls.

Each UID file string in *file_names_list* can specify either a full pathname or a filename. If a UID file string has a leading slash (/), it specifies a full pathname, and MRM opens the file as specified. Otherwise, the UID file string specifies a filename. In this case, MRM looks for the file along a search path specified by the **UIDPATH** environment variable or by a default search path, which varies depending on whether or not the **XAPPLRESDIR** environment variable is set.

The **UIDPATH** environment variable specifies a search path and naming conventions associated with UID files. It can contain the substitution field **%U**, where the UID file string from the *file_names_list* argument to **MrmOpenHierarchyPerDisplay** is substituted for **%U**. It can also contain the substitution fields accepted by **XtResolvePathname**. The substitution field **%T** is always mapped to **uid**. The entire path is first searched with **%S** mapped to **.uid**. If no file is found, it is searched again with **%S** mapped to NULL. For example, the following **UIDPATH** value and **MrmOpenHierarchy** call cause MRM to open two separate UID files:

```
UIDPATH=/uidlib/%L/%U.uid:/uidlib/%U/%L
   static char *uid_files[] = {"/usr/users/me/test.uid", "test2"};
   MrmHierarchy  *Hierarchy_id;
   MrmOpenHierarchy((MrmCount)2,uid_files, NULL, Hierarchy_id)
```

MRM opens the first file, **/usr/users/me/test.uid**, as specified in the *file_names_list* argument to **MrmOpenHierarchy**, because the UID file string in the *file_names_list* argument specifies a full pathname. MRM looks for the second file, **test2**, first as **/uidlib/%L/test2.uid** and second as **/uidlib/test2/%L**, where the display's language string is substituted for **%L**.

After **MrmOpenHierarchy** opens the UID hierarchy, you should not delete or modify the UID files until you close the UID hierarchy by calling **MrmCloseHierarchy**.

If **UIDPATH** is not set but the environment variable **XAPPLRESDIR** is set, MRM searches the following pathnames:

- **%U%S**
- **$XAPPLRESDIR/%L/uid/%N/%U%S**
- **$XAPPLRESDIR/%l/uid/%N/%U%S**
- **$XAPPLRESDIR/uid/%N/%U%S**
- **$XAPPLRESDIR/%L/uid/%U%S**
- **$XAPPLRESDIR/%l/uid/%U%S**
- **$XAPPLRESDIR/uid/%U%S**
- **$HOME/uid/%U%S**

- **$HOME/%U%S**

- **/usr/lib/X11/%L/uid/%N/%U%S**

- **/usr/lib/X11/%l/uid/%N/%U%S**

- **/usr/lib/X11/uid/%N/%U%S**

- **/usr/lib/X11/%L/uid/%U%S**

- **/usr/lib/X11/%l/uid/%U%S**

- **/usr/lib/X11/uid/%U%S**

- **/usr/include/X11/uid/%U%S**

If neither **UIDPATH** nor **XAPPLRESDIR** is set, MRM searches the following pathnames:

- **%U%S**

- **HOME/%L/uid/%N/%U%S**

- **HOME/%l/uid/%N/%U%S**

- **$HOME/uid/%N/%U%S**

- **$HOME/%L/uid/%U%S**

- **$HOME/%l/uid/%U%S**

- **$HOME/uid/%U%S**

- **$HOME/%U%S**

- **/usr/lib/X11/%L/uid/%N/%U%S**

- **/usr/lib/X11/%l/uid/%N/%U%S**

- **/usr/lib/X11/uid/%N/%U%S**

- **/usr/lib/X11/%L/uid/%U%S**

- **/usr/lib/X11/%l/uid/%U%S**

- **/usr/lib/X11/uid/%U%S**

- **/usr/include/X11/uid/%U%S**

These paths are defaults that vendors may change. For example, a vendor may use different directories for **/usr/lib/X11** and **/usr/include/X11**.

The following substitutions are used in these paths:

%U   The UID file string, from the *file_names_list* argument.

%N   The class name of the application.

%L   The display's language string.

%l   The language component of the display's language string.

%S   The suffix to the filename. The entire path is first searched with a suffix of **.uil**. If no file is found, it is searched again with a NULL suffix.

Return Value

This function returns one of the following status return constants:

MrmSUCCESS
> The function executed successfully.

MrmNOT_FOUND
> File not found.

MrmFAILURE
> The function failed.

Related Information

MrmOpenHierarchyPerDisplay(3X) and **MrmCloseHierarchy(3X)**.

MrmOpenHierarchyPerDisplay—Allocates a hierarchy ID and opens all the UID files in the hierarchy

AES Support Level

Trial-use

Synopsis

#include <Mrm/MrmPublic.h>

Cardinal MrmOpenHierarchyPerDisplay (*display, num_files, file_names_list, ancillary_structures_list, hierarchy_id*)

Display	**display*;
MrmCount	*num_files*;
String	*file_names_list*[];
MrmOsOpenParamPtr	**ancillary_structures_list*;
MrmHierarchy	**hierarchy_id*;

Description

MrmOpenHierarchyPerDisplay allows you to specify the list of UID files that MRM searches in subsequent fetch operations. All subsequent fetch operations return the first occurrence of the named item encountered while traversing the UID hierarchy from the first list element (UID file specification) to the last list element. This function also allocates a hierarchy ID and opens all the UID files in the hierarchy. It initializes the optimized search lists in the hierarchy. If **MrmOpenHierarchyPerDisplay** encounters any errors during its execution, any files that were opened are closed.

The application must call **XtAppInitialize** before calling **MrmOpenHierarchyPerDisplay**.

display   Specifies the connection to the X server and the value to pass to **XtResolvePathname**. For more information on the **Display** structure, see the Xlib function **XOpenDisplay**.

num_files   Specifies the number of files in the name list.

file_names_list
Specifies an array of character strings that identify the UID files.

ancillary_structures_list
A list of operating-system-dependent ancillary structures corresponding to items such as filenames, clobber flags, and so forth. This argument should be NULL for most operations. If you need to reference this structure, see the definition of

MrmOsOpenParamPtr in the **MrmPublic.h** header file for more information.

hierarchy_id   Returns the search hierarchy ID. The search hierarchy ID identifies the list of UID files that MRM searches (in order) when performing subsequent fetch calls.

Each UID file string in *file_names_list* can specify either a full pathname or a filename. If a UID file string has a leading / (slash), it specifies a full pathname, and MRM opens the file as specified. Otherwise, the UID file string specifies a filename. In this case MRM looks for the file along a search path specified by the **UIDPATH** environment variable or by a default search path, which varies depending on whether or not the **XAPPLRESDIR** environment variable is set.

The **UIDPATH** environment variable specifies a search path and naming conventions associated with UID files. It can contain the substitution field %U, where the UID file string from the *file_names_list* argument to **MrmOpenHierarchyPerDisplay** is substituted for %U. It can also contain the substitution fields accepted by **XtResolvePathname**. The substitution field %T is always mapped to **uid**. The entire path is searched first with %S mapped to **.uid**. If no file is found, it is searched again with %S mapped to NULL. For example, the following **UIDPATH** value and **MrmOpenHierarchyPerDisplay** call cause MRM to open two separate UID files:

```
UIDPATH=/uidlib/%L/%U.uid:/uidlib/%U/%L
   static char *uid_files[] = {"/usr/users/me/test.uid", "test2"};
   MrmHierarchy  *Hierarchy_id;
   MrmOpenHierarchyPerDisplay((MrmCount)2,uid_files, NULL, Hierarchy_id)
```

MRM opens the first file, **/usr/users/me/test.uid**, as specified in the *file_names_list* argument to **MrmOpenHierarchyPerDisplay**, because the UID file string in the *file_names_list* argument specifies a full pathname. MRM looks for the second file, **test2**, first as **/uidlib/%L/test2.uid** and second as **/uidlib/test2/%L**, where the display's language string is substituted for %L.

After **MrmOpenHierarchyPerDisplay** opens the UID hierarchy, you should not delete or modify the UID files until you close the UID hierarchy by calling **MrmCloseHierarchy**.

If **UIDPATH** is not set, but the environment variable **XAPPLRESDIR** is set, MRM searches the following pathnames:

- %U%S

- $XAPPLRESDIR/%L/uid/%N/%U%S

- $XAPPLRESDIR/%l/uid/%N/%U%S

- $XAPPLRESDIR/uid/%N/%U%S

- $XAPPLRESDIR/%L/uid/%U%S

- $XAPPLRESDIR/%l/uid/%U%S

- $XAPPLRESDIR/uid/%U%S

- $HOME/uid/%U%S

- $HOME/%U%S

- /usr/lib/X11/%L/uid/%N/%U%S

- /usr/lib/X11/%l/uid/%N/%U%S

- /usr/lib/X11/uid/%N/%U%S

- /usr/lib/X11/%L/uid/%U%S

- /usr/lib/X11/%l/uid/%U%S

- /usr/lib/X11/uid/%U%S

- /usr/include/X11/uid/%U%S

If neither **UIDPATH** nor **XAPPLRESDIR** is set, MRM searches the following pathnames:

- %U%S

- $HOME/%L/uid/%N/%U%S

- $HOME/%l/uid/%N/%U%S

- $HOME/uid/%N/%U%S

- $HOME/%L/uid/%U%S

- $HOME/%l/uid/%U%S

- $HOME/uid/%U%S

- $HOME/%U%S

- /usr/lib/X11/%L/uid/%N/%U%S

- /usr/lib/X11/%l/uid/%N/%U%S

- /usr/lib/X11/uid/%N/%U%S

- **/usr/lib/X11/%L/uid/%U%S**

- **/usr/lib/X11/%l/uid/%U%S**

- **/usr/lib/X11/uid/%U%S**

- **/usr/include/X11/uid/%U%S**

These paths are defaults that vendors may change. For example, a vendor may use different directories for **/usr/lib/X11** and **/usr/include/X11**.

The following substitutions are used in these paths:

%U   The UID file string, from the *file_names_list* argument.

%N   The class name of the application.

%L   The display's language string.

%l   The language component of the display's language string.

%S   The suffix to the filename. The entire path is first searched with a suffix of **.uil**. If no file is found, it is searched again with a NULL suffix.

Return Value

This function returns one of the following status return constants:

MrmSUCCESS
        The function executed successfully.

MrmNOT_FOUND
        File not found.

MrmFAILURE
        The function failed.

Related Information

        MrmCloseHierarchy(3X).

MrmRegisterClass—Saves the information needed for MRM to access the widget creation function for user-defined widgets

AES Support Level

Trial-use

Synopsis

#include <Mrm/MrmPublic.h>

Cardinal MrmRegisterClass(*class_code, class_name, create_name, create_proc, class_record***)**

MrmType	*class_code*;
String	*class_name*;
String	*create_name*;
Widget	(**create_proc*) ();
WidgetClass	*class_record*;

Description

The **MrmRegisterClass** function allows MRM to access user-defined widget classes. This function registers the necessary information for MRM to create widgets of this class. You must call **MrmRegisterClass** prior to fetching any user-defined class widget.

MrmRegisterClass saves the information needed to access the widget creation function and to do type conversion of argument lists by using the information in MRM databases.

class_code   This argument is ignored; it is present for compatibility with previous releases.

class_name   This argument is ignored; it is present for compatibility with previous releases.

create_name   Specifies the case-sensitive name of the low-level widget creation function for the class. An example from the Motif Toolkit is **XmCreateLabel**. Arguments are *parent_widget, name, override_arglist*, and *override_argcount*.

For user-defined widgets, *create_name* is the creation procedure in the UIL that defines this widget.

create_proc   Specifies the address of the creation function that you named in *create_name*.

class_record   Specifies a pointer to the class record.

Return Value

This function returns one of the following status return constants:

MrmSUCCESS
> The function executed successfully.

MrmFAILURE
> The function failed.

MrmRegisterNames—Registers the values associated with the names referenced in UIL (for example, UIL callback function names or UIL identifier names)

AES Support Level

Trial-use

Synopsis

#include <Mrm/MrmPublic.h>

Cardinal MrmRegisterNames(*register_list, register_count***)**
    MrmRegisterArglist   *register_list***;**
    MrmCount   *register_count***;**

Description

The **MrmRegisterNames** function registers a vector of names and associated values for access in MRM. The values can be callback functions, pointers to user-defined data, or any other values. The information provided is used to resolve symbolic references occurring in UID files to their run-time values. For callbacks, this information provides the procedure address required by the Motif Toolkit. For names used as identifiers in UIL, this information provides any run-time mapping the application needs.

This function is similar to **MrmRegisterNamesInHierarchy**, except that the scope of the names registered by **MrmRegisterNamesInHierarchy** is limited to the hierarchy specified in the call to that function, whereas the names registered by **MrmRegisterNames** have global scope. When MRM looks up a name, it first tries to find the name among those registered for the given hierarchy. If that lookup fails, it tries to find the name among those registered globally.

register_list   Specifies a list of name/value pairs for the names to be registered. Each name is a case-sensitive, NULL-terminated ASCII string. Each value is a 32-bit quantity, interpreted as a procedure address if the name is a callback function, and uninterpreted otherwise.

register_count
        Specifies the number of entries in *register_list*.

The names in the list are case-sensitive. The list can be either ordered or unordered.

Callback functions registered through **MrmRegisterNames** can be either regular or creation callbacks. Regular callbacks have declarations determined by Motif Toolkit and user requirements. Creation callbacks have the same format as any other callback:

> **void CallBackProc**(*widget_id, tag, callback_data*)
>   **Widget**   **widget_id*;
>   **Opaque**   *tag*
>   **XmAnyCallbackStruct**   **callback_data*;

widget_id   Specifies the widget ID associated with the widget performing the callback (as in any callback function).

tag   Specifies the tag value (as in any callback function).

callback_data Specifies a widget-specific data structure. This data structure has a minimum of two members: event and reason. The reason member is always set to **MrmCR_CREATE**.

Note that the widget name and parent are available from the widget record accessible through *widget_id*.

Return Value

This function returns one of the following status return constants:

MrmSUCCESS
> The function executed successfully.

MrmFAILURE
> The function failed.

MrmRegisterNamesInHierarchy—Registers the values associated with the names referenced in UIL within a single hierarchy (for example, UIL callback function names or UIL identifier names)

AES Support Level

Trial-use

Synopsis

#include <Mrm/MrmPublic.h>

Cardinal MrmRegisterNamesInHierarchy(*hierarchy_id, register_list, register_count***)**
    MrmHierarchy   *hierarchy_id***;**
    MrmRegisterArglist   *register_list***;**
    MrmCount   *register_count***;**

Description

The **MrmRegisterNamesInHierarchy** function registers a vector of names and associated values for access in MRM. The values can be callback functions, pointers to user-defined data, or any other values. The information provided is used to resolve symbolic references occurring in UID files to their run-time values. For callbacks, this information provides the procedure address required by the Motif Toolkit. For names used as identifiers in UIL, this information provides any run-time mapping the application needs.

This function is similar to **MrmRegisterNames**, except that the scope of the names registered by **MrmRegisterNamesInHierarchy** is limited to the hierarchy specified by *hierarchy_id*, whereas the names registered by **MrmRegisterNames** have global scope. When MRM looks up a name, it first tries to find the name among those registered for the given hierarchy. If that lookup fails, it tries to find the name among those registered globally.

hierarchy_id   Specifies the hierarchy with which the names are to be associated.

register_list   Specifies a list of name/value pairs for the names to be registered. Each name is a case-sensitive, NULL-terminated ASCII string. Each value is a 32-bit quantity, interpreted as a procedure address if the name is a callback function, and uninterpreted otherwise.

register_count
    Specifies the number of entries in *register_list*.

The names in the list are case-sensitive. The list can be either ordered or unordered.

Callback functions registered through **MrmRegisterNamesInHierarchy** can be either regular or creation callbacks. Regular callbacks have declarations determined by Motif Toolkit and user requirements. Creation callbacks have the same format as any other callback:

void CallBackProc(*widget_id, tag, callback_data*)
      Widget   **widget_id*;
      Opaque   *tag*;
      XmAnyCallbackStruct   **callback_data*;

widget_id   Specifies the widget ID associated with the widget performing the callback (as in any callback function).

tag   Specifies the tag value (as in any callback function).

callback_data
      Specifies a widget-specific data structure. This data structure has a minimum of two members: event and reason. The reason member is always set to **MrmCR_CREATE**.

Note that the widget name and parent are available from the widget record accessible through *widget_id*.

Return Value

This function returns one of the following status return constants:

MrmSUCCESS
      The function executed successfully.

MrmFAILURE
      The function failed.

Object—The Object widget class

AES Support Level

Full-use

Synopsis

#include <Xm/Xm.h>

Description

Object is never instantiated. Its sole purpose is as a supporting superclass for other widget classes.

Classes

The class pointer is **objectClass**.

The class name is **Object**.

New Resources

The following table defines a set of widget resources used by the programmer to specify data. The programmer can also set the resource values for the inherited classes to set attributes for this widget. To reference a resource by name or by class in a **.Xdefaults** file, remove the **XmN** or **XmC** prefix and use the remaining letters. To specify one of the defined values for a resource in a **.Xdefaults** file, remove the **Xm** prefix and use the remaining letters (in either lowercase or uppercase, but include any underscores between words). The codes in the access column indicate if the given resource can be set at creation time (C), set by using **XtSetValues** (S), retrieved by using **XtGetValues** (G), or is not applicable (N/A).

Object Resource Set		
Name	**Default**	**Access**
Class	**Type**	
XmNdestroyCallback	NULL	C
XmCCallback	XtCallbackList	

XmNdestroyCallback

Specifies a list of callbacks that is called when the gadget is destroyed.

OverrideShell—The OverrideShell widget class

AES Support Level

Full-use

Synopsis

#include <Xm/Xm.h>
#include <X11/Shell.h>

Description

OverrideShell is used for shell windows that completely bypass the window manager, for example, PopupMenu shells.

Classes

OverrideShell inherits behavior and resources from **Core**, **Composite**, and **Shell**.

The class pointer is **overrideShellWidgetClass**.

The class name is **OverrideShell**.

New Resources

OverrideShell defines no new resources, but overrides the **XmNoverrideRedirect** and **XmNsaveUnder** resources in the **Shell** class.

Inherited Resources

OverrideShell inherits behavior and resources from the following superclasses. For a complete description of each resource, refer to the reference page for that superclass.

The following table defines a set of widget resources used by the programmer to specify data. The programmer can also set the resource values for the inherited classes to set attributes for this widget. To reference a resource by name or by class in a **.Xdefaults** file, remove the **XmN** or **XmC** prefix and use the remaining letters. To specify one of the defined values for a resource in a **.Xdefaults** file, remove the **Xm** prefix and use the remaining letters (in either lowercase or uppercase, but include any underscores between words). The codes in the access column indicate if the given resource can be set at creation time (C), set by using **XtSetValues** (S), retrieved by using **XtGetValues** (G), or is not applicable (N/A).

Shell Resource Set		
Name	**Default**	**Access**
Class	**Type**	
XmNallowShellResize	False	CG
XmCAllowShellResize	Boolean	
XmNcreatePopupChildProc	NULL	CSG
XmCCreatePopupChildProc	XtCreatePopupChildProc	
XmNgeometry	NULL	CSG
XmCGeometry	String	
XmNoverrideRedirect	True	CSG
XmCOverrideRedirect	Boolean	
XmNpopdownCallback	NULL	C
XmCCallback	XtCallbackList	
XmNpopupCallback	NULL	C
XmCCallback	XtCallbackList	
XmNsaveUnder	True	CSG
XmCSaveUnder	Boolean	
XmNvisual	CopyFromParent	CSG
XmCVisual	Visual *	

Composite Resource Set		
Name	**Default**	**Access**
Class	**Type**	
XmNchildren	NULL	G
XmCReadOnly	WidgetList	
XmNinsertPosition	NULL	CSG
XmCInsertPosition	XtOrderProc	
XmNnumChildren	0	G
XmCReadOnly	Cardinal	

Core Resource Set		
Name	**Default**	**Access**
Class	**Type**	
XmNaccelerators	dynamic	CSG
XmCAccelerators	XtAccelerators	
XmNancestorSensitive	dynamic	G
XmCSensitive	Boolean	
XmNbackground	dynamic	CSG
XmCBackground	Pixel	
XmNbackgroundPixmap	XmUNSPECIFIED_PIXMAP	CSG
XmCPixmap	Pixmap	
XmNborderColor	XtDefaultForeground	CSG
XmCBorderColor	Pixel	
XmNborderPixmap	XmUNSPECIFIED_PIXMAP	CSG
XmCPixmap	Pixmap	
XmNborderWidth	1	CSG
XmCBorderWidth	Dimension	
XmNcolormap	dynamic	CG
XmCColormap	Colormap	
XmNdepth	dynamic	CG
XmCDepth	int	
XmNdestroyCallback	NULL	C
XmCCallback	XtCallbackList	
XmNheight	dynamic	CSG
XmCHeight	Dimension	
XmNinitialResourcesPersistent	True	C
XmCInitialResourcesPersistent	Boolean	
XmNmappedWhenManaged	True	CSG
XmCMappedWhenManaged	Boolean	
XmNscreen	dynamic	CG
XmCScreen	Screen *	
XmNsensitive	True	CSG
XmCSensitive	Boolean	

Name	Default	Access
Class	Type	
XmNtranslations	dynamic	CSG
XmCTranslations	XtTranslations	
XmNwidth	dynamic	CSG
XmCWidth	Dimension	
XmNx	0	CSG
XmCPosition	Position	
XmNy	0	CSG
XmCPosition	Position	

Related Information

Composite(3X), **Core(3X)**, and **Shell(3X)**.

RectObj—The RectObj widget class

AES Support Level

Full-use

Synopsis

#include <Xm/Xm.h>

Description

RectObj is never instantiated. Its sole purpose is as a supporting superclass for other widget classes.

Classes

RectObj inherits behavior and a resource from **Object**.

The class pointer is **rectObjClass**.

The class name is **RectObj**.

New Resources

The following table defines a set of widget resources used by the programmer to specify data. The programmer can also set the resource values for the inherited classes to set attributes for this widget. To reference a resource by name or by class in a **.Xdefaults** file, remove the **XmN** or **XmC** prefix and use the remaining letters. To specify one of the defined values for a resource in a **.Xdefaults** file, remove the **Xm** prefix and use the remaining letters (in either lowercase or uppercase, but include any underscores between words). The codes in the access column indicate if the given resource can be set at creation time (C), set by using **XtSetValues** (S), retrieved by using **XtGetValues** (G), or is not applicable (N/A).

<table>
<tr><th colspan="3" align="center">RectObj Resource Set</th></tr>
<tr><th>Name
Class</th><th>Default
Type</th><th>Access</th></tr>
<tr><td>XmNancestorSensitive
XmCSensitive</td><td>dynamic
Boolean</td><td>G</td></tr>
<tr><td>XmNborderWidth
XmCBorderWidth</td><td>1
Dimension</td><td>CSG</td></tr>
<tr><td>XmNheight
XmCHeight</td><td>dynamic
Dimension</td><td>CSG</td></tr>
<tr><td>XmNsensitive
XmCSensitive</td><td>True
Boolean</td><td>CSG</td></tr>
<tr><td>XmNwidth
XmCWidth</td><td>dynamic
Dimension</td><td>CSG</td></tr>
<tr><td>XmNx
XmCPosition</td><td>0
Position</td><td>CSG</td></tr>
<tr><td>XmNy
XmCPosition</td><td>0
Position</td><td>CSG</td></tr>
</table>

XmNancestorSensitive

Specifies whether the immediate parent of the gadget receives input events. Use the function **XtSetSensitive** if you are changing the argument to preserve data integrity (see **XmNsensitive**). The default is the bitwise AND of the parent's **XmNsensitive** and **XmNancestorSensitive** resources.

XmNborderWidth

Specifies the width of the border placed around the RectObj's rectangular display area.

XmNheight   Specifies the inside height (excluding the border) of the RectObj's rectangular display area.

XmNsensitive

Determines whether a RectObj receives input events. If a RectObj is sensitive, the parent dispatches to the gadget all keyboard, mouse button, motion, window enter/leave, and focus events. Insensitive gadgets do not receive these events. Use the function **XtSetSensitive** to change the sensitivity argument. Using **XtSetSensitive** ensures that if a parent widget has **XmNsensitive** set to False, the ancestor-sensitive flag of all its children is appropriately set.

XmNwidth	Specifies the inside width (excluding the border) of the RectObj's rectangular display area.
XmNx	Specifies the x-coordinate of the upper left outside corner of the RectObj's rectangular display area. The value is relative to the upper left inside corner of the parent window.
XmNy	Specifies the y-coordinate of the upper left outside corner of the RectObj's rectangular display area. The value is relative to the upper left inside corner of the parent window.

Inherited Resources

RectObj inherits behavior and a resource from **Object**. For a description of this resource, refer to the **Object** reference page.

Object Resource Set		
Name	**Default**	**Access**
Class	**Type**	
XmNdestroyCallback	NULL	C
XmCCallback	XtCallbackList	

Related Information

Object(3X).

Shell—The Shell widget class

AES Support Level

Full-use

Synopsis

#include <Xm/Xm.h>
#include <X11/Shell.h>

Description

Shell is a top-level widget (with only one managed child) that encapsulates the interaction with the window manager.

At the time the shell's child is managed, the child's width is used for both widgets if the shell is unrealized and no width has been specified for the shell. Otherwise, the shell's width is used for both widgets. The same relations hold for the height of the shell and its child.

Classes

Shell inherits behavior and resources from **Composite** and **Core**.

The class pointer is **shellWidgetClass**.

The class name is **Shell**.

New Resources

The following table defines a set of widget resources used by the programmer to specify data. The programmer can also set the resource values for the inherited classes to set attributes for this widget. To reference a resource by name or by class in a **.Xdefaults** file, remove the **XmN** or **XmC** prefix and use the remaining letters. To specify one of the defined values for a resource in a **.Xdefaults** file, remove the **Xm** prefix and use the remaining letters (in either lowercase or uppercase, but include any underscores between words). The codes in the access column indicate if the given resource can be set at creation time (C), set by using **XtSetValues** (S), retrieved by using **XtGetValues** (G), or is not applicable (N/A).

<table>
<tr><td colspan="3" align="center">Shell Resource Set</td></tr>
<tr><td>Name
   Class</td><td>Default
   Type</td><td>Access</td></tr>
<tr><td>XmNallowShellResize
   XmCAllowShellResize</td><td>False
   Boolean</td><td>CG</td></tr>
<tr><td>XmNcreatePopupChildProc
   XmCCreatePopupChildProc</td><td>NULL
   XtCreatePopupChildProc</td><td>CSG</td></tr>
<tr><td>XmNgeometry
   XmCGeometry</td><td>NULL
   String</td><td>CSG</td></tr>
<tr><td>XmNoverrideRedirect
   XmCOverrideRedirect</td><td>False
   Boolean</td><td>CSG</td></tr>
<tr><td>XmNpopdownCallback
   XmCCallback</td><td>NULL
   XtCallbackList</td><td>C</td></tr>
<tr><td>XmNpopupCallback
   XmCCallback</td><td>NULL
   XtCallbackList</td><td>C</td></tr>
<tr><td>XmNsaveUnder
   XmCSaveUnder</td><td>False
   Boolean</td><td>CSG</td></tr>
<tr><td>XmNvisual
   XmCVisual</td><td>CopyFromParent
   Visual *</td><td>CSG</td></tr>
</table>

XmNallowShellResize
> Specifies that if this resource is False, the Shell widget instance returns **XtGeometryNo** to all geometry requests from its children.

XmNcreatePopupChildProc
> Specifies the pointer to a function that is called when the Shell widget instance is popped up by **XtPopup**. The function creates the child widget when the shell is popped up instead of when the application starts up. This can be used if the child needs to be reconfigured each time the shell is popped up. The function takes one argument, the popup shell, and returns no result. It is called after the popup callbacks specified by **XmNpopupCallback**.

XmNgeometry
> Specifies the desired geometry for the widget instance. This resource is examined only when the widget instance is unrealized and the number of its managed children is changed. It is used to change the values of the **XmNx**, **XmNy**, **XmNwidth**, and **XmNheight** resources.

XmNoverrideRedirect

> If True, specifies that the widget instance is a temporary window that should be ignored by the window manager. Applications and users should not normally alter this resource.

XmNpopdownCallback

> Specifies a list of callbacks that is called when the widget instance is popped down by **XtPopdown**.

XmNpopupCallback

> Specifies a list of callbacks that is called when the widget instance is popped up by **XtPopup**.

XmNsaveUnder

> If True, specifies that it is desirable to save the contents of the screen beneath this widget instance, avoiding expose events when the instance is unmapped. This is a hint, and an implementation may save contents whenever it desires, including always or never.

XmNvisual   Specifies the visual used in creating the widget.

Inherited Resources

> Shell inherits behavior and resources from the superclass described in the following table. For a complete description of each resource, refer to the reference page for that superclass.

Composite Resource Set		
Name	**Default**	**Access**
Class	**Type**	
XmNchildren	NULL	G
XmCReadOnly	WidgetList	
XmNinsertPosition	NULL	CSG
XmCInsertPosition	XtOrderProc	
XmNnumChildren	0	G
XmCReadOnly	Cardinal	

Core Resource Set		
Name	**Default**	**Access**
Class	**Type**	
XmNaccelerators	dynamic	CSG
XmCAccelerators	XtAccelerators	
XmNancestorSensitive	dynamic	G
XmCSensitive	Boolean	
XmNbackground	dynamic	CSG
XmCBackground	Pixel	
XmNbackgroundPixmap	XmUNSPECIFIED_PIXMAP	CSG
XmCPixmap	Pixmap	
XmNborderColor	XtDefaultForeground	CSG
XmCBorderColor	Pixel	
XmNborderPixmap	XmUNSPECIFIED_PIXMAP	CSG
XmCPixmap	Pixmap	
XmNborderWidth	1	CSG
XmCBorderWidth	Dimension	
XmNcolormap	dynamic	CG
XmCColormap	Colormap	
XmNdepth	dynamic	CG
XmCDepth	int	
XmNdestroyCallback	NULL	C
XmCCallback	XtCallbackList	
XmNheight	dynamic	CSG
XmCHeight	Dimension	
XmNinitialResourcesPersistent	True	C
XmCInitialResourcesPersistent	Boolean	
XmNmappedWhenManaged	True	CSG
XmCMappedWhenManaged	Boolean	
XmNscreen	dynamic	CG
XmCScreen	Screen *	
XmNsensitive	True	CSG
XmCSensitive	Boolean	

Name	Default	Access
Class	Type	
XmNtranslations	dynamic	CSG
XmCTranslations	XtTranslations	
XmNwidth	dynamic	CSG
XmCWidth	Dimension	
XmNx	0	CSG
XmCPosition	Position	
XmNy	0	CSG
XmCPosition	Position	

Related Information

Composite(3X) and Core(3X).

TopLevelShell—The TopLevelShell widget class

AES Support Level

Full-use

Synopsis

#include <Xm/Xm.h>
#include <X11/Shell.h>

Description

TopLevelShell is used for normal top-level windows such as any additional top-level widgets an application needs.

Classes

TopLevelShell inherits behavior and resources from **Core**, **Composite**, **Shell**, **WMShell**, and **VendorShell**.

The class pointer is **topLevelShellWidgetClass**.

The class name is **TopLevelShell**.

New Resources

The following table defines a set of widget resources used by the programmer to specify data. The programmer can also set the resource values for the inherited classes to set attributes for this widget. To reference a resource by name or by class in a **.Xdefaults** file, remove the **XmN** or **XmC** prefix and use the remaining letters. To specify one of the defined values for a resource in a **.Xdefaults** file, remove the **Xm** prefix and use the remaining letters (in either lowercase or uppercase, but include any underscores between words). The codes in the access column indicate if the given resource can be set at creation time (C), set by using **XtSetValues** (S), retrieved by using **XtGetValues** (G), or is not applicable (N/A).

<table>
<tr><td colspan="3">TopLevelShell Resource Set</td></tr>
<tr><td>Name
    Class</td><td>Default
    Type</td><td>Access</td></tr>
<tr><td>XmNiconic
    XmCIconic</td><td>False
    Boolean</td><td>CSG</td></tr>
<tr><td>XmNiconName
    XmCIconName</td><td>NULL
    String</td><td>CSG</td></tr>
<tr><td>XmNiconNameEncoding
    XmCIconNameEncoding</td><td>dynamic
    Atom</td><td>CSG</td></tr>
</table>

XmNiconic   If True when the widget instance is realized, specifies that the widget instance indicates to the window manager that the application wishes to start as an icon, regardless of the **XmNinitialState** resource.

XmNiconName

Specifies the short form of the application name to be displayed by the window manager when the application is iconified.

XmNiconNameEncoding

Specifies a property type that represents the encoding of the **XmNiconName** string. If a language procedure has been set, the default is None; otherwise, the default is **XA_STRING**. When the widget is realized, if the value is None, the corresponding name is assumed to be in the current locale. The name is passed to **XmbTextListToTextProperty** with an encoding style of **XStdICCTextStyle**. The resulting encoding is **STRING** if the name is fully convertible to **STRING**, otherwise **COMPOUND_TEXT**. The values of the encoding resources are not changed; they remain None.

Inherited Resources

TopLevelShell inherits behavior and resources from the following superclasses. For a complete description of each resource, refer to the reference page for that superclass.

VendorShell Resource Set		

Name
    Class
	Default
	    Type
		Access

XmNbuttonFontList
    XmCButtonFontList
	dynamic
	    XmFontList
		CSG

XmNdefaultFontList
    XmCDefaultFontList
	dynamic
	    XmFontList
		CG

XmNdeleteResponse
    XmCDeleteResponse
	XmDESTROY
	    unsigned char
		CSG

XmNkeyboardFocusPolicy
    XmCKeyboardFocusPolicy
	XmEXPLICIT
	    unsigned char
		CSG

XmNlabelFontList
    XmCLabelFontList
	dynamic
	    XmFontList
		CSG

XmNmwmDecorations
    XmCMwmDecorations
	-1
	    int
		CSG

XmNmwmFunctions
    XmCMwmFunctions
	-1
	    int
		CSG

XmNmwmInputMode
    XmCMwmInputMode
	-1
	    int
		CSG

XmNmwmMenu
    XmCMwmMenu
	NULL
	    String
		CSG

XmNtextFontList
    XmCTextFontList
	dynamic
	    XmFontList
		CSG

WMShell Resource Set		
Name	**Default**	**Access**
Class	**Type**	
XmNbaseHeight	XtUnspecifiedShellInt	CSG
XmCBaseHeight	int	
XmNbaseWidth	XtUnspecifiedShellInt	CSG
XmCBaseWidth	int	
XmNheightInc	XtUnspecifiedShellInt	CSG
XmCHeightInc	int	
XmNiconMask	NULL	CSG
XmCIconMask	Pixmap	
XmNiconPixmap	NULL	CSG
XmCIconPixmap	Pixmap	
XmNiconWindow	NULL	CSG
XmCIconWindow	Window	
XmNiconX	-1	CSG
XmCIconX	int	
XmNiconY	-1	CSG
XmCIconY	int	
XmNinitialState	NormalState	CSG
XmCInitialState	int	
XmNinput	True	CSG
XmCInput	Boolean	
XmNmaxAspectX	XtUnspecifiedShellInt	CSG
XmCMaxAspectX	int	
XmNmaxAspectY	XtUnspecifiedShellInt	CSG
XmCMaxAspectY	int	
XmNmaxHeight	XtUnspecifiedShellInt	CSG
XmCMaxHeight	int	
XmNmaxWidth	XtUnspecifiedShellInt	CSG
XmCMaxWidth	int	
XmNminAspectX	XtUnspecifiedShellInt	CSG
XmCMinAspectX	int	

Name	Default	Access
Class	Type	
XmNminAspectY	XtUnspecifiedShellInt	CSG
XmCMinAspectY	int	
XmNminHeight	XtUnspecifiedShellInt	CSG
XmCMinHeight	int	
XmNminWidth	XtUnspecifiedShellInt	CSG
XmCMinWidth	int	
XmNtitle	dynamic	CSG
XmCTitle	String	
XmNtitleEncoding	dynamic	CSG
XmCTitleEncoding	Atom	
XmNtransient	False	CSG
XmCTransient	Boolean	
XmNwaitForWm	True	CSG
XmCWaitForWm	Boolean	
XmNwidthInc	XtUnspecifiedShellInt	CSG
XmCWidthInc	int	
XmNwindowGroup	dynamic	CSG
XmCWindowGroup	Window	
XmNwinGravity	dynamic	CSG
XmCWinGravity	int	
XmNwmTimeout	5000 ms	CSG
XmCWmTimeout	int	

Shell Resource Set		
Name	**Default**	**Access**
Class	**Type**	
XmNallowShellResize	False	CG
XmCAllowShellResize	Boolean	
XmNcreatePopupChildProc	NULL	CSG
XmCCreatePopupChildProc	XtCreatePopupChildProc	
XmNgeometry	NULL	CSG
XmCGeometry	String	
XmNoverrideRedirect	False	CSG
XmCOverrideRedirect	Boolean	
XmNpopdownCallback	NULL	C
XmCCallback	XtCallbackList	
XmNpopupCallback	NULL	C
XmCCallback	XtCallbackList	
XmNsaveUnder	False	CSG
XmCSaveUnder	Boolean	
XmNvisual	CopyFromParent	CSG
XmCVisual	Visual *	

Composite Resource Set		
Name	**Default**	**Access**
Class	**Type**	
XmNchildren	NULL	G
XmCReadOnly	WidgetList	
XmNinsertPosition	NULL	CSG
XmCInsertPosition	XtOrderProc	
XmNnumChildren	0	G
XmCReadOnly	Cardinal	

Core Resource Set		
Name	**Default**	**Access**
Class	**Type**	
XmNaccelerators	dynamic	CSG
XmCAccelerators	XtAccelerators	
XmNancestorSensitive	dynamic	G
XmCSensitive	Boolean	
XmNbackground	dynamic	CSG
XmCBackground	Pixel	
XmNbackgroundPixmap	XmUNSPECIFIED_PIXMAP	CSG
XmCPixmap	Pixmap	
XmNborderColor	XtDefaultForeground	CSG
XmCBorderColor	Pixel	
XmNborderPixmap	XmUNSPECIFIED_PIXMAP	CSG
XmCPixmap	Pixmap	
XmNborderWidth	0	CSG
XmCBorderWidth	Dimension	
XmNcolormap	dynamic	CG
XmCColormap	Colormap	
XmNdepth	dynamic	CG
XmCDepth	int	
XmNdestroyCallback	NULL	C
XmCCallback	XtCallbackList	
XmNheight	dynamic	CSG
XmCHeight	Dimension	
XmNinitialResourcesPersistent	True	C
XmCInitialResourcesPersistent	Boolean	
XmNmappedWhenManaged	True	CSG
XmCMappedWhenManaged	Boolean	
XmNscreen	dynamic	CG
XmCScreen	Screen *	
XmNsensitive	True	CSG
XmCSensitive	Boolean	

Name	Default	Access
Class	Type	
XmNtranslations	dynamic	CSG
XmCTranslations	XtTranslations	
XmNwidth	dynamic	CSG
XmCWidth	Dimension	
XmNx	0	CSG
XmCPosition	Position	
XmNy	0	CSG
XmCPosition	Position	

Related Information

Composite(3X), Core(3X), Shell(3X), WMShell(3X), and VendorShell(3X).

TransientShell—The TransientShell widget class

AES Support Level

Full-use

Synopsis

#include <Xm/Xm.h>
#include <X11/Shell.h>

Description

TransientShell is used for shell windows that can be manipulated by the window manager, but are not allowed to be iconified separately. For example, DialogBoxes make no sense without their associated application. They are iconified by the window manager only if the main application shell is iconified.

Classes

TransientShell inherits behavior and resources from **Core**, **Composite**, **Shell**, **WMShell**, and **VendorShell**.

The class pointer is **transientShellWidgetClass**.

The class name is **TransientShell**.

New Resources

The following table defines a set of widget resources used by the programmer to specify data. The programmer can also set the resource values for the inherited classes to set attributes for this widget. To reference a resource by name or by class in a **.Xdefaults** file, remove the **XmN** or **XmC** prefix and use the remaining letters. To specify one of the defined values for a resource in a **.Xdefaults** file, remove the **Xm** prefix and use the remaining letters (in either lowercase or uppercase, but include any underscores between words). The codes in the access column indicate if the given resource can be set at creation time (C), set by using **XtSetValues** (S), retrieved by using **XtGetValues** (G), or is not applicable (N/A).

In addition to these new resources, **TransientShell** overrides the **XmNsaveUnder** resource in **Shell** and the **XmNtransient** resource in **WMShell**.

TransientShell Resource Set		
Name	**Default**	**Access**
Class	**Type**	
XmNtransientFor	NULL	CSG
XmCTransientFor	Widget	

XmNtransientFor

> Specifies a widget that the shell acts as a pop-up for. If this resource is NULL or is a widget that has not been realized, the **XmNwindowGroup** is used instead.

Inherited Resources

TransientShell inherits behavior and resources from the superclasses described in the following tables, which define sets of widget resources used by the programmer to specify data. For a complete description of each resource, refer to the reference page for that superclass.

The programmer can also set the resource values for the inherited classes to set attributes for this widget. To reference a resource by name or by class in a **.Xdefaults** file, remove the **XmN** or **XmC** prefix and use the remaining letters. To specify one of the defined values for a resource in a **.Xdefaults** file, remove the **Xm** prefix and use the remaining letters (in either lowercase or uppercase, but include any underscores between words). The codes in the access column indicate if the given resource can be set at creation time (C), set by using **XtSetValues** (S), retrieved by using **XtGetValues** (G), or is not applicable (N/A).

<table>
<tr><th colspan="3">VendorShell Resource Set</th></tr>
<tr><th>Name
    Class</th><th>Default
    Type</th><th>Access</th></tr>
<tr><td>XmNbuttonFontList
    XmCButtonFontList</td><td>dynamic
    XmFontList</td><td>CSG</td></tr>
<tr><td>XmNdefaultFontList
    XmCDefaultFontList</td><td>dynamic
    XmFontList</td><td>CG</td></tr>
<tr><td>XmNdeleteResponse
    XmCDeleteResponse</td><td>XmDESTROY
    unsigned char</td><td>CSG</td></tr>
<tr><td>XmNkeyboardFocusPolicy
    XmCKeyboardFocusPolicy</td><td>XmEXPLICIT
    unsigned char</td><td>CSG</td></tr>
<tr><td>XmNlabelFontList
    XmCLabelFontList</td><td>dynamic
    XmFontList</td><td>CSG</td></tr>
<tr><td>XmNmwmDecorations
    XmCMwmDecorations</td><td>-1
    int</td><td>CSG</td></tr>
<tr><td>XmNmwmFunctions
    XmCMwmFunctions</td><td>-1
    int</td><td>CSG</td></tr>
<tr><td>XmNmwmInputMode
    XmCMwmInputMode</td><td>-1
    int</td><td>CSG</td></tr>
<tr><td>XmNmwmMenu
    XmCMwmMenu</td><td>NULL
    String</td><td>CSG</td></tr>
<tr><td>XmNtextFontList
    XmCTextFontList</td><td>dynamic
    XmFontList</td><td>CSG</td></tr>
</table>

WMShell Resource Set		
Name	**Default**	**Access**
Class	**Type**	
XmNbaseHeight	XtUnspecifiedShellInt	CSG
XmCBaseHeight	int	
XmNbaseWidth	XtUnspecifiedShellInt	CSG
XmCBaseWidth	int	
XmNheightInc	XtUnspecifiedShellInt	CSG
XmCHeightInc	int	
XmNiconMask	NULL	CSG
XmCIconMask	Pixmap	
XmNiconPixmap	NULL	CSG
XmCIconPixmap	Pixmap	
XmNiconWindow	NULL	CSG
XmCIconWindow	Window	
XmNiconX	-1	CSG
XmCIconX	int	
XmNiconY	-1	CSG
XmCIconY	int	
XmNinitialState	NormalState	CSG
XmCInitialState	int	
XmNinput	True	CSG
XmCInput	Boolean	
XmNmaxAspectX	XtUnspecifiedShellInt	CSG
XmCMaxAspectX	int	
XmNmaxAspectY	XtUnspecifiedShellInt	CSG
XmCMaxAspectY	int	
XmNmaxHeight	XtUnspecifiedShellInt	CSG
XmCMaxHeight	int	
XmNmaxWidth	XtUnspecifiedShellInt	CSG
XmCMaxWidth	int	
XmNminAspectX	XtUnspecifiedShellInt	CSG
XmCMinAspectX	int	

TransientShell(3X)

Name	Default	Access
Class	Type	
XmNminAspectY	XtUnspecifiedShellInt	CSG
XmCMinAspectY	int	
XmNminHeight	XtUnspecifiedShellInt	CSG
XmCMinHeight	int	
XmNminWidth	XtUnspecifiedShellInt	CSG
XmCMinWidth	int	
XmNtitle	dynamic	CSG
XmCTitle	String	
XmNtitleEncoding	dynamic	CSG
XmCTitleEncoding	Atom	
XmNtransient	True	CSG
XmCTransient	Boolean	
XmNwaitForWm	True	CSG
XmCWaitForWm	Boolean	
XmNwidthInc	XtUnspecifiedShellInt	CSG
XmCWidthInc	int	
XmNwindowGroup	dynamic	CSG
XmCWindowGroup	Window	
XmNwinGravity	dynamic	CSG
XmCWinGravity	int	
XmNwmTimeout	5000 ms	CSG
XmCWmTimeout	int	

Shell Resource Set		

Name
      Class
	Default
	      Type
		Access

XmNallowShellResize
      XmCAllowShellResize
	False
	      Boolean
		CG

XmNcreatePopupChildProc
      XmCCreatePopupChildProc
	NULL
	      XtCreatePopupChildProc
		CSG

XmNgeometry
      XmCGeometry
	NULL
	      String
		CSG

XmNoverrideRedirect
      XmCOverrideRedirect
	False
	      Boolean
		CSG

XmNpopdownCallback
      XmCCallback
	NULL
	      XtCallbackList
		C

XmNpopupCallback
      XmCCallback
	NULL
	      XtCallbackList
		C

XmNsaveUnder
      XmCSaveUnder
	True
	      Boolean
		CSG

XmNvisual
      XmCVisual
	CopyFromParent
	      Visual *
		CSG

Composite Resource Set		

Name
      Class
	Default
	      Type
		Access

XmNchildren
      XmCReadOnly
	NULL
	      WidgetList
		G

XmNinsertPosition
      XmCInsertPosition
	NULL
	      XtOrderProc
		CSG

XmNnumChildren
      XmCReadOnly
	0
	      Cardinal
		G

Core Resource Set		
Name	**Default**	**Access**
Class	**Type**	
XmNaccelerators	dynamic	CSG
XmCAccelerators	XtAccelerators	
XmNancestorSensitive	dynamic	G
XmCSensitive	Boolean	
XmNbackground	dynamic	CSG
XmCBackground	Pixel	
XmNbackgroundPixmap	XmUNSPECIFIED_PIXMAP	CSG
XmCPixmap	Pixmap	
XmNborderColor	XtDefaultForeground	CSG
XmCBorderColor	Pixel	
XmNborderPixmap	XmUNSPECIFIED_PIXMAP	CSG
XmCPixmap	Pixmap	
XmNborderWidth	0	CSG
XmCBorderWidth	Dimension	
XmNcolormap	dynamic	CG
XmCColormap	Colormap	
XmNdepth	dynamic	CG
XmCDepth	int	
XmNdestroyCallback	NULL	C
XmCCallback	XtCallbackList	
XmNheight	dynamic	CSG
XmCHeight	Dimension	
XmNinitialResourcesPersistent	True	C
XmCInitialResourcesPersistent	Boolean	
XmNmappedWhenManaged	True	CSG
XmCMappedWhenManaged	Boolean	
XmNscreen	dynamic	CG
XmCScreen	Screen *	
XmNsensitive	True	CSG
XmCSensitive	Boolean	

Name	Default	Access
Class	Type	
XmNtranslations	dynamic	CSG
XmCTranslations	XtTranslations	
XmNwidth	dynamic	CSG
XmCWidth	Dimension	
XmNx	0	CSG
XmCPosition	Position	
XmNy	0	CSG
XmCPosition	Position	

Related Information

Composite(3X), **Core(3X)**, **Shell(3X)**, **VendorShell(3X)**, and **WMShell(3X)**.

Uil—Invokes the UIL compiler from within an application

AES Support Level

Full-use

Synopsis

#include <uil/UilDef.h>

Uil_status_type Uil (*command_desc, compile_desc, message_cb, message_data, status_cb, status_data*)

Uil_command_type	**command_desc*;
Uil_compile_desc_type	**compile_desc*;
Uil_continue_type	*(*message_cb) ()*;
char	**message_data*;
Uil_continue_type	*(*status_cb) ()*;
char	**status_data*;

Description

The **Uil** function provides a callable entry point for the UIL compiler. The **Uil** callable interface can be used to process a UIL source file and to generate UID files, as well as return a detailed description of the UIL source module in the form of a symbol table (parse tree).

command_desc
> Specifies the **uil** command line.

compile_desc Returns the results of the compilation.

message_cb Specifies a callback function that is called when the compiler encounters errors in the UIL source.

message_data
> Specifies user data that is passed to the message callback function (*message_cb*). Note that this argument is not interpreted by UIL, and is used exclusively by the calling application.

status_cb Specifies a callback function that is called to allow X applications to service X events such as updating the screen. This function is called at various check points, which have been hard coded into the UIL compiler. The *status_update_delay* argument in *command_desc* specifies the number of check points to be passed before the *status_cb* function is invoked.

status_data   Specifies user data that is passed to the status callback function (*status_cb*). Note that this argument is not interpreted by the UIL compiler and is used exclusively by the calling application.

Following are the data structures **Uil_command_type** and **Uil_compile_desc_type**:

```
typedef struct Uil_command_type {
char *source_file;
    /* single source to compile */
char *resource_file; /* name of output file */
char *listing_file; /* name of listing file */
unsigned int *include_dir_count;
    /* number of dirs. in include_dir */
char *((*include_dir) []);
    /* dir. to search for include files */
unsigned listing_file_flag: 1;
    /* produce a listing */
unsigned resource_file_flag: 1;
    /* generate UID output */
unsigned machine_code_flag: 1;
    /* generate machine code */
unsigned report_info_msg_flag: 1;
    /* report info messages */
unsigned report_warn_msg_flag: 1;
    /* report warnings */
unsigned parse_tree_flag: 1;
    /* generate parse tree */
unsigned int status_update_delay;
    /* number of times a status point is */
    /* passed before calling status_cb */
    /* function 0 means called every time */
};
```

```
typedef struct Uil_compile_desc_type {
unsigned int compiler_version;
    /* version number of compiler */
unsigned int data_version;
    /* version number of structures */
char *parse_tree_root; /* parse tree output */
unsigned int message_count [Uil_k_max_status+1];
/* array of severity counts */
};
```

Following is a description of the message callback function specified by *message_cb*:

Uil_continue_type (**message_cb*) (*message_data, message_number, severity, msg_buffer, src_buffer, ptr_buffer, loc_buffer, message_count*)

char	**message_data*;
int	*message_number*;
int	*severity*;
char	**msg_buffer*, **src_buffer*;
char	**ptr_buffer*, **loc_buffer*;
int	*message_count*[];

This function specifies a callback function that UIL invokes instead of printing an error message when the compiler encounters an error in the UIL source. The callback should return one of the following values:

Uil_k_terminate

> Terminate processing of the source file

Uil_k_continue

> Continue processing the source file

The arguments are

message_data

> Data supplied by the application as the *message_data* argument to the **Uil** function. UIL does not interpret this data in any way; it just passes it to the callback.

message_number

> An index into a table of error messages and severities for internal use by UIL.

severity

> An integer that indicates the severity of the error. The possible values are the status constants returned by the **Uil** function. See **Return Value** for more information.

msg_buffer   A string that describes the error.

src_buffer   A string consisting of the source line where the error occurred. This string is not always available. In this case, the argument is NULL.

ptr_buffer   A string consisting of whitespace and a printing character in the character position corresponding to the column of the source line where the error occurred. This string may be printed beneath the source line to provide a visual indication of the column where the error occurred. This string is not always available. In this case, the argument is NULL.

loc_buffer   A string identifying the line number and file of the source line where the error occurred. This is not always available; the argument is then NULL.

message_count

An array of integers containing the number of diagnostic messages issued thus far for each severity level. To find the number of messages issued for the current severity level, use the *severity* argument as the index into this array.

Following is a description of the status callback function specified by *status_cb*:

Uil_continue_type (**status_cb*) (*status_data, percent_complete,*
          lines_processed, current_file, message_count)

char	**status_data*;
int	*percent_complete*;
int	*lines_processed*;
char	**current_file*;
int	*message_count*[];

This function specifies a callback function that is invoked to allow X applications to service X events such as updating the screen. The callback should return one of the following values:

Uil_k_terminate

Terminate processing of the source file

Uil_k_continue

Continue processing the source file

The arguments are

status_data

> Data supplied by the application as the *status_data* argument to the **Uil** function. UIL does not interpret this data in any way; it just passes it to the callback.

percent_complete

> An integer indicating what percentage of the current source file has been processed so far.

lines_processed

> An integer indicating how many lines of the current source file have been read so far.

current_file   A string containing the pathname of the current source file.

message_count

> An array of integers containing the number of diagnostic messages issued thus far for each severity level. To find the number of messages issued for a given severity level, use the severity level as the index into this array. The possible severity levels are the status constants returned by the **Uil** function. See **Return Value** for more information.

Return Value

This function returns one of the following status return constants:

Uil_k_success_status

> The operation succeeded.

Uil_k_info_status

> The operation succeeded. An informational message is returned.

Uil_k_warning_status

> The operation succeeded. A warning message is returned.

Uil_k_error_status

> The operation failed due to an error.

Uil_k_severe_status

> The operation failed due to an error.

VendorShell—The VendorShell widget class

AES Support Level

Full-use

History/Direction

The description of the geometry management of shells and their children has been changed (for trial-use). New resources have been added specifying font lists for button, label, and text children (for trial-use).

Synopsis

#include <Xm/Xm.h>
#include <X11/Shell.h>

Description

VendorShell is a Motif widget class used as a supporting superclass for all shell classes that are visible to the window manager and that are not override redirect. It contains resources that describe the MWM-specific look and feel. It also manages the MWM-specific communication needed by all VendorShell subclasses. See the **mwm** reference page for more information.

Setting **XmNheight**, **XmNwidth**, or **XmNborderWidth** for either a VendorShell or its managed child usually sets that resource to the same value in both the parent and the child. When an off-the-spot input method exists, the height and width of the shell may be greater than those of the managed child in order to accommodate the input method. In this case, setting **XmNheight** or **XmNwidth** for the shell does not necessarily set that resource to the same value in the managed child, and setting **XmNheight** or **XmNwidth** for the child does not necessarily set that resource to the same value in the shell.

For the managed child of a VendorShell, regardless of the value of the shell's **XmNallowShellResize**, setting **XmNx** or **XmNy** sets the corresponding resource of the parent but does not change the child's position relative to the parent. **XtGetValues** for the child's **XmNx** or **XmNy** yields the value of the corresponding resource in the parent. The x and y-coordinates of the child's upper left outside corner relative to the parent's upper left inside corner are both 0 (zero) minus the value of **XmNborderWidth**.

Note that the *Inter-Client Communication Conventions Manual* (ICCCM) allows a window manager to change or control the border width of a reparented top-level window.

Classes

VendorShell inherits behavior and resources from the **Core**, **Composite**, **Shell**, and **WMShell** classes.

The class pointer is **vendorShellWidgetClass**.

The class name is **VendorShell**.

New Resources

The following table defines a set of widget resources used by the programmer to specify data. The programmer can also set the resource values for the inherited classes to set attributes for this widget. To reference a subresource by name or by class in a **.Xdefaults** file, remove the **XmN** or **XmC** prefix and use the remaining letters. To specify one of the defined values for a subresource in a **.Xdefaults** file, remove the **Xm** prefix and use the remaining letters (in either lowercase or uppercase, but include any underscores between words). The codes in the access column indicate if the given subresource can be set at creation time (C), set by using **XtSetValues** (S), retrieved by using **XtGetValues** (G), or is not applicable (N/A).

VendorShell Resource Set		
Name	**Default**	**Access**
Class	**Type**	
XmNbuttonFontList	dynamic	CSG
XmCButtonFontList	XmFontList	
XmNdefaultFontList	dynamic	CG
XmCDefaultFontList	XmFontList	
XmNdeleteResponse	XmDESTROY	CSG
XmCDeleteResponse	unsigned char	
XmNkeyboardFocusPolicy	XmEXPLICIT	CSG
XmCKeyboardFocusPolicy	unsigned char	
XmNlabelFontList	dynamic	CSG
XmCLabelFontList	XmFontList	
XmNmwmDecorations	-1	CSG
XmCMwmDecorations	int	
XmNmwmFunctions	-1	CSG
XmCMwmFunctions	int	
XmNmwmInputMode	-1	CSG
XmCMwmInputMode	int	
XmNmwmMenu	NULL	CSG
XmCMwmMenu	String	
XmNtextFontList	dynamic	CSG
XmCTextFontList	XmFontList	

XmNbuttonFontList

Specifies the font list used for VendorShell's button descendants. If this value is NULL at initialization and if the value of **XmNdefaultFontList** is not NULL, **XmNbuttonFontList** is initialized to the value of **XmNdefaultFontList**. If the value of **XmNdefaultFontList** is NULL, the parent hierarchy of the widget is searched for an ancestor that is a subclass of the BulletinBoard, VendorShell, or MenuShell widget class. If such an ancestor is found, **XmNbuttonFontList** is initialized to the **XmNbuttonFontList** of the ancestor widget. If no such ancestor is found, the default is implementation dependent.

XmNdefaultFontList

> Specifies a default font list for VendorShell's descendants. This resource is obsolete and exists for compatibility with earlier releases. It has been replaced by **XmNbuttonFontList**, **XmNlabelFontList**, and **XmNtextFontList**.

XmNdeleteResponse

> Determines what action the shell takes in response to a **WM_DELETE_WINDOW** message. The setting can be one of three values: **XmDESTROY**, **XmUNMAP**, and **XmDO_NOTHING**. The resource is scanned, and the appropriate action is taken after the **WM_DELETE_WINDOW** callback list (if any) that is registered with the Protocol manager has been called.

XmNkeyboardFocusPolicy

> Determines allocation of keyboard focus within the widget hierarchy rooted at this shell. The X keyboard focus must be directed to somewhere in the hierarchy for this client-side focus management to take effect. Possible values are **XmEXPLICIT**, specifying a click-to-type policy, and **XmPOINTER**, specifying a pointer-driven policy.

XmNlabelFontList

> Specifies the font list used for VendorShell's label descendants (Labels and LabelGadgets). If this value is NULL at initialization and if the value of **XmNdefaultFontList** is not NULL, **XmNlabelFontList** is initialized to the value of **XmNdefaultFontList**. If the value of **XmNdefaultFontList** is NULL, the parent hierarchy of the widget is searched for an ancestor that is a subclass of the XmBulletinBoard, VendorShell, or XmMenuShell widget class. If such an ancestor is found, **XmNlabelFontList** is initialized to the **XmNlabelFontList** of the ancestor widget. If no such ancestor is found, the default is implementation dependent.

XmNmwmDecorations

Specifies the decoration flags (specific decorations to add or remove from the window manager frame) for the **_MOTIF_WM_HINTS** property. If any decoration flags are specified by the **_MOTIF_WM_HINTS** property, only decorations indicated by both that property and the MWM **clientDecoration** and **transientDecoration** resources are displayed. If no decoration flags are specified by the **_MOTIF_WM_HINTS** property, decorations indicated by the MWM **clientDecoration** and **transientDecoration** resources are displayed. The default for the **XmNmwmDecorations** resource is not to specify any decoration flags for the **_MOTIF_WM_HINTS** property.

XmNmwmFunctions

Specifies the function flags (specific window manager functions to apply or not apply to the client window) for the **_MOTIF_WM_HINTS** property. If any function flags are specified by the **_MOTIF_WM_HINTS** property, only functions indicated by both that property and the MWM **clientFunctions** and **transientFunctions** resources are applied. If no function flags are specified by the **_MOTIF_WM_HINTS** property, functions indicated by the MWM **clientFunctions** and **transientFunctions** resources are applied. The default for the **XmNmwmFunctions** resource is not to specify any function flags for the **_MOTIF_WM_HINTS** property.

XmNmwmInputMode

Specifies the input mode flag (application modal or system modal input constraints) for the **_MOTIF_WM_HINTS** property. If no input mode flag is specified by the **_MOTIF_WM_HINTS** property, no input constraints are applied, and input goes to any window. The default for the **XmNmwmInputMode** resource is not to specify any input mode flag for the **_MOTIF_WM_HINTS** property.

An application that sets input constraints on a dialog usually uses the BulletinBoard's **XmNdialogStyle** resource rather than the parent DialogShell's **XmNmwmInputMode** resource.

XmNmwmMenu

Specifies the menu items that the Motif window manager should add
to the end of the window menu. The string contains a list of items
separated by **\n** with the following format:

label [mnemonic] [accelerator] function

If more than one item is specified, the items should be separated by
a newline character.

XmNtextFontList

Specifies the font list used for VendorShell's Text and List
descendants. If this value is NULL at initialization and if the value
of **XmNdefaultFontList** is not NULL, **XmNtextFontList** is
initialized to the value of **XmNdefaultFontList**. If the value of
XmNdefaultFontList is NULL, the parent hierarchy of the widget
is searched for an ancestor that is a subclass of the BulletinBoard or
VendorShell widget class. If such an ancestor is found,
XmNtextFontList is initialized to the **XmNtextFontList** of the
ancestor widget. If no such ancestor is found, the default is
implementation dependent.

Inherited Resources

VendorShell inherits behavior and resources from the superclasses described in the
following tables. For a complete description of each resource, refer to the reference
page for that superclass.

<table>
<tr><th colspan="3">WMShell Resource Set</th></tr>
<tr><th>Name
   Class</th><th>Default
   Type</th><th>Access</th></tr>
<tr><td>XmNbaseHeight
   XmCBaseHeight</td><td>XtUnspecifiedShellInt
   int</td><td>CSG</td></tr>
<tr><td>XmNbaseWidth
   XmCBaseWidth</td><td>XtUnspecifiedShellInt
   int</td><td>CSG</td></tr>
<tr><td>XmNheightInc
   XmCHeightInc</td><td>XtUnspecifiedShellInt
   int</td><td>CSG</td></tr>
<tr><td>XmNiconMask
   XmCIconMask</td><td>NULL
   Pixmap</td><td>CSG</td></tr>
<tr><td>XmNiconPixmap
   XmCIconPixmap</td><td>NULL
   Pixmap</td><td>CSG</td></tr>
<tr><td>XmNiconWindow
   XmCIconWindow</td><td>NULL
   Window</td><td>CSG</td></tr>
<tr><td>XmNiconX
   XmCIconX</td><td>-1
   int</td><td>CSG</td></tr>
<tr><td>XmNiconY
   XmCIconY</td><td>-1
   int</td><td>CSG</td></tr>
<tr><td>XmNinitialState
   XmCInitialState</td><td>NormalState
   int</td><td>CSG</td></tr>
<tr><td>XmNinput
   XmCInput</td><td>True
   Boolean</td><td>CSG</td></tr>
<tr><td>XmNmaxAspectX
   XmCMaxAspectX</td><td>XtUnspecifiedShellInt
   int</td><td>CSG</td></tr>
<tr><td>XmNmaxAspectY
   XmCMaxAspectY</td><td>XtUnspecifiedShellInt
   int</td><td>CSG</td></tr>
<tr><td>XmNmaxHeight
   XmCMaxHeight</td><td>XtUnspecifiedShellInt
   int</td><td>CSG</td></tr>
<tr><td>XmNmaxWidth
   XmCMaxWidth</td><td>XtUnspecifiedShellInt
   int</td><td>CSG</td></tr>
<tr><td>XmNminAspectX
   XmCMinAspectX</td><td>XtUnspecifiedShellInt
   int</td><td>CSG</td></tr>
</table>

Name	Default	Access
Class	Type	
XmNminAspectY	XtUnspecifiedShellInt	CSG
XmCMinAspectY	int	
XmNminHeight	XtUnspecifiedShellInt	CSG
XmCMinHeight	int	
XmNminWidth	XtUnspecifiedShellInt	CSG
XmCMinWidth	int	
XmNtitle	dynamic	CSG
XmCTitle	String	
XmNtitleEncoding	dynamic	CSG
XmCTitleEncoding	Atom	
XmNtransient	False	CSG
XmCTransient	Boolean	
XmNwaitForWm	True	CSG
XmCWaitForWm	Boolean	
XmNwidthInc	XtUnspecifiedShellInt	CSG
XmCWidthInc	int	
XmNwindowGroup	dynamic	CSG
XmCWindowGroup	Window	
XmNwinGravity	dynamic	CSG
XmCWinGravity	int	
XmNwmTimeout	5000 ms	CSG
XmCWmTimeout	int	

Shell Resource Set		
Name	**Default**	**Access**
Class	**Type**	
XmNallowShellResize	False	CG
XmCAllowShellResize	Boolean	
XmNcreatePopupChildProc	NULL	CSG
XmCCreatePopupChildProc	XtCreatePopupChildProc	
XmNgeometry	NULL	CSG
XmCGeometry	String	
XmNoverrideRedirect	False	CSG
XmCOverrideRedirect	Boolean	
XmNpopdownCallback	NULL	C
XmCCallback	XtCallbackList	
XmNpopupCallback	NULL	C
XmCCallback	XtCallbackList	
XmNsaveUnder	False	CSG
XmCSaveUnder	Boolean	
XmNvisual	CopyFromParent	CSG
XmCVisual	Visual *	

Composite Resource Set		
Name	**Default**	**Access**
Class	**Type**	
XmNchildren	NULL	G
XmCReadOnly	WidgetList	
XmNinsertPosition	NULL	CSG
XmCInsertPosition	XtOrderProc	
XmNnumChildren	0	G
XmCReadOnly	Cardinal	

Core Resource Set		

Name
    Class
	Default
	    Type
		Access

XmNaccelerators
    XmCAccelerators
	dynamic
	    XtAccelerators
		CSG

XmNancestorSensitive
    XmCSensitive
	dynamic
	    Boolean
		G

XmNbackground
    XmCBackground
	dynamic
	    Pixel
		CSG

XmNbackgroundPixmap
    XmCPixmap
	XmUNSPECIFIED_PIXMAP
	    Pixmap
		CSG

XmNborderColor
    XmCBorderColor
	XtDefaultForeground
	    Pixel
		CSG

XmNborderPixmap
    XmCPixmap
	XmUNSPECIFIED_PIXMAP
	    Pixmap
		CSG

XmNborderWidth
    XmCBorderWidth
	0
	    Dimension
		CSG

XmNcolormap
    XmCColormap
	dynamic
	    Colormap
		CG

XmNdepth
    XmCDepth
	dynamic
	    int
		CG

XmNdestroyCallback
    XmCCallback
	NULL
	    XtCallbackList
		C

XmNheight
    XmCHeight
	dynamic
	    Dimension
		CSG

XmNinitialResourcesPersistent
    XmCInitialResourcesPersistent
	True
	    Boolean
		C

XmNmappedWhenManaged
    XmCMappedWhenManaged
	True
	    Boolean
		CSG

XmNscreen
    XmCScreen
	dynamic
	    Screen *
		CG

XmNsensitive
    XmCSensitive
	True
	    Boolean
		CSG

Name	Default	Access
Class	**Type**	
XmNtranslations	dynamic	CSG
XmCTranslations	XtTranslations	
XmNwidth	dynamic	CSG
XmCWidth	Dimension	
XmNx	0	CSG
XmCPosition	Position	
XmNy	0	CSG
XmCPosition	Position	

Related Information

Composite(3X), Core(3X), mwm(1X), Shell(3X), WMShell(3X),
XmActivateProtocol(3X), XmActivateWMProtocol(3X),
XmAddProtocolCallback(3X), XmAddWMProtocolCallback(3X),
XmAddProtocols(3X), XmAddWMProtocols(3X), XmDeactivateProtocol(3X),
XmDeactivateWMProtocol(3X), XmGetAtomName(3X), XmInternAtom(3X),
XmIsMotifWMRunning(3X), XmRemoveProtocolCallback(3X),
XmRemoveWMProtocolCallback(3X), XmRemoveProtocols(3X),
XmRemoveWMProtocols(3X), XmSetProtocolHooks(3X), and
XmSetWMProtocolHooks(3X).

WMShell—The WMShell widget class

AES Support Level

Full-use

Synopsis

#include <Xm/Xm.h>
#include <X11/Shell.h>

Description

WMShell is a top-level widget that encapsulates the interaction with the window manager.

Classes

WMShell inherits behavior and resources from the **Core**, **Composite**, and **Shell** classes.

The class pointer is **wmShellWidgetClass**.

The class name is **WMShell**.

New Resources

The following table defines a set of widget resources used by the programmer to specify data. The programmer can also set the resource values for the inherited classes to set attributes for this widget. To reference a resource by name or by class in a **.Xdefaults** file, remove the **XmN** or **XmC** prefix and use the remaining letters. To specify one of the defined values for a resource in a **.Xdefaults** file, remove the **Xm** prefix and use the remaining letters (in either lowercase or uppercase, but include any underscores between words). The codes in the access column indicate if the given resource can be set at creation time (C), set by using **XtSetValues** (S), retrieved by using **XtGetValues** (G), or is not applicable (N/A).

WMShell Resource Set		

Name
    Class
	Default
	    Type
		Access

XmNbaseHeight
    XmCBaseHeight
	XtUnspecifiedShellInt
	    int
		CSG

XmNbaseWidth
    XmCBaseWidth
	XtUnspecifiedShellInt
	    int
		CSG

XmNheightInc
    XmCHeightInc
	XtUnspecifiedShellInt
	    int
		CSG

XmNiconMask
    XmCIconMask
	NULL
	    Pixmap
		CSG

XmNiconPixmap
    XmCIconPixmap
	NULL
	    Pixmap
		CSG

XmNiconWindow
    XmCIconWindow
	NULL
	    Window
		CSG

XmNiconX
    XmCIconX
	-1
	    int
		CSG

XmNiconY
    XmCIconY
	-1
	    int
		CSG

XmNinitialState
    XmCInitialState
	NormalState
	    int
		CSG

XmNinput
    XmCInput
	False
	    Boolean
		CSG

XmNmaxAspectX
    XmCMaxAspectX
	XtUnspecifiedShellInt
	    int
		CSG

XmNmaxAspectY
    XmCMaxAspectY
	XtUnspecifiedShellInt
	    int
		CSG

XmNmaxHeight
    XmCMaxHeight
	XtUnspecifiedShellInt
	    int
		CSG

XmNmaxWidth
    XmCMaxWidth
	XtUnspecifiedShellInt
	    int
		CSG

XmNminAspectX
    XmCMinAspectX
	XtUnspecifiedShellInt
	    int
		CSG

Name	Default	Access
Class	Type	
XmNminAspectY	XtUnspecifiedShellInt	CSG
XmCMinAspectY	int	
XmNminHeight	XtUnspecifiedShellInt	CSG
XmCMinHeight	int	
XmNminWidth	XtUnspecifiedShellInt	CSG
XmCMinWidth	int	
XmNtitle	dynamic	CSG
XmCTitle	String	
XmNtitleEncoding	dynamic	CSG
XmCTitleEncoding	Atom	
XmNtransient	False	CSG
XmCTransient	Boolean	
XmNwaitForWm	True	CSG
XmCWaitForWm	Boolean	
XmNwidthInc	XtUnspecifiedShellInt	CSG
XmCWidthInc	int	
XmNwindowGroup	dynamic	CSG
XmCWindowGroup	Window	
XmNwinGravity	dynamic	CSG
XmCWinGravity	int	
XmNwmTimeout	5000 ms	CSG
XmCWmTimeout	int	

XmNbaseHeight

Specifies the base for a progression of preferred heights for the window manager to use in sizing the widget. The preferred heights are **XmNbaseHeight** plus integral multiples of **XmNheightInc**, with a minimum of **XmNminHeight** and a maximum of **XmNmaxHeight**. If an initial value is not supplied for **XmNbaseHeight** but is supplied for **XmNbaseWidth**, the value of **XmNbaseHeight** is set to 0 (zero) when the widget is realized.

XmNbaseWidth

Specifies the base for a progression of preferred widths for the window manager to use in sizing the widget. The preferred widths are **XmNbaseWidth** plus integral multiples of **XmNwidthInc**, with a minimum of **XmNminWidth** and a maximum of **XmNmaxWidth**. If an initial value is not supplied for **XmNbaseWidth** but is supplied for **XmNbaseHeight**, the value of **XmNbaseWidth** is set to 0 (zero) when the widget is realized.

XmNheightInc

Specifies the increment for a progression of preferred heights for the window manager to use in sizing the widget. The preferred heights are **XmNbaseHeight** plus integral multiples of **XmNheightInc**, with a minimum of **XmNminHeight** and a maximum of **XmNmaxHeight**. If an initial value is not supplied for **XmNheightInc** but is supplied for **XmNwidthInc**, the value of **XmNheightInc** is set to 1 when the widget is realized.

XmNiconMask

Specifies a bitmap that could be used by the window manager to clip the **XmNiconPixmap** bitmap to make the icon nonrectangular.

XmNiconPixmap

Specifies a bitmap that could be used by the window manager as the application's icon.

XmNiconWindow

Specifies the ID of a window that could be used by the window manager as the application's icon.

XmNiconX Specifies a suitable place to put the application's icon; this is a hint to the window manager in root window coordinates. Because the window manager controls icon placement policy, this resource may be ignored. If no initial value is specified, the value is set to -1 when the widget is realized.

XmNiconY Specifies a suitable place to put the application's icon; this is a hint to the window manager in root window coordinates. Because the window manager controls icon placement policy, this resource may be ignored. If no initial value is specified, the value is set to -1 when the widget is realized.

XmNinitialState

Specifies the state the application wants the widget instance to start in. It must be one of the constants **NormalState** or **IconicState**.

XmNinput Specifies the application's input model for this widget and its descendants. The meaning of a True or False value for this resource depends on the presence or absence of a WM_TAKE_FOCUS atom in the WM_PROTOCOLS property:

Input Model	XmNinput	WM_TAKE_FOCUS
No input	False	Absent
Passive	True	Absent
Locally active	True	Present
Globally active	False	Present

For more information on input models, see the X Consortium Standard *Inter-Client Communication Conventions Manual* (ICCCM).

XmNmaxAspectX

Specifies the numerator of the maximum aspect ratio (X/Y) that the application wants the widget instance to have.

XmNmaxAspectY

Specifies the denominator of the maximum aspect ratio (X/Y) that the application wants the widget instance to have.

XmNmaxHeight

Specifies the maximum height that the application wants the widget instance to have. If an initial value is not supplied for **XmNmaxHeight** but is supplied for **XmNmaxWidth**, the value of **XmNmaxHeight** is set to 32767 when the widget is realized.

XmNmaxWidth

Specifies the maximum width that the application wants the widget instance to have. If an initial value is not supplied for **XmNmaxWidth** but is supplied for **XmNmaxHeight**, the value of **XmNmaxWidth** is set to 32767 when the widget is realized.

XmNminAspectX

Specifies the numerator of the minimum aspect ratio (X/Y) that the application wants the widget instance to have.

XmNminAspectY

Specifies the denominator of the minimum aspect ratio (X/Y) that the application wants the widget instance to have.

XmNminHeight

Specifies the minimum height that the application wants the widget instance to have. If an initial value is not supplied for **XmNminHeight** but is supplied for **XmNminWidth**, the value of **XmNminHeight** is set to 1 when the widget is realized.

XmNminWidth
Specifies the minimum width that the application wants the widget instance to have. If an initial value is not supplied for **XmNminWidth** but is supplied for **XmNminHeight**, the value of **XmNminWidth** is set to 1 when the widget is realized.

XmNtitle
Specifies the application name to be displayed by the window manager. The default is the icon name, if specified; otherwise, it is the name of the application.

XmNtitleEncoding
Specifies a property type that represents the encoding of the **XmNtitle** string. If a language procedure has been set, the default is None; otherwise, the default is **XA_STRING.** When the widget is realized, if the value is None, the corresponding name is assumed to be in the current locale. The name is passed to **XmbTextListToTextProperty** with an encoding style of **XStdICCTextStyle**. The resulting encoding is **STRING** if the name is fully convertible to **STRING,**; otherwise it is **COMPOUND_TEXT**. The values of the encoding resources are not changed; they remain None.

XmNtransient
Specifies a Boolean value that is True if the widget instance is transient, typically a popup on behalf of another widget. The window manager may treat a transient widget's window differently from other windows. For example, a window manager may not iconify a transient window separately from its associated application. Applications and users should not normally alter this resource.

XmNwaitForWm
When True, specifies that the Intrinsics waits the length of time given by the **XmNwmTimeout** resource for the window manager to respond to certain actions before assuming that there is no window manager present. This resource is altered by the Intrinsics as it receives, or fails to receive, responses from the window manager.

XmNwidthInc
Specifies the base for a progression of preferred widths for the window manager to use in sizing the widget. The preferred widths are **XmNbaseWidth** plus integral multiples of **XmNwidthInc**, with a minimum of **XmNminWidth** and a maximum of **XmNmaxWidth**. If an initial value is not supplied for **XmNwidthInc** but is supplied for **XmNheightInc**, the value of **XmNwidthInc** is set to 1 when the widget is realized.

XmNwindowGroup

Specifies the ID of a window with which this widget instance is associated. By convention, this window is the "leader" of a group of windows. A window manager may treat all windows in a group in some way; for example, it may always move or iconify them together.

If no initial value is specified, the value is set to the window of the first realized ancestor widget in the parent hierarchy when the widget is realized. If a value of **XtUnspecifiedWindowGroup** is specified, no window group is set.

XmNwinGravity

Specifies the window gravity for use by the window manager in positioning the widget. If no initial value is specified, the value is set when the widget is realized. If **XmNgeometry** is not NULL, **XmNwinGravity** is set to the window gravity returned by **XWMGeometry**. Otherwise, **XmNwinGravity** is set to **NorthWestGravity**.

XmNwmTimeout

Specifies the length of time that the Intrinsics waits for the window manager to respond to certain actions before assuming that there is no window manager present. The value is in milliseconds and must not be negative.

Inherited Resources

WMShell inherits behavior and resources from the superclasses described in the following tables. For a complete description of each resource, refer to the reference page for that superclass.

Shell Resource Set		
Name	**Default**	**Access**
Class	**Type**	
XmNallowShellResize	False	CG
XmCAllowShellResize	Boolean	
XmNcreatePopupChildProc	NULL	CSG
XmCCreatePopupChildProc	XtCreatePopupChildProc	
XmNgeometry	NULL	CSG
XmCGeometry	String	
XmNoverrideRedirect	False	CSG
XmCOverrideRedirect	Boolean	
XmNpopdownCallback	NULL	C
XmCCallback	XtCallbackList	
XmNpopupCallback	NULL	C
XmCCallback	XtCallbackList	
XmNsaveUnder	False	CSG
XmCSaveUnder	Boolean	
XmNvisual	CopyFromParent	CSG
XmCVisual	Visual *	

Composite Resource Set		
Name	**Default**	**Access**
Class	**Type**	
XmNchildren	NULL	G
XmCReadOnly	WidgetList	
XmNinsertPosition	NULL	CSG
XmCInsertPosition	XtOrderProc	
XmNnumChildren	0	G
XmCReadOnly	Cardinal	

Core Resource Set		

Name
    Class
	Default
	    Type
		Access

XmNaccelerators
    XmCAccelerators
	dynamic
	    XtAccelerators
		CSG

XmNancestorSensitive
    XmCSensitive
	dynamic
	    Boolean
		G

XmNbackground
    XmCBackground
	dynamic
	    Pixel
		CSG

XmNbackgroundPixmap
    XmCPixmap
	XmUNSPECIFIED_PIXMAP
	    Pixmap
		CSG

XmNborderColor
    XmCBorderColor
	XtDefaultForeground
	    Pixel
		CSG

XmNborderPixmap
    XmCPixmap
	XmUNSPECIFIED_PIXMAP
	    Pixmap
		CSG

XmNborderWidth
    XmCBorderWidth
	1
	    Dimension
		CSG

XmNcolormap
    XmCColormap
	dynamic
	    Colormap
		CG

XmNdepth
    XmCDepth
	dynamic
	    int
		CG

XmNdestroyCallback
    XmCCallback
	NULL
	    XtCallbackList
		C

XmNheight
    XmCHeight
	dynamic
	    Dimension
		CSG

XmNinitialResourcesPersistent
    XmCInitialResourcesPersistent
	True
	    Boolean
		C

XmNmappedWhenManaged
    XmCMappedWhenManaged
	True
	    Boolean
		CSG

XmNscreen
    XmCScreen
	dynamic
	    Screen *
		CG

XmNsensitive
    XmCSensitive
	True
	    Boolean
		CSG

Name	Default	Access
Class	Type	
XmNtranslations	dynamic	CSG
XmCTranslations	XtTranslations	
XmNwidth	dynamic	CSG
XmCWidth	Dimension	
XmNx	0	CSG
XmCPosition	Position	
XmNy	0	CSG
XmCPosition	Position	

Related Information

Composite(3X), Core(3X), and Shell(3X).

XmActivateProtocol—A VendorShell function that activates a protocol

AES Support Level

Trial-use

Synopsis

#include <Xm/Xm.h>
#include <Xm/Protocols.h>

void XmActivateProtocol (*shell, property, protocol*)
    Widget   *shell*;
    Atom   *property*;
    Atom   *protocol*;

void XmActivateWMProtocol (*shell, protocol*)
    Widget   *shell*;
    Atom   *protocol*;

Description

XmActivateProtocol activates a protocol. It updates the handlers and the *property* if the *shell* is realized. It is sometimes useful to allow a protocol's state information (callback lists, and so on) to persist, even though the client may choose to temporarily resign from the interaction. This is supported by allowing a *protocol* to be in one of two states: active or inactive. If the *protocol* is active and the *shell* is realized, the *property* contains the *protocol* **Atom**. If the *protocol* is inactive, the **Atom** is not present in the *property*.

XmActivateWMProtocol is a convenience interface. It calls **XmActivateProtocol** with the property value set to the atom returned by interning **WM_PROTOCOLS**.

shell   Specifies the widget with which the protocol property is associated

property   Specifies the protocol property

protocol   Specifies the protocol **Atom** (or an **int** type cast to **Atom**)

For a complete definition of VendorShell and its associated resources, see **VendorShell(3X)**.

Related Information

VendorShell(3X), **XmActivateWMProtocol(3X)** and **XmInternAtom(3X)**.

XmActivateWMProtocol—A VendorShell convenience interface that activates a protocol

AES Support Level

Trial-use

Synopsis

#include <Xm/Xm.h>
#include <Xm/Protocols.h>

void XmActivateWMProtocol (*shell, protocol*)
    Widget   *shell*;
    Atom   *protocol*;

Description

XmActivateWMProtocol is a convenience interface. It calls **XmActivateProtocol** with the property value set to the atom returned by interning **WM_PROTOCOLS**.

shell   Specifies the widget with which the protocol property is associated

protocol   Specifies the protocol **Atom** (or an **int** type cast to **Atom**)

For a complete definition of VendorShell and its associated resources, see **VendorShell(3X)**.

Related Information

VendorShell(3X), **XmActivateProtocol(3X)**, and **XmInternAtom(3X)**.

XmAddProtocolCallback—A VendorShell function that adds client callbacks for a protocol

AES Support Level

Trial-use

Synopsis

#include <Xm/Xm.h>
#include <Xm/Protocols.h>

void XmAddProtocolCallback (*shell, property, protocol, callback, closure*)
    Widget   *shell*;
    Atom   *property*;
    Atom   *protocol*;
    XtCallbackProc   *callback*;
    XtPointer   *closure*;

void XmAddWMProtocolCallback (*shell, protocol, callback, closure*)
    Widget   *shell*;
    Atom   *protocol*;
    XtCallbackProc   *callback*;
    XtPointer   *closure*;

Description

XmAddProtocolCallback adds client callbacks for a protocol. It checks if the protocol is registered, and if it is not, calls **XmAddProtocols**. It then adds the callback to the internal list. These callbacks are called when the corresponding client message is received.

XmAddWMProtocolCallback is a convenience interface. It calls **XmAddProtocolCallback** with the property value set to the atom returned by interning **WM_PROTOCOLS**.

shell   Specifies the widget with which the protocol property is associated

property   Specifies the protocol property

protocol   Specifies the protocol **Atom** (or an **int** type cast to **Atom**)

callback   Specifies the procedure to call when a protocol message is received

closure   Specifies the client data to be passed to the callback when it is invoked

For a complete definition of VendorShell and its associated resources, see **VendorShell(3X)**.

Related Information

VendorShell(3X), **XmAddProtocols(3X)**, **XmAddWMProtocolCallback(3X)**, and **XmInternAtom(3X)**.

XmAddProtocols—A VendorShell function that adds the protocols to the protocol manager and allocates the internal tables

AES Support Level

Trial-use

Synopsis

#include <Xm/Xm.h>
#include <Xm/Protocols.h>

void XmAddProtocols (*shell, property, protocols, num_protocols*)
    Widget   *shell*;
    Atom   *property*;
    Atom   * *protocols*;
    Cardinal   *num_protocols*;

void XmAddWMProtocols (*shell, protocols, num_protocols*)
    Widget   *shell*;
    Atom   * *protocols*;
    Cardinal   *num_protocols*;

Description

XmAddProtocols adds the protocols to the protocol manager and allocates the internal tables.

XmAddWMProtocols is a convenience interface. It calls **XmAddProtocols** with the property value set to the atom returned by interning **WM_PROTOCOLS**.

shell   Specifies the widget with which the protocol property is associated

property   Specifies the protocol property

protocols   Specifies the protocol **Atoms** (or **int** types cast to **Atom**)

num_protocols
          Specifies the number of elements in *protocols*

For a complete definition of VendorShell and its associated resources, see **VendorShell(3X)**.

Related Information

VendorShell(3X), **XmAddWMProtocols(3X)**, and **XmInternAtom(3X)**.

XmAddTabGroup—A function that adds a manager or a primitive widget to the list of tab groups

AES Support Level

Full-use

History/Direction

The **XmAddTabGroup** function is scheduled for removal in revision E.

Synopsis

#include <Xm/Xm.h>

void XmAddTabGroup (*tab_group*)
    Widget   *tab_group*;

Description

This function is obsolete and its behavior is replaced by setting **XmNnavigationType** to **XmEXCLUSIVE_TAB_GROUP**. When the keyboard is used to traverse through a widget hierarchy, primitive or manager widgets are grouped together into what are known as **tab groups**. Any manager or primitive widget can be a tab group. Within a tab group, move the focus to the next widget in the tab group by using the arrow keys. To move to another tab group, use **KNextField** or **KPrevField**.

Tab groups are ordinarily specified by the **XmNnavigationType** resource. **XmAddTabGroup** is called to control the order of traversal of tab groups. The widget specified by *tab_group* is appended to the list of tab groups to be traversed, and the widget's **XmNnavigationType** is set to **XmEXCLUSIVE_TAB_GROUP**.

tab_group   Specifies the manager or primitive widget ID

Related Information

XmManager(3X), **XmPrimitive(3X)**, and **XmRemoveTabGroup(3X)**.

XmAddWMProtocolCallback—A VendorShell convenience interface that adds client callbacks for a protocol

AES Support Level

Trial-use

Synopsis

#include <Xm/Xm.h>
#include <Xm/Protocols.h>

void XmAddWMProtocolCallback (*shell, protocol, callback, closure*)
    Widget   *shell*;
    Atom   *protocol*;
    XtCallbackProc *callback*;
    XtPointer   *closure*;

Description

XmAddWMProtocolCallback is a convenience interface. It calls **XmAddProtocolCallback** with the property value set to the atom returned by interning **WM_PROTOCOLS**.

shell   Specifies the widget with which the protocol property is associated

protocol   Specifies the protocol **Atom** (or an **int** type cast to **Atom**)

callback   Specifies the procedure to call when a protocol message is received

closure   Specifies the client data to be passed to the callback when it is invoked

For a complete definition of VendorShell and its associated resources, see **VendorShell(3X)**.

Related Information

VendorShell(3X), **XmAddProtocolCallback(3X)**, and **XmInternAtom(3X)**.

XmAddWMProtocols—A VendorShell convenience interface that adds the protocols to the protocol manager and allocates the internal tables

AES Support Level

Trial-use

Synopsis

#include <Xm/Xm.h>
#include <Xm/Protocols.h>

void XmAddWMProtocols (*shell, protocols, num_protocols*)
    Widget   *shell*;
    Atom   * *protocols*;
    Cardinal   *num_protocols*;

Description

XmAddWMProtocols is a convenience interface. It calls **XmAddProtocols** with the property value set to the atom returned by interning **WM_PROTOCOLS**.

shell   Specifies the widget with which the protocol property is associated

protocols   Specifies the protocol **Atoms** (or **int** types cast to **Atom**)

num_protocols
    Specifies the number of elements in *protocols*

For a complete definition of VendorShell and its associated resources, see **VendorShell(3X)**.

Related Information

VendorShell(3X), **XmAddProtocols(3X)**, and **XmInternAtom(3X)**.

XmArrowButton—The ArrowButton widget class

AES Support Level

Full-use

Synopsis

#include <Xm/ArrowB.h>

Description

ArrowButton consists of a directional arrow surrounded by a border shadow. When it is selected, the shadow changes to give the appearance that the ArrowButton has been pressed in. When the ArrowButton is unselected, the shadow reverts to give the appearance that the ArrowButton is released, or out.

Classes

ArrowButton inherits behavior and resources from the **Core** and **XmPrimitive** classes.

The class pointer is **xmArrowButtonWidgetClass**.

The class name is **XmArrowButton**.

New Resources

The following table defines a set of widget resources used by the programmer to specify data. The programmer can also set the resource values for the inherited classes to set attributes for this widget. To reference a resource by name or by class in a **.Xdefaults** file, remove the **XmN** or **XmC** prefix and use the remaining letters. To specify one of the defined values for a resource in a **.Xdefaults** file, remove the **Xm** prefix and use the remaining letters (in either lowercase or uppercase, but include any underscores between words). The codes in the access column indicate if the given resource can be set at creation time (C), set by using **XtSetValues** (S), retrieved by using **XtGetValues** (G), or is not applicable (N/A).

XmArrowButton Resource Set		
Name	**Default**	**Access**
Class	**Type**	
XmNactivateCallback	NULL	C
XmCCallback	XtCallbackList	
XmNarmCallback	NULL	C
XmCCallback	XtCallbackList	
XmNarrowDirection	XmARROW_UP	CSG
XmCArrowDirection	unsigned char	
XmNdisarmCallback	NULL	C
XmCCallback	XtCallbackList	
XmNmultiClick	dynamic	CSG
XmCMultiClick	unsigned char	

XmNactivateCallback
> Specifies a list of callbacks that is called when the ArrowButton is activated. To activate the button, press and release **BSelect** while the pointer is inside the ArrowButton widget. Activating the ArrowButton also disarms it. The reason sent by this callback is **XmCR_ACTIVATE**.

XmNarmCallback
> Specifies a list of callbacks that is called when the ArrowButton is armed. To arm this widget, press **BSelect** while the pointer is inside the ArrowButton. The reason sent by this callback is **XmCR_ARM**.

XmNarrowDirection
> Sets the arrow direction. The values for this resource are

> - **XmARROW_UP**
> - **XmARROW_DOWN**
> - **XmARROW_LEFT**
> - **XmARROW_RIGHT**

XmNdisarmCallback
> Specifies a list of callbacks that is called when the ArrowButton is disarmed. To disarm this widget, press and release **BSelect** while the pointer is inside the ArrowButton. The reason for this callback is **XmCR_DISARM**.

XmNmultiClick

If a button click is followed by another button click within the time span specified by the display's multiclick time, and this resource is set to **XmMULTICLICK_DISCARD**, the second click. is not processed. If this resource is set to **XmMULTICLICK_KEEP**, the event is processed and *click_count* is incremented in the callback structure. When the button is not in a menu, the default value is **XmMULTICLICK_KEEP**.

Inherited Resources

ArrowButton inherits behavior and resources from the superclasses described in the following table. For a complete description of each resource, refer to the reference page for that superclass.

<table>
<thead>
<tr><th colspan="3" align="center">XmPrimitive Resource Set</th></tr>
<tr><th>Name
    Class</th><th>Default
    Type</th><th>Access</th></tr>
</thead>
<tbody>
<tr><td>XmNbottomShadowColor
    XmCBottomShadowColor</td><td>dynamic
    Pixel</td><td>CSG</td></tr>
<tr><td>XmNbottomShadowPixmap
    XmCBottomShadowPixmap</td><td>XmUNSPECIFIED_PIXMAP
    Pixmap</td><td>CSG</td></tr>
<tr><td>XmNforeground
    XmCForeground</td><td>dynamic
    Pixel</td><td>CSG</td></tr>
<tr><td>XmNhelpCallback
    XmCCallback</td><td>NULL
    XtCallbackList</td><td>C</td></tr>
<tr><td>XmNhighlightColor
    XmCHighlightColor</td><td>dynamic
    Pixel</td><td>CSG</td></tr>
<tr><td>XmNhighlightOnEnter
    XmCHighlightOnEnter</td><td>False
    Boolean</td><td>CSG</td></tr>
<tr><td>XmNhighlightPixmap
    XmCHighlightPixmap</td><td>dynamic
    Pixmap</td><td>CSG</td></tr>
<tr><td>XmNhighlightThickness
    XmCHighlightThickness</td><td>2
    Dimension</td><td>CSG</td></tr>
<tr><td>XmNnavigationType
    XmCNavigationType</td><td>XmNONE
    XmNavigationType</td><td>CSG</td></tr>
<tr><td>XmNshadowThickness
    XmCShadowThickness</td><td>2
    Dimension</td><td>CSG</td></tr>
<tr><td>XmNtopShadowColor
    XmCTopShadowColor</td><td>dynamic
    Pixel</td><td>CSG</td></tr>
<tr><td>XmNtopShadowPixmap
    XmCTopShadowPixmap</td><td>dynamic
    Pixmap</td><td>CSG</td></tr>
<tr><td>XmNtraversalOn
    XmCTraversalOn</td><td>True
    Boolean</td><td>CSG</td></tr>
<tr><td>XmNuserData
    XmCUserData</td><td>NULL
    XtPointer</td><td>CSG</td></tr>
</tbody>
</table>

Core Resource Set		

Name
    Class
	Default
	    Type
		Access

XmNaccelerators
    XmCAccelerators
	dynamic
	    XtAccelerators
		CSG

XmNancestorSensitive
    XmCSensitive
	dynamic
	    Boolean
		G

XmNbackground
    XmCBackground
	dynamic
	    Pixel
		CSG

XmNbackgroundPixmap
    XmCPixmap
	XmUNSPECIFIED_PIXMAP
	    Pixmap
		CSG

XmNborderColor
    XmCBorderColor
	XtDefaultForeground
	    Pixel
		CSG

XmNborderPixmap
    XmCPixmap
	XmUNSPECIFIED_PIXMAP
	    Pixmap
		CSG

XmNborderWidth
    XmCBorderWidth
	0
	    Dimension
		CSG

XmNcolormap
    XmCColormap
	dynamic
	    Colormap
		CG

XmNdepth
    XmCDepth
	dynamic
	    int
		CG

XmNdestroyCallback
    XmCCallback
	NULL
	    XtCallbackList
		C

XmNheight
    XmCHeight
	dynamic
	    Dimension
		CSG

XmNinitialResourcesPersistent
    XmCInitialResourcesPersistent
	True
	    Boolean
		C

XmNmappedWhenManaged
    XmCMappedWhenManaged
	True
	    Boolean
		CSG

XmNscreen
    XmCScreen
	dynamic
	    Screen *
		CG

XmNsensitive
    XmCSensitive
	True
	    Boolean
		CSG

Name	Default	Access
Class	Type	
XmNtranslations	dynamic	CSG
XmCTranslations	XtTranslations	
XmNwidth	dynamic	CSG
XmCWidth	Dimension	
XmNx	0	CSG
XmCPosition	Position	
XmNy	0	CSG
XmCPosition	Position	

Callback Information

A pointer to the following structure is passed to each callback:

```
typedef struct
{
    int         reason;
    XEvent      * event;
    int         click_count;
} XmArrowButtonCallbackStruct;
```

reason   Indicates why the callback was invoked.

event   Points to the **XEvent** that triggered the callback.

click_count This value is valid only when the reason is **XmCR_ACTIVATE**. It contains the number of clicks in the last multiclick sequence if the **XmNmultiClick** resource is set to **XmMULTICLICK_KEEP**; otherwise it contains 1. The activate callback is invoked for each click if **XmNmultiClick** is set to **XmMULTICLICK_KEEP**.

Action Routines

The **XmArrowButton** action routines are

Activate(): Draws the shadow in the unselected state. If the pointer is within the ArrowButton, calls the callbacks for **XmNactivateCallback**.

Arm(): Draws the shadow in the selected state and calls the callbacks for **XmNarmCallback**.

ArmAndActivate():
Draws the shadow in the selected state and calls the callbacks for **XmNarmCallback**. Arranges for the shadow to be drawn in the unselected state and the callbacks for **XmNactivateCallback** and **XmNdisarmCallback** to be called, either immediately or at a later time.

Disarm():
Draws the shadow in the unselected state and calls the callbacks for **XmNdisarmCallback**.

Help():
Calls the callbacks for **XmNhelpCallback** if any exist. If there are no help callbacks for this widget, this action calls the help callbacks for the nearest ancestor that has them.

MultiActivate():
If **XmNmultiClick** is **XmMULTICLICK_DISCARD**, this action does nothing.

If **XmNmultiClick** is **XmMULTICLICK_KEEP**, this action increments *click_count* in the callback structure and draws the shadow in the unselected state. If the pointer is within the ArrowButton, this action calls the callbacks for **XmNactivateCallback** and **XmNdisarmCallback**.

MultiArm(): If **XmNmultiClick** is **XmMULTICLICK_DISCARD**, this action does nothing. If **XmNmultiClick** is **XmMULTICLICK_KEEP**, this action draws the shadow in the selected state and calls the callbacks for **XmNarmCallback**.

Related Information

Core(3X), **XmCreateArrowButton(3X)**, and **XmPrimitive(3X)**.

XmArrowButtonGadget—The ArrowButtonGadget widget class

AES Support Level

Full-use

Synopsis

#include <Xm/ArrowBG.h>

Description

ArrowButtonGadget consists of a directional arrow surrounded by a border shadow. When it is selected, the shadow changes to give the appearance that the ArrowButtonGadget has been pressed in. When it is unselected, the shadow reverts to give the appearance that the button is released, or out.

Classes

ArrowButtonGadget inherits behavior and resources from the **Object**, **RectObj**, and **XmGadget** classes.

The class pointer is **xmArrowButtonGadgetClass**.

The class name is **XmArrowButtonGadget**.

New Resources

The following table defines a set of widget resources used by the programmer to specify data. The programmer can also set the resource values for the inherited classes to set attributes for this widget. To reference a resource by name or by class in a **.Xdefaults** file, remove the **XmN** or **XmC** prefix and use the remaining letters. To specify one of the defined values for a resource in a **.Xdefaults** file, remove the **Xm** prefix and use the remaining letters (in either lowercase or uppercase, but include any underscores between words). The codes in the access column indicate if the given resource can be set at creation time (C), set by using **XtSetValues** (S), retrieved by using **XtGetValues** (G), or is not applicable (N/A).

<table>
<tr><td colspan="3" align="center">ArrowButtonGadget Resource Set</td></tr>
<tr><td>Name
    Class</td><td>Default
    Type</td><td>Access</td></tr>
<tr><td>XmNactivateCallback
    XmCCallback</td><td>NULL
    XtCallbackList</td><td>C</td></tr>
<tr><td>XmNarmCallback
    XmCCallback</td><td>NULL
    XtCallbackList</td><td>C</td></tr>
<tr><td>XmNarrowDirection
    XmCArrowDirection</td><td>XmARROW_UP
    unsigned char</td><td>CSG</td></tr>
<tr><td>XmNdisarmCallback
    XmCCallback</td><td>NULL
    XtCallbackList</td><td>C</td></tr>
<tr><td>XmNmultiClick
    XmCMultiClick</td><td>dynamic
    unsigned char</td><td>CSG</td></tr>
</table>

XmNactivateCallback

Specifies a list of callbacks that is called when the ArrowButtonGadget is activated. To activate the button, press and release **BSelect** while the pointer is inside the ArrowButtonGadget. Activating the ArrowButtonGadget also disarms it. The reason sent by this callback is **XmCR_ACTIVATE**.

XmNarmCallback

Specifies a list of callbacks that is called when the ArrowButtonGadget is armed. To arm this widget, press **BSelect** while the pointer is inside the ArrowButtonGadget. The reason sent by this callback is **XmCR_ARM**.

XmNarrowDirection

Sets the arrow direction. The values for this resource are

- **XmARROW_UP**

- **XmARROW_DOWN**

- **XmARROW_LEFT**

- **XmARROW_RIGHT**

XmNdisarmCallback

Specifies a list of callbacks that is called when the ArrowButtonGadget is disarmed. To disarm this widget, press and release **BSelect** while the pointer is inside the ArrowButtonGadget. The reason sent by this callback is **XmCR_DISARM**.

XmNmultiClick

If a button click is followed by another button click within the time span specified by the display's multiclick time and this resource is set to **XmMULTICLICK_DISCARD**, the second click is not processed. If this resource is set to **XmMULTICLICK_KEEP**, the event is processed and *click_count* is incremented in the callback structure. When the ArrowButtonGadget is not in a menu, the default value is **XmMULTICLICK_KEEP**.

Inherited Resources

XmArrowButtonGadget inherits behavior and resources from the superclasses described in the following tables. For a complete description of each resource, refer to the reference page for that superclass.

XmGadget Resource Set		
Name	**Default**	**Access**
Class	**Type**	
XmNhelpCallback	NULL	C
XmCCallback	XtCallbackList	
XmNhighlightOnEnter	False	CSG
XmCHighlightOnEnter	Boolean	
XmNhighlightThickness	2	CSG
XmCHighlightThickness	Dimension	
XmNnavigationType	XmNONE	CSG
XmCNavigationType	XmNavigationType	
XmNshadowThickness	2	CSG
XmCShadowThickness	Dimension	
XmNtraversalOn	True	CSG
XmCTraversalOn	Boolean	
XmNuserData	NULL	CSG
XmCUserData	XtPointer	

XmArrowButtonGadget(3X)

<table>
<tr><td colspan="3" align="center">RectObj Resource Set</td></tr>
<tr><td>Name
    Class</td><td>Default
    Type</td><td>Access</td></tr>
<tr><td>XmNancestorSensitive
    XmCSensitive</td><td>dynamic
    Boolean</td><td>G</td></tr>
<tr><td>XmNborderWidth
    XmCBorderWidth</td><td>0
    Dimension</td><td>N/A</td></tr>
<tr><td>XmNheight
    XmCHeight</td><td>dynamic
    Dimension</td><td>CSG</td></tr>
<tr><td>XmNsensitive
    XmCSensitive</td><td>True
    Boolean</td><td>CSG</td></tr>
<tr><td>XmNwidth
    XmCWidth</td><td>dynamic
    Dimension</td><td>CSG</td></tr>
<tr><td>XmNx
    XmCPosition</td><td>0
    Position</td><td>CSG</td></tr>
<tr><td>XmNy
    XmCPosition</td><td>0
    Position</td><td>CSG</td></tr>
</table>

<table>
<tr><td colspan="3" align="center">Object Resource Set</td></tr>
<tr><td>Name
    Class</td><td>Default
    Type</td><td>Access</td></tr>
<tr><td>XmNdestroyCallback
    XmCCallback</td><td>NULL
    XtCallbackList</td><td>C</td></tr>
</table>

Callback Information

A pointer to the following structure is passed to each callback:

```
typedef struct
{
    int         reason;
    XEvent      * event;
    int         click_count;
} XmArrowButtonCallbackStruct;
```

reason   Indicates why the callback was invoked.

event   Points to the **XEvent** that triggered the callback.

click_count   This value is valid only when the reason is **XmCR_ACTIVATE**. It contains the number of clicks in the last multiclick sequence if the **XmNmultiClick** resource is set to **XmMULTICLICK_KEEP**, otherwise it contains 1. The activate callback is invoked for each click if **XmNmultiClick** is set to **XmMULTICLICK_KEEP**.

Related Information

Object(3X), **RectObj(3X)**, **XmCreateArrowButtonGadget(3X)**, and **XmGadget(3X)**.

XmBulletinBoard—The BulletinBoard widget class

AES Support Level

Full-use

History/Direction

The **XmNtextTranslations** resource is scheduled for removal in revision D.

Synopsis

#include <Xm/BulletinB.h>

Description

BulletinBoard is a composite widget that provides simple geometry management for child widgets. It does not force positioning on its children, but can be set to reject geometry requests that result in overlapping children. BulletinBoard is the base widget for most dialog widgets and is also used as a general container widget.

Modal and modeless dialogs are implemented as collections of widgets that include a DialogShell, a BulletinBoard (or subclass) child of the shell, and various dialog components (buttons, labels, and so on) that are children of BulletinBoard. BulletinBoard defines callbacks useful for dialogs (focus, map, unmap), which are available for application use. If its parent is a DialogShell, BulletinBoard passes title and input mode (based on dialog style) information to the parent, which is responsible for appropriate communication with the window manager.

Classes

BulletinBoard inherits behavior and resources from the **Core**, **Composite**, **Constraint**, and **XmManager** classes.

The class pointer is **xmBulletinBoardWidgetClass**.

The class name is **XmBulletinBoard**.

New Resources

The following table defines a set of widget resources used by the programmer to specify data. The programmer can also set the resource values for the inherited classes to set attributes for this widget. To reference a resource by name or by class in a **.Xdefaults** file, remove the **XmN** or **XmC** prefix and use the remaining letters. To specify one of the defined values for a resource in a **.Xdefaults** file, remove the **Xm** prefix and use the remaining letters (in either lowercase or uppercase, but include any underscores between words). The codes in the access column indicate if the given resource can be set at creation time (C), set by using **XtSetValues** (S), retrieved by using **XtGetValues** (G), or is not applicable (N/A).

XmBulletinBoard Resource Set		
Name	**Default**	**Access**
Class	**Type**	
XmNallowOverlap	True	CSG
XmCAllowOverlap	Boolean	
XmNautoUnmanage	True	CG
XmCAutoUnmanage	Boolean	
XmNbuttonFontList	dynamic	CSG
XmCButtonFontList	XmFontList	
XmNcancelButton	NULL	SG
XmCWidget	Widget	
XmNdefaultButton	NULL	SG
XmCWidget	Widget	
XmNdefaultPosition	True	CSG
XmCDefaultPosition	Boolean	
XmNdialogStyle	dynamic	CSG
XmCDialogStyle	unsigned char	
XmNdialogTitle	NULL	CSG
XmCDialogTitle	XmString	
XmNfocusCallback	NULL	C
XmCCallback	XtCallbackList	
XmNlabelFontList	dynamic	CSG
XmCLabelFontList	XmFontList	
XmNmapCallback	NULL	C
XmCCallback	XtCallbackList	
XmNmarginHeight	10	CSG
XmCMarginHeight	Dimension	
XmNmarginWidth	10	CSG
XmCMarginWidth	Dimension	
XmNnoResize	False	CSG
XmCNoResize	Boolean	
XmNresizePolicy	XmRESIZE_ANY	CSG
XmCResizePolicy	unsigned char	

Name	Default	Access
Class	Type	
XmNshadowType	XmSHADOW_OUT	CSG
XmCShadowType	unsigned char	
XmNtextFontList	dynamic	CSG
XmCTextFontList	XmFontList	
XmNtextTranslations	NULL	C
XmCTranslations	XtTranslations	
XmNunmapCallback	NULL	C
XmCCallback	XtCallbackList	

XmNallowOverlap

Controls the policy for overlapping child widgets. If this resource is True, BulletinBoard allows geometry requests that result in overlapping children.

XmNautoUnmanage

Controls whether or not BulletinBoard is automatically unmanaged after a button is activated. If this resource is True on initialization and if the BulletinBoard's parent is a DialogShell, BulletinBoard adds a callback to button children (PushButtons, PushButtonGadgets, and DrawnButtons) that unmanages the BulletinBoard when a button is activated. If this resource is False on initialization or if the BulletinBoard's parent is not a DialogShell, the BulletinBoard is not automatically unmanaged. For BulletinBoard subclasses with Apply or Help buttons, activating those buttons does not automatically unmanage the BulletinBoard.

XmNbuttonFontList

Specifies the font list used for BulletinBoard's button descendants. If this value is NULL at initialization, the parent hierarchy of the widget is searched for an ancestor that is a subclass of the BulletinBoard, VendorShell, or MenuShell widget class. If such an ancestor is found, the font list is initialized to the **XmNbuttonFontList** of the ancestor widget. If no such ancestor is found, the default is implementation dependent. Refer to **XmFontList(3X)** for more information on the creation and structure of a font list.

XmNcancelButton

Specifies the widget ID of the **Cancel** button. BulletinBoard's subclasses, which define a **Cancel** button, set this resource. BulletinBoard does not directly provide any behavior for that button.

XmNdefaultButton

Specifies the widget ID of the default button. Some BulletinBoard subclasses, which define a default button, set this resource. BulletinBoard defines translations and installs accelerators that activate that button when **KActivate** is pressed and the keyboard focus is not in another button.

XmNdefaultPosition

Controls whether or not the BulletinBoard is automatically positioned by its parent. If this resource is True, and the parent of the BulletinBoard is a DialogShell, the BulletinBoard is centered within or around the parent of the DialogShell when the BulletinBoard is mapped and managed. If this resource is False, the BulletinBoard is not automatically positioned.

XmNdialogStyle

Indicates the dialog style associated with the BulletinBoard. If the parent of the BulletinBoard is a DialogShell, the parent's **XmNmwmInputMode** is set according to the value of this resource. This resource can be set only if the BulletinBoard is unmanaged. Possible values for this resource include the following:

XmDIALOG_SYSTEM_MODAL

Used for dialogs that must be responded to before any other interaction in any application.

XmDIALOG_PRIMARY_APPLICATION_MODAL

Used for dialogs that must be responded to before some other interactions in ancestors of the widget.

XmDIALOG_APPLICATION_MODAL

Used for dialogs that must be responded to before some other interactions in ancestors of the widget. This value is the same as **XmDIALOG_PRIMARY_APPLICATION_MODAL**, and remains for compatibility.

XmDIALOG_FULL_APPLICATION_MODAL

Used for dialogs that must be responded to before some other interactions in the same application.

        XmDIALOG_MODELESS

                Used for dialogs that do not interrupt interaction of any application. This is the default when the parent of the BulletinBoard is a DialogShell.

        XmDIALOG_WORK_AREA

                Used for BulletinBoard widgets whose parents are not DialogShells. **XmNdialogStyle** is forced to have this value when the parent of the BulletinBoard is not a DialogShell.

XmNdialogTitle

Specifies the dialog title. If this resource is not NULL, and the parent of the BulletinBoard is a subclass of WMShell, BulletinBoard sets the **XmNtitle** and **XmNtitleEncoding** of its parent. If the only character set in **XmNdialogTitle** is ISO8859-1, **XmNtitle** is set to the string of the title, and **XmNtitleEncoding** is set to **STRING**. If **XmNdialogTitle** contains character sets other than ISO8859-1, **XmNtitle** is set to the string of the title converted to a compound text string, and **XmNtitleEncoding** is set to **COMPOUND_TEXT**.

XmNfocusCallback

Specifies the list of callbacks that is called when the BulletinBoard widget or one of its descendants accepts the input focus. The callback reason is **XmCR_FOCUS**.

XmNlabelFontList

Specifies the font list used for BulletinBoard's label descendants (Labels and LabelGadgets). If this value is NULL at initialization, the parent hierarchy of the widget is searched for an ancestor that is a subclass of the BulletinBoard, VendorShell, or MenuShell widget class. If such an ancestor is found, the font list is initialized to the **XmNlabelFontList** of the ancestor widget. If no such ancestor is found, the default is implementation dependent. Refer to **XmFontList(3X)** for more information on the creation and structure of a font list.

XmNmapCallback

Specifies the list of callbacks that is called only when the parent of the BulletinBoard is a DialogShell. In this case, this callback list is invoked when the BulletinBoard widget is mapped. The callback reason is **XmCR_MAP**. DialogShells are usually mapped when the DialogShell is managed.

XmNmarginHeight

> Specifies the minimum spacing in pixels between the top or bottom edge of BulletinBoard and any child widget.

XmNmarginWidth

> Specifies the minimum spacing in pixels between the left or right edge of BulletinBoard and any child widget.

XmNnoResize

> Controls whether or not resize controls are included in the window manager frame around the BulletinBoard's parent. If this resource is set to True, **mwm** does not include resize controls in the window manager frame containing the parent of the BulletinBoard if the parent is a subclass of VendorShell. If this resource is set to False, the window manager frame does include resize controls. Other controls provided by **mwm** can be included or excluded through the **mwm** resources provided by VendorShell.

XmNresizePolicy

> Controls the policy for resizing BulletinBoard widgets. Possible values include
>
> | | |
> |---|---|
> | **XmRESIZE_NONE** | Fixed size |
> | **XmRESIZE_ANY** | Shrink or grow as needed |
> | **XmRESIZE_GROW** | Grow only |

XmNshadowType

> Describes the shadow drawing style for BulletinBoard. This resource can have the following values:
>
> **XmSHADOW_IN**
>
> > Draws the BulletinBoard shadow so that it appears inset. This means that the bottom shadow visuals and top shadow visuals are reversed.
>
> **XmSHADOW_OUT**
>
> > Draws the BulletinBoard shadow so that it appears outset.
>
> **XmSHADOW_ETCHED_IN**
>
> > Draws the BulletinBoard shadow using a double line giving the effect of a line etched into the window, similar to the Separator widget.

        XmSHADOW_ETCHED_OUT
> Draws the BulletinBoard shadow using a double line giving the effect of a line coming out of the window, similar to the Separator widget.

XmNtextFontList
> Specifies the font list used for BulletinBoard's Text and List descendants. If this value is NULL at initialization, the parent hierarchy of the widget is searched for an ancestor that is a subclass of the XmBulletinBoard or VendorShell widget class. If such an ancestor is found, the font list is initialized to the **XmNtextFontList** of the ancestor widget. If no such ancestor is found, the default is implementation dependent. Refer to **XmFontList(3X)** for more information on the creation and structure of a font list.

XmNtextTranslations
> This resource is scheduled for removal in revision D. It adds translations to any Text widget or Text widget subclass that is added as a child of BulletinBoard.

XmNunmapCallback
> Specifies the list of callbacks that is called only when the parent of the BulletinBoard is a DialogShell. In this case, this callback list is invoked when the BulletinBoard widget is unmapped. The callback reason is **XmCR_UNMAP**. DialogShells are usually unmapped when the DialogShell is unmanaged.

Inherited Resources

BulletinBoard inherits behavior and resources from the superclasses described in the following tables. For a complete description of each resource, refer to the reference page for that superclass.

XmManager Resource Set		
Name	**Default**	**Access**
Class	**Type**	
XmNbottomShadowColor	dynamic	CSG
XmCBottomShadowColor	Pixel	
XmNbottomShadowPixmap	XmUNSPECIFIED_PIXMAP	CSG
XmCBottomShadowPixmap	Pixmap	
XmNforeground	dynamic	CSG
XmCForeground	Pixel	
XmNhelpCallback	NULL	C
XmCCallback	XtCallbackList	
XmNhighlightColor	dynamic	CSG
XmCHighlightColor	Pixel	
XmNhighlightPixmap	dynamic	CSG
XmCHighlightPixmap	Pixmap	
XmNnavigationType	XmTAB_GROUP	CSG
XmCNavigationType	XmNavigationType	
XmNshadowThickness	dynamic	CSG
XmCShadowThickness	Dimension	
XmNstringDirection	dynamic	CG
XmCStringDirection	XmStringDirection	
XmNtopShadowColor	dynamic	CSG
XmCTopShadowColor	Pixel	
XmNtopShadowPixmap	dynamic	CSG
XmCTopShadowPixmap	Pixmap	
XmNtraversalOn	True	CSG
XmCTraversalOn	Boolean	
XmNuserData	NULL	CSG
XmCUserData	XtPointer	

Composite Resource Set		
Name	**Default**	**Access**
Class	**Type**	
XmNchildren	NULL	G
XmCReadOnly	WidgetList	
XmNinsertPosition	NULL	CSG
XmCInsertPosition	XtOrderProc	
XmNnumChildren	0	G
XmCReadOnly	Cardinal	

Core Resource Set		

Name
    Class
	Default
	    Type
		Access

XmNaccelerators
    XmCAccelerators
	dynamic
	    XtAccelerators
		N/A

XmNancestorSensitive
    XmCSensitive
	dynamic
	    Boolean
		G

XmNbackground
    XmCBackground
	dynamic
	    Pixel
		CSG

XmNbackgroundPixmap
    XmCPixmap
	XmUNSPECIFIED_PIXMAP
	    Pixmap
		CSG

XmNborderColor
    XmCBorderColor
	XtDefaultForeground
	    Pixel
		CSG

XmNborderPixmap
    XmCPixmap
	XmUNSPECIFIED_PIXMAP
	    Pixmap
		CSG

XmNborderWidth
    XmCBorderWidth
	0
	    Dimension
		CSG

XmNcolormap
    XmCColormap
	dynamic
	    Colormap
		CG

XmNdepth
    XmCDepth
	dynamic
	    int
		CG

XmNdestroyCallback
    XmCCallback
	NULL
	    XtCallbackList
		C

XmNheight
    XmCHeight
	dynamic
	    Dimension
		CSG

XmNinitialResourcesPersistent
    XmCInitialResourcesPersistent
	True
	    Boolean
		C

XmNmappedWhenManaged
    XmCMappedWhenManaged
	True
	    Boolean
		CSG

XmNscreen
    XmCScreen
	dynamic
	    Screen *
		CG

XmNsensitive
    XmCSensitive
	True
	    Boolean
		CSG

Name	Default	Access
Class	Type	
XmNtranslations	dynamic	CSG
XmCTranslations	XtTranslations	
XmNwidth	dynamic	CSG
XmCWidth	Dimension	
XmNx	0	CSG
XmCPosition	Position	
XmNy	0	CSG
XmCPosition	Position	

Callback Information

A pointer to the following structure is passed to each callback:

```
typedef struct
{
    int        reason;
    XEvent     * event;
} XmAnyCallbackStruct;
```

reason   Indicates why the callback was invoked

event   Points to the **XEvent** that triggered the callback

Related Information

Composite(3X), **Constraint(3X)**, **Core(3X)**, **XmCreateBulletinBoard(3X)**,
XmCreateBulletinBoardDialog(3X), **XmDialogShell(3X),** and
XmManager(3X).

XmCascadeButton—The CascadeButton widget class

AES Support Level

Full-use

Synopsis

#include <Xm/CascadeB.h>

Description

CascadeButton links two MenuPanes or a MenuBar to a MenuPane.

It is used in menu systems and must have a RowColumn parent with its **XmNrowColumnType** resource set to **XmMENU_BAR**, **XmMENU_POPUP** or **XmMENU_PULLDOWN**.

It is the only widget that can have a Pulldown MenuPane attached to it as a submenu. The submenu is displayed when this widget is activated within a MenuBar, a PopupMenu, or a PulldownMenu. Its visuals can include a label or pixmap and a cascading indicator when it is in a Popup or Pulldown MenuPane; or it can include only a label or a pixmap when it is in a MenuBar.

The default behavior associated with a CascadeButton depends on the type of menu system in which it resides. By default, **BSelect** controls the behavior of the CascadeButton. In addition, **BMenu** controls the behavior of the CascadeButton if it resides in a PopupMenu system. The actual mouse button used is determined by its RowColumn parent.

A CascadeButton's visuals differ from most other button gadgets. When the button becomes armed, its visuals change from a 2-D to a 3-D look, and it displays the submenu that has been attached to it. If no submenu is attached, it simply changes its visuals.

When a CascadeButton within a Pulldown or Popup MenuPane is armed as the result of the user moving the mouse pointer into the widget, it does not immediately display its submenu. Instead, it waits a short amount of time to see if the arming was temporary (that is, the user was simply passing through the widget), or whether the user really wanted the submenu posted. This time delay is configurable using **XmNmappingDelay**.

CascadeButton provides a single mechanism for activating the widget from the keyboard. This mechanism is referred to as a keyboard mnemonic. If a mnemonic has been specified for the widget, the user may activate the CascadeButton by simply typing the mnemonic while the CascadeButton is visible. If the CascadeButton is in a MenuBar and the MenuBar does not have the focus, the **MAlt** modifier must be pressed with the mnemonic. Mnemonics are typically used to interact with a menu using the keyboard interface.

If the Cascadebutton is in a Pulldown or Popup MenuPane and there is a submenu attached, the **XmNmarginBottom**, **XmNmarginLeft**, **XmNmarginRight**, and **XmNmarginTop** resources may enlarge to accommodate **XmNcascadePixmap**. **XmNmarginWidth** defaults to 6 if this resource is in a MenuBar; otherwise, it takes Label's default, which is 2.

Classes

CascadeButton inherits behavior and resources from **Core**, **XmPrimitive**, and **XmLabel** classes.

The class pointer is **xmCascadeButtonWidgetClass**.

The class name is **XmCascadeButton**.

New Resources

The following table defines a set of widget resources used by the programmer to specify data. The programmer can also set the resource values for the inherited classes to set attributes for this widget. To reference a resource by name or by class in a **.Xdefaults** file, remove the **XmN** or **XmC** prefix and use the remaining letters. To specify one of the defined values for a resource in a **.Xdefaults** file, remove the **Xm** prefix and use the remaining letters (in either lowercase or uppercase, but include any underscores between words). The codes in the access column indicate if the given resource can be set at creation time (C), set by using **XtSetValues** (S), retrieved by using **XtGetValues** (G), or is not applicable (N/A).

XmCascadeButton Resource Set		
Name	**Default**	**Access**
Class	**Type**	
XmNactivateCallback	NULL	C
XmCCallback	XtCallbackList	
XmNcascadePixmap	dynamic	CSG
XmCPixmap	Pixmap	
XmNcascadingCallback	NULL	C
XmCCallback	XtCallbackList	
XmNmappingDelay	180 ms	CSG
XmCMappingDelay	int	
XmNsubMenuId	NULL	CSG
XmCMenuWidget	Widget	

XmNactivateCallback

Specifies the list of callbacks that is called when the user activates the CascadeButton widget and there is no submenu attached to pop up. The activation occurs when a mouse button is released or when the mnemonic associated with the widget is typed. The specific mouse button depends on information in the RowColumn parent. The reason sent by the callback is **XmCR_ACTIVATE**.

XmNcascadePixmap

Specifies the cascade pixmap displayed on one end of the widget when a CascadeButton is used within a Popup or Pulldown MenuPane and a submenu is attached. The Label class resources **XmNmarginBottom**, **XmNmarginLeft**, **XmNmarginRight**, and **XmNmarginTop** may be modified to ensure that room is left for the cascade pixmap. The default cascade pixmap is an arrow pointing to the side of the menu where the submenu will appear.

XmNcascadingCallback

Specifies the list of callbacks that is called just prior to the mapping of the submenu associated with CascadeButton. The reason sent by the callback is **XmCR_CASCADING**.

XmNmappingDelay

Specifies the amount of time, in milliseconds, between when a CascadeButton becomes armed and when it maps its submenu. This delay is used only when the widget is within a Popup or Pulldown MenuPane. The value must not be negative.

XmNsubMenuId

Specifies the widget ID for the Pulldown MenuPane to be associated with this CascadeButton. The specified MenuPane is displayed when the CascadeButton becomes armed. The MenuPane must have been created with the appropriate parentage depending on the type of menu used. See **XmCreateMenuBar(3X)**, **XmCreatePulldownMenu(3X)**, and **XmCreatePopupMenu(3X)** for more information on the menu systems.

Inherited Resources

CascadeButton inherits behavior and resources from the superclasses described in the following tables. For a complete description of each resource, refer to the reference page for that superclass.

XmLabel Resource Set		
Name	**Default**	**Access**
Class	**Type**	
XmNaccelerator	NULL	N/A
XmCAccelerator	String	
XmNacceleratorText	NULL	N/A
XmCAcceleratorText	XmString	
XmNalignment	dynamic	CSG
XmCAlignment	unsigned char	
XmNfontList	dynamic	CSG
XmCFontList	XmFontList	
XmNlabelInsensitivePixmap	XmUNSPECIFIED_PIXMAP	CSG
XmCLabelInsensitivePixmap	Pixmap	
XmNlabelPixmap	XmUNSPECIFIED_PIXMAP	CSG
XmCLabelPixmap	Pixmap	
XmNlabelString	dynamic	CSG
XmCXmString	XmString	
XmNlabelType	XmSTRING	CSG
XmCLabelType	unsigned char	
XmNmarginBottom	dynamic	CSG
XmCMarginBottom	Dimension	
XmNmarginHeight	2	CSG
XmCMarginHeight	Dimension	
XmNmarginLeft	0	CSG
XmCMarginLeft	Dimension	
XmNmarginRight	dynamic	CSG
XmCMarginRight	Dimension	
XmNmarginTop	dynamic	CSG
XmCMarginTop	Dimension	
XmNmarginWidth	dynamic	CSG
XmCMarginWidth	Dimension	

Name
    Class
	Default
	    Type
		Access

XmNmnemonic
    XmCMnemonic
	NULL
	    KeySym
		CSG

XmNmnemonicCharSet
    XmCMnemonicCharSet
	XmFONTLIST_DEFAULT_TAG
	    String
		CSG

XmNrecomputeSize
    XmCRecomputeSize
	True
	    Boolean
		CSG

XmNstringDirection
    XmCStringDirection
	dynamic
	    XmStringDirection
		CSG

XmPrimitive Resource Set		
Name Class	**Default** Type	**Access**
XmNbottomShadowColor XmCBottomShadowColor	dynamic Pixel	CSG
XmNbottomShadowPixmap XmCBottomShadowPixmap	XmUNSPECIFIED_PIXMAP Pixmap	CSG
XmNforeground XmCForeground	dynamic Pixel	CSG
XmNhelpCallback XmCCallback	NULL XtCallbackList	C
XmNhighlightColor XmCHighlightColor	dynamic Pixel	CSG
XmNhighlightOnEnter XmCHighlightOnEnter	False Boolean	CSG
XmNhighlightPixmap XmCHighlightPixmap	dynamic Pixmap	CSG
XmNhighlightThickness XmCHighlightThickness	0 Dimension	CSG
XmNnavigationType XmCNavigationType	XmNONE XmNavigationType	CSG
XmNshadowThickness XmCShadowThickness	2 Dimension	CSG
XmNtopShadowColor XmCTopShadowColor	dynamic Pixel	CSG
XmNtopShadowPixmap XmCTopShadowPixmap	dynamic Pixmap	CSG
XmNtraversalOn XmCTraversalOn	dynamic Boolean	G
XmNuserData XmCUserData	NULL XtPointer	CSG

Core Resource Set		
Name	**Default**	**Access**
Class	**Type**	
XmNaccelerators	dynamic	CSG
XmCAccelerators	XtAccelerators	
XmNancestorSensitive	dynamic	G
XmCSensitive	Boolean	
XmNbackground	dynamic	CSG
XmCBackground	Pixel	
XmNbackgroundPixmap	XmUNSPECIFIED_PIXMAP	CSG
XmCPixmap	Pixmap	
XmNborderColor	XtDefaultForeground	CSG
XmCBorderColor	Pixel	
XmNborderPixmap	XmUNSPECIFIED_PIXMAP	CSG
XmCPixmap	Pixmap	
XmNborderWidth	0	CSG
XmCBorderWidth	Dimension	
XmNcolormap	dynamic	CG
XmCColormap	Colormap	
XmNdepth	dynamic	CG
XmCDepth	int	
XmNdestroyCallback	NULL	C
XmCCallback	XtCallbackList	
XmNheight	dynamic	CSG
XmCHeight	Dimension	
XmNinitialResourcesPersistent	True	C
XmCInitialResourcesPersistent	Boolean	
XmNmappedWhenManaged	True	CSG
XmCMappedWhenManaged	Boolean	
XmNscreen	dynamic	CG
XmCScreen	Screen *	
XmNsensitive	True	CSG
XmCSensitive	Boolean	

Name	Default	Access
Class	**Type**	
XmNtranslations	dynamic	CSG
XmCTranslations	XtTranslations	
XmNwidth	dynamic	CSG
XmCWidth	Dimension	
XmNx	0	CSG
XmCPosition	Position	
XmNy	0	CSG
XmCPosition	Position	

Callback Information

A pointer to the following structure is passed to each callback:

typedef struct
{
    int   *reason*;
    XEvent   * *event*;
} XmAnyCallbackStruct;

reason   Indicates why the callback was invoked

event   Points to the **XEvent** that triggered the callback or is NULL if this callback was not triggered due to an **XEvent**

Action Routines

The XmCascadeButton action routines are

CleanupMenuBar():

In a MenuBar, disarms the CascadeButton and the menu and, when the shell's keyboard focus policy is **XmEXPLICT**, restores keyboard focus to the widget that had the focus before the menu was entered.

In a toplevel Pulldown MenuPane from a MenuBar, unposts the menu, disarms the MenuBar CascadeButton and the MenuBar, and, when the shell's keyboard focus policy is **XmEXPLICT**, restores keyboard focus to the widget that had the focus before the MenuBar was entered. In other Pulldown MenuPanes, unposts the menu.

In a Popup MenuPane, unposts the menu and, when the shell's keyboard focus policy is **XmEXPLICT**, restores keyboard focus to the widget from which the menu was posted.

DoSelect(): Calls the callbacks in **XmNcascadingCallback**, posts the submenu attached to the CascadeButton and enables keyboard traversal within the menu. If the CascadeButton does not have a submenu attached, this action calls the callbacks in **XmNactivateCallback**, activates the CascadeButton, and unposts all posted menus in the cascade.

Help(): Unposts all menus in the menu hierarchy and, when the shell's keyboard focus policy is **XmEXPLICT**, restores keyboard focus to the widget that had the focus before the menu system was entered. Calls the callbacks for **XmNhelpCallback** if any exist. If there are no help callbacks for this widget, this action calls the help callbacks for the nearest ancestor that has them.

KeySelect(): Calls the callbacks in **XmNcascadingCallback**, and posts the submenu attached to the CascadeButton if keyboard traversal is enabled in the menu. If the CascadeButton does not have a submenu attached, this action calls the callbacks in **XmNactivateCallback**, activates the CascadeButton, and unposts all posted menus in the cascade.

MenuBarSelect():
Unposts any menus posted by the parent menu. Arms both the CascadeButton and the MenuBar, posts the associated submenu, and enables mouse traversal. If the menu is already active, this event disables keyboard traversal for the menu and returns the menu to mouse traversal mode.

StartDrag(): Arms the CascadeButton, posts the associated submenu, and enables mouse traversal. If the menu is already active, this event disables keyboard traversal for the menu and returns the menu to mouse traversal mode.

Related Information

Core(3X), XmCascadeButtonHighlight(3X),
XmCreateCascadeButton(3X),XmCreateMenuBar(3X),
XmCreatePulldownMenu(3X), XmCreatePopupMenu(3X), XmLabel(3X),
XmPrimitive(3X), and XmRowColumn(3X).

XmCascadeButtonGadget—The CascadeButtonGadget widget class

AES Support Level

Full-use

Synopsis

#include <Xm/CascadeBG.h>

Description

CascadeButtonGadget links two MenuPanes, a MenuBar to a MenuPane, or an OptionMenu to a MenuPane.

It is used in menu systems and must have a RowColumn parent with its **XmNrowColumnType** resource set to **XmMENU_BAR**, **XmMENU_POPUP**, **XmMENU_PULLDOWN**, or **XmMENU_OPTION**.

It is the only gadget that can have a Pulldown MenuPane attached to it as a submenu. The submenu is displayed when this gadget is activated within a PopupMenu, a PulldownMenu, or an OptionMenu. Its visuals can include a label or pixmap and a cascading indicator when it is in a Popup or Pulldown MenuPane; or it can include only a label or a pixmap when it is in an OptionMenu.

The default behavior associated with a CascadeButtonGadget depends on the type of menu system in which it resides. By default, **BSelect** controls the behavior of the CascadeButtonGadget. In addition, **BMenu** controls the behavior of the CascadeButtonGadget if it resides in a PopupMenu system. The actual mouse button used is determined by its RowColumn parent.

A CascadeButtonGadget's visuals differ from most other button gadgets. When the button becomes armed, its visuals change from a 2-D to a 3-D look, and it displays the submenu that has been attached to it. If no submenu is attached, it simply changes its visuals.

When a CascadeButtonGadget within a Pulldown or Popup MenuPane is armed as the result of the user moving the mouse pointer into the gadget, it does not immediately display its submenu. Instead, it waits a short time to see if the arming was temporary (that is, the user was simply passing through the gadget), or the user really wanted the submenu posted. This delay is configurable using **XmNmappingDelay**.

CascadeButtonGadget provides a single mechanism for activating the gadget from the keyboard. This mechanism is referred to as a keyboard mnemonic. If a mnemonic has been specified for the gadget, the user may activate it by simply typing the mnemonic while the CascadeButtonGadget is visible. If the CascadeButtonGadget is in a MenuBar and the MenuBar does not have focus, the **MAlt** modifier must be pressed with the mnemonic. Mnemonics are typically used to interact with a menu using the keyboard.

If a CascadeButtonGadget is in a Pulldown or Popup MenuPane and there is a submenu attached, the **XmNmarginBottom**, **XmNmarginLeft**, **XmNmarginRight**, and **XmNmarginTop** resources may enlarge to accommodate **XmNcascadePixmap**. **XmNmarginWidth** defaults to 6 if this resource is in a MenuBar; otherwise, it takes LabelGadget's default, which is 2.

Classes

CascadeButtonGadget inherits behavior and resources from the **Object**, **RectObj**, **XmGadget**, and **XmLabelGadget** classes.

The class pointer is **xmCascadeButtonGadgetClass**.

The class name is **XmCascadeButtonGadget**.

New Resources

The following table defines a set of widget resources used by the programmer to specify data. The programmer can also set the resource values for the inherited classes to set attributes for this widget. To reference a resource by name or by class in a **.Xdefaults** file, remove the **XmN** or **XmC** prefix and use the remaining letters. To specify one of the defined values for a resource in a **.Xdefaults** file, remove the **Xm** prefix and use the remaining letters (in either lowercase or uppercase, but include any underscores between words). The codes in the access column indicate if the given resource can be set at creation time (C), set by using **XtSetValues** (S), retrieved by using **XtGetValues** (G), or is not applicable (N/A).

XmCascadeButtonGadget		
Name **Class**	**Default** **Type**	**Access**
XmNactivateCallback XmCCallback	NULL XtCallbackList	C
XmNcascadePixmap XmCPixmap	dynamic Pixmap	CSG
XmNcascadingCallback XmCCallback	NULL XtCallbackList	C
XmNmappingDelay XmCMappingDelay	180 ms int	CSG
XmNsubMenuId XmCMenuWidget	NULL Widget	CSG

XmNactivateCallback

Specifies the list of callbacks that is called when the user activates the CascadeButtonGadget, and there is no submenu attached to pop up. The activation occurs when a mouse button is released or when the mnemonic associated with the gadget is typed. The specific mouse button depends on information in the RowColumn parent. The reason sent by the callback is **XmCR_ACTIVATE**.

XmNcascadePixmap

Specifies the cascade pixmap displayed on one end of the gadget when a CascadeButtonGadget is used within a Popup or Pulldown MenuPane and a submenu is attached. The LabelGadget class resources **XmNmarginBottom**, **XmNmarginLeft**, **XmNmarginRight**, and **XmNmarginTop** may be modified to ensure that room is left for the cascade pixmap. The default cascade pixmap in menus other than option menus is an arrow pointing to the side of the menu where the submenu will appear. The default for the CascadeButtonGadget in an option menu is **XmUNSPECIFIED_PIXMAP**.

XmNcascadingCallback

Specifies the list of callbacks that is called just prior to the mapping of the submenu associated with the CascadeButtonGadget. The reason sent by the callback is **XmCR_CASCADING**.

XmNmappingDelay

Specifies the amount of time, in milliseconds, between when a CascadeButtonGadget becomes armed and when it maps its submenu. This delay is used only when the gadget is within a Popup or Pulldown MenuPane. The value must not be negative.

XmNsubMenuId

Specifies the widget ID for the Pulldown MenuPane to be associated with this CascadeButtonGadget. The specified MenuPane is displayed when the CascadeButtonGadget becomes armed. The MenuPane must have been created with the appropriate parentage depending on the type of menu used. See **XmCreatePulldownMenu(3X)**, **XmCreatePopupMenu(3X)**, and **XmCreateOptionMenu(3X)** for more information on the menu systems.

Inherited Resources

CascadeButtonGadget inherits behavior and resources from the superclasses described in the following tables. For a complete description of each resource, refer to the reference page for that superclass.

XmCascadeButtonGadget(3X)

XmLabelGadget Resource Set		

Name
    Class
	Default
	    Type
		Access

XmNaccelerator
    XmCAccelerator
	NULL
	    String
		N/A

XmNacceleratorText
    XmCAcceleratorText
	NULL
	    XmString
		N/A

XmNalignment
    XmCAlignment
	dynamic
	    unsigned char
		CSG

XmNfontList
    XmCFontList
	dynamic
	    XmFontList
		CSG

XmNlabelInsensitivePixmap
    XmCLabelInsensitivePixmap
	XmUNSPECIFIED_PIXMAP
	    Pixmap
		CSG

XmNlabelPixmap
    XmCLabelPixmap
	XmUNSPECIFIED_PIXMAP
	    Pixmap
		CSG

XmNlabelString
    XmCXmString
	dynamic
	    XmString
		CSG

XmNlabelType
    XmCLabelType
	XmSTRING
	    unsigned char
		CSG

XmNmarginBottom
    XmCMarginBottom
	dynamic
	    Dimension
		CSG

XmNmarginHeight
    XmCMarginHeight
	2
	    Dimension
		CSG

XmNmarginLeft
    XmCMarginLeft
	0
	    Dimension
		CSG

XmNmarginRight
    XmCMarginRight
	dynamic
	    Dimension
		CSG

XmNmarginTop
    XmCMarginTop
	dynamic
	    Dimension
		CSG

XmNmarginWidth
    XmCMarginWidth
	dynamic
	    Dimension
		CSG

Name	Default	Access
Class	Type	
XmNmnemonic	NULL	CSG
XmCMnemonic	KeySym	
XmNmnemonicCharSet	dynamic	CSG
XmCMnemonicCharSet	String	
XmNrecomputeSize	True	CSG
XmCRecomputeSize	Boolean	
XmNstringDirection	dynamic	CSG
XmCStringDirection	XmStringDirection	

XmGadget Resource Set		
Name	Default	Access
Class	Type	
XmNhelpCallback	NULL	C
XmCCallback	XtCallbackList	
XmNhighlightOnEnter	False	CSG
XmCHighlightOnEnter	Boolean	
XmNhighlightThickness	0	CSG
XmCHighlightThickness	Dimension	
XmNnavigationType	XmNONE	CSG
XmCNavigationType	XmNavigationType	
XmNshadowThickness	2	CSG
XmCShadowThickness	Dimension	

Name	Default	Access
Class	Type	
XmNtraversalOn	True	CSG
XmCTraversalOn	Boolean	
XmNuserData	NULL	CSG
XmCUserData	XtPointer	

RectObj Resource Set		
Name	Default	Access
Class	Type	
XmNancestorSensitive	dynamic	G
XmCSensitive	Boolean	
XmNborderWidth	0	N/A
XmCBorderWidth	Dimension	
XmNheight	dynamic	CSG
XmCHeight	Dimension	
XmNsensitive	True	CSG
XmCSensitive	Boolean	
XmNwidth	dynamic	CSG
XmCWidth	Dimension	
XmNx	0	CSG
XmCPosition	Position	
XmNy	0	CSG
XmCPosition	Position	

Object Resource Set		
Name	Default	Access
Class	Type	
XmNdestroyCallback	NULL	C
XmCCallback	XtCallbackList	

Callback Information

A pointer to the following structure is passed to each callback:

```
typedef struct
{
    int         reason;
    XEvent      * event;
} XmAnyCallbackStruct;
```

reason   Indicates why the callback was invoked

event   Points to the **XEvent** that triggered the callback or is NULL if this
                callback was not triggered by an **XEvent**

Related Information

Object(3X), **RectObj(3X)**, **XmCascadeButtonHighlight(3)**,
XmCreateCascadeButtonGadget(3X), **XmCreatePulldownMenu(3X)**,
XmCreatePopupMenu(3X), **XmCreateOptionMenu(3X)**,**XmGadget(3X)**,
XmLabelGadget(3X), and **XmRowColumn(3X)**.

XmCascadeButtonGadgetHighlight—A CascadeButtonGadget function that sets the highlight state

AES Support Level

Trial-use

History/Direction

The **XmCascadeButtonGadgetHighlight** function is scheduled for removal in revision D. The function is redundant with **XmCascadeButtonHighlight**.

Synopsis

#include <Xm/CascadeBG.h>

void XmCascadeButtonGadgetHighlight (*cascadeButtonGadget, highlight*)
    Widget   *cascadeButtonGadget*;
    Boolean   *highlight*;

Description

XmCascadeButtonGadgetHighlight either draws or erases the shadow highlight around the CascadeButtonGadget.

cascadeButtonGadget
> Specifies the CascadeButtonGadget to be highlighted or unhighlighted

highlight   Specifies whether to highlight (True) or to unhighlight (False)

For a complete definition of CascadeButtonGadget and its associated resources, see **XmCascadeButtonGadget(3X)**.

Related Information

XmCascadeButton(3X), **XmCascadeButtonGadget(3X)**, and
XmCascadeButtonHighlight(3X).

XmCascadeButtonHighlight—A CascadeButton and CascadeButtonGadget function that sets the highlight state

AES Support Level

Full-use

Synopsis

#include <Xm/CascadeB.h>
#include <Xm/CascadeBG.h>

void XmCascadeButtonHighlight (*cascadeButton, highlight*)
    Widget   *cascadeButton*;
    Boolean   *highlight*;

Description

XmCascadeButtonHighlight either draws or erases the shadow highlight around the CascadeButton or the CascadeButtonGadget.

cascadeButton
    Specifies the CascadeButton or CascadeButtonGadget to be highlighted or unhighlighted

highlight   Specifies whether to highlight (True) or to unhighlight (False)

For a complete definition of CascadeButton or CascadeButtonGadget and their associated resources, see **XmCascadeButton(3X)** or **XmCascadeButtonGadget(3X)**.

Related Information

XmCascadeButton(3X), XmCascadeButtonGadget(3X) and
XmCascadeButtonGadgetHighlight(3X).

XmClipboardCancelCopy—A clipboard function that cancels a copy to the clipboard

AES Support Level

Full-use

Synopsis

```
#include <Xm/Xm.h>
#include <Xm/CutPaste.h>

int XmClipboardCancelCopy (display, window, item_id)
    Display        * display;
    Window         window;
    long           item_id;
```

Description

XmClipboardCancelCopy cancels the copy to clipboard that is in progress and frees up temporary storage. When a copy is to be performed, **XmClipboardStartCopy** allocates temporary storage for the clipboard data. **XmClipboardCopy** copies the appropriate data into the the temporary storage. **XmClipboardEndCopy** copies the data to the clipboard structure and frees up the temporary storage structures. If **XmClipboardCancelCopy** is called, the **XmClipboardEndCopy** function does not have to be called. A call to **XmClipboardCancelCopy** is valid only after a call to **XmClipboardStartCopy** and before a call to **XmClipboardEndCopy**.

display	Specifies a pointer to the **Display** structure that was returned in a previous call to **XOpenDisplay** or **XtDisplay**.
window	Specifies a widget's window ID that relates the application window to the clipboard. The widget's window ID can be obtained through **XtWindow**. The same application instance should pass the same window ID to each of the clipboard functions that it calls.
item_id	Specifies the number assigned to this data item. This number was returned by a previous call to **XmClipboardStartCopy**.

Return Value

ClipboardSuccess
> The function was successful.

ClipboardLocked
> The function failed because the clipboard was locked by another application. The application can continue to call the function again with the same parameters until the lock goes away. This gives the application the opportunity to ask if the user wants to keep trying or to give up on the operation.

ClipboardFail
> The function failed because **XmClipboardStartCopy** was not called or because the data item contains too many formats.

Related Information
XmClipboardCopy(3X), **XmClipboardEndCopy(3X)**, and **XmClipboardStartCopy(3X)**.

XmClipboardCopy—A clipboard function that copies a data item to temporary storage for later copying to clipboard

AES Support Level

Full-use

Synopsis

#include <Xm/Xm.h>
#include <Xm/CutPaste.h>

int XmClipboardCopy (*display, window, item_id, format_name,*
            buffer, length, private_id, data_id)

Display	* *display*;
Window	*window*;
long	*item_id*;
char	* *format_name*;
XtPointer	*buffer*;
unsigned long	*length*;
long	*private_id*;
long	* *data_id*;

Description

XmClipboardCopy copies a data item to temporary storage. The data item is moved from temporary storage to the clipboard data structure when a call to **XmClipboardEndCopy** is made. Additional calls to **XmClipboardCopy** before a call to **XmClipboardEndCopy** add additional data item formats to the same data item or append data to an existing format. Formats are described in the *Inter-Client Communication Conventions Manual* (ICCCM) as targets.

NOTE: Do not call **XmClipboardCopy** before a call to **XmClipboardStartCopy** has been made. The latter function allocates temporary storage required by **XmClipboardCopy**.

If the *buffer* argument is NULL, the data is considered to be passed by name. When data that has been passed by name is later requested by another application, the application that owns the data receives a callback with a request for the data. The application that owns the data must then transfer the data to the clipboard with the **XmClipboardCopyByName** function. When a data item that was passed by name is deleted from the clipboard, the application that owns the data receives a callback stating that the data is no longer needed.

For information on the callback function, see the callback argument description for **XmClipboardStartCopy**.

display	Specifies a pointer to the **Display** structure that was returned in a previous call to **XOpenDisplay** or **XtDisplay**.
window	Specifies the window ID of a widget that relates the application window to the clipboard. The widget's window ID can be obtained through **XtWindow**. The same application instance should pass the same window ID to each of the clipboard functions that it calls.
item_id	Specifies the number assigned to this data item. This number was returned by a previous call to **XmClipboardStartCopy**.
format_name	Specifies the name of the format in which the data item is stored on the clipboard. The format was known as target in the ICCCM.
buffer	Specifies the buffer from which the clipboard copies the data.
length	Specifies the length of the data being copied to the clipboard.
private_id	Specifies the private data that the application wants to store with the data item.
data_id	Specifies an identifying number assigned to the data item that uniquely identifies the data item and the format. This argument is required only for data that is passed by name.

Return Value

ClipboardSuccess
> The function was successful.

ClipboardLocked
> The function failed because the clipboard was locked by another application. The application can continue to call the function again with the same parameters until the lock goes away. This gives the application the opportunity to ask if the user wants to keep trying or to give up on the operation.

ClipboardFail
> The function failed because **XmClipboardStartCopy** was not called or because the data item contains too many formats.

Related Information

XmClipboardCopyByName(3X), **XmClipboardEndCopy(3X)**, and
XmClipboardStartCopy(3X).

XmClipboardCopyByName—A clipboard function that copies a data item passed by name

AES Support Level

Full-use

Synopsis

#include <Xm/Xm.h>
#include <Xm/CutPaste.h>

int XmClipboardCopyByName (*display, window, data_id,*
        buffer, length, private_id)
    Display   * *display*;
    Window   *window*;
    long   *data_id*;
    XtPointer   *buffer*;
    unsigned long *length*;
    long   *private_id*;

Description

XmClipboardCopyByName copies the actual data for a data item that was previously passed by name to the clipboard. Data is considered to be passed by name when a call to **XmClipboardCopy** is made with a NULL buffer parameter. Additional calls to this function append new data to the existing data.

display   Specifies a pointer to the **Display** structure that was returned in a previous call to **XOpenDisplay** or **XtDisplay**.

window   Specifies the window ID of a widget that relates the application window to the clipboard. The widget's window ID can be obtained through **XtWindow**. The same application instance should pass the same window ID to each clipboard function it calls.

data_id   Specifies an identifying number assigned to the data item that uniquely identifies the data item and the format. This number was assigned by **XmClipboardCopy** to the data item.

buffer   Specifies the buffer from which the clipboard copies the data.

length   Specifies the number of bytes in the data item.

private_id   Specifies the private data that the application wants to store with the data item.

Return Value

ClipboardSuccess
> The function was successful.

ClipboardLocked
> The function failed because the clipboard was locked by another application. The application can continue to call the function again with the same parameters until the lock goes away. This gives the application the opportunity to ask if the user wants to keep trying or to give up on the operation.

Related Information

XmClipboardCopy(3X), **XmClipboardLock(3X)**, **XmClipboardStartCopy(3X)**, and **XmClipboardUnlock(3X)**.

XmClipboardEndCopy—A clipboard function that ends a copy to the clipboard

AES Support Level

Full-use

Synopsis

#include <Xm/Xm.h>
#include <Xm/CutPaste.h>

int XmClipboardEndCopy (*display, window, item_id*)
    Display   * *display*;
    Window   *window*;
    long   *item_id*;

Description

XmClipboardEndCopy locks the clipboard from access by other applications, places data in the clipboard data structure, and unlocks the clipboard. Data items copied to the clipboard by **XmClipboardCopy** are not actually entered in the clipboard data structure until the call to **XmClipboardEndCopy**.

This function also frees up temporary storage that was allocated by **XmClipboardStartCopy**, which must be called before **XmClipboardEndCopy**. The latter function should not be called if **XmClipboardCancelCopy** has been called.

display   Specifies a pointer to the **Display** structure that was returned in a previous call to **XOpenDisplay** or **XtDisplay**.

window   Specifies the window ID of a widget that relates the application window to the clipboard. The widget's window ID can be obtained through **XtWindow**. The same application instance should pass the same window ID to each clipboard function it calls.

item_id   Specifies the number assigned to this data item, which was returned by a previous call to **XmClipboardStartCopy**.

Return Value

ClipboardSuccess

The function was successful.

ClipboardLocked

The function failed because the clipboard was locked by another application. The application can continue to call the function again with the same parameters until the lock goes away. This gives the

application the opportunity to ask if the user wants to keep trying or
to give up on the operation.

ClipboardFail

The function failed because **XmClipboardStartCopy** was not
called.

Related Information

XmClipboardCancelCopy(3X), **XmClipboardCopy(3X)** and
XmClipboardStartCopy(3X).

XmClipboardEndRetrieve—A clipboard function that ends a copy from the clipboard

AES Support Level

Full-use

Synopsis

#include <Xm/Xm.h>
#include <Xm/CutPaste.h>

int **XmClipboardEndRetrieve** (*display, window*)
    Display   * *display*;
    Window   *window*;

Description

XmClipboardEndRetrieve suspends copying data incrementally from the clipboard. It tells the clipboard routines that the application is through copying an item from the clipboard. Until this function is called, data items can be retrieved incrementally from the clipboard with **XmClipboardRetrieve**.

display   Specifies a pointer to the **Display** structure that was returned in a previous call to **XOpenDisplay** or **XtDisplay**.

window   Specifies the window ID of a widget that relates the application window to the clipboard. The widget's window ID can be obtained with **XtWindow**. The same application instance should pass the same window ID to each of the clipboard functions that it calls.

Return Value

ClipboardSuccess

The function was successful.

ClipboardLocked

The function failed because the clipboard was locked by another application. The application can continue to call the function again with the same parameters until the lock goes away. This gives the application the opportunity to ask if the user wants to keep trying or to give up on the operation.

Related Information

XmClipboardRetrieve(3X), XmClipboardStartCopy(3X), and
XmClipboardStartRetrieve(3X).

XmClipboardInquireCount—A clipboard function that returns the number of data item formats

AES Support Level

Full-use

Synopsis

#include <Xm/Xm.h>
#include <Xm/CutPaste.h>

int XmClipboardInquireCount (*display, window, count,*
max_format_name_length)

Display	** display*;
Window	*window*;
int	** count*;
unsigned long	** max_format_name_length*;

Description

XmClipboardInquireCount returns the number of data item formats available for the data item in the clipboard. This function also returns the maximum name-length for all formats in which the data item is stored.

display   Specifies a pointer to the **Display** structure that was returned in a previous call to **XOpenDisplay** or **XtDisplay**.

window   Specifies the window ID of a widget that relates the application window to the clipboard. The widget's window ID can be obtained through **XtWindow**. The same application instance should pass the same window ID to each of the clipboard functions that it calls.

count   Returns the number of data item formats available for the data item in the clipboard. If no formats are available, this argument equals 0 (zero). The count includes the formats that were passed by name.

max_format_name_length
   Specifies the maximum length of all format names for the data item in the clipboard.

Return Value

ClipboardSuccess

The function was successful.

ClipboardLocked

The function failed because the clipboard was locked by another application. The application can continue to call the function again with the same parameters until the lock goes away. This gives the application the opportunity to ask if the user wants to keep trying or to give up on the operation.

ClipboardNoData

The function could not find data on the clipboard corresponding to the format requested. This could occur because the clipboard is empty; there is data on the clipboard, but not in the requested format; or the data in the requested format was passed by name and is no longer available.

Related Information

XmClipboardStartCopy(3X).

XmClipboardInquireFormat—A clipboard function that returns a specified format name

AES Support Level

Full-use

Synopsis

#include <Xm/Xm.h>
#include <Xm/CutPaste.h>

int XmClipboardInquireFormat (*display, window, index, format_name_buf, buffer_len, copied_len*)

Display	* *display*;
Window	*window*;
int	*index*;
XtPointer	*format_name_buf*;
unsigned long	*buffer_len*;
unsigned long	* *copied_len*;

Description

XmClipboardInquireFormat returns a specified format name for the data item in the clipboard. If the name must be truncated, the function returns a warning status.

display Specifies a pointer to the **Display** structure that was returned in a previous call to **XOpenDisplay** or **XtDisplay**.

window Specifies the window ID of a widget that relates the application window to the clipboard. The widget's window ID can be obtained through **XtWindow**. The same application instance should pass the same window ID to each of the clipboard functions that it calls.

index Specifies which of the ordered format names to obtain. If this index is greater than the number of formats for the data item, this function returns a 0 (zero) in the *copied_len* argument.

format_name_buf
Specifies the buffer that receives the format name.

buffer_len Specifies the number of bytes in the format name buffer.

copied_len Specifies the number of bytes in the string copied to the buffer. If this argument equals 0 (zero), there is no *n*th format for the data item.

Return Value

ClipboardSuccess
>The function was successful.

ClipboardLocked
>The function failed because the clipboard was locked by another application. The application can continue to call the function again with the same parameters until the lock goes away. This gives the application the opportunity to ask if the user wants to keep trying or to give up on the operation.

ClipboardTruncate
>The data returned is truncated because the user did not provide a buffer large enough to hold the data.

ClipboardNoData
>The function could not find data on the clipboard corresponding to the format requested. This could occur because the clipboard is empty; there is data on the clipboard, but not in the requested format; or the data in the requested format was passed by name and is no longer available.

Related Information

XmClipboardStartCopy(3X).

XmClipboardInquireLength—A clipboard function that returns the length of the stored data

AES Support Level

Full-use

Synopsis

#include <Xm/Xm.h>
#include <Xm/CutPaste.h>

int XmClipboardInquireLength (*display, window, format_name, length*)
    Display   * *display*;
    Window   *window*;
    char   * *format_name*;
    unsigned long * *length*;

Description

XmClipboardInquireLength returns the length of the data stored under a specified format name for the clipboard data item. If no data is found for the specified format, or if there is no item on the clipboard, this function returns a value of 0 (zero).

Any format passed by name is assumed to have *length* passed in a call to **XmClipboardCopy**, even though the data has not yet been transferred to the clipboard in that format.

display   Specifies a pointer to the **Display** structure that was returned in a previous call to **XOpenDisplay** or **XtDisplay**.

window   Specifies the window ID of a widget that relates the application window to the clipboard. The widget's window ID can be obtained through **XtWindow**. The same application instance should pass the same window ID to each of the clipboard functions that it calls.

format_name Specifies the name of the format for the data item.

length   Specifies the length of the next data item in the specified format. This argument equals 0 (zero) if no data is found for the specified format, or if there is no item on the clipboard.

Return Value

ClipboardSuccess
> The function was successful.

ClipboardLocked
> The function failed because the clipboard was locked by another application. The application can continue to call the function again with the same parameters until the lock goes away. This gives the application the opportunity to ask if the user wants to keep trying or to give up on the operation.

ClipboardNoData
> The function could not find data on the clipboard corresponding to the format requested. This could occur because the clipboard is empty; there is data on the clipboard, but not in the requested format; or the data in the requested format was passed by name and is no longer available.

Related Information

XmClipboardCopy(3X) and **XmClipboardStartCopy(3X)**.

XmClipboardInquirePendingItems—A clipboard function that returns a list of data ID/private ID pairs

AES Support Level

Full-use

Synopsis

#include <Xm/Xm.h>
#include <Xm/CutPaste.h>

int XmClipboardInquirePendingItems (*display, window, format_name, item_list, count*)
    Display   * *display*;
    Window   *window*;
    char   * *format_name*;
    XmClipboardPendingList * *item_list*;
    unsigned long   * *count*;

Description

XmClipboardInquirePendingItems returns a list of data ID/private ID pairs for the specified format name. A data item is considered pending if the application originally passed it by name, the application has not yet copied the data, and the item has not been deleted from the clipboard. The application is responsible for freeing the memory provided by this function to store the list. To free the memory, call **XtFree**.

This function is used by an application when exiting, to determine if the data that is passed by name should be sent to the clipboard.

display   Specifies a pointer to the **Display** structure that was returned in a previous call to **XOpenDisplay** or **XtDisplay**.

window   Specifies the window ID of a widget that relates the application window to the clipboard. The widget's window ID can be obtained through **XtWindow**. The same application instance should pass the same window ID to each of the clipboard functions that it calls.

format_name   Specifies a string that contains the name of the format for which the list of data ID/private ID pairs is to be obtained.

item_list   Specifies the address of the array of data ID/private ID pairs for the specified format name. This argument is a type **XmClipboardPendingList**. The application is responsible for freeing the memory provided by this function for storing the list.

<table>
<tr><td>count</td><td>Specifies the number of items returned in the list. If there is no data for the specified format name, or if there is no item on the clipboard, this argument equals 0 (zero).</td></tr>
</table>

Return Value

ClipboardSuccess
> The function was successful.

ClipboardLocked
> The function failed because the clipboard was locked by another application. The application can continue to call the function again with the same parameters until the lock goes away. This gives the application the opportunity to ask if the user wants to keep trying or to give up on the operation.

Related Information

XmClipboardStartCopy(3X).

XmClipboardLock—A clipboard function that locks the clipboard

AES Support Level

Full-use

Synopsis

#include <Xm/Xm.h>
#include <Xm/CutPaste.h>

int XmClipboardLock (*display, window*)
    Display   * *display*;
    Window   *window*;

Description

XmClipboardLock locks the clipboard from access by another application until
XmClipboardUnlock is called. All clipboard functions lock and unlock the
clipboard to prevent simultaneous access. This function allows the application to
keep the clipboard data from changing between calls to **Inquire** and other
clipboard functions. The application does not need to lock the clipboard between
calls to **XmClipboardStartCopy** and **XmClipboardEndCopy** or to
XmClipboardStartRetrieve and **XmClipboardEndRetrieve**.

If the clipboard is already locked by another application, **XmClipboardLock**
returns an error status. Multiple calls to this function by the same application
increase the lock level.

display   Specifies a pointer to the **Display** structure that was returned in a
                     previous call to **XOpenDisplay** or **XtDisplay**.

window   Specifies the window ID of a widget that relates the application
                     window to the clipboard. The widget's window ID can be obtained
                     through **XtWindow**. The same application instance should pass the
                     same window ID to each of the clipboard functions that it calls.

Return Value

ClipboardSuccess
>The function was successful.

ClipboardLocked
>The function failed because the clipboard was locked by another application. The application can continue to call the function again with the same parameters until the lock goes away. This gives the application the opportunity to ask if the user wants to keep trying or to give up on the operation.

Related Information

XmClipboardEndCopy(3X), **XmClipboardEndRetrieve(3X)**, **XmClipboardStartCopy(3X)**, **XmClipboardStartRetrieve(3X)**, and **XmClipboardUnlock(3X)**.

XmClipboardRegisterFormat—A clipboard function that registers a new format

AES Support Level

Full-use

Synopsis

#include <Xm/Xm.h>
#include <Xm/CutPaste.h>

int XmClipboardRegisterFormat (*display, format_name, format_length*)
 Display   * *display*;
 char   * *format_name*;
 int   *format_length*;

Description

XmClipboardRegisterFormat registers a new format. Each format stored on the clipboard should have a length associated with it; this length must be known to the clipboard routines. Formats are known as targets in the *Inter-Client Communication Conventions Manual* (ICCCM). All of the formats specified by the ICCCM conventions are preregistered. Any other format that the application wants to use must either be 8-bit data or be registered through this routine. Failure to register the length of the data results in incompatible applications across platforms having different byte-swapping orders.

display   Specifies a pointer to the **Display** structure that was returned in a previous call to **XOpenDisplay** or **XtDisplay**.

format_name Specifies the string name for the new format (target).

format_length Specifies the format length in bits (8, 16, or 32).

Return Value

ClipboardBadFormat

    The *format_name* must not be NULL, and the *format_length* must be 8, 16, or 32.

ClipboardSuccess

    The function was successful.

ClipboardLocked

    The function failed because the clipboard was locked by another application. The application can continue to call the function again with the same parameters until the lock goes away. This gives the application the opportunity to ask if the user wants to keep trying or to give up on the operation.

ClipboardFail

The function failed because the format was already registered with this length.

Related Information

XmClipboardStartCopy(3X).

XmClipboardRetrieve—A clipboard function that retrieves a data item from the clipboard

AES Support Level

Full-use

Synopsis

#include <Xm/Xm.h>
#include <Xm/CutPaste.h>

int XmClipboardRetrieve (*display, window, format_name,*
        buffer, length, num_bytes, private_id)

Display	* *display*;
Window	*window*;
char	* *format_name*;
XtPointer	*buffer*;
unsigned long	*length*;
unsigned long	* *num_bytes*;
long	* *private_id*;

Description

XmClipboardRetrieve retrieves the current data item from clipboard storage. It returns a warning if the clipboard is locked, if there is no data on the clipboard, or if the data needs to be truncated because the buffer length is too short.

Between a call to **XmClipboardStartRetrieve** and a call to **XmClipboardEndRetrieve**, multiple calls to **XmClipboardRetrieve** with the same format name result in data being incrementally copied from the clipboard until the data in that format has all been copied.

The return value **ClipboardTruncate** from calls to **XmClipboardRetrieve** indicates that more data remains to be copied in the given format. It is recommended that any calls to the **Inquire** functions that the application needs to make to effect the copy from the clipboard be made between the call to **XmClipboardStartRetrieve** and the first call to **XmClipboardRetrieve**. This way, the application does not need to call **XmClipboardLock** and **XmClipboardUnlock**.

display   Specifies a pointer to the **Display** structure that was returned in a previous call to **XOpenDisplay** or **XtDisplay**.

window   Specifies the window ID of a widget that relates the application window to the clipboard. The widget's window ID can be obtained through **XtWindow**. The same application instance should pass the same window ID to each of the clipboard functions that it calls.

format_name   Specifies the name of a format in which the data is stored on the clipboard.

buffer   Specifies the buffer to which the application wants the clipboard to copy the data.

length   Specifies the length of the application buffer.

num_bytes   Specifies the number of bytes of data copied into the application buffer.

private_id   Specifies the private data stored with the data item by the application that placed the data item on the clipboard. If the application did not store private data with the data item, this argument returns 0 (zero).

Return Value

ClipboardSuccess
> The function was successful.

ClipboardLocked
> The function failed because the clipboard was locked by another application. The application can continue to call the function again with the same parameters until the lock goes away. This gives the application the opportunity to ask if the user wants to keep trying or to give up on the operation.

ClipboardTruncate
> The data returned is truncated because the user did not provide a buffer large enough to hold the data.

ClipboardNoData
> The function could not find data on the clipboard corresponding to the format requested. This could occur because the clipboard is empty; there is data on the clipboard but not in the requested format; or the data in the requested format was passed by name and is no longer available.

Related Information

XmClipboardEndRetrieve(3X), XmClipboardLock(3X), XmClipboardStartCopy(3X), XmClipboardStartRetrieve(3X), and **XmClipboardUnlock(3X).**

XmClipboardStartCopy—A clipboard function that sets up a storage and data structure

AES Support Level

Full-use

Synopsis

#include <Xm/Xm.h>
#include <Xm/CutPaste.h>

int XmClipboardStartCopy (*display, window, clip_label,*
timestamp, widget, callback, item_id)
    Display   * *display*;
    Window   *window*;
    XmString   *clip_label*;
    Time   *timestamp*;
    Widget   *widget*;
    XmCutPasteProc*callback*;
    long   * *item_id*;

Description

XmClipboardStartCopy sets up storage and data structures to receive clipboard data. An application calls this function during a cut or copy operation. The data item that these structures receive then becomes the next data item in the clipboard.

Copying a large piece of data to the clipboard can take a long time. It is possible that, once the data is copied, no application will ever request that data. The Motif Toolkit provides a mechanism so that an application does not need to actually pass data to the clipboard until the data has been requested by some application.

Instead, the application passes format and length information in **XmClipboardCopy** to the clipboard functions, along with a widget ID and a callback function address that is passed in **XmClipboardStartCopy**. The widget ID is necessary for communications between the clipboard functions in the application that owns the data and the clipboard functions in the application that requests the data.

The callback functions are responsible for copying the actual data to the clipboard through **XmClipboardCopyByName**. The callback function is also called if the data item is removed from the clipboard and the actual data is no longer needed.

display   Specifies a pointer to the **Display** structure that was returned in a previous call to **XOpenDisplay** or **XtDisplay**.

window   Specifies the window ID of a widget that relates the application window to the clipboard. The widget's window ID can be obtained through **XtWindow**. The same application instance should pass the same window ID to each of the clipboard functions that it calls.

clip_label   Specifies the label to be associated with the data item. This argument is used to identify the data item, for example, in a clipboard viewer. An example of a label is the name of the application that places the data in the clipboard.

timestamp   Specifies the time of the event that triggered the copy. A valid timestamp must be supplied; it is not sufficient to use **CurrentTime**.

widget   Specifies the ID of the widget that receives messages requesting data previously passed by name. This argument must be present in order to pass data by name. Any valid widget ID in your application can be used for this purpose and all the message handling is taken care of by the cut and paste functions.

callback   Specifies the address of the callback function that is called when the clipboard needs data that was originally passed by name. This is also the callback to receive the **delete** message for items that were originally passed by name. This argument must be present in order to pass data by name.

item_id   Specifies the number assigned to this data item. The application uses this number in calls to **XmClipboardCopy**, **XmClipboardEndCopy**, and **XmClipboardCancelCopy**.

For more information on passing data by name, see **XmClipboardCopy(3X)** and **XmClipboardCopyByName(3X)**.

The *widget* and *callback* arguments must be present in order to pass data by name. The callback format is as follows:

```
void (*callback) (widget, data_id, private, reason)
    Widget      widget;
    int         *data_id;
    int         *private;
    int         *reason;
```

widget   Specifies the ID of the widget passed to this function.

data_id   Specifies the identifying number returned by **XmClipboardCopy**, which identifies the pass-by-name data.

private   Specifies the private information passed to **XmClipboardCopy**.

reason   Specifies the reason. **XmCR_CLIPBOARD_DATA_DELETE** or **XmCR_CLIPBOARD_DATA_REQUEST** are the possible values.

Return Value

ClipboardSuccess
> The function was successful.

ClipboardLocked
> The function failed because the clipboard was locked by another application. The application can continue to call the function again with the same parameters until the lock goes away. This gives the application the opportunity to ask if the user wants to keep trying or to give up on the operation.

Related Information

XmClipboardCancelCopy(3X), **XmClipboardCopy(3X)**, **XmClipboardCopyByName(3X)**, **XmClipboardEndCopy(3X)**, **XmClipboardEndRetrieve(3X)**, **XmClipboardInquireCount(3X)**, **XmClipboardInquireFormat(3X)**, **XmClipboardInquireLength(3X)**, **XmClipboardInquirePendingItems(3X)**, **XmClipboardLock(3X)**, **XmClipboardRegisterFormat(3X)**, **XmClipboardRetrieve(3X)**, **XmClipboardStartRetrieve(3X)**, **XmClipboardUndoCopy(3X)**, **XmClipboardUnlock(3X)**, and **XmClipboardWithdrawFormat(3X)**.

XmClipboardStartRetrieve—A clipboard function that starts a copy from the clipboard

AES Support Level

Full-use

Synopsis

#include <Xm/Xm.h>
#include <Xm/CutPaste.h>

int XmClipboardStartRetrieve (*display, window, timestamp*)
    Display   * *display*;
    Window   *window*;
    Time   *timestamp*;

Description

XmClipboardStartRetrieve tells the clipboard routines that the application is ready to start copying an item from the clipboard. The clipboard is locked by this routine and stays locked until **XmClipboardEndRetrieve** is called. Between a call to **XmClipboardStartRetrieve** and a call to **XmClipboardEndRetrieve**, multiple calls to **XmClipboardRetrieve** with the same format name result in data being incrementally copied from the clipboard until the data in that format has all been copied.

A return value of **ClipboardTruncate** from calls to **XmClipboardRetrieve** indicates that more data remains to be copied in the given format. It is recommended that any calls to the **Inquire** functions that the application needs to make to complete the copy from the clipboard be made between the call to **XmClipboardStartRetrieve** and the first call to **XmClipboardRetrieve**. This way, the application does not need to call **XmClipboardLock** and **XmClipboardUnlock**.

display   Specifies a pointer to the **Display** structure that was returned in a previous call to **XOpenDisplay** or **XtDisplay**.

window   Specifies the window ID of a widget that relates the application window to the clipboard. The widget's window ID can be obtained through **XtWindow**. The same application instance should pass the same window ID to each of the clipboard functions that it calls.

timestamp   Specifies the time of the event that triggered the copy. A valid timestamp must be supplied; it is not sufficient to use **CurrentTime**.

Return Value

ClipboardSuccess
> The function is successful.

ClipboardLocked
> The function failed because the clipboard was locked by another application. The application can continue to call the function again with the same parameters until the lock goes away. This gives the application the opportunity to ask if the user wants to keep trying or to give up on the operation.

Related Information

XmClipboardEndRetrieve(3X), **XmClipboardInquireCount(3X)**, **XmClipboardInquireFormat(3X)**, **XmClipboardInquireLength(3X)**, **XmClipboardInquirePendingItems(3X)**, **XmClipboardLock(3X)**, **XmClipboardRetrieve(3X)**, **XmClipboardStartCopy(3X)**, and **XmClipboardUnlock(3X)**.

XmClipboardUndoCopy—A clipboard function that deletes the last item placed on the clipboard

AES Support Level

Full-use

Synopsis

#include <Xm/Xm.h>
#include <Xm/CutPaste.h>

int XmClipboardUndoCopy (*display, window*)
  Display   * *display*;
  Window   *window*;

Description

XmClipboardUndoCopy deletes the last item placed on the clipboard if the item was placed there by an application with the passed *display* and *window* arguments. Any data item deleted from the clipboard by the original call to **XmClipboardCopy** is restored. If the *display* or *window* IDs do not match the last copied item, no action is taken, and this function has no effect.

display   Specifies a pointer to the **Display** structure that was returned in a previous call to **XOpenDisplay** or **XtDisplay**.

window   Specifies the window ID of a widget that relates the application window to the clipboard. The widget's window ID can be obtained through **XtWindow**. The same application instance should pass the same window ID to each clipboard function it calls.

Return Value

ClipboardSuccess
The function was successful.

ClipboardLocked
The function failed because the clipboard was locked by another application. The application can continue to call the function again with the same parameters until the lock goes away. This gives the application the opportunity to ask if the user wants to keep trying or to give up on the operation.

Related Information

2–227

XmClipboardLock(3X) and **XmClipboardStartCopy(3X)**.

XmClipboardUnlock—A clipboard function that unlocks the clipboard

AES Support Level

Full-use

Synopsis

#include <Xm/Xm.h>
#include <Xm/CutPaste.h>

int XmClipboardUnlock (*display, window, remove_all_locks*)
    Display   * *display*;
    Window   *window*;
    Boolean   *remove_all_locks*;

Description

XmClipboardUnlock unlocks the clipboard, enabling it to be accessed by other applications.

If multiple calls to **XmClipboardLock** have occurred, the same number of calls to **XmClipboardUnlock** is necessary to unlock the clipboard, unless *remove_all_locks* is set to True.

display
    Specifies a pointer to the **Display** structure that was returned in a previous call to **XOpenDisplay** or **XtDisplay**.

window
    Specifies the window ID of a widget that relates the application window to the clipboard. The widget's window ID can be obtained through **XtWindow**. The same application instance should pass the same window ID to each of the clipboard functions that it calls.

remove_all_locks
    When True, indicates that all nested locks should be removed. When False, indicates that only one level of lock should be removed.

Return Value

ClipboardSuccess
    The function was successful.

ClipboardFail
    The function failed because the clipboard was not locked or was locked by another application.

Related Information

XmClipboardCancelCopy(3X), **XmClipboardCopy(3X)**,
XmClipboardEndCopy(3X), **XmClipboardEndRetrieve(3X)**,
XmClipboardInquireCount(3X), **XmClipboardInquireFormat(3X)**,
XmClipboardInquireLength(3X), **XmClipboardInquirePendingItems(3X)**,
XmClipboardLock(3X), **XmClipboardRegisterFormat(3X)**,
XmClipboardRetrieve(3X), **XmClipboardStartCopy(3X)**,
XmClipboardStartRetrieve(3X), **XmClipboardUndoCopy(3X)**, and
XmClipboardWithdrawFormat(3X).

XmClipboardWithdrawFormat—A clipboard function that indicates that the application no longer wants to supply a data item

AES Support Level

Full-use

Synopsis

#include <Xm/Xm.h>
#include <Xm/CutPaste.h>

int XmClipboardWithdrawFormat (*display, window, data_id*)
    Display   * *display*;
    Window   *window*;
    long   *data_id*;

Description

XmClipboardWithdrawFormat indicates that the application no longer supplies a data item to the clipboard that the application had previously passed by name.

display   Specifies a pointer to the **Display** structure that was returned in a previous call to **XOpenDisplay** or **XtDisplay**.

window   Specifies the window ID of a widget that relates the application window to the clipboard. The widget's window ID can be obtained through **XtWindow**. The same application instance should pass the same window ID to each clipboard function it calls.

data_id   Specifies an identifying number assigned to the data item, which uniquely identifies the data item and the format. This was assigned to the item when it was originally passed by **XmClipboardCopy**.

Return Value

ClipboardSuccess
    The function was successful.

ClipboardLocked
    The function failed because the clipboard was locked by another application. The application can continue to call the function again with the same parameters until the lock goes away. This gives the application the opportunity to ask if the user wants to keep trying or to give up on the operation.

Related Information

XmClipboardCopy(3X) and **XmClipboardStartCopy(3X)**.

XmCommand—The Command widget class

AES Support Level

Full-use

Synopsis

#include <Xm/Command.h>

Description

Command is a special-purpose composite widget for command entry that provides a built-in command-history mechanism. Command includes a command-line text-input field, a command-line prompt, and a command-history list region.

One additional **WorkArea** child may be added to the Command after creation.

Whenever a command is entered, it is automatically added to the end of the command-history list and made visible. This does not change the selected item in the list, if there is one.

Many of the new resources specified for Command are actually SelectionBox resources that have been renamed for clarity and ease of use.

Classes

Command inherits behavior and resources from **Core**, **Composite**, **Constraint**, **XmManager**, **XmBulletinBoard**, and **XmSelectionBox**.

The class pointer is **xmCommandWidgetClass**.

The class name is **XmCommand**.

New Resources

The following table defines a set of widget resources used by the programmer to specify data. The programmer can also set the resource values for the inherited classes to set attributes for this widget. To reference a resource by name or by class in a **.Xdefaults** file, remove the **XmN** or **XmC** prefix and use the remaining letters. To specify one of the defined values for a resource in a **.Xdefaults** file, remove the **Xm** prefix and use the remaining letters (in either lowercase or uppercase, but include any underscores between words). The codes in the access column indicate if the given resource can be set at creation time (C), set by using **XtSetValues** (S), retrieved by using **XtGetValues** (G), or is not applicable (N/A).

XmCommand Resource Set		

Name
    Class
	Default
	    Type
		Access

XmNcommand
    XmCTextString
	""
	    XmString
		CSG

XmNcommandChangedCallback
    XmCCallback
	NULL
	    XtCallbackList
		C

XmNcommandEnteredCallback
    XmCCallback
	NULL
	    XtCallbackList
		C

XmNhistoryItems
    XmCItems
	NULL
	    XmStringTable
		CSG

XmNhistoryItemCount
    XmCItemCount
	0
	    int
		CSG

XmNhistoryMaxItems
    XmCMaxItems
	100
	    int
		CSG

XmNhistoryVisibleItemCount
    XmCVisibleItemCount
	dynamic
	    int
		CSG

XmNpromptString
    XmCPromptString
	dynamic
	    XmString
		CSG

XmNcommand

Contains the current command-line text. This is the
XmNtextString resource in SelectionBox, renamed for Command.
This resource can also be modified with **XmCommandSetValue**
and **XmCommandAppendValue** functions. The command area is
a Text widget.

XmNcommandChangedCallback

Specifies the list of callbacks that is called when the value of the
command changes. The callback reason is
XmCR_COMMAND_CHANGED. This is equivalent to the
XmNvalueChangedCallback of the Text widget, except that a
pointer to an **XmCommandCallbackStructure** is passed, and the
structure's *value* member contains the **XmString**.

XmNcommandEnteredCallback
> Specifies the list of callbacks that is called when a command is entered in the Command. The callback reason is **XmCR_COMMAND_ENTERED**. A pointer to an **XmCommandCallback** structure is passed.

XmNhistoryItems
> Lists **XmString** items that make up the contents of the history list. This is the **XmNlistItems** resource in SelectionBox, renamed for Command.

XmNhistoryItemCount
> Specifies the number of **XmStrings** in **XmNhistoryItems**. This is the **XmNlistItemCount** resource in SelectionBox, renamed for Command. The value must not be negative.

XmNhistoryMaxItems
> Specifies the maximum number of items allowed in the history list. Once this number is reached, an existing list item must be removed before a new item can be added to the list. For each command entered, the first list item is removed from the list, so the new command can be added to the list. The value must be greater than 0 (zero).

XmNhistoryVisibleItemCount
> Specifies the number of items in the history list that should be visible at one time. In effect, it sets the height (in lines) of the history list window. This is the **XmNlistVisibleItemCount** resource in SelectionBox, renamed for Command. The value must be greater than 0 (zero). The default is dynamic based on the height of the list.

XmNpromptString
> Specifies a prompt for the command line. This is the **XmNselectionLabelString** resource in SelectionBox, renamed for Command. The default may vary depending on the value of the **XmNstringDirection** resource and the locale. In the C locale the default is > (right angle bracket).

Inherited Resources

Command inherits behavior and resources from the superclasses described in the
following tables. For a complete description of each resource, refer to the reference
page for that superclass.

XmSelectionBox Resource Set		
Name **Default**		**Access**
Class **Type**		

XmNapplyCallback
    XmCCallback
	NULL
	    XtCallbackList
		N/A

XmNapplyLabelString
    XmCApplyLabelString
	dynamic
	    XmString
		N/A

XmNcancelCallback
    XmCCallback
	NULL
	    XtCallbackList
		N/A

XmNcancelLabelString
    XmCCancelLabelString
	dynamic
	    XmString
		N/A

XmNdialogType
    XmCDialogType
	XmDIALOG_COMMAND
	    unsigned char
		G

XmNhelpLabelString
    XmCHelpLabelString
	dynamic
	    XmString
		N/A

XmNlistItemCount
    XmCItemCount
	0
	    int
		CSG

XmNlistItems
    XmCItems
	NULL
	    XmStringTable
		CSG

XmNlistLabelString
    XmCListLabelString
	NULL
	    XmString
		N/A

XmNlistVisibleItemCount
    XmCVisibleItemCount
	dynamic
	    int
		CSG

XmNminimizeButtons
    XmCMinimizeButtons
	False
	    Boolean
		N/A

Name
    Class
	Default
	    Type
		Access

XmNmustMatch
    XmCMustMatch
	False
	    Boolean
		N/A

XmNnoMatchCallback
    XmCCallback
	NULL
	    XtCallbackList
		N/A

XmNokCallback
    XmCCallback
	NULL
	    XtCallbackList
		N/A

XmNokLabelString
    XmCOkLabelString
	dynamic
	    XmString
		N/A

XmNselectionLabelString
    XmCSelectionLabelString
	dynamic
	    XmString
		CSG

XmNtextAccelerators
    XmCTextAccelerators
	default
	    XtAccelerators
		C

XmNtextColumns
    XmCColumns
	dynamic
	    short
		CSG

XmNtextString
    XmCTextString
	""
	    XmString
		CSG

XmBulletinBoard Resource Set		
Name	**Default**	**Access**
Class	**Type**	
XmNallowOverlap	True	CSG
XmCAllowOverlap	Boolean	
XmNautoUnmanage	False	N/A
XmCAutoUnmanage	Boolean	
XmNbuttonFontList	dynamic	N/A
XmCButtonFontList	XmFontList	
XmNcancelButton	NULL	N/A
XmCWidget	Widget	
XmNdefaultButton	NULL	N/A
XmCWidget	Widget	
XmNdefaultPosition	False	CSG
XmCDefaultPosition	Boolean	
XmNdialogStyle	dynamic	CSG
XmCDialogStyle	unsigned char	
XmNdialogTitle	NULL	CSG
XmCDialogTitle	XmString	
XmNfocusCallback	NULL	C
XmCCallback	XtCallbackList	
XmNlabelFontList	dynamic	CSG
XmCLabelFontList	XmFontList	
XmNmapCallback	NULL	C
XmCCallback	XtCallbackList	
XmNmarginHeight	10	CSG
XmCMarginHeight	Dimension	
XmNmarginWidth	10	CSG
XmCMarginWidth	Dimension	
XmNnoResize	False	CSG
XmCNoResize	Boolean	
XmNresizePolicy	XmRESIZE_NONE	CSG
XmCResizePolicy	unsigned char	

Name	Default	Access
Class	Type	
XmNshadowType	XmSHADOW_OUT	CSG
XmCShadowType	unsigned char	
XmNtextFontList	dynamic	CSG
XmCTextFontList	XmFontList	
XmNtextTranslations	NULL	C
XmCTranslations	XtTranslations	
XmNunmapCallback	NULL	C
XmCCallback	XtCallbackList	

XmManager Resource Set		
Name	**Default**	**Access**
Class	**Type**	
XmNbottomShadowColor	dynamic	CSG
XmCBottomShadowColor	Pixel	
XmNbottomShadowPixmap	XmUNSPECIFIED_PIXMAP	CSG
XmCBottomShadowPixmap	Pixmap	
XmNforeground	dynamic	CSG
XmCForeground	Pixel	
XmNhelpCallback	NULL	C
XmCCallback	XtCallbackList	
XmNhighlightColor	dynamic	CSG
XmCHighlightColor	Pixel	
XmNhighlightPixmap	dynamic	CSG
XmCHighlightPixmap	Pixmap	
XmNnavigationType	XmTAB_GROUP	CSG
XmCNavigationType	XmNavigationType	
XmNshadowThickness	dynamic	CSG
XmCShadowThickness	Dimension	
XmNstringDirection	dynamic	CG
XmCStringDirection	XmStringDirection	
XmNtopShadowColor	dynamic	CSG
XmCTopShadowColor	Pixel	
XmNtopShadowPixmap	dynamic	CSG
XmCTopShadowPixmap	Pixmap	
XmNtraversalOn	True	CSG
XmCTraversalOn	Boolean	
XmNuserData	NULL	CSG
XmCUserData	XtPointer	

2–240

Composite Resource Set		
Name	**Default**	**Access**
Class	**Type**	
XmNchildren	NULL	G
XmCReadOnly	WidgetList	
XmNinsertPosition	NULL	CSG
XmCInsertPosition	XtOrderProc	
XmNnumChildren	0	G
XmCReadOnly	Cardinal	

Core Resource Set		
Name	**Default**	**Access**
Class	**Type**	
XmNaccelerators	dynamic	N/A
XmCAccelerators	XtAccelerators	
XmNancestorSensitive	dynamic	G
XmCSensitive	Boolean	
XmNbackground	dynamic	CSG
XmCBackground	Pixel	
XmNbackgroundPixmap	XmUNSPECIFIED_PIXMAP	CSG
XmCPixmap	Pixmap	
XmNborderColor	XtDefaultForeground	CSG
XmCBorderColor	Pixel	
XmNborderPixmap	XmUNSPECIFIED_PIXMAP	CSG
XmCPixmap	Pixmap	
XmNborderWidth	0	CSG
XmCBorderWidth	Dimension	
XmNcolormap	dynamic	CG
XmCColormap	Colormap	
XmNdepth	dynamic	CG
XmCDepth	int	
XmNdestroyCallback	NULL	C
XmCCallback	XtCallbackList	
XmNheight	dynamic	CSG
XmCHeight	Dimension	
XmNinitialResourcesPersistent	True	C
XmCInitialResourcesPersistent	Boolean	
XmNmappedWhenManaged	True	CSG
XmCMappedWhenManaged	Boolean	
XmNscreen	dynamic	CG
XmCScreen	Screen *	
XmNsensitive	True	CSG
XmCSensitive	Boolean	

Name	Default	Access
Class	**Type**	
XmNtranslations	dynamic	CSG
XmCTranslations	XtTranslations	
XmNwidth	dynamic	CSG
XmCWidth	Dimension	
XmNx	0	CSG
XmCPosition	Position	
XmNy	0	CSG
XmCPosition	Position	

Callback Information

A pointer to the following structure is passed to each callback:

typedef struct
{
    int   *reason*;
    XEvent   ** event*;
    XmString   *value*;
    int   *length*;
} XmCommandCallbackStruct;

reason   Indicates why the callback was invoked

event   Points to the **XEvent** that triggered the callback

value   Specifies the **XmString** in the CommandArea

length   Specifies the size of the command in **XmString**

Action Routines

The **XmCommand** action routines are:

SelectionBoxUpOrDown(0|1|2|3):
        When called with an argument of 0 (zero), selects the previous item in the history list and replaces the text with that item.

        When called with an argument of 1, selects the next item in the history list and replaces the text with that item.

        When called with an argument of 2, selects the first item in the history list and replaces the text with that item.

When called with an argument of 3, selects the last item in the history list and replaces the text with that item.

Calls the callbacks for **XmNcommandChangedCallback**.

Related Information

Composite(3X), **Constraint(3X)**, **Core(3X)**, **XmBulletinBoard(3X)**, **XmCommandAppendValue(3X)**, **XmCommandError(3X)**, **XmCommandGetChild(3X)**, **XmCommandSetValue(3X)**, **XmCreateCommand(3X)**, **XmManager(3X)**, and **XmSelectionBox(3X)**.

XmCommandAppendValue—A Command function that appends the passed XmString to the end of the string displayed in the command area of the widget

AES Support Level

Full-use

Synopsis

#include <Xm/Command.h>

void XmCommandAppendValue (*widget, command*)
    Widget   *widget*;
    XmString   *command*;

Description

XmCommandAppendValue appends the passed **XmString** to the end of the string displayed in the command area of the Command widget.

widget   Specifies the Command widget ID

command   Specifies the passed **XmString**

For a complete definition of Command and its associated resources, see **XmCommand(3X)**.

Related Information

XmCommand(3X).

XmCommandError—A Command function that displays an error message

AES Support Level

Full-use

Synopsis

#include <Xm/Command.h>

void XmCommandError (*widget, error*)
  Widget *widget*;
  XmString *error*;

Description

XmCommandError displays an error message in the history area of the Command widget. The **XmString** error is displayed until the next command entered occurs.

widget   Specifies the Command widget ID

error   Specifies the passed **XmString**

For a complete definition of Command and its associated resources, see **XmCommand(3X)**.

Related Information

XmCommand(3X).

XmCommandGetChild—A Command function that is used to access a component

AES Support Level

Full-use

Synopsis

#include <Xm/Command.h>

Widget XmCommandGetChild (*widget, child*)
Widget *widget*;
unsigned char *child*;

Description

XmCommandGetChild is used to access a component within a Command. The parameters given to the function are the Command widget and a value indicating which component to access.

widget   Specifies the Command widget ID.

child   Specifies a component within the Command. The following values are legal for this parameter:

- **XmDIALOG_COMMAND_TEXT**
- **XmDIALOG_PROMPT_LABEL**
- **XmDIALOG_HISTORY_LIST**
- **XmDIALOG_WORK_AREA**

For a complete definition of Command and its associated resources, see **XmCommand(3X)**.

Return Value

Returns the widget ID of the specified Command component. An application should not assume that the returned widget will be of any particular class.

Related Information

XmCommand(3X).

XmCommandSetValue—A Command function that replaces a displayed string

AES Support Level

Full-use

Synopsis

#include <Xm/Command.h>

void XmCommandSetValue (*widget, command*)
    Widget   *widget*;
    XmString   *command*;

Description

XmCommandSetValue replaces the string displayed in the command area of the Command widget with the passed **XmString**.

widget   Specifies the Command widget ID

command   Specifies the passed **XmString**

For a complete definition of Command and its associated resources, see **XmCommand(3X)**.

Related Information

XmCommand(3X).

XmConvertUnits—A function that converts a value in one unit type to another unit type

AES Support Level

Trial-use

Synopsis

#include <Xm/Xm.h>

int XmConvertUnits (*widget, orientation, from_unit_type, from_value, to_unit_type*)

Widget	*widget*;
int	*orientation*;
int	*from_unit_type*;
int	*from_value*;
int	*to_unit_type*;

Description

XmConvertUnits converts the value and returns it as the return value from the function.

widget   Specifies the widget for which the data is to be converted.

orientation Specifies whether the converter uses the horizontal or vertical screen resolution when performing the conversions. The *orientation* parameter can have values of **XmHORIZONTAL** or **XmVERTICAL**.

from_unit_type
    Specifies the current unit type of the supplied value

from_value Specifies the value to be converted

to_unit_type Converts the value to the unit type specified

The parameters *from_unit_type* and *to_unit_type* can have the following values:

XmPIXELS All values provided to the widget are treated as normal pixel values. This is the default for the resource.

Xm100TH_MILLIMETERS
    All values provided to the widget are treated as 1/100 of a millimeter.

Xm1000TH_INCHES
    All values provided to the widget are treated as 1/1000 of an inch.

Xm100TH_POINTS
> All values provided to the widget are treated as 1/100 of a point. A point is a unit typically used in text processing applications and is defined as 1/72 of an inch.

Return Value

Returns the converted value. If a NULL widget, incorrect *orientation*, or incorrect *unit_type* is supplied as parameter data, 0 (zero) is returned.

XmCreateArrowButton—The ArrowButton widget creation function

AES Support Level

Full-use

Synopsis

#include <Xm/ArrowB.h>

Widget XmCreateArrowButton (*parent, name, arglist, argcount*)
    Widget   *parent*;
    String   *name*;
    ArgList   *arglist*;
    Cardinal   *argcount*;

Description

XmCreateArrowButton creates an instance of an ArrowButton widget and returns the associated widget ID.

parent   Specifies the parent widget ID

name   Specifies the name of the created widget

arglist   Specifies the argument list

argcount   Specifies the number of attribute/value pairs in the argument list (*arglist*)

For a complete definition of ArrowButton and its associated resources, see **XmArrowButton(3X)**.

Return Value

Returns the ArrowButton widget ID.

Related Information

XmArrowButton(3X).

XmCreateArrowButtonGadget—The ArrowButtonGadget creation function

AES Support Level

Full-use

Synopsis

#include <Xm/ArrowBG.h>

Widget XmCreateArrowButtonGadget (*parent, name, arglist, argcount*)
>   **Widget**   *parent*;
>   **String**   *name*;
>   **ArgList**   *arglist*;
>   **Cardinal**   *argcount*;

Description

XmCreateArrowButtonGadget creates an instance of an ArrowButtonGadget widget and returns the associated widget ID.

parent   Specifies the parent widget ID

name   Specifies the name of the created widget

arglist   Specifies the argument list

argcount   Specifies the number of attribute/value pairs in the argument list (*arglist*)

For a complete definition of ArrowButtonGadget and its associated resources, see **XmArrowButtonGadget(3X)**.

Return Value

Returns the ArrowButtonGadget widget ID.

Related Information

XmArrowButtonGadget(3X).

XmCreateBulletinBoard—The BulletinBoard widget creation function

AES Support Level

Full-use

Synopsis

#include <Xm/BulletinB.h>

Widget XmCreateBulletinBoard (*parent, name, arglist, argcount*)
    Widget   *parent*;
    String   *name*;
    ArgList   *arglist*;
    Cardinal   *argcount*;

Description

XmCreateBulletinBoard creates an instance of a BulletinBoard widget and returns the associated widget ID.

parent   Specifies the parent widget ID

name   Specifies the name of the created widget

arglist   Specifies the argument list

argcount   Specifies the number of attribute/value pairs in the argument list (*arglist*)

For a complete definition of BulletinBoard and its associated resources, see **XmBulletinBoard(3X)**.

Return Value

Returns the BulletinBoard widget ID.

Related Information

XmBulletinBoard(3X).

XmCreateBulletinBoardDialog—The BulletinBoard BulletinBoardDialog convenience creation function

AES Support Level

Full-use

Synopsis

#include <Xm/BulletinB.h>

Widget XmCreateBulletinBoardDialog (*parent, name, arglist, argcount*)
>   **Widget**   *parent*;
>   **String**   *name*;
>   **ArgList**   *arglist*;
>   **Cardinal**   *argcount*;

Description

XmCreateBulletinBoardDialog is a convenience creation function that creates a DialogShell and an unmanaged BulletinBoard child of the DialogShell. A BulletinBoardDialog is used for interactions not supported by the standard dialog set. This function does not automatically create any labels, buttons, or other dialog components. Such components should be added by the application after the BulletinBoardDialog is created.

Use **XtManageChild** to pop up the BulletinBoardDialog (passing the BulletinBoard as the widget parameter); use **XtUnmanageChild** to pop it down.

parent   Specifies the parent widget ID

name   Specifies the name of the created widget

arglist   Specifies the argument list

argcount   Specifies the number of attribute/value pairs in the argument list (*arglist*)

For a complete definition of BulletinBoard and its associated resources, see **XmBulletinBoard(3X)**.

Return Value

Returns the BulletinBoard widget ID.

Related Information

XmBulletinBoard(3X).

XmCreateCascadeButton—The CascadeButton widget creation function

AES Support Level

Full-use

Synopsis

#include <Xm/CascadeB.h>

Widget XmCreateCascadeButton (*parent, name, arglist, argcount*)
    Widget   *parent*;
    String   *name*;
    ArgList   *arglist*;
    Cardinal   *argcount*;

Description

XmCreateCascadeButton creates an instance of a CascadeButton widget and returns the associated widget ID.

parent   Specifies the parent widget ID. The parent must be a RowColumn widget.

name   Specifies the name of the created widget

arglist   Specifies the argument list

argcount   Specifies the number of attribute/value pairs in the argument list (*arglist*)

For a complete definition of CascadeButton and its associated resources, see **XmCascadeButton(3X)**.

Return Value

Returns the CascadeButton widget ID.

Related Information

XmCascadeButton(3X).

XmCreateCascadeButtonGadget—The CascadeButtonGadget creation function

AES Support Level

Full-use

Synopsis

#include <Xm/CascadeBG.h>

Widget XmCreateCascadeButtonGadget (*parent, name, arglist, argcount*)
Widget	*parent*;
String	*name*;
ArgList	*arglist*;
Cardinal	*argcount*;

Description

XmCreateCascadeButtonGadget creates an instance of a CascadeButtonGadget and returns the associated widget ID.

parent   Specifies the parent widget ID. The parent must be a RowColumn widget.

name   Specifies the name of the created widget.

arglist   Specifies the argument list.

argcount   Specifies the number of attribute/value pairs in the argument list (*arglist*).

For a complete definition of CascadeButtonGadget and its associated resources, see **XmCascadeButtonGadget(3X)**.

Return Value

Returns the CascadeButtonGadget widget ID.

Related Information

XmCascadeButtonGadget(3X).

XmCreateCommand(3X)

XmCreateCommand—The Command widget creation function

AES Support Level

Full-use

Synopsis

#include <Xm/Command.h>

Widget XmCreateCommand (*parent, name, arglist, argcount*)
    Widget   *parent*;
    String   *name*;
    ArgList   *arglist*;
    Cardinal   *argcount*;

Description

XmCreateCommand creates an instance of a Command widget and returns the associated widget ID.

parent   Specifies the parent widget ID

name   Specifies the name of the created widget

arglist   Specifies the argument list

argcount   Specifies the number of attribute/value pairs in the argument list (*arglist*)

For a complete definition of Command and its associated resources, see **XmCommand(3X)**.

Return Value

Returns the Command widget ID.

Related Information

XmCommand(3X).

XmCreateDialogShell—The DialogShell widget creation function

AES Support Level

Full-use

Synopsis

#include <Xm/DialogS.h>

Widget XmCreateDialogShell (*parent, name, arglist, argcount*)
    Widget   *parent*;
    String   *name*;
    ArgList   *arglist*;
    Cardinal   *argcount*;

Description

XmCreateDialogShell creates an instance of a DialogShell widget and returns the associated widget ID.

parent   Specifies the parent widget ID

name   Specifies the name of the created widget

arglist   Specifies the argument list

argcount   Specifies the number of attribute/value pairs in the argument list (*arglist*)

For a complete definition of DialogShell and its associated resources, see **XmDialogShell(3X)**.

Return Value

Returns the DialogShell widget ID.

Related Information

XmDialogShell(3X).

XmCreateDrawingArea—The DrawingArea widget creation function

AES Support Level

Full-use

Synopsis

#include <Xm/DrawingA.h>

Widget XmCreateDrawingArea (*parent, name, arglist, argcount*)
> **Widget**   *parent*;
> **String**   *name*;
> **ArgList**   *arglist*;
> **Cardinal**   *argcount*;

Description

XmCreateDrawingArea creates an instance of a DrawingArea widget and returns the associated widget ID.

parent   Specifies the parent widget ID

name   Specifies the name of the created widget

arglist   Specifies the argument list

argcount   Specifies the number of attribute/value pairs in the argument list (*arglist*)

For a complete definition of DrawingArea and its associated resources, see **XmDrawingArea(3X)**.

Return Value

Returns the DrawingArea widget ID.

Related Information

XmDrawingArea(3X).

XmCreateDrawnButton—The DrawnButton widget creation function

AES Support Level

Full-use

Synopsis

#include <Xm/DrawnB.h>

Widget XmCreateDrawnButton (*parent, name, arglist, argcount*)
Widget	*parent*;
String	*name*;
ArgList	*arglist*;
Cardinal	*argcount*;

Description

XmCreateDrawnButton creates an instance of a DrawnButton widget and returns the associated widget ID.

parent Specifies the parent widget ID

name Specifies the name of the created widget

arglist Specifies the argument list

argcount Specifies the number of attribute/value pairs in the argument list (*arglist*)

For a complete definition of DrawnButton and its associated resources, see **XmDrawnButton(3X)**.

Return Value

Returns the DrawnButton widget ID.

Related Information

XmDrawnButton(3X).

XmCreateErrorDialog—The MessageBox ErrorDialog convenience creation function

AES Support Level

Full-use

Synopsis

#include <Xm/MessageB.h>

Widget XmCreateErrorDialog (*parent, name, arglist, argcount*)
    Widget   *parent*;
    String   *name*;
    ArgList   *arglist*;
    Cardinal   *argcount*;

Description

XmCreateErrorDialog is a convenience creation function that creates a DialogShell and an unmanaged MessageBox child of the DialogShell. An ErrorDialog warns the user of an invalid or potentially dangerous condition. It includes a symbol, a message, and three buttons. The default symbol is an octagon with a diagonal slash. The default button labels are **OK**, **Cancel**, and **Help**.

Use **XtManageChild** to pop up the ErrorDialog (passing the MessageBox as the widget parameter); use **XtUnmanageChild** to pop it down.

parent   Specifies the parent widget ID

name   Specifies the name of the created widget

arglist   Specifies the argument list

argcount   Specifies the number of attribute/value pairs in the argument list (*arglist*)

For a complete definition of MessageBox and its associated resources, see **XmMessageBox(3X)**.

Return Value

Returns the MessageBox widget ID.

Related Information

XmMessageBox(3X).

XmCreateFileSelectionBox—The FileSelectionBox widget creation function

AES Support Level

Full-use

Synopsis

#include <Xm/FileSB.h>

Widget XmCreateFileSelectionBox (*parent, name, arglist, argcount*)
    Widget   *parent*;
    String   *name*;
    ArgList   *arglist*;
    Cardinal *argcount*;

Description

XmCreateFileSelectionBox creates an unmanaged FileSelectionBox. A FileSelectionBox is used to select a file and includes the following:

- An editable text field for the directory mask

- A scrolling list of filenames

- An editable text field for the selected file

- Labels for the list and text fields

- Four buttons

The default button labels are **OK**, **Filter**, **Cancel**, and **Help**. One additional **WorkArea** child may be added to the FileSelectionBox after creation.

If the parent of the FileSelectionBox is a DialogShell, use **XtManageChild** to pop up the FileSelectionDialog (passing the FileSelectionBox as the widget parameter); use **XtUnmanageChild** to pop it down.

parent   Specifies the parent widget ID

name   Specifies the name of the created widget

arglist   Specifies the argument list

argcount   Specifies the number of attribute/value pairs in the argument list (*arglist*)

For a complete definition of FileSelectionBox and its associated resources, see
XmFileSelectionBox(3X).

Return Value

Returns the FileSelectionBox widget ID.

Related Information

XmFileSelectionBox(3X).

XmCreateFileSelectionDialog—The FileSelectionBox FileSelectionDialog convenience creation function

AES Support Level

Full-use

Synopsis

#include <Xm/FileSB.h>

Widget XmCreateFileSelectionDialog (*parent, name, arglist, argcount*)
    Widget   *parent*;
    String   *name*;
    ArgList   *arglist*;
    Cardinal   *argcount*;

Description

XmCreateFileSelectionDialog is a convenience creation function that creates a DialogShell and an unmanaged FileSelectionBox child of the DialogShell. A FileSelectionDialog selects a file. It includes the following:

- An editable text field for the directory mask

- A scrolling list of filenames

- An editable text field for the selected file

- Labels for the list and text fields

- Four buttons

The default button labels are **OK**, **Filter**, **Cancel**, and **Help**. One additional **WorkArea** child may be added to the FileSelectionBox after creation.

Use **XtManageChild** to pop up the FileSelectionDialog (passing the FileSelectionBox as the widget parameter); use **XtUnmanageChild** to pop it down.

parent   Specifies the parent widget ID

name   Specifies the name of the created widget

arglist   Specifies the argument list

argcount   Specifies the number of attribute/value pairs in the argument list (*arglist*)

For a complete definition of FileSelectionBox and its associated resources, see **XmFileSelectionBox(3X)**.

Return Value

Returns the FileSelectionBox widget ID.

Related Information

XmFileSelectionBox(3X).

XmCreateForm—The Form widget creation function

AES Support Level

Full-use

Synopsis

#include <Xm/Form.h>

Widget XmCreateForm (*parent, name, arglist, argcount*)
    Widget   *parent*;
    String   *name*;
    ArgList   *arglist*;
    Cardinal   *argcount*;

Description

XmCreateForm creates an instance of a Form widget and returns the associated widget ID.

parent   Specifies the parent widget ID

name   Specifies the name of the created widget

arglist   Specifies the argument list

argcount   Specifies the number of attribute/value pairs in the argument list (*arglist*)

For a complete definition of Form and its associated resources, see **XmForm(3X)**.

Return Value

Returns the Form widget ID.

Related Information

XmForm(3X).

XmCreateFormDialog(3X)

XmCreateFormDialog—A Form FormDialog convenience creation function

AES Support Level

Full-use

Synopsis

#include <Xm/Form.h>

Widget XmCreateFormDialog (*parent, name, arglist, argcount*)
    Widget   *parent*;
    String   *name*;
    ArgList   *arglist*;
    Cardinal   *argcount*;

Description

XmCreateFormDialog is a convenience creation function that creates a DialogShell and an unmanaged Form child of the DialogShell. A FormDialog is used for interactions not supported by the standard dialog set. This function does not automatically create any labels, buttons, or other dialog components. Such components should be added by the application after the FormDialog is created.

Use **XtManageChild** to pop up the FormDialog (passing the Form as the widget parameter); use **XtUnmanageChild** to pop it down.

parent   Specifies the parent widget ID

name   Specifies the name of the created widget

arglist   Specifies the argument list

argcount   Specifies the number of attribute/value pairs in the argument list (*arglist*)

For a complete definition of Form and its associated resources, see **XmForm(3X)**.

Return Value

Returns the Form widget ID.

Related Information

XmForm(3X).

XmCreateFrame—The Frame widget creation function

AES Support Level

Full-use

Synopsis

#include <Xm/Frame.h>

Widget XmCreateFrame (*parent, name, arglist, argcount*)
    Widget   *parent*;
    String   *name*;
    ArgList   *arglist*;
    Cardinal   *argcount*;

Description

XmCreateFrame creates an instance of a Frame widget and returns the associated widget ID.

parent   Specifies the parent widget ID

name   Specifies the name of the created widget

arglist   Specifies the argument list

argcount   Specifies the number of attribute/value pairs in the argument list (*arglist*)

For a complete definition of Frame and its associated resources, see **XmFrame(3X)**.

Return Value

Returns the Frame widget ID.

Related Information

XmFrame(3X).

XmCreateInformationDialog—The   MessageBox   InformationDialog
convenience creation function

AES Support Level

Full-use

Synopsis

#include <Xm/MessageB.h>

Widget XmCreateInformationDialog (*parent, name, arglist, argcount*)
    Widget   *parent*;
    String   *name*;
    ArgList   *arglist*;
    Cardinal   *argcount*;

Description

XmCreateInformationDialog is a convenience creation function that creates a
DialogShell and an unmanaged MessageBox child of the DialogShell. An
InformationDialog gives the user information, such as the status of an action. It
includes a symbol, a message, and three buttons. The default symbol is **i**. The
default button labels are **OK**, **Cancel**, and **Help**.

Use **XtManageChild** to pop up the InformationDialog (passing the MessageBox as
the widget parameter); use **XtUnmanageChild** to pop it down.

parent   Specifies the parent widget ID

name   Specifies the name of the created widget

arglist   Specifies the argument list

argcount   Specifies the number of attribute/value pairs in the argument list
                (*arglist*)

For a complete definition of MessageBox and its associated resources, see
XmMessageBox(3X).

Return Value

Returns the MessageBox widget ID.

Related Information

XmMessageBox(3X).

XmCreateLabel—The Label widget creation function

AES Support Level

Full-use

Synopsis

#include <Xm/Label.h>

Widget XmCreateLabel (*parent, name, arglist, argcount*)
    Widget   *parent*;
    String   *name*;
    ArgList   *arglist*;
    Cardinal   *argcount*;

Description

XmCreateLabel creates an instance of a Label widget and returns the associated widget ID.

parent   Specifies the parent widget ID

name   Specifies the name of the created widget

arglist   Specifies the argument list

argcount   Specifies the number of attribute/value pairs in the argument list (*arglist*)

For a complete definition of Label and its associated resources, see **XmLabel(3X)**.

Return Value

Returns the Label widget ID.

Related Information

XmLabel(3X).

XmCreateLabelGadget—The LabelGadget creation function

AES Support Level

Full-use

Synopsis

#include <Xm/LabelG.h>

Widget XmCreateLabelGadget (*parent, name, arglist, argcount*)
    Widget   *parent*;
    String   *name*;
    ArgList   *arglist*;
    Cardinal   *argcount*;

Description

XmCreateLabelGadget creates an instance of a LabelGadget widget and returns the associated widget ID.

parent   Specifies the parent widget ID

name   Specifies the name of the created widget

arglist   Specifies the argument list

argcount   Specifies the number of attribute/value pairs in the argument list (*arglist*)

For a complete definition of LabelGadget and its associated resources, see **XmLabelGadget(3X)**.

Return Value

Returns the LabelGadget widget ID.

Related Information

XmLabelGadget(3X).

XmCreateList—The List widget creation function

AES Support Level

Full-use

Synopsis

#include <Xm/List.h>

Widget XmCreateList (*parent, name, arglist, argcount*)
    Widget   *parent*;
    String   *name*;
    ArgList   *arglist*;
    Cardinal   *argcount*;

Description

XmCreateList creates an instance of a List widget and returns the associated widget ID.

parent   Specifies the parent widget ID

name   Specifies the name of the created widget

arglist   Specifies the argument list

argcount   Specifies the number of attribute/value pairs in the argument list (*arglist*)

For a complete definition of List and its associated resources, see **XmList(3X)**.

Return Value

Returns the List widget ID.

Related Information

XmList(3X).

XmCreateMainWindow—The MainWindow widget creation function

AES Support Level

Full-use

Synopsis

#include <Xm/MainW.h>

Widget XmCreateMainWindow (*parent, name, arglist, argcount*)
  Widget   *parent*;
  String   *name*;
  ArgList   *arglist*;
  Cardinal *argcount*;

Description

XmCreateMainWindow creates an instance of a MainWindow widget and returns the associated widget ID.

parent   Specifies the parent widget ID

name   Specifies the name of the created widget

arglist   Specifies the argument list

argcount   Specifies the number of attribute/value pairs in the argument list (*arglist*)

For a complete definition of MainWindow and its associated resources, see **XmMainWindow(3X)**.

Return Value

Returns the MainWindow widget ID.

Related Information

XmMainWindow(3X).

XmCreateMenuBar—A RowColumn widget convenience creation function

AES Support Level

Full-use

Synopsis

#include <Xm/RowColumn.h>

Widget XmCreateMenuBar (*parent, name, arglist, argcount*)
    Widget   *parent*;
    String   *name*;
    ArgList   *arglist*;
    Cardinal   *argcount*;

Description

XmCreateMenuBar creates an instance of a RowColumn widget of type **XmMENU_BAR** and returns the associated widget ID. It is provided as a convenience function for creating RowColumn widgets configured to operate as a MenuBar and is not implemented as a separate widget class.

The MenuBar widget is generally used for building a Pulldown menu system. Typically, a MenuBar is created and placed along the top of the application window, and several CascadeButtons are inserted as the children. Each of the CascadeButtons has a Pulldown MenuPane associated with it. These Pulldown MenuPanes must have been created as children of the MenuBar. The user interacts with the MenuBar by using either the mouse or the keyboard.

The MenuBar displays a 3-D shadow along its border. The application controls the shadow attributes using the visual-related resources supported by **XmManager**.

The MenuBar widget is homogeneous in that it accepts only children that are a subclass of **XmCascadeButton** or **XmCascadeButtonGadget**. Attempting to insert a child of a different class results in a warning message.

If the MenuBar does not have enough room to fit all of its subwidgets on a single line, the MenuBar attempts to wrap the remaining entries onto additional lines if allowed by the geometry manager of the parent widget.

parent   Specifies the parent widget ID

name   Specifies the name of the created widget

arglist   Specifies the argument list

argcount   Specifies the number of attribute/value pairs in the argument list (*arglist*)

For a complete definition of RowColumn and its associated resources, see
XmRowColumn(3X).

Return Value

Returns the RowColumn widget ID.

Related Information

XmCascadeButton(3X), XmCascadeButtonGadget(3X),
XmCreatePulldownMenu(3X), XmManager(3X), and XmRowColumn(3X).

XmCreateMenuShell—The MenuShell widget creation function

AES Support Level

Full-use

Synopsis

#include <Xm/MenuShell.h>

Widget XmCreateMenuShell (*parent, name, arglist, argcount*)
    Widget   *parent*;
    String   *name*;
    ArgList   *arglist*;
    Cardinal   *argcount*;

Description

XmCreateMenuShell creates an instance of a MenuShell widget and returns the associated widget ID.

parent   Specifies the parent widget ID

name   Specifies the name of the created widget

arglist   Specifies the argument list

argcount   Specifies the number of attribute/value pairs in the argument list (*arglist*)

For a complete definition of MenuShell and its associated resources, see **XmMenuShell(3X)**.

Return Value

Returns the MenuShell widget ID.

Related Information

XmMenuShell(3X).

XmCreateMessageBox—The MessageBox widget creation function

AES Support Level

Full-use

Synopsis

#include <Xm/MessageB.h>

Widget XmCreateMessageBox (*parent, name, arglist, argcount*)
    Widget   *parent*;
    String   *name*;
    ArgList   *arglist*;
    Cardinal   *argcount*;

Description

XmCreateMessageBox creates an unmanaged MessageBox. A MessageBox is used for common interaction tasks, which include giving information, asking questions, and reporting errors. It includes an optional symbol, a message, and three buttons.

By default, there is no symbol. The default button labels are **OK**, **Cancel**, and **Help**.

If the parent of the MessageBox is a DialogShell, use **XtManageChild** to pop up the MessageBox (passing the MessageBox as the widget parameter); use **XtUnmanageChild** to pop it down.

parent   Specifies the parent widget ID

name   Specifies the name of the created widget

arglist   Specifies the argument list

argcount   Specifies the number of attribute/value pairs in the argument list (*arglist*)

For a complete definition of MessageBox and its associated resources, see **XmMessageBox(3X)**.

Return Value

Returns the MessageBox widget ID.

Related Information

XmMessageBox(3X).

XmCreateMessageDialog—The MessageBox MessageDialog convenience creation function

AES Support Level

Full-use

Synopsis

#include <Xm/MessageB.h>

Widget XmCreateMessageDialog (*parent, name, arglist, argcount*)
    Widget   *parent*;
    String   *name*;
    ArgList   *arglist*;
    Cardinal   *argcount*;

Description

XmCreateMessageDialog is a convenience creation function that creates a DialogShell and an unmanaged MessageBox child of the DialogShell. A MessageDialog is used for common interaction tasks, which include giving information, asking questions, and reporting errors. It includes a symbol, a message, and three buttons. By default, there is no symbol. The default button labels are **OK**, **Cancel**, and **Help**.

Use **XtManageChild** to pop up the MessageDialog (passing the MessageBox as the widget parameter); use **XtUnmanageChild** to pop it down.

parent   Specifies the parent widget ID

name   Specifies the name of the created widget

arglist   Specifies the argument list

argcount   Specifies the number of attribute/value pairs in the argument list (*arglist*)

For a complete definition of MessageBox and its associated resources, see **XmMessageBox(3X)**.

Return Value

Returns the MessageBox widget ID.

Related Information

XmMessageBox(3X).

XmCreateOptionMenu—A RowColumn widget convenience creation function

AES Support Level

Full-use

Synopsis

#include <Xm/RowColumn.h>

Widget XmCreateOptionMenu (*parent, name, arglist, argcount*)
    Widget   *parent*;
    String   *name*;
    ArgList   *arglist*;
    Cardinal   *argcount*;

Description

XmCreateOptionMenu creates an instance of a RowColumn widget of type **XmMENU_OPTION** and returns the associated widget ID.

It is provided as a convenience function for creating a RowColumn widget configured to operate as an OptionMenu and is not implemented as a separate widget class.

The OptionMenu widget is a specialized RowColumn manager composed of a label, a selection area, and a single Pulldown MenuPane. When an application creates an OptionMenu widget, it supplies the label string and the Pulldown MenuPane. In order for the operation to be successful, there must be a valid **XmNsubMenuId** resource set when this function is called. When the OptionMenu is created, the Pulldown MenuPane must have been created as a child of the OptionMenu's parent and must be specified. The LabelGadget and the selection area (a CascadeButtonGadget) are created by the OptionMenu.

The OptionMenu's Pulldown MenuPane must not contain any ToggleButtons or ToggleButtonGadgets. The results of including CascadeButtons or CascadeButtonGadgets in the OptionMenu's Pulldown MenuPane are undefined.

An OptionMenu is laid out with the label displayed on one side of the widget and the selection area on the other side. The selection area has a dual purpose; it displays the label of the last item selected from the associated Pulldown MenuPane, and it provides the means for posting the Pulldown MenuPane.

The OptionMenu typically does not display any 3-D visuals around itself or the internal LabelGadget. By default, the internal CascadeButtonGadget has a visible 3-D shadow. The application may change this by getting the CascadeButtonGadget ID using **XmOptionButtonGadget**, and then calling **XtSetValues** using the standard visual-related resources.

The Pulldown MenuPane is posted when the mouse pointer is moved over the selection area and a mouse button that is defined by OptionMenu's RowColumn parent is pressed. The Pulldown MenuPane is posted and positioned so that the last selected item is directly over the selection area. The mouse is then used to arm the desired menu item. When the mouse button is released, the armed menu item is selected and the label within the selection area is changed to match that of the selected item. By default, **BSelect** is used to interact with an OptionMenu.

The OptionMenu also operates with the keyboard interface mechanism. If the application has established a mnemonic with the OptionMenu, pressing **<Alt>** with the mnemonic causes the Pulldown MenuPane to be posted with traversal enabled. The standard traversal keys can then be used to move within the MenuPane. Pressing **<Return>** or typing a mnemonic or accelerator for one of the menu items selects that item.

An application may use the **XmNmenuHistory** resource to indicate which item in the Pulldown MenuPane should be treated as the current choice and have its label displayed in the selection area. By default, the first item in the Pulldown MenuPane is used.

parent	Specifies the parent widget ID
name	Specifies the name of the created widget
arglist	Specifies the argument list
argcount	Specifies the number of attribute/value pairs in the argument list (*arglist*)

For a complete definition of RowColumn and its associated resources, see **XmRowColumn(3X)**.

Return Value

Returns the RowColumn widget ID.

Related Information

XmCascadeButtonGadget(3X), **XmCreatePulldownMenu(3X)**,
XmLabelGadget(3X), **XmOptionButtonGadget(3X)**,
XmOptionLabelGadget(3X), and **XmRowColumn(3X)**.

XmCreatePanedWindow—The PanedWindow widget creation function

AES Support Level

Full-use

Synopsis

#include <Xm/PanedW.h>

Widget XmCreatePanedWindow (*parent, name, arglist, argcount*)
    Widget   *parent*;
    String   *name*;
    ArgList   *arglist*;
    Cardinal   *argcount*;

Description

XmCreatePanedWindow creates an instance of a PanedWindow widget and returns the associated widget ID.

parent   Specifies the parent widget ID

name   Specifies the name of the created widget

arglist   Specifies the argument list

argcount   Specifies the number of attribute/value pairs in the argument list (*arglist*)

For a complete definition of PanedWindow and its associated resources, see **XmPanedWindow(3X)**.

Return Value

Returns the PanedWindow widget ID.

Related Information

XmPanedWindow(3X).

XmCreatePopupMenu—A RowColumn widget convenience creation function

AES Support Level

Full-use

Synopsis

#include <Xm/RowColumn.h>

Widget XmCreatePopupMenu (*parent, name, arglist, argcount*)
      Widget   *parent*;
      String   *name*;
      ArgList   *arglist*;
      Cardinal   *argcount*;

Description

XmCreatePopupMenu creates an instance of a RowColumn widget of type **XmMENU_POPUP** and returns the associated widget ID. When this function is used to create the Popup MenuPane, a MenuShell widget is automatically created as the parent of the MenuPane. The parent of the MenuShell widget is the widget indicated by the *parent* parameter.

XmCreatePopupMenu is provided as a convenience function for creating RowColumn widgets configured to operate as Popup MenuPanes and is not implemented as a separate widget class.

The PopupMenu is used as the first MenuPane within a PopupMenu system; all other MenuPanes are of the Pulldown type. A Popup MenuPane displays a 3-D shadow, unless the feature is disabled by the application. The shadow appears around the edge of the MenuPane.

The Popup MenuPane must be created as the child of a MenuShell widget in order to function properly when it is incorporated into a menu. If the application uses this convenience function for creating a Popup MenuPane, the MenuShell is automatically created as the real parent of the MenuPane. If the application does not use this convenience function to create the RowColumn to function as a Popup MenuPane, it is the application's responsibility to create the MenuShell widget.

To access the PopupMenu, the application must first position the widget using the **XmMenuPosition** function and then manage it using **XtManageChild**.

parent   Specifies the parent widget ID

name   Specifies the name of the created widget

> *arglist*   Specifies the argument list
>
> *argcount* Specifies the number of attribute/value pairs in the argument list (*arglist*)

For a complete definition of RowColumn and its associated resources, see **XmRowColumn(3X)**.

Return Value

Returns the RowColumn widget ID.

Related Information

XmMenuPosition(3X), **XmMenuShell(3X)**, and **XmRowColumn(3X)**.

XmCreatePromptDialog—The SelectionBox PromptDialog convenience creation function

AES Support Level

Full-use

Synopsis

#include <Xm/SelectioB.h>

Widget XmCreatePromptDialog (*parent, name, arglist, argcount*)
Widget	*parent*;
String	*name*;
ArgList	*arglist*;
Cardinal	*argcount*;

Description

XmCreatePromptDialog is a convenience creation function that creates a DialogShell and an unmanaged SelectionBox child of the DialogShell. A PromptDialog prompts the user for text input. It includes a message, a text input region, and three managed buttons. The default button labels are **OK**, **Cancel**, and **Help**. An additional button, with **Apply** as the default label, is created unmanaged; it may be explicitly managed if needed. One additional **WorkArea** child may be added to the SelectionBox after creation.

XmCreatePromptDialog forces the value of the SelectionBox resource **XmNdialogType** to **XmDIALOG_PROMPT**.

Use **XtManageChild** to pop up the PromptDialog (passing the SelectionBox as the widget parameter); use **XtUnmanageChild** to pop it down.

parent	Specifies the parent widget ID
name	Specifies the name of the created widget
arglist	Specifies the argument list
argcount	Specifies the number of attribute/value pairs in the argument list (*arglist*)

For a complete definition of SelectionBox and its associated resources, see **XmSelectionBox(3X)**.

Return Value

Returns the SelectionBox widget ID.

Related Information

XmSelectionBox(3X).

XmCreatePulldownMenu—A RowColumn widget convenience creation function

AES Support Level

Full-use

Synopsis

#include <Xm/RowColumn.h>

Widget XmCreatePulldownMenu (*parent, name, arglist, argcount*)
    Widget   *parent*;
    String   *name*;
    ArgList   *arglist*;
    Cardinal   *argcount*;

Description

XmCreatePulldownMenu creates an instance of a RowColumn widget of type **XmMENU_PULLDOWN** and returns the associated widget ID.

parent   Specifies the parent widget ID

name   Specifies the name of the created widget

arglist   Specifies the argument list

argcount   Specifies the number of attribute/value pairs in the argument list (*arglist*)

Specifies the number of attribute/value pairs in the argument list (*arglist*). When this function is used to create the Pulldown MenuPane, a MenuShell widget is automatically created as the parent of the MenuPane. If the widget specified by the *parent* parameter is a Popup or a Pulldown MenuPane, the MenuShell widget is created as a child of the *parent* MenuShell; otherwise, it is created as a child of the specified *parent* widget.

XmCreatePulldownMenu is provided as a convenience function for creating RowColumn widgets configured to operate as Pulldown MenuPanes and is not implemented as a separate widget class.

A Pulldown MenuPane displays a 3-D shadow, unless the feature is disabled by the application. The shadow appears around the edge of the MenuPane.

A Pulldown MenuPane is used with submenus that are to be attached to a CascadeButton or a CascadeButtonGadget. This is the case for all MenuPanes that are part of a PulldownMenu system (a MenuBar), the MenuPane associated with an OptionMenu, and any MenuPanes that cascade from a Popup MenuPane. Pulldown MenuPanes that are to be associated with an OptionMenu must be created before the OptionMenu is created.

XmCreatePulldownMenu(3X)

The Pulldown MenuPane must be attached to a CascadeButton or CascadeButtonGadget that resides in a MenuBar, a Popup MenuPane, a Pulldown MenuPane, or an OptionMenu. It is attached with the button resource **XmNsubMenuId**.

A MenuShell widget is required between the Pulldown MenuPane and its parent. If the application uses this convenience function for creating a Pulldown MenuPane, the MenuShell is automatically created as the real parent of the MenuPane; otherwise, it is the application's responsibility to create the MenuShell widget.

To function correctly when incorporated into a menu, the Pulldown MenuPane's hierarchy must be considered. This hierarchy depends on the type of menu system that is being built, as follows:

- If the Pulldown MenuPane is to be pulled down from a MenuBar, its *parent* must be the MenuBar.

- If the Pulldown MenuPane is to be pulled down from a Popup or another Pulldown MenuPane, its *parent* must be that Popup or Pulldown MenuPane.

- If the Pulldown MenuPane is to be pulled down from an OptionMenu, its *parent* must be the same as the OptionMenu parent.

For a complete definition of RowColumn and its associated resources, see **XmRowColumn(3X)**.

Return Value

Returns the RowColumn widget ID.

Related Information

XmCascadeButton(3X), **XmCascadeButtonGadget(3X)**, **XmCreateOptionMenu(3X)**, **XmCreatePopupMenu(3X)**, **XmMenuShell(3X)**, and **XmRowColumn(3X)**.

XmCreatePushButton—The PushButton widget creation function

AES Support Level

Full-use

Synopsis

#include <Xm/PushB.h>

Widget XmCreatePushButton (*parent, name, arglist, argcount*)
Widget	*parent*;
String	*name*;
ArgList	*arglist*;
Cardinal	*argcount*;

Description

XmCreatePushButton creates an instance of a PushButton widget and returns the associated widget ID.

parent   Specifies the parent widget ID

name   Specifies the name of the created widget

arglist   Specifies the argument list

argcount   Specifies the number of attribute/value pairs in the argument list (*arglist*)

For a complete definition of PushButton and its associated resources, see **XmPushButton(3X)**.

Return Value

Returns the PushButton widget ID.

Related Information

XmPushButton(3X).

XmCreatePushButtonGadget—The PushButtonGadget creation function

AES Support Level

Full-use

Synopsis

#include <Xm/PushBG.h>

Widget XmCreatePushButtonGadget (*parent, name, arglist, argcount*)

Widget	*parent*;
String	*name*;
ArgList	*arglist*;
Cardinal	*argcount*;

Description

XmCreatePushButtonGadget creates an instance of a PushButtonGadget widget and returns the associated widget ID.

parent   Specifies the parent widget ID

name   Specifies the name of the created widget

arglist   Specifies the argument list

argcount   Specifies the number of attribute/value pairs in the argument list (*arglist*)

For a complete definition of PushButtonGadget and its associated resources, see **XmPushButtonGadget(3X)**.

Return Value

Returns the PushButtonGadget widget ID.

Related Information

XmPushButtonGadget(3X).

XmCreateQuestionDialog—The MessageBox QuestionDialog convenience creation function

AES Support Level

Full-use

Synopsis

#include <Xm/MessageB.h>

Widget XmCreateQuestionDialog (*parent, name, arglist, argcount*)
    Widget   *parent*;
    String   *name*;
    ArgList   *arglist*;
    Cardinal   *argcount*;

Description

XmCreateQuestionDialog is a convenience creation function that creates a DialogShell and an unmanaged MessageBox child of the DialogShell. A QuestionDialog is used to get the answer to a question from the user. It includes a symbol, a message, and three buttons. The default symbol is a question mark. The default button labels are **OK**, **Cancel**, and **Help**.

Use **XtManageChild** to pop up the QuestionDialog (passing the MessageBox as the widget parameter); use **XtUnmanageChild** to pop it down.

parent   Specifies the parent widget ID

name   Specifies the name of the created widget

arglist   Specifies the argument list

argcount   Specifies the number of attribute/value pairs in the argument list (*arglist*)

For a complete definition of MessageBox and its associated resources, see **XmMessageBox(3X)**.

Return Value

Returns the MessageBox widget ID.

Related Information

XmMessageBox(3X).

XmCreateRadioBox—A RowColumn widget convenience creation function

AES Support Level

Full-use

Synopsis

#include <Xm/RowColumn.h>

Widget XmCreateRadioBox (*parent, name, arglist, argcount*)
    Widget   *parent*;
    String   *name*;
    ArgList   *arglist*;
    Cardinal   *argcount*;

Description

XmCreateRadioBox creates an instance of a RowColumn widget of type **XmWORK_AREA** and returns the associated widget ID. Typically, this is a composite widget that contains multiple ToggleButtonGadgets. The RadioBox arbitrates and ensures that at most one ToggleButtonGadget is on at any time.

Unless the application supplies other values in the *arglist*, this function provides initial values for several RowColumn resources. It initializes **XmNpacking** to **XmPACK_COLUMN**, **XmNradioBehavior** to True, **XmNisHomogeneous** to True, and **XmNentryClass** to **XmToggleButtonGadgetClass**.

In a RadioBox, the ToggleButton or ToggleButtonGadget resource **XmNindicatorType** defaults to **XmONE_OF_MANY**, and the ToggleButton or ToggleButtonGadget resource **XmNvisibleWhenOff** defaults to True.

This routine is provided as a convenience function for creating RowColumn widgets.

parent   Specifies the parent widget ID

name   Specifies the name of the created widget

arglist   Specifies the argument list

argcount   Specifies the number of attribute/value pairs in the argument list (*arglist*)

For a complete definition of RowColumn and its associated resources, see **XmRowColumn(3X)**.

Return Value

Returns the RowColumn widget ID.

Related Information

XmCreateRowColumn(3X), **XmCreateWorkArea(3X)**, and **XmRowColumn(3X)**.

XmCreateRowColumn—The RowColumn widget creation function

AES Support Level

Full-use

Synopsis

#include <Xm/RowColumn.h>

Widget XmCreateRowColumn (*parent, name, arglist, argcount*)
    Widget   *parent*;
    String   *name*;
    ArgList   *arglist*;
    Cardinal   *argcount*;

Description

XmCreateRowColumn creates an instance of a RowColumn widget and returns the associated widget ID. If **XmNrowColumnType** is not specified, then it is created with **XmWORK_AREA**, which is the default.

If this function is used to create a Popup Menu of type **XmMENU_POPUP** or a Pulldown Menu of type **XmMENU_PULLDOWN**, a MenuShell widget is not automatically created as the parent of the MenuPane. The application must first create the MenuShell by using either **XmCreateMenuShell** or the standard toolkit create function.

parent   Specifies the parent widget ID

name   Specifies the name of the created widget

arglist   Specifies the argument list

argcount   Specifies the number of attribute/value pairs in the argument list (*arglist*)

For a complete definition of RowColumn and its associated resources, see **XmRowColumn(3X)**.

Return Value

Returns the RowColumn widget ID.

Related Information

       XmCreateMenuBar(3X), **XmCreateMenuShell(3X)**,
       XmCreateOptionMenu(3X), **XmCreatePopupMenu(3X)**,
       XmCreatePulldownMenu(3X), **XmCreateRadioBox(3X)**,
       XmCreateWorkArea(3X), and **XmRowColumn(3X)**.

XmCreateScale—The Scale widget creation function

AES Support Level

Full-use

Synopsis

#include <Xm/Scale.h>

Widget XmCreateScale (*parent, name, arglist, argcount*)
  Widget   *parent*;
  String   *name*;
  ArgList   *arglist*;
  Cardinal *argcount*;

Description

XmCreateScale creates an instance of a Scale widget and returns the associated widget ID.

parent   Specifies the parent widget ID

name   Specifies the name of the created widget

arglist   Specifies the argument list

argcount Specifies the number of attribute/value pairs in the argument list (*arglist*)

For a complete definition of Scale and its associated resources, see **XmScale(3X)**.

Return Value

Returns the Scale widget ID.

Related Information

XmScale(3X).

XmCreateScrollBar—The ScrollBar widget creation function

AES Support Level

Full-use

Synopsis

#include <Xm/ScrollBar.h>

Widget XmCreateScrollBar (*parent, name, arglist, argcount*)
    Widget   *parent*;
    String   *name*;
    ArgList   *arglist*;
    Cardinal   *argcount*;

Description

XmCreateScrollBar creates an instance of a ScrollBar widget and returns the associated widget ID.

parent   Specifies the parent widget ID

name   Specifies the name of the created widget

arglist   Specifies the argument list

argcount   Specifies the number of attribute/value pairs in the argument list (*arglist*)

For a complete definition of ScrollBar and its associated resources, see **XmScrollBar(3X)**.

Return Value

Returns the ScrollBar widget ID.

Related Information

XmScrollBar(3X).

XmCreateScrolledList—The List ScrolledList convenience creation function

AES Support Level

Full-use

Synopsis

#include <Xm/List.h>

Widget XmCreateScrolledList (*parent, name, arglist, argcount*)
Widget	*parent*;
String	*name*;
ArgList	*arglist*;
Cardinal	*argcount*;

Description

XmCreateScrolledList creates an instance of a List widget that is contained within a ScrolledWindow. All ScrolledWindow subarea widgets are automatically created by this function. The ID returned by this function is that of the List widget. Use this ID for all normal List operations, as well as those that are relevant for the ScrolledList widget.

All arguments to either the List or the ScrolledWindow widget can be specified at creation time using this function. Changes to initial position and size are sent only to the ScrolledWindow widget. Other resources are sent to the List or the ScrolledWindow widget as appropriate.

This function forces the following initial values for ScrolledWindow resources:

- **XmNscrollingPolicy** is set to **XmAPPLICATION_DEFINED**.

- **XmNvisualPolicy** is set to **XmVARIABLE**.

- **XmNscrollBarDisplayPolicy** is set to **XmSTATIC**. (No initial value is forced for the List's **XmNscrollBarDisplayPolicy**.)

- **XmNshadowThickness** is set to 0 (zero).

To obtain the ID of the ScrolledWindow widget associated with the ScrolledList, use the Xt Intrinsics **XtParent** function. The name of the ScrolledWindow created by this function is formed by concatenating **SW** onto the end of the *name* specified in the parameter list.

parent   Specifies the parent widget ID

name   Specifies the name of the created widget

arglist   Specifies the argument list

argcount   Specifies the number of attribute/value pairs in the argument list
(*arglist*)

For a complete definition of List and its associated resources, see **XmList(3X)**.

Return Value

Returns the List widget ID.

Related Information

XmList(3X) and **XmScrolledWindow(3X)**.

XmCreateScrolledText—The Text ScrolledText convenience creation function

AES Support Level

Full-use

Synopsis

#include <Xm/Text.h>

Widget XmCreateScrolledText (*parent, name, arglist, argcount*)
    Widget   *parent*;
    String   *name*;
    ArgList   *arglist*;
    Cardinal   *argcount*;

Description

XmCreateScrolledText creates an instance of a Text widget that is contained within a ScrolledWindow. All ScrolledWindow subarea widgets are automatically created by this function. The ID returned by this function is that of the Text widget. Use this ID for all normal Text operations, as well as those that are relevant for the ScrolledText widget.

The Text widget defaults to single-line text edit; therefore, no ScrollBars are displayed. The Text resource **XmNeditMode** must be set to **XmMULTI_LINE_EDIT** to display the ScrollBars. The results of placing a Text widget inside a ScrolledWindow when the Text's **XmNeditMode** is **XmSINGLE_LINE_EDIT** are undefined.

All arguments to either the Text or the ScrolledWindow widget can be specified at creation time with this function. Changes to initial position and size are sent only to the ScrolledWindow widget. Other resources are sent to the Text or the ScrolledWindow widget as appropriate.

This function forces the following initial values for ScrolledWindow resources:

- **XmNscrollingPolicy** is set to **XmAPPLICATION_DEFINED**.

- **XmNvisualPolicy** is set to **XmVARIABLE**.

- **XmNscrollBarDisplayPolicy** is set to **XmSTATIC**.

- **XmNshadowThickness** is set to 0 (zero).

To obtain the ID of the ScrolledWindow widget associated with the ScrolledText, use the Xt Intrinsics **XtParent** function. The name of the ScrolledWindow created by this function is formed by concatenating the letters **SW** onto the end of the *name* specified in the parameter list.

parent   Specifies the parent widget ID

name   Specifies the name of the created widget

arglist   Specifies the argument list

argcount   Specifies the number of attribute/value pairs in the argument list (*arglist*)

For a complete definition of Text and its associated resources, see **XmText(3X)**.

Return Value

Returns the Text widget ID.

Related Information

XmScrolledWindow(3X) and **XmText(3X)**.

XmCreateScrolledWindow—The ScrolledWindow widget creation function

AES Support Level

Full-use

Synopsis

#include <Xm/ScrolledW.h>

Widget XmCreateScrolledWindow (*parent, name, arglist, argcount*)
    Widget   *parent*;
    String   *name*;
    ArgList   *arglist*;
    Cardinal   *argcount*;

Description

XmCreateScrolledWindow creates an instance of a ScrolledWindow widget and returns the associated widget ID.

parent   Specifies the parent widget ID

name   Specifies the name of the created widget

arglist   Specifies the argument list

argcount   Specifies the number of attribute/value pairs in the argument list (*arglist*)

For a complete definition of ScrolledWindow and its associated resources, see **XmScrolledWindow(3X)**.

Return Value

Returns the ScrolledWindow widget ID.

Related Information

XmScrolledWindow(3X).

XmCreateSelectionBox—The SelectionBox widget creation function

AES Support Level

Full-use

Synopsis

#include <Xm/SelectioB.h>

Widget XmCreateSelectionBox (*parent, name, arglist, argcount*)
    Widget   *parent*;
    String   *name*;
    ArgList   *arglist*;
    Cardinal   *argcount*;

Description

XmCreateSelectionBox creates an unmanaged SelectionBox. A SelectionBox is used to get a selection from a list of alternatives from the user and includes the following:

- A scrolling list of alternatives

- An editable text field for the selected alternative

- Labels for the list and text field

- Three or four buttons

The default button labels are **OK, Cancel**, and **Help**. By default, an **Apply** button is also created. If the parent of the SelectionBox is a DialogShell, it is managed; otherwise it is unmanaged. One additional **WorkArea** child may be added to the SelectionBox after creation.

parent   Specifies the parent widget ID

name   Specifies the name of the created widget

arglist   Specifies the argument list

argcount   Specifies the number of attribute/value pairs in the argument list (*arglist*)

For a complete definition of SelectionBox and its associated resources, see **XmSelectionBox(3X)**.

Return Value

Returns the SelectionBox widget ID.

Related Information

XmSelectionBox(3X).

XmCreateSelectionDialog—The SelectionBox SelectionDialog convenience creation function

AES Support Level

Full-use

Synopsis

#include <Xm/SelectioB.h>

Widget XmCreateSelectionDialog (*parent, name, arglist, argcount*)
  Widget   *parent*;
  String   *name*;
  ArgList   *arglist*;
  Cardinal   *argcount*;

Description

XmCreateSelectionDialog is a convenience creation function that creates a DialogShell and an unmanaged SelectionBox child of the DialogShell. A SelectionDialog offers the user a choice from a list of alternatives and gets a selection. It includes the following:

- A scrolling list of alternatives

- An editable text field for the selected alternative

- Labels for the text field

- Four buttons

The default button labels are **OK, Cancel**, **Apply**, and **Help**. One additional **WorkArea** child may be added to the SelectionBox after creation.

XmCreateSelectionDialog forces the value of the SelectionBox resource **XmNdialogType** to **XmDIALOG_SELECTION**.

Use **XtManageChild** to pop up the SelectionDialog (passing the SelectionBox as the widget parameter); use **XtUnmanageChild** to pop it down.

parent   Specifies the parent widget ID

name   Specifies the name of the created widget

arglist   Specifies the argument list

argcount   Specifies the number of attribute/value pairs in the argument list (*arglist*)

For a complete definition of SelectionBox and its associated resources, see
XmSelectionBox(3X).

Return Value

Returns the SelectionBox widget ID.

Related Information

XmSelectionBox(3X).

XmCreateSeparator—The Separator widget creation function

AES Support Level

Full-use

Synopsis

#include <Xm/Separator.h>

Widget XmCreateSeparator (*parent, name, arglist, argcount*)
    Widget   *parent*;
    String   *name*;
    ArgList   *arglist*;
    Cardinal   *argcount*;

Description

XmCreateSeparator creates an instance of a Separator widget and returns the associated widget ID.

parent   Specifies the parent widget ID

name   Specifies the name of the created widget

arglist   Specifies the argument list

argcount   Specifies the number of attribute/value pairs in the argument list (*arglist*)

For a complete definition of Separator and its associated resources, see **XmSeparator(3X)**.

Return Value

Returns the Separator widget ID.

Related Information

XmSeparator(3X).

XmCreateSeparatorGadget—The SeparatorGadget creation function

AES Support Level

Full-use

Synopsis

#include <Xm/SeparatoG.h>

Widget XmCreateSeparatorGadget (*parent, name, arglist, argcount*)
    Widget   *parent*;
    String   *name*;
    ArgList   *arglist*;
    Cardinal   *argcount*;

Description

XmCreateSeparatorGadget creates an instance of a SeparatorGadget widget and returns the associated widget ID.

parent   Specifies the parent widget ID

name   Specifies the name of the created widget

arglist   Specifies the argument list

argcount   Specifies the number of attribute/value pairs in the argument list (*arglist*)

For a complete definition of SeparatorGadget and its associated resources, see **XmSeparatorGadget(3X)**.

Return Value

Returns the SeparatorGadget widget ID.

Related Information

XmSeparatorGadget(3X).

XmCreateText—The Text widget creation function

AES Support Level

Full-use

Synopsis

#include <Xm/Text.h>

Widget XmCreateText (*parent, name, arglist, argcount*)
    Widget   *parent*;
    String   *name*;
    ArgList   *arglist*;
    Cardinal   *argcount*;

Description

XmCreateText creates an instance of a Text widget and returns the associated widget ID.

parent   Specifies the parent widget ID

name   Specifies the name of the created widget

arglist   Specifies the argument list

argcount   Specifies the number of attribute/value pairs in the argument list (*arglist*)

For a complete definition of Text and its associated resources, see **XmText(3X)**.

Return Value

Returns the Text widget ID.

Related Information

XmText(3X).

XmCreateTextField—The TextField widget creation function

AES Support Level

Trial-use

Synopsis

#include <Xm/TextF.h>

Widget XmCreateTextField (*parent, name, arglist, argcount*)
>   **Widget**   *parent*;
>   **String**   *name*;
>   **ArgList**   *arglist*;
>   **Cardinal**   *argcount*;

Description

XmCreateTextField creates an instance of a TextField widget and returns the associated widget ID.

parent   Specifies the parent widget ID

name   Specifies the name of the created widget

arglist   Specifies the argument list

argcount   Specifies the number of attribute/value pairs in the argument list (*arglist*)

For a complete definition of TextField and its associated resources, see **XmTextField(3X)**.

Return Value

Returns the TextField widget ID.

Related Information

XmTextField(3X).

XmCreateToggleButton—The ToggleButton widget creation function

AES Support Level

Full-use

Synopsis

#include <Xm/ToggleB.h>

Widget XmCreateToggleButton (*parent, name, arglist, argcount*)
    Widget   *parent*;
    String   *name*;
    ArgList   *arglist*;
    Cardinal   *argcount*;

Description

XmCreateToggleButton creates an instance of a ToggleButton widget and returns the associated widget ID.

parent   Specifies the parent widget ID

name   Specifies the name of the created widget

arglist   Specifies the argument list

argcount   Specifies the number of attribute/value pairs in the argument list (*arglist*)

For a complete definition of ToggleButton and its associated resources, see **XmToggleButton(3X)**.

Return Value

Returns the ToggleButton widget ID.

Related Information

XmToggleButton(3X).

XmCreateToggleButtonGadget(3X)

XmCreateToggleButtonGadget—The ToggleButtonGadget creation function

AES Support Level

Full-use

Synopsis

#include <Xm/ToggleBG.h>

Widget XmCreateToggleButtonGadget (*parent, name, arglist, argcount*)
    Widget   *parent*;
    String   *name*;
    ArgList   *arglist*;
    Cardinal   *argcount*;

Description

XmCreateToggleButtonGadget creates an instance of a ToggleButtonGadget and returns the associated widget ID.

parent   Specifies the parent widget ID

name   Specifies the name of the created widget

arglist   Specifies the argument list

argcount   Specifies the number of attribute/value pairs in the argument list (*arglist*)

For a complete definition of ToggleButtonGadget and its associated resources, see **XmToggleButtonGadget(3X)**.

Return Value

Returns the ToggleButtonGadget widget ID.

Related Information

XmToggleButtonGadget(3X).

XmCreateWarningDialog—The MessageBox WarningDialog convenience creation function

AES Support Level

Full-use

Synopsis

#include <Xm/MessageB.h>

Widget XmCreateWarningDialog (*parent, name, arglist, argcount*)
  Widget *parent*;
  String *name*;
  ArgList *arglist*;
  Cardinal *argcount*;

Description

XmCreateWarningDialog is a convenience creation function that creates a DialogShell and an unmanaged MessageBox child of the DialogShell. A WarningDialog warns users of action consequences and gives them a choice of resolutions. It includes a symbol, a message, and three buttons. The default symbol is an exclamation point. The default button labels are **OK**, **Cancel**, and **Help**.

Use **XtManageChild** to pop up the WarningDialog (passing the MessageBox as the widget parameter); use **XtUnmanageChild** to pop it down.

parent   Specifies the parent widget ID

name   Specifies the name of the created widget

arglist   Specifies the argument list

argcount   Specifies the number of attribute/value pairs in the argument list (*arglist*)

For a complete definition of MessageBox and its associated resources, see **XmMessageBox(3X)**.

Return Value

Returns the MessageBox widget ID.

Related Information

XmMessageBox(3X).

XmCreateWorkArea—A function that creates a RowColumn work area

AES Support Level

Trial-use

Synopsis

#include <Xm/RowColumn.h>

Widget XmCreateWorkArea (*parent, name, arglist, argcount*)
    Widget   *parent*;
    String   *name*;
    ArgList   *arglist*;
    Cardinal   *argcount*;

Description

XmCreateWorkArea creates an instance of a RowColumn widget and returns the associated widget ID. The widget is created with **XmNrowColumnType** set to **XmWORK_AREA**.

parent   Specifies the parent widget ID

name   Specifies the name of the created widget

arglist   Specifies the argument list

argcount   Specifies the number of attribute/value pairs in the argument list (*arglist*)

For a complete definition of RowColumn and its associated resources, see **XmRowColumn(3X)**.

Return Value

Returns the RowColumn widget ID.

Related Information

XmCreateRadioBox(3X), **XmCreateRowColumn(3X)**, and **XmRowColumn(3X)**.

XmCreateWorkingDialog—The MessageBox WorkingDialog convenience creation function

AES Support Level

Full-use

Synopsis

#include <Xm/MessageB.h>

Widget XmCreateWorkingDialog (*parent, name, arglist, argcount*)
    Widget   *parent*;
    String   *name*;
    ArgList   *arglist*;
    Cardinal   *argcount*;

Description

XmCreateWorkingDialog is a convenience creation function that creates a DialogShell and an unmanaged MessageBox child of the DialogShell. A WorkingDialog informs users that there is a time-consuming operation in progress and allows them to cancel the operation. It includes a symbol, a message, and three buttons. The default symbol is an hourglass. The default button labels are **OK**, **Cancel**, and **Help**.

Use **XtManageChild** to pop up the WorkingDialog (passing the MessageBox as the widget parameter); use **XtUnmanageChild** to pop it down.

parent   Specifies the parent widget ID

name   Specifies the name of the created widget

arglist   Specifies the argument list

argcount   Specifies the number of attribute/value pairs in the argument list (*arglist*)

For a complete definition of MessageBox and its associated resources, see **XmMessageBox(3X)**.

Return Value

Returns the MessageBox widget ID.

Related Information

XmMessageBox(3X).

XmCvtCTToXmString—A compound string function that converts compound text to a compound string

AES Support Level

Trial-use

Synopsis

#include <Xm/Xm.h>

XmString XmCvtCTToXmString (*text*)
    char   * *text*;

Description

XmCvtCTToXmString converts a (**char ***) string in compound text format to a compound string. The application must call **XtAppInitialize** before calling this function.

text   Specifies a string in compound text format to be converted to a compound string.

Return Value

Returns a compound string derived from the compound text. The compound text is assumed to be NULL-terminated; NULLs within the compound text are handled correctly. The handling of HORIZONTAL TABULATION (HT) control characters within the compound text is undefined. The compound text format is described in the X Consortium Standard *Compound Text Encoding*.

Related Information

XmCvtXmStringToCT(3X).

XmCvtXmStringToCT—A compound string function that converts a compound string to compound text

AES Support Level

Trial-use

Synopsis

#include <Xm/Xm.h>

char * XmCvtXmStringToCT (*string*)
   XmString   *string*;

Description

XmCvtXmStringToCT converts a compound string to a (**char ***) string in compound text format. The application must call **XtAppInitialize** before calling this function. The converter uses the font list tag associated with a given compound string segment to select a compound text format for that segment. A registry defines a mapping between font list tags and compound text encoding formats. The converter uses the following algorithm for each compound string segment:

1. If the compound string segment tag is mapped to **XmFONTLIST_DEFAULT_TAG** in the registry, the converter passes the text of the compound string segment to **XmbTextListToTextProperty** with an encoding style of **XCompoundTextStyle** and uses the resulting compound text for that segment.

2. If the compound string segment tag is mapped to an MIT registered charset in the registry, the converter creates the compound text for that segment using the charset (from the registry) and the text of the compound string segment as defined in the X Consortium Standard *Compound Text Encoding*.

3. If the compound string segment tag is mapped to a charset in the registry that is neither **XmFONTLIST_DEFAULT_TAG** nor an MIT registered charset, the converter creates the compound text for that segment using the charset (from the registry) and the text of the compound string segment as an "extended segment" with a variable number of octets per character.

4. If the compound string segment tag is not mapped in the registry, the result is implementation dependent.

   string   Specifies a compound string to be converted to compound text.

Return Value

Returns a (**char** *) string in compound text format. This format is described in the
X Consortium Standard *Compound Text Encoding*.

Related Information

XmCvtCTToXmString(3X), **XmFontList(3X)**, and **XmString**.

XmDeactivateProtocol—A VendorShell function that deactivates a protocol without removing it

AES Support Level

Trial-use

Synopsis

#include <Xm/Xm.h>
#include <Xm/Protocols.h>

void XmDeactivateProtocol (*shell, property, protocol*)
>   **Widget**   *shell*;
>   **Atom**   *property*;
>   **Atom**   *protocol*;

void XmDeactivateWMProtocol (*shell, protocol*)
>   **Widget**   *shell*;
>   **Atom**   *protocol*;

Description

XmDeactivateProtocol deactivates a protocol without removing it. It updates the handlers and the *property* if the *shell* is realized. It is sometimes useful to allow a protocol's state information (callback lists, and so on) to persist, even though the client may choose to temporarily resign from the interaction. The main use of this capability is to gray/ungray **f.send_msg** entries in the MWM system menu. To support this capability, *protocol* is allowed to be in one of two states: active or inactive. If *protocol* is active and *shell* is realized, *property* contains the *protocol* **Atom**. If *protocol* is inactive, **Atom** is not present in the *property*.

XmDeactivateWMProtocol is a convenience interface. It calls **XmDeactivateProtocol** with the property value set to the atom returned by interning **WM_PROTOCOLS**.

shell   Specifies the widget with which the protocol property is associated

property   Specifies the protocol property

protocol   Specifies the protocol atom (or an int type cast to **Atom**)

For a complete definition of VendorShell and its associated resources, see **VendorShell(3X)**.

Related Information

mwm(1X), **VendorShell(3X)**, **XmDeactivateWMProtocol(3X)**, and **XmInternAtom(3X)**.

XmDeactivateWMProtocol—A VendorShell convenience interface that deactivates a protocol without removing it

AES Support Level

Trial-use

Synopsis

```
#include <Xm/Xm.h>
#include <Xm/Protocols.h>

void XmDeactivateWMProtocol (shell, protocol)
        Widget          shell;
        Atom            protocol;
```

Description

XmDeactivateWMProtocol is a convenience interface. It calls **XmDeactivateProtocol** with the property value set to the atom returned by interning **WM_PROTOCOLS**.

shell   Specifies the widget with which the protocol property is associated

protocol   Specifies the protocol atom (or an int type cast to **Atom**)

For a complete definition of VendorShell and its associated resources, see **VendorShell(3X)**.

Related Information

VendorShell(3X), **XmDeactivateProtocol(3X)**, and **XmInternAtom(3X)**.

XmDestroyPixmap—A pixmap caching function that removes a pixmap from the pixmap cache

AES Support Level

Full-use

Synopsis

#include <Xm/Xm.h>

Boolean XmDestroyPixmap (*screen, pixmap*)
    Screen   * *screen*;
    Pixmap   *pixmap*;

Description

XmDestroyPixmap removes pixmaps that are no longer used. Pixmaps are completely freed only when there is no further reference to them.

screen   Specifies the display screen for which the pixmap was requested

pixmap   Specifies the pixmap to be destroyed

Return Value

Returns True when successful; returns False if there is no matching screen and pixmap in the pixmap cache.

Related Information

XmInstallImage(3X), **XmUninstallImage(3X)**, and **XmGetPixmap(3X)**.

XmDialogShell—The DialogShell widget class

AES Support Level

Full-use

History/Direction

The description of the geometry management of shells and their children has been
changed (for trial-use).

Synopsis

#include <Xm/DialogS.h>

Description

Modal and modeless dialogs use DialogShell as the Shell parent. DialogShell
widgets cannot be iconified. Instead, all secondary DialogShell widgets associated
with an ApplicationShell widget are iconified and de-iconified as a group with the
primary widget.

The client indirectly manipulates DialogShell through the convenience interfaces
during creation, and it can directly manipulate its BulletinBoard-derived child.
Much of the functionality of DialogShell assumes that its child is a BulletinBoard
subclass, although it can potentially stand alone.

Setting **XmNheight**, **XmNwidth**, or **XmNborderWidth** for either a DialogShell
or its managed child usually sets that resource to the same value in both the parent
and the child. When an off-the-spot input method exists, the height and width of
the shell may be greater than those of the managed child in order to accommodate
the input method. In this case, setting **XmNheight** or **XmNwidth** for the shell does
not necessarily set that resource to the same value in the managed child, and setting
XmNheight or **XmNwidth** for the child does not necessarily set that resource to
the same value in the shell.

For the managed child of a DialogShell, regardless of the value of the shell's
XmNallowShellResize resource, setting **XmNx** or **XmNy** sets the corresponding
resource of the parent but does not change the child's position relative to the
parent. The **XtGetValues** resource for the child's **XmNx** or **XmNy** yields the
value of the corresponding resource in the parent. The x and y-coordinates of the
child's upper left outside corner relative to the parent's upper left inside corner are
both 0 (zero) minus the value of **XmNborderWidth**.

Note that the *Inter-Client Communication Conventions Manual* (ICCCM) allows a window manager to change or control the border width of a reparented top-level window.

Classes

DialogShell inherits behavior and resources from the **Core**, **Composite**, **Shell**, **WMShell**, **VendorShell**, and **TransientShell** classes.

The class pointer is **xmDialogShellWidgetClass**.

The class name is **XmDialogShell**.

New Resources

DialogShell defines no new resources but overrides the **XmNdeleteResponse** resource in the **VendorShell** class.

Inherited Resources

DialogShell inherits behavior and resources from the superclasses described in the following tables, which define sets of widget resources used by the programmer to specify data.

For a complete description of each resource, refer to the reference page for that superclass. The programmer can also set the resource values for the inherited classes to set attributes for this widget. To reference a resource by name or by class in a **.Xdefaults** file, remove the **XmN** or **XmC** prefix and use the remaining letters. To specify one of the defined values for a resource in a **.Xdefaults** file, remove the **Xm** prefix and use the remaining letters (in either lowercase or uppercase, but include any underscores between words). The codes in the access column indicate if the given resource can be set at creation time (C), set by using **XtSetValues** (S), retrieved by using **XtGetValues** (G), or is not applicable (N/A).

TransientShell Resource Set		
Name	**Default**	**Access**
Class	**Type**	
XmNtransientFor	NULL	CSG
XmCTransientFor	Widget	

VendorShell Resource Set		

Name
    Class
	Default
	    Type
		Access

XmNbuttonFontList
    XmCButtonFontList
	dynamic
	    XmFontList
		CSG

XmNdefaultFontList
    XmCDefaultFontList
	dynamic
	    XmFontList
		CG

XmNdeleteResponse
    XmCDeleteResponse
	XmUNMAP
	    unsigned char
		CSG

XmNkeyboardFocusPolicy
    XmCKeyboardFocusPolicy
	XmEXPLICIT
	    unsigned char
		CSG

XmNlabelFontList
    XmCLabelFontList
	dynamic
	    XmFontList
		CSG

XmNmwmDecorations
    XmCMwmDecorations
	-1
	    int
		CSG

XmNmwmFunctions
    XmCMwmFunctions
	-1
	    int
		CSG

XmNmwmInputMode
    XmCMwmInputMode
	-1
	    int
		CSG

XmNmwmMenu
    XmCMwmMenu
	NULL
	    String
		CSG

XmNtextFontList
    XmCTextFontList
	dynamic
	    XmFontList
		CSG

WMShell Resource Set		

Name
  Class
	Default
	  Type
		Access

XmNbaseHeight
  XmCBaseHeight
	XtUnspecifiedShellInt
	  int
		CSG

XmNbaseWidth
  XmCBaseWidth
	XtUnspecifiedShellInt
	  int
		CSG

XmNheightInc
  XmCHeightInc
	XtUnspecifiedShellInt
	  int
		CSG

XmNiconMask
  XmCIconMask
	NULL
	  Pixmap
		CSG

XmNiconPixmap
  XmCIconPixmap
	NULL
	  Pixmap
		CSG

XmNiconWindow
  XmCIconWindow
	NULL
	  Window
		CSG

XmNiconX
  XmCIconX
	-1
	  int
		CSG

XmNiconY
  XmCIconY
	-1
	  int
		CSG

XmNinitialState
  XmCInitialState
	NormalState
	  int
		CSG

XmNinput
  XmCInput
	True
	  Boolean
		CSG

XmNmaxAspectX
  XmCMaxAspectX
	XtUnspecifiedShellInt
	  int
		CSG

XmNmaxAspectY
  XmCMaxAspectY
	XtUnspecifiedShellInt
	  int
		CSG

XmNmaxHeight
  XmCMaxHeight
	XtUnspecifiedShellInt
	  int
		CSG

XmNmaxWidth
  XmCMaxWidth
	XtUnspecifiedShellInt
	  int
		CSG

XmNminAspectX
  XmCMinAspectX
	XtUnspecifiedShellInt
	  int
		CSG

Name	Default	Access
Class	Type	
XmNminAspectY	XtUnspecifiedShellInt	CSG
XmCMinAspectY	int	
XmNminHeight	XtUnspecifiedShellInt	CSG
XmCMinHeight	int	
XmNminWidth	XtUnspecifiedShellInt	CSG
XmCMinWidth	int	
XmNtitle	dynamic	CSG
XmCTitle	String	
XmNtitleEncoding	dynamic	CSG
XmCTitleEncoding	Atom	
XmNtransient	True	CSG
XmCTransient	Boolean	
XmNwaitForWm	True	CSG
XmCWaitForWm	Boolean	
XmNwidthInc	XtUnspecifiedShellInt	CSG
XmCWidthInc	int	
XmNwindowGroup	dynamic	CSG
XmCWindowGroup	Window	
XmNwinGravity	dynamic	CSG
XmCWinGravity	int	
XmNwmTimeout	5000 ms	CSG
XmCWmTimeout	int	

Shell Resource Set		
Name	**Default**	**Access**
Class	**Type**	
XmNallowShellResize	False	CG
XmCAllowShellResize	Boolean	
XmNcreatePopupChildProc	NULL	CSG
XmCCreatePopupChildProc	XtCreatePopupChildProc	
XmNgeometry	NULL	CSG
XmCGeometry	String	
XmNoverrideRedirect	False	CSG
XmCOverrideRedirect	Boolean	
XmNpopdownCallback	NULL	C
XmCCallback	XtCallbackList	
XmNpopupCallback	NULL	C
XmCCallback	XtCallbackList	
XmNsaveUnder	True	CSG
XmCSaveUnder	Boolean	
XmNvisual	CopyFromParent	CSG
XmCVisual	Visual *	

Composite Resource Set		
Name	**Default**	**Access**
Class	**Type**	
XmNchildren	NULL	G
XmCReadOnly	WidgetList	
XmNinsertPosition	NULL	CSG
XmCInsertPosition	XtOrderProc	
XmNnumChildren	0	G
XmCReadOnly	Cardinal	

Core Resource Set		

Name
    Class
	Default
	    Type
		Access

XmNaccelerators
    XmCAccelerators
	dynamic
	    XtAccelerators
		CSG

XmNancestorSensitive
    XmCSensitive
	dynamic
	    Boolean
		G

XmNbackground
    XmCBackground
	dynamic
	    Pixel
		CSG

XmNbackgroundPixmap
    XmCPixmap
	XmUNSPECIFIED_PIXMAP
	    Pixmap
		CSG

XmNborderColor
    XmCBorderColor
	XtDefaultForeground
	    Pixel
		CSG

XmNborderPixmap
    XmCPixmap
	XmUNSPECIFIED_PIXMAP
	    Pixmap
		CSG

XmNborderWidth
    XmCBorderWidth
	0
	    Dimension
		CSG

XmNcolormap
    XmCColormap
	dynamic
	    Colormap
		CG

XmNdepth
    XmCDepth
	dynamic
	    int
		CG

XmNdestroyCallback
    XmCCallback
	NULL
	    XtCallbackList
		C

XmNheight
    XmCHeight
	dynamic
	    Dimension
		CSG

XmNinitialResourcesPersistent
    XmCInitialResourcesPersistent
	True
	    Boolean
		C

XmNmappedWhenManaged
    XmCMappedWhenManaged
	True
	    Boolean
		CSG

XmNscreen
    XmCScreen
	dynamic
	    Screen *
		CG

XmNsensitive
    XmCSensitive
	True
	    Boolean
		CSG

Name	Default	Access
Class	Type	
XmNtranslations	dynamic	CSG
XmCTranslations	XtTranslations	
XmNwidth	dynamic	CSG
XmCWidth	Dimension	
XmNx	0	CSG
XmCPosition	Position	
XmNy	0	CSG
XmCPosition	Position	

Related Information

Composite(3X), **Core(3X)**, **Shell(3X)**, **TransientShell(3X)**, **WMShell(3X)**, **VendorShell(3X)**, and **XmCreateDialogShell(3X)**.

XmDrawingArea—The DrawingArea widget class

AES Support Level

Full-use

Synopsis

#include <Xm/DrawingA.h>

Description

DrawingArea is an empty widget that is easily adaptable to a variety of purposes. It does no drawing and defines no behavior except for invoking callbacks. Callbacks notify the application when graphics need to be drawn (exposure events or widget resize) and when the widget receives input from the keyboard or mouse.

Applications are responsible for defining appearance and behavior as needed in response to DrawingArea callbacks.

DrawingArea is also a composite widget and subclass of **XmManager** that supports minimal geometry management for multiple widget or gadget children.

Classes

DrawingArea inherits behavior and resources from the **Core**, **Composite**, **Constraint**, and **XmManager** classes.

The class pointer is **xmDrawingAreaWidgetClass**.

The class name is **XmDrawingArea**.

New Resources

The following table defines a set of widget resources used by the programmer to specify data. The programmer can also set the resource values for the inherited classes to set attributes for this widget. To reference a resource by name or by class in a **.Xdefaults** file, remove the **XmN** or **XmC** prefix and use the remaining letters. To specify one of the defined values for a resource in a **.Xdefaults** file, remove the **Xm** prefix and use the remaining letters (in either lowercase or uppercase, but include any underscores between words). The codes in the access column indicate if the given resource can be set at creation time (C), set by using **XtSetValues** (S), retrieved by using **XtGetValues** (G), or is not applicable (N/A).

XmDrawingArea Resource Set		
Name	**Default**	**Access**
Class	**Type**	
XmNexposeCallback	NULL	C
XmCCallback	XtCallbackList	
XmNinputCallback	NULL	C
XmCCallback	XtCallbackList	
XmNmarginHeight	10	CSG
XmCMarginHeight	Dimension	
XmNmarginWidth	10	CSG
XmCMarginWidth	Dimension	
XmNresizeCallback	NULL	C
XmCCallback	XtCallbackList	
XmNresizePolicy	XmRESIZE_ANY	CSG
XmCResizePolicy	unsigned char	

XmNexposeCallback

Specifies the list of callbacks that is called when DrawingArea receives an exposure event. The callback reason is **XmCR_EXPOSE**. The callback structure also includes the exposure event.

XmNinputCallback

Specifies the list of callbacks that is called when the DrawingArea receives a keyboard or mouse event (key or button, up or down). The callback reason is **XmCR_INPUT**. The callback structure also includes the input event.

XmNmarginHeight

Specifies the minimum spacing in pixels between the top or bottom edge of DrawingArea and any child widget.

XmNmarginWidth

Specifies the minimum spacing in pixels between the left or right edge of DrawingArea and any child widget.

XmNresizeCallback
> Specifies the list of callbacks that is called when the DrawingArea is resized. The callback reason is **XmCR_RESIZE**.

XmNresizePolicy
> Controls the policy for resizing DrawingArea widgets. Possible values include **XmRESIZE_NONE** (fixed size), **XmRESIZE_ANY** (shrink or grow as needed), and **XmRESIZE_GROW** (grow only).

Inherited Resources

DrawingArea inherits behavior and resources from the following superclasses. For a complete description of each resource, refer to the reference page for that superclass.

XmManager Resource Set		

Name
    Class
	Default
	    Type
		Access

XmNbottomShadowColor
    XmCBottomShadowColor
	dynamic
	    Pixel
		CSG

XmNbottomShadowPixmap
    XmCBottomShadowPixmap
	XmUNSPECIFIED_PIXMAP
	    Pixmap
		CSG

XmNforeground
    XmCForeground
	dynamic
	    Pixel
		CSG

XmNhelpCallback
    XmCCallback
	NULL
	    XtCallbackList
		C

XmNhighlightColor
    XmCHighlightColor
	dynamic
	    Pixel
		CSG

XmNhighlightPixmap
    XmCHighlightPixmap
	dynamic
	    Pixmap
		CSG

XmNnavigationType
    XmCNavigationType
	XmTAB_GROUP
	    XmNavigationType
		CSG

XmNshadowThickness
    XmCShadowThickness
	0
	    Dimension
		CSG

XmNstringDirection
    XmCStringDirection
	dynamic
	    XmStringDirection
		CG

XmNtopShadowColor
    XmCTopShadowColor
	dynamic
	    Pixel
		CSG

XmNtopShadowPixmap
    XmCTopShadowPixmap
	dynamic
	    Pixmap
		CSG

XmNtraversalOn
    XmCTraversalOn
	True
	    Boolean
		CSG

XmNuserData
    XmCUserData
	NULL
	    XtPointer
		CSG

Composite Resource Set		
Name	**Default**	**Access**
Class	**Type**	
XmNchildren	NULL	G
XmCReadOnly	WidgetList	
XmNinsertPosition	NULL	CSG
XmCInsertPosition	XtOrderProc	
XmNnumChildren	0	G
XmCReadOnly	Cardinal	

Core Resource Set		
Name	**Default**	**Access**
Class	**Type**	
XmNaccelerators	dynamic	CSG
XmCAccelerators	XtAccelerators	
XmNancestorSensitive	dynamic	G
XmCSensitive	Boolean	
XmNbackground	dynamic	CSG
XmCBackground	Pixel	
XmNbackgroundPixmap	XmUNSPECIFIED_PIXMAP	CSG
XmCPixmap	Pixmap	
XmNborderColor	XtDefaultForeground	CSG
XmCBorderColor	Pixel	
XmNborderPixmap	XmUNSPECIFIED_PIXMAP	CSG
XmCPixmap	Pixmap	
XmNborderWidth	0	CSG
XmCBorderWidth	Dimension	
XmNcolormap	dynamic	CG
XmCColormap	Colormap	
XmNdepth	dynamic	CG
XmCDepth	int	
XmNdestroyCallback	NULL	C
XmCCallback	XtCallbackList	
XmNheight	dynamic	CSG
XmCHeight	Dimension	
XmNinitialResourcesPersistent	True	C
XmCInitialResourcesPersistent	Boolean	
XmNmappedWhenManaged	True	CSG
XmCMappedWhenManaged	Boolean	
XmNscreen	dynamic	CG
XmCScreen	Screen *	
XmNsensitive	True	CSG
XmCSensitive	Boolean	

Name	Default	Access
Class	Type	
XmNtranslations	dynamic	CSG
XmCTranslations	XtTranslations	
XmNwidth	dynamic	CSG
XmCWidth	Dimension	
XmNx	0	CSG
XmCPosition	Position	
XmNy	0	CSG
XmCPosition	Position	

Callback Information

A pointer to the following structure is passed to each callback:

typedef struct
{
    int   *reason*;
    XEvent   * *event*;
    Window   *window*;
} XmDrawingAreaCallbackStruct;

reason   Indicates why the callback was invoked.

event   Points to the **XEvent** that triggered the callback. This is NULL for the **XmNresizeCallback**.

window   Is set to the widget window.

Action Routines

The **XmDrawingArea** action routines are

DrawingAreaInput():
Unless the event takes place in a gadget, calls the callbacks for **XmNinputCallback**

ManagerGadgetKeyInput():
Causes the current gadget to process a keyboard event

Related Information

Composite(3X), **Constraint(3X)**, **Core(3X)**, **XmCreateDrawingArea(3X)**, and **XmManager(3X)**.

XmDrawnButton—The DrawnButton widget class

AES Support Level

Full-use

Synopsis

#include <Xm/DrawnB.h>

Description

The DrawnButton widget consists of an empty widget window surrounded by a shadow border. It provides the application developer with a graphics area that can have PushButton input semantics.

Callback types are defined for widget exposure and widget resize to allow the application to redraw or reposition its graphics. If the DrawnButton widget has a highlight and shadow thickness, the application should not draw in that area. To avoid drawing in the highlight and shadow area, create the graphics context with a clipping rectangle for drawing in the widget. The clipping rectangle should take into account the size of the widget's highlight thickness and shadow.

Classes

DrawnButton inherits behavior and resources from the **Core**, **XmPrimitive**, and **XmLabel** classes.

The class pointer is **xmDrawnButtonWidgetClass**.

The class name is **XmDrawnButton**.

New Resources

The following table defines a set of widget resources used by the programmer to specify data. The programmer can also set the resource values for the inherited classes to set attributes for this widget. To reference a resource by name or by class in a **.Xdefaults** file, remove the **XmN** or **XmC** prefix and use the remaining letters. To specify one of the defined values for a resource in a **.Xdefaults** file, remove the **Xm** prefix and use the remaining letters (in either lowercase or uppercase, but include any underscores between words). The codes in the access column indicate if the given resource can be set at creation time (C), set by using **XtSetValues** (S), retrieved by using **XtGetValues** (G), or is not applicable (N/A).

XmDrawnButton Resource Set		

Name
  Class
	Default
	  Type
		Access

XmNactivateCallback
  XmCCallback
	NULL
	  XtCallbackList
		C

XmNarmCallback
  XmCCallback
	NULL
	  XtCallbackList
		C

XmNdisarmCallback
  XmCCallback
	NULL
	  XtCallbackList
		C

XmNexposeCallback
  XmCCallback
	NULL
	  XtCallbackList
		C

XmNmultiClick
  XmCMultiClick
	dynamic
	  unsigned char
		CSG

XmNpushButtonEnabled
  XmCPushButtonEnabled
	False
	  Boolean
		CSG

XmNresizeCallback
  XmCCallback
	NULL
	  XtCallbackList
		C

XmNshadowType
  XmCShadowType
	XmSHADOW_ETCHED_IN
	  unsigned char
		CSG

XmNactivateCallback

Specifies the list of callbacks that is called when the widget becomes selected. The reason sent by the callback is **XmCR_ACTIVATE**.

XmNarmCallback

Specifies the list of callbacks that is called when the widget becomes armed. The reason sent by the callback is **XmCR_ARM**.

XmNdisarmCallback

Specifies the list of callbacks that is called when the widget becomes disarmed. The reason sent by the callback is **XmCR_DISARM**.

XmNexposeCallback

Specifies the list of callbacks that is called when the widget receives an exposure event. The reason sent by the callback is **XmCR_EXPOSE**.

XmNmultiClick

If a button click is followed by another button click within the time span specified by the display's multiclick time, and this resource is set to **XmMULTICLICK_DISCARD**, the second click is not processed. If this resource is set to **XmMULTICLICK_KEEP**, the event is processed and *click_count* is incremented in the callback structure. When the button is not in a menu, the default value is **XmMULTICLICK_KEEP**.

XmNpushButtonEnabled
Enables or disables the 3-dimensional shadow drawing as in PushButton.

XmNresizeCallback
Specifies the list of callbacks that is called when the widget receives a resize event. The reason sent by the callback is **XmCR_RESIZE**. The event returned for this callback is NULL.

XmNshadowType
Describes the drawing style for the DrawnButton. This resource can have the following values:

XmSHADOW_IN
Draws the DrawnButton so that the shadow appears inset. This means that the bottom shadow visuals and top shadow visuals are reversed.

XmSHADOW_OUT
Draws the DrawnButton so that the shadow appears outset.

XmSHADOW_ETCHED_IN
Draws the DrawnButton using a double line. This gives the effect of a line etched into the window. The thickness of the double line is equal to the value of **XmNshadowThickness**.

XmSHADOW_ETCHED_OUT
Draws the DrawnButton using a double line. This gives the effect of a line coming out of the window. The thickness of the double line is equal to the value of **XmNshadowThickness**.

Inherited Resources

DrawnButton inherits behavior and resources from the superclasses described in the following tables. For a complete description of each resource, refer to the reference page for that superclass.

XmLabel Resource Set		
Name **Class**	**Default** **Type**	**Access**
XmNaccelerator XmCAccelerator	NULL String	N/A
XmNacceleratorText XmCAcceleratorText	NULL XmString	N/A
XmNalignment XmCAlignment	dynamic unsigned char	CSG
XmNfontList XmCFontList	dynamic XmFontList	CSG
XmNlabelInsensitivePixmap XmCLabelInsensitivePixmap	XmUNSPECIFIED_PIXMAP Pixmap	CSG
XmNlabelPixmap XmCLabelPixmap	XmUNSPECIFIED_PIXMAP Pixmap	CSG
XmNlabelString XmCXmString	"\0" XmString	CSG
XmNlabelType XmCLabelType	XmSTRING unsigned char	CSG
XmNmarginBottom XmCMarginBottom	0 Dimension	CSG
XmNmarginHeight XmCMarginHeight	2 Dimension	CSG
XmNmarginLeft XmCMarginLeft	0 Dimension	CSG
XmNmarginRight XmCMarginRight	0 Dimension	CSG
XmNmarginTop XmCMarginTop	0 Dimension	CSG
XmNmarginWidth XmCMarginWidth	2 Dimension	CSG
XmNmnemonic XmCMnemonic	NULL KeySym	N/A

Name	Default	Access
Class	Type	
XmNmnemonicCharSet	XmFONTLIST_DEFAULT_TAG	N/A
XmCMnemonicCharSet	String	
XmNrecomputeSize	True	CSG
XmCRecomputeSize	Boolean	
XmNstringDirection	dynamic	CSG
XmCStringDirection	XmStringDirection	

XmPrimitive Resource Set		
Name	**Default**	**Access**
Class	**Type**	
XmNbottomShadowColor	dynamic	CSG
XmCBottomShadowColor	Pixel	
XmNbottomShadowPixmap	XmUNSPECIFIED_PIXMAP	CSG
XmCBottomShadowPixmap	Pixmap	
XmNforeground	dynamic	CSG
XmCForeground	Pixel	
XmNhelpCallback	NULL	C
XmCCallback	XtCallbackList	
XmNhighlightColor	dynamic	CSG
XmCHighlightColor	Pixel	
XmNhighlightOnEnter	False	CSG
XmCHighlightOnEnter	Boolean	
XmNhighlightPixmap	dynamic	CSG
XmCHighlightPixmap	Pixmap	
XmNhighlightThickness	2	CSG
XmCHighlightThickness	Dimension	
XmNnavigationType	XmNONE	CSG
XmCNavigationType	XmNavigationType	
XmNshadowThickness	2	CSG
XmCShadowThickness	Dimension	
XmNtopShadowColor	dynamic	CSG
XmCTopShadowColor	Pixel	
XmNtopShadowPixmap	dynamic	CSG
XmCTopShadowPixmap	Pixmap	
XmNtraversalOn	True	CSG
XmCTraversalOn	Boolean	
XmNuserData	NULL	CSG
XmCUserData	XtPointer	

Core Resource Set		
Name	**Default**	**Access**
Class	**Type**	
XmNaccelerators	dynamic	CSG
XmCAccelerators	XtAccelerators	
XmNancestorSensitive	dynamic	G
XmCSensitive	Boolean	
XmNbackground	dynamic	CSG
XmCBackground	Pixel	
XmNbackgroundPixmap	XmUNSPECIFIED_PIXMAP	CSG
XmCPixmap	Pixmap	
XmNborderColor	XtDefaultForeground	CSG
XmCBorderColor	Pixel	
XmNborderPixmap	XmUNSPECIFIED_PIXMAP	CSG
XmCPixmap	Pixmap	
XmNborderWidth	0	CSG
XmCBorderWidth	Dimension	
XmNcolormap	dynamic	CG
XmCColormap	Colormap	
XmNdepth	dynamic	CG
XmCDepth	int	
XmNdestroyCallback	NULL	C
XmCCallback	XtCallbackList	
XmNheight	dynamic	CSG
XmCHeight	Dimension	
XmNinitialResourcesPersistent	True	C
XmCInitialResourcesPersistent	Boolean	
XmNmappedWhenManaged	True	CSG
XmCMappedWhenManaged	Boolean	
XmNscreen	dynamic	CG
XmCScreen	Screen *	
XmNsensitive	True	CSG
XmCSensitive	Boolean	

Name	Default	Access
Class	Type	
XmNtranslations	dynamic	CSG
XmCTranslations	XtTranslations	
XmNwidth	dynamic	CSG
XmCWidth	Dimension	
XmNx	0	CSG
XmCPosition	Position	
XmNy	0	CSG
XmCPosition	Position	

Callback Information

A pointer to the following structure is passed to each callback:

```
typedef struct
{
    int         reason;
    XEvent      * event;
    Window      window;
    int         click_count;
} XmDrawnButtonCallbackStruct;
```

reason   Indicates why the callback was invoked.

event   Points to the **XEvent** that triggered the callback. This is NULL for **XmNresizeCallback**.

window   Is set to the window ID in which the event occurred.

click_count   Contains the number of clicks in the last multiclick sequence if the **XmNmultiClick** resource is set to **XmMULTICLICK_KEEP**, otherwise it contains 1. The activate callback is invoked for each click if **XmNmultiClick** is set to **XmMULTICLICK_KEEP**.

Action Routines

The **XmDrawnButton** action routines are

Activate():   If **XmNpushButtonEnabled** is True, redraws the shadow in the unselected state; otherwise, redraws the shadow according to **XmNshadowType**. If the pointer is within the DrawnButton, calls the **XmNactivateCallback** callbacks.

Arm():   If **XmNpushButtonEnabled** is True, redraws the shadow in the selected state; otherwise, redraws the shadow according to **XmNshadowType**. Calls the callbacks for **XmNarmCallback**.

ArmAndActivate():

If **XmNpushButtonEnabled** is True, redraws the shadow in the selected state; otherwise, redraws the shadow according to **XmNshadowType**. Calls the callbacks for **XmNarmCallback**.

If **XmNpushButtonEnabled** is True, the shadow is redrawn in the unselected state; otherwise, the shadow is redrawn according to **XmNshadowType**. The callbacks for **XmNactivateCallback** and **XmNdisarmCallback** are called. These actions happen either immediately or at a later time.

Disarm():   Marks the DrawnButton as unselected and calls the callbacks for **XmNdisarmCallback**.

Help():   Calls the callbacks for **XmNhelpCallback** if any exist. If there are no help callbacks for this widget, this action calls the help callbacks for the nearest ancestor that has them.

MultiActivate():

If **XmNmultiClick** is **XmMULTICLICK_DISCARD**, this action does nothing.

If **XmNmultiClick** is **XmMULTICLICK_KEEP**, this action increments *click_count* in the callback structure. If **XmNpushButtonEnabled** is True, this action redraws the shadow in the unselected state; otherwise, it redraws the shadow according to **XmNshadowType**. If the pointer is within the DrawnButton, this action calls the **XmNactivateCallback** callbacks and calls the callbacks for **XmNdisarmCallback**.

MultiArm():   If **XmNmultiClick** is **XmMULTICLICK_DISCARD**, this action does nothing.

If **XmNmultiClick** is **XmMULTICLICK_KEEP** and if **XmNpushButtonEnabled** is True, this action redraws the shadow in the selected state; otherwise, it redraws the shadow according to **XmNshadowType** and calls the callbacks for **XmNarmCallback**.

Related Information

Core(3X), XmCreateDrawnButton, XmLabel(3X), XmPrimitive(3X), XmPushButton, and XmSeparator(3X).

XmFileSelectionBox—The FileSelectionBox widget class

AES Support Level

Full-use

Synopsis

#include <Xm/FileSB.h>

Description

FileSelectionBox traverses through directories, views the files and subdirectories in them, and then selects files.

A FileSelectionBox has five main areas:

- A text input field for displaying and editing a directory mask used to select the files to be displayed

- A scrollable list of filenames

- A scrollable list of subdirectories

- A text input field for displaying and editing a filename

- A group of PushButtons, labeled **OK**, **Filter**, **Cancel**, and **Help**

Additional children may be added to the FileSelectionBox after creation. To remove the list of filenames, the list of subdirectories, or both from the FileSelectionBox after creation, unmanage the appropriate widgets and their labels. The list and label widgets are obtained through a call to the **XmFileSelectionBoxGetChild** function. To remove either the directory list or the file list, unmanage the parent of the appropriate list widget and unmanage the corresponding label.

The directory mask is a string specifying the base directory to be examined and a search pattern. Ordinarily, the directory list displays the subdirectories of the base directory, as well as the base directory itself and its parent directory. The file list ordinarily displays all files and/or subdirectories in the base directory that match the search pattern.

A procedure specified by the **XmNqualifySearchDataProc** resource extracts the base directory and search pattern from the directory mask. If the directory specification is empty, the current working directory is used. If the search pattern is empty, a pattern that matches all files is used.

An application can supply its own **XmNqualifySearchDataProc** as well as its own procedures to search for subdirectories and files. The default **XmNqualifySearchDataProc** works as follows: The directory mask is a pathname that can contain zero or more *wildcard* characters in its directory portion, its file portion, or both. The directory components of the directory mask — up to, but not including, the first component with a wildcard character — specify the directory to be searched, relative to the current working directory. The remaining components specify the search pattern. If the directory mask is empty or if its first component contains a wildcard character, the current working directory is searched. If no component of the directory mask contains a wildcard character, the entire directory mask is the directory specification, and all files in that directory are matched.

The user can select a new directory to examine by scrolling through the list of directories and selecting the desired directory or by editing the directory mask. Selecting a new directory from the directory list does not change the search pattern. A user can select a new search pattern by editing the directory mask. Double clicking or pressing **KActivate** on a directory in the directory list initiates a search for files and subdirectories in the new directory, using the current search pattern.

The user can select a file by scrolling through the list of filenames and selecting the desired file or by entering the filename directly into the text edit area. Selecting a file from the list causes that filename to appear in the file selection text edit area.

The user may select a new file as many times as desired. The application is not notified until the user takes one of the following actions:

- Selects the **OK** PushButton

- Presses **KActivate** while the selection text edit area has the keyboard focus

- Double clicks or presses **KActivate** on an item in the file list

FileSelectionBox initiates a directory and file search when any of the following occurs:

- The FileSelectionBox is initialized

- The function **XtSetValues** is used to change **XmNdirMask**, **XmNdirectory**, **XmNpattern**, or **XmNfileTypeMask**

- The user activates the **Filter** PushButton

- The user double clicks or presses **KActivate** on an item in the directory list

- The application calls **XmFileSelectionDoSearch**

- The user presses **KActivate** while the directory mask text edit area has the keyboard focus

When a file search is initiated, the FileSelectionBox takes the following actions:

- Constructs an **XmFileSelectionBoxCallbackStruct** structure with values appropriate for the action that initiated the search

- Calls the **XmNqualifySearchDataProc** with the callback structure as the data input argument

- Sets **XmNdirectoryValid** and **XmNlistUpdated** to False

- Calls the **XmNdirSearchProc** with the qualified data returned by the **XmNqualifySearchDataProc**

If **XmNdirectoryValid** is True, the FileSelectionBox takes the following additional actions:

- Sets **XmNlistUpdated** to False

- Calls the **XmNfileSearchProc** with the qualified data returned by the **XmNqualifySearchDataProc** (and possibly modified by the **XmNdirSearchProc**)

- If **XmNlistUpdated** is True and the file list is empty, displays the **XmNnoMatchString** in the file list and clears the selection text and **XmNdirSpec**

- If **XmNlistUpdated** is True and the file list is not empty, sets the selection text and **XmNdirSpec** to the qualified *dir* returned by the **XmNqualifySearchDataProc** (and possibly modified by the **XmNdirSearchProc**)

- Sets the directory mask text and **XmNdirMask** to the qualified *mask* returned by the **XmNqualifySearchDataProc** (and possibly modified by the **XmNdirSearchProc**)

- Sets **XmNdirectory** to the qualified *dir* returned by the **XmNqualifySearchDataProc** (and possibly modified by the **XmNdirSearchProc**)

- Sets **XmNpattern** to the qualified *pattern* returned by the **XmNqualifySearchDataProc** (and possibly modified by the **XmNdirSearchProc**)

Classes

FileSelectionBox inherits behavior and resources from **Core**, **Composite**, **Constraint**, **XmManager**, **XmBulletinBoard**, and **XmSelectionBox**.

The class pointer is **xmFileSelectionBoxWidgetClass**.

The class name is **XmFileSelectionBox**.

New Resources

The following table defines a set of widget resources used by the programmer to specify data. The programmer can also set the resource values for the inherited classes to set attributes for this widget. To reference a resource by name or by class in a **.Xdefaults** file, remove the **XmN** or **XmC** prefix and use the remaining letters. To specify one of the defined values for a resource in a **.Xdefaults** file, remove the **Xm** prefix and use the remaining letters (in either lowercase or uppercase, but include any underscores between words). The codes in the access column indicate if the given resource can be set at creation time (C), set by using **XtSetValues** (S), retrieved by using **XtGetValues** (G), or is not applicable (N/A).

XmFileSelectionBox Resource Set		
Name	**Default**	**Access**
Class	**Type**	
XmNdirectory	dynamic	CSG
XmCDirectory	XmString	
XmNdirectoryValid	dynamic	SG
XmCDirectoryValid	Boolean	
XmNdirListItems	dynamic	SG
XmCDirListItems	XmStringTable	
XmNdirListItemCount	dynamic	SG
XmCDirListItemCount	int	
XmNdirListLabelString	dynamic	CSG
XmCDirListLabelString	XmString	
XmNdirMask	dynamic	CSG
XmCDirMask	XmString	
XmNdirSearchProc	default procedure	CSG
XmCDirSearchProc	XmSearchProc	
XmNdirSpec	dynamic	CSG
XmCDirSpec	XmString	
XmNfileListItems	dynamic	SG
XmCItems	XmStringTable	
XmNfileListItemCount	dynamic	SG
XmCItemCount	int	
XmNfileListLabelString	dynamic	CSG
XmCFileListLabelString	XmString	
XmNfileSearchProc	default procedure	CSG
XmCFileSearchProc	XmSearchProc	
XmNfileTypeMask	XmFILE_REGULAR	CSG
XmCFileTypeMask	unsigned char	
XmNfilterLabelString	dynamic	CSG
XmCFilterLabelString	XmString	
XmNlistUpdated	dynamic	SG
XmCListUpdated	Boolean	

Name	Default	Access
Class	**Type**	
XmNnoMatchString	" [ ] "	CSG
XmCNoMatchString	XmString	
XmNpattern	dynamic	CSG
XmCPattern	XmString	
XmNqualifySearchDataProc	default procedure	CSG
XmCQualifySearchDataProc	XmQualifyProc	

XmNdirectory

    Specifies the base directory used in combination with **XmNpattern** in determining the files and directories to be displayed. The default value is determined by the **XmNqualifySearchDataProc** and depends on the initial values of **XmNdirMask**, **XmNdirectory**, and **XmNpattern**. If the default is NULL or empty, the current working directory is used.

XmNdirectoryValid

    Specifies an attribute that is set only by the directory search procedure. The value is set to True if the directory passed to the directory search procedure can actually be searched. If this value is False the file search procedure is not called, and **XmNdirMask**, **XmNdirectory**, and **XmNpattern** are not changed.

XmNdirListItems

    Specifies the items in the directory list.

XmNdirListItemCount

    Specifies the number of items in the directory list. The value must not be negative.

XmNdirListLabelString

    Specifies the label string of the directory list. The default for this resource depends on the locale. In the C locale the default is **Directories**.

XmNdirMask

    Specifies the directory mask used in determining the files and directories to be displayed. The default value is determined by the **XmNqualifySearchDataProc** and depends on the initial values of **XmNdirMask, XmNdirectory**, and **XmNpattern**.

XmNdirSearchProc

Specifies a directory search procedure to replace the default directory search procedure. FileSelectionBox's default directory search procedure fulfills the needs of most applications. Because it is impossible to cover the requirements of all applications, you can replace the default search procedure.

The directory search procedure is called with two arguments: the FileSelectionBox widget and a pointer to an **XmFileSelectionBoxCallbackStruct** structure. The callback structure is generated by the **XmNqualifySearchDataProc** and contains all information required to conduct a directory search, including the directory mask and a qualified base directory and search pattern. Once called, it is up to the search routine to generate a new list of directories and update the FileSelectionBox widget by using **XtSetValues**.

The search procedure must set **XmNdirectoryValid** and **XmNlistUpdated**. If it generates a new list of directories, it must also set **XmNdirListItems** and **XmNdirListItemCount**.

If the search procedure cannot search the specified directory, it must warn the user and set **XmNdirectoryValid** and **XmNlistUpdated** to False, unless it prompts and subsequently obtains a valid directory. If the directory is valid but is the same as the current **XmNdirectory**, the search procedure must set **XmNdirectoryValid** to True, but it may elect not to generate a new list of directories. In this case, it must set **XmNlistUpdated** to False.

If the search procedure generates a new list of directories, it must set **XmNdirListItems** to the new list of directories and **XmNdirListItemCount** to the number of items in the list. If there are no directories, it sets **XmNdirListItems** to NULL and **XmNdirListItemCount** to 0 (zero). In either case, it must set **XmNdirectoryValid** and **XmNlistUpdated** to True.

The search procedure ordinarily should not change the callback structure. But if the original directory is not valid, the search procedure may obtain a new directory from the user. In this case, it should set the *dir* member of the callback structure to the new directory, call the **XmNqualifySearchDataProc** with the callback struct as the input argument, and copy the qualified data returned by the **XmNqualifySearchDataProc** into the callback struct.

XmNdirSpec Specifies the full file path specification. This is the **XmNtextString** resource in SelectionBox, renamed for FileSelectionBox. The default value is determined by the FileSelectionBox after conducting the initial directory and file search.

XmNfileListItems

Specifies the items in the file list. This is the **XmNlistItems** resource in SelectionBox, renamed for FileSelectionBox.

XmNfileListItemCount

Specifies the number of items in the file list. This is the **XmNlistItemCount** resource in SelectionBox, renamed for FileSelectionBox. The value must not be negative.

XmNfileListLabelString

Specifies the label string of the file list. This is the **XmNlistLabelString** resource in SelectionBox, renamed for FileSelectionBox. The default for this resource depends on the locale. In the C locale the default is **Files**.

XmNfileSearchProc

Specifies a file search procedure to replace the default file search procedure. FileSelectionBox's default file search procedure fulfills the needs of most applications. Because it is impossible to cover the requirements of all applications, you can replace the default search procedure.

The file search procedure is called with two arguments: the FileSelectionBox widget and a pointer to an **XmFileSelectionBoxCallbackStruct** structure. The callback structure is generated by the **XmNqualifySearchDataProc** (and possibly modified by the **XmNdirSearchProc**). It contains all information required to conduct a file search, including the directory mask and a qualified base directory and search pattern. Once this procedure is called, it is up to the search routine to generate a new list of files and update the FileSelectionBox widget by using **XtSetValues**.

The search procedure must set **XmNlistUpdated**. If it generates a new list of files, it must also set **XmNfileListItems** and **XmNfileListItemCount**.

It is recommended that the search procedure always generate a new list of files. If the *mask* member of the callback structure is the same as the *mask* member of the callback struct in the preceding call to the search procedure, the procedure may elect not to generate a new list of files. In this case it must set **XmNlistUpdated** to False.

If the search procedure generates a new list of files, it must set **XmNfileListItems** to the new list of files and **XmNfileListItemCount** to the number of items in the list. If there are no files, it sets **XmNfileListItems** to NULL and **XmNfileListItemCount** to 0 (zero). In either case it must set **XmNlistUpdated** to True.

In constructing the list of files, the search procedure should include only files of the types specified by the widget's **XmNfileTypeMask**.

Setting **XmNdirSpec** is optional, but recommended. Set this attribute to the full file specification of the directory searched. The directory specification is displayed below the directory and file lists.

XmNfileTypeMask
Specifies the type of files listed in the file list. The possible values are

XmFILE_REGULAR
Restricts the file list to contain only regular files.

XmFILE_DIRECTORY
Restricts the file list to contain only directories.

XmFILE_ANY_TYPE
Allows the list to contain all file types including directories.

XmNfilterLabelString
Specifies the label string for the text entry field for the directory mask. The default for this resource depends on the locale. In the C locale the default is **Filter**.

XmNlistUpdated
Specifies an attribute that is set only by the directory and file search procedures. This resource is set to True if the search procedure updated the directory or file list.

XmNnoMatchString
Specifies a string to be displayed in the file list if the list of files is empty.

XmNpattern Specifies the search pattern used in combination with **XmNdirectory** in determining the files and directories to be displayed. The default value is determined by **XmNqualifySearchDataProc** and depends on the initial values of **XmNdirMask**, **XmNdirectory**, and **XmNpattern**. If the default is NULL or empty, a pattern that matches all files is used.

XmNqualifySearchDataProc

Specifies a search data qualification procedure to replace the default data qualification procedure. FileSelectionBox's default data qualification procedure fulfills the needs of most applications. Because it is impossible to cover the requirements of all applications, you can replace the default procedure.

The data qualification procedure is called to generate a qualified directory mask, base directory, and search pattern for use by the directory and file search procedures. It is called with three arguments: the FileSelectionBox widget and pointers to two **XmFileSelectionBoxCallbackStruct** structures. The first callback structure contains the input data. The second callback structure contains the output data, to be filled in by the data qualification procedure.

If the input *dir* and *pattern* members are not NULL, the procedure must copy them to the corresponding members of the output callback structure.

If the input *dir* is NULL, the procedure constructs the output *dir* as follows: If the input *mask* member is NULL, the procedure uses the widget's **XmNdirectory** as the output *dir*; otherwise, it extracts the output *dir* from the input *mask*. If the resulting output *dir* is empty, the procedure uses the current working directory instead.

If the input *pattern* is NULL, the procedure constructs the output *pattern* as follows: If the input *mask* member is NULL, the procedure uses the widget's **XmNpattern** as the output *pattern*; otherwise, it extracts the output *pattern* from the input *mask*. If the resulting output *pattern* is empty, the procedure uses a pattern that matches all files instead.

The data qualification procedure constructs the output *mask* from the output *dir* and *pattern*. The procedure must ensure that the output *dir*, *pattern*, and *mask* are fully qualified.

If the input *value* member is not NULL, the procedure must copy it to the output *value* member; otherwise, the procedure must copy the widget's **XmNdirSpec** to the output *value*.

The data qualification procedure must calculate the lengths of the output *value*, *mask*, *dir*, and *pattern* members and must fill in the corresponding length members of the output callback struct.

The data qualification procedure must copy the input *reason* and *event* members to the corresponding output members.

The values of the **XmNdirSearchProc** and **XmNfileSearchProc** are procedure pointers of type **XmSearchProc**, defined as follows:

void (* XmSearchProc) (*w, search_data*)
    Widget   *w*;
    XtPointer *search_data*;

w   The FileSelectionBox widget

search_data   Pointer to an **XmFileSelectionBoxCallbackStruct** containing information for conducting a search

The value of the **XmNqualifySearchDataProc** resource is a procedure pointer of type **XmQualifyProc**, defined as follows:

void (* XmQualifyProc) (*w, input_data, output_data*)
    Widget   *w*;
    XtPointer *input_data*;
    XtPointer *output_data*;

w   The FileSelectionBox widget

input_data   Pointer to an **XmFileSelectionBoxCallbackStruct** containing input data to be qualified

output_data   Pointer to an **XmFileSelectionBoxCallbackStruct** containing output data to be filled in by the qualification procedure

Inherited Resources

FileSelectionBox inherits behavior and resources from the superclasses described in the following tables. For a complete description of each resource, refer to the reference page for that superclass.

XmSelectionBox Resource Set		

Name
    Class
	Default
	    Type
		Access

XmNapplyCallback
    XmCCallback
	NULL
	    XtCallbackList
		C

XmNapplyLabelString
    XmCApplyLabelString
	dynamic
	    XmString
		CSG

XmNcancelCallback
    XmCCallback
	NULL
	    XtCallbackList
		C

XmNcancelLabelString
    XmCCancelLabelString
	dynamic
	    XmString
		CSG

XmNdialogType
    XmCDialogType
	XmDIALOG_FILE_SELECTION
	    unsigned char
		G

XmNhelpLabelString
    XmCHelpLabelString
	dynamic
	    XmString
		CSG

XmNlistItemCount
    XmCItemCount
	dynamic
	    int
		CSG

XmNlistItems
    XmCItems
	dynamic
	    XmStringTable
		CSG

XmNlistLabelString
    XmCListLabelString
	dynamic
	    XmString
		CSG

XmNlistVisibleItemCount
    XmCVisibleItemCount
	dynamic
	    int
		CSG

XmNminimizeButtons
    XmCMinimizeButtons
	False
	    Boolean
		CSG

XmNmustMatch
    XmCMustMatch
	False
	    Boolean
		CSG

XmNnoMatchCallback
    XmCCallback
	NULL
	    XtCallbackList
		C

XmNokCallback
    XmCCallback
	NULL
	    XtCallbackList
		C

Name	Default	Access
Class	Type	
XmNokLabelString	dynamic	CSG
XmCOkLabelString	XmString	
XmNselectionLabelString	dynamic	CSG
XmCSelectionLabelString	XmString	
XmNtextAccelerators	default	C
XmCTextAccelerators	XtAccelerators	
XmNtextColumns	dynamic	CSG
XmCColumns	short	
XmNtextString	dynamic	CSG
XmCTextString	XmString	

XmBulletinBoard Resource Set		
Name **Class**	**Default** **Type**	**Access**
XmNallowOverlap XmCAllowOverlap	True Boolean	CSG
XmNautoUnmanage XmCAutoUnmanage	False Boolean	CG
XmNbuttonFontList XmCButtonFontList	dynamic XmFontList	CSG
XmNcancelButton XmCWidget	Cancel button Widget	SG
XmNdefaultButton XmCWidget	OK button Widget	SG
XmNdefaultPosition XmCDefaultPosition	True Boolean	CSG
XmNdialogStyle XmCDialogStyle	dynamic unsigned char	CSG
XmNdialogTitle XmCDialogTitle	NULL XmString	CSG
XmNfocusCallback XmCCallback	NULL XtCallbackList	C
XmNlabelFontList XmCLabelFontList	dynamic XmFontList	CSG
XmNmapCallback XmCCallback	NULL XtCallbackList	C
XmNmarginHeight XmCMarginHeight	10 Dimension	CSG
XmNmarginWidth XmCMarginWidth	10 Dimension	CSG
XmNnoResize XmCNoResize	False Boolean	CSG
XmNresizePolicy XmCResizePolicy	XmRESIZE_ANY unsigned char	CSG

Name	Default	Access
Class	Type	
XmNshadowType	XmSHADOW_OUT	CSG
XmCShadowType	unsigned char	
XmNtextFontList	dynamic	CSG
XmCTextFontList	XmFontList	
XmNtextTranslations	NULL	C
XmCTranslations	XtTranslations	
XmNunmapCallback	NULL	C
XmCCallback	XtCallbackList	

XmManager Resource Set		

Name
  Class
	Default
	  Type
		Access

XmNbottomShadowColor
  XmCBottomShadowColor
	dynamic
	  Pixel
		CSG

XmNbottomShadowPixmap
  XmCBottomShadowPixmap
	XmUNSPECIFIED_PIXMAP
	  Pixmap
		CSG

XmNforeground
  XmCForeground
	dynamic
	  Pixel
		CSG

XmNhelpCallback
  XmCCallback
	NULL
	  XtCallbackList
		C

XmNhighlightColor
  XmCHighlightColor
	dynamic
	  Pixel
		CSG

XmNhighlightPixmap
  XmCHighlightPixmap
	dynamic
	  Pixmap
		CSG

XmNnavigationType
  XmCNavigationType
	XmTAB_GROUP
	  XmNavigationType
		CSG

XmNshadowThickness
  XmCShadowThickness
	dynamic
	  Dimension
		CSG

XmNstringDirection
  XmCStringDirection
	dynamic
	  XmStringDirection
		CG

XmNtopShadowColor
  XmCTopShadowColor
	dynamic
	  Pixel
		CSG

XmNtopShadowPixmap
  XmCTopShadowPixmap
	dynamic
	  Pixmap
		CSG

XmNtraversalOn
  XmCTraversalOn
	True
	  Boolean
		CSG

XmNuserData
  XmCUserData
	NULL
	  XtPointer
		CSG

Composite Resource Set		
Name	**Default**	**Access**
Class	**Type**	
XmNchildren	NULL	G
XmCReadOnly	WidgetList	
XmNinsertPosition	NULL	CSG
XmCInsertPosition	XtOrderProc	
XmNnumChildren	0	G
XmCReadOnly	Cardinal	

Core Resource Set		
Name	**Default**	**Access**
Class	**Type**	
XmNaccelerators	dynamic	N/A
XmCAccelerators	XtAccelerators	
XmNancestorSensitive	dynamic	G
XmCSensitive	Boolean	
XmNbackground	dynamic	CSG
XmCBackground	Pixel	
XmNbackgroundPixmap	XmUNSPECIFIED_PIXMAP	CSG
XmCPixmap	Pixmap	
XmNborderColor	XtDefaultForeground	CSG
XmCBorderColor	Pixel	
XmNborderPixmap	XmUNSPECIFIED_PIXMAP	CSG
XmCPixmap	Pixmap	
XmNborderWidth	0	CSG
XmCBorderWidth	Dimension	
XmNcolormap	dynamic	CG
XmCColormap	Colormap	
XmNdepth	dynamic	CG
XmCDepth	int	
XmNdestroyCallback	NULL	C
XmCCallback	XtCallbackList	
XmNheight	dynamic	CSG
XmCHeight	Dimension	
XmNinitialResourcesPersistent	True	C
XmCInitialResourcesPersistent	Boolean	
XmNmappedWhenManaged	True	CSG
XmCMappedWhenManaged	Boolean	
XmNscreen	dynamic	CG
XmCScreen	Screen *	
XmNsensitive	True	CSG
XmCSensitive	Boolean	

Name	Default	Access
Class	Type	
XmNtranslations	dynamic	CSG
XmCTranslations	XtTranslations	
XmNwidth	dynamic	CSG
XmCWidth	Dimension	
XmNx	0	CSG
XmCPosition	Position	
XmNy	0	CSG
XmCPosition	Position	

Callback Information

A pointer to the following structure is passed to each callback:

```
typedef struct
{
    int          reason;
    XEvent       * event;
    XmString     value;
    int          length;
    XmString     mask;
    int          mask_length;
    XmString     dir;
    int          dir_length;
    XmString     pattern;
    int          pattern_length;
} XmFileSelectionBoxCallbackStruct;
```

reason	Indicates why the callback was invoked
event	Points to the **XEvent** that triggered the callback
value	Specifies the current value of **XmNdirSpec**
length	Specifies the number of bytes in *value*
mask	Specifies the current value of **XmNdirMask**
mask_length	Specifies the number of bytes in *mask*
dir	Specifies the current base directory
dir_length	Specifies the number of bytes in *dir*

pattern   Specifies the current search pattern

pattern_length

          Specifies the number of bytes in *pattern*

Action Routines

The XmFileSelectionBox action routines are

SelectionBoxUpOrDown(0|1|2|3):

          If neither the selection text nor the directory mask (filter) text has
          the focus, this action does nothing.

          If the selection text has the focus, the term *list* in the following
          description refers to the file list, and the term *text* refers to the
          selection text. If the directory mask text has the focus, *list* refers to
          the directory list, and *text* refers to the directory mask text.

          When called with an argument of 0 (zero), this action selects the
          previous item in the list and replaces the text with that item.

          When called with an argument of 1, this action selects the next item
          in the list and replaces the text with that item.

          When called with an argument of 2, this action selects the first item
          in the list and replaces the text with that item.

          When called with an argument of 3, this action selects the last item
          in the list and replaces the text with that item.

SelectionBoxRestore():

          If neither the selection text nor the directory mask (filter) text has
          the focus, this action does nothing.

          If the selection text has the focus, this action replaces the selection
          text with the selected item in the file list. If no item in the file list is
          selected, it clears the selection text.

          If the directory mask text has the focus, this action replaces the
          directory mask text with a new directory mask constructed from the
          XmNdirectory and **XmNpattern** resources.

Related Information

**Composite(3X), Constraint(3X), Core(3X), XmBulletinBoard(3X),
XmCreateFileSelectionBox(3X), XmCreateFileSelectionDialog(3X),
XmFileSelectionBoxGetChild(3X), XmFileSelectionDoSearch(3X),
XmManager(3X), and XmSelectionBox(3X).**

XmFileSelectionBoxGetChild—A FileSelectionBox function used to access a component

AES Support Level

Full-use

Synopsis

#include <Xm/FileSB.h>

Widget XmFileSelectionBoxGetChild (*widget, child*)
    Widget   *widget*;
    unsigned char *child*;

Description

XmFileSelectionBoxGetChild is used to access a component within a FileSelectionBox. The parameters given to the function are the FileSelectionBox widget and a value indicating which component to access.

widget   Specifies the FileSelectionBox widget ID.

child   Specifies a component within the FileSelectionBox. The following are legal values for this parameter:

- **XmDIALOG_APPLY_BUTTON**
- **XmDIALOG_CANCEL_BUTTON**
- **XmDIALOG_DEFAULT_BUTTON**
- **XmDIALOG_DIR_LIST**
- **XmDIALOG_DIR_LIST_LABEL**
- **XmDIALOG_FILTER_LABEL**
- **XmDIALOG_FILTER_TEXT**
- **XmDIALOG_HELP_BUTTON**
- **XmDIALOG_LIST**
- **XmDIALOG_LIST_LABEL**
- **XmDIALOG_OK_BUTTON**
- **XmDIALOG_SELECTION_LABEL**
- **XmDIALOG_SEPARATOR**

- **XmDIALOG_TEXT**

- **XmDIALOG_WORK_AREA**

For a complete definition of FileSelectionBox and its associated resources, see **XmFileSelectionBox(3X)**.

Return Value

Returns the widget ID of the specified FileSelectionBox component. An application should not assume that the returned widget will be of any particular class.

Related Information

XmFileSelectionBox(3X).

XmFileSelectionDoSearch—A FileSelectionBox function that initiates a directory search

AES Support Level

Full-use

Synopsis

#include <Xm/FileSB.h>

void XmFileSelectionDoSearch (*widget, dirmask*)
    Widget   *widget*;
    XmString   *dirmask*;

Description

XmFileSelectionDoSearch initiates a directory and file search in a FileSelectionBox widget. For a description of the actions that the FileSelectionBox takes when doing a search, see **XmFileSelectionBox(3X)**.

widget   Specifies the FileSelectionBox widget ID.

dirmask   Specifies the directory mask used in determining the directories and files displayed in the FileSelectionBox lists. This value is used as the *mask* member of the input data **XmFileSelectionBoxCallbackStruct** structure passed to the FileSelectionBox's **XmNqualifySearchDataProc**. The *dir* and *pattern* members of that structure are NULL.

For a complete definition of FileSelectionBox and its associated resources, see **XmFileSelectionBox(3X)**.

Related Information

XmFileSelectionBox(3X).

XmFontList—Data type for a font list

AES Support Level

Full-use

History/Direction

Font lists have been enhanced in revision C to contain font sets as well as fonts (for trial-use).

Synopsis

#include <Xm/Xm.h>

Description

XmFontList is the data type for a font list. A font list consists of font list entries. Each entry contains a font or a font set (a group of fonts) and is identified with a tag, which is optional. If this tag is NULL, the tag is set to **XmFONTLIST_DEFAULT_TAG**.

When a compound string is displayed, the font list element tag of the compound string segment is matched with a font list entry tag in the font list and the matching font list entry is used to display the compound string. A font list entry is chosen as follows:

- The first font list entry whose tag matches the tag of the compound string segment is used.

- If no match has been found, the first entry in the font list is used.

The font list interface consists of the routines listed in **Related Information**.

Font lists are specified in resource files with the following syntax:

resource_spec: *font_entry* [, *font_entry*]+

The resource value string consists of one or more font list entries separated by commas. Each *font_entry* identifies a font or font set and an optional font list entry tag. A tag specified for a single font follows the font name and is separated by = (equals sign); otherwise, in a font set the tag is separated by a colon. The colon is required whether a tag is specified or not. A font entry uses the following syntax to specify a single font:

font_name ['=' *tag*]

For example, the following entry specifies a 10 point Times Italic font without a font list entry tag;

```
*fontList:   -Adobe-Times-Medium-I-Normal--10*
```

A font entry containing a font set is similar, except a semicolon separates multiple font names and the specification ends with a colon followed by an optional tag:

font_name [';' *font_name*]+ ':' [*tag*]

A *font_name* is an X Logical Font Description (XLFD) string and *tag* is any set of characters from ISO646IRV except space, comma, colon, equal sign and semicolon. Following is an example of a font set entry. It consists of three fonts (except for charsets), and an explicit font list entry tag.

```
*fontList : -Adobe-Courier-Bold-R-Normal--25-180-100-100-M-150;\
-JIS-Fixed-Medium-R-Normal--26-180-100-100-C-240;\
-JIS-Fixed-Medium-R-Normal--26-180-100-100-C-120:MY_TAG
```

Related Information

XmFontListAdd(3X), **XmFontListAppendEntry(3X)**, **XmFontListCopy(3X)**, **XmFontListCreate(3X)**, **XmFontListEntryCreate(3X)**, **XmFontListEntryFree(3X)**, **XmFontListEntryGetFont(3X)**, **XmFontListEntryGetTag(3X)**, **XmFontListEntryLoad(3X)**, **XmFontListFree(3X)**, **XmFontListFreeFontContext(3X)**, **XmFontListInitFontContext(3X)**, **XmFontListNextEntry(3X)**, **XmFontListRemoveEntry(3X)**, and **XmString(3X)**.

XmFontListAdd—A font list function that creates a new font list

AES Support Level

Trial-use

History/Direction

XmFontListAdd is scheduled for removal in revision D.

Synopsis

#include <Xm/Xm.h>

XmFontList XmFontListAdd (*oldlist, font, charset*)
    XmFontList   *oldlist*;
    XFontStruct   ******font*;
    XmStringCharSet *charset*;

Description

XmFontListAdd creates a new font list consisting of the contents of *oldlist* and the new font list element being added. This function deallocates *oldlist* after extracting the required information; therefore, do not reference *oldlist* thereafter.

NOTE: This function is obsolete and exists for compatibility with previous releases. It has been replaced by **XmFontListAppendEntry**.

oldlist   Specifies a pointer to the font list to which an entry will be added.

font   Specifies a pointer to a font structure for which the new font list is generated. This is the structure returned by the XLib **XLoadQueryFont** function.

charset   Specifies the character set identifier for the font.

Return Value

Returns NULL if *oldlist* is NULL; returns *oldlist* if *font* or *charset* is NULL; otherwise, returns a new font list.

Related Information

XmFontList(3X) and **XmFontListAppendEntry(3X)**.

XmFontListAppendEntry—A font list function that appends an entry to a font list

AES Support Level

Trial-use

Synopsis

#include <Xm/Xm.h>

XmFontList XmFontListAppendEntry (*oldlist, entry*)
    XmFontList   *oldlist*;
    XmFontListEntry *entry*;

Description

XmFontListAppendEntry creates a new font list that contains the contents of *oldlist*. This function copies the contents of the font list entry being added into this new font list. If *oldlist* is NULL, **XmFontListAppendEntry** creates a new font list containing only the single entry specified.

This function deallocates the original font list after extracting the required information. The caller must free the font list entry by using **XmFontListEntryFree**.

oldlist   Specifies the font list to be added to

entry   Specifies the font list entry to be added

Return Value

If *entry* is NULL, returns *oldlist*; otherwise, returns a new font list.

Related Information

XmFontList(3X), XmFontListEntryCreate(3X), XmFontListEntryFree(3X), XmFontListEntryLoad(3X), XmFontListFree(3X), and **XmFontListRemoveEntry(3X)**.

XmFontListCopy—A font list function that copies a font list

AES Support Level

Trial-use

Synopsis

#include <Xm/Xm.h>

XmFontList XmFontListCopy (*fontlist*)
    XmFontList   *fontlist*;

Description

XmFontListCopy creates a new font list consisting of the contents of the *fontlist* argument.

fontlist   Specifies a font list to be copied

Return Value

Returns NULL if *fontlist* is NULL; otherwise, returns a new font list.

Related Information

XmFontList(3X) and **XmFontListFree(3X)**.

XmFontListCreate(3X)

XmFontListCreate—A font list function that creates a font list

AES Support Level

Trial-use

History/Direction

XmFontListCreate is scheduled for removal in revision D.

Synopsis

#include <Xm/Xm.h>

XmFontList XmFontListCreate (*font, charset*)
    XFontStruct   * *font*;
    XmStringCharSet *charset*;

Description

XmFontListCreate creates a new font list with a single element specified by the provided font and character set. It also allocates the space for the font list.

NOTE: This function is obsolete and exists for compatibility with previous releases. It is replaced by **XmFontListAppendEntry**.

font   Specifies a pointer to a font structure for which the new font list is generated. This is the structure returned by the XLib **XLoadQueryFont** function.

charset   Specifies the character set identifier for the font.

Return Value

Returns NULL if *font* or *charset* is NULL; otherwise, returns a new font list.

Related Information

XmFontList(3X) and **XmFontListAppendEntry(3X)**.

XmFontListEntryCreate—A font list function that creates a font list entry

AES Support Level

Trial-use

Synopsis

#include <Xm/Xm.h>

XmFontListEntry XmFontListEntryCreate (*tag, type, font*)
    char   **tag*;
    XmFontType   *type*;
    XtPointer   *font*;

Description

XmFontListEntryCreate creates a font list entry that contains either a font or font set and is identified by a tag.

   tag   Specifies a NULL terminated string for the tag of the font list entry. The tag may be specified as **XmFONTLIST_DEFAULT_TAG**, which is used to identify the default font list element in a font list.

   type   Specifies whether the *font* argument is a font structure or a font set. Valid values are **XmFONT_IS_FONT** and **XmFONT_IS_FONTSET**.

   font   Specifies either an **XFontSet** returned by **XCreateFontSet** or a pointer to an **XFontStruct** returned by **XLoadQueryFont**.

The toolkit does not copy the X Font structure specified by the *font* argument. Therefore, an application programmer must not free **XFontStruct** or **XFontSet** until all font lists and/or font entries that reference it have been freed.

Return Value

Returns a font list entry.

Related Information

XmFontList(3X), **XmFontListAppendEntry(3X)**, **XmFontListEntryFree(3X)**, **XmFontListEntryGetFont(3X)**, **XmFontListEntryGetTag(3X)**, **XmFontListEntryLoad(3X)**, and **XmFontListRemoveEntry(3X)**.

XmFontListEntryFree—A font list function that recovers memory used by a font list entry

AES Support Level

Trial-use

Synopsis

#include <Xm/Xm.h>

void XmFontListEntryFree (*entry*)
    XmFontListEntry **entry*;

Description

XmFontListEntryFree recovers memory used by a font list entry. This routine does not free the **XFontSet** or **XFontStruct** associated with the font list entry.

entry   Specifies the font list entry to be freed

Related Information

**XmFontList(3X), XmFontListAppendEntry(3X),
XmFontListEntryCreate(3X), XmFontListEntryLoad(3X),
XmFontListNextEntry(3X),** and **XmFontListRemoveEntry(3X).**

XmFontListEntryGetFont—A font list function that retrieves font information from a font list entry

AES Support Level

Trial-use

Synopsis

#include <Xm/Xm.h>

XtPointer XmFontListEntryGetFont (*entry, type_return*)
    XmFontListEntry *entry*;
    XmFontType   **type_return*;

Description

XmFontListEntryGetFont retrieves font information for a specified font list entry. If the font list entry contains a font, *type_return* returns **XmFONT_IS_FONT** and the function returns a pointer to an **XFontStruct**. If the font list entry contains a font set, *type_return* returns **XmFONT_IS_FONTSET** and the function returns the **XFontSet**.

entry   Specifies the font list entry.

type_return   Specifies a pointer to the type of the font element for the current entry. Valid values are **XmFONT_IS_FONT** and **XmFONT_IS_FONTSET**.

The returned **XFontSet** or **XFontStruct** is not a copy of the toolkit data and must not be freed.

Return Value

Returns an **XFontSet** or a pointer to an **XFontStruct** structure.

Related Information

XmFontList(3X), **XmFontListEntryCreate(3X)**, **XmFontListEntryGetTag(3X)**
XmFontListEntryLoad(3X), and **XmFontListNextEntry(3X)**.

XmFontListEntryGetTag(3X)

XmFontListEntryGetTag—A font list function that retrieves the tag of a font list entry

AES Support Level

Trial-use

Synopsis

#include <Xm/Xm.h>

char* XmFontListEntryGetTag (*entry*)
XmFontListEntry *entry*;

Description

XmFontListEntryGetTag retrieves a copy of the tag of the specified font list entry. This routine allocates memory for the tag string that must be freed by the application.

entry   Specifies the font list entry

Return Value

Returns the tag for the font list entry.

Related Information

**XmFontList(3X), XmFontListEntryCreate(3X),
XmFontListEntryGetFont(3X), XmFontListEntryLoad(3X)**, and
XmFontListNextEntry(3X).

XmFontListEntryLoad—A font list function that loads a font or creates a font set and creates an accompanying font list entry

AES Support Level

Trial-use

Synopsis

#include <Xm/Xm.h>

XmFontListEntry XmFontListEntryLoad (*display, font_name, type, tag*)
    Display   **display*;
    char   **font_name*;
    XmFontType *type*;
    char   **tag*;

Description

XmFontListEntryLoad loads a font or creates a font set based on the value of the *type* argument. It creates and returns a font list entry that contains the font or font set and the specified tag.

If the value of *type* is **XmFONT_IS_FONT**, the function uses the **XtCvtStringToFontStruct** routine to convert the value of *font_name* to a font struct. If the value of *type* is **XmFONT_IS_FONTSET**, the function uses the **XtCvtStringToFontSet** converter to create a font set in the current locale. **XmFontListEntryLoad** creates a font list entry that contains the font or font set derived from the converter. For more information about **XtCvtStringToFontStruct** and **XtCvtStringToFontSet**, see *X Toolkit Intrinsics— C Language Interface*.

display   Specifies the display where the font list will be used.

font_name   Specifies an X Logical Font Description (XLFD) string, which is interpreted either as a font name or as a base font name list. A base font name list is a comma-separated and NULL-terminated string.

type   Specifies whether the *font_name* argument refers to a font name or to a base font name list. Valid values are **XmFONT_IS_FONT** and **XmFONT_IS_FONTSET**.

tag   Specifies the tag of the font list entry to be created. The tag may be specified as **XmFONTLIST_DEFAULT_TAG**, which is used to identify the default font list element in a font list when specified as part of a resource.

Return Value

If the specified font is not found, or the specified font set cannot be created, returns NULL; otherwise, returns a font list entry.

Related Information

XmFontList(3X), **XmFontListAppendEntry(3X)**, **XmFontListEntryCreate(3X)**, **XmFontListEntryFree(3X)**, **XmFontListEntryGetFont(3X)**, **XmFontListEntryGetTag(3X)**, and **XmFontListRemoveEntry(3X)**.

XmFontListFree—A font list function that recovers memory used by a font list

AES Support Level

Full-use

Synopsis

#include <Xm/Xm.h>

void XmFontListFree (*list*)
    XmFontList   *list*;

Description

XmFontListFree recovers memory used by a font list. This routine does not free the XFontSet or XFontStruct associated with the specified font list.

list   Specifies the font list to be freed

Related Information

XmFontList(3X), **XmFontListAppendEntry(3X)**, **XmFontListCopy(3X)**, and **XmFontListRemoveEntry(3X)**.

XmFontListFreeFontContext—A font list function that instructs the toolkit that the font list context is no longer needed

AES Support Level

Trial-use

Synopsis

#include <Xm/Xm.h>

void XmFontListFreeFontContext (*context*)
    XmFontContext   *context*;

Description

XmFontListFreeFontContext instructs the toolkit that the context is no longer needed and will not be used without reinitialization.

context   Specifies the font list context structure that was allocated by the **XmFontListInitFontContext** function

Related Information

XmFontListInitFontContext(3X) and **XmFontListNextEntry(3X)**.

XmFontListInitFontContext—A font list function that allows applications to access the entries in a font list

AES Support Level

Trial-use

Synopsis

#include <Xm/Xm.h>

Boolean XmFontListInitFontContext (*context, fontlist*)
    XmFontContext   **context*;
    XmFontList   *fontlist*;

Description

XmFontListInitFontContext establishes a context to allow applications to access the contents of a font list. This context is used when reading the font list entry tag, font, or font set associated with each entry in the font list. A Boolean status is returned to indicate whether or not the font list is valid.

context   Specifies a pointer to the allocated context

fontlist   Specifies the font list

Return Value

Returns True if the context was allocated; otherwise, returns False.

Related Information

XmFontList(3X), **XmFontListFreeFontContext(3X)**, and **XmFontListNextEntry(3X)**.

XmFontListNextEntry(3X)

XmFontListNextEntry—A font list function that returns the next entry in a font list

AES Support Level

Trial-use

Synopsis

#include <Xm/Xm.h>

XmFontListEntry XmFontListNextEntry (*context*)
    XmFontContext   *context*;

Description

XmFontListNextEntry returns the next entry in the font list. The application uses the **XmFontListInitFontContext** routine to create a font list context. The first call to **XmFontListNextEntry** sets the context to the first entry in the font list. The application then calls **XmFontListNextEntry** repeatedly with the same context. Each succeeding call accesses the next entry of the font list. When finished, the application calls **XmFontListFreeFontContext** to free the allocated font list context.

context   Specifies the font list context

Return Value

Returns NULL if the context does not refer to a valid entry or if it is at the end of the font list; otherwise, it returns a font list entry.

Related Information

XmFontList(3X), XmFontListEntryFree(3X), XmFontListEntryGetFont(3X), XmFontListEntryGetTag(3X), XmFontListFreeFontContext(3X), and **XmFontListInitFontContext(3X).**

XmFontListRemoveEntry—A font list function that removes a font list entry from a font list

AES Support Level

Trial-use

Synopsis

#include <Xm/Xm.h>

XmFontList XmFontListRemoveEntry (*oldlist, entry*)
    XmFontList   *oldlist*;
    XmFontListEntry *entry*;

Description

XmFontListRemoveEntry creates a new font list that contains the contents of *oldlist* minus those entries specified in *entry*. The routine removes any entries from *oldlist* that match the components (tag, type font/font set) of the specified entry. The function deallocates the original font list after extracting the required information. The caller uses **XmFontListEntryFree** to recover memory allocated for the specified entry. This routine does not free the **XFontSet** or **XFontStruct** associated with the font list entry that is removed.

oldlist   Specifies the font list

entry   Specifies the font list entry to be removed

Return Value

If *oldlist* is NULL, the function returns NULL. If *entry* is NULL or no entries are removed, the function returns *oldlist*. Otherwise, it returns a new font list.

Related Information

XmFontList(3X), XmFontListAppendEntry(3X),
XmFontListEntryCreate(3X), XmFontListEntryFree(3X),
XmFontListEntryLoad(3X), and **XmFontListFree(3X).**

XmForm—The Form widget class

AES Support Level

Full-use

Synopsis

#include <Xm/Form.h>

Description

Form is a container widget with no input semantics of its own. Constraints are placed on children of the Form to define attachments for each of the child's four sides. These attachments can be to the Form, to another child widget or gadget, to a relative position within the Form, or to the initial position of the child. The attachments determine the layout behavior of the Form when resizing occurs.

Following are some important considerations in using a Form:

- Every child must have an attachment on either the left or the right. If initialization or **XtSetValues** leaves a widget without such an attachment, the result depends upon the value of **XmNrubberPositioning**.

  If **XmNrubberPositioning** is False, the child is given an **XmNleftAttachment** of **XmATTACH_FORM** and an **XmNleftOffset** equal to its current x value.

  If **XmNrubberPositioning** is True, the child is given an **XmNleftAttachment** of **XmATTACH_POSITION** and an **XmNleftPosition** proportional to the current x value divided by the width of the Form.

  In either case, if the child has not been previously given an x value, its x value is taken to be 0 (zero), which places the child at the left side of the Form.

- If you want to create a child without any attachments, and then later (for example, after creating and managing it, but before realizing it) give it a right attachment through **XtSetValues**, you must set its **XmNleftAttachment** to **XmATTACH_NONE** at the same time.

- The **XmNresizable** resource controls only whether a geometry request by the child will be granted. It has no effect on whether the child's size can be changed because of changes in geometry of the Form or of other children.

- Every child has a preferred width, based on geometry requests it makes (whether they are granted or not).

- If a child has attachments on both the left and the right sides, its size is completely controlled by the Form. It can be shrunk below its preferred width or enlarged above it, if necessary, due to other constraints. In addition, the child's geometry requests to change its own width may be refused.

- If a child has attachments on only its left or right side, it will always be at its preferred width (if resizable, otherwise at is current width). This may cause it to be clipped by the Form or by other children.

- If a child's left (or right) attachment is set to **XmATTACH_SELF**, its corresponding left (or right) offset is forced to 0 (zero). The attachment is then changed to **XmATTACH_POSITION**, with a position that corresponds to the x value of the child's left (or right) edge. To fix the position of a side at a specific x value, use **XmATTACH_FORM** or **XmATTACH_OPPOSITE_FORM** with the x value as the left (or right) offset.

- Unmapping a child has no effect on the Form except that the child is not mapped.

- Unmanaging a child unmaps it. If no other child is attached to it, or if all children attached to it and all children recursively attached to them are also all unmanaged, all of those children are treated as if they did not exist in determining the size of the Form.

- When using **XtSetValues** to change the **XmNx** resource of a child, you must simultaneously set its left attachment to either **XmATTACH_SELF** or **XmATTACH_NONE**. Otherwise, the request is not granted. If **XmNresizable** is False, the request is granted only if the child's size can remain the same.

- A left (or right) attachment of **XmATTACH_WIDGET**, where **XmNleftWidget** (or **XmNrightWidget**) is NULL, acts like an attachment of **XmATTACH_FORM**.

- If an attachment is made to a widget that is not a child of the Form, but an ancestor of the widget is a child of the Form, the attachment is made to the ancestor.

All these considerations are true of top and bottom attachments as well, with top acting like left, bottom acting like right, y acting like x, and height acting like width.

Classes

Form inherits behavior and resources from **Core**, **Composite**, **Constraint**, **XmManager**, and **XmBulletinBoard**.

The class pointer is **xmFormWidgetClass**.

The class name is **XmForm**.

New Resources

The following table defines a set of widget resources used by the programmer to specify data. The programmer can also set the resource values for the inherited classes to set attributes for this widget. To reference a resource by name or by class in a **.Xdefaults** file, remove the **XmN** or **XmC** prefix and use the remaining letters. To specify one of the defined values for a resource in a **.Xdefaults** file, remove the **Xm** prefix and use the remaining letters (in either lowercase or uppercase, but include any underscores between words). The codes in the access column indicate if the given resource can be set at creation time (C), set by using **XtSetValues** (S), retrieved by using **XtGetValues** (G), or is not applicable (N/A).

XmForm Resource Set		
Name	**Default**	**Access**
Class	**Type**	
XmNfractionBase	100	CSG
XmCMaxValue	int	
XmNhorizontalSpacing	0	CSG
XmCSpacing	Dimension	
XmNrubberPositioning	False	CSG
XmCRubberPositioning	Boolean	
XmNverticalSpacing	0	CSG
XmCSpacing	Dimension	

XmNfractionBase

Specifies the denominator used in calculating the relative position of a child widget using **XmATTACH_POSITION** constraints. The value must not be 0 (zero).

If the value of a child's **XmNleftAttachment** (or **XmNrightAttachment**) is **XmATTACH_POSITION**, the position of the left (or right) side of the child is relative to the left side of the Form and is a fraction of the width of the Form. This fraction is the value of the child's **XmNleftPosition** (or **XmNrightPosition**) resource divided by the value of the Form's **XmNfractionBase**.

If the value of a child's **XmNtopAttachment** (or **XmNbottomAttachment**) is **XmATTACH_POSITION**, the position of the top (or bottom) side of the child is relative to the top side of the Form and is a fraction of the height of the Form. This fraction is the value of the child's **XmNtopPosition** (or **XmNbottomPosition**) resource divided by the value of the Form's **XmNfractionBase**.

XmNhorizontalSpacing

Specifies the offset for right and left attachments. This resource is only used if no offset resource is specified (when attaching to a widget), or if no margin resource is specified (when attaching to the Form).

XmNrubberPositioning

Indicates the default near (left) and top attachments for a child of the Form. (Note that whether this resource actually applies to the left or right side of the child and its attachment may depend on the value of the **XmNstringDirection** resource.)

The default left attachment is applied whenever initialization or **XtSetValues** leaves the child without either a left or right attachment. The default top attachment is applied whenever initialization or **XtSetValues** leaves the child without either a top or bottom attachment.

If this Boolean resource is set to False, **XmNleftAttachment** and **XmNtopAttachment** default to **XmATTACH_FORM**, **XmNleftOffset** defaults to the current x value of the left side of the child, and **XmNtopOffset** defaults to the current y value of the child. The effect is to position the child according to its absolute distance from the left or top side of the Form.

If this resource is set to True, **XmNleftAttachment** and **XmNtopAttachment** default to **XmATTACH_POSITION**, **XmNleftPosition** defaults to a value proportional to the current x value of the left side of the child divided by the width of the Form, and **XmNtopPosition** defaults to a value proportional to the current y value of the child divided by the height of the Form. The effect is to position the child relative to the left or top side of the Form and in proportion to the width or height of the Form.

XmNverticalSpacing

Specifies the offset for top and bottom attachments. This resource is only used if no offset resource is specified (when attaching to a widget), or if no margin resource is specified (when attaching to the Form).

XmForm Constraint Resource Set		
Name	**Default**	**Access**
Class	**Type**	
XmNbottomAttachment	XmATTACH_NONE	CSG
XmCAttachment	unsigned char	
XmNbottomOffset	0	CSG
XmCOffset	int	
XmNbottomPosition	0	CSG
XmCAttachment	int	
XmNbottomWidget	NULL	CSG
XmCWidget	Widget	
XmNleftAttachment	XmATTACH_NONE	CSG
XmCAttachment	unsigned char	
XmNleftOffset	0	CSG
XmCOffset	int	
XmNleftPosition	0	CSG
XmCAttachment	int	
XmNleftWidget	NULL	CSG
XmCWidget	Widget	
XmNresizable	True	CSG
XmCBoolean	Boolean	
XmNrightAttachment	XmATTACH_NONE	CSG
XmCAttachment	unsigned char	
XmNrightOffset	0	CSG
XmCOffset	int	
XmNrightPosition	0	CSG
XmCAttachment	int	
XmNrightWidget	NULL	CSG
XmCWidget	Widget	
XmNtopAttachment	XmATTACH_NONE	CSG
XmCAttachment	unsigned char	

Name	Default	Access
Class	Type	
XmNtopOffset	0	CSG
XmCOffset	int	
XmNtopPosition	0	CSG
XmCAttachment	int	
XmNtopWidget	NULL	CSG
XmCWidget	Widget	

XmNbottomAttachment

Specifies attachment of the bottom side of the child. It can have the following values:

XmATTACH_NONE

Do not attach the bottom side of the child.

Attach the bottom side of the child to the bottom side of the Form.

XmATTACH_OPPOSITE_FORM

Attach the bottom side of the child to the top side of the Form. **XmNbottomOffset** can be used to determine the visibility of the child.

XmATTACH_WIDGET

Attach the bottom side of the child to the top side of the widget or gadget specified in the **XmNbottomWidget** resource. If **XmNbottomWidget** is NULL, **XmATTACH_WIDGET** is replaced by **XmATTACH_FORM**, and the child is attached to the bottom side of the Form.

XmATTACH_OPPOSITE_WIDGET

Attach the bottom side of the child to the bottom side of the widget or gadget specified in the **XmNbottomWidget** resource.

XmATTACH_POSITION

Attach the bottom side of the child to a position that is relative to the top side of the Form and in proportion to the height of the Form. This position is determined by the **XmNbottomPosition** and **XmNfractionBase** resources.

XmATTACH_SELF

Attach the bottom side of the child to a position that is proportional to the current *y* value of the bottom of the child divided by the height of the Form. This position is determined by the **XmNbottomPosition** and **XmNfractionBase** resources. **XmNbottomPosition** is set to a value proportional to the current *y* value of the bottom of the child divided by the height of the Form.

XmNbottomOffset

Specifies the constant offset between the bottom side of the child and the object to which it is attached. The effect of a nonzero value for this resource is undefined if **XmNbottomAttachment** is set to **XmATTACH_POSITION**. The relationship established remains, regardless of any resizing operations that occur. When this resource is explicitly set, the value of **XmNverticalSpacing** is ignored.

XmNbottomPosition

This resource is used to determine the position of the bottom side of the child when the child's **XmNbottomAttachment** is set to **XmATTACH_POSITION**. In this case the position of the bottom side of the child is relative to the top side of the Form and is a fraction of the height of the Form. This fraction is the value of the child's **XmNbottomPosition** resource divided by the value of the Form's **XmNfractionBase**. For example, if the child's **XmNbottomPosition** is 50, the Form's **XmNfractionBase** is 100, and the Form's height is 200, the position of the bottom side of the child is 100.

XmNbottomWidget

Specifies the widget or gadget to which the bottom side of the child is attached. This resource is used if the **XmNbottomAttachment** resource is set to either **XmATTACH_WIDGET** or **XmATTACH_OPPOSITE_WIDGET**.

XmNleftAttachment

Specifies attachment of the near (left) side of the child. (Note that whether this resource actually applies to the left or right side of the child and its attachment may depend on the value of the **XmNstringDirection** resource.) It can have the following values:

XmATTACH_NONE

Do not attach the left side of the child. If **XmNrightAttachment** is also

XmATTACH_NONE, this value is ignored and the child is given a default left attachment.

XmATTACH_FORM

Attach the left side of the child to the left side of the Form.

XmATTACH_OPPOSITE_FORM

Attach the left side of the child to the right side of the Form. **XmNleftOffset** can be used to determine the visibility of the child.

XmATTACH_WIDGET

Attach the left side of the child to the right side of the widget or gadget specified in the **XmNleftWidget** resource. If **XmNleftWidget** is NULL, **XmATTACH_WIDGET** is replaced by **XmATTACH_FORM**, and the child is attached to the left side of the Form.

XmATTACH_OPPOSITE_WIDGET

Attach the left side of the child to the left side of the widget or gadget specified in the **XmNleftWidget** resource.

XmATTACH_POSITION

Attach the left side of the child to a position that is relative to the left side of the Form and in proportion to the width of the Form. This position is determined by the **XmNleftPosition** and **XmNfractionBase** resources.

XmATTACH_SELF

Attach the left side of the child to a position that is proportional to the current x value of the left side of the child divided by the width of the Form. This position is determined by the **XmNleftPosition** and **XmNfractionBase** resources. **XmNleftPosition** is set to a value proportional to the current x value of the left side of the child divided by the width of the Form.

XmNleftOffset

Specifies the constant offset between the near (left) side of the child and the object to which it is attached. (Note that whether this resource actually applies to the left or right side of the child and its attachment may depend on the value of the **XmNstringDirection** resource.) The effect of a nonzero value for this resource is undefined if **XmNleftAttachment** is set to **XmATTACH_POSITION**. The relationship established remains, regardless of any resizing operations that occur. When this resource is explicitly set, the value of **XmNhorizontalSpacing** is ignored.

XmNleftPosition

This resource is used to determine the position of the near (left) side of the child when the child's **XmNleftAttachment** is set to **XmATTACH_POSITION**. (Note that whether this resource actually applies to the left or right side of the child and its attachment may depend on the value of the **XmNstringDirection** resource.)

In this case, the position of the left side of the child is relative to the left side of the Form and is a fraction of the width of the Form. This fraction is the value of the child's **XmNleftPosition** resource divided by the value of the Form's **XmNfractionBase**. For example, if the child's **XmNleftPosition** is 50, the Form's **XmNfractionBase** is 100, and the Form's width is 200, the position of the left side of the child is 100.

XmNleftWidget

Specifies the widget or gadget to which the near (left) side of the child is attached. (Note that whether this resource actually applies to the left or right side of the child and its attachment may depend on the value of the **XmNstringDirection** resource.) The **XmNleftWidget** resource is used if the **XmNleftAttachment** resource is set to either **XmATTACH_WIDGET** or **XmATTACH_OPPOSITE_WIDGET**.

XmNresizable

This Boolean resource specifies whether or not a child's request for a new size is (conditionally) granted by the Form. If this resource is set to True the request is granted if possible. If this resource is set to False the request is always refused.

If a child has both left and right attachments, its width is completely controlled by the Form, regardless of the value of the child's **XmNresizable** resource. If a child has a left or right attachment but not both, the child's **XmNwidth** is used in setting its width if the value of the child's **XmNresizable** resource is True. These conditions are also true for top and bottom attachments, with height acting like width.

XmNrightAttachment

Specifies attachment of the far (right) side of the child. (Note that whether this resource actually applies to the left or right side of the child and its attachment may depend on the value of the **XmNstringDirection** resource.) It can have the following values:

XmATTACH_NONE

Do not attach the right side of the child.

XmATTACH_FORM

Attach the right side of the child to the right side of the Form.

XmATTACH_OPPOSITE_FORM

Attach the right side of the child to the left side of the Form. **XmNrightOffset** can be used to determine the visibility of the child.

XmATTACH_WIDGET

Attach the right side of the child to the left side of the widget or gadget specified in the **XmNrightWidget** resource. If **XmNrightWidget** is NULL, **XmATTACH_WIDGET** is replaced by **XmATTACH_FORM**, and the child is attached to the right side of the Form.

XmATTACH_OPPOSITE_WIDGET

Attach the right side of the child to the right side of the widget or gadget specified in the **XmNrightWidget** resource.

XmATTACH_POSITION

Attach the right side of the child to a position that is relative to the left side of the Form and in proportion to the width of the Form. This position is determined by the **XmNrightPosition** and **XmNfractionBase** resources.

XmATTACH_SELF

Attach the right side of the child to a position that is proportional to the current x value of the right side of the child divided by the width of the Form. This position is determined by the **XmNrightPosition** and **XmNfractionBase** resources. **XmNrightPosition** is set to a value proportional to the current x value of the right side of the child divided by the width of the Form.

XmNrightOffset

Specifies the constant offset between the far (right) side of the child and the object to which it is attached. (Note that whether this resource actually applies to the left or right side of the child and its attachment may depend on the value of the **XmNstringDirection** resource.) The effect of a nonzero value for this resource is undefined if **XmNrightAttachment** is set to **XmATTACH_POSITION**. The relationship established remains, regardless of any resizing operations that occur. When this resource is explicitly set, the value of **XmNhorizontalSpacing** is ignored.

XmNrightPosition

This resource is used to determine the position of the far (right) side of the child when the child's **XmNrightAttachment** is set to **XmATTACH_POSITION**. (Note that whether this resource actually applies to the left or right side of the child and its attachment may depend on the value of the **XmNstringDirection** resource.)

In this case the position of the right side of the child is relative to the left side of the Form and is a fraction of the width of the Form. This fraction is the value of the child's **XmNrightPosition** resource divided by the value of the Form's **XmNfractionBase**. For example, if the child's **XmNrightPosition** is 50, the Form's **XmNfractionBase** is 100, and the Form's width is 200, the position of the right side of the child is 100.

XmNrightWidget

Specifies the widget or gadget to which the far (right) side of the child is attached. (Note that whether this resource actually applies to the left or right side of the child and its attachment may depend on the value of the **XmNstringDirection** resource.) The **XmNrightWidget** resource is used if the **XmNrightAttachment** resource is set to either **XmATTACH_WIDGET** or **XmATTACH_OPPOSITE_WIDGET**.

XmNtopAttachment

Specifies attachment of the top side of the child. It can have following values:

XmATTACH_NONE

Do not attach the top side of the child. If the **XmNbottomAttachment** resource is also **XmATTACH_NONE**, this value is ignored and the child is given a default top attachment.

XmATTACH_FORM

Attach the top side of the child to the top side of the Form.

XmATTACH_OPPOSITE_FORM

Attach the top side of the child to the bottom side of the Form. **XmNtopOffset** can be used to determine the visibility of the child.

XmATTACH_WIDGET

Attach the top side of the child to the bottom side of the widget or gadget specified in the **XmNtopWidget** resource. If **XmNtopWidget** is NULL, **XmATTACH_WIDGET** is replaced by **XmATTACH_FORM** and the child is attached to the top side of the Form.

XmATTACH_OPPOSITE_WIDGET

Attach the top side of the child to the top side of the widget or gadget specified in the **XmNtopWidget** resource.

XmATTACH_POSITION

Attach the top side of the child to a position that is relative to the top side of the Form and in proportion to the height of the Form. This position is determined by the **XmNtopPosition** and **XmNfractionBase** resources.

XmATTACH_SELF

Attach the top side of the child to a position that is proportional to the current y value of the child divided by the height of the Form. This position is determined by the **XmNtopPosition** and **XmNfractionBase** resources. **XmNtopPosition** is set to a value proportional to the current *y* value of the child divided by the height of the Form.

XmNtopOffset

Specifies the constant offset between the top side of the child and the object to which it is attached. The effect of a nonzero value for this resource is undefined if **XmNtopAttachment** is set to **XmATTACH_POSITION**. The relationship established remains, regardless of any resizing operations that occur. When this resource is explicitly set, the value of **XmNverticalSpacing** is ignored.

XmNtopPosition

This resource is used to determine the position of the top side of the child when the child's **XmNtopAttachment** is set to **XmATTACH_POSITION**. In this case, the position of the top side of the child is relative to the top side of the Form and is a fraction of the height of the Form. This fraction is the value of the child's **XmNtopPosition** resource divided by the value of the Form's **XmNfractionBase**. For example, if the child's **XmNtopPosition** is 50, the Form's **XmNfractionBase** is 100, and the Form's height is 200, the position of the top side of the child is 100.

XmNtopWidget

Specifies the widget or gadget to which the top side of the child is attached. This resource is used if **XmNtopAttachment** is set to a value of either **XmATTACH_WIDGET** or **XmATTACH_OPPOSITE_WIDGET**.

Inherited Resources

Form inherits behavior and resources from the superclasses described in the following tables. For a complete description of each resource, refer to the reference page for that superclass.

XmBulletinBoard Resource Set		
Name	**Default**	**Access**
Class	**Type**	
XmNallowOverlap	True	CSG
XmCAllowOverlap	Boolean	
XmNautoUnmanage	True	CG
XmCAutoUnmanage	Boolean	
XmNbuttonFontList	dynamic	CSG
XmCButtonFontList	XmFontList	
XmNcancelButton	NULL	SG
XmCWidget	Widget	
XmNdefaultButton	NULL	SG
XmCWidget	Widget	
XmNdefaultPosition	True	CSG
XmCDefaultPosition	Boolean	
XmNdialogStyle	dynamic	CSG
XmCDialogStyle	unsigned char	
XmNdialogTitle	NULL	CSG
XmCDialogTitle	XmString	
XmNfocusCallback	NULL	C
XmCCallback	XtCallbackList	
XmNlabelFontList	dynamic	CSG
XmCLabelFontList	XmFontList	
XmNmapCallback	NULL	C
XmCCallback	XtCallbackList	
XmNmarginHeight	0	CSG
XmCMarginHeight	Dimension	
XmNmarginWidth	0	CSG
XmCMarginWidth	Dimension	
XmNnoResize	False	CSG
XmCNoResize	Boolean	
XmNresizePolicy	XmRESIZE_ANY	CSG
XmCResizePolicy	unsigned char	

Name Class	Default Type	Access
XmNshadowType XmCShadowType	XmSHADOW_OUT unsigned char	CSG
XmNtextFontList XmCTextFontList	dynamic XmFontList	CSG
XmNtextTranslations XmCTranslations	NULL XtTranslations	C
XmNunmapCallback XmCCallback	NULL XtCallbackList	C

XmManager Resource Set		
Name	**Default**	**Access**
Class	**Type**	
XmNbottomShadowColor	dynamic	CSG
XmCBottomShadowColor	Pixel	
XmNbottomShadowPixmap	XmUNSPECIFIED_PIXMAP	CSG
XmCBottomShadowPixmap	Pixmap	
XmNforeground	dynamic	CSG
XmCForeground	Pixel	
XmNhelpCallback	NULL	C
XmCCallback	XtCallbackList	
XmNhighlightColor	dynamic	CSG
XmCHighlightColor	Pixel	
XmNhighlightPixmap	dynamic	CSG
XmCHighlightPixmap	Pixmap	
XmNnavigationType	XmTAB_GROUP	CSG
XmCNavigationType	XmNavigationType	
XmNshadowThickness	dynamic	CSG
XmCShadowThickness	Dimension	
XmNstringDirection	dynamic	CG
XmCStringDirection	XmStringDirection	
XmNtopShadowColor	dynamic	CSG
XmCTopShadowColor	Pixel	
XmNtopShadowPixmap	dynamic	CSG
XmCTopShadowPixmap	Pixmap	
XmNtraversalOn	True	CSG
XmCTraversalOn	Boolean	
XmNuserData	NULL	CSG
XmCUserData	XtPointer	

Composite Resource Set		
Name	**Default**	**Access**
Class	**Type**	
XmNchildren	NULL	G
XmCReadOnly	WidgetList	
XmNinsertPosition	NULL	CSG
XmCInsertPosition	XtOrderProc	
XmNnumChildren	0	G
XmCReadOnly	Cardinal	

Core Resource Set		
Name	**Default**	**Access**
Class	**Type**	
XmNaccelerators	dynamic	N/A
XmCAccelerators	XtAccelerators	
XmNancestorSensitive	dynamic	G
XmCSensitive	Boolean	
XmNbackground	dynamic	CSG
XmCBackground	Pixel	
XmNbackgroundPixmap	XmUNSPECIFIED_PIXMAP	CSG
XmCPixmap	Pixmap	
XmNborderColor	XtDefaultForeground	CSG
XmCBorderColor	Pixel	
XmNborderPixmap	XmUNSPECIFIED_PIXMAP	CSG
XmCPixmap	Pixmap	
XmNborderWidth	0	CSG
XmCBorderWidth	Dimension	
XmNcolormap	dynamic	CG
XmCColormap	Colormap	
XmNdepth	dynamic	CG
XmCDepth	int	
XmNdestroyCallback	NULL	C
XmCCallback	XtCallbackList	
XmNheight	dynamic	CSG
XmCHeight	Dimension	
XmNinitialResourcesPersistent	True	C
XmCInitialResourcesPersistent	Boolean	
XmNmappedWhenManaged	True	CSG
XmCMappedWhenManaged	Boolean	
XmNscreen	dynamic	CG
XmCScreen	Screen *	
XmNsensitive	True	CSG
XmCSensitive	Boolean	

Name	Default	Access
Class	Type	
XmNtranslations	dynamic	CSG
XmCTranslations	XtTranslations	
XmNwidth	dynamic	CSG
XmCWidth	Dimension	
XmNx	0	CSG
XmCPosition	Position	
XmNy	0	CSG
XmCPosition	Position	

Related Information

Composite(3X), **Constraint(3X)**, **Core(3X)**, **XmBulletinBoard(3X)**, **XmCreateForm**, **XmCreateFormDialog(3X)**, and **XmManager(3X)**.

XmFrame—The Frame widget class

AES Support Level

Full-use

Synopsis

#include <Xm/Frame.h>

Description

Frame is a very simple manager used to enclose a single child in a border drawn by Frame. It uses the Manager class resources for border drawing and performs geometry management so that its size always matches its child's outer size plus the Frame's margins and shadow thickness.

Frame is most often used to enclose other managers when the application developer wants the manager to have the same border appearance as the primitive widgets. Frame can also be used to enclose primitive widgets that do not support the same type of border drawing. This gives visual consistency when you develop applications using diverse widget sets.

If the Frame's parent is a Shell widget, the **XmNshadowType** resource defaults to **XmSHADOW_OUT**, and the Manager's **XmNshadowThickness** resource defaults to 1.

If the Frame's parent is not a Shell widget, the **XmNshadowType** resouce defaults to **XmSHADOW_ETCHED_IN**, and the Manager's **XmNshadowThickness** resource defaults to 2.

Classes

Frame inherits behavior and resources from the **Core**, **Composite**, **Constraint**, and **XmManager** classes.

The class pointer is **xmFrameWidgetClass**.

The class name is **XmFrame**.

New Resources

The following table defines a set of widget resources used by the programmer to specify data. The programmer can also set the resource values for the inherited classes to set attributes for this widget. To reference a resource by name or by class in a **.Xdefaults** file, remove the **XmN** or **XmC** prefix and use the remaining letters. To specify one of the defined values for a resource in a **.Xdefaults** file, remove the **Xm** prefix and use the remaining letters (in either lowercase or uppercase, but include any underscores between words). The codes in the access column indicate if the given resource can be set at creation time (C), set by using **XtSetValues** (S), retrieved by using **XtGetValues** (G), or is not applicable (N/A).

XmFrame Resource Set		
Name	**Default**	**Access**
Class	**Type**	
XmNmarginWidth	0	CSG
XmCMarginWidth	Dimension	
XmNmarginHeight	0	CSG
XmCMarginHeight	Dimension	
XmNshadowType	dynamic	CSG
XmCShadowType	unsigned char	

XmNmarginWidth

Specifies the padding space on the left and right sides between Frame's child and Frame's shadow drawing.

XmNmarginHeight

Specifies the padding space on the top and bottom sides between Frame's child and Frame's shadow drawing.

XmNshadowType

Describes the drawing style for Frame. This resource can have the following values:

XmSHADOW_IN

Draws Frame so that it appears inset. This means that the bottom shadow visuals and top shadow visuals are reversed.

XmSHADOW_OUT

Draws Frame so that it appears outset. This is the default if Frame's parent is a Shell widget.

XmSHADOW_ETCHED_IN

Draws Frame using a double line giving the effect of a line etched into the window. The thickness of the double line is equal to the value of **XmNshadowThickness**. This is the default when Frame's parent is not a Shell widget.

XmSHADOW_ETCHED_OUT

Draws Frame using a double line giving the effect of a line coming out of the window. The thickness of the double line is equal to the value of **XmNshadowThickness**.

Inherited Resources

Frame inherits behavior and resources from the following superclasses. For a complete description of each resource, refer to the reference page for that superclass.

XmManager Resource Set		
Name	**Default**	**Access**
Class	**Type**	
XmNbottomShadowColor	dynamic	CSG
XmCBottomShadowColor	Pixel	
XmNbottomShadowPixmap	XmUNSPECIFIED_PIXMAP	CSG
XmCBottomShadowPixmap	Pixmap	
XmNforeground	dynamic	CSG
XmCForeground	Pixel	
XmNhelpCallback	NULL	C
XmCCallback	XtCallbackList	
XmNhighlightColor	dynamic	CSG
XmCHighlightColor	Pixel	
XmNhighlightPixmap	dynamic	CSG
XmCHighlightPixmap	Pixmap	
XmNnavigationType	XmTAB_GROUP	CSG
XmCNavigationType	XmNavigationType	
XmNshadowThickness	dynamic	CSG
XmCShadowThickness	Dimension	
XmNstringDirection	dynamic	CG
XmCStringDirection	XmStringDirection	
XmNtopShadowColor	dynamic	CSG
XmCTopShadowColor	Pixel	
XmNtopShadowPixmap	dynamic	CSG
XmCTopShadowPixmap	Pixmap	
XmNtraversalOn	True	CSG
XmCTraversalOn	Boolean	
XmNuserData	NULL	CSG
XmCUserData	XtPointer	

Composite Resource Set		
Name	**Default**	**Access**
Class	**Type**	
XmNchildren	NULL	G
XmCReadOnly	WidgetList	
XmNinsertPosition	NULL	CSG
XmCInsertPosition	XtOrderProc	
XmNnumChildren	0	G
XmCReadOnly	Cardinal	

Core Resource Set		
Name	**Default**	**Access**
Class	**Type**	
XmNaccelerators	dynamic	CSG
XmCAccelerators	XtAccelerators	
XmNancestorSensitive	dynamic	G
XmCSensitive	Boolean	
XmNbackground	dynamic	CSG
XmCBackground	Pixel	
XmNbackgroundPixmap	XmUNSPECIFIED_PIXMAP	CSG
XmCPixmap	Pixmap	
XmNborderColor	XtDefaultForeground	CSG
XmCBorderColor	Pixel	
XmNborderPixmap	XmUNSPECIFIED_PIXMAP	CSG
XmCPixmap	Pixmap	
XmNborderWidth	0	CSG
XmCBorderWidth	Dimension	
XmNcolormap	dynamic	CG
XmCColormap	Colormap	
XmNdepth	dynamic	CG
XmCDepth	int	
XmNdestroyCallback	NULL	C
XmCCallback	XtCallbackList	
XmNheight	dynamic	CSG
XmCHeight	Dimension	
XmNinitialResourcesPersistent	True	C
XmCInitialResourcesPersistent	Boolean	
XmNmappedWhenManaged	True	CSG
XmCMappedWhenManaged	Boolean	
XmNscreen	dynamic	CG
XmCScreen	Screen *	
XmNsensitive	True	CSG
XmCSensitive	Boolean	

Name	Default	Access
Class	Type	
XmNtranslations	dynamic	CSG
XmCTranslations	XtTranslations	
XmNwidth	dynamic	CSG
XmCWidth	Dimension	
XmNx	0	CSG
XmCPosition	Position	
XmNy	0	CSG
XmCPosition	Position	

Related Information

Composite(3X), Constraint(3X), Core(3X), XmCreateFrame(3X), and XmManager(3X).

XmGadget—The Gadget widget class

AES Support Level

Full-use

Synopsis

#include <Xm/Xm.h>

Description

Gadget is a widget class used as a supporting superclass for other gadget classes. It handles shadow-border drawing and highlighting, traversal activation and deactivation, and various callback lists needed by gadgets.

The color and pixmap resources defined by **XmManager** are directly used by gadgets. If **XtSetValues** is used to change one of the resources for a manager widget, all of the gadget children within the manager also change.

Classes

Gadget inherits behavior and resources from **Object** and **RectObj**.

The class pointer is **xmGadgetClass**.

The class name is **XmGadget**.

New Resources

The following table defines a set of widget resources used by the programmer to specify data. The programmer can also set the resource values for the inherited classes to set attributes for this widget. To reference a resource by name or by class in a .Xdefaults file, remove the **XmN** or **XmC** prefix and use the remaining letters. To specify one of the defined values for a resource in a .Xdefaults file, remove the **Xm** prefix and use the remaining letters (in either lowercase or uppercase, but include any underscores between words). The codes in the access column indicate if the given resource can be set at creation time (C), set by using **XtSetValues** (S), retrieved by using **XtGetValues** (G), or is not applicable (N/A).

XmGadget Resource Set		
Name	**Default**	**Access**
Class	**Type**	
XmNhelpCallback	NULL	C
XmCCallback	XtCallbackList	
XmNhighlightOnEnter	False	CSG
XmCHighlightOnEnter	Boolean	
XmNhighlightThickness	2	CSG
XmCHighlightThickness	Dimension	
XmNnavigationType	XmNONE	CSG
XmCNavigationType	XmNavigationType	
XmNshadowThickness	2	CSG
XmCShadowThickness	Dimension	
XmNtraversalOn	True	CSG
XmCTraversalOn	Boolean	
XmNuserData	NULL	CSG
XmCUserData	XtPointer	

XmNhelpCallback

> Specifies the list of callbacks that is called when the help key
> sequence is pressed. The reason sent by the callback is
> **XmCR_HELP**.

XmNhighlightOnEnter

> Specifies if the highlighting rectangle is drawn when the cursor
> moves into the widget. If the shell's focus policy is **XmEXPLICIT**,
> this resource is ignored, and the widget is highlighted when it has
> the focus. If the shell's focus policy is **XmPOINTER** and if this
> resource is True, the highlighting rectangle is drawn when the the
> cursor moves into the widget. If the shell's focus policy is
> **XmPOINTER** and if this resource is False, the highlighting
> rectangle is not drawn when the the cursor moves into the widget.
> The default is False.

XmNhighlightThickness

> Specifies the thickness of the highlighting rectangle.

XmNnavigationType

Determines whether the widget is a tab group.

XmNONE   Indicates that the widget is not a tab group.

XmTAB_GROUP

Indicates that the widget is a tab group, unless the **XmNnavigationType** of another widget in the hierarchy is **XmEXCLUSIVE_TAB_GROUP**.

XmSTICKY_TAB_GROUP

Indicates that the widget is a tab group, even if the **XmNnavigationType** of another widget in the hierarchy is **XmEXCLUSIVE_TAB_GROUP**.

XmEXCLUSIVE_TAB_GROUP

Indicates that the widget is a tab group and that widgets in the hierarchy whose **XmNnavigationType** is **XmTAB_GROUP** are not tab groups.

When a parent widget has an **XmNnavigationType** of **XmEXCLUSIVE_TAB_GROUP**, traversal of non-tab-group widgets within the group is based on the order of those widgets in their parent's **XmNchildren** list.

XmNshadowThickness

Specifies the size of the drawn border shadow.

XmNtraversalOn

Specifies traversal activation for this gadget.

XmNuserData

Allows the application to attach any necessary specific data to the gadget. This is an internally unused resource.

Inherited Resources

Gadget inherits resources from the superclass described in the following table. For a complete description of each resource, refer to the reference page for that superclass.

<table>
<tr><th colspan="3">RectObj Resource Set</th></tr>
<tr><th>Name
   Class</th><th>Default
   Type</th><th>Access</th></tr>
<tr><td>XmNancestorSensitive
   XmCSensitive</td><td>dynamic
   Boolean</td><td>G</td></tr>
<tr><td>XmNborderWidth
   XmCBorderWidth</td><td>0
   Dimension</td><td>N/A</td></tr>
<tr><td>XmNheight
   XmCHeight</td><td>dynamic
   Dimension</td><td>CSG</td></tr>
<tr><td>XmNsensitive
   XmCSensitive</td><td>True
   Boolean</td><td>CSG</td></tr>
<tr><td>XmNwidth
   XmCWidth</td><td>dynamic
   Dimension</td><td>CSG</td></tr>
<tr><td>XmNx
   XmCPosition</td><td>0
   Position</td><td>CSG</td></tr>
<tr><td>XmNy
   XmCPosition</td><td>0
   Position</td><td>CSG</td></tr>
</table>

<table>
<tr><th colspan="3">Object Resource Set</th></tr>
<tr><th>Name
   Class</th><th>Default
   Type</th><th>Access</th></tr>
<tr><td>XmNdestroyCallback
   XmCCallback</td><td>NULL
   XtCallbackList</td><td>C</td></tr>
</table>

Callback Information

A pointer to the following structure is passed to each callback:

```
typedef struct
{
    int             reason;
    XEvent          * event;
} XmAnyCallbackStruct;
```

reason   Indicates why the callback was invoked. For this callback, *reason* is set to **XmCR_HELP**.

event   Points to the **XEvent** that triggered the callback.

Related Information
        Object(3X), **RectObj(3X)**, and **XmManager(3X)**.

XmGetAtomName—A function that returns the string representation for an atom

AES Support Level

Full-use

History/Direction

The include file **AtomMgr.h** moved from the **X11** directory to the **Xm** directory. In revision B this include file will be accessible from either directory. In future revisions it will only be accessible from the **Xm** directory.

Synopsis

#include <Xm/Xm.h>
#include <Xm/AtomMgr.h>

String XmGetAtomName (*display, atom*)
    Display   * *display*;
    Atom   *atom*;

Description

XmGetAtomName returns the string representation for an atom. It mirrors the **Xlib** interfaces for atom management but provides client-side caching. When and where caching is provided in **Xlib**, the routines will become pseudonyms for the **Xlib** routines.

display   Specifies the connection to the X server

atom   Specifies the atom for the property name you want returned

Return Value

Returns a string.

XmGetColors—A function that generates foreground, select, and shadow colors

AES Support Level

Trial-use

Synopsis

#include <Xm/Xm.h>

void XmGetColors (*screen, colormap, background, foreground, top_shadow, bottom_shadow, select*)

Screen	* *screen*;
Colormap	*colormap*;
Pixel	*background*;
Pixel	* *foreground*;
Pixel	* *top_shadow*;
Pixel	* *bottom_shadow*;
Pixel	* *select*;

Description

XmGetColors takes a screen, a colormap, and a background pixel, and returns pixel values for foreground, select, and shadow colors.

screen   Specifies the screen for which these colors should be allocated.

colormap   Specifies the colormap from which these colors should be allocated.

background   Specifies the background on which the colors should be based.

foreground   Specifies a pointer to the returned foreground pixel value. If this argument is NULL no value is returned for this color.

top_shadow Specifies a pointer to the returned top shadow pixel value. If this argument is NULL, no value is returned for this color.

bottom_shadow

                Specifies a pointer to the returned bottom shadow pixel value. If this argument is NULL, no value is returned for this color.

select   Specifies a pointer to the returned select pixel value. If this argument is NULL, no value is returned for this color.

XmGetMenuCursor—A RowColumn function that returns the cursor ID for the current menu cursor

AES Support Level

Full-use

Synopsis

#include <Xm/Xm.h>

Cursor XmGetMenuCursor (*display*)
    Display   * *display*;

Description

XmGetMenuCursor queries the menu cursor currently being used by this client on the specified display and returns the cursor ID.

display   Specifies the display whose menu cursor is to be queried

For a complete definition of the menu cursor resource, see **XmRowColumn(3X)**.

Return Value

Returns the cursor ID for the current menu cursor or the value None if a cursor is not yet defined. A cursor will not be defined if the application makes this call before the client has created any menus on the specified display.

Related Information

XmRowColumn(3X).

XmGetPixmap—A pixmap caching function that generates a pixmap, stores it in a pixmap cache, and returns the pixmap

AES Support Level

Full-use

Synopsis

#include <Xm/Xm.h>

Pixmap XmGetPixmap (*screen, image_name, foreground, background*)
    Screen   **screen*;
    char   **image_name*;
    Pixel   *foreground*;
    Pixel   *background*;

Description

XmGetPixmap uses the parameter data to perform a lookup in the pixmap cache to see if a pixmap has already been generated that matches the data. If one is found, a reference count is incremented and the pixmap is returned. Applications should use **XmDestroyPixmap** when the pixmap is no longer needed.

screen   Specifies the display screen on which the pixmap is to be drawn. The depth of the pixmap is the default depth for this screen.

image_name   Specifies the name of the image to be used to generate the pixmap

foreground   Combines the image with the *foreground* color to create the pixmap if the image referenced is a bit-per-pixel image

background   Combines the image with the *background* color to create the pixmap if the image referenced is a bit-per-pixel image

If a pixmap is not found, *image_name* is used to perform a lookup in the image cache. If an image is found, it is used to generate the pixmap, which is then cached and returned.

If an image is not found, the *image_name* is used as a filename, and a search is made for an **X10** or **X11** bitmap file. If it is found, the file is read, converted into an image, and cached in the image cache. The image is then used to generate a pixmap, which is cached and returned.

If *image_name* has a leading slash (/), it specifies a full pathname, and **XmGetPixmap** opens the file as specified. Otherwise, *image_name* specifies a filename. In this case, **XmGetPixmap** looks for the file along a search path specified by the **XBMLANGPATH** environment variable or by a default search path, which varies depending on whether or not the **XAPPLRESDIR** environment variable is set.

The **XBMLANGPATH** environment variable specifies a search path for X bitmap files. It can contain the substitution field **%B**, where the *image_name* argument to **XmGetPixmap** is substituted for **%B**. It can also contain the substitution fields accepted by **XtResolvePathname**. The substitution field **%T** is always mapped to **bitmaps**, and **%S** is always mapped to NULL.

If **XBMLANGPATH** is not set but the environment variable **XAPPLRESDIR** is set, the following pathnames are searched:

- **%B**

- **$XAPPLRESDIR/%L/bitmaps/%N/%B**

- **$XAPPLRESDIR/%l/bitmaps/%N/%B**

- **$XAPPLRESDIR/bitmaps/%N/%B**

- **$XAPPLRESDIR/%L/bitmaps/%B**

- **$XAPPLRESDIR/%l/bitmaps/%B**

- **$XAPPLRESDIR/bitmaps/%B**

- **$HOME/bitmaps/%B**

- **$HOME/%B**

- **/usr/lib/X11/%L/bitmaps/%N/%B**

- **/usr/lib/X11/%l/bitmaps/%N/%B**

- **/usr/lib/X11/bitmaps/%N/%B**

- **/usr/lib/X11/%L/bitmaps/%B**

- **/usr/lib/X11/%l/bitmaps/%B**

- **/usr/lib/X11/bitmaps/%B**

- **/usr/include/X11/bitmaps/%B**

If neither **XBMLANGPATH** nor **XAPPLRESDIR** is set, the following pathnames are searched:

- **%B**

- **$HOME/%L/bitmaps/%N/%B**

- **$HOME/%l/bitmaps/%N/%B**

- **$HOME/bitmaps/%N/%B**

- **$HOME/%L/bitmaps/%B**

- **$HOME/%l/bitmaps/%B**

- **$HOME/bitmaps/%B**

- **$HOME/%B**

- **/usr/lib/X11/%L/bitmaps/%N/%B**

- **/usr/lib/X11/%l/bitmaps/%N/%B**

- **/usr/lib/X11/bitmaps/%N/%B**

- **/usr/lib/X11/%L/bitmaps/%B**

- **/usr/lib/X11/%l/bitmaps/%B**

- **/usr/lib/X11/bitmaps/%B**

- **/usr/include/X11/bitmaps/%B**

These paths are defaults that vendors may change. For example, a vendor may use different directories for **/usr/lib/X11** and **/usr/include/X11**.

The following substitutions are used in these paths:

%B	The image name, from the *image_name* argument
%N	The class name of the application
%L	The display's language string
%l	The language component of the display's language string

Return Value

Returns a pixmap when successful; returns **XmUNSPECIFIED_PIXMAP** if the image corresponding to *image_name* cannot be found.

Related Information

XmDestroyPixmap(3X), **XmInstallImage(3X)**, and **XmUninstallImage(3X)**.

XmGetPostedFromWidget—A RowColumn function that returns the widget from which a menu was posted

AES Support Level

Trial-use

Synopsis

#include <Xm/RowColumn.h>

Widget XmGetPostedFromWidget (*menu*)
    Widget   *menu***;**

Description

XmGetPostedFromWidget returns the widget from which a menu was posted. An application can use this routine during the activate callback to determine the context in which the menu callback should be interpreted.

menu   Specifies the widget ID of the menu

For a complete definition of RowColumn and its associated resources, see **XmRowColumn(3X)**.

Return Value

Returns the widget ID of the widget from which the menu was posted. If the menu is a Popup Menu, the returned widget is the widget from which the menu was popped up. If the menu is a Pulldown Menu, the returned widget is the MenuBar or OptionMenu from which the widget was pulled down.

Related Information

XmRowColumn(3X).

XmInstallImage—A pixmap caching function that adds an image to the image cache

AES Support Level

Full-use

Synopsis

#include <Xm/Xm.h>

Boolean XmInstallImage (*image, image_name*)
    XImage   * *image*;
    char   * *image_name*;

Description

XmInstallImage stores an image in an image cache that can later be used to generate a pixmap. Part of the installation process is to extend the resource converter used to reference these images. The resource converter is given the image name so that the image can be referenced in a **.Xdefaults** file. Since an image can be referenced by a widget through its pixmap resources, it is up to the application to ensure that the image is installed before the widget is created.

image   Points to the image structure to be installed. The installation process does not make a local copy of the image. Therefore, the application should not destroy the image until it is uninstalled from the caching functions.

image_name   Specifies a string that the application uses to name the image. After installation, this name can be used in **.Xdefaults** for referencing the image. A local copy of the name is created by the image caching functions.

The image caching functions provide a set of eight preinstalled images. These names can be used within a **.Xdefaults** file for generating pixmaps for the resource for which they are provided.

Image Name	Description
background	A tile of solid background
25_foreground	A tile of 25% foreground, 75% background
50_foreground	A tile of 50% foreground, 50% background
75_foreground	A tile of 75% foreground, 25% background
horizontal	A tile of horizontal lines of the two colors
vertical	A tile of vertical lines of the two colors
slant_right	A tile of slanting lines of the two colors
slant_left	A tile of slanting lines of the two colors

Return Value

Returns True when successful; returns False if NULL *image*, NULL *image_name*, or duplicate *image_name* is used as a parameter value.

Related Information

XmUninstallImage(3X), **XmGetPixmap(3X)**, and **XmDestroyPixmap(3X)**.

XmInternAtom—A function that returns an atom for a given name

AES Support Level

Full-use

History/Direction

The include file **AtomMgr.h** moved from the **X11** directory to the **Xm** directory. In revision B this include file will be accessible from either directory. In future revisions it will only be accessible from the **Xm** directory.

Synopsis

#include <Xm/Xm.h>
#include <Xm/AtomMgr.h>

Atom XmInternAtom (*display, name, only_if_exists*)
    Display   * *display*;
    String   *name*;
    Boolean   *only_if_exists*;

Description

XmInternAtom returns an atom for a given name. It mirrors the **Xlib** interfaces for atom management, but provides client-side caching. When and where caching is provided in **Xlib**, the routines will become pseudonyms for the **Xlib** routines.

display   Specifies the connection to the X server

name   Specifies the name associated with the atom you want returned

only_if_exists

            Specifies a Boolean value that indicates whether **XInternAtom** creates the atom

Return Value

Returns an atom.

XmIsMotifWMRunning—A function that determines whether the window manager is running

AES Support Level

Full-use

History/Direction

The include file for this function has changed from **X11/Shell.h** to **Xm/Xm.h**.

Synopsis

#include <Xm/Xm.h>

Boolean XmIsMotifWMRunning (*shell*)
    Widget   *shell*;

Description

XmIsMotifWMRunning lets a user know whether the Motif Window Manager is running on a screen that contains a specific widget hierarchy. This function first sees whether the **_MOTIF_WM_INFO** property is present on the root window of the shell's screen. If it is, its window field is used to query for the presence of the specified window as a child of root.

shell   Specifies the shell whose screen will be tested for **mwm**'s presence.

Return Value

Returns True if MWM is running.

XmLabel—The Label widget class

AES Support Level

Full-use

History/Direction

Changes have been made in the determination of default label strings (for trial-use).

Synopsis

#include <Xm/Label.h>

Description

Label is an instantiable widget and is also used as a superclass for other button widgets, such as PushButton and ToggleButton. The Label widget does not accept any button or key input, and the help callback is the only callback defined. Label also receives enter and leave events.

Label can contain either text or a pixmap. Label text is a compound string. Refer to the *OSF/Motif Programmer's Guide* for more information on compound strings. The text can be multilingual, multiline, and/or multifont. When a Label is insensitive, its text is stippled, or the user-supplied insensitive pixmap is displayed.

Label supports both accelerators and mnemonics primarily for use in Label subclass widgets that are contained in menus. Mnemonics are available in a menu system when the button is visible. Accelerators in a menu system are accessible even when the button is not visible. The Label widget displays the mnemonic by underlining the first matching character in the text string. The accelerator is displayed as a text string adjacent to the label text or pixmap.

Label consists of many margin fields surrounding the text or pixmap. These margin fields are resources that may be set by the user, but Label subclasses and Manager parents also modify some of these fields. They tend to modify the **XmNmarginLeft**, **XmNmarginRight**, **XmNmarginTop**, and **XmNmarginBottom** resources and leave the **XmNmarginWidth** and **XmNmarginHeight** resources as set by the application.

In a Label, **XmNtraversalOn** and **XmNhighlightOnEnter** are forced to False inside Popup MenuPanes, Pulldown MenuPanes, and OptionMenus. Otherwise, these resources default to False.

Classes

Label inherits behavior and resources from **Core** and **XmPrimitive**.

The class pointer is **xmLabelWidgetClass**.

The class name is **XmLabel**.

New Resources

The following table defines a set of widget resources used by the programmer to specify data. The programmer can also set the resource values for the inherited classes to set attributes for this widget. To reference a resource by name or by class in a **.Xdefaults** file, remove the **XmN** or **XmC** prefix and use the remaining letters. To specify one of the defined values for a resource in a **.Xdefaults** file, remove the **Xm** prefix and use the remaining letters (in either lowercase or uppercase, but include any underscores between words). The codes in the access column indicate if the given resource can be set at creation time (C), set by using **XtSetValues** (S), retrieved by using **XtGetValues** (G), or is not applicable (N/A).

XmLabel(3X)

XmLabel Resource Set		
Name	**Default**	**Access**
Class	**Type**	
XmNaccelerator	NULL	CSG
XmCAccelerator	String	
XmNacceleratorText	NULL	CSG
XmCAcceleratorText	XmString	
XmNalignment	dynamic	CSG
XmCAlignment	unsigned char	
XmNfontList	dynamic	CSG
XmCFontList	XmFontList	
XmNlabelInsensitivePixmap	XmUNSPECIFIED_PIXMAP	CSG
XmCLabelInsensitivePixmap	Pixmap	
XmNlabelPixmap	XmUNSPECIFIED_PIXMAP	CSG
XmCLabelPixmap	Pixmap	
XmNlabelString	dynamic	CSG
XmCXmString	XmString	
XmNlabelType	XmSTRING	CSG
XmCLabelType	unsigned char	
XmNmarginBottom	0	CSG
XmCMarginBottom	Dimension	
XmNmarginHeight	2	CSG
XmCMarginHeight	Dimension	
XmNmarginLeft	0	CSG
XmCMarginLeft	Dimension	
XmNmarginRight	0	CSG
XmCMarginRight	Dimension	
XmNmarginTop	0	CSG
XmCMarginTop	Dimension	
XmNmarginWidth	2	CSG
XmCMarginWidth	Dimension	
XmNmnemonic	NULL	CSG
XmCMnemonic	KeySym	

Name	Default	Access
Class	**Type**	
XmNmnemonicCharSet	XmFONTLIST_DEFAULT_TAG	CSG
XmCMnemonicCharSet	String	
XmNrecomputeSize	True	CSG
XmCRecomputeSize	Boolean	
XmNstringDirection	dynamic	CSG
XmCStringDirection	XmStringDirection	

XmNaccelerator

Sets the accelerator on a button widget in a menu, which activates a visible or invisible, but managed, button from the keyboard. This resource is a string that describes a set of modifiers and the key that may be used to select the button. The format of this string is identical to that used by the translations manager, with the exception that only a single event may be specified and only **KeyPress** events are allowed.

Accelerators for buttons are supported only for PushButton and ToggleButton in Pulldown and Popup MenuPanes.

XmNacceleratorText

Specifies the text displayed for the accelerator. The text is displayed adjacent to the label string or pixmap. Accelerator text for buttons is displayed only for PushButtons and ToggleButtons in Pulldown and Popup Menus.

XmNalignment

Specifies the label alignment for text or pixmap.

XmALIGNMENT_BEGINNING (left alignment)

Causes the left sides of the lines of text to be vertically aligned with the left edge of the widget window. For a pixmap, its left side is vertically aligned with the left edge of the widget window.

XmALIGNMENT_CENTER (center alignment)

Causes the centers of the lines of text to be vertically aligned in the center of the widget window. For a pixmap, its center is vertically aligned with the center of the widget window.

XmALIGNMENT_END (right alignment)
> Causes the right sides of the lines of text to be vertically aligned with the right edge of the widget window. For a pixmap, its right side is vertically aligned with the right edge of the widget window.

The preceding descriptions for text are correct when **XmNstringDirection** is **XmSTRING_DIRECTION_L_TO_R**. When that resource is **XmSTRING_DIRECTION_R_TO_L**, the descriptions for **XmALIGNMENT_BEGINNING** and **XmALIGNMENT_END** are switched.

If the parent is a RowColumn whose **XmNisAligned** resource is True, **XmNalignment** is forced to the same value as the RowColumn's **XmNentryAlignment** if the RowColumn's **XmNrowColumnType** is **XmWORK_AREA** or if the widget is a subclass of XmLabel. Otherwise, the default is **XmALIGNMENT_CENTER**.

XmNfontList Specifies the font of the text used in the widget. If this value is NULL at initialization, the parent hierarchy of the widget is searched for an ancestor that is a subclass of the XmBulletinBoard, VendorShell, or XmMenuShell widget class. If such an ancestor is found, the font list is initialized to the **XmNbuttonFontList** (for button subclasses) or **XmNlabelFontList** of the ancestor widget. If no such ancestor is found, the default is implementation dependent. Refer to **XmFontList(3X)** for more information on the creation and structure of a font list.

XmNlabelInsensitivePixmap
> Specifies a pixmap used as the button face if **XmNlabelType** is **XmPIXMAP** and the button is insensitive.

XmNlabelPixmap
> Specifies the pixmap when **XmNlabelType** is **XmPIXMAP**.

XmNlabelString
> Specifies the compound string when **XmNlabelType** is **XmSTRING**. If this value is NULL, it is initialized by converting the name of the widget to a compound string. Refer to **XmString(3X)** for more information on the creation and structure of compound strings.

XmNlabelType

Specifies the label type.

XmSTRING Text displays **XmNlabelString**.

XmPIXMAP Icon data in pixmap displays **XmNlabelPixmap** or **XmNlabelInsensitivePixmap**.

XmNmarginBottom

Specifies the amount of spacing between the bottom of the label text and the top of the bottom margin specified by **XmNmarginHeight**. This may be modified by Label's subclasses. For example, CascadeButton may increase this field to make room for the cascade pixmap.

XmNmarginHeight

Specifies the amount of spacing between the top of the label (specified by **XmNmarginTop**) and the bottom edge of the top shadow, and the amount of spacing between the bottom of the label (specified by **XmNmarginBottom**) and the top edge of the bottom shadow.

XmNmarginLeft

Specifies the amount of spacing between the left edge of the label text and the right side of the left margin (specified by **XmNmarginWidth**). This may be modified by Label's subclasses. For example, ToggleButton may increase this field to make room for the toggle indicator and for spacing between the indicator and label. Whether this actually applies to the left or right side of the label may depend on the value of **XmNstringDirection**.

XmNmarginRight

Specifies the amount of spacing between the right edge of the label text and the left side of the right margin (specified by **XmNmarginWidth**). This may be modified by Label's subclasses. For example, CascadeButton may increase this field to make room for the cascade pixmap. Whether this actually applies to the left or right side of the label may depend on the value of **XmNstringDirection**.

XmNmarginTop

Specifies the amount of spacing between the top of the label text and the bottom of the top margin (specified by **XmNmarginHeight**). This may be modified by Label's subclasses. For example, CascadeButton may increase this field to make room for the cascade pixmap.

XmNmarginWidth
> Specifies the amount of spacing between the left side of the label (specified by **XmNmarginLeft**) and the right edge of the left shadow, and the amount of spacing between the right side of the label (specified by **XmNmarginRight**) and the left edge of the right shadow.

XmNmnemonic
> Provides the user with an alternate means of selecting a button. A button in a MenuBar, a Popup MenuPane, or a Pulldown MenuPane can have a mnemonic.
>
> This resource contains a keysym as listed in the X11 keysym table. The first character in the label string that exactly matches the mnemonic in the character set specified in **XmNmnemonicCharSet** is underlined when the button is displayed.
>
> When a mnemonic has been specified, the user activates the button by pressing the mnemonic key while the button is visible. If the button is a CascadeButton in a MenuBar and the MenuBar does not have the focus, the user must use the **MAlt** modifier while pressing the mnemonic. The user can activate the button by pressing either the shifted or the unshifted mnemonic key.

XmNmnemonicCharSet
> Specifies the character set of the mnemonic for the label. The default is **XmFONTLIST_DEFAULT_TAG**.

XmNrecomputeSize
> Specifies a Boolean value that indicates whether the widget attempts to be big enough to contain the label. If True, an **XtSetValues** with a resource value that would change the size of the widget causes the widget to shrink or expand to exactly fit the label string or pixmap. If False, the widget never attempts to change size on its own.

XmNstringDirection
> Specifies the direction in which the string is to be drawn:
>
> **XmSTRING_DIRECTION_L_TO_R**   Left to right
>
> **XmSTRING_DIRECTION_R_TO_L**   Right to left
>
> The default for this resource is determined at creation time. If no value is specified for this resource and the widget's parent is a manager, the value is inherited from the parent; otherwise, it defaults to **XmSTRING_DIRECTION_L_TO_R**.

Inherited Resources

Label inherits behavior and resources from the following superclasses. For a complete description of each resource, refer to the reference page for that superclass.

XmPrimitive Resource Set		
Name	**Default**	**Access**
Class	**Type**	
XmNbottomShadowColor	dynamic	CSG
XmCBottomShadowColor	Pixel	
XmNbottomShadowPixmap	XmUNSPECIFIED_PIXMAP	CSG
XmCBottomShadowPixmap	Pixmap	
XmNforeground	dynamic	CSG
XmCForeground	Pixel	
XmNhelpCallback	NULL	C
XmCCallback	XtCallbackList	
XmNhighlightColor	dynamic	CSG
XmCHighlightColor	Pixel	
XmNhighlightOnEnter	False	CSG
XmCHighlightOnEnter	Boolean	
XmNhighlightPixmap	dynamic	CSG
XmCHighlightPixmap	Pixmap	
XmNhighlightThickness	0	CSG
XmCHighlightThickness	Dimension	
XmNnavigationType	XmNONE	CSG
XmCNavigationType	XmNavigationType	
XmNshadowThickness	0	CSG
XmCShadowThickness	Dimension	
XmNtopShadowColor	dynamic	CSG
XmCTopShadowColor	Pixel	

XmLabel(3X)

Name	Default	Access
Class	Type	
XmNtopShadowPixmap	dynamic	CSG
XmCTopShadowPixmap	Pixmap	
XmNtraversalOn	False	CSG
XmCTraversalOn	Boolean	
XmNuserData	NULL	CSG
XmCUserData	XtPointer	

Core Resource Set		
Name	Default	Access
Class	Type	
XmNaccelerators	dynamic	CSG
XmCAccelerators	XtAccelerators	
XmNancestorSensitive	dynamic	G
XmCSensitive	Boolean	
XmNbackground	dynamic	CSG
XmCBackground	Pixel	
XmNbackgroundPixmap	XmUNSPECIFIED_PIXMAP	CSG
XmCPixmap	Pixmap	
XmNborderColor	XtDefaultForeground	CSG
XmCBorderColor	Pixel	
XmNborderPixmap	XmUNSPECIFIED_PIXMAP	CSG
XmCPixmap	Pixmap	
XmNborderWidth	0	CSG
XmCBorderWidth	Dimension	
XmNcolormap	dynamic	CG
XmCColormap	Colormap	
XmNdepth	dynamic	CG
XmCDepth	int	
XmNdestroyCallback	NULL	C
XmCCallback	XtCallbackList	
XmNheight	dynamic	CSG
XmCHeight	Dimension	

Name
    Class
	Default
	    Type
		Access

XmNinitialResourcesPersistent
    XmCInitialResourcesPersistent
	True
	    Boolean
		C

XmNmappedWhenManaged
    XmCMappedWhenManaged
	True
	    Boolean
		CSG

XmNscreen
    XmCScreen
	dynamic
	    Screen *
		CG

XmNsensitive
    XmCSensitive
	True
	    Boolean
		CSG

XmNtranslations
    XmCTranslations
	dynamic
	    XtTranslations
		CSG

XmNwidth
    XmCWidth
	dynamic
	    Dimension
		CSG

XmNx
    XmCPosition
	0
	    Position
		CSG

XmNy
    XmCPosition
	0
	    Position
		CSG

Action Routines

The **XmLabel** action routines are

Help():   In a Popup or Pulldown MenuPane, unposts all menus in the menu hierarchy and, when the shell's keyboard focus policy is **XmEXPLICIT**, restores keyboard focus to the widget that had the focus before the menu system was entered. Calls the callbacks for **XmNhelpCallback** if any exist. If there are no help callbacks for this widget, this action calls the help callbacks for the nearest ancestor that has them.

MenuEscape():

In a MenuBar, disarms the CascadeButton and the menu and, when the shell's keyboard focus policy is **XmEXPLICIT**, restores keyboard focus to the widget that had the focus before the menu was entered.

In a top-level Pulldown MenuPane from a MenuBar, unposts the menu, disarms the MenuBar CascadeButton and the MenuBar, and, when the shell's keyboard focus policy is **XmEXPLICIT**, restores keyboard focus to the widget that had the focus before the MenuBar was entered. In other Pulldown MenuPanes, unposts the menu and moves the focus to its CascadeButton.

In a Popup MenuPane, unposts the menu and, when the shell's keyboard focus policy is **XmEXPLICIT**, restores keyboard focus to the widget from which the menu was posted.

MenuTraverseDown():

If the current menu item has a submenu and is in a MenuBar, then this action posts the submenu, disarms the current menu item, and arms the submenu's first traversable menu item.

If the current menu item is in a MenuPane, then this action disarms the current menu item and arms the item below it. This action wraps within the MenuPane. When the current menu item is at the MenuPane's bottom edge, then this action wraps to the topmost menu item in the column to the right, if one exists. When the current menu item is at the bottom, rightmost corner of the MenuPane, then this action wraps to the tear-off control, if present, or to the top, leftmost menu item.

MenuTraverseLeft():

When the current menu item is in a MenuBar, then this action disarms the current item and arms the MenuBar item to the left. This action wraps within the MenuBar.

In MenuPanes, if the current menu item is not at the left edge of a MenuPane, this action disarms the current item and arms the item to its left. If the current menu item is at the left edge of a submenu attached to a MenuBar item, then this action unposts the submenu and traverses to the MenuBar item to the left, wrapping if necessary. If that MenuBar item has a submenu, it posts the submenu and arms the first traversable item in the submenu. If the current menu item is at the left edge of a submenu not directly attached to a MenuBar item, then this action unposts the current submenu only.

In Popup or Torn-off MenuPanes, when the current menu item is at the left edge, this action wraps within the MenuPane. If the current menu item is at the left edge of the MenuPane and not in the top row, this action wraps to the rightmost menu item in the row above. If the current menu item is in the upper, leftmost corner, this action wraps to the tear-off control, if present, or else it wraps to the bottom, rightmost menu item in the MenuPane.

MenuTraverseRight():

If the current menu item is in a MenuBar, then this action disarms the current item and arms the MenuBar item to the right. This action wraps within the MenuBar.

In MenuPanes, if the current menu item is a CascadeButton, then this action posts its associated submenu. If the current menu item is not a CascadeButton and is not at the right edge of a MenuPane, this action disarms the current item and arms the item to its right, wrapping if necessary. If the current menu item is not a CascadeButton and is at the right edge of a submenu that is a descendent of a MenuBar, then this action unposts all submenus and traverses to the MenuBar item to the right. If that MenuBar item has a submenu, it posts the submenu and arms the submenu's first traversable item.

In Popup or Torn-off menus, if the current menu item is not a CascadeButton and is at the right edge of a row (except the bottom row), this action wraps to the leftmost menu item in the row below. If the current menu item is not a CascadeButton and is in the bottom, rightmost corner of a Popup or Pulldown MenuPane, this action wraps to the tear-off control, if present, or else it wraps to the top, leftmost menu item of the MenuPane.

MenuTraverseUp():
When the current menu item is in a MenuPane, then this action disarms the current menu item and arms the item above it. This action wraps within the MenuPane. When the current menu item is at the MenuPane's top edge, then this action wraps to the bottommost menu item in the column to the left, if one exists. When the current menu item is at the top, leftmost corner of the MenuPane, then this action wraps to the tear-off control, if present, or to the bottom, rightmost menu item.

Related Information

Core(3X), **XmCreateLabel(3X)**, **XmFontListAppendEntry(3X)**, **XmStringCreate(3X)**, **XmStringCreateLtoR(3X)**, and **XmPrimitive(3X)**.

XmLabelGadget—The LabelGadget widget class

AES Support Level

Full-use

History/Direction

Changes have been made in the determination of default label strings (for trial-use).

Synopsis

#include <Xm/LabelG.h>

Description

LabelGadget is an instantiable widget and is also used as a superclass for other button gadgets, such as PushButtonGadget and ToggleButtonGadget.

LabelGadget can contain either text or a pixmap. LabelGadget text is a compound string. Refer to the *OSF/Motif Programmer's* Guide for more information on compound strings. The text can be multilingual, multiline, and/or multifont. When a LabelGadget is insensitive, its text is stippled, or the user-supplied insensitive pixmap is displayed.

LabelGadget supports both accelerators and mnemonics primarily for use in LabelGadget subclass widgets that are contained in menus. Mnemonics are available in a menu system when the button is visible. Accelerators in a menu system are accessible even when the button is not visible. The LabelGadget displays the mnemonic by underlining the first matching character in the text string. The accelerator is displayed as a text string adjacent to the label text or pixmap.

LabelGadget consists of many margin fields surrounding the text or pixmap. These margin fields are resources that may be set by the user, but LabelGadget subclasses and Manager parents also modify some of these fields. They tend to modify the **XmNmarginLeft**, **XmNmarginRight**, **XmNmarginTop**, and **XmNmarginBottom** resources and leave the **XmNmarginWidth** and **XmNmarginHeight** resources as set by the application.

In a LabelGadget, **XmNtraversalOn** and **XmNhighlightOnEnter** are forced to False inside Popup MenuPanes, Pulldown MenuPanes, and OptionMenus. Otherwise these resources default to False.

Classes

LabelGadget inherits behavior and resources from **Object**, **RectObj** and **XmGadget**.

The class pointer is **xmLabelGadgetClass**.

The class name is **XmLabelGadget**.

New Resources

The following table defines a set of widget resources used by the programmer to specify data. The programmer can also set the resource values for the inherited classes to set attributes for this widget. To reference a resource by name or by class in a **.Xdefaults** file, remove the **XmN** or **XmC** prefix and use the remaining letters. To specify one of the defined values for a resource in a **.Xdefaults** file, remove the **Xm** prefix and use the remaining letters (in either lowercase or uppercase, but include any underscores between words). The codes in the access column indicate if the given resource can be set at creation time (C), set by using **XtSetValues** (S), retrieved by using **XtGetValues** (G), or is not applicable (N/A).

XmLabelGadget Resource Set		
Name	**Default**	**Access**
Class	**Type**	
XmNaccelerator	NULL	CSG
XmCAccelerator	String	
XmNacceleratorText	NULL	CSG
XmCAcceleratorText	XmString	
XmNalignment	dynamic	CSG
XmCAlignment	unsigned char	
XmNfontList	dynamic	CSG
XmCFontList	XmFontList	
XmNlabelInsensitivePixmap	XmUNSPECIFIED_PIXMAP	CSG
XmCLabelInsensitivePixmap	Pixmap	
XmNlabelPixmap	XmUNSPECIFIED_PIXMAP	CSG
XmCLabelPixmap	Pixmap	
XmNlabelString	dynamic	CSG
XmCXmString	XmString	
XmNlabelType	XmSTRING	CSG
XmCLabelType	unsigned char	
XmNmarginBottom	0	CSG
XmCMarginBottom	Dimension	
XmNmarginHeight	2	CSG
XmCMarginHeight	Dimension	
XmNmarginLeft	0	CSG
XmCMarginLeft	Dimension	
XmNmarginRight	0	CSG
XmCMarginRight	Dimension	
XmNmarginTop	0	CSG
XmCMarginTop	Dimension	
XmNmarginWidth	2	CSG
XmCMarginWidth	Dimension	

Name	Default	Access
Class	Type	
XmNmnemonic	NULL	CSG
XmCMnemonic	KeySym	
XmNmnemonicCharSet	dynamic	CSG
XmCMnemonicCharSet	String	
XmNrecomputeSize	True	CSG
XmCRecomputeSize	Boolean	
XmNstringDirection	dynamic	CSG
XmCStringDirection	XmStringDirection	

XmNaccelerator

Sets the accelerator on a button widget in a menu, which activates a visible or invisible, but managed, button from the keyboard. This resource is a string that describes a set of modifiers and the key that may be used to select the button. The format of this string is identical to that used by the translations manager, with the exception that only a single event may be specified and only **KeyPress** events are allowed.

Accelerators for buttons are supported only for PushButtonGadget and ToggleButtonGadget in Pulldown and Popup menus.

XmNacceleratorText

Specifies the text displayed for the accelerator. The text is displayed adjacent to the label string or pixmap. Accelerator text for buttons is displayed only for PushButtonGadgets and ToggleButtonGadgets in Pulldown and Popup Menus.

XmNalignment

Specifies the label alignment for text or pixmap.

XmALIGNMENT_BEGINNING (left alignment)

Causes the left sides of the lines of text to be vertically aligned with the left edge of the gadget. For a pixmap, its left side is vertically aligned with the left edge of the gadget.

XmALIGNMENT_CENTER (center alignment)

Causes the centers of the lines of text to be vertically aligned in the center of the gadget. For a pixmap, its center is vertically aligned with the center of the gadget.

XmALIGNMENT_END (right alignment)

Causes the right sides of the lines of text to be vertically aligned with the right edge of the gadget. For a pixmap, its right side is vertically aligned with the right edge of the gadget.

The preceding descriptions for text are correct when **XmNstringDirection** is **XmSTRING_DIRECTION_L_TO_R**; the descriptions for **XmALIGNMENT_BEGINNING** and **XmALIGNMENT_END** are switched when the resource is **XmSTRING_DIRECTION_R_TO_L**.

If the parent is a RowColumn whose **XmNisAligned** resource is True, **XmNalignment** is forced to the same value as the RowColumn's **XmNentryAlignment** if the RowColumn's **XmNrowColumnType** is **XmWORK_AREA** or if the gadget is a subclass of **XmLabelGadget**. Otherwise, the default is **XmALIGNMENT_CENTER**.

XmNfontList Specifies the font of the text used in the gadget. If this value is NULL at initialization, the parent hierarchy of the widget is searched for an ancestor that is a subclass of the **XmBulletinBoard**, **VendorShell**, or **XmMenuShell** widget class. If such an ancestor is found, the font list is initialized to the **XmNbuttonFontList** (for button gadget subclasses) or **XmNlabelFontList** of the ancestor widget. If no such ancestor is found, the default is implementation dependent. Refer to **XmFontList(3X)** for more information on the creation and structure of a font list.

XmNlabelInsensitivePixmap

Specifies a pixmap used as the button face if **XmNlabelType** is **XmPIXMAP** and the button is insensitive.

XmNlabelPixmap

Specifies the pixmap when **XmNlabelType** is **XmPIXMAP**.

XmNlabelString

Specifies the compound string when **XmNlabelType** is **XmSTRING**. If the value of this resource is NULL, it is initialized to name of the gadget converted to a compound string. Refer to **XmString(3X)** for more information on the creation and the structure of compound strings.

XmNlabelType

Specifies the label type.

XmSTRING Text displays **XmNlabelString**

XmPIXMAP Icon data in pixmap displays **XmNlabelPixmap** or **XmNlabelInsensitivePixmap**

XmNmarginBottom

>Specifies the amount of spacing between the bottom of the label text and the top of the bottom margin (specified by **XmNmarginHeight**). This may be modified by LabelGadget's subclasses. For example, CascadeButtonGadget may increase this field to make room for the cascade pixmap.

XmNmarginHeight

>Specifies the amount of spacing between the top of the label (specified by **XmNmarginTop**) and the bottom edge of the top shadow, and the amount of spacing between the bottom of the label (specified by **XmNmarginBottom**) and the top edge of the bottom shadow.

XmNmarginLeft

>Specifies the amount of spacing between the left edge of the label text and the right side of the left margin (specified by **XmNmarginWidth**). This may be modified by LabelGadget's subclasses. For example, ToggleButtonGadget may increase this field to make room for the toggle indicator and for spacing between the indicator and label. Whether this actually applies to the left or right side of the label may depend on the value of **XmNstringDirection**.

XmNmarginRight

>Specifies the amount of spacing between the right edge of the label text and the left side of the right margin (specified by **XmNmarginWidth**). This may be modified by LabelGadget's subclasses. For example, CascadeButtonGadget may increase this field to make room for the cascade pixmap. Whether this actually applies to the left or right side of the label may depend on the value of **XmNstringDirection**.

XmNmarginTop

>Specifies the amount of spacing between the top of the label text and the bottom of the top margin (specified by **XmNmarginHeight**). This may be modified by LabelGadget's subclasses. For example, CascadeButtonGadget may increase this field to make room for the cascade pixmap.

XmNmarginWidth

Specifies the amount of spacing between the left side of the label (specified by **XmNmarginLeft**) and the right edge of the left shadow, and the amount of spacing between the right side of the label (specified by **XmNmarginRight**) and the left edge of the right shadow.

XmNmnemonic

Provides the user with an alternate means of selecting a button. A button in a MenuBar, a Popup MenuPane, or a Pulldown MenuPane can have a mnemonic.

This resource contains a keysym as listed in the X11 keysym table. The first character in the label string that exactly matches the mnemonic in the character set specified in **XmNmnemonicCharSet** is underlined when the button is displayed.

When a mnemonic has been specified, the user activates the button by pressing the mnemonic key while the button is visible. If the button is a CascadeButtonGadget in a MenuBar and the MenuBar does not have the focus, the user must use the **MAlt** modifier while pressing the mnemonic. The user can activate the button by pressing either the shifted or the unshifted mnemonic key.

XmNmnemonicCharSet

Specifies the character set of the mnemonic for the label. The default is **XmFONTLIST_DEFAULT_TAG**.

XmNrecomputeSize

Specifies a Boolean value that indicates whether the gadget attempts to be big enough to contain the label. If True, an **XtSetValues** with a resource value that would change the size of the gadget causes the gadget to shrink or expand to exactly fit the label string or pixmap. If False, the gadget never attempts to change size on its own.

XmNstringDirection

Specifies the direction in which the string is to be drawn.

XmSTRING_DIRECTION_L_TO_R   Left to right

XmSTRING_DIRECTION_R_TO_L   Right to left

The default for this resource is determined at creation time. If no value is specified for this resource and the widget's parent is a manager, the value is inherited from the parent; otherwise, it defaults to **XmSTRING_DIRECTION_L_TO_R**.

Inherited Resources

LabelGadget inherits behavior and resources from the superclasses described in the following tables. For a complete description of each resource, refer to the reference page for that superclass.

XmGadget Resource Set		
Name	**Default**	**Access**
Class	**Type**	
XmNhelpCallback	NULL	C
XmCCallback	XtCallbackList	
XmNhighlightOnEnter	False	CSG
XmCHighlightOnEnter	Boolean	
XmNhighlightThickness	0	CSG
XmCHighlightThickness	Dimension	
XmNnavigationType	XmNONE	CSG
XmCNavigationType	XmNavigationType	
XmNshadowThickness	0	CSG
XmCShadowThickness	Dimension	
XmNtraversalOn	False	CSG
XmCTraversalOn	Boolean	
XmNuserData	NULL	CSG
XmCUserData	XtPointer	

RectObj Resource Set		
Name	**Default**	**Access**
Class	**Type**	
XmNancestorSensitive	dynamic	G
XmCSensitive	Boolean	
XmNborderWidth	0	N/A
XmCBorderWidth	Dimension	
XmNheight	dynamic	CSG
XmCHeight	Dimension	
XmNsensitive	True	CSG
XmCSensitive	Boolean	
XmNwidth	dynamic	CSG
XmCWidth	Dimension	
XmNx	0	CSG
XmCPosition	Position	
XmNy	0	CSG
XmCPosition	Position	

Object Resource Set		
Name	**Default**	**Access**
Class	**Type**	
XmNdestroyCallback	NULL	C
XmCCallback	XtCallbackList	

Related Information

Object(3X), **RectObj(3X)**, **XmCreateLabelGadget(3X)**,
XmFontListCreate(3X), **XmStringCreate(3X)**, **XmStringCreateLtoR(3X)**, and
XmGadget(3X).

XmList—The List widget class

AES Support Level

Full-use

History/Direction

The visible item count default value is now dynamic (for trial-use). The valid return fields in the **XmListCallbackStruct** for the reason **XmCR_DEFAULT_ACTION** are being extended in revision D to include *selected_items*, *selected_item_count*, and *selected_item_positions*.

Synopsis

#include <Xm/List.h>

Description

List allows a user to select one or more items from a group of choices. Items are selected from the list in a variety of ways, using both the pointer and the keyboard. List operates on an array of compound strings that are defined by the application. Each compound string becomes an item in the List, with the first compound string becoming the item in position 1, the second becoming the item in position 2, and so on.

Specifying the number of items that are visible sets the size of the List. If the number of visible items is not specified, the height of the list controls the number of visible items. Each item assumes the height of the tallest element in the list. To create a list that allows the user to scroll easily through a large number of items, use the **XmCreateScrolledList** convenience function.

To select items, move the pointer or cursor to the desired item and press the **BSelect** mouse button or the key defined as **KSelect**. There are several styles of selection behavior, and they all highlight the selected item or items by displaying them in inverse colors. An appropriate callback is invoked to notify the application of the user's choice. The application then takes whatever action is required for the specified selection.

Selection

Each list has one of four selection models:

- Single Select

- Browse Select

- Multiple Select

- Extended Select

In Single Select and Browse Select, at most one item is selected at a time. In Single Select, pressing **BSelect** on an item toggles its selection state and deselects any other selected item. In Browse Select, pressing **BSelect** on an item selects it and deselects any other selected item; dragging **BSelect** moves the selection along with the cursor.

In Multiple Select, any number of items can be selected at a time. Pressing **BSelect** on an item toggles its selection state but does not deselect any other selected items.

In Extended Select, any number of items can be selected at a time, and the user can easily select ranges of items. Pressing **BSelect** on an item selects it and deselects any other selected item. Dragging **BSelect** or pressing or dragging **BExtend** following a **BSelect** action selects all items between the item under the pointer and the item on which **BSelect** was pressed. This action also deselects any other selected items outside that range.

Extended Select also allows the user to select and deselect discontiguous ranges of items. Pressing **BToggle** on an item toggles its selection state but does not deselect any other selected items. Dragging **BToggle** or pressing or dragging **BExtend** following a **BToggle** action sets the selection state of all items between the item under the pointer and the item on which **BToggle** was pressed to the state of the item on which **BToggle** was pressed. This action does not deselect any other selected items outside that range.

All selection operations available from the mouse are also available from the keyboard. List has two keyboard selection modes, Normal Mode and Add Mode. In Normal Mode, navigation operations and **KSelect** select the item at the location cursor and deselect any other selected items. In Add Mode, navigation operations have no effect on selection, and **KSelect** toggles the selection state of the item at the location cursor without deselecting any other selected items, except in Single Select.

Single and Multiple Select use Add Mode, and Browse Select uses Normal Mode.

Extended Select can use either mode; the user changes modes by pressing **KAddMode**. In Extended Select Normal Mode, pressing **KSelect** has the same effect as pressing **BSelect**; **KExtend** and shifted navigation have the same effect as pressing **BExtend** following a **BSelect** action. In Extended Select Add Mode, pressing **KSelect** has the same effect as pressing **BToggle**; **KExtend** and shifted navigation have the same effect as pressing **BExtend** following a **BToggle** action.

Normal Mode is indicated by a solid location cursor, and Add Mode is indicated by a dashed location cursor.

Classes

List inherits behavior and resources from **Core** and **XmPrimitive**.

The class pointer is **xmListWidgetClass**.

The class name is **XmList**.

New Resources

The following table defines a set of widget resources used by the programmer to specify data. The programmer can also set the resource values for the inherited classes to set attributes for this widget. To reference a resource by name or by class in a **.Xdefaults** file, remove the **XmN** or **XmC** prefix and use the remaining letters. To specify one of the defined values for a resource in a **.Xdefaults** file, remove the **Xm** prefix and use the remaining letters (in either lowercase or uppercase, but include any underscores between words). The codes in the access column indicate if the given resource can be set at creation time (C), set by using **XtSetValues** (S), retrieved by using **XtGetValues** (G), or is not applicable (N/A).

XmList Resource Set		
Name	**Default**	**Access**
Class	**Type**	
XmNautomaticSelection	False	CSG
XmCAutomaticSelection	Boolean	
XmNbrowseSelectionCallback	NULL	C
XmCCallback	XtCallbackList	
XmNdefaultActionCallback	NULL	C
XmCCallback	XtCallbackList	
XmNextendedSelectionCallback	NULL	C
XmCCallback	XtCallbackList	
XmNfontList	dynamic	CSG
XmCFontList	XmFontList	
XmNitemCount	0	CSG
XmCItemCount	int	
XmNitems	NULL	CSG
XmCItems	XmStringTable	
XmNlistMarginHeight	0	CSG
XmCListMarginHeight	Dimension	
XmNlistMarginWidth	0	CSG
XmCListMarginWidth	Dimension	
XmNlistSizePolicy	XmVARIABLE	CG
XmCListSizePolicy	unsigned char	
XmNlistSpacing	0	CSG
XmCListSpacing	Dimension	
XmNmultipleSelectionCallback	NULL	C
XmCCallback	XtCallbackList	
XmNscrollBarDisplayPolicy	XmAS_NEEDED	CSG
XmCScrollBarDisplayPolicy	unsigned char	
XmNselectedItemCount	0	CSG
XmCSelectedItemCount	int	

Name	Default	Access
Class	Type	
XmNselectedItems	NULL	CSG
XmCSelectedItems	XmStringTable	
XmNselectionPolicy	XmBROWSE_SELECT	CSG
XmCSelectionPolicy	unsigned char	
XmNsingleSelectionCallback	NULL	C
XmCCallback	XtCallbackList	
XmNstringDirection	dynamic	CSG
XmCStringDirection	XmStringDirection	
XmNtopItemPosition	1	CSG
XmCTopItemPosition	int	
XmNvisibleItemCount	dynamic	CSG
XmCVisibleItemCount	int	

XmNautomaticSelection

Invokes either **XmNbrowseSelectionCallback** or **XmNextendedSelectionCallback** when BSelect is pressed and the items that are shown as selected change if the value is True and the selection mode is either **XmBROWSE_SELECT** or **XmEXTENDED_SELECT** respectively. If False, no selection callbacks are invoked until the user releases the mouse button. See **Behavior** for further details on the interaction of this resource with the selection modes.

XmNbrowseSelectionCallback

Specifies a list of callbacks that is called when an item is selected in the browse selection mode. The reason is **XmCR_BROWSE_SELECT**.

XmNdefaultActionCallback

Specifies a list of callbacks that is called when an item is double clicked. The reason is **XmCR_DEFAULT_ACTION**.

XmNextendedSelectionCallback

Specifies a list of callbacks that is called when items are selected using the extended selection mode. The reason is **XmCR_EXTENDED_SELECT**.

XmNfontList Specifies the font list associated with the list items. This is used in conjunction with the **XmNvisibleItemCount** resource to determine the height of the List widget. If this value is NULL at initialization, the parent hierarchy of the widget is searched for an ancestor that is a subclass of the XmBulletinBoard or VendorShell widget class. If such an ancestor is found, the font list is initialized to the **XmNtextFontList** of the ancestor widget. If no such ancestor is found, the default is implementation dependent. Refer to **XmFontList(3X)** for more information on a font list structure.

XmNitemCount

Specifies the total number of items. The value must be the number of items in **XmNitems** and must not be negative. It is automatically updated by the list whenever an item is added to or deleted from the list.

XmNitems Points to an array of compound strings that are to be displayed as the list items. Refer to **XmString(3X)** for more information on the creation and structure of compound strings.

XmNlistMarginHeight

Specifies the height of the margin between the list border and the items.

XmNlistMarginWidth

Specifies the width of the margin between the list border and the items.

XmNlistSizePolicy

Controls the reaction of the List when an item grows horizontally beyond the current size of the list work area. If the value is **XmCONSTANT**, the list viewing area does not grow, and a horizontal ScrollBar is added for a ScrolledList. If this resource is set to **XmVARIABLE**, the List grows to match the size of the longest item, and no horizontal ScrollBar appears.

When the value of this resource is **XmRESIZE_IF_POSSIBLE**, the List attempts to grow or shrink to match the width of the widest item. If it cannot grow to match the widest size, a horizontal ScrollBar is added for a ScrolledList if the longest item is wider than the list viewing area.

The size policy must be set at the time the List widget is created. It cannot be changed at a later time through **XtSetValues**.

XmNlistSpacing

Specifies the spacing between list items. This spacing increases by the value of the **XmNhighlightThickness** resource in Primitive.

XmNmultipleSelectionCallback

Specifies a list of callbacks that is called when an item is selected in multiple selection mode. The reason is **XmCR_MULTIPLE_SELECT**.

XmNscrollBarDisplayPolicy

Controls the display of vertical ScrollBars in a ScrolledList. When the value of this resource is **XmAS_NEEDED**, a vertical ScrollBar is displayed only when the number of items in the List exceeds the number of visible items. When the value is **XmSTATIC**, a vertical ScrollBar is always displayed.

XmNselectedItemCount

Specifies the number of strings in the selected items list. The value must be the number of items in **XmNselectedItems** and must not be negative.

XmNselectedItems

Points to an array of compound strings that represents the list items that are currently selected, either by the user or by the application.

XmNselectionPolicy

Defines the interpretation of the selection action. This can be one of the following:

XmSINGLE_SELECT

Allows only single selections

XmMULTIPLE_SELECT

Allows multiple selections

XmEXTENDED_SELECT

Allows extended selections

XmBROWSE_SELECT

Allows drag-and-browse functionality

XmNsingleSelectionCallback

Specifies a list of callbacks that is called when an item is selected in single selection mode. The reason is **XmCR_SINGLE_SELECT**.

XmNstringDirection

Specifies the initial direction to draw the string. The values for this resource are **XmSTRING_DIRECTION_L_TO_R** and **XmSTRING_DIRECTION_R_TO_L**. The value of this resource is determined at creation time. If the widget's parent is a manager, this value is inherited from the widget's parent; otherwise it is set to **XmSTRING_DIRECTION_L_TO_R**.

XmNtopItemPosition

Specifies the position of the item that is the first visible item in the list. Setting this resource is equivalent to calling the **XmListSetPos** function. The position of the first item in the list is 1; the position of the second item is 2; and so on. A position of 0 (zero) specifies the last item in the list. The value must not be negative.

XmNvisibleItemCount

Specifies the number of items that can fit in the visible space of the list work area. The List uses this value to determine its height. The value must be greater than 0 (zero).

Inherited Resources

List inherits behavior and resources from the superclasses described in the following tables. For a complete description of each resource, refer to the reference page for that superclass.

XmPrimitive Resource Set		

Name
   Class
	Default
	   Type
		Access

XmNbottomShadowColor
   XmCBottomShadowColor
	dynamic
	   Pixel
		CSG

XmNbottomShadowPixmap
   XmCBottomShadowPixmap
	XmUNSPECIFIED_PIXMAP
	   Pixmap
		CSG

XmNforeground
   XmCForeground
	dynamic
	   Pixel
		CSG

XmNhelpCallback
   XmCCallback
	NULL
	   XtCallbackList
		C

XmNhighlightColor
   XmCHighlightColor
	dynamic
	   Pixel
		CSG

XmNhighlightOnEnter
   XmCHighlightOnEnter
	False
	   Boolean
		CSG

XmNhighlightPixmap
   XmCHighlightPixmap
	dynamic
	   Pixmap
		CSG

XmNhighlightThickness
   XmCHighlightThickness
	2
	   Dimension
		CSG

XmNnavigationType
   XmCNavigationType
	XmTAB_GROUP
	   XmNavigationType
		CSG

XmNshadowThickness
   XmCShadowThickness
	2
	   Dimension
		CSG

XmNtopShadowColor
   XmCTopShadowColor
	dynamic
	   Pixel
		CSG

XmNtopShadowPixmap
   XmCTopShadowPixmap
	dynamic
	   Pixmap
		CSG

XmNtraversalOn
   XmCTraversalOn
	True
	   Boolean
		CSG

XmNuserData
   XmCUserData
	NULL
	   XtPointer
		CSG

Core Resource Set		
Name	**Default**	**Access**
Class	**Type**	
XmNaccelerators	dynamic	CSG
XmCAccelerators	XtAccelerators	
XmNancestorSensitive	dynamic	G
XmCSensitive	Boolean	
XmNbackground	dynamic	CSG
XmCBackground	Pixel	
XmNbackgroundPixmap	XmUNSPECIFIED_PIXMAP	CSG
XmCPixmap	Pixmap	
XmNborderColor	XtDefaultForeground	CSG
XmCBorderColor	Pixel	
XmNborderPixmap	XmUNSPECIFIED_PIXMAP	CSG
XmCPixmap	Pixmap	
XmNborderWidth	0	CSG
XmCBorderWidth	Dimension	
XmNcolormap	dynamic	CG
XmCColormap	Colormap	
XmNdepth	dynamic	CG
XmCDepth	int	
XmNdestroyCallback	NULL	C
XmCCallback	XtCallbackList	
XmNheight	dynamic	CSG
XmCHeight	Dimension	
XmNinitialResourcesPersistent	True	C
XmCInitialResourcesPersistent	Boolean	
XmNmappedWhenManaged	True	CSG
XmCMappedWhenManaged	Boolean	
XmNscreen	dynamic	CG
XmCScreen	Screen *	
XmNsensitive	True	CSG
XmCSensitive	Boolean	

Name	Default	Access
Class	Type	
XmNtranslations	dynamic	CSG
XmCTranslations	XtTranslations	
XmNwidth	dynamic	CSG
XmCWidth	Dimension	
XmNx	0	CSG
XmCPosition	Position	
XmNy	0	CSG
XmCPosition	Position	

Callback Information

List defines a new callback structure. The application must first look at the reason field and use only the structure members that are valid for that particular reason, because not all fields are relevant for every possible reason. The callback structure is defined as follows:

```
typedef struct
{
    int           reason;
    XEvent        *event;
    XmString      item;
    int           item_length;
    int           item_position;
    XmString      *selected_items;
    int           selected_item_count;
    int           *selected_item_positions;
    char          selection_type;
} XmListCallbackStruct;
```

reason　　　　Indicates why the callback was invoked.

event　　　　Points to the **XEvent** that triggered the callback. It can be NULL.

item　　　　The last item selected at the time of the *event* that caused the callback. *item* points to a temporary storage space that is reused after the callback is finished. Therefore, if an application needs to save the item, it should copy the item into its own data space.

item_length　　The length in bytes of *item*.

item_position

　　　　The position of *item* in the List's **XmNitems** array.

selected_items

> A list of items selected at the time of the *event* that caused the callback. *selected_items* points to a temporary storage space that is reused after the callback is finished. Therefore, if an application needs to save the selected list, it should copy the list into its own data space.

selected_item_count

> The number of items in the *selected_items* list. This number must be non-negative.

selected_item_positions

> An array of integers, one for each selected item, representing the position of each selected item in the List's **XmNitems** array. *selected_item_positions* points to a temporary storage space that is reused after the callback is finished. Therefore, if an application needs to save this array, it should copy the array into its own data space.

selection_type

> Indicates that the most recent extended selection was the initial selection (**XmINITIAL**), a modification of an existing selection (**XmMODIFICATION**), or an additional noncontiguous selection (**XmADDITION**).

The following table describes the reasons for which the individual callback structure fields are valid.

Reason	Valid Fields
XmCR_SINGLE_SELECT	*reason, event, item, item_length, item_position*
XmCR_DEFAULT_ACTION	*reason, event, item, item_length, item_position*
XmCR_BROWSE_SELECT	*reason, event, item, item_length, item_position*
XmCR_MULTIPLE_SELECT	*reason, event, item, item_length, item_position, selected_items, selected_item_count, selected_item_positions*
XmCR_EXTENDED_SELECT	*reason, event, item, item_length, item_position, selected_items, selected_item_count, selected_item_positions, selection_type*

Action Routines

The **XmList** action routines are described in the following list. The current selection is always shown with inverted colors.

ListAddMode():
> Toggles the state of Add Mode for keyboard selection.

ListBeginData():
> Moves the location cursor to the first item in the list. In Normal Mode, this also deselects any current selection, selects the first item in the list, and calls the appropriate selection callbacks (**XmNbrowseSelectionCallback** when **XmNselectionPolicy** is set to **XmBROWSE_SELECT**, **XmNextendedSelectionCallback** when **XmNselectionPolicy** is set to **XmEXTENDED_SELECT**).

ListBeginDataExtend():
> If **XmNselectionPolicy** is set to **XmMULTIPLE_SELECT** or **XmEXTENDED_SELECT**, this action moves the location cursor to the first item in the list.

> If **XmNselectionPolicy** is set to **XmEXTENDED_SELECT**, this action does the following: If an extended selection has been made from the current anchor point, restores the selection state of the items in that range to their state before the extended selection was done; changes the selection state of the first item and all items between it and the current anchor point to the state of the item at the current anchor point; calls the **XmNextendedSelectionCallback** callbacks.

ListBeginExtend():
> If **XmNselectionPolicy** is set to **XmEXTENDED_SELECT**, this action does the following: If an extended selection has been made from the current anchor point, restores the selection state of the items in that range to their state before the extended selection was done, and changes the selection state of the item under the pointer and all items between it and the current anchor point to the state of the item at the current anchor point. If **XmNautomaticSelection** is set to True, this action calls the **XmNextendedSelectionCallback** callbacks.

ListBeginLine():
> Moves the horizontal scroll region to the beginning of the line.

ListBeginSelect():
> If **XmNselectionPolicy** is set to **XmSINGLE_SELECT**, deselects any current selection and toggles the selection state of the item under the pointer.

> If **XmNselectionPolicy** is set to **XmBROWSE_SELECT**, deselects any current selection and selects the item under the

pointer. If **XmNautomaticSelection** is set to True, calls the **XmNbrowseSelectionCallback** callbacks.

If **XmNselectionPolicy** is set to **XmMULTIPLE_SELECT**, toggles the selection state of the item under the pointer. Any previous selections remain.

If **XmNselectionPolicy** is set to **XmEXTENDED_SELECT**, this action deselects any current selection, selects the item under the pointer, and sets the current anchor at that item. If **XmNautomaticSelection** is set to True, this action calls the **XmNextendedSelectionCallback** callbacks.

ListBeginToggle():

If **XmNselectionPolicy** is set to **XmEXTENDED_SELECT**, this action moves the current anchor to the item under the pointer without changing the current selection. If the item is unselected, this action selects it; if the item is selected, this action unselects it. If **XmNautomaticSelection** is set to True, this action calls the **XmNextendedSelectionCallback** callbacks.

ListButtonMotion():

If **XmNselectionPolicy** is set to **XmBROWSE_SELECT**, this action deselects any current selection and selects the item under the pointer. If **XmNautomaticSelection** is set to True and the pointer has entered a new list item, this action calls the **XmNbrowseSelectionCallback** callbacks.

If **XmNselectionPolicy** is set to **XmEXTENDED_SELECT**, this action does the following: If an extended selection is being made and an extended selection has previously been made from the current anchor point, restores the selection state of the items in that range to their state before the previous extended selection was done and changes the selection state of the item under the pointer and all items between it and the current anchor point to the state of the item at the current anchor point. If **XmNautomaticSelection** is set to True and the pointer has entered a new list item, calls the **XmNextendedSelectionCallback** callbacks.

If the pointer leaves a scrolled list, this action scrolls the list in the direction of the pointer motion.

ListEndData():

Moves the location cursor to the last item in the list. In Normal Mode, this also deselects any current selection, selects the last item in the list, and calls the appropriate selection callbacks (**XmNbrowseSelectionCallback** when **XmNselectionPolicy** is set to **XmBROWSE_SELECT**, **XmNextendedSelectionCallback** when **XmNselectionPolicy** is set to **XmEXTENDED_SELECT**).

ListEndDataExtend():

If **XmNselectionPolicy** is set to **XmMULTIPLE_SELECT** or **XmEXTENDED_SELECT**, this action moves the location cursor to the last item in the list.

If **XmNselectionPolicy** is set to **XmEXTENDED_SELECT**, this action does the following: If an extended selection has been made from the current anchor point, restores the selection state of the items in that range to their state before the extended selection was done; changes the selection state of the last item and all items between it and the current anchor point to the state of the item at the current anchor point; calls the **XmNextendedSelectionCallback** callbacks.

ListEndExtend():

If **XmNselectionPolicy** is set to **XmEXTENDED_SELECT**, this action moves the location cursor to the last item selected or deselected and, if **XmNautomaticSelection** is set to False, calls the **XmNextendedSelectionCallback** callbacks.

ListEndLine():

Moves the horizontal scroll region to the end of the line.

ListEndSelect():

If **XmNselectionPolicy** is set to **XmSINGLE_SELECT** or **XmMULTIPLE_SELECT**, this action moves the location cursor to the last item selected or deselected and calls the appropriate selection callbacks (**XmNsingleSelectionCallback** when **XmNselectionPolicy** is set to **XmSINGLE_SELECT**, **XmNmultipleSelectionCallback** when **XmNselectionPolicy** is set to **XmMULTIPLE_SELECT**).

If **XmNselectionPolicy** is set to **XmBROWSE_SELECT** or **XmEXTENDED_SELECT**, moves the location cursor to the last item selected or deselected and, if **XmNautomaticSelection** is set to False, calls the appropriate selection callbacks (**XmNbrowseSelectionCallback** when **XmNselectionPolicy** is set to **XmBROWSE_SELECT**, **XmNextendedSelectionCallback** when **XmNselectionPolicy** is set to **XmEXTENDED_SELECT**).

ListEndToggle():

If **XmNselectionPolicy** is set to **XmEXTENDED_SELECT**, moves the location cursor to the last item selected or deselected and, if **XmNautomaticSelection** is set to False, calls the **XmNextendedSelectionCallback** callbacks.

ListExtendNextItem():

If **XmNselectionPolicy** is set to **XmEXTENDED_SELECT**, this action does the following: If an extended selection has been made from the current anchor point, restores the selection state of the items in that range to their state before the extended selection was done; moves the location cursor to the next item and changes the selection state of the item and all items between it and the current anchor point to the state of the item at the current anchor point; calls the **XmNextendedSelectionCallback** callbacks.

ListExtendPrevItem():

If **XmNselectionPolicy** is set to **XmEXTENDED_SELECT**, this action does the following: If an extended selection has been made from the current anchor point, restores the selection state of the items in that range to their state before the extended selection was done; moves the location cursor to the previous item and changes the selection state of the item and all items between it and the current anchor point to the state of the item at the current anchor point; calls the **XmNextendedSelectionCallback** callbacks.

ListKbdActivate():

Calls the callbacks for **XmNdefaultActionCallback**. If the List's parent is a manager, this action passes the event to the parent.

ListKbdBeginExtend():

If **XmNselectionPolicy** is set to **XmEXTENDED_SELECT**, does the following: If an extended selection has been made from the current anchor point, restores the selection state of the items in that range to their state before the extended selection was done; changes the selection state of the item at the location cursor and all items between it and the current anchor point to the state of the item at the current anchor point. If **XmNautomaticSelection** is set to True, this action calls the **XmNextendedSelectionCallback** callbacks.

ListKbdBeginSelect():

If the **XmNselectionPolicy** is set to **XmSINGLE_SELECT**, deselects any current selection and toggles the state of the item at the location cursor.

If the **XmNselectionPolicy** is set to **XmBROWSE_SELECT**, deselects any current selection and selects the item at the location cursor. If **XmNautomaticSelection** is set to True, calls the **XmNbrowseSelectionCallback** callbacks.

If the **XmNselectionPolicy** is set to **XmMULTIPLE_SELECT**, toggles the selection state of the item at the location cursor. Any previous selections remain.

If the **XmNselectionPolicy** is set to **XmEXTENDED_SELECT**, moves the current anchor to the item at the location cursor. In Normal Mode, this action deselects any current selection and selects the item at the location cursor. In Add Mode, this action toggles the selection state of the item at the location cursor and leaves the current selection unchanged. If **XmNautomaticSelection** is set to True, this action calls the **XmNextendedSelectionCallback** callbacks.

ListKbdCancel():

If **XmNselectionPolicy** is set to **XmEXTENDED_SELECT** and an extended selection is being made from the current anchor point, this action cancels the new selection and restores the selection state of the items in that range to their state before the extended selection was done. If **XmNautomaticSelection** is set to True, this action calls the **XmNextendedSelectionCallback** callbacks; otherwise, if the parent is a manager, it passes the event to the parent.

ListKbdDeSelectAll():

If the **XmNselectionPolicy** is set to **XmSINGLE_SELECT**, **XmMULTIPLE_SELECT**, or **XmEXTENDED_SELECT** in Add Mode, this action deselects all items in the list. If the **XmNselectionPolicy** is set to **XmEXTENDED_SELECT** in Normal Mode, this action deselects all items in the list (except the item at the location cursor if the shell's **XmNkeyboardFocusPolicy** is **XmEXPLICIT**). This action also calls the appropriate selection callbacks (**XmNsingleSelectionCallback** when **XmNselectionPolicy** is set to **XmSINGLE_SELECT**, **XmNmultipleSelectionCallback** when **XmNselectionPolicy** is set to **XmMULTIPLE_SELECT**, **XmNextendedSelectionCallback** when **XmNselectionPolicy** is set to **XmEXTENDED_SELECT**).

ListKbdEndExtend():

If **XmNselectionPolicy** is set to **XmEXTENDED_SELECT** and if **XmNautomaticSelection** is set to False, this action calls the **XmNextendedSelectionCallback** callbacks.

ListKbdEndSelect():

If **XmNselectionPolicy** is set to **XmSINGLE_SELECT** or **XmMULTIPLE_SELECT** or if **XmNautomaticSelection** is set to False, calls the appropriate selection callbacks (**XmNsingleSelectionCallback** when **XmNselectionPolicy** is set to

XmSINGLE_SELECT, XmNbrowseSelectionCallback when **XmNselectionPolicy** is set to **XmBROWSE_SELECT**, **XmNmultipleSelectionCallback** when **XmNselectionPolicy** is set to **XmMULTIPLE_SELECT**, **XmNextendedSelectionCallback** when **XmNselectionPolicy** is set to **XmEXTENDED_SELECT**).

ListKbdSelectAll():

If **XmNselectionPolicy** is set to **XmSINGLE_SELECT** or **XmBROWSE_SELECT**, this action selects the item at the location cursor. If **XmNselectionPolicy** is set to **XmEXTENDED_SELECT** or **XmMULTIPLE_SELECT**, it selects all items in the list. This action also calls the appropriate selection callbacks (**XmNsingleSelectionCallback** when **XmNselectionPolicy** is set to **XmSINGLE_SELECT**, **XmNbrowseSelectionCallback** when **XmNselectionPolicy** is set to **XmBROWSE_SELECT**, **XmNmultipleSelectionCallback** when **XmNselectionPolicy** is set to **XmMULTIPLE_SELECT**, **XmNextendedSelectionCallback** when **XmNselectionPolicy** is set to **XmEXTENDED_SELECT**).

ListLeftChar():

Scrolls the list one character to the left.

ListLeftPage():

Scrolls the list one page to the left.

ListNextItem():

Moves the location cursor to the next item in the list.

If the **XmNselectionPolicy** is set to **XmBROWSE_SELECT**, this action also selects the next item, deselects any current selection, and calls the **XmNbrowseSelectionCallback** callbacks.

If the **XmNselectionPolicy** is set to **XmEXTENDED_SELECT**, this action in Normal Mode also selects the next item, deselects any current selection, moves the current anchor to the next item, and calls the **XmNextendedSelectionCallback** callbacks. In Add Mode, this action does not affect the selection or the anchor.

ListNextPage():

Scrolls the list to the next page, moving the location cursor to a new item.

If the **XmNselectionPolicy** is set to **XmBROWSE_SELECT**, this action also selects the new item, deselects any current selection, and calls the **XmNbrowseSelectionCallback** callbacks.

If the **XmNselectionPolicy** is set to **XmEXTENDED_SELECT**, this action in Normal Mode also selects the new item, deselects any current selection, moves the current anchor to the new item, and calls the **XmNextendedSelectionCallback** callbacks. In Add Mode, this action does not affect the selection or the anchor.

ListPrevItem():
Moves the location cursor to the previous item in the list.

If the **XmNselectionPolicy** is set to **XmBROWSE_SELECT**, this action also selects the previous item, deselects any current selection, and calls the **XmNbrowseSelectionCallback** callbacks.

If the **XmNselectionPolicy** is set to **XmEXTENDED_SELECT**, this action in Normal Mode also selects the previous item, deselects any current selection, moves the current anchor to the previous item, and calls the **XmNextendedSelectionCallback** callbacks. In Add Mode, this action does not affect the selection or the anchor.

ListPrevPage():
Scrolls the list to the previous page, moving the location cursor to a new item.

If the **XmNselectionPolicy** is set to **XmBROWSE_SELECT**, this action also selects the new item, deselects any current selection, and calls the **XmNbrowseSelectionCallback** callbacks.

If the **XmNselectionPolicy** is set to **XmEXTENDED_SELECT**, this action in Normal Mode also selects the new item, deselects any current selection, moves the current anchor to the new item, and calls the **XmNextendedSelectionCallback** callbacks. In Add Mode this action does not affect the selection or the anchor.

ListRightChar():
Scrolls the list one character to the right.

ListRightPage():
Scrolls the list one page to the right.

PrimitiveHelp():
Calls the callbacks for **XmNhelpCallback** if any exist. If there are no help callbacks for this widget, this action calls the help callbacks for the nearest ancestor that has them.

PrimitiveNextTabGroup():
> Moves the focus to the first item contained within the next tab group. If the current tab group is the last entry in the tab group list, it wraps to the beginning of the tab group list.

PrimitivePrevTabGroup():
> Moves the focus to the first item contained within the previous tab group. If the beginning of the tab group list is reached, it wraps to the end of the tab group list.

Related Information

Core(3X), **XmCreateList(3X)**, **XmCreateScrolledList(3X)**, **XmFontListCreate(3X)**, **XmFontListAppendEntry(3X)**, **XmListAddItem(3X)**, **XmListAddItems(3X)**, **XmListAddItemUnselected(3X)**, **XmListDeleteAllItems(3X)**, **XmListDeleteItem(3X)**, **XmListDeleteItems(3X)**, **XmListDeleteItemsPos(3X)**, **XmListDeletePos(3X)**, **XmListDeselectAllItems(3X)**, **XmListDeselectItem(3X)**, **XmListDeselectPos(3X)**, **XmListGetMatchPos(3X)**, **XmListGetSelectedPos(3X)**, **XmListItemExists(3X)**, **XmListItemPos(3X)**, **XmListReplaceItems(3X)**, **XmListReplaceItemsPos(3X)**, **XmListSelectItem(3X)**, **XmListSelectPos(3X)**, **XmListSetAddMode(3X)**, **XmListSetBottomItem(3X)**, **XmListSetBottomPos(3X)**, **XmListSetHorizPos(3X)**, **XmListSetItem(3X)**, **XmListSetPos(3X)**, **XmPrimitive(3X)** and **XmStringCreate(3X)**.

XmListAddItem—A List function that adds an item to the list

AES Support Level

Full-use

Synopsis

#include <Xm/List.h>

void XmListAddItem (*widget, item, position*)
    Widget   *widget*;
    XmString   *item*;
    int   *position*;

Description

XmListAddItem adds an item to the list at the given position. When the item is inserted into the list, it is compared with the current **XmNselectedItems** list. If the new item matches an item on the selected list, it appears selected.

widget   Specifies the ID of the List to which an item is added.

item   Specifies the item to be added to the list.

position   Specifies the position of the new item in the list. A value of 1 makes the new item the first item in the list; a value of 2 makes it the second item; and so on. A value of 0 (zero) makes the new item the last item in the list.

For a complete definition of List and its associated resources, see **XmList(3X)**.

Related Information

XmList(3X).

XmListAddItemUnselected—A List function that adds an item to the list

AES Support Level

Full-use

Synopsis

#include <Xm/List.h>

void XmListAddItemUnselected (*widget, item, position*)
    Widget   *widget*;
    XmString   *item*;
    int   *position*;

Description

XmListAddItemUnselected adds an item to the list at the given position. The item does not appear selected, even if it matches an item in the current **XmNselectedItems** list.

widget   Specifies the ID of the List from whose list an item is added.

item   Specifies the item to be added to the list.

position   Specifies the position of the new item in the list. A value of 1 makes the new item the first item in the list; a value of 2 makes it the second item; and so on. A value of 0 (zero) makes the new item the last item in the list.

For a complete definition of List and its associated resources, see **XmList(3X)**.

Related Information

XmList(3X).

XmListAddItems—A List function that adds items to the list

AES Support Level

Full-use

Synopsis

#include <Xm/List.h>

void XmListAddItems (*widget, items, item_count, position*)
    Widget   *widget*;
    XmString   **items*;
    int   *item_count*;
    int   *position*;

Description

XmListAddItems adds the specified items to the list at the given position. The first *item_count* items of the *items* array are added to the list. When the items are inserted into the list, they are compared with the current **XmNselectedItems** list. If any of the new items matches an item on the selected list, it appears selected.

widget   Specifies the ID of the List to which an item is added.

items   Specifies a pointer to the items to be added to the list.

item_count Specifies the number of items in *items*. This number must be nonnegative.

position   Specifies the position of the first new item in the list. A value of 1 makes the first new item the first item in the list; a value of 2 makes it the second item; and so on. A value of 0 (zero) makes the first new item follow the last item in the list.

For a complete definition of List and its associated resources, see **XmList(3X)**.

Related Information

XmList(3X).

XmListDeleteAllItems—A List function that deletes all items from the list

AES Support Level

Full-use

Synopsis

#include <Xm/List.h>

void **XmListDeleteAllItems** (*widget*)
    Widget   *widget*;

Description

XmListDeleteAllItems deletes all items from the list.

widget   Specifies the ID of the List from whose list the items are deleted

For a complete definition of List and its associated resources, see **XmList(3X)**.

Related Information

XmList(3X).

XmListDeleteItem—A List function that deletes an item from the list

AES Support Level

Full-use

Synopsis

#include <Xm/List.h>

void XmListDeleteItem (*widget, item*)
    Widget   *widget*;
    XmString   *item*;

Description

XmListDeleteItem deletes the first item in the list that matches *item*. A warning message appears if the item does not exist.

widget   Specifies the ID of the List from whose list an item is deleted

item   Specifies the text of the item to be deleted from the list

For a complete definition of List and its associated resources, see **XmList(3X)**.

Related Information

XmList(3X).

XmListDeleteItems—A List function that deletes items from the list

AES Support Level

Full-use

Synopsis

#include <Xm/List.h>

void XmListDeleteItems (*widget, items, item_count*)
    Widget   *widget*;
    XmString   *items*;
    int   *item_count*;

Description

XmListDeleteItems deletes the specified items from the list. For each element of *items*, the first item in the list that matches that element is deleted. A warning message appears if any of the items do not exist.

widget   Specifies the ID of the List from whose list an item is deleted

items   Specifies a pointer to items to be deleted from the list

item_count Specifies the number of elements in *items* This number must be nonnegative.

For a complete definition of List and its associated resources, see **XmList(3X)**.

Related Information

XmList(3X).

XmListDeleteItemsPos—A List function that deletes items from the list starting at the given position

AES Support Level

Full-use

Synopsis

#include <Xm/List.h>

void XmListDeleteItemsPos (*widget, item_count, position*)
    Widget   *widget*;
    int   *item_count*;
    int   *position*;

Description

XmListDeleteItemsPos deletes the specified number of items from the list starting at the specified position.

widget   Specifies the ID of the List from whose list an item is deleted.

item_count   Specifies the number of items to be deleted. This number must be nonnegative.

position   Specifies the position in the list of the first item to be deleted. A value of 1 indicates that the first deleted item is the first item in the list; a value of 2 indicates that it is the second item; and so on.

For a complete definition of List and its associated resources, see **XmList(3X)**.

Related Information

XmList(3X).

XmListDeletePos—A List function that deletes an item from a list at a specified position

AES Support Level

Full-use

Synopsis

#include <Xm/List.h>

void XmListDeletePos (*widget, position*)
    Widget   *widget*;
    int   *position*;

Description

XmListDeletePos deletes an item at a specified position. A warning message appears if the position does not exist.

widget   Specifies the ID of the List from which an item is to be deleted.

position   Specifies the position of the item to be deleted. A value of 1 indicates that the first item in the list is deleted; a value of 2 indicates that the second item is deleted; and so on. A value of 0 (zero) indicates that the last item in the list is deleted.

For a complete definition of List and its associated resources, see **XmList(3X)**.

Related Information

XmList(3X).

XmListDeselectAllItems—A List function that unhighlights and removes all items
from the selected list

AES Support Level

Full-use

Synopsis

#include <Xm/List.h>

void XmListDeselectAllItems (*widget*)
    Widget   *widget*;

Description

XmListDeselectAllItems unhighlights and removes all items from the selected list.

widget   Specifies the ID of the List widget from whose list all selected items
                are deselected

For a complete definition of List and its associated resources, see **XmList(3X)**.

Related Information

XmList(3X).

XmListDeselectItem—A List function that deselects the specified item from the selected list

AES Support Level

Full-use

Synopsis

#include <Xm/List.h>

void XmListDeselectItem (*widget, item*)
    Widget   *widget*;
    XmString   *item*;

Description

XmListDeselectItem unhighlights and removes from the selected list the first item in the list that matches *item*.

widget   Specifies the ID of the List from whose list an item is deselected

item   Specifies the item to be deselected from the list

For a complete definition of List and its associated resources, see **XmList(3X)**.

Related Information

XmList(3X).

XmListDeselectPos—A List function that deselects an item at a specified position in the list

AES Support Level

Full-use

Synopsis

#include <Xm/List.h>

void XmListDeselectPos (*widget, position*)
    Widget   *widget*;
    int   *position*;

Description

XmListDeselectPos unhighlights the item at the specified position and deletes it from the list of selected items.

widget   Specifies the ID of the List widget

position   Specifies the position of the item to be deselected. A value of 1 indicates that the first item in the list is deselected; a value of 2 indicates that the second item is deselected; and so on. A value of 0 (zero) indicates that the last item in the list is deselected.

For a complete definition of List and its associated resources, see **XmList(3X)**.

Related Information

XmList(3X).

XmListGetMatchPos—A List function that returns all instances of an item in the list

AES Support Level

Full-use

Synopsis

#include <Xm/List.h>

Boolean XmListGetMatchPos (*widget, item, position_list, position_count*)
    Widget   *widget*;
    XmString   *item*;
    int   ***position_list*;
    int   **position_count*;

Description

XmListGetMatchPos is a Boolean function that returns an array of positions where a specified item is found in a List.

widget   Specifies the ID of the List widget.

item   Specifies the item to search for.

position_list   Returns an array of positions at which the item occurs in the List. The position of the first item in the list is 1; the position of the second item is 2; and so on. When the return value is True, **XmListGetMatchPos** allocates memory for this array. The caller is responsible for freeing this memory.

position_count
           Returns the number of elements in the *position_list*.

For a complete definition of List and its associated resources, see **XmList(3X)**.

Return Value

Returns True if the specified item is present in the list, and False if it is not.

Related Information

XmList(3X).

XmListGetSelectedPos—A List function that returns the position of every selected item in the list

AES Support Level

Full-use

Synopsis

#include <Xm/List.h>

Boolean XmListGetSelectedPos (*widget, position_list, position_count*)
Widget	*widget*;
int	***position_list*;
int	**position_count*;

Description

XmListGetSelectedPos is a Boolean function that returns an array of the positions of the selected items in a List.

widget   Specifies the ID of the List widget.

position_list Returns an array of the positions of the selected items in the List. The position of the first item in the list is 1; the position of the second item is 2; and so on. When the return value is True, **XmListGetSelectedPos** allocates memory for this array. The caller is responsible for freeing this memory.

position_count
        Returns the number of elements in the *position_list*.

For a complete definition of List and its associated resources, see **XmList(3X)**.

Return Value

Returns True if the list has any selected items, and False if it does not.

Related Information

XmList(3X).

XmListItemExists—A List function that checks if a specified item is in the list

AES Support Level

Full-use

Synopsis

#include <Xm/List.h>

Boolean XmListItemExists (*widget, item*)
    Widget   *widget*;
    XmString   *item*;

Description

XmListItemExists is a Boolean function that checks if a specified item is present in the list.

widget   Specifies the ID of the List widget

item   Specifies the item whose presence is checked

For a complete definition of List and its associated resources, see **XmList(3X)**.

Return Value

Returns True if the specified item is present in the list.

Related Information

XmList(3X).

XmListItemPos—A List function that returns the position of an item in the list

AES Support Level

Trial-use

Synopsis

#include <Xm/List.h>

int XmListItemPos (*widget, item*)
    Widget   *widget*;
    XmString   *item*;

Description

XmListItemPos returns the position of the first instance of the specified item in a list.

widget   Specifies the ID of the List widget

item   Specifies the item whose position is returned

For a complete definition of List and its associated resources, see **XmList(3X)**.

Return Value

Returns the position in the list of the first instance of the specified item. The position of the first item in the list is 1; the position of the second item is 2; and so on. This function returns 0 (zero) if the item is not found.

Related Information

XmList(3X).

XmListReplaceItems—A List function that replaces the specified elements in the list

AES Support Level

Full-use

Synopsis

#include <Xm/List.h>

void XmListReplaceItems (*widget, old_items, item_count, new_items*)
    Widget   *widget*;
    XmString   **old_items*;
    int   *item_count*;
    XmString   **new_items*;

Description

XmListReplaceItems replaces each specified item of the list with a corresponding new item.

widget   Specifies the ID of the List widget.

old_items   Specifies the items to be replaced.

item_count   Specifies the number of items in *old_items* and *new_items*. This number must be nonnegative.

new_items   Specifies the replacement items.

Every occurrence of each element of *old_items* is replaced with the corresponding element from *new_items*.

For a complete definition of List and its associated resources, see **XmList(3X)**.

Related Information

XmList(3X).

XmListReplaceItemsPos—A List function that replaces the specified elements in the list

AES Support Level

Full-use

Synopsis

#include <Xm/List.h>

void XmListReplaceItemsPos (*widget, new_items, item_count, position*)
    Widget   *widget*;
    XmString   *new_items*;
    int   *item_count*;
    int   *position*;

Description

XmListReplaceItemsPos replaces the specified number of items of the List with new items, starting at the specified position in the List.

widget   Specifies the ID of the List widget.

new_items   Specifies the replacement items.

item_count   Specifies the number of items in *new_items* and the number of items in the list to replace. This number must be nonnegative.

position   Specifies the position of the first item in the list to be replaced. A value of 1 indicates that the first item replaced is the first item in the list; a value of 2 indicates that it is the second item; and so on.

           Beginning with the item specified in *position*, *item_count* items in the list are replaced with the corresponding elements from *new_items*.

For a complete definition of List and its associated resources, see **XmList(3X)**.

Related Information

XmList(3X).

XmListSelectItem—A List function that selects an item in the list

AES Support Level
Full-use

Synopsis
#include <Xm/List.h>

void XmListSelectItem (*widget, item, notify*)
    Widget   *widget*;
    XmString   *item*;
    Boolean   *notify*;

Description
XmListSelectItem highlights and adds to the selected list the first item in the list that matches *item*.

widget   Specifies the ID of the List widget from whose list an item is selected.

item   Specifies the item to be selected in the List widget.

notify   Specifies a Boolean value that when True invokes the selection callback for the current mode. From an application interface view, calling this function with *notify* True is indistinguishable from a user-initiated selection action.

For a complete definition of List and its associated resources, see **XmList(3X)**.

Related Information
XmList(3X).

XmListSelectPos—A List function that selects an item at a specified position in the list

AES Support Level

Full-use

Synopsis

#include <Xm/List.h>

void XmListSelectPos (*widget, position, notify*)
    Widget   *widget*;
    int   *position*;
    Boolean   *notify*;

Description

XmListSelectPos highlights a List item at the specified position and adds it to the list of selected items.

widget   Specifies the ID of the List widget.

position   Specifies the position of the item to be selected. A value of 1 indicates that the first item in the list is selected; a value of 2 indicates that the second item is selected; and so on. A value of 0 (zero) indicates that the last item in the list is selected.

notify   Specifies a Boolean value that when True invokes the selection callback for the current mode. From an application interface view, calling this function with *notify* True is indistinguishable from a user-initiated selection action.

For a complete definition of List and its associated resources, see **XmList(3X)**.

Related Information

XmList(3X).

XmListSetAddMode—A List function that sets add mode in the list

AES Support Level

Trial-use

Synopsis

#include <Xm/List.h>

void **XmListSetAddMode** (*widget, state*)
    Widget   *widget*;
    Boolean   *state*;

Description

XmListSetAddMode allows applications control over Add Mode in the extended selection model.

widget   Specifies the ID of the List widget

state   Specifies whether to activate or deactivate Add Mode. If *state* is True, Add Mode is activated. If *state* is False, Add Mode is deactivated.

For a complete definition of List and its associated resources, see **XmList(3X)**.

Related Information

XmList(3X).

XmListSetBottomItem—A List function that makes an existing item the last visible item in the list

AES Support Level

Full-use

Synopsis

#include <Xm/List.h>

void XmListSetBottomItem (*widget, item*)
    Widget   *widget*;
    XmString   *item*;

Description

XmListSetBottomItem makes the first item in the list that matches *item* the last visible item in the list.

widget   Specifies the ID of the List widget from whose list an item is made the last visible

item   Specifies the item

For a complete definition of List and its associated resources, see **XmList(3X)**.

Related Information

XmList(3X).

XmListSetBottomPos—A List function that makes a specified item the last visible item in the list

AES Support Level

Full-use

Synopsis

#include <Xm/List.h>

void **XmListSetBottomPos** (*widget, position*)
    Widget   *widget*;
    int   *position*;

Description

XmListSetBottomPos makes the item at the specified position the last visible item in the List.

widget   Specifies the ID of the List widget.

position   Specifies the position of the item to be made the last visible item in the list. A value of 1 indicates that the first item in the list is the last visible item; a value of 2 indicates that the second item is the last visible item; and so on. A value of 0 (zero) indicates that the last item in the list is the last visible item.

For a complete definition of List and its associated resources, see **XmList(3X)**.

Related Information

XmList(3X).

XmListSetHorizPos—A List function that scrolls to the specified position in the list

AES Support Level

Full-use

Synopsis

#include <Xm/List.h>

void XmListSetHorizPos (*widget, position*)
    Widget   *widget*;
    int   *position*;

Description

XmListSetHorizPos sets the **XmNvalue** resource of the horizontal ScrollBar to the specified position and updates the visible portion of the list with the new value if the List widget's **XmNlistSizePolicy** is set to **XmCONSTANT** or **XmRESIZE_IF_POSSIBLE** and the horizontal ScrollBar is currently visible. This is equivalent to moving the horizontal ScrollBar to the specified position.

widget   Specifies the ID of the List widget

position   Specifies the horizontal position

For a complete definition of List and its associated resources, see **XmList(3X)**.

Related Information

XmList(3X).

XmListSetItem—A List function that makes an existing item the first visible item in the list

AES Support Level

Full-use

Synopsis

#include <Xm/List.h>

void XmListSetItem (*widget, item*)
    Widget   *widget*;
    XmString   *item*;

Description

XmListSetItem makes the first item in the list that matches *item* the first visible item in the list.

widget   Specifies the ID of the List widget from whose list an item is made the first visible

item   Specifies the item

For a complete definition of List and its associated resources, see **XmList(3X)**.

Related Information

XmList(3X).

XmListSetPos—A List function that makes the item at the given position the first visible position in the list

AES Support Level

Full-use

Synopsis

#include <Xm/List.h>

void XmListSetPos (*widget, position*)
    Widget   *widget*;
    int   *position*;

Description

XmListSetPos makes the item at the given position the first visible position in the list.

widget   Specifies the ID of the List widget.

position   Specifies the position of the item to be made the first visible item in the list. A value of 1 indicates that the first item in the list is the first visible item; a value of 2 indicates that the second item is the first visible item; and so on. A value of 0 (zero) indicates that the last item in the list is the first visible item.

For a complete definition of List and its associated resources, see **XmList(3X)**.

Related Information

XmList(3X).

XmMainWindow—The MainWindow widget class

AES Support Level

Full-use

Synopsis

#include <Xm/MainW.h>

Description

MainWindow provides a standard layout for the primary window of an application. This layout includes a MenuBar, a CommandWindow, a work region, a MessageWindow, and ScrollBars. Any or all of these areas are optional. The work region and ScrollBars in the MainWindow behave identically to the work region and ScrollBars in the ScrolledWindow widget. The user can think of the MainWindow as an extended ScrolledWindow with an optional MenuBar and optional CommandWindow and MessageWindow.

In a fully loaded MainWindow, the MenuBar spans the top of the window horizontally. The CommandWindow spans the MainWindow horizontally just below the MenuBar, and the work region lies below the CommandWindow. The MessageWindow is below the work region. Any space remaining below the MessageWindow is managed in a manner identical to ScrolledWindow. The behavior of ScrolledWindow can be controlled by the ScrolledWindow resources. To create a MainWindow, first create the work region elements, a MenuBar, a CommandWindow, a MessageWindow, a horizontal ScrollBar, and a vertical ScrollBar widget, and then call **XmMainWindowSetAreas** with those widget IDs.

MainWindow can also create three Separator widgets that provide a visual separation of MainWindow's four components.

Classes

MainWindow inherits behavior and resources from **Core**, **Composite**, **Constraint**, **XmManager**, and **ScrolledWindow**.

The class pointer is **xmMainWindowWidgetClass**.

The class name is **XmMainWindow**.

New Resources

The following table defines a set of widget resources used by the programmer to specify data. The programmer can also set the resource values for the inherited classes to set attributes for this widget. To reference a resource by name or by class in a **.Xdefaults** file, remove the **XmN** or **XmC** prefix and use the remaining letters. To specify one of the defined values for a resource in a **.Xdefaults** file, remove the **Xm** prefix and use the remaining letters (in either lowercase or uppercase, but include any underscores between words). The codes in the access

column indicate if the given resource can be set at creation time (C), set by using
XtSetValues (S), retrieved by using **XtGetValues** (G), or is not applicable (N/A).

XmMainWindow Resource Set		
Name	**Default**	**Access**
Class	**Type**	
XmNcommandWindow	NULL	CSG
XmCCommandWindow	Widget	
XmNcommandWindowLocation	ABOVE (SeeDesc.)	CG
XmCCommandWindowLocation	unsigned char	
XmNmainWindowMarginHeight	0	CSG
XmCMainWindowMarginHeight	Dimension	
XmNmainWindowMarginWidth	0	CSG
XmCMainWindowMarginWidth	Dimension	
XmNmenuBar	NULL	CSG
XmCMenuBar	Widget	
XmNmessageWindow	NULL	CSG
XmCMessageWindow	Widget	
XmNshowSeparator	False	CSG
XmCShowSeparator	Boolean	

XmNcommandWindow

    Specifies the widget to be laid out as the CommandWindow. This
widget must have been previously created and managed as a child of
MainWindow.

XmNcommandWindowLocation

    Controls the position of the command window.
XmCOMMAND_ABOVE_WORKSPACE locates the command
window between the menu bar and the work window.
XmCOMMAND_BELOW_WORKSPACE locates the command
window between the work window and the message window.

XmNmainWindowMarginHeight

    Specifies the margin height on the top and bottom of MainWindow.
This resource overrides any setting of the ScrolledWindow resource
XmNscrolledWindowMarginHeight.

XmNmainWindowMarginWidth

    Specifies the margin width on the right and left sides of
MainWindow. This resource overrides any setting of the
ScrolledWindow resource **XmNscrolledWindowMarginWidth**.

XmNmenuBar

Specifies the widget to be laid out as the MenuBar. This widget must have been previously created and managed as a child of MainWindow.

XmNmessageWindow

Specifies the widget to be laid out as the MessageWindow. This widget must have been previously created and managed as a child of MainWindow. The MessageWindow is positioned at the bottom of the MainWindow. If this value is NULL, no message window is included in the MainWindow.

XmNshowSeparator

Displays separators between the components of the MainWindow when set to True. If set to False, no separators are displayed.

Inherited Resources

MainWindow inherits behavior and resources from the superclasses described in the following table. For a complete description of each resource, refer to the reference page for that superclass.

XmScrolledWindow Resource Set		

Name
    Class
	Default
	    Type
		Access

XmNclipWindow
    XmCClipWindow
	dynamic
	    Widget
		G

XmNhorizontalScrollBar
    XmCHorizontalScrollBar
	dynamic
	    Widget
		CSG

XmNscrollBarDisplayPolicy
    XmCScrollBarDisplayPolicy
	dynamic
	    unsigned char
		CSG

XmNscrollBarPlacement
    XmCScrollBarPlacement
	XmBOTTOM_RIGHT
	    unsigned char
		CSG

XmNscrolledWindowMarginHeight
    XmCScrolledWindowMarginHeight
	0
	    Dimension
		N/A

XmNscrolledWindowMarginWidth
    XmCScrolledWindowMarginWidth
	0
	    Dimension
		N/A

XmNscrollingPolicy
    XmCScrollingPolicy
	XmAPPLICATION_DEFINED
	    unsigned char
		CG

XmNspacing
    XmCSpacing
	4
	    Dimension
		CSG

XmNverticalScrollBar
    XmCVerticalScrollBar
	dynamic
	    Widget
		CSG

XmNvisualPolicy
    XmCVisualPolicy
	dynamic
	    unsigned char
		G

XmNworkWindow
    XmCWorkWindow
	NULL
	    Widget
		CSG

XmManager Resource Set		
Name	**Default**	**Access**
Class	**Type**	
XmNbottomShadowColor	dynamic	CSG
XmCBottomShadowColor	Pixel	
XmNbottomShadowPixmap	XmUNSPECIFIED_PIXMAP	CSG
XmCBottomShadowPixmap	Pixmap	
XmNforeground	dynamic	CSG
XmCForeground	Pixel	
XmNhelpCallback	NULL	C
XmCCallback	XtCallbackList	
XmNhighlightColor	dynamic	CSG
XmCHighlightColor	Pixel	
XmNhighlightPixmap	dynamic	CSG
XmCHighlightPixmap	Pixmap	
XmNnavigationType	XmTAB_GROUP	CSG
XmCNavigationType	XmNavigationType	
XmNshadowThickness	0	CSG
XmCShadowThickness	Dimension	
XmNstringDirection	dynamic	CG
XmCStringDirection	XmStringDirection	
XmNtopShadowColor	dynamic	CSG
XmCTopShadowColor	Pixel	
XmNtopShadowPixmap	dynamic	CSG
XmCTopShadowPixmap	Pixmap	
XmNtraversalOn	True	CSG
XmCTraversalOn	Boolean	
XmNuserData	NULL	CSG
XmCUserData	XtPointer	

Composite Resource Set		
Name	**Default**	**Access**
Class	**Type**	
XmNchildren	NULL	G
XmCReadOnly	WidgetList	
XmNinsertPosition	NULL	CSG
XmCInsertPosition	XtOrderProc	
XmNnumChildren	0	G
XmCReadOnly	Cardinal	

Core Resource Set		
Name	**Default**	**Access**
Class	**Type**	
XmNaccelerators	dynamic	CSG
XmCAccelerators	XtAccelerators	
XmNancestorSensitive	dynamic	G
XmCSensitive	Boolean	
XmNbackground	dynamic	CSG
XmCBackground	Pixel	
XmNbackgroundPixmap	XmUNSPECIFIED_PIXMAP	CSG
XmCPixmap	Pixmap	
XmNborderColor	XtDefaultForeground	CSG
XmCBorderColor	Pixel	
XmNborderPixmap	XmUNSPECIFIED_PIXMAP	CSG
XmCPixmap	Pixmap	
XmNborderWidth	0	CSG
XmCBorderWidth	Dimension	
XmNcolormap	dynamic	CG
XmCColormap	Colormap	
XmNdepth	dynamic	CG
XmCDepth	int	
XmNdestroyCallback	NULL	C
XmCCallback	XtCallbackList	
XmNheight	dynamic	CSG
XmCHeight	Dimension	
XmNinitialResourcesPersistent	True	C
XmCInitialResourcesPersistent	Boolean	
XmNmappedWhenManaged	True	CSG
XmCMappedWhenManaged	Boolean	
XmNscreen	dynamic	CG
XmCScreen	Screen *	
XmNsensitive	True	CSG
XmCSensitive	Boolean	

Name	Default	Access
Class	Type	
XmNtranslations	dynamic	CSG
XmCTranslations	XtTranslations	
XmNwidth	dynamic	CSG
XmCWidth	Dimension	
XmNx	0	CSG
XmCPosition	Position	
XmNy	0	CSG
XmCPosition	Position	

Related Information

Composite(3X), **Constraint(3X)**, **Core(3X)**, **XmCreateMainWindow(3X)**,
XmMainWindowSep1(3X), **XmMainWindowSep2(3X)**,
XmMainWindowSep3(3X), **XmMainWindowSetAreas(3X)**, **XmManager(3X)**,
and **XmScrolledWindow(3X)**

XmMainWindowSep1—A MainWindow function that returns the widget ID of the first Separator widget

AES Support Level

Full-use

History/Direction

The **XmMainWindowSep1** function is scheduled for removal in revision E.

Synopsis

#include <Xm/MainW.h>

Widget XmMainWindowSep1 (*widget*)
    Widget   *widget*;

Description

XmMainWindowSep1 returns the widget ID of the first Separator widget in the MainWindow. The first Separator widget is located between the MenuBar and the Command widget. This Separator is visible only when **XmNshowSeparator** is True.

widget   Specifies the MainWindow widget ID

For a complete definition of MainWindow and its associated resources, see **XmMainWindow(3X)**.

Return Value

Returns the widget ID of the first Separator.

Related Information

XmMainWindow(3X).

XmMainWindowSep2—A MainWindow function that returns the widget ID of the second Separator widget

AES Support Level

Full-use

History/Direction

The **XmMainWindowSep2** function is scheduled for removal in revision E.

Synopsis

#include <Xm/MainW.h>

Widget XmMainWindowSep2 (*widget*)
    Widget   *widget*;

Description

XmMainWindowSep2 returns the widget ID of the second Separator widget in the MainWindow. The second Separator widget is located between the Command widget and the ScrolledWindow. This Separator is visible only when **XmNshowSeparator** is True.

widget   Specifies the MainWindow widget ID

For a complete definition of MainWindow and its associated resources, see **XmMainWindow(3X)**.

Return Value

Returns the widget ID of the second Separator.

Related Information

XmMainWindow(3X).

XmMainWindowSep3—A MainWindow function that returns the widget ID of the third Separator widget

AES Support Level

Full-use

History/Direction

The **XmMainWindowSep3** function is scheduled for removal in revision E.

Synopsis

#include <Xm/MainW.h>

Widget XmMainWindowSep3 (*widget*)
    Widget   *widget*;

Description

XmMainWindowSep3 returns the widget ID of the third Separator widget in the MainWindow. The third Separator widget is located between the message window and the widget above it. This Separator is visible only when **XmNshowSeparator** is True.

widget   Specifies the MainWindow widget ID

For a complete definition of MainWindow and its associated resources, see **XmMainWindow(3X)**.

Return Value

Returns the widget ID of the third Separator.

Related Information

XmMainWindow(3X).

XmMainWindowSetAreas—A MainWindow function that identifies manageable children for each area

AES Support Level

Full-use

Synopsis

#include <Xm/MainW.h>

void XmMainWindowSetAreas (*widget, menu_bar, command_window, horizontal_scrollbar, vertical_scrollbar, work_region*)

Widget	*widget*;
Widget	*menu_bar*;
Widget	*command_window*;
Widget	*horizontal_scrollbar*;
Widget	*vertical_scrollbar*;
Widget	*work_region*;

Description

XmMainWindowSetAreas identifies which of the valid children for each area (such as the MenuBar and work region) are to be actively managed by MainWindow. This function also sets up or adds the MenuBar, work window, command window, and ScrollBar widgets to the application's main window widget.

Each area is optional; therefore, the user can pass NULL to one or more of the following arguments. The window manager provides the title bar.

widget   Specifies the MainWindow widget ID.

menu_bar   Specifies the widget ID for the MenuBar to be associated with the MainWindow widget. Set this ID only after creating an instance of the MainWindow widget. The attribute name associated with this argument is **XmNmenuBar**.

command_window

Specifies the widget ID for the command window to be associated with the MainWindow widget. Set this ID only after creating an instance of the MainWindow widget. The attribute name associated with this argument is **XmNcommandWindow**.

horizontal_scrollbar
> Specifies the ScrollBar widget ID for the horizontal ScrollBar to be associated with the MainWindow widget. Set this ID only after creating an instance of the MainWindow widget. The attribute name associated with this argument is **XmNhorizontalScrollBar**.

vertical_scrollbar
> Specifies the ScrollBar widget ID for the vertical ScrollBar to be associated with the MainWindow widget. Set this ID only after creating an instance of the MainWindow widget. The attribute name associated with this argument is **XmNverticalScrollBar**.

work_region
> Specifies the widget ID for the work window to be associated with the MainWindow widget. Set this ID only after creating an instance of the MainWindow widget. The attribute name associated with this argument is **XmNworkWindow**.

For a complete definition of MainWindow and its associated resources, see **XmMainWindow(3X)**.

Related Information

XmMainWindow(3X).

XmManager—The Manager widget class

AES Support Level

Full-use

Synopsis

#include <Xm/Xm.h>

Description

Manager is a widget class used as a supporting superclass for other widget classes. It supports the visual resources, graphics contexts, and traversal resources necessary for the graphics and traversal mechanisms.

Classes

Manager inherits behavior and resources from **Core**, **Composite**, and **Constraint**.

The class pointer is **xmManagerWidgetClass**.

The class name is **XmManager**.

New Resources

The following table defines a set of widget resources used by the programmer to specify data. The programmer can also set the resource values for the inherited classes to set attributes for this widget. To reference a resource by name or by class in a **.Xdefaults** file, remove the **XmN** or **XmC** prefix and use the remaining letters. To specify one of the defined values for a resource in a **.Xdefaults** file, remove the **Xm** prefix and use the remaining letters (in either lowercase or uppercase, but include any underscores between words). The codes in the access column indicate if the given resource can be set at creation time (C), set by using **XtSetValues** (S), retrieved by using **XtGetValues** (G), or is not applicable (N/A).

XmManager Resource Set		
Name	**Default**	**Access**
Class	**Type**	
XmNbottomShadowColor	dynamic	CSG
XmCBottomShadowColor	Pixel	
XmNbottomShadowPixmap	XmUNSPECIFIED_PIXMAP	CSG
XmCBottomShadowPixmap	Pixmap	
XmNforeground	dynamic	CSG
XmCForeground	Pixel	
XmNhelpCallback	NULL	C
XmCCallback	XtCallbackList	
XmNhighlightColor	dynamic	CSG
XmCHighlightColor	Pixel	
XmNhighlightPixmap	dynamic	CSG
XmCHighlightPixmap	Pixmap	
XmNnavigationType	XmTAB_GROUP	CSG
XmCNavigationType	XmNavigationType	
XmNshadowThickness	0	CSG
XmCShadowThickness	Dimension	
XmNstringDirection	dynamic	CG
XmCStringDirection	XmStringDirection	
XmNtopShadowColor	dynamic	CSG
XmCTopShadowColor	Pixel	
XmNtopShadowPixmap	dynamic	CSG
XmCTopShadowPixmap	Pixmap	
XmNtraversalOn	True	CSG
XmCTraversalOn	Boolean	
XmNuserData	NULL	CSG
XmCUserData	XtPointer	

XmNbottomShadowColor

Specifies the color to use to draw the bottom and right sides of the border shadow. This color is used if the **XmNbottomShadowPixmap** resource is NULL.

XmNbottomShadowPixmap

Specifies the pixmap to use to draw the bottom and right sides of the border shadow.

XmNforeground

Specifies the foreground drawing color used by manager widgets.

XmNhelpCallback

Specifies the list of callbacks that are called when the help key sequence is pressed. The reason sent by this callback is **XmCR_HELP**.

XmNhighlightColor

Specifies the color of the highlighting rectangle. This color is used if the highlight pixmap resource is **XmUNSPECIFIED_PIXMAP**.

XmNhighlightPixmap

Specifies the pixmap used to draw the highlighting rectangle.

XmNnavigationType

Determines whether the widget is a tab group.

XmNONE   Indicates that the widget is not a tab group.

XmTAB_GROUP

Indicates that the widget is a tab group, unless the **XmNnavigationType** of another widget in the hierarchy is **XmEXCLUSIVE_TAB_GROUP**.

XmSTICKY_TAB_GROUP

Indicates that the widget is a tab group, even if the **XmNnavigationType** of another widget in the hierarchy is **XmEXCLUSIVE_TAB_GROUP**.

XmEXCLUSIVE_TAB_GROUP

Indicates that the widget is a tab group and that widgets in the hierarchy whose **XmNnavigationType** is **XmTAB_GROUP** are not tab groups.

When a parent widget has an **XmNnavigationType** of **XmEXCLUSIVE_TAB_GROUP**, traversal of non-tab-group widgets within the group is based on the order of those widgets in their parent's **XmNchildren** list.

XmNshadowThickness

Specifies the thickness of the drawn border shadow. **XmBulletinBoard** and its descendants set this value dynamically. If the widget is a top-level window, this value is set to 1. If it is not a top-level window, this value is set to 0 (zero).

XmNstringDirection

Specifies the initial direction to draw strings. The values for this resource are **XmSTRING_DIRECTION_L_TO_R** and **XmSTRING_DIRECTION_R_TO_L**. The value of this resource is determined at creation time. If the widget's parent is a manager, this value is inherited from the widget's parent, otherwise it is set to **XmSTRING_DIRECTION_L_TO_R**.

XmNtopShadowColor

Specifies the color to use to draw the top and left sides of the border shadow. This color is used if the **XmNtopShadowPixmap** resource is NULL.

XmNtopShadowPixmap

Specifies the pixmap to use to draw the top and left sides of the border shadow.

XmNtraversalOn

Specifies whether traversal is activated for this widget.

XmNuserData

Allows the application to attach any necessary specific data to the widget. This is an internally unused resource.

Dynamic Color Defaults

The foreground, background, top shadow, and bottom shadow resources are dynamically defaulted. If no color data is specified, the colors are automatically generated. On a single-plane system, a black and white color scheme is generated. Otherwise, four colors are generated, which display the correct shading for the 3-D visuals. If the background is the only color specified for a widget, the top shadow, bottom shadow, and foreground colors are generated to give the 3-D appearance.

Colors are generated only at creation. Resetting the background through **XtSetValues** does not regenerate the other colors.

Inherited Resources

Manager inherits resources from the superclasses described in the following tables. For a complete description of each resource, refer to the reference page for that superclass.

Composite Resource Set		
Name	**Default**	**Access**
Class	**Type**	
XmNchildren	NULL	G
XmCReadOnly	WidgetList	
XmNinsertPosition	NULL	CSG
XmCInsertPosition	XtOrderProc	
XmNnumChildren	0	G
XmCReadOnly	Cardinal	

Core Resource Set		
Name	**Default**	**Access**
Class	**Type**	
XmNaccelerators	dynamic	CSG
XmCAccelerators	XtAccelerators	
XmNancestorSensitive	dynamic	G
XmCSensitive	Boolean	
XmNbackground	dynamic	CSG
XmCBackground	Pixel	
XmNbackgroundPixmap	XmUNSPECIFIED_PIXMAP	CSG
XmCPixmap	Pixmap	
XmNborderColor	XtDefaultForeground	CSG
XmCBorderColor	Pixel	
XmNborderPixmap	XmUNSPECIFIED_PIXMAP	CSG
XmCPixmap	Pixmap	
XmNborderWidth	0	CSG
XmCBorderWidth	Dimension	
XmNcolormap	dynamic	CG
XmCColormap	Colormap	
XmNdepth	dynamic	CG
XmCDepth	int	
XmNdestroyCallback	NULL	C
XmCCallback	XtCallbackList	
XmNheight	dynamic	CSG
XmCHeight	Dimension	
XmNinitialResourcesPersistent	True	C
XmCInitialResourcesPersistent	Boolean	
XmNmappedWhenManaged	True	CSG
XmCMappedWhenManaged	Boolean	
XmNscreen	dynamic	CG
XmCScreen	Screen *	
XmNsensitive	True	CSG
XmCSensitive	Boolean	

Name	Default	Access
Class	Type	
XmNtranslations	dynamic	CSG
XmCTranslations	XtTranslations	
XmNwidth	dynamic	CSG
XmCWidth	Dimension	
XmNx	0	CSG
XmCPosition	Position	
XmNy	0	CSG
XmCPosition	Position	

Callback Information

A pointer to the following structure is passed to each callback:

typedef struct
{
    int   *reason*;
    XEvent   * *event*;
} XmAnyCallbackStruct;

reason   Indicates why the callback was invoked. For this callback, *reason* is set to **XmCR_HELP**.

event   Points to the **XEvent** that triggered the callback.

Action Routines

The **XmManager** action routines are

ManagerGadgetActivate():
    Causes the current gadget to be activated.

ManagerGadgetArm():
    Causes the current gadget to be armed.

    Causes the current gadget to process a mouse motion event.

ManagerGadgetHelp():
    Calls the callbacks for the current gadget's **XmNhelpCallback** if any exist. If there are no help callbacks for this widget, this action calls the help callbacks for the nearest ancestor that has them.

ManagerGadgetKeyInput():
    Causes the current gadget to process a keyboard event.

ManagerGadgetMultiActivate():
> Causes the current gadget to process a multiple mouse click.

ManagerGadgetMultiArm():
> Causes the current gadget to process a multiple mouse button press.

ManagerGadgetNextTabGroup():
> Traverses to the first item in the next tab group. If the current tab group is the last entry in the tab group list, it wraps to the beginning of the tab group list.

ManagerGadgetPrevTabGroup():
> Traverses to the first item in the previous tab group. If the beginning of the tab group list is reached, it wraps to the end of the tab group list.

ManagerGadgetSelect():
> Causes the current gadget to be armed and activated.

ManagerGadgetTraverseDown():
> Traverses to the next item below the current gadget in the current tab group, wrapping if necessary.

ManagerGadgetTraverseHome():
> Traverses to the first widget or gadget in the current tab group.

ManagerGadgetTraverseLeft():
> Traverses to the next item to the left of the current gadget in the current tab group, wrapping if necessary.

ManagerGadgetTraverseNext():
> Traverses to the next item in the current tab group, wrapping if necessary.

ManagerGadgetTraversePrev():
> Traverses to the previous item in the current tab group, wrapping if necessary.

ManagerGadgetTraverseRight()
> Traverses to the next item to the right of the current gadget in the current tab group, wrapping if necessary.

ManagerGadgetTraverseUp():
> Traverses to the next item above the current gadget in the current tab group, wrapping if necessary.

ManagerParentActivate():
> If the parent is a manager, passes the **KActivate** event received by the current widget/gadget to its parent.

ManagerParentCancel():
> If the parent is a manager, passes the **KCancel** event received by the current widget/gadget to its parent.

Related Information

Composite(3X), **Constraint(3X)**, **Core(3X)**, and **XmGadget(3X)**.

XmMenuPosition—A RowColumn function that positions a Popup MenuPane

AES Support Level

Full-use

Synopsis

#include <Xm/RowColumn.h>

void XmMenuPosition (*menu, event*)
    Widget   *menu*;
    XButtonPressedEvent * *event*;

Description

XmMenuPosition positions a Popup MenuPane using the information in the specified event. Unless an application is positioning the MenuPane itself, it must first invoke this function before managing the PopupMenu. The *x_root* and *y_root* values in the specified event are used to determine the menu position.

menu   Specifies the PopupMenu to be positioned

event   Specifies the event passed to the action procedure which manages the PopupMenu

For a complete definition of RowColumn and its associated resources, see **XmRowColumn(3X)**.

Related Information

XmRowColumn(3X).

XmMenuShell—The MenuShell widget class

AES Support Level

Full-use

History/Direction

The description of the geometry management of shells and their children has been changed (for trial-use). New resources have been added specifying font lists for button and label children (for trial-use).

Synopsis

#include <Xm/MenuShell.h>

Description

The MenuShell widget is a custom OverrideShell widget. An OverrideShell widget bypasses **mwm** when displaying itself. It is designed specifically to contain Popup or Pulldown MenuPanes.

Most application writers never encounter this widget if they use the menu-system convenience functions, **XmCreatePopupMenu** or **XmCreatePulldown Menu**, to create a Popup or Pulldown MenuPane. The convenience functions automatically create a MenuShell widget as the parent of the MenuPane. However, if the convenience functions are not used, the application programmer must create the required MenuShell. In this case, it is important to note that the parent of the MenuShell depends on the type of menu system being built.

- If the MenuShell is for the top-level Popup MenuPane, the MenuShell's parent must be the widget from which the Popup MenuPane is popped up.

- If the MenuShell is for a MenuPane that is pulled down from a Popup or another Pulldown MenuPane, the MenuShell's parent must be the Popup or Pulldown MenuPane.

- If the MenuShell is for a MenuPane that is pulled down from a MenuBar, the MenuShell's parent must be the MenuBar.

- If the MenuShell is for a Pulldown MenuPane in an OptionMenu, the MenuShell's parent must be the OptionMenu's parent.

Setting **XmNheight**, **XmNwidth**, or **XmNborderWidth** for either a MenuShell or its child sets that resource to the same value in both the parent and the child. An application should always specify these resources for the child, not the parent.

For the managed child of a MenuShell, regardless of the value of the shell's **XmNallowShellResize**, setting **XmNx** or **XmNy** sets the corresponding resource of the parent but does not change the child's position relative to the parent. **XtGetValues** for the child's **XmNx** or **XmNy** yields the value of the corresponding resource in the parent. The x and y-coordinates of the child's upper left outside corner relative to the parent's upper left inside corner are both 0 (zero) minus the value of **XmNborderWidth**.

Classes

MenuShell inherits behavior and resources from **Core**, **Composite**, **Shell**, and **OverrideShell**.

The class pointer is **xmMenuShellWidgetClass**.

The class name is **XmMenuShell**.

New Resources

MenuShell overrides the **XmNallowShellResize** resource in Shell. The following table defines a set of widget resources used by the programmer to specify data. The programmer can also set the resource values for the inherited classes to set attributes for this widget. To reference a resource by name or by class in a **.Xdefaults** file, remove the **XmN** or **XmC** prefix and use the remaining letters. To specify one of the defined values for a resource in a **.Xdefaults** file, remove the **Xm** prefix and use the remaining letters (in either lowercase or uppercase, but include any underscores between words). The codes in the access column indicate if the given resource can be set at creation time (C), set by using **XtSetValues** (S), retrieved by using **XtGetValues** (G), or is not applicable (N/A).

XmMenuShell Resource Set		
Name	**Default**	**Access**
Class	**Type**	
XmNbuttonFontList	dynamic	CSG
XmCButtonFontList	XmFontList	
XmNdefaultFontList	dynamic	CG
XmCDefaultFontList	XmFontList	
XmNlabelFontList	dynamic	CSG
XmCLabelFontList	XmFontList	

XmNbuttonFontList

Specifies the font list used for MenuShell's button descendants. If this value is NULL at initialization and if the value of **XmNdefaultFontList** is not NULL, **XmNbuttonFontList** is initialized to the value of **XmNdefaultFontList**. If the value of **XmNdefaultFontList** is NULL, **XmNbuttonFontList** is initialized by looking up the parent hierarchy of the widget for an ancestor that is a subclass of the BulletinBoard, VendorShell, or MenuShell widget class. If such an ancestor is found, **XmNbuttonFontList** is initialized to the **XmNbuttonFontList** of the ancestor widget. If no such ancestor is found, the default is implementation dependent.

XmNdefaultFontList

Specifies a default font list for MenuShell's descendants. This resource is obsolete and exists for compatibility with earlier releases. It has been replaced by **XmNbuttonFontList** and **XmNlabelFontList**.

XmNlabelFontList

Specifies the font list used for MenuShell's label descendants (Labels and LabelGadgets). If this value is NULL at initialization and if the value of **XmNdefaultFontList** is not NULL, **XmNlabelFontList** is initialized to the value of **XmNdefaultFontList**. If the value of **XmNdefaultFontList** is NULL, the parent hierarchy of the widget is searched for an ancestor that is a subclass of the XmBulletinBoard, VendorShell, or XmMenuShell widget class. If such an ancestor is found, **XmNlabelFontList** is initialized to the **XmNlabelFontList** of the ancestor widget. If no such ancestor is found, the default is implementation dependent.

Inherited Resources

MenuShell inherits behavior and resources from the superclasses described in the following tables. For a complete description of each resource, refer to the reference page for that superclass. The programmer can set the resource values for these inherited classes to set attributes for this widget. To reference a resource by name or by class in a **.Xdefaults** file, remove the **XmN** or **XmC** prefix and use the remaining letters. To specify one of the defined values for a resource in a **.Xdefaults** file, remove the **Xm** prefix and use the remaining letters (in either lowercase or uppercase, but include any underscores between words). The codes in the access column indicate if the given resource can be set at creation time (C), set by using **XtSetValues** (S), retrieved by using **XtGetValues** (G), or is not applicable (N/A).

Shell Resource Set		
Name	**Default**	**Access**
Class	**Type**	
XmNallowShellResize	True	G
XmCAllowShellResize	Boolean	
XmNcreatePopupChildProc	NULL	CSG
XmCCreatePopupChildProc	XtCreatePopupChildProc	
XmNgeometry	NULL	CSG
XmCGeometry	String	
XmNoverrideRedirect	True	CSG
XmCOverrideRedirect	Boolean	
XmNpopdownCallback	NULL	C
XmCCallback	XtCallbackList	
XmNpopupCallback	NULL	C
XmCCallback	XtCallbackList	
XmNsaveUnder	True	CSG
XmCSaveUnder	Boolean	
XmNvisual	CopyFromParent	CSG
XmCVisual	Visual *	

Composite Resource Set		
Name	**Default**	**Access**
Class	**Type**	
XmNchildren	NULL	G
XmCReadOnly	WidgetList	
XmNinsertPosition	NULL	CSG
XmCInsertPosition	XtOrderProc	
XmNnumChildren	0	G
XmCReadOnly	Cardinal	

Core Resource Set		

Name
    Class
	Default
	    Type
		Access

XmNaccelerators
    XmCAccelerators
	dynamic
	    XtAccelerators
		CSG

XmNancestorSensitive
    XmCSensitive
	dynamic
	    Boolean
		G

XmNbackground
    XmCBackground
	dynamic
	    Pixel
		CSG

XmNbackgroundPixmap
    XmCPixmap
	XmUNSPECIFIED_PIXMAP
	    Pixmap
		CSG

XmNborderColor
    XmCBorderColor
	XtDefaultForeground
	    Pixel
		CSG

XmNborderPixmap
    XmCPixmap
	XmUNSPECIFIED_PIXMAP
	    Pixmap
		CSG

XmNborderWidth
    XmCBorderWidth
	0
	    Dimension
		CSG

XmNcolormap
    XmCColormap
	dynamic
	    Colormap
		CG

XmNdepth
    XmCDepth
	dynamic
	    int
		CG

XmNdestroyCallback
    XmCCallback
	NULL
	    XtCallbackList
		C

XmNheight
    XmCHeight
	dynamic
	    Dimension
		CSG

XmNinitialResourcesPersistent
    XmCInitialResourcesPersistent
	True
	    Boolean
		C

XmNmappedWhenManaged
    XmCMappedWhenManaged
	True
	    Boolean
		CSG

XmNscreen
    XmCScreen
	dynamic
	    Screen *
		CG

XmNsensitive
    XmCSensitive
	True
	    Boolean
		CSG

Name	Default	Access
Class	Type	
XmNtranslations	dynamic	CSG
XmCTranslations	XtTranslations	
XmNwidth	dynamic	CSG
XmCWidth	Dimension	
XmNx	0	CSG
XmCPosition	Position	
XmNy	0	CSG
XmCPosition	Position	

Action Routines

The **XmMenuShell** action routines are

ClearTraversal():

Disables keyboard traversal for the menu, enables mouse traversal, and unposts any menus posted by this menu.

MenuShellPopdownDone():

Unposts the menu hierarchy and, when the shell's keyboard focus policy is **XmEXPLICIT**, restores focus to the widget that had the focus before the menu system was entered.

MenuShellPopdownOne():

In a top-level Pulldown MenuPane from a MenuBar, this action unposts the menu, disarms the MenuBar CascadeButton and the MenuBar, and, when the shell's keyboard focus policy is **XmEXPLICT**, restores keyboard focus to the widget that had the focus before the MenuBar was entered. In other Pulldown MenuPanes, this action unposts the menu.

In a Popup MenuPane, this action unposts the menu, and, when the shell's keyboard focus policy is **XmEXPLICT**, restores keyboard focus to the widget from which the menu was posted.

Related Information

Composite(3X), **Core(3X)**, **OverrideShell(3X)**, **Shell(3X)**, **XmCreateMenuShell(3X)**, **XmCreatePopupMenu(3X)**, **XmCreatePulldown(3X)**, and **XmRowColumn(3X)**.

XmMessageBox—The MessageBox widget class

AES Support Level

Full-use

Synopsis

#include <Xm/MessageB.h>

Description

MessageBox is a dialog class used for creating simple message dialogs. Convenience dialogs based on MessageBox are provided for several common interaction tasks, which include giving information, asking questions, and reporting errors.

A MessageBox dialog is typically transient in nature, displayed for the duration of a single interaction. MessageBox is a subclass of BulletinBoard and depends on it for much of its general dialog behavior.

A typical MessageBox contains a message symbol, a message, and up to three standard default PushButtons: **OK, Cancel**, and **Help**. It is laid out with the symbol and message on top and the PushButtons on the bottom. The **Help** button is positioned to the side of the other push buttons. You can localize the default symbols and button labels for MessageBox convenience dialogs.

A MessageBox can also be customized by creating and managing new children that are added to the MessageBox children created automatically by the convenience dialogs.

At initialization, MessageBox looks for the following bitmap files:

- **xm_error**

- **xm_information**

- **xm_question**

- **xm_working**

- **xm_warning**

See **XmGetPixmap(3X)** for a list of the paths that are searched for these files.

Classes

MessageBox inherits behavior and resources from **Core**, **Composite**, **Constraint**, **XmManager**, and **XmBulletinBoard**.

The class pointer is **xmMessageBoxWidgetClass**.

The class name is **XmMessageBox**.

New Resources

The following table defines a set of widget resources used by the programmer to specify data. The programmer can also set the resource values for the inherited classes to set attributes for this widget. To reference a resource by name or by class in a **.Xdefaults** file, remove the **XmN** or **XmC** prefix and use the remaining letters. To specify one of the defined values for a resource in a **.Xdefaults** file, remove the **Xm** prefix and use the remaining letters (in either lowercase or uppercase, but include any underscores between words). The codes in the access column indicate if the given resource can be set at creation time (C), set by using **XtSetValues** (S), retrieved by using **XtGetValues** (G), or is not applicable (N/A).

XmMessageBox Resource Set		

Name
    Class
	Default
	    Type
		Access

XmNcancelCallback
    XmCCallback
	NULL
	    XtCallbackList
		C

XmNcancelLabelString
    XmCCancelLabelString
	dynamic
	    XmString
		CSG

XmNdefaultButtonType
    XmCDefaultButtonType
	XmDIALOG_OK_BUTTON
	    unsigned char
		CSG

XmNdialogType
    XmCDialogType
	XmDIALOG_MESSAGE
	    unsigned char
		CSG

XmNhelpLabelString
    XmCHelpLabelString
	dynamic
	    XmString
		CSG

XmNmessageAlignment
    XmCAlignment
	XmALIGNMENT_BEGINNING
	    unsigned char
		CSG

XmNmessageString
    XmCMessageString
	""
	    XmString
		CSG

XmNminimizeButtons
    XmCMinimizeButtons
	False
	    Boolean
		CSG

XmNokCallback
    XmCCallback
	NULL
	    XtCallbackList
		C

XmNokLabelString
    XmCOkLabelString
	dynamic
	    XmString
		CSG

XmNsymbolPixmap
    XmCPixmap
	dynamic
	    Pixmap
		CSG

XmNcancelCallback
Specifies the list of callbacks that is called when the user clicks on the cancel button. The reason sent by the callback is **XmCR_CANCEL**.

XmNcancelLabelString
Specifies the string label for the cancel button. The default for this resource depends on the locale. In the C locale the default is **Cancel**.

XmNdefaultButtonType
Specifies the default PushButton. A value of **XmDIALOG_NONE** means that there should be no default PushButton. The following types are valid:

- **XmDIALOG_CANCEL_BUTTON**

- **XmDIALOG_OK_BUTTON**

- **XmDIALOG_HELP_BUTTON**

- **XmDIALOG_NONE**

XmNdialogType
Specifies the type of MessageBox dialog, which determines the default message symbol. The following are the possible values for this resource:

XmDIALOG_ERROR
Indicates an ErrorDialog.

XmDIALOG_INFORMATION
Indicates an InformationDialog.

XmDIALOG_MESSAGE
Indicates a MessageDialog. This is the default MessageBox dialog type. The default message symbol is NULL.

XmDIALOG_QUESTION
Indicates a QuestionDialog.

XmDIALOG_WARNING
Indicates a WarningDialog.

XmDIALOG_WORKING
Indicates a WorkingDialog.

If this resource is changed with **XtSetValues**, the symbol bitmap is modified to the new **XmNdialogType** bitmap unless **XmNsymbolPixmap** is also being set in the call to **XtSetValues**.

XmNhelpLabelString
> Specifies the string label for the help button. The default for this resource depends on the locale. In the C locale the default is **Help**.

XmNmessageAlignment
> Controls the alignment of the message Label. Possible values include the following:

> - **XmALIGNMENT_BEGINNING** (default)
> - **XmALIGNMENT_CENTER**
> - **XmALIGNMENT_END**

XmNmessageString
> Specifies the string to be used as the message.

XmNminimizeButtons
> Sets the buttons to the width of the widest button and height of the tallest button if False. If this resource is True, button width and height are set to the preferred size of each button.

XmNokCallback
> Specifies the list of callbacks that is called when the user clicks on the OK button. The reason sent by the callback is **XmCR_OK**.

XmNokLabelString
> Specifies the string label for the OK button. The default for this resource depends on the locale. In the C locale the default is **OK**.

XmNsymbolPixmap
> Specifies the pixmap label to be used as the message symbol.

Inherited Resources

MessageBox inherits behavior and resources from the superclasses described in the following tables. For a complete description of each resource, refer to the reference page for that superclass.

XmMessageBox(3X)

XmBulletinBoard Resource Set		
Name	**Default**	**Access**
Class	**Type**	
XmNallowOverlap	True	CSG
XmCAllowOverlap	Boolean	
XmNautoUnmanage	True	CG
XmCAutoUnmanage	Boolean	
XmNbuttonFontList	dynamic	CSG
XmCButtonFontList	XmFontList	
XmNcancelButton	Cancel button	SG
XmCWidget	Widget	
XmNdefaultButton	dynamic	SG
XmCWidget	Widget	
XmNdefaultPosition	True	CSG
XmCDefaultPosition	Boolean	
XmNdialogStyle	dynamic	CSG
XmCDialogStyle	unsigned char	
XmNdialogTitle	NULL	CSG
XmCDialogTitle	XmString	
XmNfocusCallback	NULL	C
XmCCallback	XtCallbackList	
XmNlabelFontList	dynamic	CSG
XmCLabelFontList	XmFontList	
XmNmapCallback	NULL	C
XmCCallback	XtCallbackList	
XmNmarginHeight	10	CSG
XmCMarginHeight	Dimension	
XmNmarginWidth	10	CSG
XmCMarginWidth	Dimension	
XmNnoResize	False	CSG
XmCNoResize	Boolean	
XmNresizePolicy	XmRESIZE_ANY	CSG
XmCResizePolicy	unsigned char	

Name	Default	Access
Class	Type	
XmNshadowType	XmSHADOW_OUT	CSG
XmCShadowType	unsigned char	
XmNtextFontList	dynamic	CSG
XmCTextFontList	XmFontList	
XmNtextTranslations	NULL	C
XmCTranslations	XtTranslations	
XmNunmapCallback	NULL	C
XmCCallback	XtCallbackList	

XmManager Resource Set		
Name	**Default**	**Access**
Class	**Type**	
XmNbottomShadowColor	dynamic	CSG
XmCBottomShadowColor	Pixel	
XmNbottomShadowPixmap	XmUNSPECIFIED_PIXMAP	CSG
XmCBottomShadowPixmap	Pixmap	
XmNforeground	dynamic	CSG
XmCForeground	Pixel	
XmNhelpCallback	NULL	C
XmCCallback	XtCallbackList	
XmNhighlightColor	dynamic	CSG
XmCHighlightColor	Pixel	
XmNhighlightPixmap	dynamic	CSG
XmCHighlightPixmap	Pixmap	
XmNnavigationType	XmTAB_GROUP	CSG
XmCNavigationType	XmNavigationType	
XmNshadowThickness	dynamic	CSG
XmCShadowThickness	Dimension	
XmNstringDirection	dynamic	CG
XmCStringDirection	XmStringDirection	
XmNtopShadowColor	dynamic	CSG
XmCTopShadowColor	Pixel	
XmNtopShadowPixmap	dynamic	CSG
XmCTopShadowPixmap	Pixmap	
XmNtraversalOn	True	CSG
XmCTraversalOn	Boolean	
XmNuserData	NULL	CSG
XmCUserData	XtPointer	

Composite Resource Set		
Name	**Default**	**Access**
Class	**Type**	
XmNchildren	NULL	G
XmCReadOnly	WidgetList	
XmNinsertPosition	NULL	CSG
XmCInsertPosition	XtOrderProc	
XmNnumChildren	0	G
XmCReadOnly	Cardinal	

Core Resource Set		
Name **Class**	**Default** **Type**	**Access**
XmNaccelerators XmCAccelerators	dynamic XtAccelerators	N/A
XmNancestorSensitive XmCSensitive	dynamic Boolean	G
XmNbackground XmCBackground	dynamic Pixel	CSG
XmNbackgroundPixmap XmCPixmap	XmUNSPECIFIED_PIXMAP Pixmap	CSG
XmNborderColor XmCBorderColor	XtDefaultForeground Pixel	CSG
XmNborderPixmap XmCPixmap	XmUNSPECIFIED_PIXMAP Pixmap	CSG
XmNborderWidth XmCBorderWidth	0 Dimension	CSG
XmNcolormap XmCColormap	dynamic Colormap	CG
XmNdepth XmCDepth	dynamic int	CG
XmNdestroyCallback XmCCallback	NULL XtCallbackList	C
XmNheight XmCHeight	dynamic Dimension	CSG
XmNinitialResourcesPersistent XmCInitialResourcesPersistent	True Boolean	C
XmNmappedWhenManaged XmCMappedWhenManaged	True Boolean	CSG
XmNscreen XmCScreen	dynamic Screen *	CG
XmNsensitive XmCSensitive	True Boolean	CSG

Name	Default	Access
Class	Type	
XmNtranslations	dynamic	CSG
XmCTranslations	XtTranslations	
XmNwidth	dynamic	CSG
XmCWidth	Dimension	
XmNx	0	CSG
XmCPosition	Position	
XmNy	0	CSG
XmCPosition	Position	

Callback Information

A pointer to the following structure is passed to each callback:

```
typedef struct
{
    int            reason;
    XEvent         * event;
} XmAnyCallbackStruct;
```

reason   Indicates why the callback was invoked

event   Points to the **XEvent** that triggered the callback

Related Information

Composite(3X), **Constraint(3X)**, **Core(3X)**, **XmBulletinBoard(3X)**,
XmCreateErrorDialog(3X), **XmCreateInformationDialog(3X)**,
XmCreateMessageBox(3X), **XmCreateMessageDialog(3X)**,
XmCreateQuestionDialog(3X), **XmCreateWarningDialog(3X)**,
XmCreateWorkingDialog(3X), **XmManager(3X)**, and
XmMessageBoxGetChild(3X).

XmMessageBoxGetChild—A MessageBox function that is used to access a component

AES Support Level

Full-use

Synopsis

#include <Xm/MessageB.h>

Widget XmMessageBoxGetChild (*widget, child*)
    Widget   *widget*;
    unsigned char *child*;

Description

XmMessageBoxGetChild is used to access a component within a MessageBox. The parameters given to the function are the MessageBox widget and a value indicating which component to access.

widget   Specifies the MessageBox widget ID.

child   Specifies a component within the MessageBox. The following are legal values for this parameter:

- **XmDIALOG_CANCEL_BUTTON**

- **XmDIALOG_DEFAULT_BUTTON**

- **XmDIALOG_HELP_BUTTON**

- **XmDIALOG_MESSAGE_LABEL**

- **XmDIALOG_OK_BUTTON**

- **XmDIALOG_SEPARATOR**

- **XmDIALOG_SYMBOL_LABEL**

For a complete definition of MessageBox and its associated resources, see **XmMessageBox(3X)**.

Return Value

Returns the widget ID of the specified MessageBox component. An application should not assume that the returned widget will be of any particular class.

Related Information

XmMessageBox(3X).

XmOptionButtonGadget(3X)

XmOptionButtonGadget—A RowColumn function that obtains the widget ID for the CascadeButtonGadget in an OptionMenu

AES Support Level

Full-use

Synopsis

#include <Xm/RowColumn.h>

Widget XmOptionButtonGadget (*option_menu*)
    Widget   *option_menu*;

Description

XmOptionButtonGadget provides the application with the means for obtaining the widget ID for the internally created CascadeButtonGadget. Once the application has obtained the widget ID, it can adjust the visuals for the CascadeButtonGadget, if desired.

When an application creates an instance of the OptionMenu widget, the widget creates two internal gadgets. One is a LabelGadget that is used to display RowColumn's **XmNlabelString** resource. The other is a CascadeButtonGadget that displays the current selection and provides the means for posting the OptionMenu's submenu.

option_menu   Specifies the OptionMenu widget ID

For a complete definition of RowColumn and its associated resources, see **XmRowColumn(3X)**.

Return Value

Returns the widget ID for the internal button.

Related Information

XmCreateOptionMenu(3X), **XmCascadeButtonGadget(3X)**,
XmOptionLabelGadget(3X), and **XmRowColumn(3X)**.

XmOptionLabelGadget—A RowColumn function that obtains the widget ID for the LabelGadget in an OptionMenu

AES Support Level

Full-use

Synopsis

#include <Xm/RowColumn.h>

Widget XmOptionLabelGadget (*option_menu*)
    Widget   *option_menu*;

Description

XmOptionLabelGadget provides the application with the means for obtaining the widget ID for the internally created LabelGadget. Once the application has obtained the widget ID, it can adjust the visuals for the LabelGadget, if desired.

option_menu   Specifies the OptionMenu widget ID

When an application creates an instance of the OptionMenu widget, the widget creates two internal gadgets. One is a LabelGadget that is used to display RowColumn's **XmNlabelString** resource. The other is a CascadeButtonGadget that displays the current selection and provides the means for posting the OptionMenu's submenu.

For a complete definition of RowColumn and its associated resources, see **XmRowColumn(3X)**.

Return Value

Returns the widget ID for the internal label.

Related Information

XmCreateOptionMenu(3X), **XmLabelGadget(3X)**,
XmOptionButtonGadget(3X), and **XmRowColumn(3X)**.

XmPanedWindow—The PanedWindow widget class

AES Support Level

Full-use

Synopsis

#include <Xm/PanedW.h>

Description

PanedWindow is a composite widget that lays out children in a vertically tiled format. Children appear in top-to-bottom fashion, with the first child inserted appearing at the top of the PanedWindow and the last child inserted appearing at the bottom. The PanedWindow grows to match the width of its widest child and all other children are forced to this width. The height of the PanedWindow is equal to the sum of the heights of all its children, the spacing between them, and the size of the top and bottom margins.

The user can also adjust the size of the panes. To facilitate this adjustment, a pane control sash is created for most children. The sash appears as a square box positioned on the bottom of the pane that it controls. The user can adjust the size of a pane by using the mouse or keyboard.

The PanedWindow is also a constraint widget, which means that it creates and manages a set of constraints for each child. You can specify a minimum and maximum size for each pane. The PanedWindow does not allow a pane to be resized below its minimum size or beyond its maximum size. Also, when the minimum size of a pane is equal to its maximum size, no control sash is presented for that pane or for the lowest pane.

The default **XmNinsertPosition** procedure for PanedWindow causes sashes to be inserted at the end of the list of children and causes nonsash widgets to be inserted after other nonsash children but before any sashes.

Classes

PanedWindow inherits behavior and resources from the **Core**, **Composite**, **Constraint**, and **XmManager** classes.

The class pointer is **xmPanedWindowWidgetClass**.

The class name is **XmPanedWindow**.

New Resources

The following table defines a set of widget resources used by the programmer to specify data. The programmer can also set the resource values for the inherited classes to set attributes for this widget. To reference a resource by name or by class in a **.Xdefaults** file, remove the **XmN** or **XmC** prefix and use the remaining letters. To specify one of the defined values for a resource in a **.Xdefaults** file, remove the **Xm** prefix and use the remaining letters (in either lowercase or uppercase, but include any underscores between words). The codes in the access column indicate if the given resource can be set at creation time (C), set by using **XtSetValues** (S), retrieved by using **XtGetValues** (G), or is not applicable (N/A).

XmPanedWindow Resource Set		
Name	**Default**	**Access**
Class	**Type**	
XmNmarginHeight	3	CSG
XmCMarginHeight	Dimension	
XmNmarginWidth	3	CSG
XmCMarginWidth	Dimension	
XmNrefigureMode	True	CSG
XmCBoolean	Boolean	
XmNsashHeight	10	CSG
XmCSashHeight	Dimension	
XmNsashIndent	-10	CSG
XmCSashIndent	Position	
XmNsashShadowThickness	dynamic	CSG
XmCShadowThickness	Dimension	
XmNsashWidth	10	CSG
XmCSashWidth	Dimension	
XmNseparatorOn	True	CSG
XmCSeparatorOn	Boolean	
XmNspacing	8	CSG
XmCSpacing	Dimension	

XmNmarginHeight

Specifies the distance between the top and bottom edges of the PanedWindow and its children.

XmNmarginWidth

Specifies the distance between the left and right edges of the PanedWindow and its children.

XmNrefigureMode

Determines whether the panes' positions are recomputed and repositioned when programmatic changes are being made to the PanedWindow. Setting this resource to True resets the children to their appropriate positions.

XmNsashHeight
> Specifies the height of the sash.

XmNsashIndent
> Specifies the horizontal placement of the sash along each pane. A positive value causes the sash to be offset from the near (left) side of the PanedWindow, and a negative value causes the sash to be offset from the far (right) side of the PanedWindow. If the offset is greater than the width of the PanedWindow minus the width of the sash, the sash is placed flush against the near side of the PanedWindow.
>
> Whether the placement actually corresponds to the left or right side of the PanedWindow may depend on the value of the **XmNstringDirection** resource.

XmNsashShadowThickness
> Specifies the thickness of the shadows of the sashes.

XmNsashWidth
> Specifies the width of the sash.

XmNseparatorOn
> Determines whether a separator is created between each of the panes. Setting this resource to True creates a Separator at the midpoint between each of the panes.

XmNspacing Specifies the distance between each child pane.

XmPanedWindow Constraint Resource Set		
Name	**Default**	**Access**
Class	**Type**	
XmNallowResize	False	CSG
XmCBoolean	Boolean	
XmNpaneMaximum	1000	CSG
XmCPaneMaximum	Dimension	
XmNpaneMinimum	1	CSG
XmCPaneMinimum	Dimension	
XmNskipAdjust	False	CSG
XmCBoolean	Boolean	

XmNallowResize
> Allows an application to specify whether the PanedWindow should allow a pane to request to be resized. This flag has an effect only after the PanedWindow and its children have been realized. If this

flag is set to True, the PanedWindow tries to honor requests to alter the height of the pane. If False, it always denies pane requests to resize.

XmNpaneMaximum

Allows an application to specify the maximum size to which a pane may be resized. This value must be greater than the specified minimum.

XmNpaneMinimum

Allows an application to specify the minimum size to which a pane may be resized. This value must be greater than 0 (zero).

XmNskipAdjust

When set to True, this Boolean resource allows an application to specify that the PanedWindow should not automatically resize this pane.

Inherited Resources

PanedWindow inherits behavior and resources from the superclasses described in the following tables. For a complete description of each resource, refer to the reference page for that superclass.

XmManager Resource Set		

Name
  Class
	Default
	  Type
		Access

XmNbottomShadowColor
  XmCBottomShadowColor
	dynamic
	  Pixel
		CSG

XmNbottomShadowPixmap
  XmCBottomShadowPixmap
	XmUNSPECIFIED_PIXMAP
	  Pixmap
		CSG

XmNforeground
  XmCForeground
	dynamic
	  Pixel
		CSG

XmNhelpCallback
  XmCCallback
	NULL
	  XtCallbackList
		C

XmNhighlightColor
  XmCHighlightColor
	dynamic
	  Pixel
		CSG

XmNhighlightPixmap
  XmCHighlightPixmap
	dynamic
	  Pixmap
		CSG

XmNnavigationType
  XmCNavigationType
	XmTAB_GROUP
	  XmNavigationType
		CSG

XmNshadowThickness
  XmCShadowThickness
	2
	  Dimension
		CSG

XmNstringDirection
  XmCStringDirection
	dynamic
	  XmStringDirection
		CG

XmNtopShadowColor
  XmCTopShadowColor
	dynamic
	  Pixel
		CSG

XmNtopShadowPixmap
  XmCTopShadowPixmap
	dynamic
	  Pixmap
		CSG

XmNtraversalOn
  XmCTraversalOn
	True
	  Boolean
		CSG

XmNuserData
  XmCUserData
	NULL
	  XtPointer
		CSG

Core Resource Set		
Name	**Default**	**Access**
Class	**Type**	
XmNaccelerators	dynamic	CSG
XmCAccelerators	XtAccelerators	
XmNancestorSensitive	dynamic	G
XmCSensitive	Boolean	
XmNbackground	dynamic	CSG
XmCBackground	Pixel	
XmNbackgroundPixmap	XmUNSPECIFIED_PIXMAP	CSG
XmCPixmap	Pixmap	
XmNborderColor	XtDefaultForeground	CSG
XmCBorderColor	Pixel	
XmNborderPixmap	XmUNSPECIFIED_PIXMAP	CSG
XmCPixmap	Pixmap	
XmNborderWidth	0	CSG
XmCBorderWidth	Dimension	
XmNcolormap	dynamic	CG
XmCColormap	Colormap	
XmNdepth	dynamic	CG
XmCDepth	int	
XmNdestroyCallback	NULL	C
XmCCallback	XtCallbackList	
XmNheight	dynamic	CSG
XmCHeight	Dimension	
XmNinitialResourcesPersistent	True	C
XmCInitialResourcesPersistent	Boolean	
XmNmappedWhenManaged	True	CSG
XmCMappedWhenManaged	Boolean	
XmNscreen	dynamic	CG
XmCScreen	Screen *	
XmNsensitive	True	CSG
XmCSensitive	Boolean	

Name	Default	Access
Class	Type	
XmNtranslations	dynamic	CSG
XmCTranslations	XtTranslations	
XmNwidth	dynamic	CSG
XmCWidth	Dimension	
XmNx	0	CSG
XmCPosition	Position	
XmNy	0	CSG
XmCPosition	Position	

Composite Resource Set		
Name	Default	Access
Class	Type	
XmNchildren	NULL	G
XmCReadOnly	WidgetList	
XmNinsertPosition	default procedure	CSG
XmCInsertPosition	XtOrderProc	
XmNnumChildren	0	G
XmCReadOnly	Cardinal	

Action Routines

The **XmPanedWindow** action routines are

Help(): Calls the callbacks for **XmNhelpCallback** if any exist. If there are no help callbacks for this widget, this action calls the help callbacks for the nearest ancestor that has them.

NextTabGroup():
Moves the keyboard focus to the next tab group. By default, each pane and sash is a tab group.

PrevTabGroup():
Moves the keyboard focus to the previous tab group. By default, each pane and sash is a tab group.

SashAction(*action*) or **SashAction**(**Key,***increment***,***direction***):**
> The **Start** action activates the interactive placement of the pane's borders. The **Move** action causes the sash to track the position of the pointer. If one of the panes reaches its minimum or maximum size, adjustment continues with the next adjustable pane. The **Commit** action ends sash motion.
>
> When sash action is caused by a keyboard event, the sash with the keyboard focus is moved according to the *increment* and *direction* specified. **DefaultIncr** adjusts the sash by one line. **LargeIncr** adjusts the sash by one view region. The *direction* is specified as either **Up** or **Down**.
>
> Note that the SashAction action routine is not a direct action routine of the **XmPanedWindow,** but rather an action of the Sash control created by the **XmPanedWindow.**

Virtual Bindings
> The bindings for virtual keys are vendor specific.

Related Information

> **Composite(3X)**, **Constraint(3X)**, **Core(3X)**, **XmCreatePanedWindow(3X)**, and **XmManager(3X)**.

XmPrimitive—The Primitive widget class

AES Support Level

Full-use

Synopsis

#include <Xm/Xm.h>

Description

Primitive is a widget class used as a supporting superclass for other widget classes. It handles border drawing and highlighting, traversal activation and deactivation, and various callback lists needed by Primitive widgets.

Classes

Primitive inherits behavior and resources from **Core**.

The class pointer is **xmPrimitiveWidgetClass**.

The class name is **XmPrimitive**.

New Resources

The following table defines a set of widget resources used by the programmer to specify data. The programmer can also set the resource values for the inherited classes to set attributes for this widget. To reference a resource by name or by class in a **.Xdefaults** file, remove the **XmN** or **XmC** prefix and use the remaining letters. To specify one of the defined values for a resource in a **.Xdefaults** file, remove the **Xm** prefix and use the remaining letters (in either lowercase or uppercase, but include any underscores between words). The codes in the access column indicate if the given resource can be set at creation time (C), set by using **XtSetValues** (S), retrieved by using **XtGetValues** (G), or is not applicable (N/A).

XmPrimitive Resource Set		

Name
    Class
	Default
	    Type
		Access

XmNbottomShadowColor
    XmCBottomShadowColor
	dynamic
	    Pixel
		CSG

XmNbottomShadowPixmap
    XmCBottomShadowPixmap
	XmUNSPECIFIED_PIXMAP
	    Pixmap
		CSG

XmNforeground
    XmCForeground
	dynamic
	    Pixel
		CSG

XmNhelpCallback
    XmCCallback
	NULL
	    XtCallbackList
		C

XmNhighlightColor
    XmCHighlightColor
	dynamic
	    Pixel
		CSG

XmNhighlightOnEnter
    XmCHighlightOnEnter
	False
	    Boolean
		CSG

XmNhighlightPixmap
    XmCHighlightPixmap
	dynamic
	    Pixmap
		CSG

XmNhighlightThickness
    XmCHighlightThickness
	2
	    Dimension
		CSG

XmNnavigationType
    XmCNavigationType
	XmNONE
	    XmNavigationType
		CSG

XmNshadowThickness
    XmCShadowThickness
	2
	    Dimension
		CSG

XmNtopShadowColor
    XmCTopShadowColor
	dynamic
	    Pixel
		CSG

XmNtopShadowPixmap
    XmCTopShadowPixmap
	dynamic
	    Pixmap
		CSG

XmNtraversalOn
    XmCTraversalOn
	True
	    Boolean
		CSG

XmNuserData
    XmCUserData
	NULL
	    XtPointer
		CSG

XmNbottomShadowColor

>Specifies the color to use to draw the bottom and right sides of the border shadow. This color is used if the **XmNtopShadowPixmap** resource is unspecified.

XmNbottomShadowPixmap

>Specifies the pixmap to use to draw the bottom and right sides of the border shadow.

XmNforeground

Specifies the foreground drawing color used by Primitive widgets.

XmNhelpCallback

Specifies the list of callbacks that is called when the help key is pressed. The reason sent by the callback is **XmCR_HELP**.

XmNhighlightColor

Specifies the color of the highlighting rectangle. This color is used if the highlight pixmap resource is **XmUNSPECIFIED_PIXMAP**.

XmNhighlightOnEnter

Specifies if the highlighting rectangle is drawn when the cursor moves into the widget. If the shell's focus policy is **XmEXPLICIT**, this resource is ignored, and the widget is highlighted when it has the focus. If the shell's focus policy is **XmPOINTER** and if this resource is True, the highlighting rectangle is drawn when the cursor moves into the widget. If the shell's focus policy is **XmPOINTER** and if this resource is False, the highlighting rectangle is not drawn when the the cursor moves into the widget. The default is False.

XmNhighlightPixmap

Specifies the pixmap used to draw the highlighting rectangle.

XmNhighlightThickness

Specifies the thickness of the highlighting rectangle.

XmNnavigationType

Determines whether the widget is a tab group.

XmNONE   Indicates that the widget is not a tab group.

XmTAB_GROUP

Indicates that the widget is a tab group, unless the **XmNnavigationType** of another widget in the hierarchy is **XmEXCLUSIVE_TAB_GROUP**.

XmSTICKY_TAB_GROUP

Indicates that the widget is a tab group, even if the **XmNnavigationType** of another widget in the hierarchy is **XmEXCLUSIVE_TAB_GROUP**.

XmEXCLUSIVE_TAB_GROUP

Indicates that the widget is a tab group and that widgets in the hierarchy whose **XmNnavigationType** is **XmTAB_GROUP** are not tab groups.

When a parent widget has an **XmNnavigationType**

of **XmEXCLUSIVE_TAB_GROUP**, traversal of non-tab-group widgets within the group is based on the order of those widgets in their parent's **XmNchildren** list.

XmNshadowThickness

Specifies the size of the drawn border shadow.

XmNtopShadowColor

Specifies the color to use to draw the top and left sides of the border shadow. This color is used if the **XmNtopShadowPixmap** resource is unspecified.

XmNtopShadowPixmap

Specifies the pixmap to use to draw the top and left sides of the border shadow.

XmNtraversalOn

Specifies if traversal is activated for this widget. In CascadeButton and CascadeButtonGadget, this resource is forced to True unless the parent is an OptionMenu.

XmNuserData

Allows the application to attach any necessary specific data to the widget. It is an internally unused resource.

Dynamic Color Defaults

The foreground, background, top shadow, and bottom shadow resources are dynamically defaulted. If no color data is specified, the colors are automatically generated. On a single-plane system, a black and white color scheme is generated. Otherwise, four colors are generated, which display the correct shading for the 3-D visuals. If the background is the only color specified for a widget, the top shadow, bottom shadow, and foreground colors are generated to give the 3-D appearance.

Colors are generated only at creation. Resetting the background through **XtSetValues** does not regenerate the other colors.

Inherited Resources

Primitive inherits behavior and resources from the superclass described in the following table. For a complete description of each resource, refer to the reference page for that superclass.

Core Resource Set		
Name	**Default**	**Access**
Class	**Type**	
XmNaccelerators	dynamic	CSG
XmCAccelerators	XtAccelerators	
XmNancestorSensitive	dynamic	G
XmCSensitive	Boolean	
XmNbackground	dynamic	CSG
XmCBackground	Pixel	
XmNbackgroundPixmap	XmUNSPECIFIED_PIXMAP	CSG
XmCPixmap	Pixmap	
XmNborderColor	XtDefaultForeground	CSG
XmCBorderColor	Pixel	
XmNborderPixmap	XmUNSPECIFIED_PIXMAP	CSG
XmCPixmap	Pixmap	
XmNborderWidth	0	CSG
XmCBorderWidth	Dimension	
XmNcolormap	dynamic	CG
XmCColormap	Colormap	
XmNdepth	dynamic	CG
XmCDepth	int	
XmNdestroyCallback	NULL	C
XmCCallback	XtCallbackList	
XmNheight	dynamic	CSG
XmCHeight	Dimension	
XmNinitialResourcesPersistent	True	C
XmCInitialResourcesPersistent	Boolean	
XmNmappedWhenManaged	True	CSG
XmCMappedWhenManaged	Boolean	
XmNscreen	dynamic	CG
XmCScreen	Screen *	
XmNsensitive	True	CSG
XmCSensitive	Boolean	

Name	Default	Access
Class	Type	
XmNtranslations	dynamic	CSG
XmCTranslations	XtTranslations	
XmNwidth	dynamic	CSG
XmCWidth	Dimension	
XmNx	0	CSG
XmCPosition	Position	
XmNy	0	CSG
XmCPosition	Position	

Callback Information

A pointer to the following structure is passed to each callback:

typedef struct
{
    int   *reason*;
    XEvent   ** event*;
} XmAnyCallbackStruct;

reason   Indicates why the callback was invoked. For this callback, *reason* is set to **XmCR_HELP**.

event   Points to the **XEvent** that triggered the callback.

Action Routines

The **XmPrimitive** action routines are

PrimitiveHelp():

Calls the callbacks for **XmNhelpCallback** if any exist. If there are no help callbacks for this widget, this action calls the help callbacks for the nearest ancestor that has them.

PrimitiveNextTabGroup():

Traverses to the first item in the next tab group. If the current tab group is the last entry in the tab group list, it wraps to the beginning of the tab group list.

PrimitiveParentActivate():

If the parent is a manager, passes the **KActivate** event received by the widget to the parent.

PrimitiveParentCancel():
If the parent is a manager, passes the **KCancel** event received by the widget to the parent.

PrimitivePrevTabGroup():
Traverses to the first item in the previous tab group. If the beginning of the tab group list is reached, it wraps to the end of the tab group list.

PrimitiveTraverseDown():
Traverses to the next item below the current widget in the current tab group, wrapping if necessary.

PrimitiveTraverseHome():
Traverses to the first widget or gadget in the current tab group.

PrimitiveTraverseLeft():
Traverses to the next item to the left of the current widget in the current tab group, wrapping if necessary.

PrimitiveTraverseNext():
Traverses to the next item in the current tab group, wrapping if necessary.

PrimitiveTraversePrev():
Traverses to the previous item in the current tab group, wrapping if necessary.

PrimitiveTraverseRight():
Traverses to the next item to the right of the current gadget in the current tab group, wrapping if necessary.

PrimitiveTraverseUp():
Traverses to the next item above the current gadget in the current tab group, wrapping if necessary.

Related Information

Core(3X).

XmProcessTraversal—A function that determines which component receives keyboard events when a widget has the focus

AES Support Level

Full-use

Synopsis

#include <Xm/Xm.h>

Boolean XmProcessTraversal (*widget, direction*)
    Widget   *widget*;
    XmTraversalDirection *direction*;

Description

XmProcessTraversal determines which component of a hierarchy receives keyboard events when the hierarchy that contains the given widget has keyboard focus. It is not possible to use **XmProcessTraversal** to traverse to MenuBars, Pulldown MenuPanes, or Popup MenuPanes.

widget   Specifies the widget ID of the widget whose hierarchy is to be traversed. The hierarchy is only traversed up to the top of the shell. If that shell does not currently have the focus, any changes to the element with focus within that shell will not occur until the next time the shell recieves focus.

direction   Specifies the direction of traversal

The *direction* parameter can have the following values, which cause the routine to take the corresponding actions:

XmTRAVERSE_CURRENT
    Finds the hierarchy and the tab group that contain *widget*. If this tab group is not the active tab group, this action makes it the active tab group. If *widget* is an item in the active tab group, this action makes it the active item. If *widget* is the active tab group, this action makes the first traversable item in the tab group the active item.

XmTRAVERSE_DOWN
    Finds the hierarchy that contains *widget*, finds the active item in the active tab group, and makes the item below it the active item. If there is no item below, it wraps.

XmTRAVERSE_HOME

    Finds the hierarchy that contains *widget* and finds the active item in the active tab group and makes the first traversable item in the tab group the active item.

XmTRAVERSE_LEFT

    Finds the hierarchy that contains *widget*, finds the active item in the active tab group, and makes the item to the left the active item. If there is no item to the left, this action wraps.

XmTRAVERSE_NEXT

    Finds the hierarchy that contains *widget*, finds the active item in the active tab group, and makes the next item in child order the active item.

XmTRAVERSE_NEXT_TAB_GROUP

    Finds the hierarchy that contains *widget*, finds the active tab group (if any), and makes the next tab group the active tab group in the hierarchy.

XmTRAVERSE_PREV

    Finds the hierarchy that contains *widget*, finds the active item in the active tab group, and makes the previous item in child order the active item.

XmTRAVERSE_PREV_TAB_GROUP

    Finds the hierarchy that contains *widget*, finds the active tab group (if any), and makes the previous tab group the active tab group in the hierarchy.

XmTRAVERSE_RIGHT

    Finds the hierarchy that contains *widget*, finds the active item in the active tab group, and makes the item to the right the active item. If there is no item to the right, this action wraps.

XmTRAVERSE_UP

    Finds the hierarchy that contains *widget*, finds the active item in the active tab group, and makes the item above it the active item. If there is no item above, this action wraps.

Return Value

Returns True if the setting succeeded. Returns False if the keyboard focus policy is not **XmEXPLICIT**, if there are no traversable items, or if the call to the routine has invalid parameters.

XmPushButton—The PushButton widget class

AES Support Level

Full-use

Synopsis

#include <Xm/PushB.h>

Description

PushButton issues commands within an application. It consists of a text label or pixmap surrounded by a border shadow. When a PushButton is selected, the shadow changes to give the appearance that it has been pressed in. When a PushButton is unselected, the shadow changes to give the appearance that it is out.

The default behavior associated with a PushButton in a menu depends on the type of menu system in which it resides. By default, **BSelect** controls the behavior of the PushButton. In addition, **BMenu** controls the behavior of the PushButton if it resides in a PopupMenu system. The actual mouse button used is determined by its RowColumn parent.

Thickness for a second shadow, used when the PushButton is the default button, may be specified with the **XmNshowAsDefault** resource. If it has a nonzero value, the Label's resources **XmNmarginLeft**, **XmNmarginRight**, **XmNmarginTop**, and **XmNmarginBottom** may be modified to accommodate the second shadow.

If an initial value is specified for **XmNarmPixmap** but not for **XmNlabelPixmap**, the **XmNarmPixmap** value is used for **XmNlabelPixmap**.

Classes

PushButton inherits behavior and resources from **Core**, **XmPrimitive**, and **XmLabel**.

The class pointer is **xmPushButtonWidgetClass**.

The class name is **XmPushButton**.

New Resources

The following table defines a set of widget resources used by the programmer to specify data. The programmer can also set the resource values for the inherited classes to set attributes for this widget. To reference a resource by name or by class in a **.Xdefaults** file, remove the **XmN** or **XmC** prefix and use the remaining letters. To specify one of the defined values for a resource in a **.Xdefaults** file, remove the **Xm** prefix and use the remaining letters (in either lowercase or uppercase, but include any underscores between words). The codes in the access column indicate if the given resource can be set at creation time (C), set by using **XtSetValues** (S), retrieved by using **XtGetValues** (G), or is not applicable (N/A).

XmPushButton Resource Set		
Name	**Default**	**Access**
Class	**Type**	
XmNactivateCallback	NULL	C
XmCCallback	XtCallbackList	
XmNarmCallback	NULL	C
XmCCallback	XtCallbackList	
XmNarmColor	dynamic	CSG
XmCArmColor	Pixel	
XmNarmPixmap	XmUNSPECIFIED_PIXMAP	CSG
XmCArmPixmap	Pixmap	
XmNdefaultButtonShadowThickness	dynamic	CSG
XmCDefaultButtonShadowThickness	Dimension	
XmNdisarmCallback	NULL	C
XmCCallback	XtCallbackList	
XmNfillOnArm	True	CSG
XmCFillOnArm	Boolean	
XmNmultiClick	dynamic	CSG
XmCMultiClick	unsigned char	
XmNshowAsDefault	0	CSG
XmCShowAsDefault	Dimension	

XmNactivateCallback

Specifies the list of callbacks that is called when PushButton is activated. PushButton is activated when the user presses and releases the active mouse button while the pointer is inside that widget. Activating the PushButton also disarms it. For this callback, the reason is **XmCR_ACTIVATE**.

XmNarmCallback

Specifies the list of callbacks that is called when PushButton is armed. PushButton is armed when the user presses the active mouse button while the pointer is inside that widget. For this callback, the reason is **XmCR_ARM**.

XmNarmColor

Specifies the color with which to fill the armed button. **XmNfillOnArm** must be set to True for this resource to have an effect. The default for a color display is a color between the background and the bottom shadow color. For a monochrome display, the default is set to the foreground color, and any text in the label appears in the background color when the button is armed.

XmNarmPixmap

Specifies the pixmap to be used as the button face if **XmNlabelType** is **XmPIXMAP** and PushButton is armed. This resource is disabled when the PushButton is in a menu.

XmNdefaultButtonShadowThickness

This resource specifies the width of the default button indicator shadow. If this resource is 0 (zero), the width of the shadow comes from the value of the **XmNshowAsDefault** resource. If this resource is greater than 0, the **XmNshowAsDefault** resource is only used to specify whether this button is the default. The default value is the initial value of **XmNshowAsDefault**.

XmNdisarmCallback

Specifies the list of callbacks that is called when PushButton is disarmed. PushButton is disarmed when the user presses and releases the active mouse button while the pointer is inside that widget. For this callback, the reason is **XmCR_DISARM**.

XmNfillOnArm

Forces the PushButton to fill the background of the button with the color specified by **XmNarmColor** when the button is armed and when this resource is set to True. If False, only the top and bottom shadow colors are switched. When the PushButton is in a menu, this resource is ignored and assumed to be False.

XmNmultiClick

If a button click is followed by another button click within the time span specified by the display's multiclick time, and this resource is set to **XmMULTICLICK_DISCARD**, do not process the second click. If this resource is set to **XmMULTICLICK_KEEP**, process the event and increment *click_count* in the callback structure. When the button is not in a menu, the default value is **XmMULTICLICK_KEEP**.

XmNshowAsDefault

If **XmNdefaultButtonShadowThickness** is greater than 0 (zero), a value greater than 0 in this resource specifies to mark this button as the default button. If **XmNdefaultButtonShadowThickness** is 0, a value greater than 0 in this resource specifies to mark this button as the default button with the shadow thickness specified by this resource. The space between the shadow and the default shadow is equal to the sum of both shadows. The default value is 0. When this value is not 0, the Label resources **XmNmarginLeft**, **XmNmarginRight**, **XmNmarginTop**, and **XmNmarginBottom** may be modified to accommodate the second shadow. This resource is disabled when the PushButton is in a menu.

Inherited Resources

PushButton inherits behavior and resources from the superclasses described the following tables. For a complete description of each resource, refer to the reference page for that superclass.

<table>
<thead>
<tr><th colspan="3" align="center">XmLabel Resource Set</th></tr>
<tr><th>Name
   Class</th><th>Default
   Type</th><th>Access</th></tr>
</thead>
<tbody>
<tr><td>XmNaccelerator
   XmCAccelerator</td><td>NULL
   String</td><td>CSG</td></tr>
<tr><td>XmNacceleratorText
   XmCAcceleratorText</td><td>NULL
   XmString</td><td>CSG</td></tr>
<tr><td>XmNalignment
   XmCAlignment</td><td>dynamic
   unsigned char</td><td>CSG</td></tr>
<tr><td>XmNfontList
   XmCFontList</td><td>dynamic
   XmFontList</td><td>CSG</td></tr>
<tr><td>XmNlabelInsensitivePixmap
   XmCLabelInsensitivePixmap</td><td>XmUNSPECIFIED_PIXMAP
   Pixmap</td><td>CSG</td></tr>
<tr><td>XmNlabelPixmap
   XmCLabelPixmap</td><td>dynamic
   Pixmap</td><td>CSG</td></tr>
<tr><td>XmNlabelString
   XmCXmString</td><td>dynamic
   XmString</td><td>CSG</td></tr>
<tr><td>XmNlabelType
   XmCLabelType</td><td>XmSTRING
   unsigned char</td><td>CSG</td></tr>
<tr><td>XmNmarginBottom
   XmCMarginBottom</td><td>dynamic
   Dimension</td><td>CSG</td></tr>
<tr><td>XmNmarginHeight
   XmCMarginHeight</td><td>2
   Dimension</td><td>CSG</td></tr>
<tr><td>XmNmarginLeft
   XmCMarginLeft</td><td>dynamic
   Dimension</td><td>CSG</td></tr>
<tr><td>XmNmarginRight
   XmCMarginRight</td><td>dynamic
   Dimension</td><td>CSG</td></tr>
<tr><td>XmNmarginTop
   XmCMarginTop</td><td>dynamic
   Dimension</td><td>CSG</td></tr>
<tr><td>XmNmarginWidth
   XmCMarginWidth</td><td>2
   Dimension</td><td>CSG</td></tr>
<tr><td>XmNmnemonic
   XmCMnemonic</td><td>NULL
   KeySym</td><td>CSG</td></tr>
</tbody>
</table>

Name	Default	Access
Class	Type	
XmNmnemonicCharSet	XmFONTLIST_DEFAULT_TAG	CSG
XmCMnemonicCharSet	String	
XmNrecomputeSize	True	CSG
XmCRecomputeSize	Boolean	
XmNstringDirection	dynamic	CSG
XmCStringDirection	XmStringDirection	

XmPrimitive Resource Set		
Name	**Default**	**Access**
Class	**Type**	
XmNbottomShadowColor	dynamic	CSG
XmCBottomShadowColor	Pixel	
XmNbottomShadowPixmap	XmUNSPECIFIED_PIXMAP	CSG
XmCBottomShadowPixmap	Pixmap	
XmNforeground	dynamic	CSG
XmCForeground	Pixel	
XmNhelpCallback	NULL	C
XmCCallback	XtCallbackList	
XmNhighlightColor	dynamic	CSG
XmCHighlightColor	Pixel	
XmNhighlightOnEnter	False	CSG
XmCHighlightOnEnter	Boolean	
XmNhighlightPixmap	dynamic	CSG
XmCHighlightPixmap	Pixmap	
XmNhighlightThickness	2	CSG
XmCHighlightThickness	Dimension	
XmNnavigationType	XmNONE	CSG
XmCNavigationType	XmNavigationType	
XmNshadowThickness	2	CSG
XmCShadowThickness	Dimension	
XmNtopShadowColor	dynamic	CSG
XmCTopShadowColor	Pixel	
XmNtopShadowPixmap	dynamic	CSG
XmCTopShadowPixmap	Pixmap	
XmNtraversalOn	True	CSG
XmCTraversalOn	Boolean	
XmNuserData	NULL	CSG
XmCUserData	XtPointer	

Core Resource Set		
Name	**Default**	**Access**
Class	**Type**	
XmNaccelerators	dynamic	CSG
XmCAccelerators	XtAccelerators	
XmNancestorSensitive	dynamic	G
XmCSensitive	Boolean	
XmNbackground	dynamic	CSG
XmCBackground	Pixel	
XmNbackgroundPixmap	XmUNSPECIFIED_PIXMAP	CSG
XmCPixmap	Pixmap	
XmNborderColor	XtDefaultForeground	CSG
XmCBorderColor	Pixel	
XmNborderPixmap	XmUNSPECIFIED_PIXMAP	CSG
XmCPixmap	Pixmap	
XmNborderWidth	0	CSG
XmCBorderWidth	Dimension	
XmNcolormap	dynamic	CG
XmCColormap	Colormap	
XmNdepth	dynamic	CG
XmCDepth	int	
XmNdestroyCallback	NULL	C
XmCCallback	XtCallbackList	
XmNheight	dynamic	CSG
XmCHeight	Dimension	
XmNinitialResourcesPersistent	True	C
XmCInitialResourcesPersistent	Boolean	
XmNmappedWhenManaged	True	CSG
XmCMappedWhenManaged	Boolean	
XmNscreen	dynamic	CG
XmCScreen	Screen *	
XmNsensitive	True	CSG
XmCSensitive	Boolean	

Name	Default	Access
Class	Type	
XmNtranslations	dynamic	CSG
XmCTranslations	XtTranslations	
XmNwidth	dynamic	CSG
XmCWidth	Dimension	
XmNx	0	CSG
XmCPosition	Position	
XmNy	0	CSG
XmCPosition	Position	

Callback Information

A pointer to the following structure is passed to each callback:

typedef struct
{
    int   *reason*;
    XEvent   ** event*;
    int   *click_count*;
} XmPushButtonCallbackStruct;

reason   Indicates why the callback was invoked.

event   Points to the **XEvent** that triggered the callback.

click_count   This value is valid only when the reason is **XmCR_ACTIVATE**. It contains the number of clicks in the last multiclick sequence if the **XmNmultiClick** resource is set to **XmMULTICLICK_KEEP**, otherwise it contains 1. The activate callback is invoked for each click if **XmNmultiClick** is set to **XmMULTICLICK_KEEP**.

Action Routines

The **XmPushButton** action routines are

Activate():   This action draws the shadow in the unarmed state. If the button is not in a menu and if **XmNfillOnArm** is set to True, the background color reverts to the unarmed color. If **XmNlabelType** is **XmPIXMAP**, **XmNlabelPixmap** is used for the button face. If the pointer is still within the button, this action calls the callbacks for **XmNactivateCallback**.

Arm():   This action arms the PushButton. It draws the shadow in the armed state. If the button is not in a menu and if **XmNfillOnArm** is set to True, it fills the button with the color specified by **XmNarmColor**.

If **XmNlabelType** is **XmPIXMAP**, the **XmNarmPixmap** is used for the button face. It calls the **XmNarmCallback** callbacks.

ArmAndActivate():

In a menu, unposts all menus in the menu hierarchy and, unless the button is already armed, calls the **XmNarmCallback** callbacks. This action calls the **XmNactivateCallback** and **XmNdisarmCallback** callbacks.

Outside a menu, draws the shadow in the armed state and, if **XmNfillOnArm** is set to True, fills the button with the color specified by **XmNarmColor**. If **XmNlabelType** is **XmPIXMAP**, **XmNarmPixmap** is used for the button face. This action calls the **XmNarmCallback** callbacks.

Outside a menu, this action also arranges for the following to happen, either immediately or at a later time: the shadow is drawn in the unarmed state and, if **XmNfillOnArm** is set to True, the background color reverts to the unarmed color. If **XmNlabelType** is **XmPIXMAP**, **XmNlabelPixmap** is used for the button face. The **XmNactivateCallback** and **XmNdisarmCallback** callbacks are called.

BtnDown(): This action unposts any menus posted by the PushButton's parent menu, disables keyboard traversal for the menu, and enables mouse traversal for the menu. It draws the shadow in the armed state and, unless the button is already armed, calls the **XmNarmCallback** callbacks.

BtnUp(): This action unposts all menus in the menu hierarchy and activates the PushButton. It calls the **XmNactivateCallback** callbacks and then the **XmNdisarmCallback** callbacks.

Disarm(): Calls the callbacks for **XmNdisarmCallback**.

Help(): In a Pulldown or Popup MenuPane, unposts all menus in the menu hierarchy and, when the shell's keyboard focus policy is **XmEXPLICT**, restores keyboard focus to the widget that had the focus before the menu system was entered. This action calls the callbacks for **XmNhelpCallback** if any exist. If there are no help callbacks for this widget, this action calls the help callbacks for the nearest ancestor that has them.

MenuShellPopdownOne():

In a top-level Pulldown MenuPane from a MenuBar, unposts the menu, disarms the MenuBar CascadeButton and the MenuBar; and, when the shell's keyboard focus policy is **XmEXPLICT**, restores keyboard focus to the widget that had the focus before the MenuBar was entered. In other Pulldown MenuPanes, it unposts the menu.

In a Popup MenuPane, this action unposts the menu and restores keyboard focus to the widget from which the menu was posted.

MultiActivate():

If **XmNmultiClick** is **XmMULTICLICK_DISCARD**, this action does nothing.

If **XmNmultiClick** is **XmMULTICLICK_KEEP**, this action increments *click_count* in the callback structure and draws the shadow in the unarmed state. If the button is not in a menu and if **XmNfillOnArm** is set to True, the background color reverts to the unarmed color. If **XmNlabelType** is **XmPIXMAP**, the **XmNlabelPixmap** is used for the button face. If the pointer is within the PushButton, calls the callbacks for **XmNactivateCallback** and **XmNdisarmCallback**.

MultiArm(): If **XmNmultiClick** is **XmMULTICLICK_DISCARD**, this action does nothing.

If **XmNmultiClick** is **XmMULTICLICK_KEEP**, this action draws the shadow in the armed state. If the button is not in a menu and if **XmNfillOnArm** is set to True, this action fills the button with the color specified by **XmNarmColor**. If **XmNlabelType** is **XmPIXMAP**, the **XmNarmPixmap** is used for the button face. This action calls the **XmNarmCallback** callbacks.

Related Information

Core(3X), **XmCreatePushButton(3X)**, **XmLabel(3X)**, **XmPrimitive(3X)**, and **XmRowColumn(3X)**.

XmPushButtonGadget—The PushButtonGadget widget class

AES Support Level

Full-use

Synopsis

#include <Xm/PushBG.h>

Description

PushButtonGadget issues commands within an application. It consists of a text label or pixmap surrounded by a border shadow. When PushButtonGadget is selected, the shadow changes to give the appearance that the PushButtonGadget has been pressed in. When PushButtonGadget is unselected, the shadow changes to give the appearance that the PushButtonGadget is out.

The default behavior associated with a PushButtonGadget in a menu depends on the type of menu system in which it resides. By default, **BSelect** controls the behavior of the PushButtonGadget. In addition, **BMenu** controls the behavior of the PushButtonGadget if it resides in a PopupMenu system. The actual mouse button used is determined by its RowColumn parent.

Thickness for a second shadow may be specified with the **XmNshowAsDefault** resource. If it has a nonzero value, the Label's **XmNmarginLeft**, **XmNmarginRight**, **XmNmarginTop**, and **XmNmarginBottom** resources may be modified to accommodate the second shadow.

If an initial value is specified for **XmNarmPixmap** but not for **XmNlabelPixmap**, the **XmNarmPixmap** value is used for **XmNlabelPixmap**.

Classes

PushButtonGadget inherits behavior and resources from **Object**, **RectObj**, **XmGadget** and **XmLabelGadget**.

The class pointer is **xmPushButtonGadgetClass**.

The class name is **XmPushButtonGadget**.

New Resources

The following table defines a set of widget resources used by the programmer to specify data. The programmer can also set the resource values for the inherited classes to set attributes for this widget. To reference a resource by name or by class in a **.Xdefaults** file, remove the **XmN** or **XmC** prefix and use the remaining letters. To specify one of the defined values for a resource in a **.Xdefaults** file, remove the **Xm** prefix and use the remaining letters (in either lowercase or uppercase, but include any underscores between words). The codes in the access column indicate if the given resource can be set at creation time (C), set by using **XtSetValues** (S), retrieved by using **XtGetValues** (G), or is not applicable (N/A).

<table>
<tr><th colspan="3" style="text-align:center">XmPushButtonGadget</th></tr>
<tr><th>Name
   Class</th><th>Default
   Type</th><th>Access</th></tr>
<tr><td>XmNactivateCallback
   XmCCallback</td><td>NULL
   XtCallbackList</td><td>C</td></tr>
<tr><td>XmNarmCallback
   XmCCallback</td><td>NULL
   XtCallbackList</td><td>C</td></tr>
<tr><td>XmNarmColor
   XmCArmColor</td><td>dynamic
   Pixel</td><td>CSG</td></tr>
<tr><td>XmNarmPixmap
   XmCArmPixmap</td><td>XmUNSPECIFIED_PIXMAP
   Pixmap</td><td>CSG</td></tr>
<tr><td>XmNdefaultButtonShadowThickness
   XmCdefaultButtonShadowThickness</td><td>dynamic
   Dimension</td><td>CSG</td></tr>
<tr><td>XmNdisarmCallback
   XmCCallback</td><td>NULL
   XtCallbackList</td><td>C</td></tr>
<tr><td>XmNfillOnArm
   XmCFillOnArm</td><td>True
   Boolean</td><td>CSG</td></tr>
<tr><td>XmNmultiClick
   XmCMultiClick</td><td>dynamic
   unsigned char</td><td>CSG</td></tr>
<tr><td>XmNshowAsDefault
   XmCShowAsDefault</td><td>0
   Dimension</td><td>CSG</td></tr>
</table>

XmNactivateCallback

Specifies the list of callbacks that is called when the PushButtonGadget is activated. It is activated when the user presses and releases the active mouse button while the pointer is inside the PushButtonGadget. Activating PushButtonGadget also disarms it. For this callback, the reason is **XmCR_ACTIVATE**.

XmNarmCallback

Specifies the list of callbacks that is called when PushButtonGadget is armed. It is armed when the user presses the active mouse button while the pointer is inside the PushButtonGadget. For this callback, the reason is **XmCR_ARM**.

XmNarmColor
> Specifies the color with which to fill the armed button. **XmNfillOnArm** must be set to True for this resource to have an effect. The default for a color display is a color between the background and the bottom shadow color. For a monochrome display, the default is set to the foreground color, and any text in the label appears in the background color when the button is armed.

XmNarmPixmap
> Specifies the pixmap to be used as the button face if **XmNlabeltype** is **XmPIXMAP** and PushButtonGadget is armed. This resource is disabled when the PushButtonGadget is in a menu.

XmNdefaultButtonShadowThickness
> This resource specifies the width of the default button indicator shadow. If this resource is 0 (zero), the width of the shadow comes from the value of the **XmNshowAsDefault** resource. If this resource is greater than zero, the **XmNshowAsDefault** resource is only used to specify whether this button is the default. The default value is the initial value of **XmNshowAsDefault**.

XmNdisarmCallback
> Specifies the list of callbacks that is called when the PushButtonGadget is disarmed. PushButtonGadget is disarmed when the user presses and releases the active mouse button while the pointer is inside that gadget. For this callback, the reason is **XmCR_DISARM**.

XmNfillOnArm
> Forces the PushButtonGadget to fill the background of the button with the color specified by **XmNarmColor** when the button is armed and when this resource is set to True. If it is False, only the top and bottom shadow colors are switched. When the PushButtonGadget is in a menu, this resource is ignored and assumed to be False.

XmNmultiClick
> If a button click is followed by another button click within the time span specified by the display's multiclick time, and this resource is set to **XmMULTICLICK_DISCARD**, the second click is not processed. If this resource is set to **XmMULTICLICK_KEEP**, the event is processed and *click_count* is incremented in the callback structure. When the PushButtonGadget is not in a menu, the default value is **XmMULTICLICK_KEEP**.

XmNshowAsDefault

If **XmNdefaultButtonShadowThickness** is greater than 0 (zero), a value greater than zero in this resource specifies to mark this button as the default button. If **XmNdefaultButtonShadowThickness** is 0, a value greater than 0 in this resource specifies to mark this button as the default button with the shadow thickness specified by this resource. The space between the shadow and the default shadow is equal to the sum of both shadows. The default value is 0. When this value is not 0, the Label **XmNmarginLeft**, **XmNmarginRight**, **XmNmarginTop**, and **XmNmarginBottom** resources may be modified to accommodate the second shadow. This resource is disabled when the PushButton is in a menu.

Inherited Resources

PushButtonGadget inherits behavior and resources from the superclasses described in the following tables. For a complete description of each resource, refer to the reference page for that superclass.

XmLabelGadget Resource Set		
Name **Class**	**Default** **Type**	**Access**
XmNaccelerator XmCAccelerator	NULL String	CSG
XmNacceleratorText XmCAcceleratorText	NULL XmString	CSG
XmNalignment XmCAlignment	dynamic unsigned char	CSG
XmNfontList XmCFontList	dynamic XmFontList	CSG
XmNlabelInsensitivePixmap XmCLabelInsensitivePixmap	XmUNSPECIFIED_PIXMAP Pixmap	CSG
XmNlabelPixmap XmCLabelPixmap	dynamic Pixmap	CSG
XmNlabelString XmCXmString	dynamic XmString	CSG
XmNlabelType XmCLabelType	XmSTRING unsigned char	CSG
XmNmarginBottom XmCMarginBottom	dynamic Dimension	CSG
XmNmarginHeight XmCMarginHeight	2 Dimension	CSG
XmNmarginLeft XmCMarginLeft	dynamic Dimension	CSG
XmNmarginRight XmCMarginRight	dynamic Dimension	CSG
XmNmarginTop XmCMarginTop	dynamic Dimension	CSG
XmNmarginWidth XmCMarginWidth	2 Dimension	CSG

Name	Default	Access
Class	**Type**	
XmNmnemonic	NULL	CSG
XmCMnemonic	KeySym	
XmNmnemonicCharSet	dynamic	CSG
XmCMnemonicCharSet	String	
XmNrecomputeSize	True	CSG
XmCRecomputeSize	Boolean	
XmNstringDirection	dynamic	CSG
XmCStringDirection	XmStringDirection	

XmGadget Resource Set		
Name	**Default**	**Access**
Class	**Type**	
XmNhelpCallback	NULL	C
XmCCallback	XtCallbackList	
XmNhighlightOnEnter	False	CSG
XmCHighlightOnEnter	Boolean	
XmNhighlightThickness	2	CSG
XmCHighlightThickness	Dimension	
XmNnavigationType	XmNONE	CSG
XmCNavigationType	XmNavigationType	
XmNshadowThickness	2	CSG
XmCShadowThickness	Dimension	
XmNtraversalOn	True	CSG
XmCTraversalOn	Boolean	
XmNuserData	NULL	CSG
XmCUserData	XtPointer	

RectObj Resource Set		
Name	**Default**	**Access**
Class	**Type**	
XmNancestorSensitive	dynamic	G
XmCSensitive	Boolean	
XmNborderWidth	0	N/A
XmCBorderWidth	Dimension	
XmNheight	dynamic	CSG
XmCHeight	Dimension	
XmNsensitive	True	CSG
XmCSensitive	Boolean	
XmNwidth	dynamic	CSG
XmCWidth	Dimension	
XmNx	0	CSG
XmCPosition	Position	
XmNy	0	CSG
XmCPosition	Position	

Object Resource Set		
Name	**Default**	**Access**
Class	**Type**	
XmNdestroyCallback	NULL	C
XmCCallback	XtCallbackList	

Callback Information

A pointer to the following structure is passed to each callback:

```
typedef struct
{
    int        reason;
    XEvent     * event;
    int        click_count;
} XmPushButtonCallbackStruct;
```

reason   Indicates why the callback was invoked.

event   Points to the **XEvent** that triggered the callback.

click_count Valid only when the reason is **XmCR_ACTIVATE**. It contains the number of clicks in the last multiclick sequence if the **XmNmultiClick** resource is set to **XmMULTICLICK_KEEP**;

XmPushButtonGadget(3X)

otherwise it contains 1. The activate callback is invoked for each click if **XmNmultiClick** is set to **XmMULTICLICK_KEEP**.

Related Information

Object(3X), RectObj(3X), XmCreatePushButtonGadget(3X), XmGadget(3X), XmLabelGadget(3X), and XmRowColumn(3X).

XmRemoveProtocolCallback—A VendorShell function that removes a callback from the internal list

AES Support Level

Trial-use

Synopsis

#include <Xm/Xm.h>
#include <Xm/Protocols.h>

void XmRemoveProtocolCallback (*shell, property, protocol, callback, closure*)
> **Widget**   *shell*;
> **Atom**   *property*;
> **Atom**   *protocol*;
> **XtCallbackProc** *callback*;
> **XtPointer**   *closure*;

void XmRemoveWMProtocolCallback (*shell, protocol, callback, closure*)
> **Widget**   *shell*;
> **Atom**   *protocol*;
> **XtCallbackProc** *callback*;
> **XtPointer**   *closure*;

Description

XmRemoveProtocolCallback removes a callback from the internal list.

XmRemoveWMProtocolCallback is a convenience interface. It calls **XmRemoveProtocolCallback** with the property value set to the atom returned by interning **WM_PROTOCOLS**.

shell   Specifies the widget with which the protocol property is associated

property   Specifies the protocol property

protocol   Specifies the protocol atom (or an int cast to Atom)

callback   Specifies the procedure to call when a protocol message is received

closure   Specifies the client data to be passed to the callback when it is invoked

For a complete definition of VendorShell and its associated resources, see **VendorShell(3X)**.

Related Information

**VendorShell(3X), XmInternAtom(3X), and
XmRemoveWMProtocolCallback(3X).**

XmRemoveProtocols—A VendorShell function that removes the protocols from the protocol manager and deallocates the internal tables

AES Support Level

Trial-use

Synopsis

#include <Xm/Xm.h>
#include <Xm/Protocols.h>

void XmRemoveProtocols (*shell, property, protocols, num_protocols*)
    Widget   *shell*;
    Atom   *property*;
    Atom   ** protocols*;
    Cardinal   *num_protocols*;

void XmRemoveWMProtocols (*shell, protocols, num_protocols*)
    Widget   *shell*;
    Atom   ** protocols*;
    Cardinal   *num_protocols*;

Description

XmRemoveProtocols removes the protocols from the protocol manager and deallocates the internal tables. If any of the protocols are active, it will update the handlers and update the property if *shell* is realized.

XmRemoveWMProtocols is a convenience interface. It calls **XmRemoveProtocols** with the property value set to the atom returned by interning **WM_PROTOCOLS**.

shell   Specifies the widget with which the protocol property is associated

property   Specifies the protocol property

protocols   Specifies the protocol atoms (or ints cast to Atom)

num_protocols
          Specifies the number of elements in protocols

For a complete definition of VendorShell and its associated resources, see **VendorShell(3X)**.

Related Information

VendorShell(3X), **XmInternAtom(3X)**, and **XmRemoveWMProtocols(3X)**.

XmRemoveTabGroup—A function that removes a tab group

AES Support Level

Full-use

History/Direction

The **XmRemoveTabGroup** function is scheduled for removal in revision E.

Synopsis

#include <Xm/Xm.h>

void **XmRemoveTabGroup** (*tab_group*)
    Widget   *tab_group*;

Description

This function is obsolete and its behavior is replaced by setting **XmNnavigationType** to **XmNONE**. **XmRemoveTabGroup** removes a widget from the list of tab groups associated with a particular widget hierarchy and sets the widget's **XmNnavigationType** to **XmNONE**.

tab_group   Specifies the widget ID

Related Information

XmAddTabGroup(3X), **XmManager(3X)**, and **XmPrimitive(3X)**.

XmRemoveWMProtocolCallback—A VendorShell convenience interface that removes a callback from the internal list

AES Support Level

Trial-use

Synopsis

#include <Xm/Xm.h>
#include <Xm/Protocols.h>

void XmRemoveWMProtocolCallback (*shell, protocol, callback, closure*)
    Widget   *shell*;
    Atom   *protocol*;
    XtCallbackProc *callback*;
    XtPointer   *closure*;

Description

XmRemoveWMProtocolCallback is a convenience interface. It calls **XmRemoveProtocolCallback** with the property value set to the atom returned by interning **WM_PROTOCOLS**.

shell   Specifies the widget with which the protocol property is associated

protocol   Specifies the protocol atom (or an **int** type cast to **Atom**)

callback   Specifies the procedure to call when a protocol message is received

closure   Specifies the client data to be passed to the callback when it is invoked

For a complete definition of VendorShell and its associated resources, see **VendorShell(3X)**.

Related Information

VendorShell(3X), **XmInternAtom(3X)**, and **XmRemoveProtocolCallback(3X)**.

XmRemoveWMProtocols—A VendorShell convenience interface that removes the protocols from the protocol manager and deallocates the internal tables

AES Support Level

Trial-use

Synopsis

#include <Xm/Xm.h>
#include <Xm/Protocols.h>

void XmRemoveWMProtocols (*shell, protocols, num_protocols*)
    Widget   *shell*;
    Atom   * *protocols*;
    Cardinal   *num_protocols*;

Description

XmRemoveWMProtocols is a convenience interface. It calls **XmRemoveProtocols** with the property value set to the atom returned by interning **WM_PROTOCOLS**.

shell   Specifies the widget with which the protocol property is associated

protocols   Specifies the protocol atoms (or **ints** cast to **Atom**)

num_protocols
          Specifies the number of elements in protocols

For a complete definition of VendorShell and its associated resources, see **VendorShell(3X)**.

Related Information

VendorShell(3X), **XmInternAtom(3X)**, and **XmRemoveProtocols(3X)**.

XmResolvePartOffsets—A function that allows writing of upward-compatible applications and widgets

AES Support Level

Full-use

Synopsis

#include <Xm/XmP.h>

void XmResolvePartOffsets (*widget_class, offset*)
    WidgetClass *widget_class*;
    XmOffsetPtr * *offset*;

Description

The use of offset records requires one extra global variable per widget class. The variable consists of a pointer to an array of offsets into the widget record for each part of the widget structure. The **XmResolvePartOffsets** function allocates the offset records needed by an application to guarantee upward-compatible access to widget instance records by applications and widgets. These offset records are used by the widget to access all of the widget's variables. A widget needs to take the steps described in the following paragraphs.

Instead of creating a resource list, the widget creates an offset resource list. To accomplish this, use the **XmPartResource** structure and the **XmPartOffset** macro. The **XmPartResource** data structure looks just like a resource list, but instead of having one integer for its offset, it has two shorts. This structure is put into the class record as if it were a normal resource list. Instead of using **XtOffset** for the offset, the widget uses **XmPartOffset**.

```
XmPartResource resources[] = {
  { BarNxyz, BarCXyz, XmRBoolean,
    sizeof(Boolean), XmPartOffset(Bar,xyz),
    XmRImmediate, (XtPointer)False }
};
```

Instead of putting the widget size in the class record, the widget puts the widget part size in the same field.

Instead of putting **XtVersion** in the class record, the widget puts **XtVersionDontCheck** in the class record.

The widget defines a variable, of type **XmOffsetPtr**, to point to the offset record. This can be part of the widget's class record or a separate global variable.

In class initialization, the widget calls **XmResolvePartOffsets**, passing it a pointer to contain the address of the offset record and the class record. This does several things:

- Adds the superclass (which, by definition, has already been initialized) size field to the part size field

- Allocates an array based upon the number of superclasses

- Fills in the offsets of all the widget parts with the appropriate values, determined by examining the size fields of all superclass records

- Uses the part offset array to modify the offset entries in the resource list to be real offsets, in place

The widget defines a constant that will be the index to its part structure in the offsets array. The value should be 1 greater than the index of the widget's superclass. Constants defined for all **Xm** widgets can be found in **XmP.h**.

```
#define BarIndex (XmBulletinBIndex + 1)
```

Instead of accessing fields directly, the widget must always go through the offset table. The **XmField** macro helps you access these fields. Because the **XmPartOffset** and **XmField** macros concatenate things together, you must ensure that there is no space after the part argument. For example, the following macros do not work because of the space after the part (Label) argument:

```
XmField(w, offset, Label , text, char *)
XmPartOffset(Label , text)
```

Therefore, you must not have any spaces after the part (Label) argument, as illustrated here:

```
XmField(w, offset, Label, text, char *)
```

You can define macros for each field to make this easier. Assume an integer field *xyz*:

```
#define BarXyz(w) (*(int *)(((char *) w) + \
    offset[BarIndex] + XtOffset(BarPart,xyz)))
```

The parameters for **XmResolvePartOffsets** are

widget_class   Specifies the widget class pointer for the created widget

offset   Returns the offset record

XmRowColumn—The RowColumn widget class

AES Support Level

Full-use

Synopsis

#include <Xm/RowColumn.h>

Description

The RowColumn widget is a general purpose RowColumn manager capable of containing any widget type as a child. In general, it requires no special knowledge about how its children function and provides nothing beyond support for several different layout styles. However, it can be configured as a menu, in which case, it expects only certain children, and it configures to a particular layout. The menus supported are MenuBar, Pulldown or Popup MenuPanes, and OptionMenu.

The type of layout performed is controlled by how the application has set the various layout resources. It can be configured to lay out its children in either rows or columns. In addition, the application can specify how the children are laid out, as follows:

- The children are packed tightly together into either rows or columns

- Each child is placed in an identically sized box (producing a symmetrical look)

- A specific layout (the current x and y positions of the children control their location)

In addition, the application has control over both the spacing that occurs between each row and column and the margin spacing present between the edges of the RowColumn widget and any children that are placed against it.

In a MenuBar, Pulldown MenuPane, or Popup MenuPane the default for the **XmNshadowThickness** resource is 2. In an OptionMenu or a WorkArea, (such as a RadioBox or CheckBox) this resource is not applicable and its use is undefined. If an application wishes to place a 3-D shadow around an OptionMenu or WorkArea, it can create the RowColumn as a child of a Frame widget.

In a MenuBar, Pulldown MenuPane, or Popup MenuPane the **XmNnavigationType** resource is not applicable and its use is undefined. In a WorkArea, the default for **XmNnavigationType** is **XmTAB_GROUP**. In an OptionMenu the default for **XmNnavigationType** is **XmNONE**.

In a MenuBar, Pulldown MenuPane, or Popup MenuPane the **XmNtraversalOn** resource is not applicable and its use is undefined. In an OptionMenu or WorkArea, the default for **XmNtraversalOn** is True.

If the parent of the RowColumn is a MenuShell, the **XmNmappedWhenManaged** resource is forced to False when the widget is realized.

Classes

RowColumn inherits behavior and resources from **Core**, **Composite**, **Constraint**, and **XmManager** classes.

The class pointer is **xmRowColumnWidgetClass**.

The class name is **XmRowColumn**.

New Resources

The following table defines a set of widget resources used by the programmer to specify data. The programmer can also set the resource values for the inherited classes to set attributes for this widget. To reference a resource by name or by class in a **.Xdefaults** file, remove the **XmN** or **XmC** prefix and use the remaining letters. To specify one of the defined values for a resource in a **.Xdefaults** file, remove the **Xm** prefix and use the remaining letters (in either lowercase or uppercase, but include any underscores between words). The codes in the access column indicate if the given resource can be set at creation time (C), set by using **XtSetValues** (S), retrieved by using **XtGetValues** (G), or is not applicable (N/A).

XmRowColumn Resource Set		

Name
    Class
	Default
	    Type
		Access

XmNadjustLast
    XmCAdjustLast
	True
	    Boolean
		CSG

XmNadjustMargin
    XmCAdjustMargin
	True
	    Boolean
		CSG

XmNentryAlignment
    XmCAlignment
	XmALIGNMENT_BEGINNING
	    unsigned char
		CSG

XmNentryBorder
    XmCEntryBorder
	0
	    Dimension
		CSG

XmNentryCallback
    XmCCallback
	NULL
	    XtCallbackList
		C

XmNentryClass
    XmCEntryClass
	dynamic
	    WidgetClass
		CSG

XmNisAligned
    XmCIsAligned
	True
	    Boolean
		CSG

XmNisHomogeneous
    XmCIsHomogeneous
	dynamic
	    Boolean
		CG

XmNlabelString
    XmCXmString
	NULL
	    XmString
		C

XmNmapCallback
    XmCCallback
	NULL
	    XtCallbackList
		C

XmNmarginHeight
    XmCMarginHeight
	dynamic
	    Dimension
		CSG

XmNmarginWidth
    XmCMarginWidth
	dynamic
	    Dimension
		CSG

XmNmenuAccelerator
    XmCAccelerators
	dynamic
	    String
		CSG

XmNmenuHelpWidget
    XmCMenuWidget
	NULL
	    Widget
		CSG

XmNmenuHistory
    XmCMenuWidget
	NULL
	    Widget
		CSG

XmNmnemonic
    XmCMnemonic
	NULL
	    KeySym
		CSG

XmNmnemonicCharSet
    XmCMnemonicCharSet
	XmFONTLIST_DEFAULT_TAG
	    String
		CSG

XmNnumColumns
    XmCNumColumns
	1
	    short
		CSG

XmNorientation
    XmCOrientation
	dynamic
	    unsigned char
		CSG

XmNpacking
    XmCPacking
	dynamic
	    unsigned char
		CSG

XmNpopupEnabled
    XmCPopupEnabled
	True
	    Boolean
		CSG

XmNradioAlwaysOne
    XmCRadioAlwaysOne
	True
	    Boolean
		CSG

XmNradioBehavior
    XmCRadioBehavior
	False
	    Boolean
		CSG

XmNresizeHeight
    XmCResizeHeight
	True
	    Boolean
		CSG

XmNresizeWidth
    XmCResizeWidth
	True
	    Boolean
		CSG

XmNrowColumnType
    XmCRowColumnType
	XmWORK_AREA
	    unsigned char
		CG

XmNspacing
    XmCSpacing
	dynamic
	    Dimension
		CSG

XmNsubMenuId
    XmCMenuWidget
	NULL
	    Widget
		CSG

XmNunmapCallback
    XmCCallback
	NULL
	    XtCallbackList
		C

XmNadjustLast

> Extends the last row of children to the bottom edge of RowColumn (when **XmNorientation** is **XmHORIZONTAL**) or extends the last column to the right edge of RowColumn (when **XmNorientation** is **XmVERTICAL**). Setting **XmNadjustLast** to False disables this feature.

XmNadjustMargin

> Specifies whether the inner minor margins of all items contained within the RowColumn widget are forced to the same value. The inner minor margin corresponds to the **XmNmarginLeft**, **XmNmarginRight**, **XmNmarginTop**, and **XmNmarginBottom** resources supported by **XmLabel** and **XmLabelGadget**.

A horizontal orientation causes **XmNmarginTop** and **XmNmarginBottom** for all items in a particular row to be forced to the same value; the value is the largest margin specified for one of the Label items.

A vertical orientation causes **XmNmarginLeft** and **XmNmarginRight** for all items in a particular column to be forced to the same value; the value is the largest margin specified for one of the Label items.

This keeps all text within each row or column lined up with all other text in its row or column. If **XmNrowColumnType** is either **XmMENU_POPUP** or **XmMENU_PULLDOWN** and this resource is True, only button children have their margins adjusted.

XmNentryAlignment

Specifies the alignment type for children that are subclasses of **XmLabel** or **XmLabelGadget** when **XmNisAligned** is enabled. The following are textual alignment types:

- **XmALIGNMENT_BEGINNING** (default)

- **XmALIGNMENT_CENTER**

- **XmALIGNMENT_END**

See the description of **XmNalignment** in the **XmLabel(3X)** reference page for an explanation of these actions.

XmNentryBorder

Imposes a uniform border width upon all RowColumn's children. The default value is 0 (zero), which disables the feature.

XmNentryCallback

Disables the **XmNactivateCallback** and **XmNvalueChangedCallback** callbacks for all CascadeButton, DrawnButton, PushButton, and ToggleButton widgets and gadgets contained within the RowColumn widget. If the application supplies this resource, the **XmNactivateCallback** and **XmNvalueChangedCallback** callbacks are then revectored to the **XmNentryCallback** callbacks. This allows an application to supply a single callback routine for handling all items contained in a RowColumn widget. The callback reason is **XmCR_ACTIVATE**. If the application does not supply this resource, the **XmNactivateCallback** and **XmNvalueChangedCallback** callbacks for each item in the RowColumn widget work as normal.

The application must supply this resource when this widget is created. Changing this resource using the **XtSetValues** is not supported.

XmNentryClass

Specifies the only widget class that can be added to the RowColumn widget; this resource is meaningful only when the **XmNisHomogeneous** resource is set to True. Both widget and gadget variants of the specified class may be added to the widget.

When **XmCreateRadioBox** is called or when **XmNrowColumnType** is set to **XmWORK_AREA** and **XmNradioBehavior** is True, the default value of **XmNentryClass** is **xmToggleButtonGadgetClass**. When **XmNrowColumnType** is set to **XmMENU_BAR**, the value of **XmNentryClass** is forced to **xmCascadeButtonWidgetClass**.

XmNisAligned

Specifies text alignment for each item within the RowColumn widget; this applies only to items that are subclasses of **XmLabel** or **XmLabelGadget**. However, if the item is a Label widget or gadget and its parent is either a Popup MenuPane or a Pulldown MenuPane, alignment is not performed; the Label is treated as the title within the MenuPane, and the alignment set by the application is not overridden. **XmNentryAlignment** controls the type of textual alignment.

XmNisHomogeneous

Indicates whether the RowColumn widget should enforce exact homogeneity among the items it contains; if this resource is set to True, only the widgets that are of the class indicated by **XmNentryClass** are allowed as children of the RowColumn widget. This is most often used when creating a MenuBar. Attempting to insert a child that is not a member of the specified class generates a warning message.

In a MenuBar, the value of **XmNisHomogeneous** is forced to True. In an OptionMenu, the value is forced to False. When **XmCreateRadioBox** is called the default value is True. Otherwise, the default value is False.

XmNlabelString

Points to a text string that displays the label to one side of the selection area when **XmNrowColumnType** is set to **XmMENU_OPTION**. This resource is not meaningful for all other RowColumn types. If the application wishes to change the label after creation, it must get the LabelGadget ID (**XmOptionLabelGadget**) and call **XtSetValues** on the LabelGadget directly. The default value is no label.

XmNmapCallback

Specifies a widget-specific callback function that is invoked when the window associated with the RowColumn widget is about to be mapped. The callback reason is **XmCR_MAP**.

XmNmarginHeight

Specifies the amount of blank space between the top edge of the RowColumn widget and the first item in each column, and the bottom edge of the RowColumn widget and the last item in each column. The default value is 0 (zero) for Pulldown and Popup MenuPanes, and 3 pixels for other RowColumn types.

XmNmarginWidth

Specifies the amount of blank space between the left edge of the RowColumn widget and the first item in each row, and the right edge of the RowColumn widget and the last item in each row. The default value is 0 (zero) for Pulldown and Popup MenuPanes, and 3 pixels for other RowColumn types.

XmNmenuAccelerator

This resource is useful only when the RowColumn widget has been configured to operate as a Popup MenuPane or a MenuBar. The format of this resource is similar to the left side specification of a translation string, with the limitation that it must specify a key event. For a Popup MenuPane, when the accelerator is typed by the user, the Popup MenuPane is posted. For a MenuBar, when the accelerator is typed by the user, the first item in the MenuBar is highlighted, and traversal is enabled in the MenuBar. The default for a Popup MenuPane is **KMenu**. The default for a MenuBar is **KMenuBar**. Setting the **XmNpopupEnabled** resource to False disables the accelerator.

XmNmenuHelpWidget

Specifies the widget ID for the CascadeButton, which is treated as the Help widget if **XmNrowColumnType** is set to **XmMENU_BAR**. The MenuBar always places the Help widget at the bottom right corner (in a left to right environment) of the

MenuBar. If the RowColumn widget is any type other than **XmMENU_BAR**, this resource is not meaningful.

XmNmenuHistory

Specifies the widget ID of the last menu entry to be activated. It is also useful for specifying the current selection for an OptionMenu. If **XmNrowColumnType** is set to **XmMENU_OPTION**, the specified menu item is positioned under the cursor when the menu is displayed.

If the RowColumn widget has the **XmNradioBehavior** resource set to True, the widget field associated with this resource contains the widget ID of the last ToggleButton or ToggleButtonGadget to change from unselected to selected. The default value is the widget ID of the first child in the widget.

XmNmnemonic

This resource is useful only when **XmNrowColumnType** is set to **XmMENU_OPTION**. It specifies a keysym for a key that, when pressed by the user along with the **MAlt** modifier, posts the associated Pulldown MenuPane. The first character in the OptionMenu label string that exactly matches the mnemonic in the character set specified in **XmNmnemonicCharSet** is underlined. The user can post the menu by pressing either the shifted or the unshifted mnemonic key. The default is no mnemonic.

XmNmnemonicCharSet

Specifies the character set of the mnemonic for an OptionMenu. The default is **XmFONTLIST_DEFAULT_TAG**. If the RowColumn widget is any type other than **XmMENU_OPTION**, this resource is not meaningful.

XmNnumColumns

Specifies the number of minor dimension extensions that are made to accommodate the entries; this attribute is meaningful only when **XmNpacking** is set to **XmPACK_COLUMN**.

For vertically oriented RowColumn widgets, this attribute indicates how many columns are built; the number of entries per column is adjusted to maintain this number of columns, if possible.

For horizontally oriented RowColumn widgets, this attribute indicates how many rows are built.

The default value is 1. In an OptionMenu the value is forced to 1. The value must be greater than 0 (zero).

XmNorientation

Determines whether RowColumn layouts are row-major or column-major. In a column-major layout, the children of the RowColumn are laid out in columns top to bottom within the widget. In a row-major layout the children of the RowColumn are laid out in rows. The **XmVERTICAL** resource value selects a column-major layout. **XmHORIZONTAL** selects a row-major layout.

When creating a MenuBar or an OptionMenu, the default is **XmHORIZONTAL**. Otherwise, the default value is **XmVERTICAL**. The results of specifying a value of **XmVERTICAL** for a MenuBar are undefined.

XmNpacking Specifies how to pack the items contained within a RowColumn widget. This can be set to **XmPACK_TIGHT, XmPACK_COLUMN** or **XmPACK_NONE**. When a RowColumn widget packs the items it contains, it determines its major dimension using the value of the **XmNorientation** resource.

XmPACK_TIGHT indicates that given the current major dimension (for example, vertical if **XmNorientation** is **XmVERTICAL**), entries are placed one after the other until the RowColumn widget must wrap. RowColumn wraps when there is no room left for a complete child in that dimension. Wrapping occurs by beginning a new row or column in the next available space. Wrapping continues, as often as necessary, until all of the children are laid out. In the vertical dimension (columns), boxes are set to the same width; in the horizontal dimension (rows), boxes are set to the same depth. Each entry's position in the major dimension is left unaltered (for example, **XmNy** is left unchanged when **XmNorientation** is **XmVERTICAL**); its position in the minor dimension is set to the same value as the greatest entry in that particular row or column. The position in the minor dimension of any particular row or column is independent of all other rows or columns.

XmPACK_COLUMN indicates that all entries are placed in identically sized boxes. The boxes are based on the largest height and width values of all the children widgets. The value of the **XmNnumColumns** resource determines how many boxes are placed in the major dimension, before extending in the minor dimension.

XmPACK_NONE indicates that no packing is performed. The *x* and *y* attributes of each entry are left alone, and the RowColumn widget attempts to become large enough to enclose all entries.

When **XmCreateRadioBox** is called or when **XmNrowColumnType** is set to **XmWORK_AREA** and **XmNradioBehavior** is True, the default value of **XmNpacking** is **XmPACK_COLUMN**. In an OptionMenu the value is initialized to **XmPACK_TIGHT**. Otherwise, the value defaults to **XmPACK_TIGHT**.

XmNpopupEnabled

Allows the menu system to enable keyboard input (accelerators and mnemonics) defined for the Popup MenuPane and any of its submenus. The Popup MenuPane needs to be informed whenever its accessibility to the user changes because posting of the Popup MenuPane is controlled by the application. The default value of this resource is True (keyboard input—accelerators and mnemonics—defined for the Popup MenuPane and any of its submenus is enabled).

XmNradioAlwaysOne

If True, forces the active ToggleButton or ToggleButtonGadget to be automatically selected after having been unselected (if no other toggle was activated). If False, the active toggle may be unselected. The default value is True. This resource is important only when **XmNradioBehavior** is True.

The application can always add and subtract toggles from RowColumn regardless of the selected/unselected state of the toggle. The application can also manage and unmanage toggle children of RowColumn at any time regardless of state. Therefore, the application can sometimes create a RowColumn that has **XmNradioAlwaysOne** set to True and none of the toggle children selected. The result is undefined if the value of this resource is True and the application sets more than one ToggleButton at a time.

XmNradioBehavior

Specifies a Boolean value that when True, indicates that the RowColumn widget should enforce a RadioBox-type behavior on all of its children that are ToggleButtons or ToggleButtonGadgets.

When the value of this resource is True, **XmNindicatorType** defaults to **XmONE_OF_MANY** for ToggleButton and ToggleButtonGadget children.

RadioBox behavior dictates that when one toggle is selected and the user selects another toggle, the first toggle is unselected automatically. The RowColumn usually does not enforce this behavior if the application, rather than the user, changes the state of a toggle. The RowColumn does enforce this behavior if a toggle child is selected with **XmToggleButtonSetState** or **XmToggleButtonGadgetSetState** with a *notify* argument of True.

When **XmCreateRadioBox** is called, the default value of **XmNradioBehavior** is True. Otherwise, the default value is False.

XmNresizeHeight

Requests a new height if necessary, when set to True. When this resource is set to False, the widget does not request a new height regardless of any changes to the widget or its children.

XmNresizeWidth

Requests a new width if necessary, when set to True. When set to False, the widget does not request a new width regardless of any changes to the widget or its children.

XmNrowColumnType

Specifies the type of RowColumn widget to be created. It is a nonstandard resource that cannot be changed after it is set. If an application uses any of the convenience routines, except **XmCreateRowColumn**, this resource is automatically forced to the appropriate value by the convenience routine. If an application uses the Xt Intrinsics API to create its RowColumn widgets, it must specify this resource itself. The set of possible settings for this resource are

- **XmWORK_AREA** (default)

- **XmMENU_BAR**

- **XmMENU_PULLDOWN**

- **XmMENU_POPUP**

- **XmMENU_OPTION**

This resource cannot be changed after the RowColumn widget is created. Any changes attempted through **XtSetValues** are ignored.

The value of this resource is used to determine the value of a number of other resources. The descriptions of RowColumn resources explain this when it is the case. The resource **XmNnavigationType**, inherited from **XmManager**, is changed to **XmNONE** if **XmNrowColumnType** is **XmMENU_OPTION**.

XmNspacing Specifies the horizontal and vertical spacing between items contained within the RowColumn widget. The default value is 3 pixels for **XmOPTION_MENU** and **XmWORK_AREA** and 0 (zero) for other RowColumn types.

XmNsubMenuId

Specifies the widget ID for the Pulldown MenuPane to be associated with an OptionMenu. This resource is useful only when **XmNrowColumnType** is set to **XmMENU_OPTION**. The default value is NULL.

XmNunmapCallback

Specifies a list of callbacks that is called after the window associated with the RowColumn widget has been unmapped. The callback reason is **XmCR_UNMAP**. The default value is NULL.

Display Resource		
Name **Class**	**Default** **Type**	**Access**
XmNmenuCursor XmCCursor	arrow String	C

XmNmenuCursor

Sets a variable that controls the cursor used whenever this application posts a menu. This resource can be specified only once at application startup time, either by placing it within a defaults file or by using the **-xrm** command line argument.

The menu cursor can also be selected programmatically with the **XmSetMenuCursor** function. The following is a list of acceptable cursor names. If the application does not specify a cursor or if an invalid name is supplied, the default cursor (an arrow pointing up and to the right) is used.

X_cursor   **leftbutton**

arrow   **ll_angle**

based_arrow_down   **lr_angle**

based_arrow_up	**man**
boat	**middlebutton**
bogosity	**mouse**
bottom_left_corner	**pencil**
bottom_right_corner	**pirate**
bottom_side	**plus**
bottom_tee	**question_arrow**
box_spiral	**right_ptr**
center_ptr	**right_side**
circle	**right_tee**
clock	**rightbutton**
coffee_mug	**rtl_logo**
cross	**sailboat**
cross_reverse	**sb_down_arrow**
crosshair	**sb_h_double_arrow**
diamond_cross	**sb_left_arrow**
dot	**sb_right_arrow**
dotbox	**sb_up_arrow**
double_arrow	**sb_v_double_arrow**
draft_large	**shuttle**
draft_small	**sizing**
draped_box	**spider**
exchange	**spraycan**
fleur	**star**
gobbler	**target**
gumby	**tcross**

hand1	**top_left_arrow**
hand2	**top_left_corner**
heart	**top_right_corner**
icon	**top_side**
iron_cross	**left_ptr**
left_side	**top_tee**
left_tee	**trek**
ul_angle	**umbrella**
ur_angle	**watch**
xterm	

Inherited Resources

RowColumn inherits behavior and resources from the superclasses described in the following tables. For a complete description of each resource, refer to the reference page for that superclass.

XmManager Resource Set		

Name
    Class
	Default
	    Type
		Access

XmNbottomShadowColor
    XmCBottomShadowColor
	dynamic
	    Pixel
		CSG

XmNbottomShadowPixmap
    XmCBottomShadowPixmap
	XmUNSPECIFIED_PIXMAP
	    Pixmap
		CSG

XmNforeground
    XmCForeground
	dynamic
	    Pixel
		CSG

XmNhelpCallback
    XmCCallback
	NULL
	    XtCallbackList
		C

XmNhighlightColor
    XmCHighlightColor
	dynamic
	    Pixel
		CSG

XmNhighlightPixmap
    XmCHighlightPixmap
	dynamic
	    Pixmap
		CSG

XmNnavigationType
    XmCNavigationType
	dynamic
	    XmNavigationType
		CSG

XmNshadowThickness
    XmCShadowThickness
	dynamic
	    Dimension
		CSG

XmNstringDirection
    XmCStringDirection
	dynamic
	    XmStringDirection
		CG

XmNtopShadowColor
    XmCTopShadowColor
	dynamic
	    Pixel
		CSG

XmNtopShadowPixmap
    XmCTopShadowPixmap
	dynamic
	    Pixmap
		CSG

XmNtraversalOn
    XmCTraversalOn
	dynamic
	    Boolean
		CSG

XmNuserData
    XmCUserData
	NULL
	    XtPointer
		CSG

Composite Resource Set		
Name	**Default**	**Access**
Class	**Type**	
XmNchildren	NULL	G
XmCReadOnly	WidgetList	
XmNinsertPosition	default procedure	CSG
XmCInsertPosition	XtOrderProc	
XmNnumChildren	0	G
XmCReadOnly	Cardinal	

Core Resource Set		
Name	**Default**	**Access**
Class	**Type**	
XmNaccelerators	dynamic	CSG
XmCAccelerators	XtAccelerators	
XmNancestorSensitive	dynamic	G
XmCSensitive	Boolean	
XmNbackground	dynamic	CSG
XmCBackground	Pixel	
XmNbackgroundPixmap	XmUNSPECIFIED_PIXMAP	CSG
XmCPixmap	Pixmap	
XmNborderColor	XtDefaultForeground	CSG
XmCBorderColor	Pixel	
XmNborderPixmap	XmUNSPECIFIED_PIXMAP	CSG
XmCPixmap	Pixmap	
XmNborderWidth	0	CSG
XmCBorderWidth	Dimension	
XmNcolormap	dynamic	CG
XmCColormap	Colormap	
XmNdepth	dynamic	CG
XmCDepth	int	
XmNdestroyCallback	NULL	C
XmCCallback	XtCallbackList	
XmNheight	dynamic	CSG
XmCHeight	Dimension	
XmNinitialResourcesPersistent	True	C
XmCInitialResourcesPersistent	Boolean	
XmNmappedWhenManaged	True	CSG
XmCMappedWhenManaged	Boolean	
XmNscreen	dynamic	CG
XmCScreen	Screen *	
XmNsensitive	True	CSG
XmCSensitive	Boolean	

Name	Default	Access
Class	Type	
XmNtranslations	dynamic	CSG
XmCTranslations	XtTranslations	
XmNwidth	dynamic	CSG
XmCWidth	Dimension	
XmNx	0	CSG
XmCPosition	Position	
XmNy	0	CSG
XmCPosition	Position	

Callback Information

A pointer to the following structure is passed to each callback:

```
typedef struct
{
    int         reason;
    XEvent      * event;
    Widget      widget;
    char        * data;
    char        * callbackstruct;
} XmRowColumnCallbackStruct;
```

reason   Indicates why the callback was invoked

event   Points to the **XEvent** that triggered the callback

The following fields apply only when the callback reason is **XmCR_ACTIVATE**; for all other callback reasons, these fields are set to NULL. The **XmCR_ACTIVATE** callback reason is generated only when the application has supplied an entry callback, which overrides any activation callbacks registered with the individual RowColumn items.

widget   Is set to the widget ID of the RowColumn item that has been activated

data   Contains the client-data value supplied by the application when the RowColumn item's activation callback was registered

callbackstruct

    Points to the callback structure generated by the RowColumn item's activation callback

Action Routines

The **XmRowColumn** action routines are

Help(): Calls the callbacks for **XmNhelpCallback** if any exist. If there are no help callbacks for this widget, this action calls the help callbacks for the nearest ancestor that has them.

ManagerGadgetSelect():
When a gadget child of the menu has the focus, invokes the gadget child's behavior associated with **KSelect**. This generally has the effect of unposting the menu hierarchy and arming and activating the gadget, except that, for a CascadeButtonGadget with a submenu, it posts the submenu.

MenuBtnDown():
When a gadget child of the menu has focus, invokes the gadget child's behavior associated with **BSelect Press**. This generally has the effect of unposting any menus posted by the parent menu, enabling mouse traversal in the menu, and arming the gadget. For a CascadeButtonGadget with a submenu, it also posts the associated submenu.

MenuBtnUp():
When a gadget child of the menu has focus, invokes the gadget child's behavior associated with **BSelect Release**. This generally has the effect of unposting the menu hierarchy and activating the gadget, except that for a CascadeButtonGadget with a submenu, it posts the submenu and enables keyboard traversal in the menu.

MenuGadgetEscape():
In a top-level Pulldown MenuPane from a MenuBar, unposts the menu, disarms the MenuBar CascadeButton and the MenuBar, and, when the shell's keyboard focus policy is **XmEXPLICIT**, restores keyboard focus to the widget that had the focus before the MenuBar was entered. In other Pulldown MenuPanes, unposts the menu.

In a Popup MenuPane, unposts the menu and, when the shell's keyboard focus policy is **XmEXPLICIT**, restores keyboard focus to the widget from which the menu was posted.

MenuGadgetTraverseDown():
If the current menu item has a submenu and is in a MenuBar, then this action posts the submenu, disarms the current menu item, and arms the submenu's first traversable menu item.

If the current menu item is in a MenuPane, then this action disarms the current menu item and arms the item below it. This action wraps within the MenuPane. When the current menu item is at the MenuPane's bottom edge, then this action wraps to the topmost menu item in the column to the right, if one exists. When the current menu item is at the bottom, rightmost corner of the MenuPane, then this action wraps to the tear-off control, if present, or to the top, leftmost menu item.

MenuGadgetTraverseLeft():

When the current menu item is in a MenuBar, this action disarms the current item and arms the MenuBar item to the left. This action wraps within the MenuBar.

In MenuPanes, if the current menu item is not at the left edge of a MenuPane, this action disarms the current item and arms the item to its left. If the current menu item is at the left edge of a submenu attached to a MenuBar item, then this action unposts the submenu and traverses to the MenuBar item to the left, wrapping if necessary. If that MenuBar item has a submenu, it posts the submenu and arms the first traversable item in the submenu. If the current menu item is at the left edge of a submenu not directly attached to a MenuBar item, then this action unposts the current submenu only.

In Popup or Torn-off MenuPanes, when the current menu item is at the left edge, this action wraps within the MenuPane. If the current menu item is at the left edge of the MenuPane and not in the top row, this action wraps to the rightmost menu item in the row above. If the current menu item is in the upper, leftmost corner, this action wraps to the tear-off control, if present, or else it wraps to the bottom, rightmost menu item in the MenuPane.

MenuGadgetTraverseRight():

If the current menu item is in a MenuBar, then this action disarms the current item and arms the MenuBar item to the right. This action wraps within the MenuBar.

In MenuPanes, if the current menu item is a CascadeButton, then this action posts its associated submenu. If the current menu item is not a CascadeButton and is not at the right edge of a MenuPane, this action disarms the current item and arms the item to its right, wrapping if necessary. If the current menu item is not a CascadeButton and is at the right edge of a submenu that is a descendent of a MenuBar, then this action unposts all submenus and traverses to the MenuBar item to the right. If that MenuBar item has a submenu, it posts the submenu and arms the submenu's first traversable item.

In Popup or Torn-off menus, if the current menu item is not a CascadeButton and is at the right edge of a row (except the bottom row), this action wraps to the leftmost menu item in the row below. If the current menu item is not a CascadeButton and is in the bottom, rightmost corner of a Popup or Pulldown MenuPane, this action wraps to the tear-off control, if present, or else it wraps to the top, leftmost menu item of the MenuPane.

MenuGadgetTraverseUp():

When the current menu item is in a MenuPane, then this action disarms the current menu item and arms the item above it. This action wraps within the MenuPane. When the current menu item is at the MenuPane's top edge, then this action wraps to the bottommost menu item in the column to the left, if one exists. When the current menu item is at the top, leftmost corner of the MenuPane, then this action wraps to the tear-off control, if present, or to the bottom, rightmost menu item.

Related Information

Composite(3X), **Constraint(3X)**, **Core(3X)**, **XmCreateMenuBar(3X)**, **XmCreateOptionMenu(3X)**, **XmCreatePopupMenu(3X)**, **XmCreatePulldownMenu(3X)**, **XmCreateRadioBox(3X)**, **XmCreateRowColumn(3X)**, **XmCreateWorkArea(3X)**, **XmGetMenuCursor(3X)**, **XmGetPostedFromWidget(3X)**, **XmLabel(3X)**, **XmManager(3X)**, **XmMenuPosition(3X)**, **XmOptionButtonGadget(3X)**, **XmOptionLabelGadget(3X)**, **XmSetMenuCursor(3X)**, and **XmUpdateDisplay(3X)**.

XmScale—The Scale widget class

AES Support Level

Full-use

Synopsis

#include <Xm/Scale.h>

Description

Scale is used by an application to indicate a value from within a range of values, and it allows the user to input or modify a value from the same range.

A Scale has an elongated rectangular region similar to a ScrollBar. A slider inside this region indicates the current value along the Scale. The user can also modify the Scale's value by moving the slider within the rectangular region of the Scale. A Scale can also include a label set located outside the Scale region. These can indicate the relative value at various positions along the scale.

A Scale can be either input/output or output only. An input/output Scale's value can be set by the application and also modified by the user with the slider. An output-only Scale is used strictly as an indicator of the current value of something and cannot be modified interactively by the user. The **Core** resource **XmNsensitive** specifies whether the user can interactively modify the Scale's value.

Classes

Scale inherits behavior and resources from **Core**, **Composite**, **Constraint**, and **XmManager** classes.

The class pointer is **xmScaleWidgetClass**.

The class name is **XmScale**.

New Resources

The following table defines a set of widget resources used by the programmer to specify data. The programmer can also set the resource values for the inherited classes to set attributes for this widget. To reference a resource by name or by class in a **.Xdefaults** file, remove the **XmN** or **XmC** prefix and use the remaining letters. To specify one of the defined values for a resource in a **.Xdefaults** file, remove the **Xm** prefix and use the remaining letters (in either lowercase or uppercase, but include any underscores between words). The codes in the access column indicate if the given resource can be set at creation time (C), set by using **XtSetValues** (S), retrieved by using **XtGetValues** (G), or is not applicable (N/A).

XmScale Resource Set		
Name	**Default**	**Access**
Class	**Type**	
XmNdecimalPoints	0	CSG
XmCDecimalPoints	short	
XmNdragCallback	NULL	C
XmCCallback	XtCallbackList	
XmNfontList	dynamic	CSG
XmCFontList	XmFontList	
XmNhighlightOnEnter	False	CSG
XmCHighlightOnEnter	Boolean	
XmNhighlightThickness	2	CSG
XmCHighlightThickness	Dimension	
XmNmaximum	100	CSG
XmCMaximum	int	
XmNminimum	0	CSG
XmCMinimum	int	
XmNorientation	XmVERTICAL	CSG
XmCOrientation	unsigned char	
XmNprocessingDirection	dynamic	CSG
XmCProcessingDirection	unsigned char	
XmNscaleHeight	0	CSG
XmCScaleHeight	Dimension	
XmNscaleMultiple	dynamic	CSG
XmCScaleMultiple	int	
XmNscaleWidth	0	CSG
XmCScaleWidth	Dimension	
XmNshowValue	False	CSG
XmCShowValue	Boolean	

Name	Default	Access
Class	Type	
XmNtitleString	NULL	CSG
XmCTitleString	XmString	
XmNvalue	dynamic	CSG
XmCValue	int	
XmNvalueChangedCallback	NULL	C
XmCCallback	XtCallbackList	

XmNdecimalPoints

Specifies the number of decimal points to shift the slider value when displaying it. For example, a slider value of 2,350 and an **XmdecimalPoints** value of 2 results in a display value of 23.50. The value must not be negative.

XmNdragCallback

Specifies the list of callbacks that is called when the slider position changes as the slider is being dragged. The reason sent by the callback is **XmCR_DRAG**.

XmNfontList Specifies the font list to use for the title text string specified by **XmNtitleString**, and the label displayed when **XmNshowValue** is True. If this value is NULL at initialization, the parent hierarchy is searched for an ancestor that is a subclass of the BulletinBoard, VendorShell, or MenuShell widget class. If such an ancestor is found, the font list is initialized to the **XmNlabelFontList** of the ancestor widget. If no such ancestor is found, the default is implementation dependent. Refer to **XmFontList(3X)** for more information on the creation and structure of a font list.

XmNhighlightOnEnter

Specifies whether the highlighting rectangle is drawn when the cursor moves into the widget. If the shell's focus policy is **XmEXPLICIT**, this resource is ignored, and the widget is highlighted when it has the focus. If the shell's focus policy is **XmPOINTER** and if this resource is True, the highlighting rectangle is drawn when the the cursor moves into the widget. If the shell's focus policy is **XmPOINTER** and if this resource is False, the highlighting rectangle is not drawn when the the cursor moves into the widget. The default is False.

XmNhighlightThickness

Specifies the size of the slider's border drawing rectangle used for enter window and traversal highlight drawing.

XmNmaximum

Specifies the slider's maximum value. **XmNmaximum** must be greater than **XmNminimum**.

XmNminimum

Specifies the slider's minimum value. **XmNmaximum** must be greater than **XmNminimum**.

XmNorientation

Displays Scale vertically or horizontally. This resource can have values of **XmVERTICAL** and **XmHORIZONTAL**.

XmNprocessingDirection

Specifies whether the value for **XmNmaximum** is on the right or left side of **XmNminimum** for horizontal Scales or above or below **XmNminimum** for vertical Scales. This resource can have values of **XmMAX_ON_TOP**, **XmMAX_ON_BOTTOM**, **XmMAX_ON_LEFT**, and **XmMAX_ON_RIGHT**. If the Scale is oriented vertically, the default value is **XmMAX_ON_TOP**. If the XmScale is oriented horizontally, the default value may depend on the value of the **XmNstringDirection** resource.

XmNscaleHeight

Specifies the height of the slider area. The value should be in the specified unit type (the default is pixels). If no value is specified a default height is computed.

XmNscaleMultiple

Specifies the amount to move the slider when the user takes an action that moves the slider by a multiple increment. The default is (**XmNmaximum** - **XmNminimum**) divided by 10, with a minimum of 1.

XmNscaleWidth
> Specifies the width of the slider area. The value should be in the specified unit type (the default is pixels). If no value is specified a default width is computed.

XmNshowValue
> Specifies whether a label for the current slider value should be displayed next to the slider. If the value is True, the current slider value is displayed.

XmNtitleString
> Specifies the title text string to appear in the Scale widget window.

XmNvalue
> Specifies the slider's current position along the scale, between **XmNminimum** and **XmNmaximum**. The value is constrained to be within these inclusive bounds. The initial value of this resource is the larger of 0 (zero) and **XmNminimum**.

XmNvalueChangedCallback
> Specifies the list of callbacks that is called when the value of the slider has changed. The reason sent by the callback is **XmCR_VALUE_CHANGED**.

Inherited Resources

Scale inherits behavior and resources from the superclasses described in the following tables. For a complete description of each resource, refer to the reference page for that superclass.

XmManager Resource Set		

Name
    Class
	Default
	    Type
		Access

XmNbottomShadowColor
    XmCBottomShadowColor
	dynamic
	    Pixel
		CSG

XmNbottomShadowPixmap
    XmCBottomShadowPixmap
	XmUNSPECIFIED_PIXMAP
	    Pixmap
		CSG

XmNforeground
    XmCForeground
	dynamic
	    Pixel
		CSG

XmNhelpCallback
    XmCCallback
	NULL
	    XtCallbackList
		C

XmNhighlightColor
    XmCHighlightColor
	dynamic
	    Pixel
		CSG

XmNhighlightPixmap
    XmCHighlightPixmap
	dynamic
	    Pixmap
		CSG

XmNnavigationType
    XmCNavigationType
	XmTAB_GROUP
	    XmNavigationType
		CSG

XmNshadowThickness
    XmCShadowThickness
	2
	    Dimension
		CSG

XmNstringDirection
    XmCStringDirection
	dynamic
	    XmStringDirection
		CG

XmNtopShadowColor
    XmCTopShadowColor
	dynamic
	    Pixel
		CSG

XmNtopShadowPixmap
    XmCTopShadowPixmap
	dynamic
	    Pixmap
		CSG

XmNtraversalOn
    XmCTraversalOn
	True
	    Boolean
		CSG

XmNuserData
    XmCUserData
	NULL
	    XtPointer
		CSG

Composite Resource Set		
Name	**Default**	**Access**
Class	**Type**	
XmNchildren	NULL	G
XmCReadOnly	WidgetList	
XmNinsertPosition	NULL	CSG
XmCInsertPosition	XtOrderProc	
XmNnumChildren	0	G
XmCReadOnly	Cardinal	

Core Resource Set		

Name
    Class
	Default
	    Type
		Access

XmNaccelerators
    XmCAccelerators
	dynamic
	    XtAccelerators
		CSG

XmNancestorSensitive
    XmCSensitive
	dynamic
	    Boolean
		G

XmNbackground
    XmCBackground
	dynamic
	    Pixel
		CSG

XmNbackgroundPixmap
    XmCPixmap
	XmUNSPECIFIED_PIXMAP
	    Pixmap
		CSG

XmNborderColor
    XmCBorderColor
	XtDefaultForeground
	    Pixel
		CSG

XmNborderPixmap
    XmCPixmap
	XmUNSPECIFIED_PIXMAP
	    Pixmap
		CSG

XmNborderWidth
    XmCBorderWidth
	0
	    Dimension
		CSG

XmNcolormap
    XmCColormap
	dynamic
	    Colormap
		CG

XmNdepth
    XmCDepth
	dynamic
	    int
		CG

XmNdestroyCallback
    XmCCallback
	NULL
	    XtCallbackList
		C

XmNheight
    XmCHeight
	dynamic
	    Dimension
		CSG

XmNinitialResourcesPersistent
    XmCInitialResourcesPersistent
	True
	    Boolean
		C

XmNmappedWhenManaged
    XmCMappedWhenManaged
	True
	    Boolean
		CSG

XmNscreen
    XmCScreen
	dynamic
	    Screen *
		CG

XmNsensitive
    XmCSensitive
	True
	    Boolean
		CSG

Name	Default	Access
Class	Type	
XmNtranslations	dynamic	CSG
XmCTranslations	XtTranslations	
XmNwidth	dynamic	CSG
XmCWidth	Dimension	
XmNx	0	CSG
XmCPosition	Position	
XmNy	0	CSG
XmCPosition	Position	

Callback Information

A pointer to the following structure is passed to each callback:

typedef struct
{
    int   *reason*;
    XEvent   * *event*;
    int   *value*;
} XmScaleCallbackStruct;

reason   Indicates why the callback was invoked

event   Points to the **XEvent** that triggered the callback

value   Is the new slider value

Behavior

XmScale has the following behavior:

BSelect Press or **BTransfer Press**:
> **In the region between an end of the Scale and the slider**:
> Moves the slider by one multiple increment in the direction of the end of the Scale and calls the **XmNvalueChangedCallback** callbacks. If **XmNprocessingDirection** is **XmMAX_ON_RIGHT** or **XmMAX_ON_BOTTOM**, movement toward the right or bottom increments the Scale value, and movement toward the left or top decrements the Scale value. If **XmNprocessingDirection** is **XmMAX_ON_LEFT** or **XmMAX_ON_TOP**, movement toward the right or bottom decrements the Scale value, and movement toward the left or top increments the Scale value. If the button is held down longer than a delay period, the slider is moved again by the same increment and the same callbacks are called.

In slider:
Activates the interactive dragging of the slider.

BSelect Motion or **BTransfer Motion**:
If the button press occurs within the slider, the subsequent motion events move the slider to the position of the pointer and call the callbacks for **XmNdragCallback**.

BSelect Release or **BTransfer Release**:
If the button press occurs within the slider and the slider position is changed, the callbacks for **XmNvalueChangedCallback** are called.

MCtrl BSelect Press:
In the region between an end of the Scale and the slider:
Moves the slider to that end of the Scale and calls the **XmNvalueChangedCallback** callbacks. If **XmNprocessingDirection** is **XmMAX_ON_RIGHT** or **XmMAX_ON_BOTTOM**, movement toward the right or bottom increments the Scale value, and movement toward the left or top decrements the Scale value. If **XmNprocessingDirection** is **XmMAX_ON_LEFT** or **XmMAX_ON_TOP**, movement toward the right or bottom decrements the Scale value, and movement toward the left or top increments the Scale value.

KUp:
For vertical Scales, moves the slider up one increment and calls the **XmNvalueChangedCallback** callbacks. If **XmNprocessingDirection** is **XmMAX_ON_TOP**, movement toward the top increments the Scale value. If **XmNprocessingDirection** is **XmMAX_ON_BOTTOM**, movement toward the top decrements the Scale value.

KDown:
For vertical Scales, moves the slider down one increment and calls the **XmNvalueChangedCallback** callbacks. If **XmNprocessingDirection** is **XmMAX_ON_BOTTOM**, movement toward the bottom increments the Scale value. If **XmNprocessingDirection** is **XmMAX_ON_TOP**, movement toward the bottom decrements the Scale value.

KLeft:
For horizontal Scales, moves the slider one increment to the left and calls the **XmNvalueChangedCallback** callbacks. If **XmNprocessingDirection** is **XmMAX_ON_LEFT**, movement toward the left increments the Scale value. If **XmNprocessingDirection** is **XmMAX_ON_RIGHT**, movement toward the left decrements the Scale value.

KRight: For horizontal Scales, moves the slider one increment to the right and calls the **XmNvalueChangedCallback** callbacks. If **XmNprocessingDirection** is **XmMAX_ON_RIGHT**, movement toward the right increments the Scale value. If **XmNprocessingDirection** is **XmMAX_ON_LEFT**, movement toward the right decrements the Scale value.

MCtrl KUp or **KPageUp:**
For vertical Scales, moves the slider up one multiple increment and calls the **XmNvalueChangedCallback** callbacks. If **XmNprocessingDirection** is **XmMAX_ON_TOP**, movement toward the top increments the Scale value. If **XmNprocessingDirection** is **XmMAX_ON_BOTTOM**, movement toward the top decrements the Scale value.

MCtrl KDown or **KPageDown:**
For vertical Scales, moves the slider down one multiple increment and calls the **XmNvalueChangedCallback** callbacks. If **XmNprocessingDirection** is **XmMAX_ON_BOTTOM**, movement toward the bottom increments the Scale value. If **XmNprocessingDirection** is **XmMAX_ON_TOP**, movement toward the bottom decrements the Scale value.

MCtrl KLeft or **KPageLeft:**
For horizontal Scales, moves the slider one multiple increment to the left and calls the **XmNvalueChangedCallback** callbacks. If **XmNprocessingDirection** is **XmMAX_ON_LEFT**, movement toward the left increments the Scale value. If **XmNprocessingDirection** is **XmMAX_ON_RIGHT**, movement toward the left decrements the Scale value.

MCtrl KRight or **KPageRight:**
For horizontal Scales, moves the slider one multiple increment to the right and calls the **XmNvalueChangedCallback** callbacks. If **XmNprocessingDirection** is **XmMAX_ON_RIGHT**, movement toward the right increments the Scale value. If **XmNprocessingDirection** is **XmMAX_ON_LEFT**, movement toward the right decrements the Scale value.

KBeginLine or **KBeginData:**
Moves the slider to the minimum value and calls the **XmNvalueChangedCallback** callbacks.

KEndLine or **KEndData**:
> Moves the slider to the maximum value and calls the **XmNvalueChangedCallback** callbacks.

KNextField: Traverses to the first item in the next tab group. If the current tab group is the last entry in the tab group list, it wraps to the beginning of the tab group list.

KPrevField: Traverses to the first item in the previous tab group. If the beginning of the tab group list is reached, it wraps to the end of the tab group list.

KHelp: Calls the callbacks for **XmNhelpCallback** if any exist. If there are no help callbacks for this widget, this action calls the help callbacks for the nearest ancestor that has them.

Virtual Bindings

The bindings for virtual keys are vendor specific.

Related Information

Composite(3X), **Constraint(3X)**, **Core(3X)**, **XmCreateScale(3X)**,
XmManager(3X), **XmScaleGetValue(3X)**, and **XmScaleSetValue(3X)**.

XmScaleGetValue(3X)

XmScaleGetValue—A Scale function that returns the current slider position

AES Support Level

Full-use

Synopsis

#include <Xm/Scale.h>

void **XmScaleGetValue** (*widget, value_return*)
    Widget   *widget*;
    int   * *value_return*;

Description

XmScaleGetValue returns the current slider position value displayed in the scale.

widget   Specifies the Scale widget ID

value_return   Returns the current slider position value

For a complete definition of Scale and its associated resources, see **XmScale(3X)**.

Related Information

XmScale(3X).

XmScaleSetValue—A Scale function that sets a slider value

AES Support Level

Full-use

Synopsis

#include <Xm/Scale.h>

void XmScaleSetValue (*widget, value*)
    Widget   *widget*;
    int   *value*;

Description

XmScaleSetValue sets the slider *value* within the Scale widget.

widget   Specifies the Scale widget ID.

value   Specifies the slider position along the scale. This sets the **XmNvalue** resource.

For a complete definition of Scale and its associated resources, see **XmScale(3X)**.

Related Information

XmScale(3X).

XmScrollBar—The ScrollBar widget class

AES Support Level

Full-use

Synopsis

#include <Xm/ScrollBar.h>

Description

The ScrollBar widget allows the user to view data that is too large to be displayed all at once. ScrollBars are usually located inside a ScrolledWindow and adjacent to the widget that contains the data to be viewed. When the user interacts with the ScrollBar, the data within the other widget scrolls.

A ScrollBar consists of two arrows placed at each end of a rectangle. The rectangle is called the scroll region. A smaller rectangle, called the slider, is placed within the scroll region. The data is scrolled by clicking either arrow, selecting on the scroll region, or dragging the slider. When an arrow is selected, the slider within the scroll region is moved in the direction of the arrow by an amount supplied by the application. If the mouse button is held down, the slider continues to move at a constant rate.

The ratio of the slider size to the scroll region size typically corresponds to the relationship between the size of the visible data and the total size of the data. For example, if 10 percent of the data is visible, the slider typically occupies 10 percent of the scroll region. This provides the user with a visual clue to the size of the invisible data.

Classes

ScrollBar inherits behavior and resources from the **Core** and **XmPrimitive** classes.

The class pointer is **xmScrollBarWidgetClass**.

The class name is **XmScrollBar**.

New Resources

The following table defines a set of widget resources used by the programmer to specify data. The programmer can also set the resource values for the inherited classes to set attributes for this widget. To reference a resource by name or by class in a **.Xdefaults** file, remove the **XmN** or **XmC** prefix and use the remaining letters. To specify one of the defined values for a resource in a **.Xdefaults** file, remove the **Xm** prefix and use the remaining letters (in either lowercase or uppercase, but include any underscores between words). The codes in the access column indicate if the given resource can be set at creation time (C), set by using **XtSetValues** (S), retrieved by using **XtGetValues** (G), or is not applicable (N/A).

XmScrollBar Resource Set		
Name	**Default**	**Access**
Class	**Type**	
XmNdecrementCallback	NULL	C
XmCCallback	XtCallbackList	
XmNdragCallback	NULL	C
XmCCallback	XtCallbackList	
XmNincrement	1	CSG
XmCIncrement	int	
XmNincrementCallback	NULL	C
XmCCallback	XtCallbackList	
XmNinitialDelay	250 ms	CSG
XmCInitialDelay	int	
XmNmaximum	dynamic	CSG
XmCMaximum	int	
XmNminimum	0	CSG
XmCMinimum	int	
XmNorientation	XmVERTICAL	CSG
XmCOrientation	unsigned char	
XmNpageDecrementCallback	NULL	C
XmCCallback	XtCallbackList	
XmNpageIncrement	10	CSG
XmCPageIncrement	int	
XmNpageIncrementCallback	NULL	C
XmCCallback	XtCallbackList	
XmNprocessingDirection	dynamic	CSG
XmCProcessingDirection	unsigned char	
XmNrepeatDelay	50 ms	CSG
XmCRepeatDelay	int	
XmNshowArrows	True	CSG
XmCShowArrows	Boolean	
XmNsliderSize	dynamic	CSG
XmCSliderSize	int	

Name	Default	Access
Class	Type	
XmNtoBottomCallback	NULL	C
XmCCallback	XtCallbackList	
XmNtoTopCallback	NULL	C
XmCCallback	XtCallbackList	
XmNtroughColor	dynamic	CSG
XmCTroughColor	Pixel	
XmNvalue	dynamic	CSG
XmCValue	int	
XmNvalueChangedCallback	NULL	C
XmCCallback	XtCallbackList	

XmNdecrementCallback

Specifies the list of callbacks that is called when the user takes an action that moves the ScrollBar by one increment and the value decreases. The reason passed to the callback is **XmCR_DECREMENT**.

XmNdragCallback

Specifies the list of callbacks that is called on each incremental change of position when the slider is being dragged. The reason sent by the callback is **XmCR_DRAG**.

XmNincrement

Specifies the amount by which the value increases or decreases when the user takes an action that moves the slider by one increment. The actual change in value is the lesser of **XmNincrement** and (previous **XmNvalue** - **XmNminimum**) when the slider moves to the end of the ScrollBar with the minimum value, and the lesser of **XmNincrement** and (**XmNmaximum-XmNsliderSize** - previous **XmNvalue**) when the slider moves to the end of the ScrollBar with the maximum value. The value of this resource must be greater than 0 (zero).

XmNincrementCallback

Specifies the list of callbacks that is called when the user takes an action that moves the ScrollBar by one increment and the value increases. The reason passed to the callback is **XmCR_INCREMENT**.

XmNinitialDelay

Specifies the amount of time in milliseconds to wait before starting continuous slider movement while a button is pressed in an arrow or the scroll region. The value of this resource must be greater than 0 (zero).

XmNmaximum

Specifies the slider's maximum value. ScrollBars contained within ScrolledWindows have a maximum equal to the size of ScrollBar (that is, the height if it is vertical, or the width if it is horizontal). **XmNmaximum** must be greater than **XmNminimum**.

XmNminimum

Specifies the slider's minimum value. **XmNmaximum** must be greater than **XmNminimum**.

XmNorientation

Specifies whether the ScrollBar is displayed vertically or horizontally. This resource can have values of **XmVERTICAL** and **XmHORIZONTAL**.

XmNpageDecrementCallback

Specifies the list of callbacks that is called when the user takes an action that moves the ScrollBar by one page increment and the value decreases. The reason passed to the callback is **XmCR_PAGE_DECREMENT**.

XmNpageIncrement

Specifies the amount by which the value increases or decreases when the user takes an action that moves the slider by one page increment. The actual change in value is the lesser of **XmNpageIncrement** and (previous **XmNvalue** - **XmNminimum**) when the slider moves to the end of the ScrollBar with the minimum value, and the lesser of **XmNpageIncrement** and (**XmNmaximum-XmNsliderSize** - previous **XmNvalue**) when the slider moves to the end of the ScrollBar with the maximum value. The value of this resource must be greater than 0 (zero).

XmNpageIncrementCallback
Specifies the list of callbacks that is called when the user takes an action that moves the ScrollBar by one page increment and the value increases. The reason passed to the callback is **XmCR_PAGE_INCREMENT**.

XmNprocessingDirection
Specifies whether the value for **XmNmaximum** should be on the right or left side of **XmNminimum** for horizontal ScrollBars or above or below **XmNminimum** for vertical ScrollBars. This resource can have values of **XmMAX_ON_TOP,** **XmMAX_ON_BOTTOM,** **XmMAX_ON_LEFT,** and **XmMAX_ON_RIGHT**. If the ScrollBar is oriented vertically, the default value is **XmMAX_ON_BOTTOM**. If the ScrollBar is oriented horizontally, the default value may depend on the value of the **XmNstringDirection** resource.

XmNrepeatDelay
Specifies the amount of time in milliseconds to wait between subsequent slider movements after the **XmNinitialDelay** has been processed. The value of this resource must be greater than 0 (zero).

XmNshowArrows
Specifies whether the arrows are displayed.

XmNsliderSize
Specifies the length of the slider between the values of 1 and (**XmNmaximum** - **XmNminimum**). The value is constrained to be within these inclusive bounds. The default value is (**XmNmaximum** - **XmNminimum**) divided by 10, with a minimum of 1.

XmNtoBottomCallback
> Specifies the list of callbacks that is called when the user takes an action that moves the slider to the end of the ScrollBar with the maximum value. The reason passed to the callback is **XmCR_TO_BOTTOM**.

XmNtoTopCallback
> Specifies the list of callbacks that is called when the user takes an action that moves the slider to the end of the ScrollBar with the minimum value. The reason passed to the callback is **XmCR_TO_TOP**.

XmNtroughColor
> Specifies the color of the slider trough.

XmNvalue
> Specifies the slider's position, between **XmNminimum** and (**XmNmaximum** - **XmNsliderSize**). The value is constrained to be within these inclusive bounds. The initial value of this resource is the larger of 0 (zero) and **XmNminimum**.

XmNvalueChangedCallback
> Specifies the list of callbacks that is called when the slider is released after being dragged. These callbacks are also called in place of **XmNincrementCallback**, **XmNdecrementCallback**, **XmNpageIncrementCallback**, **XmNpageDecrementCallback**, **XmNtoTopCallback**, or **XmNtoBottomCallback** when one of these callback lists would normally be called but the value of the corresponding resource is NULL. The reason passed to the callback is **XmCR_VALUE_CHANGED**.

Inherited Resources

ScrollBar inherits behavior and resources from the superclasses described in the following tables. For a complete description of each resource, refer to the reference page for that superclass.

<table>
<tr><th colspan="3">XmPrimitive Resource Set</th></tr>
<tr><td>Name
   Class</td><td>Default
   Type</td><td>Access</td></tr>
<tr><td>XmNbottomShadowColor
   XmCBottomShadowColor</td><td>dynamic
   Pixel</td><td>CSG</td></tr>
<tr><td>XmNbottomShadowPixmap
   XmCBottomShadowPixmap</td><td>XmUNSPECIFIED_PIXMAP
   Pixmap</td><td>CSG</td></tr>
<tr><td>XmNforeground
   XmCForeground</td><td>dynamic
   Pixel</td><td>CSG</td></tr>
<tr><td>XmNhelpCallback
   XmCCallback</td><td>NULL
   XtCallbackList</td><td>C</td></tr>
<tr><td>XmNhighlightColor
   XmCHighlightColor</td><td>dynamic
   Pixel</td><td>CSG</td></tr>
<tr><td>XmNhighlightOnEnter
   XmCHighlightOnEnter</td><td>False
   Boolean</td><td>CSG</td></tr>
<tr><td>XmNhighlightPixmap
   XmCHighlightPixmap</td><td>dynamic
   Pixmap</td><td>CSG</td></tr>
<tr><td>XmNhighlightThickness
   XmCHighlightThickness</td><td>dynamic
   Dimension</td><td>CSG</td></tr>
<tr><td>XmNnavigationType
   XmCNavigationType</td><td>XmSTICKY_TAB_GROUP
   XmNavigationType</td><td>CSG</td></tr>
<tr><td>XmNshadowThickness
   XmCShadowThickness</td><td>2
   Dimension</td><td>CSG</td></tr>
<tr><td>XmNtopShadowColor
   XmCTopShadowColor</td><td>dynamic
   Pixel</td><td>CSG</td></tr>
<tr><td>XmNtopShadowPixmap
   XmCTopShadowPixmap</td><td>dynamic
   Pixmap</td><td>CSG</td></tr>
<tr><td>XmNtraversalOn
   XmCTraversalOn</td><td>dynamic
   Boolean</td><td>CSG</td></tr>
<tr><td>XmNuserData
   XmCUserData</td><td>NULL
   XtPointer</td><td>CSG</td></tr>
</table>

Core Resource Set		
Name	**Default**	**Access**
Class	**Type**	
XmNaccelerators	dynamic	CSG
XmCAccelerators	XtAccelerators	
XmNancestorSensitive	dynamic	G
XmCSensitive	Boolean	
XmNbackground	dynamic	CSG
XmCBackground	Pixel	
XmNbackgroundPixmap	XmUNSPECIFIED_PIXMAP	CSG
XmCPixmap	Pixmap	
XmNborderColor	XtDefaultForeground	CSG
XmCBorderColor	Pixel	
XmNborderPixmap	XmUNSPECIFIED_PIXMAP	CSG
XmCPixmap	Pixmap	
XmNborderWidth	0	CSG
XmCBorderWidth	Dimension	
XmNcolormap	dynamic	CG
XmCColormap	Colormap	
XmNdepth	dynamic	CG
XmCDepth	int	
XmNdestroyCallback	NULL	C
XmCCallback	XtCallbackList	
XmNheight	dynamic	CSG
XmCHeight	Dimension	
XmNinitialResourcesPersistent	True	C
XmCInitialResourcesPersistent	Boolean	
XmNmappedWhenManaged	True	CSG
XmCMappedWhenManaged	Boolean	
XmNscreen	dynamic	CG
XmCScreen	Screen *	
XmNsensitive	True	CSG
XmCSensitive	Boolean	

Name	Default	Access
Class	Type	
XmNtranslations	dynamic	CSG
XmCTranslations	XtTranslations	
XmNwidth	dynamic	CSG
XmCWidth	Dimension	
XmNx	0	CSG
XmCPosition	Position	
XmNy	0	CSG
XmCPosition	Position	

Callback Information

A pointer to the following structure is passed to each callback:

typedef struct
{
    int   *reason*;
    XEvent   ** event*;
    int   *value*;
    int   *pixel*;
} XmScrollBarCallbackStruct;

reason	Indicates why the callback was invoked.
event	Points to the **XEvent** that triggered the callback.
value	Contains the new slider location value.
pixel	Is used only for **XmNtoTopCallback** and **XmNtoBottomCallback**. For horizontal ScrollBars, it contains the x coordinate of where the mouse button selection occurred. For vertical ScrollBars, it contains the y coordinate.

Action Routines

The ScrollBar action routines are

CancelDrag():

    If the key press occurs during scrolling, cancels the scroll and returns the slider to its previous location in the scrollbar, otherwise, and if the parent is a manager, it passes the event to the parent.

IncrementDownOrRight(0|1):

    With an argument of 0 (zero), moves the slider down by one increment. With an argument of 1, it moves the slider right by one increment. If **XmNprocessingDirection** is **XmMAX_ON_RIGHT** or **XmMAX_ON_BOTTOM**, movement toward the right or bottom calls the callbacks for **XmNincrementCallback**. If **XmNprocessingDirection** is **XmMAX_ON_LEFT** or **XmMAX_ON_TOP**, movement toward the right or bottom calls the callbacks for **XmNdecrementCallback**. The **XmNvalueChangedCallback** is called if the **XmNincrementCallback** or **XmNdecrementCallback** is NULL.

IncrementUpOrLeft(0|1):
> With an argument of 0 (zero), moves the slider up by one increment. With an argument of 1, it moves the slider left by one increment. If **XmNprocessingDirection** is **XmMAX_ON_RIGHT** or **XmMAX_ON_BOTTOM**, movement to the left or top calls the callbacks for **XmNdecrementCallback**. If **XmNprocessingDirection** is **XmMAX_ON_LEFT** or **XmMAX_ON_TOP**, movement to the left or top calls the callbacks for **XmNincrementCallback**. The **XmNvalueChangedCallback** is called if the **XmNincrementCallback** or **XmNdecrementCallback** is NULL.

Moved():
> If the button press occurs within the slider, the subsequent motion events move the slider to the position of the pointer and call the callbacks for **XmNdragCallback**.

PageDownOrRight(0|1):
> With an argument of 0 (zero), moves the slider down by one page increment. With an argument of 1, moves the slider right by one page increment. If **XmNprocessingDirection** is **XmMAX_ON_RIGHT** or **XmMAX_ON_BOTTOM**, movement toward the right or bottom calls the callbacks for **XmNpageIncrementCallback**. If **XmNprocessingDirection** is **XmMAX_ON_LEFT** or **XmMAX_ON_TOP**, movement toward the right or bottom calls the **XmNpageDecrementCallback** callbacks. The **XmNvalueChangedCallback** is called if the **XmNpageIncrementCallback** or **XmNpageDecrementCallback** is NULL.

PageUpOrLeft(0|1):
> With an argument of 0 (zero), moves the slider up by one page increment. With an argument of 1, it moves the slider left by one page increment. If **XmNprocessingDirection** is **XmMAX_ON_RIGHT** or **XmMAX_ON_BOTTOM**, movement to the left or top calls the callbacks for **XmNpageDecrementCallback**. If **XmNprocessingDirection** is

        XmMAX_ON_LEFT or **XmMAX_ON_TOP**, movement to the left or top calls the **XmNpageIncrementCallback** callbacks. The **XmNvalueChangedCallback** is called if the **XmNpageIncrementCallback** or **XmNpageDecrementCallback** is NULL.

PrimitiveHelp():
        Calls the callbacks for **XmNhelpCallback** if any exist. If there are no help callbacks for this widget, this action calls the help callbacks for the nearest ancestor that has them.

PrimitiveNextTabGroup():
        Traverses to the first item in the next tab group. If the current tab group is the last entry in the tab group list, it wraps to the beginning of the tab group list.

PrimitiveParentActivate():
        If the parent is a manager, passes the event to the parent.

PrimitivePrevTabGroup():
        Traverses to the first item in the previous tab group. If the beginning of the tab group list is reached, it wraps to the end of the tab group list.

Release():   If the button press occurs within the slider and the slider position is changed, the callbacks for **XmNvalueChangedCallback** are called.

Select():   **In arrow**:
        Moves the slider by one increment in the direction of the arrow. If **XmNprocessingDirection** is **XmMAX_ON_RIGHT** or **XmMAX_ON_BOTTOM**, movement toward the right or bottom calls the callbacks for **XmNincrementCallback**, and movement to the left or top calls the callbacks for **XmNdecrementCallback**. If **XmNprocessingDirection** is **XmMAX_ON_LEFT** or **XmMAX_ON_TOP**, movement toward the right or bottom calls the callbacks for **XmNdecrementCallback**, and movement to the left or top calls the callbacks for **XmNincrementCallback**. The **XmNvalueChangedCallback** is called if the **XmNincrementCallback** or **XmNdecrementCallback** is NULL.

        In scroll region between an arrow and the slider:
        Moves the slider by one page increment in the direction of the arrow. If **XmNprocessingDirection** is **XmMAX_ON_RIGHT** or **XmMAX_ON_BOTTOM**, movement toward the right or bottom calls the callbacks for **XmNpageIncrementCallback**, and movement to the left or top calls the callbacks for

XmNpageDecrementCallback. If **XmNprocessingDirection** is **XmMAX_ON_LEFT** or **XmMAX_ON_TOP**, movement toward the right or bottom calls the callbacks for **XmNpageDecrementCallback**, and movement to the left or top calls the callbacks for **XmNpageIncrementCallback**. The **XmNvalueChangedCallback** is called if the **XmNpageIncrementCallback** or **XmNpageDecrementCallback** is NULL.

In slider:
Activates the interactive dragging of the slider.

If the button is held down in either the arrows or the scroll region longer than the **XmNinitialDelay** resource, the slider is moved again by the same increment and the same callbacks are called. After the initial delay has been used, the time delay changes to the time defined by the resource **XmNrepeatDelay**.

TopOrBottom():

MCtrl BSelect Press in an arrow or in the scroll region between an arrow and the slider moves the slider as far as possible in the direction of the arrow. If **XmNprocessingDirection** is **XmMAX_ON_RIGHT** or **XmMAX_ON_BOTTOM**, movement toward the right or bottom calls the callbacks for **XmNtoBottomCallback**, and movement to the left or top calls the callbacks for **XmNtoTopCallback**. If **XmNprocessingDirection** is **XmMAX_ON_LEFT** or **XmMAX_ON_TOP**, movement toward the right or bottom calls the callbacks for **XmNtoTopCallback**, and movement to the left or top calls the callbacks for **XmNtoBottomCallback**. The **XmNvalueChangedCallback** is called if the **XmNtoTopCallback** or **XmNtoBottomCallback** is NULL. Pressing **KBeginLine** or **KBeginData** moves the slider to the minimum value and invokes the **XmNtoTopCallback**. Pressing **KEndLine** or **KEndData** moves the slider to the maximum value and invokes the **XmNtoBottomCallback**.

Related Information

Core(3X), **XmCreateScrollBar(3X)**, **XmPrimitive(3X)**, **XmScrollBarGetValues(3X)**, and **XmScrollBarSetValues(3X)**.

XmScrollBarGetValues—A ScrollBar function that returns the ScrollBar's increment values

AES Support Level

Full-use

Synopsis

#include <Xm/ScrollBar.h>

void XmScrollBarGetValues (*widget, value_return, slider_size_return, increment_return, page_increment_return*)

Widget	*widget*;
int	** value_return*;
int	** slider_size_return*;
int	** increment_return*;
int	** page_increment_return*;

Description

XmScrollBarGetValues returns the the ScrollBar's increment values. The scroll region is overlaid with a slider bar that is adjusted in size and position using the main ScrollBar or set slider function attributes.

widget   Specifies the ScrollBar widget ID.

value_return Returns the ScrollBar's slider position between the **XmNminimum** and **XmNmaximum** resources.

slider_size_return

    Returns the size of the slider as a value between 0 (zero) and the absolute value of **XmNmaximum** minus **XmNminimum**. The size of the slider varies, depending on how much of the slider scroll area it represents.

increment_return

    Returns the amount of increment and decrement.

page_increment_return

    Returns the amount of page increment and decrement.

For a complete definition of ScrollBar and its associated resources, see **XmScrollBar(3X)**.

Return Value

Returns the ScrollBar's increment values.

Related Information

XmScrollBar(3X).

XmScrollBarSetValues—A ScrollBar function that changes ScrollBar's increment values and the slider's size and position

AES Support Level

Full-use

Synopsis

#include <Xm/ScrollBar.h>

void XmScrollBarSetValues (*widget, value, slider_size, increment, page_increment, notify*)

Widget	*widget*;
int	*value*;
int	*slider_size*;
int	*increment*;
int	*page_increment*;
Boolean	*notify*;

Description

XmSetScrollBarValues changes the ScrollBar's increment values and the slider's size and position. The scroll region is overlaid with a slider bar that is adjusted in size and position using the main ScrollBar or set slider function attributes.

widget　　　　Specifies the ScrollBar widget ID.

value　　　　Specifies the ScrollBar's slider position between **XmNminimum** and **XmNmaximum**. The resource name associated with this argument is **XmNvalue**.

slider_size　　Specifies the size of the slider as a value between 0 (zero) and the absolute value of **XmNmaximum** minus **XmNminimum**. The size of the slider varies, depending on how much of the slider scroll area it represents. This sets the **XmNsliderSize** resource associated with ScrollBar.

increment　　Specifies the amount of button increment and decrement. If this argument is not 0 (zero), the ScrollBar widget automatically adjusts the slider when an increment or decrement action occurs. This sets the **XmNincrement** resource associated with ScrollBar.

page_increment

　　　　　　　Specifies the amount of page increment and decrement. If this argument is not 0 (zero), the ScrollBar widget automatically adjusts the slider when an increment or decrement action occurs. This sets the **XmNpageIncrement** resource associated with ScrollBar.

notify   Specifies a Boolean value that, when True, indicates a change in the ScrollBar value and also specifies that the ScrollBar widget automatically activates the **XmNvalueChangedCallback** with the recent change. If it is set to False, it specifies any change that has occurred in the ScrollBar's value, but does not activate **XmNvalueChangedCallback**.

For a complete definition of ScrollBar and its associated resources, see **XmScrollBar(3X)**.

Related Information

XmScrollBar(3X).

XmScrolledWindow—The ScrolledWindow widget class

AES Support Level

Full-use

History/Direction

The **XmNvisualPolicy** resource is obsolete and will be removed in favor of the **XmNscrollingPolicy** resource in revision E.

Synopsis

#include <Xm/ScrolledW.h>

Description

The ScrolledWindow widget combines one or two ScrollBar widgets and a viewing area to implement a visible window onto some other (usually larger) data display. The visible part of the window can be scrolled through the larger display by the use of ScrollBars.

To use ScrolledWindow, an application first creates a ScrolledWindow widget, any needed ScrollBar widgets, and a widget capable of displaying any desired data as the work area of ScrolledWindow. ScrolledWindow positions the work area widget and displays the ScrollBars if so requested. When the user performs some action on the ScrollBar, the application is notified through the normal ScrollBar callback interface.

ScrolledWindow can be configured to operate automatically so that it performs all scrolling and display actions with no need for application program involvement. It can also be configured to provide a minimal support framework in which the application is responsible for processing all user input and making all visual changes to the displayed data in response to that input.

When ScrolledWindow is performing automatic scrolling, it creates a clipping window. Conceptually, this window becomes the viewport through which the user examines the larger underlying data area. The application simply creates the desired data, then makes that data the work area of the ScrolledWindow. When the user moves the slider to change the displayed data, the workspace is moved under the viewing area so that a new portion of the data becomes visible.

Sometimes it is impractical for an application to create a large data space and simply display it through a small clipping window. For example, in a text editor, creating a single data area that consisted of a large file would involve an undesirable amount of overhead. The application needs to use a ScrolledWindow (a small viewport onto some larger data), but needs to be notified when the user scrolls the viewport so it can bring in more data from storage and update the display area. For these cases, the ScrolledWindow can be configured so that it provides only visual layout support. No clipping window is created, and the application must maintain the data displayed in the work area, as well as respond to user input on the ScrollBars.

Classes

ScrolledWindow inherits behavior and resources from **Core**, **Composite**, **Constraint**, and **XmManager**.

The class pointer is **xmScrolledWindowWidgetClass**.

The class name is **XmScrolledWindow**.

New Resources

The following table defines a set of widget resources used by the programmer to specify data. The programmer can also set the resource values for the inherited classes to set attributes for this widget. To reference a resource by name or by class in a **.Xdefaults** file, remove the **XmN** or **XmC** prefix and use the remaining letters. To specify one of the defined values for a resource in a **.Xdefaults** file, remove the **Xm** prefix and use the remaining letters (in either lowercase or uppercase, but include any underscores between words). The codes in the access column indicate if the given resource can be set at creation time (C), set by using **XtSetValues** (S), retrieved by using **XtGetValues** (G), or is not applicable (N/A).

XmScrolledWindow Resource Set		
Name	**Default**	**Access**
Class	**Type**	
XmNclipWindow	dynamic	G
XmCClipWindow	Widget	
XmNhorizontalScrollBar	dynamic	CSG
XmCHorizontalScrollBar	Widget	
XmNscrollBarDisplayPolicy	dynamic	CSG
XmCScrollBarDisplayPolicy	unsigned char	
XmNscrollBarPlacement	XmBOTTOM_RIGHT	CSG
XmCScrollBarPlacement	unsigned char	
XmNscrolledWindowMarginHeight	0	CSG
XmCScrolledWindowMarginHeight	Dimension	
XmNscrolledWindowMarginWidth	0	CSG
XmCScrolledWindowMarginWidth	Dimension	
XmNscrollingPolicy	XmAPPLICATION_DEFINED	CG
XmCScrollingPolicy	unsigned char	
XmNspacing	4	CSG
XmCSpacing	Dimension	
XmNverticalScrollBar	dynamic	CSG
XmCVerticalScrollBar	Widget	
XmNvisualPolicy	dynamic	G
XmCVisualPolicy	unsigned char	
XmNworkWindow	NULL	CSG
XmCWorkWindow	Widget	

XmNclipWindow

Specifies the widget ID of the clipping area. This is automatically
created by ScrolledWindow when the **XmNvisualPolicy** resource is
set to **XmCONSTANT** and can only be read by the application.
Any attempt to set this resource to a new value causes a warning
message to be printed by the scrolled window. If the
XmNvisualPolicy resource is set to **XmVARIABLE**, this resource
is set to NULL, and no clipping window is created.

XmNhorizontalScrollBar

Specifies the widget ID of the horizontal ScrollBar. This is
automatically created by ScrolledWindow when the
XmNscrollingPolicy is initialized to **XmAUTOMATIC**; otherwise,
the default is NULL.

XmNscrollBarDisplayPolicy

Controls the automatic placement of the ScrollBars. If it is set to **XmAS_NEEDED** and if **XmNscrollingPolicy** is set to **XmAUTOMATIC**, ScrollBars are displayed only if the workspace exceeds the clip area in one or both dimensions. A resource value of **XmSTATIC** causes the ScrolledWindow to display the ScrollBars whenever they are managed, regardless of the relationship between the clip window and the work area. This resource must be **XmSTATIC** when **XmNscrollingPolicy** is **XmAPPLICATION_DEFINED**. The default is **XmAS_NEEDED** when **XmNscrollingPolicy** is **XmAUTOMATIC**, and **XmSTATIC** otherwise.

XmNscrollBarPlacement

Specifies the positioning of the ScrollBars in relation to the work window. The the values are

XmTOP_LEFT

The horizontal ScrollBar is placed above the work window; the vertical ScrollBar to is placed the left.

XmBOTTOM_LEFT

The horizontal ScrollBar is placed below the work window; the vertical ScrollBar to is placed the left.

XmTOP_RIGHT

The horizontal ScrollBar is placed above the work window; the vertical ScrollBar to is placed the right.

XmBOTTOM_RIGHT

The horizontal ScrollBar is placed below the work window; the vertical ScrollBar to is placed the right.

The default value may depend on the value of the **XmNstringDirection** resource.

XmNscrolledWindowMarginHeight

Specifies the margin height on the top and bottom of the ScrolledWindow.

XmNscrolledWindowMarginWidth

Specifies the margin width on the right and left sides of the ScrolledWindow.

XmNscrollingPolicy

Performs automatic scrolling of the work area with no application interaction. If the value of this resource is **XmAUTOMATIC**,

XmScrolledWindow(3X)

ScrolledWindow automatically creates the ScrollBars; attaches callbacks to the ScrollBars; sets the visual policy to **XmCONSTANT**; and automatically moves the work area through the clip window in response to any user interaction with the ScrollBars. An application can also add its own callbacks to the ScrollBars. This allows the application to be notified of a scroll event without having to perform any layout procedures.

NOTE: Since the ScrolledWindow adds callbacks to the ScrollBars, an application should not perform an **XtRemoveAllCallbacks** on any of the ScrollBar widgets.

When **XmNscrollingPolicy** is set to **XmAPPLICATION_DEFINED**, the application is responsible for all aspects of scrolling. The ScrollBars must be created by the application, and it is responsible for performing any visual changes in the work area in response to user input.

This resource must be set to the desired policy at the time the ScrolledWindow is created. It cannot be changed through **SetValues**.

XmNspacing Specifies the distance that separates the ScrollBars from the work window.

XmNverticalScrollBar

Specifies the widget ID of the vertical ScrollBar. This is automatically created by ScrolledWindow when the **XmNscrollingPolicy** is initialized to **XmAUTOMATIC**; otherwise, the default is NULL.

XmNvisualPolicy

Enlarges the ScrolledWindow to match the size of the work area. It can also be used as a static viewport onto a larger data space. If the visual policy is **XmVARIABLE**, the ScrolledWindow forces the ScrollBar display policy to **XmSTATIC** and allows the work area to grow or shrink at any time and adjusts its layout to accommodate the new size. When the policy is **XmCONSTANT**, the work area grows or shrinks as requested, but a clipping window forces the size of the visible portion to remain constant. The only time the viewing area can grow is in response to a resize from the ScrolledWindow's parent. The default is **XmCONSTANT** when **XmNscrollingPolicy** is **XmAUTOMATIC**, and **XmVARIABLE** otherwise.

XmNworkWindow
> Specifies the widget ID of the viewing area.

Inherited Resources
> ScrolledWindow inherits behavior and resources from the superclasses described in the following tables. For a complete description of each resource, refer to the reference page for that superclass.

XmManager Resource Set		
Name	**Default**	**Access**
Class	**Type**	
XmNbottomShadowColor	dynamic	CSG
XmCBottomShadowColor	Pixel	
XmNbottomShadowPixmap	XmUNSPECIFIED_PIXMAP	CSG
XmCBottomShadowPixmap	Pixmap	
XmNforeground	dynamic	CSG
XmCForeground	Pixel	
XmNhelpCallback	NULL	C
XmCCallback	XtCallbackList	
XmNhighlightColor	dynamic	CSG
XmCHighlightColor	Pixel	
XmNhighlightPixmap	dynamic	CSG
XmCHighlightPixmap	Pixmap	
XmNnavigationType	XmTAB_GROUP	CSG
XmCNavigationType	XmNavigationType	

Name	Default	Access
Class	Type	
XmNshadowThickness	dynamic	CSG
XmCShadowThickness	Dimension	
XmNstringDirection	dynamic	CG
XmCStringDirection	XmStringDirection	
XmNtopShadowColor	dynamic	CSG
XmCTopShadowColor	Pixel	
XmNtopShadowPixmap	dynamic	CSG
XmCTopShadowPixmap	Pixmap	
XmNtraversalOn	True	CSG
XmCTraversalOn	Boolean	
XmNuserData	NULL	CSG
XmCUserData	XtPointer	

Composite Resource Set		
Name	Default	Access
Class	Type	
XmNchildren	NULL	G
XmCReadOnly	WidgetList	
XmNinsertPosition	NULL	CSG
XmCInsertPosition	XtOrderProc	
XmNnumChildren	0	G
XmCReadOnly	Cardinal	

Core Resource Set		
Name	**Default**	**Access**
Class	**Type**	
XmNaccelerators	dynamic	CSG
XmCAccelerators	XtAccelerators	
XmNancestorSensitive	dynamic	G
XmCSensitive	Boolean	
XmNbackground	dynamic	CSG
XmCBackground	Pixel	
XmNbackgroundPixmap	XmUNSPECIFIED_PIXMAP	CSG
XmCPixmap	Pixmap	
XmNborderColor	XtDefaultForeground	CSG
XmCBorderColor	Pixel	
XmNborderPixmap	XmUNSPECIFIED_PIXMAP	CSG
XmCPixmap	Pixmap	
XmNborderWidth	0	CSG
XmCBorderWidth	Dimension	
XmNcolormap	dynamic	CG
XmCColormap	Colormap	
XmNdepth	dynamic	CG
XmCDepth	int	
XmNdestroyCallback	NULL	C
XmCCallback	XtCallbackList	
XmNheight	dynamic	CSG
XmCHeight	Dimension	
XmNinitialResourcesPersistent	True	C
XmCInitialResourcesPersistent	Boolean	
XmNmappedWhenManaged	True	CSG
XmCMappedWhenManaged	Boolean	
XmNscreen	dynamic	CG
XmCScreen	Screen *	
XmNsensitive	True	CSG
XmCSensitive	Boolean	

Name	Default	Access
Class	Type	
XmNtranslations	dynamic	CSG
XmCTranslations	XtTranslations	
XmNwidth	dynamic	CSG
XmCWidth	Dimension	
XmNx	0	CSG
XmCPosition	Position	
XmNy	0	CSG
XmCPosition	Position	

Callback Information

ScrolledWindow defines no new callback structures. The application must use the ScrollBar callbacks to be notified of user input.

Related Information

Composite(3X), **Constraint(3X)**, **Core(3X)**, **XmCreateScrolledWindow(3X)**, **XmManager(3X)**, and **XmScrolledWindowSetAreas(3X)**.

XmScrolledWindowSetAreas—A ScrolledWindow function that adds or changes a window work region and a horizontal or vertical ScrollBar widget to the ScrolledWindow widget

AES Support Level

Full-use

Synopsis

#include <Xm/ScrolledW.h>

void XmScrolledWindowSetAreas (*widget, horizontal_scrollbar, vertical_scrollbar, work_region*)

Widget	*widget*;
Widget	*horizontal_scrollbar*;
Widget	*vertical_scrollbar*;
Widget	*work_region*;

Description

XmScrolledWindowSetAreas adds or changes a window work region and a horizontal or vertical ScrollBar widget to the ScrolledWindow widget for the application. Each widget is optional and may be passed as NULL.

widget   Specifies the ScrolledWindow widget ID.

horizontal_scrollbar

> Specifies the ScrollBar widget ID for the horizontal ScrollBar to be associated with the ScrolledWindow widget. Set this ID only after creating an instance of the ScrolledWindow widget. The resource name associated with this argument is **XmNhorizontalScrollBar**.

vertical_scrollbar

> Specifies the ScrollBar widget ID for the vertical ScrollBar to be associated with the ScrolledWindow widget. Set this ID only after creating an instance of the ScrolledWindow widget. The resource name associated with this argument is **XmNverticalScrollBar**.

work_region   Specifies the widget ID for the work window to be associated with the ScrolledWindow widget. Set this ID only after creating an instance of the ScrolledWindow widget. The attribute name associated with this argument is **XmNworkWindow**.

For a complete definition of ScrolledWindow and its associated resources, see **XmScrolledWindow(3X)**.

Related Information
XmScrolledWindow(3X).

XmSelectionBox—The SelectionBox widget class

AES Support Level

Full-use

Synopsis

#include <Xm/SelectioB.h>

Description

SelectionBox is a general dialog widget that allows the user to select one item from a list. By default, a SelectionBox includes the following:

- A scrolling list of alternatives

- An editable text field for the selected alternative

- Labels for the list and text field

- Three or four buttons

The default button labels are **OK**, **Cancel**, and **Help**. By default an **Apply** button is also created; if the parent of the SelectionBox is a DialogShell, it is managed; otherwise it is unmanaged. Additional children may be added to the SelectionBox after creation.

The user can select an item in two ways: by scrolling through the list and selecting the desired item or by entering the item name directly into the text edit area. Selecting an item from the list causes that item name to appear in the selection text edit area.

The user may select a new item as many times as desired. The item is not actually selected until the user presses the **OK** PushButton.

The default value for the **XmBulletinBoard** resource **XmNcancelButton** is the Cancel button, unless **XmNdialogType** is **XmDIALOG_COMMAND**, when the default is NULL. The default value for the **XmBulletinBoard** **XmNdefaultButton** resource is the OK button, unless **XmNdialogType** is **XmDIALOG_COMMAND**, when the default is NULL.

Classes

SelectionBox inherits behavior and resources from **Core**, **Composite**, **Constraint**, **XmManager**, and **XmBulletinBoard**.

The class pointer is **xmSelectionBoxWidgetClass**.

The class name is **XmSelectionBox**.

New Resources

The following table defines a set of widget resources used by the programmer to specify data. The programmer can also set the resource values for the inherited classes to set attributes for this widget. To reference a resource by name or by class in a **.Xdefaults** file, remove the **XmN** or **XmC** prefix and use the remaining letters. To specify one of the defined values for a resource in a **.Xdefaults** file, remove the **Xm** prefix and use the remaining letters (in either lowercase or uppercase, but include any underscores between words). The codes in the access column indicate if the given resource can be set at creation time (C), set by using **XtSetValues** (S), retrieved by using **XtGetValues** (G), or is not applicable (N/A).

XmSelectionBox Resource Set		
Name **Class**	**Default** **Type**	**Access**
XmNapplyCallback XmCCallback	NULL XtCallbackList	C
XmNapplyLabelString XmCApplyLabelString	dynamic XmString	CSG
XmNcancelCallback XmCCallback	NULL XtCallbackList	C
XmNcancelLabelString XmCCancelLabelString	dynamic XmString	CSG
XmNdialogType XmCDialogType	dynamic unsigned char	CG
XmNhelpLabelString XmCHelpLabelString	dynamic XmString	CSG
XmNlistItemCount XmCItemCount	0 int	CSG
XmNlistItems XmCItems	NULL XmStringTable	CSG
XmNlistLabelString XmCListLabelString	dynamic XmString	CSG
XmNlistVisibleItemCount XmCVisibleItemCount	dynamic int	CSG
XmNminimizeButtons XmCMinimizeButtons	False Boolean	CSG
XmNmustMatch XmCMustMatch	False Boolean	CSG
XmNnoMatchCallback XmCCallback	NULL XtCallbackList	C
XmNokCallback XmCCallback	NULL XtCallbackList	C

Name	Default	Access
Class	Type	
XmNokLabelString	dynamic	CSG
XmCOkLabelString	XmString	
XmNselectionLabelString	dynamic	CSG
XmCSelectionLabelString	XmString	
XmNtextAccelerators	default	C
XmCTextAccelerators	XtAccelerators	
XmNtextColumns	dynamic	CSG
XmCColumns	short	
XmNtextString	""	CSG
XmCTextString	XmString	

XmNapplyCallback

> Specifies the list of callbacks called when the user activates the **Apply** button. The callback reason is **XmCR_APPLY**.

XmNapplyLabelString

> Specifies the string label for the **Apply** button. The default for this resource depends on the locale. In the C locale the default is **Apply**.

XmNcancelCallback

> Specifies the list of callbacks called when the user activates the **Cancel** button. The callback reason is **XmCR_CANCEL**.

XmNcancelLabelString

> Specifies the string label for the **Cancel** button. The default for this resource depends on the locale. In the C locale the default is **Cancel**.

XmNdialogType

> Determines the set of SelectionBox children widgets that are created and managed at initialization. The possible values are

> **XmDIALOG_PROMPT**
>
> > All standard children except the list and list label are created, and all except the **Apply** button are managed

> **XmDIALOG_COMMAND**
>
> > Only the list, the selection label, and the text field are created and managed

XmDIALOG_SELECTION

All standard children are created and managed

XmDIALOG_FILE_SELECTION

All standard children are created and managed

XmDIALOG_WORK_AREA

All standard children are created, and all except the **Apply** button are managed

If the parent of the SelectionBox is a DialogShell, the default is **XmDIALOG_SELECTION**; otherwise, the default is **XmDIALOG_WORK_AREA**. **XmCreatePromptDialog** and **XmCreateSelectionDialog** set and append this resource to the creation *arglist* supplied by the application. This resource cannot be modified after creation.

XmNhelpLabelString

Specifies the string label for the **Help** button. The default for this resource depends on the locale. In the C locale the default is **Help**.

XmNlistItems

Specifies the items in the SelectionBox list.

XmNlistItemCount

Specifies the number of items in the SelectionBox list. The value must not be negative.

XmNlistLabelString

Specifies the string label to appear above the SelectionBox list containing the selection items. The default for this resource depends on the locale. In the C locale the default is **Items** unless **XmNdialogType** is **XmDIALOG_PROMPT**; in this case the default is NULL.

XmNlistVisibleItemCount

Specifies the number of items displayed in the SelectionBox list. The value must be greater than 0 (zero) unless **XmNdialogType** is **XmDIALOG_PROMPT**; in this case, the value is always 0. The default is dynamic based on the height of the list.

XmNminimizeButtons

Sets the buttons to the width of the widest button and height of the tallest button if False. If True, button width and height are not modified.

XmNmustMatch

Specifies whether the selection widget should check if the user's selection in the text edit field has an exact match in the SelectionBox list when the **OK** button is activated. If the selection does not have an exact match, and **XmNmustMatch** is True, the **XmNnoMatchCallback** callbacks are called. If the selection does have an exact match or if **XmNmustMatch** is False, **XmNokCallback** callbacks are called.

XmNnoMatchCallback

Specifies the list of callbacks called when the user makes a selection from the text edit field that does not have an exact match with any of the items in the list box. The callback reason is **XmCR_NO_MATCH**. Callbacks in this list are called only if **XmNmustMatch** is true.

XmNokCallback

Specifies the list of callbacks called when the user activates the **OK** button. The callback reason is **XmCR_OK**. If the selection text does not match a list item, and **XmNmustMatch** is True, the **XmNnoMatchCallback** callbacks are called instead.

XmNokLabelString

Specifies the string label for the **OK** button. The default for this resource depends on the locale. In the C locale the default is **OK**.

XmNselectionLabelString

Specifies the string label for the selection text edit field. The default for this resource depends on the locale. In the C locale the default is **Selection**.

XmNtextAccelerators

Specifies translations added to the Text widget child of the SelectionBox. The default includes bindings for the up and down keys for auto selection of list items. This resource is ignored if **XmNaccelerators** is initialized to a nondefault value.

XmNtextColumns

Specifies the number of columns in the Text widget. The value must be greater than 0 (zero).

XmNtextString

Specifies the text in the text edit selection field.

Inherited Resources

SelectionBox inherits behavior and resources from the superclasses in the following tables. For a complete description of each resource, refer to the reference page for that superclass.

XmBulletinBoard Resource Set		

Name
    Class
	Default
	    Type
		Access

XmNallowOverlap
    XmCAllowOverlap
	True
	    Boolean
		CSG

XmNautoUnmanage
    XmCAutoUnmanage
	True
	    Boolean
		CG

XmNbuttonFontList
    XmCButtonFontList
	dynamic
	    XmFontList
		CSG

XmNcancelButton
    XmCWidget
	dynamic
	    Widget
		SG

XmNdefaultButton
    XmCWidget
	dynamic
	    Widget
		SG

XmNdefaultPosition
    XmCDefaultPosition
	True
	    Boolean
		CSG

XmNdialogStyle
    XmCDialogStyle
	dynamic
	    unsigned char
		CSG

XmNdialogTitle
    XmCDialogTitle
	NULL
	    XmString
		CSG

XmNfocusCallback
    XmCCallback
	NULL
	    XtCallbackList
		C

XmNlabelFontList
    XmCLabelFontList
	dynamic
	    XmFontList
		CSG

XmNmapCallback
    XmCCallback
	NULL
	    XtCallbackList
		C

XmNmarginHeight
    XmCMarginHeight
	10
	    Dimension
		CSG

XmNmarginWidth
    XmCMarginWidth
	10
	    Dimension
		CSG

XmNnoResize
    XmCNoResize
	False
	    Boolean
		CSG

XmNresizePolicy
    XmCResizePolicy
	XmRESIZE_ANY
	    unsigned char
		CSG

Name Class	Default Type	Access
XmNshadowType XmCShadowType	XmSHADOW_OUT unsigned char	CSG
XmNtextFontList XmCTextFontList	dynamic XmFontList	CSG
XmNtextTranslations XmCTranslations	NULL XtTranslations	C
XmNunmapCallback XmCCallback	NULL XtCallbackList	C

XmManager Resource Set		

Name
    Class
	Default
	    Type
		Access

XmNbottomShadowColor
    XmCBottomShadowColor
	dynamic
	    Pixel
		CSG

XmNbottomShadowPixmap
    XmCBottomShadowPixmap
	XmUNSPECIFIED_PIXMAP
	    Pixmap
		CSG

XmNforeground
    XmCForeground
	dynamic
	    Pixel
		CSG

XmNhelpCallback
    XmCCallback
	NULL
	    XtCallbackList
		C

XmNhighlightColor
    XmCHighlightColor
	dynamic
	    Pixel
		CSG

XmNhighlightPixmap
    XmCHighlightPixmap
	dynamic
	    Pixmap
		CSG

XmNnavigationType
    XmCNavigationType
	XmTAB_GROUP
	    XmNavigationType
		CSG

XmNshadowThickness
    XmCShadowThickness
	dynamic
	    Dimension
		CSG

XmNstringDirection
    XmCStringDirection
	dynamic
	    XmStringDirection
		CG

XmNtopShadowColor
    XmCTopShadowColor
	dynamic
	    Pixel
		CSG

XmNtopShadowPixmap
    XmCTopShadowPixmap
	dynamic
	    Pixmap
		CSG

XmNtraversalOn
    XmCTraversalOn
	True
	    Boolean
		CSG

XmNuserData
    XmCUserData
	NULL
	    XtPointer
		CSG

Composite Resource Set		
Name	**Default**	**Access**
Class	**Type**	
XmNchildren	NULL	G
XmCReadOnly	WidgetList	
XmNinsertPosition	NULL	CSG
XmCInsertPosition	XtOrderProc	
XmNnumChildren	0	G
XmCReadOnly	Cardinal	

Core Resource Set		
Name	**Default**	**Access**
Class	**Type**	
XmNaccelerators	dynamic	N/A
XmCAccelerators	XtAccelerators	
XmNancestorSensitive	dynamic	G
XmCSensitive	Boolean	
XmNbackground	dynamic	CSG
XmCBackground	Pixel	
XmNbackgroundPixmap	XmUNSPECIFIED_PIXMAP	CSG
XmCPixmap	Pixmap	
XmNborderColor	XtDefaultForeground	CSG
XmCBorderColor	Pixel	
XmNborderPixmap	XmUNSPECIFIED_PIXMAP	CSG
XmCPixmap	Pixmap	
XmNborderWidth	0	CSG
XmCBorderWidth	Dimension	
XmNcolormap	dynamic	CG
XmCColormap	Colormap	
XmNdepth	dynamic	CG
XmCDepth	int	
XmNdestroyCallback	NULL	C
XmCCallback	XtCallbackList	
XmNheight	dynamic	CSG
XmCHeight	Dimension	
XmNinitialResourcesPersistent	True	C
XmCInitialResourcesPersistent	Boolean	
XmNmappedWhenManaged	True	CSG
XmCMappedWhenManaged	Boolean	
XmNscreen	dynamic	CG
XmCScreen	Screen *	
XmNsensitive	True	CSG
XmCSensitive	Boolean	

| Name | Default | Access |
Class	Type	
XmNtranslations	dynamic	CSG
XmCTranslations	XtTranslations	
XmNwidth	dynamic	CSG
XmCWidth	Dimension	
XmNx	0	CSG
XmCPosition	Position	
XmNy	0	CSG
XmCPosition	Position	

Callback Information

A pointer to the following structure is passed to each callback:

typedef struct
{
    int   *reason*;
    XEvent   * *event*;
    XmString   *value*;
    int   *length*;
} XmSelectionBoxCallbackStruct;

reason   Indicates why the callback was invoked

event   Points to the **XEvent** that triggered the callback

value   Indicates the **XmString** value selected by the user from the SelectionBox list or entered into the SelectionBox text field

length   Indicates the size in bytes of the **XmString** value

Action Routines

The XmSelectionBox action routines are

SelectionBoxUpOrDown(0|1|2|3):
When called with an argument of 0 (zero), selects the previous item in the list and replaces the text with that item.

When called with an argument of 1, selects the next item in the list and replaces the text with that item.

When called with an argument of 2, selects the first item in the list and replaces the text with that item.

When called with an argument of 3, selects the last item in the list
and replaces the text with that item.

SelectionBoxRestore():
> Replaces the text value with the list selection. If no item in the list
> is selected, clears the text.

Related Information

Composite(3X), **Constraint(3X)**, **Core(3X)**, **XmBulletinBoard(3X)**,
XmCreateSelectionBox(3X), **XmCreateSelectionDialog(3X)**,
XmCreatePromptDialog(3X), **XmManager(3X)**, and
XmSelectionBoxGetChild(3X).

XmSelectionBoxGetChild—A SelectionBox function that is used to access a component

AES Support Level

Full-use

Synopsis

#include <Xm/SelectioB.h>

Widget XmSelectionBoxGetChild (*widget, child*)
    Widget   *widget*;
    unsigned char *child*;

Description

XmSelectionBoxGetChild is used to access a component within a SelectionBox. The parameters given to the function are the SelectionBox widget and a value indicating which component to access.

widget   Specifies the SelectionBox widget ID.

child   Specifies a component within the SelectionBox. The following values are legal for this parameter:

- **XmDIALOG_APPLY_BUTTON**
- **XmDIALOG_CANCEL_BUTTON**
- **XmDIALOG_DEFAULT_BUTTON**
- **XmDIALOG_HELP_BUTTON**
- **XmDIALOG_LIST**
- **XmDIALOG_LIST_LABEL**
- **XmDIALOG_OK_BUTTON**
- **XmDIALOG_SELECTION_LABEL**
- **XmDIALOG_SEPARATOR**
- **XmDIALOG_TEXT**
- **XmDIALOG_WORK_AREA**

For a complete definition of SelectionBox and its associated resources, see **XmSelectionBox(3X)**.

Return Value

Returns the widget ID of the specified SelectionBox component. An application should not assume that the returned widget will be of any particular class.

Related Information

XmSelectionBox(3X).

XmSeparator—The Separator widget class

AES Support Level

Full-use

Synopsis

#include <Xm/Separator.h>

Description

Separator is a primitive widget that separates items in a display. Several different line drawing styles are provided, as well as horizontal or vertical orientation.

The Separator line drawing is automatically centered within the height of the widget for a horizontal orientation and centered within the width of the widget for a vertical orientation. An **XtSetValues** with a new **XmNseparatorType** resizes the widget to its minimal height (for horizontal orientation) or its minimal width (for vertical orientation) unless height or width is explicitly set in the **XtSetValues** call.

Separator does not draw shadows around the separator. The Primitive resource **XmNshadowThickness** is used for the Separator's thickness when **XmNseparatorType** is **XmSHADOW_ETCHED_IN** or **XmSHADOW_ETCHED_OUT**.

Separator does not highlight and allows no traversing. The primitive resource **XmNtraversalOn** is forced to False.

The **XmNseparatorType** of **XmNO_LINE** provides an escape to the application programmer who needs a different style of drawing. A pixmap the height of the widget can be created and used as the background pixmap by building an argument list using the **XmNbackgroundPixmap** argument type as defined by **Core**. Whenever the widget is redrawn, its background is displayed containing the desired separator drawing.

Classes

Separator inherits behavior and resources from **Core** and **XmPrimitive**.

The class pointer is **xmSeparatorWidgetClass**.

The class name is **XmSeparator**.

New Resources

The following table defines a set of widget resources used by the programmer to specify data. The programmer can also set the resource values for the inherited classes to set attributes for this widget. To reference a resource by name or by class in a **.Xdefaults** file, remove the **XmN** or **XmC** prefix and use the remaining letters. To specify one of the defined values for a resource in a **.Xdefaults** file, remove the **Xm** prefix anduse the remaining letters (in either lowercase or uppercase, but include any underscores between words). The codes in the access column indicate if the given resource can be set at creation time (C), set by using **XtSetValues** (S), retrieved by using **XtGetValues** (G), or is not applicable (N/A).

XmSeparator Resource Set		
Name	**Default**	**Access**
Class	**Type**	
XmNmargin	0	CSG
XmCMargin	Dimension	
XmNorientation	XmHORIZONTAL	CSG
XmCOrientation	unsigned char	
XmNseparatorType	XmSHADOW_ETCHED_IN	CSG
XmCSeparatorType	unsigned char	

XmNmargin For horizontal orientation, specifies the space on the left and right sides between the border of the Separator and the line drawn. For vertical orientation, specifies the space on the top and bottom between the border of the Separator and the line drawn.

XmNorientation

Displays Separator vertically or horizontally. This resource can have values of **XmVERTICAL** and **XmHORIZONTAL**.

XmNseparatorType

Specifies the type of line drawing to be done in the Separator widget.

XmSINGLE_LINE

Single line

XmDOUBLE_LINE

Double line

XmSINGLE_DASHED_LINE

Single-dashed line

XmDOUBLE_DASHED_LINE

Double-dashed line

XmNO_LINE

No line

XmSHADOW_ETCHED_IN

Double line giving the effect of a line etched into the

window. The thickness of the double line is equal to the value of **XmNshadowThickness**. For horizontal orientation, the top line is drawn in **XmNtopShadowColor** and the bottom line is drawn in **XmNbottomShadowColor**. For vertical orientation, the left line is drawn in **XmNtopShadowColor** and the right line is drawn in **XmNbottomShadowColor**.

XmSHADOW_ETCHED_OUT
Double line giving the effect of an etched line coming out from the window. The thickness of the double line is equal to the value of **XmNshadowThickness**. For horizontal orientation, the top line is drawn in **XmNbottomShadowColor** and the bottom line is drawn in **XmNtopShadowColor**. For vertical orientation, the left line is drawn in **XmNbottomShadowColor** and the right line is drawn in **XmNtopShadowColor**.

Inherited Resources

Separator inherits behavior and resources from the superclasses in the following table. For a complete description of each resource, refer to the reference page for that superclass.

XmPrimitive Resource Set		
Name	**Default**	**Access**
Class	**Type**	
XmNbottomShadowColor	dynamic	CSG
XmCBottomShadowColor	Pixel	
XmNbottomShadowPixmap	XmUNSPECIFIED_PIXMAP	CSG
XmCBottomShadowPixmap	Pixmap	
XmNforeground	dynamic	CSG
XmCForeground	Pixel	
XmNhelpCallback	NULL	C
XmCCallback	XtCallbackList	
XmNhighlightColor	dynamic	CSG
XmCHighlightColor	Pixel	
XmNhighlightOnEnter	False	CSG
XmCHighlightOnEnter	Boolean	
XmNhighlightPixmap	dynamic	CSG
XmCHighlightPixmap	Pixmap	
XmNhighlightThickness	0	CSG
XmCHighlightThickness	Dimension	
XmNnavigationType	XmNONE	CSG
XmCNavigationType	XmNavigationType	
XmNshadowThickness	2	CSG
XmCShadowThickness	Dimension	
XmNtopShadowColor	dynamic	CSG
XmCTopShadowColor	Pixel	
XmNtopShadowPixmap	dynamic	CSG
XmCTopShadowPixmap	Pixmap	
XmNtraversalOn	False	G
XmCTraversalOn	Boolean	
XmNuserData	NULL	CSG
XmCUserData	XtPointer	

Core Resource Set		
Name	**Default**	**Access**
Class	**Type**	
XmNaccelerators	dynamic	CSG
XmCAccelerators	XtAccelerators	
XmNancestorSensitive	dynamic	G
XmCSensitive	Boolean	
XmNbackground	dynamic	CSG
XmCBackground	Pixel	
XmNbackgroundPixmap	XmUNSPECIFIED_PIXMAP	CSG
XmCPixmap	Pixmap	
XmNborderColor	XtDefaultForeground	CSG
XmCBorderColor	Pixel	
XmNborderPixmap	XmUNSPECIFIED_PIXMAP	CSG
XmCPixmap	Pixmap	
XmNborderWidth	0	CSG
XmCBorderWidth	Dimension	
XmNcolormap	dynamic	CG
XmCColormap	Colormap	
XmNdepth	dynamic	CG
XmCDepth	int	
XmNdestroyCallback	NULL	C
XmCCallback	XtCallbackList	
XmNheight	dynamic	CSG
XmCHeight	Dimension	
XmNinitialResourcesPersistent	True	C
XmCInitialResourcesPersistent	Boolean	
XmNmappedWhenManaged	True	CSG
XmCMappedWhenManaged	Boolean	
XmNscreen	dynamic	CG
XmCScreen	Screen *	
XmNsensitive	True	CSG
XmCSensitive	Boolean	

Name	Default	Access
Class	Type	
XmNtranslations	dynamic	CSG
XmCTranslations	XtTranslations	
XmNwidth	dynamic	CSG
XmCWidth	Dimension	
XmNx	0	CSG
XmCPosition	Position	
XmNy	0	CSG
XmCPosition	Position	

Related Information

Core(3X), **XmCreateSeparator(3X)**, and **XmPrimitive(3X)**.

XmSeparatorGadget—The SeparatorGadget widget class

AES Support Level

Full-use

Synopsis

#include <Xm/SeparatoG.h>

Description

SeparatorGadget separates items in a display. Several line drawing styles are provided, as well as horizontal or vertical orientation.

Lines drawn within the SeparatorGadget are automatically centered within the height of the gadget for a horizontal orientation and centered within the width of the gadget for a vertical orientation. An **XtSetValues** with a new **XmNseparatorType** resizes the widget to its minimal height (for horizontal orientation) or its minimal width (for vertical orientation) unless height or width is explicitly set in the **XtSetValues** call.

SeparatorGadget does not draw shadows around the separator. The Gadget resource **XmNshadowThickness** is used for the SeparatorGadget's thickness when **XmNseparatorType** is **XmSHADOW_ETCHED_IN** or **XmSHADOW_ETCHED_OUT**.

SeparatorGadget does not highlight and allows no traversing. The Gadget resource **XmNtraversalOn** is forced to False.

Classes

SeparatorGadget inherits behavior and resources from **Object**, **RectObj**, and **XmGadget**.

The class pointer is **xmSeparatorGadgetClass**.

The class name is **XmSeparatorGadget**.

New Resources

The following table defines a set of widget resources used by the programmer to specify data. The programmer can also set the resource values for the inherited classes to set attributes for this widget. To reference a resource by name or by class in a **.Xdefaults** file, remove the **XmN** or **XmC** prefix and use the remaining letters. To specify one of the defined values for a resource in a **.Xdefaults** file, remove the **Xm** prefix and use the remaining letters (in either lowercase or uppercase, but include any underscores between words). The codes in the access column indicate if the given resource can be set at creation time (C), set by using **XtSetValues** (S), retrieved by using **XtGetValues** (G), or is not applicable (N/A).

XmSeparatorGadget Resource Set		
Name	**Default**	**Access**
Class	**Type**	
XmNmargin	0	CSG
XmCMargin	Dimension	
XmNorientation	XmHORIZONTAL	CSG
XmCOrientation	unsigned char	
XmNseparatorType	XmSHADOW_ETCHED_IN	CSG
XmCSeparatorType	unsigned char	

XmNmargin   For horizontal orientation, specifies the space on the left and right sides between the border of SeparatorGadget and the line drawn. For vertical orientation, specifies the space on the top and bottom between the border of SeparatorGadget and the line drawn.

XmNorientation

Specifies whether SeparatorGadget is displayed vertically or horizontally. This resource can have values of **XmVERTICAL** and **XmHORIZONTAL**.

XmNseparatorType

Specifies the type of line drawing to be done in the Separator widget.

XmSINGLE_LINE

Single line.

XmDOUBLE_LINE

Double line.

XmSINGLE_DASHED_LINE

Single-dashed line.

XmDOUBLE_DASHED_LINE

Double-dashed line.

XmNO_LINE

No line.

XmSHADOW_ETCHED_IN

Double line giving the effect of a line etched into the window. The thickness of the double line is equal to the value of **XmNshadowThickness**. For horizontal orientation, the top line is drawn in

XmNtopShadowColor and the bottom line is drawn in **XmNbottomShadowColor**. For vertical orientation, the left line is drawn in **XmNtopShadowColor** and the right line is drawn in **XmNbottomShadowColor**.

XmSHADOW_ETCHED_OUT

Double line giving the effect of an etched line coming out from the window. The thickness of the double line is equal to the value of **XmNshadowThickness**. For horizontal orientation, the top line is drawn in **XmNbottomShadowColor** and the bottom line is drawn in **XmNtopShadowColor**. For vertical orientation, the left line is drawn in **XmNbottomShadowColor** and the right line is drawn in **XmNtopShadowColor**.

Inherited Resources

SeparatorGadget inherits behavior and resources from the superclasses in the following tables. For a complete description of each resource, refer to the reference page for that superclass.

XmGadget Resource Set		
Name	**Default**	**Access**
Class	**Type**	
XmNhelpCallback	NULL	C
XmCCallback	XtCallbackList	
XmNhighlightOnEnter	False	CSG
XmCHighlightOnEnter	Boolean	
XmNhighlightThickness	0	CSG
XmCHighlightThickness	Dimension	
XmNnavigationType	XmNONE	CSG
XmCNavigationType	XmNavigationType	
XmNshadowThickness	2	CSG
XmCShadowThickness	Dimension	
XmNtraversalOn	False	G
XmCTraversalOn	Boolean	
XmNuserData	NULL	CSG
XmCUserData	XtPointer	

RectObj Resource Set		
Name **Class**	**Default** **Type**	**Access**
XmNancestorSensitive XmCSensitive	dynamic Boolean	G
XmNborderWidth XmCBorderWidth	0 Dimension	N/A
XmNheight XmCHeight	dynamic Dimension	CSG
XmNsensitive XmCSensitive	True Boolean	CSG
XmNwidth XmCWidth	dynamic Dimension	CSG
XmNx XmCPosition	0 Position	CSG
XmNy XmCPosition	0 Position	CSG

Object Resource Set		
Name **Class**	**Default** **Type**	**Access**
XmNdestroyCallback XmCCallback	NULL XtCallbackList	C

Related Information

Object(3X), RectObject(3X), XmCreateSeparatorGadget(3X), and XmGadget(3X).

XmSetMenuCursor—A RowColumn function that modifies the menu cursor for a client

AES Support Level

Full-use

Synopsis

#include <Xm/Xm.h>

void XmSetMenuCursor (*display, cursorId*)
  Display   * *display*;
  Cursor   *cursorId*;

Description

XmSetMenuCursor programmatically modifies the menu cursor for a client; after the cursor has been created by the client, this function registers the cursor with the menu system. After calling this function, the specified cursor is displayed whenever this client displays a Motif menu on the indicated display. The client can then specify different cursors on different displays.

display   Specifies the display to which the cursor is to be associated

cursorId   Specifies the **X** cursor ID

For a complete definition of the menu cursor resource, see **XmRowColumn(3X)**.

Related Information

XmRowColumn(3X).

XmSetProtocolHooks—A VendorShell function that allows preactions and postactions to be executed when a protocol message is received from MWM

AES Support Level

Trial-use

Synopsis

#include <Xm/Xm.h>
#include <Xm/Protocols.h>

void XmSetProtocolHooks (*shell, property, protocol, prehook, pre_closure, posthook, post_closure*)

Widget	*shell*;
Atom	*property*;
Atom	*protocol*;
XtCallbackProc	*prehook*;
XtPointer	*pre_closure*;
XtCallbackProc	*posthook*;
XtPointer	*post_closure*;

void XmSetWMProtocolHooks (*shell, protocol, prehook, pre_closure, posthook, post_closure*)

Widget	*shell*;
Atom	*protocol*;
XtCallbackProc	*prehook*;
XtPointer	*pre_closure*;
XtCallbackProc	*posthook*;
XtPointer	*post_closure*;

Description

XmSetProtocolHooks is used by shells that want to have preactions and postactions executed when a protocol message is received from MWM. Since there is no guaranteed ordering in execution of event handlers or callback lists, this allows the shell to control the flow while leaving the protocol manager structures opaque.

XmSetWMProtocolHooks is a convenience interface. It calls **XmSetProtocolHooks** with the property value set to the atom returned by interning **WM_PROTOCOLS**.

shell   Specifies the widget with which the protocol property is associated

property   Specifies the protocol property

protocol   Specifies the protocol atom (or an **int** cast to **Atom**) *prehook*   Specifies the procedure to call before calling entries on the client callback list

pre_closure   Specifies the client data to be passed to the prehook when it is invoked

posthook   Specifies the procedure to call after calling entries on the client callback list

post_closure   Specifies the client data to be passed to the posthook when it is invoked

For a complete definition of VendorShell and its associated resources, see **VendorShell(3X)**.

Related Information

VendorShell(3X), **XmInternAtom(3X)**, and **XmSetWMProtocolHooks(3X)**.

XmSetWMProtocolHooks—A VendorShell convenience interface that allows preactions and postactions to be executed when a protocol message is received from the window manager

AES Support Level

Trial-use

Synopsis

#include <Xm/Xm.h>
#include <Xm/Protocols.h>

void XmSetWMProtocolHooks (*shell, protocol, prehook, pre_closure, posthook, post_closure*)

Widget	*shell*;
Atom	*protocol*;
XtCallbackProc	*prehook*;
XtPointer	*pre_closure*;
XtCallbackProc	*posthook*;
XtPointer	*post_closure*;

Description

XmSetWMProtocolHooks is a convenience interface. It calls **XmSetProtocolHooks** with the property value set to the atom returned by interning **WM_PROTOCOLS**.

shell　　　Specifies the widget with which the protocol property is associated

protocol　　　Specifies the protocol atom (or an **int** cast to **Atom**)

prehook　　　Specifies the procedure to call before calling entries on the client callback list

pre_closure　　　Specifies the client data to be passed to the prehook when it is invoked

posthook　　　Specifies the procedure to call after calling entries on the client callback list

post_closure　　　Specifies the client data to be passed to the posthook when it is invoked

For a complete definition of VendorShell and its associated resources, see **VendorShell(3X)**.

Related Information

VendorShell(3X), **XmInternAtom(3X)**, and **XmSetProtocolHooks(3X)**.

XmString—Data type for a compound string

AES Support Level

Full-use

Synopsis

#include <Xm/Xm.h>

Description

XmString is the data type for a compound string. Compound strings include one or more segments, each of which may contain a font list element tag, string direction, and text component. When a compound string is displayed, the font list element tag and the direction are used to determine how to display the text.

Calling **XtGetValues** for a resource whose type is **XmString** yields a copy of the compound string resource value. The application is responsible for using **XmStringFree** to free the memory allocated for the copy.

Refer to the **XmFontList** reference page for a description of the algorithm that associates the font list element tag of a compound string segment with a font list entry in a font list.

The compound string interface consists of the routines listed in **Related Information**.

Related Information

XmStringBaseline(3X), **XmStringByteCompare(3X)**, **XmStringCompare(3X)**, **XmStringConcat(3X)**, **XmStringCopy(3X)**, **XmStringCreate(3X)**, **XmStringCreateLtoR(3X)**, **XmStringCreateLocalized(3X)**, **XmStringCreateSimple(3X)**, **XmStringDirection(3X)**, **XmStringDraw(3X)**, **XmStringDrawImage(3X)**, **XmStringDrawUnderline(3X)**, **XmStringEmpty(3X)**, **XmStringExtent(3X)**, **XmStringFree(3X)**, **XmStringFreeContext(3X)**, **XmStringGetLtoR(3X)**, **XmStringGetNextComponent(3X)**, **XmStringGetNextSegment(3X)**, **XmStringHasSubstring(3X)**, **XmStringHeight(3X)**, **XmStringInitContext(3X)**, **XmStringLength(3X)**, **XmStringLineCount(3X)**, **XmStringNConcat(3X)**, **XmStringNCopy(3X)**, **XmStringSegmentCreate(3X)**, **XmStringSeparatorCreate(3X)**, **XmStringTable(3X)**, and **XmStringWidth(3X)**.

XmStringBaseline—A compound string function that returns the number of pixels between the top of the character box and the baseline of the first line of text

AES Support Level

Trial-use

Synopsis

#include <Xm/Xm.h>

Dimension XmStringBaseline (*fontlist, string*)
    XmFontList   *fontlist*;
    XmString   *string*;

Description

XmStringBaseline returns the number of pixels between the top of the character box and the baseline of the first line of text in the provided compound string.

When *string* has been created with **XmStringCreateSimple**, the font associated with the character set derived from the current language environment must appear at the front of *fontlist*. Otherwise, the result of the function is undefined.

fontlist   Specifies the font list

string   Specifies the string

Return Value

Returns the number of pixels between the top of the character box and the baseline of the first line of text.

Related Information

XmStringCreate(3X) and **XmStringCreateSimple(3X)**.

XmStringByteCompare—A compound string function that indicates the results of a byte-by-byte comparison

AES Support Level

Trial-use

Synopsis

#include <Xm/Xm.h>

Boolean XmStringByteCompare (*s1, s2*)
    XmString   *s1*;
    XmString   *s2*;

Description

XmStringByteCompare returns a Boolean indicating the results of a byte-by-byte comparison of two compound strings.

In general, if two compound strings are created with the same (**char ***) string using **XmStringCreateLocalized** in the same language environment, the compound strings compare as equal. If two compound strings are created with the same (**char ***) string and the same font list element tag set other than **XmFONTLIST_DEFAULT_TAG** using **XmStringCreate**, the strings compare as equal.

In some cases, once a compound string is put into a widget, that string is converted into an internal form to allow faster processing. Part of the conversion process strips out unnecessary or redundant information. If an application then does an **XtGetValues** to retrieve a compound string from a widget (specifically, Label and all of its subclasses), it is not guaranteed that the compound string returned is byte-for-byte the same as the string given to the widget originally.

s1   Specifies a compound string to be compared with *s2*

s2   Specifies a compound string to be compared with *s1*

Return Value

Returns True if two compound strings are identical byte-by-byte.

Related Information

XmStringCreate(3X) and **XmStringCreateLocalized(3X)**.

XmStringCompare—A compound string function that compares two strings

AES Support Level

Trial-use

Synopsis

#include <Xm/Xm.h>

Boolean XmStringCompare (*s1, s2*)
    XmString   *s1*;
    XmString   *s2*;

Description

XmStringCompare returns a Boolean value indicating the results of a semantically equivalent comparison of two compound strings.

Semantically equivalent means that the strings have the same text components, font list element tags, directions, and separators. In general, if two compound strings are created with the same (**char ***) string using **XmStringCreateLocalized** in the same language environment, the compound strings compare as equal. If two compound strings are created with the same (**char ***) string and the same font list element tag other than **XmFONTLIST_DEFAULT_TAG** using **XmStringCreate**, the strings compare as equal.

s1   Specifies a compound string to be compared with *s2*

s2   Specifies a compound string to be compared with *s1*

Return Value

Returns True if two compound strings are equivalent.

Related Information

XmStringCreate(3X) and **XmStringCreateLocalized(3X)**.

XmStringConcat—A compound string function that appends one string to another

AES Support Level

Trial-use

Synopsis

#include <Xm/Xm.h>

XmString XmStringConcat (*s1, s2*)
    XmString   *s1*;
    XmString   *s2*;

Description

XmStringConcat copies *s2* to the end of *s1* and returns a copy of the resulting compound string. The original strings are preserved. The space for the resulting compound string is allocated within the function. After using this function, free this space by calling **XmStringFree**.

s1   Specifies the compound string to which a copy of *s2* is appended

s2   Specifies the compound string that is appended to the end of *s1*

Return Value

Returns a new compound string.

Related Information

XmStringCreate(3X) and **XmStringFree(3X)**.

XmStringCopy(3X)

XmStringCopy—A compound string function that makes a copy of a string

AES Support Level

Trial-use

Synopsis

#include <Xm/Xm.h>

XmString XmStringCopy (*s1*)
    XmString   *s1*;

Description

XmStringCopy makes a copy of a compound string. The space for the resulting compound string is allocated within the function. The application is responsible for managing the allocated space. The memory can be recovered with **XmStringFree**.

s1   Specifies the compound string to be copied

Return Value

Returns a new compound string.

Related Information

XmStringCreate(3X) and **XmStringFree(3X)**.

XmStringCreate—A compound string function that creates a compound string

AES Support Level

Trial-use

Synopsis

#include <Xm/Xm.h>

XmString XmStringCreate (*text, tag*)
    char   **text*;
    char   **tag*;

Description

XmStringCreate creates a compound string with two components: text and a font list element tag.

text   Specifies a NULL-terminated string to be used as the text component of the compound string.

tag   Specifies the font list element tag to be associated with the given text. The value **XmFONTLIST_DEFAULT_TAG** identifies a locale text segment.

Return Value

Returns a new compound string.

Related Information

XmFontList(3X), XmFontListAdd(3X), XmFontListAppendEntry(3X), XmFontListCopy(3X), XmFontListCreate(3X), XmFontListEntryCreate(3X), XmFontListEntryFree(3X), XmFontListEntryGetFont(3X), XmFontListEntryGetTag(3X), XmFontListEntryLoad(3X), XmFontListFree(3X), XmFontListFreeFontContext(3X), XmFontListInitFontContext(3X), XmFontListNextEntry(3X), XmFontListRemoveEntry(3X), XmString(3X), XmStringBaseline(3X), XmStringByteCompare(3X), XmStringCompare(3X), XmStringConcat(3X), XmStringCopy(3X), XmStringCreateLocalized(3X), XmStringCreateLtoR(3X), XmStringCreateSimple(3X), XmStringDirection(3X), XmStringDraw(3X), XmStringDrawImage(3X), XmStringDrawUnderline(3X), XmStringEmpty(3X), XmStringExtent(3X), XmStringFree(3X), XmStringFreeContext(3X), XmStringGetLtoR(3X), XmStringGetNextComponent(3X), XmStringGetNextSegment(3X), XmStringHasSubstring(3X), XmStringHeight(3X), XmStringInitContext(3X), XmStringLength(3X), XmStringLineCount(3X), XmStringNConcat(3X),

XmStringCreate(3X)

XmStringNCopy(3X), **XmStringSegmentCreate(3X)**, **XmStringSeparatorCreate(3X)**, **XmStringTable(3X)**, and **XmStringWidth(3X)**.

XmStringCreateLocalized—A compound string function that creates a compound string in the current locale

AES Support Level

Temporary-use

Synopsis

#include <Xm/Text.h>

XmString XmStringCreateLocalized (*text*)
        char   ****text*;

Description

XmStringCreateLocalized creates a compound string containing the specified text and assigns **XmFONTLIST_DEFAULT_TAG** as the font list entry tag. An identical compound string would result from the function **XmStringCreate** called with **XmFONTLIST_DEFAULT_TAG** explicitly as the font list entry tag.

text   Specifies a NULL-terminated string of text encoded in the current locale to be used as the text component of the compound string

Return Value

Returns a new compound string.

Related Information

XmStringCreate(3X).

XmStringCreateSimple—A compound string function that creates a compound string in the language environment of a widget

AES Support Level

Trial-use

History/Direction

The **XmStringCreateSimple** function is scheduled for removal in revision D.

Synopsis

#include <Xm/Xm.h>

XmString XmStringCreateSimple (*text*)
    char   * *text*;

Description

XmStringCreateSimple creates a compound string with two components: text and a character set. It derives the character set from the current language environment.

NOTE: This routine is obsolete and exists for compatibility with previous releases. It has been replaced by **XmStringCreateLocalized**.

text   Specifies a NULL-terminated string to be used as the text component of the compound string.

Return Value

Returns a new compound string.

Related Information

XmStringCreate(3X). **XmStringCreate(3X)** and
XmStringCreateLocalized(3X).

XmStringDirection—Data type for the direction of display in a string

AES Support Level

Full-use

Synopsis

#include <Xm/Xm.h>

Description

XmStringDirection is the data type for specifying the direction in which the system displays characters of a string, or characters of a segment of a compound string. This is an enumeration with two possible values:

XmSTRING_DIRECTION_L_TO_R
> Specifies left to right display

XmSTRING_DIRECTION_R_TO_L
> Specifies right to left display

Related Information

XmString(3X).

XmStringDraw—A compound string function that draws a compound string in an X window

AES Support Level

Trial-use

Synopsis

#include <Xm/Xm.h>

void XmStringDraw (*d, w, fontlist, string, gc, x, y, width, alignment, layout_direction, clip*)

Display	* *d*;
Window	*w*;
XmFontList	*fontlist*;
XmString	*string*;
GC	*gc*;
Position	*x*;
Position	*y*;
Dimension	*width*;
unsigned char	*alignment*;
unsigned char	*layout_direction*;
XRectangle	* *clip*;

Description

XmStringDraw draws a compound string in an X Window.

When *string* has been created with **XmStringCreateSimple**, the font associated with the character set derived from the current language environment must appear at the front of *fontlist*. Otherwise, the result of the function is undefined.

d	Specifies the display.
w	Specifies the window.
fontlist	Specifies the font list.
string	Specifies the string.
gc	Specifies the graphics context to use.
x	Specifies a coordinate of the rectangle that will contain the displayed compound string.
y	Specifies a coordinate of the rectangle that will contain the displayed compound string.
width	Specifies the width of the rectangle that will contain the displayed compound string.

alignment   Specifies how the string will be aligned within the specified rectangle. It is either **XmALIGNMENT_BEGINNING**, **XmALIGNMENT_CENTER**, or **XmALIGNMENT_END**.

layout_direction
Controls the direction in which the segments of the compound string will be laid out. It also determines the meaning of the *alignment* parameter.

clip   Allows the application to restrict the area into which the compound string will be drawn. If the value is NULL, no clipping will be done.

Related Information
XmStringCreate(3X) and **XmStringCreateSimple(3X)**.

XmStringDrawImage—A compound string function that draws a compound string in an X Window and creates an image

AES Support Level

Trial-use

Synopsis

#include <Xm/Xm.h>

void XmStringDrawImage (*d, w, fontlist, string, gc, x, y, width, alignment, layout_direction, clip*)

Display	* *d*;
Window	*w*;
XmFontList	*fontlist*;
XmString	*string*;
GC	*gc*;
Position	*x*;
Position	*y*;
Dimension	*width*;
unsigned char	*alignment*;
unsigned char	*layout_direction*;
XRectangle	* *clip*;

Description

XmStringDrawImage draws a compound string in an X Window and paints both the foreground and background bits of each character.

When *string* has been created with **XmStringCreateSimple**, the font associated with the character set derived from the current language environment must appear at the front of *fontlist*. Otherwise, the result of the function is undefined.

d	Specifies the display.
w	Specifies the window.
fontlist	Specifies the font list.
string	Specifies the string.
gc	Specifies the graphics context to use.
x	Specifies a coordinate of the rectangle that will contain the displayed compound string.
y	Specifies a coordinate of the rectangle that will contain the displayed compound string.

width Specifies the width of the rectangle that will contain the displayed compound string.

alignment Specifies how the string will be aligned within the specified rectangle. It is either **XmALIGNMENT_BEGINNING**, **XmALIGNMENT_CENTER**, or **XmALIGNMENT_END**.

layout_direction
Controls the direction in which the segments of the compound string will be laid out. It also determines the meaning of the *alignment* parameter.

clip Allows the application to restrict the area into which the compound string will be drawn. If NULL, no clipping will be done.

Related Information

XmStringCreate(3X) and **XmStringCreateSimple(3X)**.

XmStringDrawUnderline(3X)

XmStringDrawUnderline—A compound string function that underlines a string drawn in an X Window

AES Support Level

Trial-use

Synopsis

#include <Xm/Xm.h>

void XmStringDrawUnderline (*d, w, fontlist, string, gc, x, y, width, alignment, layout_direction, clip, underline*)

Display	* *d*;
Window	*w*;
XmFontList	*fontlist*;
XmString	*string*;
GC	*gc*;
Position	*x*;
Position	*y*;
Dimension	*width*;
unsigned char	*alignment*;
unsigned char	*layout_direction*;
XRectangle	* *clip*;
XmString	*underline*;

Description

XmStringDrawUnderline draws a compound string in an X Window. If the substring identified by *underline* can be matched in *string*, the substring will be underlined. Once a match has occurred, no further matches or underlining will be done.

When *string* has been created with **XmStringCreateSimple**, the font associated with the character set derived from the current language environment must appear at the front of *fontlist*. Otherwise, the result of the function is undefined.

d	Specifies the display.
w	Specifies the window.
fontlist	Specifies the font list.
string	Specifies the string.
gc	Specifies the graphics context to use.
x	Specifies a coordinate of the rectangle that will contain the displayed compound string.

y Specifies a coordinate of the rectangle that will contain the displayed compound string.

width Specifies the width of the rectangle that will contain the displayed compound string.

alignment Specifies how the string will be aligned within the specified rectangle. It is one of **XmALIGNMENT_BEGINNING**, **XmALIGNMENT_CENTER**, or **XmALIGNMENT_END**.

layout_direction

Controls the direction in which the segments of the compound string will be laid out. It also determines the meaning of the *alignment* parameter.

clip Allows the application to restrict the area into which the compound string will be drawn. If it is NULL, no clipping will be done.

underline Specifies the substring to be underlined.

Related Information

XmStringCreate(3X) and **XmStringCreateSimple(3X)**.

XmStringEmpty—A compound string function that provides information on the existence of non-zero-length text components

AES Support Level

Trial-use

Synopsis

#include <Xm/Xm.h>

Boolean XmStringEmpty (*s1***)**
        XmString   *s1***;**

Description

XmStringEmpty returns a Boolean value indicating whether any non-zero-length text components exist in the provided compound string. It returns True if there are no text segments in the string. If this routine is passed NULL as the string, it returns True.

s1   Specifies the compound string

Return Value

Returns True if there are no text segments in the string. If this routine is passed NULL as the string, it returns True.

Related Information

XmStringCreate(3X).

XmStringExtent—A compound string function that determines the size of the smallest rectangle that will enclose the compound string

AES Support Level

Trial-use

Synopsis

#include <Xm/Xm.h>

void XmStringExtent (*fontlist, string, width, height*)
    XmFontList   *fontlist*;
    XmString   *string*;
    Dimension   **width*;
    Dimension   **height*;

Description

XmStringExtent determines the width and height, in pixels, of the smallest rectangle that will enclose the provided compound string.

When *string* has been created with **XmStringCreateSimple**, the font associated with the character set derived from the current language environment must appear at the front of *fontlist*. Otherwise, the result of the function is undefined.

fontlist   Specifies the font list

string   Specifies the string

width   Specifies a pointer to the width of the rectangle

height   Specifies a pointer to the height of the rectangle

Related Information

XmStringCreate(3X) and **XmStringCreateSimple(3X)**.

XmStringFree—A compound string function that recovers memory

AES Support Level

Trial-use

Synopsis

#include <Xm/Xm.h>

void XmStringFree (*string*)
    XmString   *string*;

Description

XmStringFree recovers memory used by a compound string.

string   Specifies the compound string to be freed

Related Information

XmStringCreate(3X).

XmStringFreeContext—A compound string function that instructs the toolkit that the context is no longer needed

AES Support Level

Trial-use

Synopsis

#include <Xm/Xm.h>

void XmStringFreeContext (*context*)
  XmStringContext *context*;

Description

XmStringFreeContext instructs the toolkit that the context is no longer needed and will not be used without reinitialization.

context Specifies the string context structure that was allocated by the **XmStringInitContext** function

Related Information

XmStringCreate(3X) and **XmStringInitContext(3X)**.

XmStringGetNextSegment—A compound string function that fetches the octets in the next segment of a compound string

AES Support Level

Trial-use

Synopsis

#include <Xm/Xm.h>

Boolean XmStringGetNextSegment (*context, text, tag, direction, separator*)
    XmStringContext   *context*;
    char   ***text*;
    XmStringCharSet   *tag*;
    XmStringDirection   *direction*;
    Boolean   *separator*;

Description

XmStringGetNextSegment fetches the octets in the next segment; repeated calls fetch sequential segments. The *text*, *tag*, and *direction* of the fetched segment are returned each time. A Boolean status is returned to indicate whether a valid segment was successfully parsed.

context   Specifies the string context structure which was allocated by the **XmStringInitContext** function

text   Specifies a pointer to a NULL-terminated string

tag   Specifies a pointer to the font list element tag associated with the text

direction   Specifies a pointer to the direction of the text

separator   Specifies whether the next component of the compound string is a separator

Return Value

Returns True if a valid segment is found.

Related Information

XmStringCreate(3X) and **XmStringInitContext(3X)**.

XmStringHasSubstring—A compound string function that indicates whether one compound string is contained within another

AES Support Level

Trial-use

Synopsis

#include <Xm/Xm.h>

Boolean XmStringHasSubstring (*string, substring*)
    XmString   *string*;
    XmString   *substring*;

Description

XmStringHasSubstring indicates whether or not one compound string is contained within another.

string   Specifies the compound string to be searched

substring   Specifies the compound string to be searched for

Return Value

Returns True if *substring* has a single segment and if its text is completely contained within any single segment of *string*; otherwise, it returns False. If two compound strings created using **XmStringCreateLocalized** in the same language environment satisfy this condition, the function returns True. If two compound strings created with the same character set using **XmStringCreate** satisfy this condition, the function returns True.

Related Information

XmStringCreate(3X) and **XmStringCreateSimple(3X)**.
XmStringCreateLocalized(3X).

XmStringHeight(3X)

XmStringHeight—A compound string function that returns the line height of the given compound string

AES Support Level
Trial-use

Synopsis
#include <Xm/Xm.h>

Dimension XmStringHeight (*fontlist, string*)
    XmFontList   *fontlist*;
    XmString   *string*;

Description
XmStringHeight returns the height, in pixels, of the sum of all the line heights of the given compound string. Separator components delimit lines.

When *string* has been created with **XmStringCreateSimple**, the font associated with the character set derived from the current language environment must appear at the front of *fontlist*. Otherwise, the result of the function is undefined.

fontlist   Specifies the font list

string   Specifies the string

Return Value
Returns the height of the specified string.

Related Information
XmStringCreate(3X) and **XmStringCreateSimple(3X)**.

XmStringInitContext—A compound string function that allows applications to read out the content segment by segment

AES Support Level

Trial-use

Synopsis

#include <Xm/Xm.h>

Boolean XmStringInitContext (*context, string*)
    XmStringContext * *context*;
    XmString   *string*;

Description

XmStringInitContext maintains a context to allow applications to read out the contents of a compound string segment by segment. This function establishes the context for this read out. This context is used when reading subsequent segments out of the string. A Boolean status is returned to indicate if the input string could be parsed.

context   Specifies a pointer to the allocated context

string   Specifies the string

Return Value

Returns True if the context was allocated

Related Information

XmStringCreate(3X).

XmStringLength(3X)

XmStringLength—A compound string function that obtains the length of a compound string

AES Support Level

Trial-use

Synopsis

#include <Xm/Xm.h>

int XmStringLength (*s1***)**
     XmString   *s1***;**

Description

XmStringLength obtains the length of a compound string. It returns the number of bytes in *s1* including all tags, direction indicators, and separators. If the compound string has an invalid structure, 0 (zero) is returned.

s1   Specifies the compound string

Return Value

Returns the length of the compound string.

Related Information

XmStringCreate(3X).

XmStringLineCount—A compound string function that returns the number of separators plus one in the provided compound string

AES Support Level

Trial-use

Synopsis

#include <Xm/Xm.h>

int XmStringLineCount (*string*)
    XmString   *string*;

Description

XmStringLineCount returns the number of separators plus one in the provided compound string. In effect, it counts the lines of text.

string   Specifies the string

Return Value

Returns the number of lines in the compound string

Related Information

XmStringCreate(3X).

XmStringNConcat—A compound string function that appends a specified number of bytes to a compound string

AES Support Level

Trial-use

History/Direction

The **XmStringNConcat** function is scheduled for removal in revision D.

Synopsis

#include <Xm/Xm.h>

XmString XmStringNConcat (*s1, s2, num_bytes*)
      XmString   *s1*;
      XmString   *s2*;
      int   *num_bytes*;

Description

XmStringNConcat appends a specified number of bytes from *s2* to the end of *s1*, including tags, directional indicators, and separators. It then returns the resulting compound string. The original strings are preserved. The space for the resulting compound string is allocated within the function. The application is responsible for managing the allocated space. The memory can be recovered with **XmStringFree**.

s1   Specifies the compound string to which a copy of *s2* is appended.

s2   Specifies the compound string that is appended to the end of *s1*.

num_bytes   Specifies the number of bytes of *s2* to append to *s1*. If this value is less than the length of *s2*, as many bytes as possible, but possibly fewer than this value, will be appended to *s1* such that the resulting string is still a valid compound string.

Return Value

Returns a new compound string.

Related Information

XmStringCreate(3X) and **XmStringFree(3X)**.

XmStringNCopy—A compound string function that creates a copy of a compound string

AES Support Level

Trial-use

History/Direction

The **XmStringNCopy** function is scheduled for removal in revision D.

Synopsis

#include <Xm/Xm.h>

XmString XmStringNCopy (*s1, num_bytes*)
    XmString   *s1*;
    int   *num_bytes*;

Description

XmStringNCopy creates a copy of *s1* that contains a specified number of bytes, including tags, directional indicators, and separators. It then returns the resulting compound string. The original strings are preserved. The space for the resulting compound string is allocated within the function. The application is responsible for managing the allocated space. The memory can be recovered by calling **XmStringFree**.

s1   Specifies the compound string.

num_bytes   Specifies the number of bytes of *s1* to copy. If this value is less than the length of *s1*, as many bytes as possible, but possibly fewer than this value, will be appended to *s1* such that the resulting string is still a valid compound string.

Return Value

Returns a new compound string.

Related Information

XmStringCreate(3X) and **XmStringFree(3X)**.

XmStringSegmentCreate—A compound string function that creates a compound string

AES Support Level

Trial-use

Synopsis

#include <Xm/Xm.h>

XmString XmStringSegmentCreate (*text, tag, direction, separator*)
    char   * *text*;
    char   **tag*;
    XmStringDirection*direction*;
    Boolean   *separator*;

Description

XmStringSegmentCreate is a high-level function that assembles a compound string consisting of a font list element tag, a direction component, a text component, and an optional separator component.

text   Specifies a NULL-terminated string to be used as the text component of the compound string.

tag   Specifies the font list element tag to be associated with the text. The value **XmFONTLIST_DEFAULT_TAG** identifies a locale text segment.

direction   Specifies the direction of the text.

separator   Specifies separator addition. A value of False means the compound string does not have a separator at the end. A value of True, means a separator immediately follows the text component.

Return Value

Returns a new compound string.

Related Information

XmStringCreate(3X).

XmStringSeparatorCreate—A compound string function that creates a compound string

AES Support Level

Trial-use

Synopsis

#include <Xm/Xm.h>

XmString XmStringSeparatorCreate ()

Description

XmStringSeparatorCreate creates a compound string with a single component, a separator.

Return Value

Returns a new compound string.

Related Information

XmStringCreate(3X).

XmStringTable—Data type for an array of compound strings

AES Support Level

Full-use

Synopsis

#include <Xm/Xm.h>

Description

XmStringTable is the data type for an array of compound strings (objects of type **XmString**).

Related Information

XmString(3X).

XmStringWidth—A compound string function that returns the width of the longest sequence of text components in a compound string

AES Support Level

Trial-use

Synopsis

#include <Xm/Xm.h>

Dimension XmStringWidth (*fontlist, string*)
 XmFontList *fontlist*;
 XmString *string*;

Description

XmStringWidth returns the width, in pixels, of the longest sequence of text components in the provided compound string. Separator components are used to delimit sequences of text components.

When *string* has been created with **XmStringCreateSimple**, the font associated with the character set derived from the current language environment must appear at the front of *fontlist*. Otherwise, the result of the function is undefined.

fontlist   Specifies the font list

string   Specifies the string

Return Value

Returns the width of the compound string.

Related Information

XmStringCreate(3X) and **XmStringCreateSimple(3X)**.

XmText(3X)

XmText—The Text widget class

AES Support Level

Full-use

History/Direction

In normal mode, deletion actions now delete any non-null primary selection (for trial-use).

Synopsis

#include <Xm/Text.h>

Description

Text provides a single-line and multiline text editor for customizing both user and programmatic interfaces. It can be used for single-line string entry, forms entry with verification procedures, and full-window editing. It provides an application with a consistent editing system for textual data. The screen's textual data adjusts to the application writer's needs.

Text provides separate callback lists to verify movement of the insert cursor, modification of the text, and changes in input focus. Each of these callbacks provides the verification function with the widget instance, the event that caused the callback, and a data structure specific to the verification type. From this information, the function can verify if the application considers this to be a legitimate state change and can signal the widget whether to continue with the action.

The user interface tailors a new set of translations. The default translations provide key bindings for insert cursor movement, deletion, insertion, and selection of text.

Text allows the user to select regions of text. Selection is based on the model specified in the *Inter-Client Communication Conventions Manual* (ICCCM). Text supports primary and secondary selection.

Mouse Selection

The Text widget allows text to be edited, inserted, and selected. The user can cut, copy, and paste text using the clipboard, primary transfer, or secondary transfer.

The insertion cursor, displayed as an I-beam, shows where input is inserted. Input is inserted just before the insertion cursor.

Classes

Text inherits behavior and resources from **Core** and **Primitive**.

The class pointer is **xmTextWidgetClass**.

The class name is **XmText**.

New Resources

The following table defines a set of widget resources used by the programmer to specify data. The programmer can also set the resource values for the inherited classes to set attributes for this widget. To reference a resource by name or by class in a **.Xdefaults** file, remove the **XmN** or **XmC** prefix and use the remaining letters. To specify one of the defined values for a resource in a **.Xdefaults** file, remove the **Xm** prefix and use the remaining letters (in either lowercase or uppercase, but include any underscores between words). The codes in the access column indicate if the given resource can be set at creation time (C), set by using **XtSetValues** (S), retrieved by using **XtGetValues** (G), or is not applicable (N/A).

<table>
<tr><th colspan="3">XmText Resource Set</th></tr>
<tr><th>Name
    Class</th><th>Default
    Type</th><th>Access</th></tr>
<tr><td>XmNactivateCallback
    XmCCallback</td><td>NULL
    XtCallbackList</td><td>C</td></tr>
<tr><td>XmNautoShowCursorPosition
    XmCAutoShowCursorPosition</td><td>True
    Boolean</td><td>CSG</td></tr>
<tr><td>XmNcursorPosition
    XmCCursorPosition</td><td>0
    XmTextPosition</td><td>CSG</td></tr>
<tr><td>XmNeditable
    XmCEditable</td><td>True
    Boolean</td><td>CSG</td></tr>
<tr><td>XmNeditMode
    XmCEditMode</td><td>XmSINGLE_LINE_EDIT
    int</td><td>CSG</td></tr>
<tr><td>XmNfocusCallback
    XmCCallback</td><td>NULL
    XtCallbackList</td><td>C</td></tr>
<tr><td>XmNgainPrimaryCallback
    XmCCallback</td><td>NULL
    XtCallbackList</td><td>C</td></tr>
<tr><td>XmNlosePrimaryCallback
    XmCCallback</td><td>NULL
    XtCallbackList</td><td>C</td></tr>
<tr><td>XmNlosingFocusCallback
    XmCCallback</td><td>NULL
    XtCallbackList</td><td>C</td></tr>
<tr><td>XmNmarginHeight
    XmCMarginHeight</td><td>5
    Dimension</td><td>CSG</td></tr>
<tr><td>XmNmarginWidth
    XmCMarginWidth</td><td>5
    Dimension</td><td>CSG</td></tr>
<tr><td>XmNmaxLength
    XmCMaxLength</td><td>largest integer
    int</td><td>CSG</td></tr>
<tr><td>XmNmodifyVerifyCallback
    XmCCallback</td><td>NULL
    XtCallbackList</td><td>C</td></tr>
<tr><td>XmNmotionVerifyCallback
    XmCCallback</td><td>NULL
    XtCallbackList</td><td>C</td></tr>
<tr><td>XmNsource
    XmCSource</td><td>Default source
    XmTextSource</td><td>CSG</td></tr>
</table>

Name	Default	Access
Class	Type	
XmNtopCharacter	0	CSG
XmCTextPosition	XmTextPosition	
XmNvalue	""	CSG
XmCValue	String	
XmNvalueChangedCallback	NULL	C
XmCCallback	XtCallbackList	
XmNverifyBell	dynamic	CSG
XmCVerifyBell	Boolean	

XmNactivateCallback

Specifies the list of callbacks that is called when the user invokes an event that calls the **Activate()** function. The type of the structure whose address is passed to this callback is **XmAnyCallbackStruct**. The reason sent by the callback is **XmCR_ACTIVATE**.

XmNautoShowCursorPosition

Ensures that the visible text contains the insert cursor when set to True. If the insert cursor changes, the contents of Text may scroll in order to bring the insertion point into the window.

XmNcursorPosition

Indicates the position in the text where the current insert cursor is to be located. Position is determined by the number of characters from the beginning of the text. The first character position is 0 (zero).

XmNeditable When set to True, indicates that the user can edit the text string. Prohibits the user from editing the text when set to False.

XmNeditMode

Specifies the set of keyboard bindings used in Text. The default, **XmSINGLE_LINE_EDIT**, provides the set of key bindings to be used in editing single-line text. **XmMULTI_LINE_EDIT** provides the set of key bindings to be used in editing multiline text.

The results of placing a Text widget inside a ScrolledWindow when the Text's **XmNeditMode** is **XmSINGLE_LINE_EDIT** are undefined.

XmNfocusCallback
Specifies the list of callbacks called when Text accepts input focus.
The type of the structure whose address is passed to this callback is
XmAnyCallbackStruct. The reason sent by the callback is
XmCR_FOCUS.

XmNgainPrimaryCallback
Specifies the list of callbacks called when an event causes the Text
widget to gain ownership of the primary selection. The reason sent
by the callback is **XmCR_GAIN_PRIMARY**.

XmNlosePrimaryCallback
Specifies the list of callbacks called when an event causes the Text
widget to lose ownership of the primary selection. The reason sent
by the callback is **XmCR_LOSE_PRIMARY**.

XmNlosingFocusCallback
Specifies the list of callbacks called before Text loses input focus.
The type of the structure whose address is passed to this callback is
XmTextVerifyCallbackStruct. The reason sent by the callback is
XmCR_LOSING_FOCUS.

XmNmarginHeight
Specifies the distance between the top edge of the widget window
and the text, and between the bottom edge of the widget window
and the text.

XmNmarginWidth
Specifies the distance between the left edge of the widget window
and the text, and between the right edge of the widget window and
the text.

XmNmaxLength
Specifies the maximum length of the text string that can be entered
into text from the keyboard. This value must be nonnegative.
Strings that are entered using the **XmNvalue** resource or the
XmTextSetString function ignore this resource.

XmNmodifyVerifyCallback
Specifies the list of callbacks called before text is deleted from or
inserted into Text. The type of the structure whose address is passed
to this callback is **XmTextVerifyCallbackStruct**. The reason sent
by the callback is **XmCR_MODIFYING_TEXT_VALUE**. When
multiple Text widgets share the same source, only the widget that
initiates the source change will generate the
XmNmodifyVerifyCallback.

XmNmotionVerifyCallback

Specifies the list of callbacks called before the insert cursor is moved to a new position. The type of the structure whose address is passed to this callback is **XmTextVerifyCallbackStruct**. The reason sent by the callback is **XmCR_MOVING_INSERT_CURSOR**. It is possible for more than one **XmNmotionVerifyCallback** to be generated from a single action.

XmNsource   Specifies the source with which the widget displays text. If no source is specified, the widget creates a default string source. This resource can be used to share text sources between Text widgets.

XmNtopCharacter

Displays the position of text at the top of the window. Position is determined by the number of characters from the beginning of the text. The first character position is 0 (zero).

If the **XmNeditMode** is **XmMULTI_LINE_EDIT**, the line of text that contains the top character is displayed at the top of the widget without shifting the text left or right. **XtGetValues** for **XmNtopCharacter** returns the position of the first character in the line that is displayed at the top of the widget.

XmNvalue   Displays the string value. **XtGetValues** returns the value of the internal buffer and **XtSetValues** copies the string values into the internal buffer.

XmNvalueChangedCallback

Specifies the list of callbacks called after text is deleted from or inserted into Text. The type of the structure whose address is passed to this callback is **XmAnyCallbackStruct**. The reason sent by the callback is **XmCR_VALUE_CHANGED**. When multiple Text widgets share the same source, only the widget that initiates the source change will generate the **XmNvalueChangedCallback**. This callback represents a change in the source in the Text, not in the Text widget. The **XmNvalueChangedCallback** should occur only in pairs with an **XmNmodifyVerifyCallback**, assuming that the *doit* flag in the callback structure of the **XmNmodifyVerifyCallback** is not set to False.

XmNverifyBell

Specifies whether the bell should sound when the verification returns without continuing the action.

<table>
<tr><td colspan="3" align="center">XmText Input Resource Set</td></tr>
<tr><td>Name
    Class</td><td>Default
    Type</td><td>Access</td></tr>
<tr><td>XmNpendingDelete
    XmCPendingDelete</td><td>True
    Boolean</td><td>CSG</td></tr>
<tr><td>XmNselectionArray
    XmCSelectionArray</td><td>default array
    XtPointer</td><td>CSG</td></tr>
<tr><td>XmNselectionArrayCount
    XmCSelectionArrayCount</td><td>4
    int</td><td>CSG</td></tr>
<tr><td>XmNselectThreshold
    XmCSelectThreshold</td><td>5
    int</td><td>CSG</td></tr>
</table>

XmNpendingDelete
> Indicates that pending delete mode is on when the Boolean value is True. Pending deletion is defined as deletion of the selected text when an insertion is made.

XmNselectionArray
> Defines the actions for multiple mouse clicks. The value of the resource is an array of **XmTextScanType** elements. **XmTextScanType** is an enumeration indicating possible actions. Each mouse click performed within half a second of the previous mouse click increments the index into this array and performs the defined action for that index. The possible actions in the order they occur in the default array are

XmSELECT_POSITION
> Resets the insert cursor position

XmSELECT_WORD
> Selects a word

XmSELECT_LINE
> Selects a line of text

XmSELECT_ALL
> Selects all of the text

XmNselectionArrayCount
> Indicates the number of elements in the **XmNselectionArray** resource. The value must not be negative.

XmNselectThreshold

>   Specifies the number of pixels of motion that is required to select the next character when selection is performed using the click-drag mode of selection. The value must not be negative.

XmText Output Resource Set		
Name	**Default**	**Access**
Class	**Type**	
XmNblinkRate	500	CSG
XmCBlinkRate	int	
XmNcolumns	dynamic	CSG
XmCColumns	short	
XmNcursorPositionVisible	True	CSG
XmCCursorPositionVisible	Boolean	
XmNfontList	dynamic	CSG
XmCFontList	XmFontList	
XmNresizeHeight	False	CSG
XmCResizeHeight	Boolean	
XmNresizeWidth	False	CSG
XmCResizeWidth	Boolean	
XmNrows	dynamic	CSG
XmCRows	short	
XmNwordWrap	False	CSG
XmCWordWrap	Boolean	

XmNblinkRate

>   Specifies the blink rate of the text cursor in milliseconds. The time indicated in the blink rate relates to the time the cursor is visible and the time the cursor is invisible (that is, the time it takes to blink the insertion cursor on and off is twice the blink rate). The cursor does not blink when the blink rate is set to 0 (zero). The value must not be negative.

XmNcolumns

>   Specifies the initial width of the text window measured in character spaces. The value must be greater than 0 (zero). The default value depends on the value of the **XmNwidth** resource. If no width is specified the default is 20.

XmNcursorPositionVisible
Indicates that the insert cursor position is marked by a blinking text cursor when the Boolean value is True.

XmNfontList Specifies the font list to be used for Text. If this value is NULL at initialization, the parent hierarchy of the widget is searched for an ancestor that is subclass of the BulletinBoard or VendorShell widget class. If such an ancestor is found, the font list is initialized to the **XmNtextFontList** of the ancestor widget. If no such ancestor is found, the default is implementation dependent.

Text searches the font list for the first occurrence of a font set that has an **XmFONTLIST_DEFAULT_TAG**. If a default element is not found, the first font set in the font list is used. If the list contains no font sets, the first font in the font list will be used. Refer to **XmFontList(3X)** for more information on a font list structure.

XmNresizeHeight
Indicates that Text will attempt to resize its height to accommodate all the text contained in the widget when the Boolean value is True. If the Boolean value is set to True, the text is always displayed starting from the first position in the source, even if instructed otherwise. This attribute is ignored when the application uses a ScrolledText widget and when **XmNscrollVertical** is True.

XmNresizeWidth
Indicates that Text attempts to resize its width to accommodate all the text contained in the widget when the Boolean value is True. This attribute is ignored if **XmNwordWrap** is True.

XmNrows Specifies the initial height of the text window measured in character heights. This attribute is ignored if the text widget resource **XmNeditMode** is **XmSINGLE_LINE_EDIT**. The value must be greater than 0 (zero). The default value depends on the value of the **XmNheight** resource. If no height is specified the default is 1.

XmNwordWrap
Indicates that lines are to be broken at word breaks (that is, the text does not go off the right edge of the window) when the Boolean value is True. Words are defined as a sequence of characters separated by white space. White space is defined as a space, tab, or newline. This attribute is ignored if the text widget resource **XmNeditMode** is **XmSINGLE_LINE_EDIT**.

The following resources are used only when text is created in a ScrolledWindow. See the reference page for **XmCreateScrolledText**.

XmText ScrolledText Resource Set		
Name	**Default**	**Access**
Class	**Type**	
XmNscrollHorizontal	True	CG
XmCScroll	Boolean	
XmNscrollLeftSide	dynamic	CG
XmCScrollSide	Boolean	
XmNscrollTopSide	False	CG
XmCScrollSide	Boolean	
XmNscrollVertical	True	CG
XmCScroll	Boolean	

XmNscrollHorizontal

Adds a ScrollBar that allows the user to scroll horizontally through text when the Boolean value is True. This resource is forced to False when the Text widget is placed in a ScrolledWindow with **XmNscrollingPolicy** set to **XmAUTOMATIC**.

XmNscrollLeftSide

Indicates that the vertical ScrollBar should be placed on the left side of the scrolled text window when the Boolean value is True. This attribute is ignored if **XmNscrollVertical** is False or the Text resource **XmNeditMode** is **XmSINGLE_LINE_EDIT**. The default value may depend on the value of the **XmNstringDirection** resource.

XmNscrollTopSide

Indicates that the horizontal ScrollBar should be placed on the top side of the scrolled text window when the Boolean value is True.

XmNscrollVertical

Adds a ScrollBar that allows the user to scroll vertically through text when the Boolean value is True. This attribute is ignored if the Text resource **XmNeditMode** is **XmSINGLE_LINE_EDIT**. This resource is forced to False when the Text widget is placed in a ScrolledWindow with **XmNscrollingPolicy** set to **XmAUTOMATIC**.

Inherited Resources

Text inherits behavior and resources from the superclasses described in the following tables. For a complete description of each resource, refer to the reference page for that superclass.

XmPrimitive Resource Set		

Name
    Class
	Default
	    Type
		Access

XmNbottomShadowColor
    XmCBottomShadowColor
	dynamic
	    Pixel
		CSG

XmNbottomShadowPixmap
    XmCBottomShadowPixmap
	XmUNSPECIFIED_PIXMAP
	    Pixmap
		CSG

XmNforeground
    XmCForeground
	dynamic
	    Pixel
		CSG

XmNhelpCallback
    XmCCallback
	NULL
	    XtCallbackList
		C

XmNhighlightColor
    XmCHighlightColor
	dynamic
	    Pixel
		CSG

XmNhighlightOnEnter
    XmCHighlightOnEnter
	False
	    Boolean
		CSG

XmNhighlightPixmap
    XmCHighlightPixmap
	dynamic
	    Pixmap
		CSG

XmNhighlightThickness
    XmCHighlightThickness
	2
	    Dimension
		CSG

XmNnavigationType
    XmCNavigationType
	XmTAB_GROUP
	    XmNavigationType
		CSG

XmNshadowThickness
    XmCShadowThickness
	2
	    Dimension
		CSG

XmNtopShadowColor
    XmCTopShadowColor
	dynamic
	    Pixel
		CSG

XmNtopShadowPixmap
    XmCTopShadowPixmap
	dynamic
	    Pixmap
		CSG

XmNtraversalOn
    XmCTraversalOn
	True
	    Boolean
		CSG

XmNuserData
    XmCUserData
	NULL
	    XtPointer
		CSG

Core Resource Set		

Name
  Class
	Default
	  Type
		Access

XmNaccelerators
  XmCAccelerators
	dynamic
	  XtAccelerators
		CSG

XmNancestorSensitive
  XmCSensitive
	dynamic
	  Boolean
		G

XmNbackground
  XmCBackground
	dynamic
	  Pixel
		CSG

XmNbackgroundPixmap
  XmCPixmap
	XmUNSPECIFIED_PIXMAP
	  Pixmap
		CSG

XmNborderColor
  XmCBorderColor
	XtDefaultForeground
	  Pixel
		CSG

XmNborderPixmap
  XmCPixmap
	XmUNSPECIFIED_PIXMAP
	  Pixmap
		CSG

XmNborderWidth
  XmCBorderWidth
	0
	  Dimension
		CSG

XmNcolormap
  XmCColormap
	dynamic
	  Colormap
		CG

XmNdepth
  XmCDepth
	dynamic
	  int
		CG

XmNdestroyCallback
  XmCCallback
	NULL
	  XtCallbackList
		C

XmNheight
  XmCHeight
	dynamic
	  Dimension
		CSG

XmNinitialResourcesPersistent
  XmCInitialResourcesPersistent
	True
	  Boolean
		C

XmNmappedWhenManaged
  XmCMappedWhenManaged
	True
	  Boolean
		CSG

XmNscreen
  XmCScreen
	dynamic
	  Screen *
		CG

XmNsensitive
  XmCSensitive
	True
	  Boolean
		CSG

Name	Default	Access
Class	Type	
XmNtranslations	dynamic	CSG
XmCTranslations	XtTranslations	
XmNwidth	dynamic	CSG
XmCWidth	Dimension	
XmNx	0	CSG
XmCPosition	Position	
XmNy	0	CSG
XmCPosition	Position	

Callback Information

A pointer to the following structure is passed to each callback:

typedef struct
{
    int   *reason***;**
    XEvent   ** event***;**
} XmAnyCallbackStruct;

reason   Indicates why the callback was invoked

event   Points to the **XEvent** that triggered the callback

The Text widget defines a new callback structure for use with verification callbacks. Note that not all fields are relevant for every callback reason. The application must first look at the *reason* field and use only the structure members that are valid for the particular reason. The values *startPos*, *endPos*, and *text* in the callback structure **XmTextVerifyCallbackStruct** may be modified when the callback is received, and these changes will be reflected as changes made to the source of the Text widget. (For example, all keystrokes can be converted to spaces or NULL characters when a password is entered into a Text widget.) The application programmer should not overwrite the *text* field, but should attach data to that pointer.

A pointer to the following structure is passed to callbacks for **XmNlosingFocusCallback**, **XmNmodifyVerifyCallback**, and **XmNmotionVerifyCallback**:

```
typedef struct
{
    int                reason;
    XEvent             * event;
    Boolean            doit;
    XmTextPosition     currInsert, newInsert;
    XmTextPosition     startPos, endPos;
    XmTextBlock        text;
} XmTextVerifyCallbackStruct, *XmTextVerifyPtr;
```

reason   Indicates why the callback was invoked.

event   Points to the **XEvent** that triggered the callback.

doit   Indicates whether the action that invoked the callback is performed. Setting *doit* to False negates the action.

currInsert   Indicates the current position of the insert cursor.

newInsert   Indicates the position at which the user attempts to position the insert cursor.

startPos   Indicates the starting position of the text to modify. If the callback is not a modify verification callback, this value is the same as *currInsert*.

endPos   Indicates the ending position of the text to modify. If no text is replaced or deleted, the value is the same as *startPos*. If the callback is not a modify verification callback, this value is the same as *currInsert*.

text   Points to a structure of type **XmTextBlockRec**. This structure holds the textual information to be inserted.

```
typedef struct
{
    char              *ptr;
    int               length;
    XmTextFormat      format;
} XmTextBlockRec, *XmTextBlock;
```

        ptr   Points to the text to be inserted.

        length   Specifies the length of the text to be inserted.

        format   Specifies the format of the text, either **XmFMT_8_BIT** or **XmFMT_16_BIT**.

The following table describes the reasons why the individual verification callback structure fields are valid.

Reason	Valid Fields
XmCR_LOSING_FOCUS	*reason, event, doit, currInsert, newInsert, startPos, endPos*
XmCR_MODIFYING_TEXT_VALUE	*reason, event, doit, currInsert, newInsert, startPos, endPos, text*
XmCR_MOVING_INSERT_CURSOR	*reason, event, doit, currInsert, newInsert*

Action Routines

The **XmText** action routines are

activate(): Calls the callbacks for **XmNactivateCallback**. If the parent is a manager, passes the event to the parent.

backward-character():
Moves the insertion cursor one character to the left. This action may have different behavior in a right-to-left language environment.

backward-paragraph(*extend*):
If **XmNeditMode** is **XmMULTI_LINE_EDIT** and this action is called with no argument, moves the insertion cursor to the first non-whitespace character following the first previous blank line or beginning of the text. If the insertion cursor is already at the beginning of a paragraph, moves the insertion cursor to the beginning of the previous paragraph.

If **XmNeditMode** is **XmMULTI_LINE_EDIT** and this action is called with an argument of **extend**, moves the insertion cursor as in the case of no argument and extends the current selection.

backward-word(*extend*):
If this action is called with no argument, moves the insertion cursor to the first non-whitespace character after the first whitespace character to the left or after the beginning of the line. If the insertion cursor is already at the beginning of a word, moves the insertion cursor to the beginning of the previous word. This action may have different behavior in a locale other than the C locale.

If called with an argument of **extend**, moves the insertion cursor as in the case of no argument and extends the current selection.

beep(): Causes the terminal to beep.

beginning-of-file(*extend*):
> If this action is called with no argument, moves the insertion cursor to the beginning of the text.
>
> If called with an argument of **extend**, moves the insertion cursor as in the case of no argument and extends the current selection.

beginning-of-line(*extend*):
> If this action is called with no argument, moves the insertion cursor to the beginning of the line.
>
> If called with an argument of **extend**, moves the insertion cursor as in the case of no argument and extends the current selection.

clear-selection():
> Clears the current selection by replacing each character except **<Return>** with a **<space>** character.

copy-clipboard():
> Copies the current selection to the clipboard.

copy-primary():
> Copies the primary selection to just before the insertion cursor.

copy-to(): If a secondary selection exists, copies the secondary selection to just before the insertion cursor. If no secondary selection exists, copies the primary selection to the pointer location.

cut-clipboard():
> Cuts the current selection to the clipboard.

cut-primary():
> Cuts the primary selection to just before the insertion cursor.

delete-next-character():
> In normal mode, if there is a nonnull selection, deletes the selection; otherwise, deletes the character following the insertion cursor. In add mode, if there is a nonnull selection, the cursor is not disjoint from the selection, and **XmNpendingDelete** is set to True, deletes the selection; otherwise, deletes the character following the insertion cursor. This may impact the selection.

delete-next-word():
> In normal mode, if there is a nonnull selection, deletes the selection; otherwise, deletes the characters following the insertion cursor to the next space, tab or end-of-line character. In add mode, if there is a nonnull selection, the cursor is not disjoint from the selection, and **XmNpendingDelete** is set to True, deletes the selection; otherwise,

deletes the characters following the insertion cursor to the next space, tab or end-of-line character. This may impact the selection. This action may have different behavior in a locale other than the C locale.

delete-previous-character():

In normal mode, if there is a nonnull selection, deletes the selection; otherwise, deletes the character of text immediately preceding the insertion cursor. In add mode, if there is a nonnull selection, the cursor is not disjoint from the selection, and **XmNpendingDelete** is set to True, deletes the selection; otherwise, deletes the character of text immediately preceding the insertion cursor. This may impact the selection.

delete-previous-word():

In normal mode, if there is a nonnull selection, deletes the selection; otherwise, deletes the characters preceding the insertion cursor to the next space, tab or beginning-of-line character. In add mode, if there is a nonnull selection, the cursor is not disjoint from the selection, and **XmNpendingDelete** is set to True, deletes the selection; otherwise, deletes the characters preceding the insertion cursor to the next space, tab or beginning-of-line character. This may impact the selection. This action may have different behavior in a locale other than the C locale.

delete-selection():

Deletes the current selection.

delete-to-end-of-line():

In normal mode, if there is a nonnull selection, deletes the selection; otherwise, deletes the characters following the insertion cursor to the next end of line character. In add mode, if there is a nonnull selection, the cursor is not disjoint from the selection, and **XmNpendingDelete** is set to True, deletes the selection; otherwise, deletes the characters following the insertion cursor to the next end of line character. This may impact the selection.

delete-to-start-of-line():

In normal mode, if there is a nonnull selection, deletes the selection; otherwise, deletes the characters preceding the insertion cursor to the previous beginning-of-line character. In add mode, if there is a nonnull selection, the cursor is not disjoint from the selection, and **XmNpendingDelete** is set to True, deletes the selection; otherwise, deletes the characters preceding the insertion cursor to the previous beginning-of-line character. This may impact the selection.

deselect-all():
> Deselects the current selection.

do-quick-action():
> Marks the end of a secondary selection. Performs the quick action initiated by the **quick-copy-set** or **quick-cut-set** action.

end-of-file(*extend*):
> If this action is called with no argument, moves the insertion cursor to the end of the text.
>
> If called with an argument of **extend**, moves the insertion cursor as in the case of no argument and extends the current selection.

end-of-line(*extend*):
> If this action is called with no argument, moves the insertion cursor to the end of the line. If called with an argument of **extend**, moves the insertion cursor as in the case of no argument and extends the current selection.

extend-adjust():
> Selects text from the anchor to the pointer position and deselects text outside that range. Moving the pointer over several lines selects text from the anchor to the end of each line the pointer moves over and up to the pointer position on the current line.

extend-end():
> Moves the insertion cursor to the position of the pointer.

extend-start():
> Adjusts the anchor using the balance-beam method. Selects text from the anchor to the pointer position and deselects text outside that range.

forward-character():
> Moves the insertion cursor one character to the right. This action may have different behavior in a right-to-left language environment.

forward-paragraph(*extend*):
> If **XmNeditMode** is **XmMULTI_LINE_EDIT**, and this action is called with no argument, moves the insertion cursor to the first non-whitespace character following the next blank line. If the insertion cursor is already at the beginning of a paragraph, moves the insertion cursor to the beginning of the next paragraph.
>
> If **XmNeditMode** is **XmMULTI_LINE_EDIT** and this action is called with an argument of **extend**, moves the insertion cursor as in the case of no argument and extends the current selection.

forward-word(*extend*):

If this action is called with no argument, moves the insertion cursor to the first whitespace character or end-of-line following the next non-whitespace character. If the insertion cursor is already at the end of a word, moves the insertion cursor to the end of the next word. This action may have different behavior in a locale other than the C locale.

If called with an argument of **extend**, moves the insertion cursor as in the case of no argument and extends the current selection.

grab-focus(): This key binding performs the action defined in the **XmNselectionArray**, depending on the number of multiple mouse clicks. The default selection array ordering is one click to move the insertion cursor to the pointer position, two clicks to select a word, three clicks to select a line of text, and four clicks to select all text. A single click also deselects any selected text and sets the anchor at the pointer position. This action may have different behavior in a locale other than the C locale.

Help(): Calls the callbacks for **XmNhelpCallback** if any exist. If there are no help callbacks for this widget, this action calls the help callbacks for the nearest ancestor that has them.

insert-string(*string*):

If **XmNpendingDelete** is True and the cursor is not disjoint from the current selection, deletes the entire selection. Inserts *string* before the insertion cursor.

key-select(*direction*):

If called with an argument of **right**, moves the insertion cursor one character to the right and extends the current selection. If called with an argument of **left**, moves the insertion cursor one character to the left and extends the current selection. If called with no argument, extends the current selection.

kill-next-character():

In normal mode, if there is a nonnull selection, deletes the selection; otherwise, kills the character following the insertion cursor and stores the character in the cut buffer. In add mode, if there is a nonnull selection, the cursor is not disjoint from the selection, and **XmNpendingDelete** is set to True, deletes the selection; otherwise, kills the character following the insertion cursor and stores the character in the cut buffer. This may impact the selection.

kill-next-word():

> In normal mode, if there is a nonnull selection, deletes the selection; otherwise, kills the characters following the insertion cursor to the next space, tab or end-of-line character, and stores the characters in the cut buffer. In add mode, if there is a nonnull selection, the cursor is not disjoint from the selection, and **XmNpendingDelete** is set to True, deletes the selection; otherwise, kills the characters following the insertion cursor to the next space, tab or end-of-line character, and stores the characters in the cut buffer. This may impact the selection. This action may have different behavior in a locale other than the C locale.

kill-previous-character():

> In normal mode, if there is a nonnull selection, deletes the selection; otherwise, kills the character immediately preceding the insertion cursor and stores the character in the cut buffer. In add mode, if there is a nonnull selection, the cursor is not disjoint from the selection, and **XmNpendingDelete** is set to True, deletes the selection; otherwise, kills the character immediately preceding the insertion cursor and stores the character in the cut buffer. This may impact the selection.

kill-previous-word():

> In normal mode, if there is a nonnull selection, deletes the selection; otherwise, kills the characters preceding the insertion cursor up to the next space, tab or beginning-of-line character, and stores the characters in the cut buffer. In add mode, if there is a nonnull selection, the cursor is not disjoint from the selection, and **XmNpendingDelete** is set to True, deletes the selection; otherwise, kills the characters preceding the insertion cursor up to the next space, tab or beginning-of-line character, and stores the characters in the cut buffer. This may impact the selection. This action may have different behavior in a locale other than the C locale.

kill-selection():

> Kills the currently selected text and stores the text in the cut buffer.

kill-to-end-of-line():

> In normal mode, if there is a nonnull selection, deletes the selection; otherwise, kills the characters following the insertion cursor to the next end-of-line character and stores the characters in the cut buffer.

In add mode, if there is a nonnull selection, the cursor is not disjoint from the selection, and **XmNpendingDelete** is set to True, deletes the selection; otherwise, kills the characters following the insertion cursor to the next end of line character and stores the characters in the cut buffer. This may impact the selection.

kill-to-start-of-line():
In normal mode, if there is a nonnull selection, deletes the selection; otherwise, kills the characters preceding the insertion cursor to the next beginning-of-line character and stores the characters in the cut buffer. In add mode, if there is a nonnull selection, the cursor is not disjoint from the selection, and **XmNpendingDelete** is set to True, deletes the selection; otherwise, kills the characters preceding the insertion cursor to the next beginning-of-line character and stores the characters in the cut buffer. This may impact the selection.

move-destination():
Moves the insertion cursor to the pointer position without changing any existing current selection. If there is no current selection, sets the widget as the destination widget.

move-to():   If a secondary selection exists, cuts the secondary selection to the insertion cursor. If no secondary selection exists, cuts the primary selection to the pointer location.

newline():   If **XmNpendingDelete** is True and the cursor is not disjoint from the current selection, deletes the entire selection. Inserts a newline before the insertion cursor.

newline-and-backup():
If **XmNpendingDelete** is True and the cursor is not disjoint from the current selection, deletes the entire selection. Inserts a newline just before the insertion cursor and repositions the insertion cursor to the end of the line before the newline.

newline-and-indent():
If **XmNpendingDelete** is True and the cursor is not disjoint from the current selection, deletes the entire selection. Inserts a newline and then the same number of whitespace characters as at the beginning of the previous line.

next-line():   Moves the insertion cursor to the next line.

next-page(*extend***)**:
If this action is called with no argument, moves the insertion cursor forward one page.

If this action is called with an argument of **extend**, it moves the insertion cursor as in the case of no argument and extends the current selection.

next-tab-group():
　　　　　Traverses to the next tab group.

page-left():　Scrolls the viewing window left one page of text.

page-right():　Scrolls the viewing window right one page of text.

paste-clipboard():
　　　　　Pastes the contents of the clipboard before the insertion cursor.

prev-tab-group():
　　　　　Traverses to the previous tab group.

previous-line():
　　　　　Moves the insertion cursor to the previous line.

previous-page(*extend*):
　　　　　If this action is called with no argument, moves the insertion cursor back one page.

　　　　　If this action is called with an argument of **extend**, it fmoves the insertion cursor as in the case of no argument and extends the current selection.

process-cancel():
　　　　　Cancels the current **extend-adjust**() or **secondary-adjust**() operation and leaves the selection state as it was before the operation; otherwise, and if the parent is a manager, passes the event to the parent.

process-down():
　　　　　If **XmNeditMode** is **XmSINGLE_LINE_EDIT**, and **XmNnavigationType** is **XmNONE**, traverses to the widget below the current one in the tab group.

　　　　　If **XmNeditMode** is **XmMULTI_LINE_EDIT**, moves the insertion cursor down one line.

process-home():
　　　　　Moves the insertion cursor to the beginning of the line. For other effects, see the description of navigation operations in **Keyboard Selection**.

process-return():
> If **XmNeditMode** is **XmSINGLE_LINE_EDIT**, calls the callbacks for **XmNactivateCallback**, and if the parent is a manager, passes the event to the parent. If **XmNeditMode** is **XmMULTI_LINE_EDIT**, inserts a newline.

process-shift-down():
> If **XmNeditMode** is **XmMULTI_LINE_EDIT**, moves the insertion cursor down one line.

process-shift-up():
> If **XmNeditMode** is **XmMULTI_LINE_EDIT**, moves the insertion cursor up one line.

process-tab():
> If **XmNeditMode** is **XmSINGLE_LINE_EDIT**, traverses to the next tab group. If **XmNeditMode** is **XmMULTI_LINE_EDIT**, inserts a tab.

process-up(): If **XmNeditMode** is **XmSINGLE_LINE_EDIT** and **XmNnavigationType** is **XmNONE**, traverses to the widget above the current one in the tab group.

> If **XmNeditMode** is **XmMULTI_LINE_EDIT**, moves the insertion cursor up one line.

quick-copy-set():
> Marks the beginning of a secondary selection for use in quick copy.

quick-cut-set():
> Marks the beginning of a secondary selection for use in quick cut.

redraw-display():
> Redraws the contents of the text window.

scroll-one-line-down():
> Scrolls the text area down one line.

scroll-one-line-up():
> Scrolls the text area up one line.

secondary-adjust():
> Extends the secondary selection to the pointer position.

secondary-notify():
> Copies the secondary selection to the insertion cursor of the destination widget.

secondary-start():
> Marks the beginning of a secondary selection.

select-adjust():
> Extends the current selection. The amount of text selected depends on the number of mouse clicks, as specified by the **XmNselectionArray** resource.

select-all(): Selects all text.

select-end(): Extends the current selection. The amount of text selected depends on the number of mouse clicks, as specified by the **XmNselectionArray** resource.

select-start(): Marks the beginning of a new selection region.

self-insert(): If **XmNpendingDelete** is True and the cursor is not disjoint from the current selection, deletes the entire selection. Inserts the character associated with the key pressed at the insertion cursor.

set-anchor(): Resets the anchor point for extended selections. Resets the destination of secondary selection actions.

set-insertion-point():
> Sets the insertion position.

set-selection-hint():
> Sets the text source and location of the current selection.

toggle-add-mode():
> Toggles the state of Add Mode.

traverse-home():
> Traverses to the first widget in the tab group.

traverse-next():
> Traverses to the next widget in the tab group.

traverse-prev():
Traverses to the previous widget in the tab group.

unkill(): Restores last killed text to the position of the insertion cursor.

Related Information

Core(3X), XmCreateScrolledText(3X), XmCreateText(3X), XmFontList(3X), XmFontListAppendEntry(3X), XmPrimitive(3X), XmTextClearSelection(3X), XmTextCopy(3X), XmTextCut(3X), XmTextField(3X), XmTextGetBaseline(3X), XmTextGetEditable(3X), XmTextGetInsertionPosition(3X), XmTextGetLastPosition(3X), XmTextGetMaxLength(3X), XmTextGetSelection(3X), XmTextGetSelectionPosition(3X), XmTextGetSource(3X), XmTextGetString(3X), XmTextGetTopCharacter(3X), XmTextInsert(3X), XmTextPaste(3X), XmTextPosToXY(3X), XmTextPosition(3X), XmTextRemove(3X), XmTextReplace(3X), XmTextScroll(3X), XmTextSetAddMode(3X), XmTextSetEditable(3X), XmTextSetHighlight(3X), XmTextSetInsertionPosition(3X), XmTextSetMaxLength(3X), XmTextSetSelection(3X), XmTextSetSource(3X), XmTextSetString(3X), XmTextSetTopCharacter(3X), XmTextShowPosition(3X), and XmTextXYToPos(3X).

XmTextClearSelection—A Text function that clears the primary selection

AES Support Level

Full-use

Synopsis

#include <Xm/Text.h>

void XmTextClearSelection (*widget, time*)
    Widget   *widget*;
    Time   *time*;

Description

XmTextClearSelection clears the primary selection in the Text widget.

widget   Specifies the Text widget ID.

time   Specifies the server time at which the selection value is desired. This should be the time of the event that triggered this request.

For a complete definition of Text and its associated resources, see **XmText(3X)**.

Related Information

XmText(3X).

XmTextCopy—A Text function that copies the primary selection to the clipboard

AES Support Level

Full-use

Synopsis

#include <Xm/Text.h>

Boolean XmTextCopy (*widget, time*)
    Widget   *widget*;
    Time   *time*;

Description

XmTextCopy copies the primary selected text to the clipboard.

widget   Specifies the Text widget ID.

time   Specifies the server time at which the selection value is to be modified. This should be the time of the event which triggered this request.

For a complete definition of Text and its associated resources, see **XmText(3X)**.

Return Value

This function returns False if the primary selection is NULL, if the *widget* does not own the primary selection, or if the function is unable to gain ownership of the clipboard selection. Otherwise, it returns True.

Related Information

XmText(3X).

XmTextCut—A Text function that copies the primary selection to the clipboard and deletes the selected text

AES Support Level

Full-use

Synopsis

#include <Xm/Text.h>

Boolean XmTextCut (*widget, time*)
    Widget   *widget*;
    Time   *time*;

Description

XmTextCut copies the primary selected text to the clipboard and then deletes the primary selected text. This routine also calls the widget's **XmNmodifyVerifyCallback** and **XmNvalueChangedCallback** callbacks.

widget   Specifies the Text widget ID.

time   Specifies the server time at which the selection value is to be modified. This should be the time of the event that triggered this request.

For a complete definition of Text and its associated resources, see **XmText(3X)**.

Return Value

This function returns False if the primary selection is NULL, if the *widget* does not own the primary selection, or if the function is unable to gain ownership of the clipboard selection. Otherwise, it returns True.

Related Information

XmText(3X).

XmTextField—The TextField class

AES Support Level

Trial-use

Synopsis

#include <Xm/TextF.h>

Description

The TextField widget provides a single line text editor for customizing both user and programmatic interfaces. It is used for single-line string entry, and forms entry with verification procedures. It provides an application with a consistent editing system for textual data.

TextField provides separate callback lists to verify movement of the insert cursor, modification of the text, and changes in input focus. Each of these callbacks provides the verification function with the widget instance, the event that caused the callback, and a data structure specific to the verification type. From this information, the function can verify if the application considers this to be a legitimate state change and can signal the widget whether to continue with the action.

The user interface tailors a new set of actions. The key bindings have been added for insert cursor movement, deletion, insertion, and selection of text.

TextField allows the user to select regions of text. Selection is based on the model specified in the *Inter-Client Communication Conventions Manual* (ICCCM). TextField supports primary and secondary selection.

Classes

TextField widget inherits behavior and resources from **Core** and **Primitive**.

The class pointer is **xmTextFieldWidgetClass**.

The class name is **XmTextField**.

New Resources

The following table defines a set of widget resources used by the programmer to specify data. The programmer can also set the resource values for the inherited classes to set attributes for this widget. To reference a resource by name or by class in a **.Xdefaults** file, remove the **XmN** or **XmC** prefix and use the remaining letters. To specify one of the defined values for a resource in a **.Xdefaults** file, remove the **Xm** prefix and use the remaining letters (in either lower case or upper case, but include any underscores between words). The codes in the access column indicate if the given resource can be set at creation time (C), set by using **XtSetValues** (S), retrieved by using **XtGetValues** (G), or is not applicable (N/A).

XmTextFieldResource Set		

Name
    Class
	Default
	    Type
		Access

XmNactivateCallback
    XmCCallback
	NULL
	    XtCallbackList
		C

XmNblinkRate
    XmCBlinkRate
	500
	    int
		CSG

XmNcolumns
    XmCColumns
	dynamic
	    short
		CSG

XmNcursorPosition
    XmCCursorPosition
	0
	    XmTextPosition
		CSG

XmNcursorPositionVisible
    XmCCursorPositionVisible
	True
	    Boolean
		CSG

XmNeditable
    XmCEditable
	True
	    Boolean
		CSG

XmNfocusCallback
    XmCCallback
	NULL
	    XtCallbackList
		C

XmNfontList
    XmCFontList
	dynamic
	    XmFontList
		CSG

XmNgainPrimaryCallback
    XmCCallback
	NULL
	    XtCallbackList
		C

XmNlosePrimaryCallback
    XmCCallback
	NULL
	    XtCallbackList
		C

XmNlosingFocusCallback
    XmCCallback
	NULL
	    XtCallbackList
		C

XmNmarginHeight
    XmCMarginHeight
	5
	    Dimension
		CSG

Name	Default	Access
Class	Type	
XmNmarginWidth	5	CSG
XmCMarginWidth	Dimension	
XmNmaxLength	largest integer	CSG
XmCMaxLength	int	
XmNmodifyVerifyCallback	NULL	C
XmCCallback	XtCallbackList	
XmNmotionVerifyCallback	NULL	C
XmCCallback	XtCallbackList	
XmNpendingDelete	True	CSG
XmCPendingDelete	Boolean	
XmNresizeWidth	False	CSG
XmCResizeWidth	Boolean	
XmNselectionArray	default array	CSG
XmCSelectionArray	XtPointer	
XmNselectionArrayCount	3	CSG
XmCSelectionArrayCount	int	
XmNselectThreshold	5	CSG
XmCSelectThreshold	int	
XmNvalue	""	CSG
XmCValue	String	
XmNvalueChangedCallback	NULL	C
XmCCallback	XtCallbackList	
XmNverifyBell	dynamic	CSG
XmCVerifyBell	Boolean	

XmNactivateCallback

Specifies the list of callbacks that is called when the user invokes an event that calls the **Activate()** function. The type of the structure whose address is passed to this callback is **XmAnyCallbackStruct**. The reason sent by the callback is **XmCR_ACTIVATE**.

XmNblinkRate

Specifies the blink rate of the text cursor in milliseconds. The time indicated in the blink rate relates to the length of time the cursor is visible and the time the cursor is invisible (that is, the time it will take to blink the insertion cursor on and off will be two times the blink rate). The cursor will not blink when the blink rate is set to 0 (zero). The value must not be negative.

XmNcolumns

> Specifies the initial width of the text window as an integer number of characters. The width equals the number of characters specified by this resource multiplied by the maximum character width of the associated font. For proportionate fonts, the actual number of characters that fit on a given line may be greater than the value specified. The value must be greater than 0 (zero). The default value depends on the value of the **XmNwidth** resource. If no width is specified the default is 20.

XmNcursorPosition

> Indicates the position in the text where the current insert cursor is to be located. Position is determined by the number of characters from the beginning of the text.

XmNcursorPositionVisible

> Indicates that the insert cursor position is marked by a blinking text cursor when the Boolean is True.

XmNeditable When set to True, indicates that the user can edit the text string. A false value will prohibit the user from editing the text.

XmNfocusCallback

> Specifies the list of callbacks called when TextField accepts input focus. The type of the structure whose address is passed to this callback is **XmAnyCallbackStruct**. The reason sent by the callback is **XmCR_FOCUS**.

XmNfontList Specifies the font list to be used for TextField. If this value is NULL at initialization, the parent hierarchy of the widget is searched for an ancestor that is a subclass of the BulletinBoard or VendorShell widget class. If such an ancestor is found, the font list is initialized to the **XmNtextFontList** of the ancestor widget. If no such ancestor is found, the default is implementation dependent. Refer to **XmFontList(3X)** for more information on a font list structure.

> TextField searches the font list for the first occurrence of a font set that has an **XmFONTLIST_DEFAULT_TAG**. If a default element is not found, the first font set in the font list is used. If the list contains no font sets, the first font in the font list is used.

XmNgainPrimaryCallback

> Specifies the list of callbacks that are called when the user invokes an event that causes the text widget to gain ownership of the primary selection. The callback reason for this callback is **XmCR_GAIN_PRIMARY**.

XmNlosePrimaryCallback

> Specifies the list of callbacks that are called when the user invokes an event that cause the text widget to lose ownership of the primary selection. The callback reason for this callback is **XmCR_LOSE_PRIMARY**.

XmNlosingFocusCallback

> Specifies the list of callbacks that are called before TextField widget loses input focus. The type of the structure whose address is passed to this callback is **XmTextVerifyCallbackStruct**. The reason sent by the callback is **XmCR_LOSING_FOCUS**.

XmNmarginHeight

> Specifies the distance between the top edge of the widget window and the text, and the bottom edge of the widget window and the text.

XmNmarginWidth

> Specifies the distance between the left edge of the widget window and the text, and the right edge of the widget window and the text.

XmNmaxLength

> Specifies the maximum length of the text string that can be entered into text from the keyboard. This value must be nonnegative. Strings that are entered using the **XmNvalue** resource or the **XmTextFieldSetString** function ignore this resource.

XmNmodifyVerifyCallback

> Specifies the list of callbacks that is called before text is deleted from or inserted into TextField. The type of the structure whose address is passed to this callback is **XmTextVerifyCallbackStruct**. The reason sent by the callback is **XmCR_MODIFYING_TEXT_VALUE**. When multiple TextField widgets share the same source, only the widget that initiates the source change will generate the **XmNmodifyVerifyCallback**.

XmNmotionVerifyCallback

> Specifies the list of callbacks that is called before the insert cursor is moved to a new position. The type of the structure whose address is passed to this callback is **XmTextVerifyCallbackStruct**. The reason sent by the callback is **XmCR_MOVING_INSERT_CURSOR**. It is possible for more than one **XmNmotionVerifyCallback**s to be generated from a single action.

XmNpendingDelete

Indicates that pending delete mode is on when the Boolean is True. Pending deletion is defined as deletion of the selected text when an insertion is made.

XmNresizeWidth

Indicates that the TextField widget will attempt to resize its width to accommodate all the text contained in the widget when Boolean is True.

XmNselectionArray

Defines the actions for multiple mouse clicks. Each mouse click performed within a half of a second of the previous mouse click will increment the index into this array and perform the defined action for that index. The possible actions are

XmSELECT_POSITION

Resets the insert cursor position

XmSELECT_WORD

Selects a word

XmSELECT_LINE

Selects a line of text

XmNselectionArrayCount

Specifies the number of actions that are defined in the **XmNselectionArray** resource. The value must not be negative.

XmNselectThreshold

Specifies the number of pixels of motion that is required to select the next character when selection is performed using the click-drag mode of selection. The value must not be negative.

XmNvalue Displays the string value. **XtGetValues** returns the value of the internal buffer and **XtSetValues** copies the string values into the internal buffer.

XmNvalueChangedCallback

Specifies the list of callbacks that is called after text is deleted from or inserted into TextField. The type of the structure whose address is passed to this callback is **XmAnyCallbackStruct**. The reason sent by the callback is **XmCR_VALUE_CHANGED**. When multiple TextField widgets share the same source, only the widget that initiates the source change will generate the **XmNvalueChangedCallback**. This callback represents a change in the source in the TextField, not in the TextField widget. The

XmNvalueChangedCallback should occur only in pairs with a **XmNmodifyVerifyCallback**, assuming that the *doit* flag in the callback structure of the **XmNmodifyVerifyCallback** is not set to False.

XmNverifyBell

Specifies whether a bell will sound when an action is reversed during a verification callback.

Inherited Resources

TextField widget inherits behavior and resources from the superclasses in the following tables. For a complete description of these resources, refer to the reference page for that superclass.

<table>
<tr><th colspan="3">XmPrimitive Resource Set</th></tr>
<tr><th>Name
Class</th><th>Default
Type</th><th>Access</th></tr>
<tr><td>XmNbottomShadowColor
XmCBottomShadowColor</td><td>dynamic
Pixel</td><td>CSG</td></tr>
<tr><td>XmNbottomShadowPixmap
XmCBottomShadowPixmap</td><td>XmUNSPECIFIED_PIXMAP
Pixmap</td><td>CSG</td></tr>
<tr><td>XmNforeground
XmCForeground</td><td>dynamic
Pixel</td><td>CSG</td></tr>
<tr><td>XmNhelpCallback
XmCCallback</td><td>NULL
XtCallbackList</td><td>C</td></tr>
<tr><td>XmNhighlightColor
XmCHighlightColor</td><td>dynamic
Pixel</td><td>CSG</td></tr>
<tr><td>XmNhighlightOnEnter
XmCHighlightOnEnter</td><td>False
Boolean</td><td>CSG</td></tr>
<tr><td>XmNhighlightPixmap
XmCHighlightPixmap</td><td>dynamic
Pixmap</td><td>CSG</td></tr>
<tr><td>XmNhighlightThickness
XmCHighlightThickness</td><td>2
Dimension</td><td>CSG</td></tr>
<tr><td>XmNnavigationType
XmCNavigationType</td><td>XmTAB_GROUP
XmNavigationType</td><td>CSG</td></tr>
<tr><td>XmNshadowThickness
XmCShadowThickness</td><td>2
Dimension</td><td>CSG</td></tr>
<tr><td>XmNtopShadowColor
XmCTopShadowColor</td><td>dynamic
Pixel</td><td>CSG</td></tr>
<tr><td>XmNtopShadowPixmap
XmCTopShadowPixmap</td><td>dynamic
Pixmap</td><td>CSG</td></tr>
<tr><td>XmNtraversalOn
XmCTraversalOn</td><td>Truc
Boolean</td><td>CSG</td></tr>
<tr><td>XmNuserData
XmCUserData</td><td>NULL
XtPointer</td><td>CSG</td></tr>
</table>

Core Resource Set		

Name
  Class
	Default
	  Type
		Access

XmNaccelerators
  XmCAccelerators
	dynamic
	  XtAccelerators
		CSG

XmNancestorSensitive
  XmCSensitive
	dynamic
	  Boolean
		G

XmNbackground
  XmCBackground
	dynamic
	  Pixel
		CSG

XmNbackgroundPixmap
  XmCPixmap
	XmUNSPECIFIED_PIXMAP
	  Pixmap
		CSG

XmNborderColor
  XmCBorderColor
	XtDefaultForeground
	  Pixel
		CSG

XmNborderPixmap
  XmCPixmap
	XmUNSPECIFIED_PIXMAP
	  Pixmap
		CSG

XmNborderWidth
  XmCBorderWidth
	0
	  Dimension
		CSG

XmNcolormap
  XmCColormap
	dynamic
	  Colormap
		CG

XmNdepth
  XmCDepth
	dynamic
	  int
		CG

XmNdestroyCallback
  XmCCallback
	NULL
	  XtCallbackList
		C

XmNheight
  XmCHeight
	dynamic
	  Dimension
		CSG

XmNinitialResourcesPersistent
  XmCInitialResourcesPersistent
	True
	  Boolean
		C

XmNmappedWhenManaged
  XmCMappedWhenManaged
	True
	  Boolean
		CSG

XmNscreen
  XmCScreen
	dynamic
	  Screen *
		CG

XmNsensitive
  XmCSensitive
	True
	  Boolean
		CSG

Name	Default	Access
Class	Type	
XmNtranslations	dynamic	CSG
XmCTranslations	XtTranslations	
XmNwidth	dynamic	CSG
XmCWidth	Dimension	
XmNx	0	CSG
XmCPosition	Position	
XmNy	0	CSG
XmCPosition	Position	

Callback Information

A pointer to the following structure is passed to each callback:

```
typedef struct
{
    int             reason;
    XEvent          * event;
} XmAnyCallbackStruct;
```

reason   Indicates why the callback was invoked

event   Points to the **XEvent** that triggered the callback

The TextField widget defines a new callback structure for use with verification callbacks. Note that not all of the fields are relevant for every callback reason. The application must first look at the *reason* field and use only the structure members that are valid for the particular reason. The values *startPos*, *endPos*, and *text* in the callback structure **XmTextVerifyCallbackStruct** may be modified upon receiving the callback, and these changes will be reflected as the change made to the source of the TextField widget. (For example, all keystrokes can be converted to spaces or NULL characters when a password is entered into a TextField widget.) The application programmer should not overwrite the *text* field, but should attach data to that pointer.

A pointer to the following structure is passed to the callbacks for **XmNlosingFocusCallback**, **XmNmodifyVerifyCallback**, and **XmNmotionVerifyCallback**.

```
typedef struct
{
    int                reason;
    XEvent             *event;
    Boolean            doit;
    XmTextPosition     currInsert, newInsert;
    XmTextPosition     startPos, endPos;
    XmTextBlock        text;
} XmTextVerifyCallbackStruct, *XmTextVerifyPtr;
```

reason   Indicates why the callback was invoked.

event   Points to the **XEvent** the triggered the callback. It can be NULL. For example, changes made to the Text widget programmatically do not have an event that can be passed to the associated callback.

doit   Indicates whether the action that invoked the callback will be performed. Setting *doit* to False negates the action.

currInsert   Indicates the current position of the insert cursor.

newInsert   Indicates the position at which the user attempts to position the insert cursor.

startPos   Indicates the starting position of the text to modify. If the callback is not a modify verification callback, this value is the same as *currInsert*.

endPos   Indicates the ending position of the text to modify. If no text is replaced or deleted, then the value is the same as *startPos*. If the callback is not a modify verification callback, this value is the same as *currInsert*.

text   Points to the following structure of type **XmTextBlockRec**. This structure holds the textual information to be inserted.

```
typedef struct
{
    char               *ptr;
    int                length;
    XmTextFormat       format
} XmTextBlockRec, *XmTextBlock;
```

> *ptr* The text to be inserted. *ptr* points to a temporary storage space that is reused after the callback is finished. Therefore, if an application needs to save the text to be inserted, it should copy the text into its own data space.
>
> *length* Specifies the length of the text to be inserted.
>
> *format* Specifies the format of the text, either **XmFMT_8_BIT** or **XmFMT_16_BIT**.

The following table describes the reasons for which the individual verification callback structure fields are valid.

Reason	Valid Fields
XmCR_LOSING_FOCUS	*reason, event, doit*
XmCR_MODIFYING_TEXT_VALUE	*reason, event, doit, currInsert, newInsert, startPos, endPos, text*
XmCR_MOVING_INSERT_CURSOR	*reason, event, doit, currInsert, newInsert*

Action Routines

The **XmText** action routines are

activate(): Calls the callbacks for **XmNactivateCallback**. If the parent is a manager, passes the event to the parent.

backward-character():

Moves the insertion cursor one character to the left. This action may have different behavior in a right-to-left language environment.

backward-word(*extend*):

If this action is called with no argument, moves the insertion cursor to the first non-whitespace character after the first whitespace character to the left or after the beginning of the line. If the insertion cursor is already at the beginning of a word, moves the insertion cursor to the beginning of the previous word. This action may have different behavior in a locale other than the C locale.

If called with an argument of **extend**, moves the insertion cursor as in the case of no argument and extends the current selection.

beginning-of-line(*extend*):

If this action is called with no argument, moves the insertion cursor to the beginning of the line.

If called with an argument of **extend**, moves the insertion cursor as in the case of no argument and extends the current selection.

clear-selection():

Clears the current selection by replacing each character except **<Return>** with a **<space>** character.

copy-clipboard():

Copies the current selection to the clipboard.

copy-primary():

Copies the primary selection to just before the insertion cursor.

copy-to():   If a secondary selection exists, copies the secondary selection to just before the insertion cursor. If no secondary selection exists, copies the primary selection to the pointer location.

cut-clipboard():

Cuts the current selection to the clipboard.

cut-primary():

Cuts the primary selection to just before the insertion cursor.

delete-next-character():

In normal mode, if there is a nonnull selection, deletes the selection; otherwise, deletes the character following the insertion cursor. In add mode, if there is a nonnull selection, the cursor is not disjoint from the selection and **XmNpendingDelete** is set to True, deletes the selection; otherwise, deletes the character following the insertion cursor. This may impact the selection.

delete-next-word():

In normal mode, if there is a nonnull selection, deletes the selection; otherwise, deletes the characters following the insertion cursor to the next space, tab or end-of-line character. In add mode, if there is a nonnull selection, the cursor is not disjoint from the selection and **XmNpendingDelete** is set to True, deletes the selection; otherwise, deletes the characters following the insertion cursor to the next space, tab or end-of-line character. This may impact the selection. This action may have different behavior in a locale other than the C locale.

delete-previous-character():

In normal mode, if there is a nonnull selection, deletes the selection; otherwise, deletes the character of text immediately preceding the insertion cursor. In add mode, if there is a nonnull selection, the cursor is not disjoint from the selection and **XmNpendingDelete** is set to True, deletes the selection; otherwise, deletes the character of text immediately preceding the insertion cursor. This may impact the selection.

delete-previous-word():

In normal mode, if there is a nonnull selection, deletes the selection; otherwise, deletes the characters preceding the insertion cursor to the next space, tab or beginning-of-line character. In add mode, if there is a nonnull selection, the cursor is not disjoint from the selection and **XmNpendingDelete** is set to True, deletes the selection; otherwise, deletes the characters preceding the insertion cursor to the next space, tab or beginning-of-line character. This may impact the selection. This action may have different behavior in a locale other than the C locale.

delete-selection():

Deletes the current selection.

delete-to-end-of-line():

In normal mode, if there is a nonnull selection, deletes the selection; otherwise, deletes the characters following the insertion cursor to the next end of line character. In add mode, if there is a nonnull selection, the cursor is not disjoint from the selection and **XmNpendingDelete** is set to True, deletes the selection; otherwise, deletes the characters following the insertion cursor to the next end of line character. This may impact the selection.

delete-to-start-of-line():

In normal mode, if there is a nonnull selection, deletes the selection; otherwise, deletes the characters preceding the insertion cursor to the previous beginning-of-line character. In add mode, if there is a nonnull selection, the cursor is not disjoint from the selection and **XmNpendingDelete** is set to True, deletes the selection; otherwise, deletes the characters preceding the insertion cursor to the previous beginning-of-line character. This may impact the selection.

deselect-all():

Deselects the current selection.

end-of-line(*extend***):**

If this action is called with no argument, moves the insertion cursor to the end of the line. If called with an argument of **extend**, moves the insertion cursor as in the case of no argument and extends the current selection.

extend-adjust():
Selects text from the anchor to the pointer position and deselects text outside that range.

extend-end():
Moves the insertion cursor to the position of the pointer.

extend-start():
Adjusts the anchor using the balance-beam method. Selects text from the anchor to the pointer position and deselects text outside that range.

forward-character():
Moves the insertion cursor one character to the right. This action may have different behavior in a right-to-left language environment.

forward-word(*extend***)**:
If this action is called with no argument, moves the insertion cursor to the first whitespace character or end-of-line following the next non-whitespace character. If the insertion cursor is already at the end of a word, moves the insertion cursor to the end of the next word. This action may have different behavior in a locale other than the C locale.

If called with an argument of **extend**, moves the insertion cursor as in the case of no argument and extends the current selection.

grab-focus(): This key binding performs the action defined in the **XmNselectionArray**, depending on the number of multiple mouse clicks. The default selection array ordering is one click to move the insertion cursor to the pointer position, two clicks to select a word, three clicks to select a line of text, and four clicks to select all text. A single click also deselects any selected text and sets the anchor at the pointer position. This action may have different behavior in a locale other than the C locale.

Help():
Calls the callbacks for **XmNhelpCallback** if any exist. If there are no help callbacks for this widget, this action calls the help callbacks for the nearest ancestor that has them.

key-select(*direction***)**:
If called with an argument of **right**, moves the insertion cursor one character to the right and extends the current selection. If called with an argument of **left**, moves the insertion cursor one character to the left and extends the current selection. If called with no argument, extends the current selection.

move-destination():
> Moves the insertion cursor to the pointer position without changing any existing current selection. If there is no current selection, sets the widget as the destination widget.

move-to(): If a secondary selection exists, cuts the secondary selection to just before the insertion cursor. If no secondary selection exists, cuts the primary selection to the pointer location.

next-tab-group():
> Traverses to the next tab group.

page-left(): Scrolls the viewing window left one page of text.

page-right(): Scrolls the viewing window right one page of text.

paste-clipboard():
> Pastes the contents of the clipboard before the insertion cursor.

prev-tab-group():
> Traverses to the previous tab group.

process-cancel():
> Cancels the current **extend-adjust**() or **secondary-adjust**() operation and leaves the selection state as it was before the operation; otherwise, and the parent is a manager, it passes the event to the parent.

secondary-adjust():
> Extends the secondary selection to the pointer position.

secondary-start():
> Marks the beginning of a secondary selection.

select-all(): Selects all text.

self-insert(): If **XmNpendingDelete** is True and the cursor is not disjoint from the current selection, deletes the entire selection. Inserts the character associated with the key pressed before the insertion cursor.

set-anchor(): Resets the anchor point for extended selections. Resets the destination of secondary selection actions.

toggle-add-mode():
> Toggles the state of Add Mode.

traverse-home():
> Traverses to the first widget in the tab group.

traverse-next():
>   Traverses to the next widget in the tab group.

traverse-prev():
>   Traverses to the previous widget in the tab group.

Related Information

Core(3X), XmCreateTextField(3X), XmFontList(3X),
XmFontListAppendEntry(3X), XmPrimitive(3X),
XmTextFieldClearSelection(3X), XmTextFieldCopy(3X),
XmTextFieldCut(3X), XmTextFieldGetBaseline(3X),
XmTextFieldGetEditable(3X), XmTextFieldGetInsertionPosition(3X),
XmTextFieldGetLastPosition(3X), XmTextFieldGetMaxLength(3X),
XmTextFieldGetSelection(3X), XmTextFieldGetSelectionPosition(3X),
XmTextFieldGetString(3X), XmTextFieldGetSubstring(3X),
XmTextFieldInsert(3X), XmTextFieldPaste(3X), XmTextFieldPosToXY(3X),
XmTextFieldRemove(3X), XmTextFieldReplace(3X),
XmTextFieldSetAddMode(3X), XmTextFieldSetEditable(3X),
XmTextFieldSetHighlight(3X), XmTextFieldSetInsertionPosition(3X),
XmTextFieldSetMaxLength(3X), XmTextFieldSetSelection(3X),
XmTextFieldSetString(3X), XmTextFieldShowPosition(3X), and
XmTextFieldXYToPos(3X).

XmTextFieldClearSelection—A TextField function that clears the primary selection

AES Support Level

Trial-use

Synopsis

#include <Xm/TextF.h>

void XmTextFieldClearSelection (*widget, time*)
    Widget   *widget*;
    Time   *time*;

Description

XmTextFieldClearSelection clears the primary selection in the TextField widget.

widget   Specifies the TextField widget ID.

time   Specifies the time at which the selection value is desired. This should be the time of the event that triggered this request.

For a complete definition of TextField and its associated resources, see **XmTextField(3X)**.

Related Information

XmTextField(3X).

XmTextFieldCopy—A TextField function that copies the primary selection to the clipboard

AES Support Level

Trial-use

Synopsis

#include <Xm/TextF.h>

Boolean XmTextFieldCopy (*widget, time*)
    Widget   *widget*;
    Time   *time*;

Description

XmTextFieldCopy copies the primary selected text to the clipboard.

widget   Specifies the TextField widget ID.

time   Specifies the time at which the selection value is to be modified. This should be the time of the event that triggered this request.

For a complete definition of TextField and its associated resources, see **XmTextField(3X)**.

Return Value

This function returns False if the primary selection is NULL, if the *widget* does not own the primary selection, or if the function is unable to gain ownership of the clipboard selection. Otherwise, it returns True.

Related Information

XmTextField(3X).

XmTextFieldCut—A TextField function that copies the primary selection to the clipboard and deletes the selected text

AES Support Level

Trial-use

Synopsis

#include <Xm/TextF.h>

Boolean XmTextFieldCut (*widget, time*)
    Widget   *widget*;
    Time   *time*;

Description

XmTextFieldCut copies the primary selected text to the clipboard and then deletes the primary selected text. This routine also calls the widget's **XmNmodifyVerifyCallback** and **XmNvalueChangedCallback** callbacks.

widget   Specifies the TextField widget ID.

time   Specifies the time at which the selection value is to be modified. This should be the time of the event that triggered this request.

For a complete definition of TextField and its associated resources, see **XmTextField(3X)**.

Return Value

This function returns False if the primary selection is NULL, if the *widget* does not own the primary selection, or if the function is unable to gain ownership of the clipboard selection. Otherwise, it returns True.

Related Information

XmTextField(3X).

XmTextFieldGetBaseline—A TextField function that accesses the *x* position of the first baseline

AES Support Level

Trial-use

Synopsis

#include <Xm/TextF.h>

int XmTextFieldGetBaseline (*widget*)
    Widget   *widget*;

Description

XmTextFieldGetBaseline accesses the *x* position of the first baseline in the TextField widget, relative to the *x* position of the top of the widget.

widget   Specifies the TextField widget ID

For a complete definition of TextField and its associated resources, see **XmTextField(3X)**.

Return Value

Returns an integer value that indicates the *x* position of the first baseline in the TextField widget. The calculation takes into account the margin height, shadow thickness, highlight thickness, and font ascent of the first font in the fontlist. In this calculation, the *x* position of the top of the widget is 0 (zero).

Related Information

XmTextField(3X).

XmTextFieldGetEditable—A TextField function that accesses the edit permission
state

AES Support Level

Trial-use

Synopsis

#include <Xm/TextF.h>

Boolean XmTextFieldGetEditable (*widget*)
> **Widget** *widget*;

Description

XmTextFieldGetEditable accesses the edit permission state of the TextField
widget.

widget Specifies the TextField widget ID

For a complete definition of TextField and its associated resources, see
XmTextField(3X).

Return Value

Returns a Boolean value that indicates the state of the **XmNeditable** resource.

Related Information

XmTextField(3X).

XmTextFieldGetInsertionPosition—A TextField function that accesses the position of the insertion cursor

AES Support Level

Trial-use

Synopsis

#include <Xm/TextF.h>

XmTextPosition XmTextFieldGetInsertionPosition (*widget*)
    Widget   *widget*;

Description

XmTextFieldGetInsertionPosition accesses the insertion cursor position of the TextField widget.

widget   Specifies the TextField widget ID

For a complete definition of TextField and its associated resources, see **XmTextField(3X)**.

Return Value

Returns an **XmTextPosition** value that indicates the state of the **XmNcursorPosition** resource. This is an integer number of characters from the beginning of the text buffer. The first character position is 0 (zero).

Related Information

XmTextField(3X).

XmTextFieldGetLastPosition—A TextField function that accesses the position of the last text character

AES Support Level

Trial-use

Synopsis

#include <Xm/TextF.h>

XmTextPosition XmTextFieldGetLastPosition (*widget*)
    Widget   *widget*;

Description

XmTextFieldGetLastPosition accesses the position of the last character in the text buffer of the TextField widget.

widget   Specifies the TextField widget ID

For a complete definition of TextField and its associated resources, see **XmTextField(3X)**.

Return Value

Returns an **XmTextPosition** value that indicates the position of the last character in the text buffer. This is an integer number of characters from the beginning of the buffer. The first character position is 0 (zero).

Related Information

XmTextField(3X).

XmTextFieldGetMaxLength—A TextField function that accesses the value of the
current maximum allowable length of a text string entered from the keyboard

AES Support Level

Trial-use

Synopsis

#include <Xm/TextF.h>

int XmTextFieldGetMaxLength (*widget*)
    Widget   *widget*;

Description

XmTextFieldGetMaxLength accesses the value of the current maximum
allowable length of the text string in the TextField widget entered from the
keyboard. The maximum allowable length prevents the user from entering a text
string larger than this limit.

widget   Specifies the TextField widget ID

For a complete definition of TextField and its associated resources, see
XmTextField(3X).

Return Value

Returns the integer value that indicates the string's maximum allowable length that
can be entered from the keyboard.

Related Information

XmTextField(3X).

XmTextFieldGetSelection—A TextField function that retrieves the value of the primary selection

AES Support Level

Trial-use

Synopsis

#include <Xm/TextF.h>

char * XmTextFieldGetSelection (*widget*)
    Widget   *widget*;

Description

XmTextFieldGetSelection retrieves the value of the primary selection. It returns a NULL pointer if no text is selected in the widget. The application is responsible for freeing the storage associated with the string by calling **XtFree**.

widget   Specifies the TextField widget ID

For a complete definition of TextField and its associated resources, see **XmTextField(3X)**.

Return Value

Returns a character pointer to the string that is associated with the primary selection.

Related Information

XmTextField(3X).

XmTextFieldGetSelectionPosition—A TextField function that accesses the position of the primary selection

AES Support Level

Trial-use

Synopsis

#include <Xm/TextF.h>

Boolean XmTextFieldGetSelectionPosition (*widget, left, right*)
 Widget *widget*;
 XmTextPosition**left*;
 XmTextPosition**right*;

Description

XmTextFieldGetSelectionPosition accesses the left and right position of the primary selection in the text buffer of the TextField widget.

widget Specifies the TextField widget ID

left Specifies the pointer in which the position of the left boundary of the primary selection is returned. This is an integer number of characters from the beginning of the buffer. The first character position is 0 (zero).

right Specifies the pointer in which the position of the right boundary of the primary selection is returned. This is an integer number of characters from the beginning of the buffer. The first character position is 0 (zero).

For a complete definition of TextField and its associated resources, see **XmTextField(3X)**.

Return Value

This function returns True if the widget owns the primary selection; otherwise, it returns False.

Related Information

XmTextField(3X).

XmTextFieldGetString—A TextField function that accesses the string value

AES Support Level

Trial-use

Synopsis

#include <Xm/TextF.h>

char * XmTextFieldGetString (*widget*)
    Widget   *widget*;

Description

XmTextFieldGetString accesses the string value of the TextField widget. The application is responsible for freeing the storage associated with the string by calling **XtFree**.

widget   Specifies the TextField widget ID

For a complete definition of TextField and its associated resources, see **XmTextField(3X)**.

Return Value

Returns a character pointer to the string value of the TextField widget. Returns an empty string if the length of the TextField widget's string is 0 (zero).

Related Information

XmTextField(3X).

XmTextFieldInsert—A TextField function that inserts a character string into a text string

AES Support Level

Trial-use

Synopsis

#include <Xm/TextF.h>

void XmTextFieldInsert (*widget, position, value*)
    Widget   *widget*;
    XmTextPosition *position*;
    char   * *value*;

Description

XmTextFieldInsert inserts a character string into the text string in the TextField widget. The character positions begin at 0 (zero) and are numbered sequentially from the beginning of the text. For example, to insert a string after the fourth character, the *position* parameter must be 4.

This routine also calls the widget's **XmNmodifyVerifyCallback** and **XmNvalueChangedCallback** callbacks.

widget   Specifies the TextField widget ID

position   Specifies the position in the text string where the character string is to be inserted

value   Specifies the character string value to be added to the text widget

For a complete definition of TextField and its associated resources, see **XmTextField(3X)**.

Related Information

XmTextField(3X).

XmTextFieldPaste—A TextField function that inserts the clipboard selection

AES Support Level

Trial-use

Synopsis

#include <Xm/TextF.h>

Boolean XmTextFieldPaste (*widget*)
    Widget   *widget*;

Description

XmTextFieldPaste inserts the clipboard selection at the insertion cursor of the destination widget. If **XmNpendingDelete** is True and the insertion cursor is inside the current selection, the clipboard selection replaces the selected text. This routine calls the widget's **XmNvalueChangedCallback** and **XmNmodifyVerifyCallback**.

widget   Specifies the TextField widget ID.

For a complete definition of TextField and its associated resources, see **XmTextField(3X)**.

Return Value

This function returns False if the *widget* does not own the primary selection. Otherwise, it returns True.

Related Information

XmTextField(3X).

XmTextFieldPosToXY—A TextField function that accesses the x and y position of a character position

AES Support Level

Trial-use

Synopsis

#include <Xm/TextF.h>

Boolean XmTextFieldPosToXY (*widget, position, x, y*)
    Widget   *widget*;
    XmTextPosition*position*;
    Position   **x*;
    Position   **y*;

Description

XmTextFieldPosToXY accesses the x and y position, relative to the upper left corner of the TextField widget, of a given character position in the text buffer.

widget   Specifies the TextField widget ID

position   Specifies the character position in the text for which the x and y position is accessed. This is an integer number of characters from the beginning of the buffer. The first character position is 0.

x   Specifies the pointer in which the x position, relative to the upper left corner of the widget, is returned. This value is meaningful only if the function returns True.

y   Specifies the pointer in which the y position, relative to the upper left corner of the widget, is returned. This value is meaningful only if the function returns True.

For a complete definition of TextField and its associated resources, see **XmTextField(3X)**.

Return Value

This function returns True if the character position is displayed in the TextField widget; otherwise, it returns False, and no x or y value is returned.

Related Information

XmTextField(3X).

XmTextFieldRemove—A TextField function that deletes the primary selection

AES Support Level

Trial-use

Synopsis

#include <Xm/TextF.h>

Boolean XmTextFieldRemove (*widget*)
  Widget *widget*;

Description

XmTextFieldRemove deletes the primary selected text. This routine also calls the widget's **XmNmodifyVerifyCallback** and **XmNvalueChangedCallback** callbacks if there is a selection.

widget Specifies the TextField widget ID.

For a complete definition of TextField and its associated resources, see **XmTextField(3X)**.

Return Value

This function returns False if the primary selection is NULL or if the *widget* does not own the primary selection. Otherwise, it returns True.

Related Information

XmTextField(3X).

XmTextFieldReplace—A TextField function that replaces part of a text string

AES Support Level

Trial-use

Synopsis

#include <Xm/TextF.h>

void XmTextFieldReplace (*widget, from_pos, to_pos, value*)
    Widget   *widget*;
    XmTextPosition *from_pos*;
    XmTextPosition *to_pos*;
    char   * *value*;

Description

XmTextFieldReplace replaces part of the text string in the TextField widget. The character positions begin at 0 (zero) and are numbered sequentially from the beginning of the text.

An example text replacement would be to replace the second and third characters in the text string. To accomplish this, the parameter *from_pos* must be 1 and *to_pos* must be 3. To insert a string after the fourth character, both parameters, *from_pos* and *to_pos*, must be 4.

This routine also calls the widget's **XmNmodifyVerifyCallback** and **XmNvalueChangedCallback** callbacks.

widget   Specifies the TextField widget ID

from_pos   Specifies the start position of the text to be replaced

to_pos   Specifies the end position of the text to be replaced

value   Specifies the character string value to be added to the text widget

For a complete definition of TextField and its associated resources, see **XmTextField(3X)**.

Related Information

XmTextField(3X).

XmTextFieldSetAddMode—A TextField function that sets the state of Add mode

AES Support Level

Trial-use

Synopsis

#include <Xm/TextF.h>

void XmTextFieldSetAddMode (*widget, state*)
    Widget   *widget*;
    Boolean   *state*;

Description

XmTextFieldSetAddMode controls whether or not the TextField widget is in Add mode. When the widget is in Add mode, the insert cursor can be moved without disturbing the primary selection.

widget   Specifies the TextField widget ID

state   Specifies whether or not the widget is in Add mode. A value of True turns on Add mode; a value of False turns off Add mode.

For a complete definition of TextField and its associated resources, see **XmTextField(3X)**.

Related Information

XmTextField(3X).

XmTextFieldSetEditable—A TextField function that sets the edit permission

AES Support Level

Trial-use

Synopsis

#include <Xm/TextF.h>

void XmTextFieldSetEditable (*widget, editable*)
    Widget   *widget*;
    Boolean   *editable*;

Description

XmTextFieldSetEditable sets the edit permission state of the TextField widget. When set to True, the text string can be edited.

widget   Specifies the TextField widget ID

editable   Specifies a Boolean value that when True allows text string edits

For a complete definition of TextField and its associated resources, see **XmTextField(3X)**.

Related Information

XmTextField(3X).

XmTextFieldSetHighlight—A TextField function that highlights text

AES Support Level

Trial-use

Synopsis

#include <Xm/TextF.h>

void XmTextFieldSetHighlight (*widget, left, right, mode*)
    Widget   *widget*;
    XmTextPosition*left*;
    XmTextPosition*right*;
    XmHighlightMode*mode*;

Description

XmTextFieldSetHighlight highlights text between the two specified character positions. The *mode* parameter determines the type of highlighting. Highlighting text merely changes the visual appearance of the text; it does not set the selection.

widget   Specifies the TextField widget ID

left   Specifies the position of the left boundary of text to be highlighted. This is an integer number of characters from the beginning of the text buffer. The first character position is 0 (zero).

right   Specifies the position of the right boundary of text to be highlighted. This is an integer number of characters from the beginning of the text buffer. The first character position is 0 (zero).

mode   Specifies the type of highlighting to be done. A value of **XmHIGHLIGHT_NORMAL** removes highlighting. A value of **XmHIGHLIGHT_SELECTED** highlights the test using reverse video. A value of **XmHIGHLIGHT_SECONDARY_SELECTED** highlights the text using underlining.

For a complete definition of TextField and its associated resources, see **XmTextField(3X)**.

Related Information

XmTextField(3X).

XmTextFieldSetInsertionPosition—A TextField function that sets the position of the insertion cursor

AES Support Level

Trial-use

Synopsis

#include <Xm/TextF.h>

void XmTextFieldSetInsertionPosition (*widget, position*)
  Widget   *widget*;
  XmTextPosition*position*;

Description

XmTextFieldSetInsertionPosition sets the insertion cursor position of the TextField widget. This routine also calls the widget's **XmNmotionVerifyCallback** callbacks if the insertion cursor position changes.

widget   Specifies the TextField widget ID

position   Specifies the position of the insert cursor. This is an integer number of characters from the beginning of the text buffer. The first character position is 0 (zero).

For a complete definition of TextField and its associated resources, see **XmTextField(3X)**.

Related Information

XmTextField(3X).

XmTextFieldSetMaxLength—A TextField function that sets the value of the current maximum allowable length of a text string entered from the keyboard

AES Support Level

Trial-use

Synopsis

#include <Xm/TextF.h>

void XmTextFieldSetMaxLength (*widget, max_length*)
    Widget   *widget*;
    int   *max_length*;

Description

XmTextFieldSetMaxLength sets the value of the current maximum allowable length of the text string in the TextField widget. The maximum allowable length prevents the user from entering a text string from the keyboard that is larger than this limit. Strings that are entered using the **XmNvalue** resource or the **XmTextSetString** function ignore this resource.

widget   Specifies the TextField widget ID

max_length   Specifies the maximum allowable length of the text string

For a complete definition of TextField and its associated resources, see **XmTextField(3X)**.

Related Information

XmText(3X), and **XmTextFieldSetString(3X)**.

XmTextFieldSetSelection—A TextField function that sets the primary selection of the text

AES Support Level

Trial-use

Synopsis

#include <Xm/TextF.h>

void XmTextFieldSetSelection (*widget, first, last, time*)
    Widget   *widget*;
    XmTextPosition *first*;
    XmTextPosition *last*;
    Time   *time*;

Description

XmTextFieldSetSelection sets the primary selection of the text in the widget. It also sets the insertion cursor position to the last position of the selection and calls the widget's **XmNmotionVerifyCallback** callbacks.

widget   Specifies the TextField widget ID

first   Marks the first character position of the text to be selected

last   Marks the last position of the text to be selected

time   Specifies the time at which the selection value is desired. This should be the same as the time of the event that triggered this request.

For a complete definition of TextField and its associated resources, see **XmTextField(3X)**.

Related Information

XmTextField(3X).

XmTextFieldSetString—A TextField function that sets the string value

AES Support Level

Trial-use

Synopsis

#include <Xm/TextF.h>

void XmTextFieldSetString (*widget, value*)
    Widget   *widget*;
    char   * *value*;

Description

XmTextFieldSetString sets the string value of the TextField widget. This routine calls the widget's **XmNmodifyVerifyCallback** and **XmNvalueChangedCallback** callbacks. It also sets the insertion cursor position to the beginning of the string and calls the widget's **XmNmotionVerifyCallback** callbacks.

widget   Specifies the TextField widget ID

value   Specifies the character pointer to the string value and places the string into the text edit window

For a complete definition of TextField and its associated resources, see **XmTextField(3X)**.

Related Information

XmTextField(3X).

XmTextFieldShowPosition—A TextField function that forces text at a given position to be displayed

AES Support Level

Trial-use

Synopsis

#include <Xm/TextF.h>

void XmTextFieldShowPosition (*widget, position*)
    Widget   *widget*;
    XmTextPosition*position*;

Description

XmTextFieldShowPosition forces text at the specified position to be displayed. If the **XmNautoShowCursorPosition** resource is True, the application should also set the insert cursor to this position.

widget   Specifies the TextField widget ID

position   Specifies the character position to be displayed. This is an integer number of characters from the beginning of the text buffer. The first character position is 0 (zero).

For a complete definition of TextField and its associated resources, see **XmTextField(3X)**.

Related Information

XmTextField(3X).

XmTextFieldXYToPos—A TextField function that accesses the character position nearest an x and y position

AES Support Level

Trial-use

Synopsis

#include <Xm/TextF.h>

XmTextPosition XmTextFieldXYToPos (*widget, x, y*)
    Widget   *widget*;
    Position   *x*;
    Position   *y*;

Description

XmTextFieldXYToPos accesses the character position nearest to the specified x and y position, relative to the upper left corner of the TextField widget.

widget   Specifies the TextField widget ID

x   Specifies the x position, relative to the upper left corner of the widget.

y   Specifies the y position, relative to the upper left corner of the widget.

For a complete definition of TextField and its associated resources, see **XmTextField(3X)**.

Return Value

Returns the character position in the text nearest the x and y position specified. This is an integer number of characters from the beginning of the buffer. The first character position is 0 (zero).

Related Information

XmTextField(3X).

XmTextGetBaseline—A Text function that accesses the x position of the first baseline

AES Support Level

Full-use

Synopsis

#include <Xm/Text.h>

int XmTextGetBaseline (*widget*)
    Widget   *widget*;

Description

XmTextGetBaseline accesses the x position of the first baseline in the Text widget, relative to the x position of the top of the widget.

widget   Specifies the Text widget ID

For a complete definition of Text and its associated resources, see **XmText(3X)**.

Return Value

Returns an integer value that indicates the x position of the first baseline in the Text widget. The calculation takes into account the margin height, shadow thickness, highlight thickness, and font ascent of the first font in the fontlist. In this calculation the x position of the top of the widget is 0 (zero).

Related Information

XmText(3X).

XmTextGetEditable—A Text function that accesses the edit permission state

AES Support Level

Full-use

Synopsis

#include <Xm/Text.h>

Boolean XmTextGetEditable (*widget*)
    Widget   *widget*;

Description

XmTextGetEditable accesses the edit permission state of the Text widget.

widget   Specifies the Text widget ID

For a complete definition of Text and its associated resources, see **XmText(3X)**.

Return Value

Returns a Boolean value that indicates the state of the **XmNeditable** resource.

Related Information

XmText(3X).

XmTextGetInsertionPosition—A Text function that accesses the position of the insert cursor

AES Support Level

Full-use

Synopsis

#include <Xm/Text.h>

XmTextPosition XmTextGetInsertionPosition (*widget*)
    Widget   *widget*;

Description

XmTextGetInsertionPosition accesses the insertion cursor position of the Text widget.

widget   Specifies the Text widget ID

For a complete definition of Text and its associated resources, see **XmText(3X)**.

Return Value

Returns an **XmTextPosition** value that indicates the state of the **XmNcursorPosition** resource. This is an integer number of characters from the beginning of the text buffer. The first character position is 0 (zero).

Related Information

XmText(3X).

XmTextGetLastPosition—A Text function that accesses the last position in the text

AES Support Level

Full-use

Synopsis

#include <Xm/Text.h>

XmTextPosition XmTextGetLastPosition (*widget*)
    Widget   *widget*;

Description

XmTextGetLastPosition accesses the last position in the text buffer of the Text widget. This is an integer number of characters from the beginning of the buffer, and represents the position that text added to the end of the buffer is placed after. The first character position is 0 (zero). The last character position is equal to the number of characters in the text buffer.

widget   Specifies the Text widget ID

For a complete definition of Text and its associated resources, see **XmText(3X)**.

Return Value

Returns an **XmTextPosition** value that indicates the last position in the text buffer.

Related Information

XmText(3X).

XmTextGetMaxLength—A Text function that accesses the value of the current maximum allowable length of a text string entered from the keyboard

AES Support Level

Full-use

Synopsis

#include <Xm/Text.h>

int XmTextGetMaxLength (*widget*)
    Widget   *widget*;

Description

XmTextGetMaxLength accesses the value of the current maximum allowable length of the text string in the Text widget entered from the keyboard. The maximum allowable length prevents the user from entering a text string larger than this limit.

widget   Specifies the Text widget ID

For a complete definition of Text and its associated resources, see **XmText(3X)**.

Return Value

Returns the integer value that indicates the string's maximum allowable length that can be entered from the keyboard.

Related Information

XmText(3X).

XmTextGetSelection—A Text function that retrieves the value of the primary selection

AES Support Level

Full-use

Synopsis

#include <Xm/Text.h>

char * XmTextGetSelection (*widget*)
    Widget   *widget*;

Description

XmTextGetSelection retrieves the value of the primary selection. It returns a NULL pointer if no text is selected in the widget. The application is responsible for freeing the storage associated with the string by calling **XtFree**.

widget   Specifies the Text widget ID

For a complete definition of Text and its associated resources, see **XmText(3X)**.

Return Value

Returns a character pointer to the string that is associated with the primary selection.

Related Information

XmText(3X).

XmTextGetSelectionPosition—A Text function that accesses the position of the primary selection

AES Support Level

Full-use

Synopsis

#include <Xm/Text.h>

Boolean XmTextGetSelectionPosition (*widget, left, right*)
    Widget   *widget*;
    XmTextPosition**left*;
    XmTextPosition**right*;

Description

XmTextGetSelectionPosition accesses the left and right position of the primary selection in the text buffer of the Text widget.

widget   Specifies the Text widget ID

left   Specifies the pointer in which the position of the left boundary of the primary selection is returned. This is an integer number of characters from the beginning of the buffer. The first character position is 0 (zero).

right   Specifies the pointer in which the position of the right boundary of the primary selection is returned. This is an integer number of characters from the beginning of the buffer. The first character position is 0 (zero).

For a complete definition of Text and its associated resources, see **XmText(3X)**.

Return Value

This function returns True if the widget owns the primary selection; otherwise, it returns False.

Related Information

XmText(3X).

XmTextGetSource—A Text function that accesses the source of the widget

AES Support Level

Trial-use

Synopsis

#include <Xm/Text.h>

XmTextSource XmTextGetSource (*widget*)
    Widget   *widget*;

Description

XmTextGetSource accesses the source of the Text widget. Text widgets can share sources of text so that editing in one widget is reflected in another. This function accesses the source of one widget so that it can be made the source of another widget, using the function **XmTextSetSource(3X)**.

Setting a new text source destroys the old text source if no other Text widgets are using that source. To replace a text source but keep it for later use, create an unmanaged Text widget and set its source to the text source you want to keep.

widget   Specifies the Text widget ID

For a complete definition of Text and its associated resources, see **XmText(3X)**.

Return Value

Returns an **XmTextSource** value that represents the source of the Text widget.

Related Information

XmText(3X).

XmTextGetString—A Text function that accesses the string value

AES Support Level

Full-use

Synopsis

#include <Xm/Text.h>

char * XmTextGetString (*widget*)
    Widget   *widget*;

Description

XmTextGetString accesses the string value of the Text widget. The application is responsible for freeing the storage associated with the string by calling **XtFree**.

widget   Specifies the Text widget ID

For a complete definition of Text and its associated resources, see **XmText(3X)**.

Return Value

Returns a character pointer to the string value of the text widget. Returns an empty string if the length of the Text widget's string is 0 (zero).

Related Information

XmText(3X).

XmTextGetTopCharacter—A Text function that accesses the position of the first character displayed

AES Support Level

Full-use

Synopsis

#include <Xm/Text.h>

XmTextPosition XmTextGetTopCharacter (*widget*)
   Widget   *widget*;

Description

XmTextGetTopCharacter accesses the position of the text at the top of the Text widget.

widget   Specifies the Text widget ID

For a complete definition of Text and its associated resources, see **XmText(3X)**.

Return Value

Returns an **XmTextPosition** value that indicates the state of the **XmNtopCharacter** resource. This is an integer number of characters from the beginning of the text buffer. The first character position is 0 (zero).

Related Information

XmText(3X).

XmTextInsert—A Text function that inserts a character string into a text string

AES Support Level

Full-use

Synopsis

#include <Xm/Text.h>

void XmTextInsert(*widget, position, value*)
    Widget   *widget*;
    XmTextPosition   *position*;
    char   * *value*;

Description

XmTextInsert inserts a character string into the text string in the Text widget. The character positions begin at 0 (zero) and are numbered sequentially from the beginning of the text. For example, to insert a string after the fourth character, the parameter *position* must be 4.

This routine also calls the widget's **XmNmodifyVerifyCallback** and **XmNvalueChangedCallback** callbacks.

widget   Specifies the Text widget ID.

position   Specifies the position in the text string where the character string is to be inserted.

value   Specifies the character string value to be added to the text widget.

For a complete definition of Text and its associated resources, see **XmText(3X)**.

Related Information

XmText(3X).

XmTextPaste—A Text function that inserts the clipboard selection

AES Support Level

Full-use

Synopsis

#include <Xm/Text.h>

Boolean XmTextPaste (*widget*)
    Widget   *widget*;

Description

XmTextPaste inserts the clipboard selection at the insertion cursor of the destination widget. If **XmNpendingDelete** is True and the insertion cursor is inside the current selection, the clipboard selection replaces the selected text. This routine calls the widget's **XmNvalueChangedCallback** and **XmNmodifyVerifyCallback**.

widget   Specifies the Text widget ID.

For a complete definition of Text and its associated resources, see **XmText(3X)**.

Return Value

This function returns False if the *widget* does not own the primary selection. Otherwise, it returns True.

Related Information

XmText(3X).

XmTextPosToXY—A Text function that accesses the *x* and *y* position of a character position

AES Support Level

Full-use

Synopsis

#include <Xm/Text.h>

Boolean XmTextPosToXY (*widget, position, x, y*)
> **Widget**   *widget*;
> **XmTextPosition***position*;
> **Position**   **x*;
> **Position**   **y*;

Description

XmTextPosToXY accesses the *x* and *y* position, relative to the upper left corner of the Text widget, of a given character position in the text buffer.

widget   Specifies the Text widget ID

position   Specifies the character position in the text for which the *x* and *y* position is accessed. This is an integer number of characters from the beginning of the buffer. The first character position is 0 (zero).

x   Specifies the pointer in which the *x* position, relative to the upper left corner of the widget, is returned. This value is meaningful only if the function returns True.

y   Specifies the pointer in which the *y* position, relative to the upper left corner of the widget, is returned. This value is meaningful only if the function returns True.

For a complete definition of Text and its associated resources, see **XmText(3X)**.

Return Value

This function returns True if the character position is displayed in the Text widget; otherwise, it returns False, and no *x* or *y* value is returned.

Related Information

XmText(3X).

XmTextPosition—Data type for a character position within a text string

AES Support Level

Full-use

Synopsis

#include <Xm/Xm.h>

Description

XmTextPosition is the data type for a character position within a text string. The text position is an integer representing the number of characters from the beginning of the string. The first character position in the string is 0 (zero).

Related Information

XmText(3X).

XmTextRemove—A Text function that deletes the primary selection

AES Support Level

Full-use

Synopsis

#include <Xm/Text.h>

Boolean XmTextRemove (*widget*)
    Widget   *widget*;

Description

XmTextRemove deletes the primary selected text. This routine also calls the widget's **XmNmodifyVerifyCallback** and **XmNvalueChangedCallback** callbacks if there is a selection.

widget   Specifies the Text widget ID.

For a complete definition of Text and its associated resources, see **XmText(3X)**.

Return Value

This function returns False if the primary selection is NULL or if the *widget* does not own the primary selection. Otherwise, it returns True.

Related Information

XmText(3X).

XmTextReplace—A Text function that replaces part of a text string

AES Support Level

Full-use

Synopsis

#include <Xm/Text.h>

void XmTextReplace (*widget, from_pos, to_pos, value*)
    Widget   *widget*;
    XmTextPosition *from_pos*;
    XmTextPosition *to_pos*;
    char   * *value*;

Description

XmTextReplace replaces part of the text string in the Text widget. The character positions begin at 0 (zero) and are numbered sequentially from the beginning of the text.

An example text replacement would be to replace the second and third characters in the text string. To accomplish this, the parameter *from_pos* must be 1 and *to_pos* must be 3. To insert a string after the fourth character, both parameters, *from_pos* and *to_pos*, must be 4.

This routine also calls the widget's **XmNmodifyVerifyCallback** and **XmNvalueChangedCallback** callbacks.

widget   Specifies the Text widget ID

from_pos   Specifies the start position of the text to be replaced

to_pos   Specifies the end position of the text to be replaced

value   Specifies the character string value to be added to the text widget

For a complete definition of Text and its associated resources, see **XmText(3X)**.

Related Information

XmText(3X).

XmTextScroll—A Text function that scrolls text

AES Support Level

Full-use

Synopsis

#include <Xm/Text.h>

void XmTextScroll (*widget, lines*)
    Widget   *widget*;
    int   *lines*;

Description

XmTextScroll scrolls text in a Text widget.

widget   Specifies the Text widget ID

lines   Specifies the number of lines of text to scroll. A positive value causes text to scroll upward; a negative value causes text to scroll downward.

For a complete definition of Text and its associated resources, see **XmText(3X)**.

Related Information

XmText(3X).

XmTextSetAddMode—A Text function that sets the state of Add mode

AES Support Level

Trial-use

Synopsis

#include <Xm/Text.h>

void XmTextSetAddMode (*widget, state*)
    Widget   *widget*;
    Boolean   *state*;

Description

XmTextSetAddMode controls whether or not the Text widget is in Add mode. When the widget is in Add mode, the insert cursor can be moved without disturbing the primary selection.

widget   Specifies the Text widget ID

state   Specifies whether or not the widget is in Add mode. A value of True turns on Add mode; a value of False turns off Add mode.

For a complete definition of Text and its associated resources, see **XmText(3X)**.

Related Information

XmText(3X).

XmTextSetEditable—A Text function that sets the edit permission

AES Support Level

Full-use

Synopsis

#include <Xm/Text.h>

void XmTextSetEditable (*widget, editable*)
    Widget   *widget*;
    Boolean   *editable*;

Description

XmTextSetEditable sets the edit permission state of the Text widget. When set to True, the text string can be edited.

widget   Specifies the Text widget ID

editable   Specifies a Boolean value that when True allows text string edits

For a complete definition of Text and its associated resources, see **XmText(3X)**.

Related Information

XmText(3X).

XmTextSetHighlight—A Text function that highlights text

AES Support Level

Full-use

Synopsis

#include <Xm/Text.h>

void XmTextSetHighlight (*widget, left, right, mode*)
    Widget   *widget*;
    XmTextPosition*left*;
    XmTextPosition*right*;
    XmHighlightMode*mode*;

Description

XmTextSetHighlight highlights text between the two specified character positions. The *mode* parameter determines the type of highlighting. Highlighting text merely changes the visual appearance of the text; it does not set the selection.

widget   Specifies the Text widget ID

left   Specifies the position of the left boundary of text to be highlighted. This is an integer number of characters from the beginning of the text buffer. The first character position is 0 (zero).

right   Specifies the position of the right boundary of text to be highlighted. This is an integer number of characters from the beginning of the text buffer. The first character position is 0 (zero).

mode   Specifies the type of highlighting to be done. A value of **XmHIGHLIGHT_NORMAL** removes highlighting. A value of **XmHIGHLIGHT_SELECTED** highlights the text using reverse video. A value of **XmHIGHLIGHT_SECONDARY_SELECTED** highlights the text using underlining.

For a complete definition of Text and its associated resources, see **XmText(3X)**.

Related Information

XmText(3X).

XmTextSetInsertionPosition—A Text function that sets the position of the insert cursor

AES Support Level

Full-use

Synopsis

#include <Xm/Text.h>

void XmTextSetInsertionPosition (*widget, position*)
    Widget   *widget*;
    XmTextPosition*position*;

Description

XmTextSetInsertionPosition sets the insertion cursor position of the Text widget. This routine also calls the widget's **XmNmotionVerifyCallback** callbacks if the insertion cursor position changes.

widget   Specifies the Text widget ID

position   Specifies the position of the insertion cursor. This is an integer number of characters from the beginning of the text buffer. The first character position is 0 (zero).

For a complete definition of Text and its associated resources, see **XmText(3X)**.

Related Information

XmText(3X).

XmTextSetMaxLength—A Text function that sets the value of the current maximum allowable length of a text string entered from the keyboard

AES Support Level

Full-use

Synopsis

#include <Xm/Text.h>

void XmTextSetMaxLength (*widget, max_length*)
    Widget   *widget*;
    int   *max_length*;

Description

XmTextSetMaxLength sets the value of the current maximum allowable length of the text string in the Text widget. The maximum allowable length prevents the user from entering a text string from the keyboard that is larger than this limit. Strings that are entered using the **XmNvalue** resource or the **XmTextSetString** function ignore this resource.

widget   Specifies the Text widget ID

max_length   Specifies the maximum allowable length of the text string

For a complete definition of Text and its associated resources, see **XmText(3X)**.

Related Information

XmText(3X) and **XmTextSetString(3X)**.

XmTextSetSelection—A Text function that sets the primary selection of the text

AES Support Level

Full-use

Synopsis

#include <Xm/Text.h>

void XmTextSetSelection (*widget, first, last, time*)
    Widget   *widget*;
    XmTextPosition *first*;
    XmTextPosition *last*;
    Time   *time*;

Description

XmTextSetSelection sets the primary selection of the text in the widget. It also sets the insertion cursor position to the last position of the selection and calls the widget's **XmNmotionVerifyCallback** callbacks.

widget   Specifies the Text widget ID

first   Marks the first character position of the text to be selected

last   Marks the last position of the text to be selected

time   Specifies the time at which the selection value is desired. This should be the same as the time of the event that triggered this request.

For a complete definition of Text and its associated resources, see **XmText(3X)**.

Related Information

XmText(3X).

XmTextSetSource—A Text function that sets the source of the widget

AES Support Level

Trial-use

Synopsis

#include <Xm/Text.h>

void XmTextSetSource (*widget, source, top_character, cursor_position*)
    Widget   *widget*;
    XmTextSource *source*;
    XmTextPosition*top_character*;
    XmTextPosition*cursor_position*;

Description

XmTextSetSource sets the source of the Text widget. Text widgets can share sources of text so that editing in one widget is reflected in another. This function sets the source of one widget so that it can share the source of another widget.

Setting a new text source destroys the old text source if no other Text widgets are using that source. To replace a text source but keep it for later use, create an unmanaged Text widget and set its source to the text source you want to keep.

widget   Specifies the Text widget ID.

source   Specifies the source with which the widget displays text. This can be a value returned by the **XmTextGetSource(3X)** function. If no source is specified, the widget creates a default string source.

top_character Specifies the position in the text to display at the top of the widget. This is an integer number of characters from the beginning of the text buffer. The first character position is 0 (zero).

cursor_position
        Specifies the position in the text at which the insert cursor is located. This is an integer number of characters from the beginning of the text buffer. The first character position is 0 (zero).

For a complete definition of Text and its associated resources, see **XmText(3X)**.

Related Information

XmText(3X).

XmTextSetString—A Text function that sets the string value

AES Support Level

Full-use

Synopsis

#include <Xm/Text.h>

void XmTextSetString (*widget, value*)
    Widget   *widget*;
    char   * *value*;

Description

XmTextSetString sets the string value of the Text widget. This routine calls the widget's **XmNmodifyVerifyCallback** and **XmNvalueChangedCallback** callbacks. This function also sets the insertion cursor position to the beginning of the string and calls the widget's **XmNmotionVerifyCallback** callbacks.

widget   Specifies the Text widget ID

value   Specifies the character pointer to the string value and places the string into the text edit window

For a complete definition of Text and its associated resources, see **XmText(3X)**.

Related Information

XmText(3X).

XmTextSetTopCharacter—A Text function that sets the position of the first character displayed

AES Support Level

Full-use

Synopsis

#include <Xm/Text.h>

void XmTextSetTopCharacter (*widget, top_character*)
    Widget   *widget*;
    XmTextPosition*top_character*;

Description

XmTextSetTopCharacter sets the position of the text at the top of the Text widget. If the **XmNeditMode** is **XmMULTI_LINE_EDIT,** the line of text that contains *top_character* is displayed at the top of the widget without the text shifting left or right.

widget   Specifies the Text widget ID

top_character Specifies the position in the text to display at the top of the widget. This is an integer number of characters from the beginning of the text buffer. The first character position is 0 (zero).

For a complete definition of Text and its associated resources, see **XmText(3X)**.

Related Information

XmText(3X).

XmTextShowPosition—A Text function that forces text at a given position to be displayed

AES Support Level

Full-use

Synopsis

#include <Xm/Text.h>

void XmTextShowPosition (*widget, position*)
 Widget *widget*;
 XmTextPosition*position*;

Description

XmTextShowPosition forces text at the specified position to be displayed. If the **XmNautoShowCursorPosition** resource is True, the application should also set the insert cursor to this position.

widget Specifies the Text widget ID

position Specifies the character position to be displayed. This is an integer number of characters from the beginning of the text buffer. The first character position is 0 (zero).

For a complete definition of Text and its associated resources, see **XmText(3X)**.

Related Information

XmText(3X).

XmTextXYToPos—A Text function that accesses the character position nearest an *x* and *y* position

AES Support Level

Full-use

Synopsis

#include <Xm/Text.h>

XmTextPosition XmTextXYToPos (*widget, x, y*)
    Widget   *widget*;
    Position   *x*;
    Position   *y*;

Description

XmTextXYToPos accesses the character position nearest to the specified *x* and *y* position, relative to the upper left corner of the Text widget.

widget   Specifies the Text widget ID

x   Specifies the *x* position, relative to the upper left corner of the widget

y   Specifies the *y* position, relative to the upper left corner of the widget

For a complete definition of Text and its associated resources, see **XmText(3X)**.

Return Value

Returns the character position in the text nearest the *x* and *y* position specified. This is an integer number of characters from the beginning of the buffer. The first character position is 0 (zero).

Related Information

XmText(3X).

XmToggleButton—The ToggleButton widget class

AES Support Level

Full-use

History/Direction

The way background color is calculated based on **XmNindicatorOn** and **XmNfillOnSelect** has been changed (for trial-use).

Synopsis

#include <Xm/ToggleB.h>

Description

ToggleButton sets nontransitory state data within an application. Usually this widget consists of an indicator (square or diamond) with either text or a pixmap on one side of it. However, it can also consist of just text or a pixmap without the indicator.

The toggle graphics display a **1-of-many** or **N-of-many** selection state. When a toggle indicator is displayed, a square indicator shows an **N-of-many** selection state and a diamond indicator shows a **1-of-many** selection state.

ToggleButton implies a selected or unselected state. In the case of a label and an indicator, an empty indicator (square or diamond shaped) indicates that ToggleButton is unselected, and a filled indicator shows that it is selected. In the case of a pixmap toggle, different pixmaps are used to display the selected/unselected states.

The default behavior associated with a ToggleButton in a menu depends on the type of menu system in which it resides. By default, **BSelect** controls the behavior of the ToggleButton. In addition, **BMenu** controls the behavior of the ToggleButton if it resides in a PopupMenu system. The actual mouse button used is determined by its RowColumn parent.

Label's resource **XmNmarginLeft** may be increased to accommodate the toggle indicator when it is created.

Classes

 ToggleButton inherits behavior and resources from **Core**, **XmPrimitive**, and **XmLabel**.

 The class pointer is **xmToggleButtonWidgetClass**.

 The class name is **XmToggleButton**.

New Resources

 The following table defines a set of widget resources used by the programmer to specify data. The programmer can also set the resource values for the inherited classes to set attributes for this widget. To reference a resource by name or by class in a **.Xdefaults** file, remove the **XmN** or **XmC** prefix and use the remaining letters. To specify one of the defined values for a resource in a **.Xdefaults** file, remove the **Xm** prefix and use the remaining letters (in either lowercase or uppercase, but include any underscores between words). The codes in the access column indicate if the given resource can be set at creation time (C), set by using **XtSetValues** (S), retrieved by using **XtGetValues** (G), or is not applicable (N/A).

XmToggleButton Resource Set		
Name	**Default**	**Access**
Class	**Type**	
XmNarmCallback	NULL	C
XmCArmCallback	XtCallbackList	
XmNdisarmCallback	NULL	C
XmCDisarmCallback	XtCallbackList	
XmNfillOnSelect	dynamic	CSG
XmCFillOnSelect	Boolean	
XmNindicatorOn	True	CSG
XmCIndicatorOn	Boolean	
XmNindicatorSize	dynamic	CSG
XmCIndicatorSize	Dimension	
XmNindicatorType	dynamic	CSG
XmCIndicatorType	unsigned char	
XmNselectColor	dynamic	CSG
XmCSelectColor	Pixel	
XmNselectInsensitivePixmap	XmUNSPECIFIED_PIXMAP	CSG
XmCSelectInsensitivePixmap	Pixmap	
XmNselectPixmap	XmUNSPECIFIED_PIXMAP	CSG
XmCSelectPixmap	Pixmap	
XmNset	False	CSG
XmCSet	Boolean	
XmNspacing	4	CSG
XmCSpacing	Dimension	
XmNvalueChangedCallback	NULL	C
XmCValueChangedCallback	XtCallbackList	
XmNvisibleWhenOff	dynamic	CSG
XmCVisibleWhenOff	Boolean	

XmNarmCallback

>Specifies the list of callbacks called when the ToggleButton is armed. To arm this widget, press the active mouse button while the pointer is inside the ToggleButton. For this callback, the reason is **XmCR_ARM**.

XmNdisarmCallback

>Specifies the list of callbacks called when ToggleButton is disarmed. To disarm this widget, press and release the active mouse

button while the pointer is inside the ToggleButton. This widget is also disarmed when the user moves out of the widget and releases the mouse button when the pointer is outside the widget. For this callback, the reason is **XmCR_DISARM**.

XmNfillOnSelect

Fills the indicator with the color specified in **XmNselectColor** and switches the top and bottom shadow colors when set to True. Otherwise, it switches only the top and bottom shadow colors. The default is set to the value of **XmNindicatorOn**. When **XmNindicatorOn** is False, and **XmNfillOnSelect** is set explicitly to True, the background is filled with the color specified by **XmNselectColor**.

XmNindicatorOn

Specifies that a toggle indicator is drawn to one side of the toggle text or pixmap when set to True. When set to False, no space is allocated for the indicator, and it is not displayed. If **XmNindicatorOn** is True, the indicator shadows are switched when the button is selected or unselected, but, any shadows around the entire widget are not switched. However, if **XmNindicatorOn** is False, any shadows around the entire widget are switched when the toggle is selected or unselected.

XmNindicatorSize

Sets the size of the indicator. If no value is specified, the size of the indicator is based on the size of the label string or pixmap. If the label string or pixmap changes, the size of the indicator is recomputed based on the size of the label string or pixmap. Once a value has been specified for **XmNindicatorSize**, the indicator has that size, regardless of the size of the label string or pixmap, until a new value is specified.

XmNindicatorType

Specifies if the indicator is a **1-of** or **N-of** indicator. For the **1-of** indicator, the value is **XmONE_OF_MANY**. For the **N-of** indicator, the value is **XmN_OF_MANY**. The **N-of-many** indicator is square. The **1-of-many** indicator is diamond shaped. This resource specifies only the visuals and does not enforce the behavior. When the ToggleButton is in a RadioBox, the default is **XmONE_OF_MANY**; otherwise, the default is **XmN_OF_MANY**.

XmNselectColor

Allows the application to specify what color fills the center of the square or diamond-shaped indicator when it is set. If this color is the same as either the top or the bottom shadow color of the indicator, a one-pixel-wide margin is left between the shadows and the fill; otherwise, it is filled completely. This resource's default for a color display is a color between the background and the bottom shadow color. For a monochrome display, the default is set to the foreground color. To set the background of the button to **XmNselectColor** when **XmNindicatorOn** is False, the value of **XmNfillOnSelect** must be explicitly set to True.

XmNselectInsensitivePixmap
> Specifies a pixmap used as the button face when the ToggleButton is selected, the button is insensitive, and the Label resource **XmNlabelType** is set to **XmPIXMAP**. If the ToggleButton is unselected and the button is insensitive, the pixmap in **XmNlabelInsensitivePixmap** is used as the button face. If no value is specified for **XmNlabelInsensitivePixmap**, that resource is set to the value specified for **XmNselectInsensitivePixmap**.

XmNselectPixmap
> Specifies the pixmap to be used as the button face when **XmNlabelType** is **XmPIXMAP** and the ToggleButton is selected. When the ToggleButton is unselected, the pixmap specified in the Label's **XmNlabelPixmap** is used. If no value is specified for **XmNlabelPixmap**, that resource is set to the value specified for **XmNselectPixmap**.

XmNset
> Represents the state of the ToggleButton. A value of False indicates that the ToggleButton is not set. A value of True indicates that the ToggleButton is set. Setting this resource sets the state of the ToggleButton.

XmNspacing
> Specifies the amount of spacing between the toggle indicator and the toggle label (text or pixmap).

XmNvalueChangedCallback
> Specifies the list of callbacks called when the ToggleButton value is changed. To change the value, press and release the active mouse button while the pointer is inside the ToggleButton. This action also causes this widget to be disarmed. For this callback, the reason is **XmCR_VALUE_CHANGED**.

XmNvisibleWhenOff
> Indicates that the toggle indicator is visible in the unselected state when the Boolean value is True. When the ToggleButton is in a menu, the default value is False. When the ToggleButton is in a RadioBox, the default value is True.

Inherited Resources

ToggleButton inherits behavior and resources from the superclasses described in the following tables. For a complete description of each resource, refer to the reference page for that superclass.

XmLabel Resource Set		

Name
    Class
	Default
	    Type
		Access

XmNaccelerator
    XmCAccelerator
	NULL
	    String
		CSG

XmNacceleratorText
    XmCAcceleratorText
	NULL
	    XmString
		CSG

XmNalignment
    XmCAlignment
	dynamic
	    unsigned char
		CSG

XmNfontList
    XmCFontList
	dynamic
	    XmFontList
		CSG

XmNlabelInsensitivePixmap
    XmCLabelInsensitivePixmap
	XmUNSPECIFIED_PIXMAP
	    Pixmap
		CSG

XmNlabelPixmap
    XmCLabelPixmap
	XmUNSPECIFIED_PIXMAP
	    Pixmap
		CSG

XmNlabelString
    XmCXmString
	dynamic
	    XmString
		CSG

XmNlabelType
    XmCLabelType
	XmSTRING
	    unsigned char
		CSG

XmNmarginBottom
    XmCMarginBottom
	dynamic
	    Dimension
		CSG

XmNmarginHeight
    XmCMarginHeight
	2
	    Dimension
		CSG

XmNmarginLeft
    XmCMarginLeft
	dynamic
	    Dimension
		CSG

XmNmarginRight
    XmCMarginRight
	0
	    Dimension
		CSG

XmNmarginTop
    XmCMarginTop
	dynamic
	    Dimension
		CSG

XmNmarginWidth
    XmCMarginWidth
	2
	    Dimension
		CSG

XmNmnemonic
    XmCMnemonic
	NULL
	    KeySym
		CSG

XmToggleButton(3X)

Name	Default	Access
Class	Type	
XmNmnemonicCharSet	XmFONTLIST_DEFAULT_TAG	CSG
XmCMnemonicCharSet	String	
XmNrecomputeSize	True	CSG
XmCRecomputeSize	Boolean	
XmNstringDirection	dynamic	CSG
XmCStringDirection	XmStringDirection	

XmPrimitive Resource Set		

Name
    Class
	Default
	    Type
		Access

XmNbottomShadowColor
    XmCBottomShadowColor
	dynamic
	    Pixel
		CSG

XmNbottomShadowPixmap
    XmCBottomShadowPixmap
	XmUNSPECIFIED_PIXMAP
	    Pixmap
		CSG

XmNforeground
    XmCForeground
	dynamic
	    Pixel
		CSG

XmNhelpCallback
    XmCCallback
	NULL
	    XtCallbackList
		C

XmNhighlightColor
    XmCHighlightColor
	dynamic
	    Pixel
		CSG

XmNhighlightOnEnter
    XmCHighlightOnEnter
	False
	    Boolean
		CSG

XmNhighlightPixmap
    XmCHighlightPixmap
	dynamic
	    Pixmap
		CSG

XmNhighlightThickness
    XmCHighlightThickness
	2
	    Dimension
		CSG

XmNnavigationType
    XmCNavigationType
	XmNONE
	    XmNavigationType
		CSG

XmNshadowThickness
    XmCShadowThickness
	dynamic
	    Dimension
		CSG

XmNtopShadowColor
    XmCTopShadowColor
	dynamic
	    Pixel
		CSG

XmNtopShadowPixmap
    XmCTopShadowPixmap
	dynamic
	    Pixmap
		CSG

XmNtraversalOn
    XmCTraversalOn
	True
	    Boolean
		CSG

XmNuserData
    XmCUserData
	NULL
	    XtPointer
		CSG

Core Resource Set		
Name	**Default**	**Access**
Class	**Type**	
XmNaccelerators	dynamic	CSG
XmCAccelerators	XtAccelerators	
XmNancestorSensitive	dynamic	G
XmCSensitive	Boolean	
XmNbackground	dynamic	CSG
XmCBackground	Pixel	
XmNbackgroundPixmap	XmUNSPECIFIED_PIXMAP	CSG
XmCPixmap	Pixmap	
XmNborderColor	XtDefaultForeground	CSG
XmCBorderColor	Pixel	
XmNborderPixmap	XmUNSPECIFIED_PIXMAP	CSG
XmCPixmap	Pixmap	
XmNborderWidth	0	CSG
XmCBorderWidth	Dimension	
XmNcolormap	dynamic	CG
XmCColormap	Colormap	
XmNdepth	dynamic	CG
XmCDepth	int	
XmNdestroyCallback	NULL	C
XmCCallback	XtCallbackList	
XmNheight	dynamic	CSG
XmCHeight	Dimension	
XmNinitialResourcesPersistent	True	C
XmCInitialResourcesPersistent	Boolean	
XmNmappedWhenManaged	True	CSG
XmCMappedWhenManaged	Boolean	
XmNscreen	dynamic	CG
XmCScreen	Screen *	
XmNsensitive	True	CSG
XmCSensitive	Boolean	

Name	Default	Access
Class	Type	
XmNtranslations	dynamic	CSG
XmCTranslations	XtTranslations	
XmNwidth	dynamic	CSG
XmCWidth	Dimension	
XmNx	0	CSG
XmCPosition	Position	
XmNy	0	CSG
XmCPosition	Position	

Callback Information

A pointer to the following structure is passed to each callback:

```
typedef struct
{
    int               reason;
    XEvent            * event;
    int               set;
} XmToggleButtonCallbackStruct;
```

reason   Indicates why the callback was invoked

event   Points to the **XEvent** that triggered the callback

set   Reflects the ToggleButton's current state when the callback
                  occurred, either True (selected) or False (unselected)

Action Routines

The **XmToggleButton** action routines are

Arm():   If the button was previously unset, this action does the following: if
                  XmNindicatorOn is True, it draws the indicator shadow so that the
                  indicator looks pressed; if **XmNfillOnSelect** is True, it fills the
                  indicator with the color specified by **XmNselectColor**. If
                  XmNindicatorOn is False, it draws the button shadow so that the

button looks pressed. If **XmNlabelType** is **XmPIXMAP**, the **XmNselectPixmap** is used as the button face. This action calls the **XmNarmCallback** callbacks.

If the button was previously set, this action does the following: if both **XmNindicatorOn** and **XmNvisibleWhenOff** are True, it draws the indicator shadow so that the indicator looks raised; if **XmNfillOnSelect** is True, it fills the indicator with the background color. If **XmNindicatorOn** is False, it draws the button shadow so that the button looks raised. If **XmNlabelType** is **XmPIXMAP**, the **XmNlabelPixmap** is used as the button face. This action calls the **XmNarmCallback** callbacks.

ArmAndActivate():

If the ToggleButton was previously set, unsets it; if the ToggleButton was previously unset, sets it.

In a menu, this action unposts all menus in the menu hierarchy. Unless the button is already armed, it calls the **XmNarmCallback** callbacks. This action calls the **XmNvalueChangedCallback** and **XmNdisarmCallback** callbacks.

Outside a menu, if the button was previously unset, this action does the following: if **XmNindicatorOn** is True, it draws the indicator shadow so that the indicator looks pressed; if **XmNfillOnSelect** is True, it fills the indicator with the color specified by **XmNselectColor**. If **XmNindicatorOn** is False, it draws the button shadow so that the button looks pressed. If **XmNlabelType** is **XmPIXMAP**, the **XmNselectPixmap** is used as the button face. This action calls the **XmNarmCallback**, **XmNvalueChangedCallback**, and **XmNdisarmCallback** callbacks.

Outside a menu, if the button was previously set, this action does the following: if both **XmNindicatorOn** and **XmNvisibleWhenOff** are True, it draws the indicator shadow so that the indicator looks raised; if **XmNfillOnSelect** is True, it fills the indicator with the background color. If **XmNindicatorOn** is False, it draws the button shadow so that the button looks raised. If **XmNlabelType** is **XmPIXMAP**, the **XmNlabelPixmap** is used as the button face. This action calls the **XmNarmCallback**, **XmNvalueChangedCallback**, and **XmNdisarmCallback** callbacks.

BtnDown(): This action unposts any menus posted by the ToggleButton's parent menu, disables keyboard traversal for the menu, and enables mouse traversal for the menu. It draws the shadow in the armed state and, unless the button is already armed, calls the **XmNarmCallback** callbacks.

BtnUp(): This action unposts all menus in the menu hierarchy. If the ToggleButton was previously set, unsets it; if the ToggleButton was previously unset, sets it. It calls the **XmNvalueChangedCallback** callbacks and then the **XmNdisarmCallback** callbacks.

Disarm(): Calls the callbacks for **XmNdisarmCallback**.

Help(): In a Pulldown or Popup MenuPane, unposts all menus in the menu hierarchy and restores keyboard focus to the tab group that had the focus before the menu system was entered. Calls the callbacks for **XmNhelpCallback** if any exist. If there are no help callbacks for this widget, this action calls the help callbacks for the nearest ancestor that has them.

MenuShellPopdownOne():
In a toplevel Pulldown MenuPane from a MenuBar, unposts the menu, disarms the MenuBar CascadeButton and the MenuBar, and restores keyboard focus to the tab group that had the focus before the MenuBar was entered. In other Pulldown MenuPanes, unposts the menu.

In a Popup MenuPane, unposts the menu and restores keyboard focus to the widget from which the menu was posted.

Select(): If the pointer is within the button, takes the following actions: If the button was previously unset, sets it; if the button was previously set, unsets it. This action calls the **XmNvalueChangedCallback** callbacks.

Related Information

Core(3X), **XmCreateRadioBox(3X)**, **XmCreateToggleButton(3X)**,
XmLabel(3X), **XmPrimitive(3X)**, **XmRowColumn(3X)**,
XmToggleButtonGetState(3X), and **XmToggleButtonSetState(3X)**.

XmToggleButtonGadget—The ToggleButtonGadget widget class

AES Support Level

Full-use

History/Direction

Changed the way background color is selected based on **XmNindicatorOn** and **XmNfillOnSelect** (for Trial-use).

Synopsis

#include <Xm/ToggleBG.h>

Description

ToggleButtonGadget sets nontransitory state data within an application. Usually this gadget consists of an indicator (square or diamond-shaped) with either text or a pixmap on one side of it. However, it can also consist of just text or a pixmap without the indicator.

The toggle graphics display a **1-of-many** or **N-of-many** selection state. When a toggle indicator is displayed, a square indicator shows an **N-of-many** selection state and a diamond-shaped indicator shows a **1-of-many** selection state.

ToggleButtonGadget implies a selected or unselected state. In the case of a label and an indicator, an empty indicator (square or diamond-shaped) indicates that ToggleButtonGadget is unselected, and a filled indicator shows that it is selected. In the case of a pixmap toggle, different pixmaps are used to display the selected/unselected states.

The default behavior associated with a ToggleButtonGadget in a menu depends on the type of menu system in which it resides. By default, **BSelect** controls the behavior of the ToggleButtonGadget. In addition, **BMenu** controls the behavior of the ToggleButtonGadget if it resides in a PopupMenu system. The actual mouse button used is determined by its RowColumn parent.

Label's resource **XmNmarginLeft** may be increased to accommodate the toggle indicator when it is created.

Classes

> ToggleButtonGadget inherits behavior and resources from **Object**, **RectObj**, **XmGadget** and **XmLabelGadget**.
>
> The class pointer is **xmToggleButtonGadgetClass**.
>
> The class name is **XmToggleButtonGadget**.

New Resources

> The following table defines a set of widget resources used by the programmer to specify data. The programmer can also set the resource values for the inherited classes to set attributes for this widget. To reference a resource by name or by class in a **.Xdefaults** file, remove the **XmN** or **XmC** prefix and use the remaining letters. To specify one of the defined values for a resource in a **.Xdefaults** file, remove the **Xm** prefix and use the remaining letters (in either lowercase or uppercase, but include any underscores between words). The codes in the access column indicate if the given resource can be set at creation time (C), set by using **XtSetValues** (S), retrieved by using **XtGetValues** (G), or is not applicable (N/A).

XmToggleButtonGadget Resource Set		

Name
    Class
	Default
	    Type
		Access

XmNarmCallback
    XmCArmCallback
	NULL
	    XtCallbackList
		C

XmNdisarmCallback
    XmCDisarmCallback
	NULL
	    XtCallbackList
		C

XmNfillOnSelect
    XmCFillOnSelect
	dynamic
	    Boolean
		CSG

XmNindicatorOn
    XmCIndicatorOn
	True
	    Boolean
		CSG

XmNindicatorSize
    XmCIndicatorSize
	dynamic
	    Dimension
		CSG

XmNindicatorType
    XmCIndicatorType
	dynamic
	    unsigned char
		CSG

XmNselectColor
    XmCSelectColor
	dynamic
	    Pixel
		CSG

XmNselectInsensitivePixmap
    XmCSelectInsensitivePixmap
	XmUNSPECIFIED_PIXMAP
	    Pixmap
		CSG

XmNselectPixmap
    XmCSelectPixmap
	XmUNSPECIFIED_PIXMAP
	    Pixmap
		CSG

XmNset
    XmCSet
	False
	    Boolean
		CSG

XmNspacing
    XmCSpacing
	4
	    Dimension
		CSG

XmNvalueChangedCallback
    XmCValueChangedCallback
	NULL
	    XtCallbackList
		C

XmNvisibleWhenOff
    XmCVisibleWhenOff
	dynamic
	    Boolean
		CSG

XmNarmCallback

Specifies a list of callbacks that is called when the ToggleButtonGadget is armed. To arm this gadget, press the active mouse button while the pointer is inside the ToggleButtonGadget. For this callback, the reason is **XmCR_ARM**.

XmNdisarmCallback

Specifies a list of callbacks called when ToggleButtonGadget is disarmed. To disarm this gadget, press and release the active mouse button while the pointer is inside the ToggleButtonGadget. The gadget is also disarmed when the user moves out of the gadget and releases the mouse button when the pointer is outside the gadget. For this callback, the reason is **XmCR_DISARM**.

XmNfillOnSelect

Fills the indicator with the color specified in **XmNselectColor** and switches the top and bottom shadow colors when set to True. Otherwise, it switches only the top and bottom shadow colors. The default is set to the value of **XmNindicatorOn**. When **XmNindicatorOn** is False, and **XmNfillOnSelect** is set explicitly to True, the background is filled with the color specified by **XmNselectColor**.

XmNindicatorOn

Specifies that a toggle indicator is drawn to one side of the toggle text or pixmap when set to True. When set to False, no space is allocated for the indicator, and it is not displayed. If **XmNindicatorOn** is True, the indicator shadows are switched when the button is selected or unselected, but any shadows around the entire gadget are not switched. However, if **XmNindicatorOn** is False, any shadows around the entire gadget are switched when the toggle is selected or unselected.

XmNindicatorSize

Sets the size of the indicator. If no value is specified, the size of the indicator is based on the size of the label string or pixmap. If the label string or pixmap changes, the size of the indicator is recomputed based on the size of the label string or pixmap. Once a value has been specified for **XmNindicatorSize**, the indicator has that size, regardless of the size of the label string or pixmap, until a new value is specified.

XmNindicatorType

Specifies if the indicator is a **1-of** or an **N-of** indicator. For the **1-of** indicator, the value is **XmONE_OF_MANY**. For the **N-of** indicator, the value is **XmN_OF_MANY**. The **N-of-many** indicator is square. The **1-of-many** indicator is diamond-shaped. This resource specifies only the visuals and does not enforce the behavior. When the ToggleButtonGadget is in a RadioBox, the default is **XmONE_OF_MANY**; otherwise, the default is **XmN_OF_MANY**.

XmNselectColor

Allows the application to specify what color fills the center of the square or diamond-shaped indicator when it is set. If this color is the same as either the top or the bottom shadow color of the indicator, a one-pixel-wide margin is left between the shadows and the fill; otherwise, it is filled completely. This resource's default for a color display is a color between the background and the bottom shadow color. For a monochrome display, the default is set to the foreground color. The meaning of this resource is undefined when **XmNindicatorOn** is False.

XmNselectInsensitivePixmap

Specifies a pixmap used as the button face when the ToggleButtonGadget is selected, the button is insensitive, and the LabelGadget resource **XmNlabelType** is **XmPIXMAP**. If the ToggleButtonGadget is unselected and the button is insensitive, the pixmap in **XmNlabelInsensitivePixmap** is used as the button face. If no value is specified for **XmNlabelInsensitivePixmap**, that resource is set to the value specified for **XmNselectInsensitivePixmap**.

XmNselectPixmap

Specifies the pixmap to be used as the button face if **XmNlabelType** is **XmPIXMAP** and the ToggleButtonGadget is selected. When the ToggleButtonGadget is unselected, the pixmap specified in LabelGadget's **XmNlabelPixmap** is used. If no value is specified for **XmNlabelPixmap**, that resource is set to the value specified for **XmNselectPixmap**.

XmNset
Represents the state of the ToggleButton. A value of false indicates that the ToggleButton is not set. A value of true indicates that the ToggleButton is set. Setting this resource sets the state of the ToggleButton.

XmNspacing Specifies the amount of spacing between the toggle indicator and the toggle label (text or pixmap).

XmNvalueChangedCallback
> Specifies a list of callbacks called when the ToggleButtonGadget value is changed. To change the value, press and release the active mouse button while the pointer is inside the ToggleButtonGadget. This action also causes the gadget to be disarmed. For this callback, the reason is **XmCR_VALUE_CHANGED**.

XmNvisibleWhenOff
> Indicates that the toggle indicator is visible in the unselected state when the Boolean value is True. When the ToggleButtonGadget is in a menu, the default value is False. When the ToggleButtonGadget is in a RadioBox, the default value is True.

Inherited Resources

ToggleButtonGadget inherits behavior and resources from the superclasses described in the following tables. For a complete description of each resource, refer to the reference page for that superclass.

XmToggleButtonGadget(3X)

XmLabelGadget Resource Set		

Name
    Class
	Default
	    Type
		Access

XmNaccelerator
    XmCAccelerator
	NULL
	    String
		CSG

XmNacceleratorText
    XmCAcceleratorText
	NULL
	    XmString
		CSG

XmNalignment
    XmCAlignment
	dynamic
	    unsigned char
		CSG

XmNfontList
    XmCFontList
	dynamic
	    XmFontList
		CSG

XmNlabelInsensitivePixmap
    XmCLabelInsensitivePixmap
	XmUNSPECIFIED_PIXMAP
	    Pixmap
		CSG

XmNlabelPixmap
    XmCLabelPixmap
	XmUNSPECIFIED_PIXMAP
	    Pixmap
		CSG

XmNlabelString
    XmCXmString
	dynamic
	    XmString
		CSG

XmNlabelType
    XmCLabelType
	XmSTRING
	    unsigned char
		CSG

XmNmarginBottom
    XmCMarginBottom
	dynamic
	    Dimension
		CSG

XmNmarginHeight
    XmCMarginHeight
	2
	    Dimension
		CSG

XmNmarginLeft
    XmCMarginLeft
	dynamic
	    Dimension
		CSG

XmNmarginRight
    XmCMarginRight
	0
	    Dimension
		CSG

XmNmarginTop
    XmCMarginTop
	dynamic
	    Dimension
		CSG

XmNmarginWidth
    XmCMarginWidth
	2
	    Dimension
		CSG

| Name | Default | Access |
Class	Type	
XmNmnemonic	NULL	CSG
XmCMnemonic	KeySym	
XmNmnemonicCharSet	dynamic	CSG
XmCMnemonicCharSet	String	
XmNrecomputeSize	True	CSG
XmCRecomputeSize	Boolean	
XmNstringDirection	dynamic	CSG
XmCStringDirection	XmStringDirection	

XmGadget Resource Set		
Name	Default	Access
Class	Type	
XmNhelpCallback	NULL	C
XmCCallback	XtCallbackList	
XmNhighlightOnEnter	False	CSG
XmCHighlightOnEnter	Boolean	
XmNhighlightThickness	2	CSG
XmCHighlightThickness	Dimension	
XmNnavigationType	XmNONE	CSG
XmCNavigationType	XmNavigationType	
XmNshadowThickness	dynamic	CSG
XmCShadowThickness	Dimension	
XmNtraversalOn	True	CSG
XmCTraversalOn	Boolean	
XmNuserData	NULL	CSG
XmCUserData	XtPointer	

XmToggleButtonGadget(3X)

<table>
<tr><td colspan="3" align="center">RectObj Resource Set</td></tr>
<tr><td>Name
Class</td><td>Default
Type</td><td>Access</td></tr>
<tr><td>XmNancestorSensitive
XmCSensitive</td><td>dynamic
Boolean</td><td>G</td></tr>
<tr><td>XmNborderWidth
XmCBorderWidth</td><td>0
Dimension</td><td>N/A</td></tr>
<tr><td>XmNheight
XmCHeight</td><td>dynamic
Dimension</td><td>CSG</td></tr>
<tr><td>XmNsensitive
XmCSensitive</td><td>True
Boolean</td><td>CSG</td></tr>
<tr><td>XmNwidth
XmCWidth</td><td>dynamic
Dimension</td><td>CSG</td></tr>
<tr><td>XmNx
XmCPosition</td><td>0
Position</td><td>CSG</td></tr>
<tr><td>XmNy
XmCPosition</td><td>0
Position</td><td>CSG</td></tr>
</table>

<table>
<tr><td colspan="3" align="center">Object Resource Set</td></tr>
<tr><td>Name
Class</td><td>Default
Type</td><td>Access</td></tr>
<tr><td>XmNdestroyCallback
XmCCallback</td><td>NULL
XtCallbackList</td><td>C</td></tr>
</table>

Callback Information

A pointer to the following structure is passed to each callback:

```
typedef struct
{
    int            reason;
    XEvent         * event;
    int            set;
} XmToggleButtonCallbackStruct;
```

reason   Indicates why the callback was invoked

event   Points to the **XEvent** that triggered the callback

set   Reflects the ToggleButtonGadget's current state when the callback
                occurred, either True (selected) or False (unselected)

Related Information

Object(3X), **RectObj(3X)**, **XmCreateRadioBox(3X)**,
XmCreateToggleButtonGadget(3X), **XmGadget(3X)**, **XmLabelGadget(3X)**,
XmRowColumn(3X), **XmToggleButtonGadgetGetState(3X)**, and
XmToggleButtonGadgetSetState(3X).

XmToggleButtonGadgetGetState—A ToggleButtonGadget function that obtains the state of a ToggleButtonGadget

AES Support Level

Full-use

Synopsis

#include <Xm/ToggleBG.h>

Boolean XmToggleButtonGadgetGetState (*widget*)
    Widget   *widget*;

Description

XmToggleButtonGadgetGetState obtains the state of a ToggleButtonGadget.

widget   Specifies the ToggleButtonGadget ID

For a complete definition of ToggleButtonGadget and its associated resources, see **XmToggleButtonGadget(3X)**.

Return Value

Returns True if the button is selected and False if the button is unselected.

Related Information

XmToggleButtonGadget(3X).

XmToggleButtonGadgetSetState—A ToggleButtonGadget function that sets or changes the current state

AES Support Level

Full-use

Synopsis

#include <Xm/ToggleBG.h>

void XmToggleButtonGadgetSetState (*widget, state, notify*)
    Widget   *widget*;
    Boolean   *state*;
    Boolean   *notify*;

Description

XmToggleButtonGadgetSetState sets or changes the ToggleButtonGadget's current state.

widget   Specifies the ToggleButtonGadget widget ID.

state   Specifies a Boolean value that indicates whether the ToggleButtonGadget state is selected or unselected. If the value is True, the button state is selected; if it is False, the button state is unselected.

notify   Indicates whether **XmNvalueChangedCallback** is called; it can be either True or False. The **XmNvalueChangedCallback** is only called when this function changes the state of the ToggleButtonGadget. When this argument is True and the ToggleButtonGadget is a child of a RowColumn widget whose **XmNradioBehavior** is True, setting the ToggleButtonGadget causes other ToggleButton and ToggleButtonGadget children of the RowColumn to be unselected.

For a complete definition of ToggleButtonGadget and its associated resources, see **XmToggleButtonGadget(3X)**.

Related Information

XmToggleButtonGadget(3X).

XmToggleButtonGetState(3X)

XmToggleButtonGetState—A ToggleButton function that obtains the state of a ToggleButton

AES Support Level

Full-use

Synopsis

#include <Xm/ToggleB.h>

Boolean XmToggleButtonGetState (*widget*)
        Widget   *widget*;

Description

XmToggleButtonGetState obtains the state of a ToggleButton.

widget   Specifies the ToggleButton widget ID

For a complete definition of ToggleButton and its associated resources, see **XmToggleButton(3X)**.

Return Value

Returns True if the button is selected and False if the button is unselected.

Related Information

XmToggleButton(3X).

XmToggleButtonSetState—A ToggleButton function that sets or changes the current state

AES Support Level

Full-use

Synopsis

#include <Xm/ToggleB.h>

void XmToggleButtonSetState (*widget, state, notify*)
    Widget   *widget*;
    Boolean   *state*;
    Boolean   *notify*;

Description

XmToggleButtonSetState sets or changes the ToggleButton's current state.

widget   Specifies the ToggleButton widget ID.

state   Specifies a Boolean value that indicates whether the ToggleButton state is selected or unselected. If the value is True, the button state is selected; if it is False, the button state is unselected.

notify   Indicates whether **XmNvalueChangedCallback** is called; it can be either True or False. The **XmNvalueChangedCallback** is only called when this function changes the state of the ToggleButton. When this argument is True and the ToggleButton is a child of a RowColumn widget whose **XmNradioBehavior** is True, setting the ToggleButton causes other ToggleButton and ToggleButtonGadget children of the RowColumn to be unselected.

For a complete definition of ToggleButton and its associated resources, see **XmToggleButton(3X)**.

Related Information

XmToggleButton(3X).

XmTrackingLocate—A Toolkit function that provides a modal interaction

AES Support Level

Trial-use

Synopsis

#include <Xm/Xm.h>

Widget XmTrackingLocate (*widget, cursor, confine_to*)
    Widget   *widget*;
    Cursor   *cursor*;
    Boolean   *confine_to*;

Description

XmTrackingLocate provides a modal interface for selection of a component. It is intended to support context help. The function grabs the pointer and returns the widget in which a button press occurs.

widget   Specifies the widget ID of a widget to use as the basis of the modal interaction. That is, the widget within which the interaction must occur, usually a top-level shell.

cursor   Specifies the cursor to be used for the pointer during the interaction. This is a standard X cursor name.

confine_to   Specifies whether or not the cursor should be confined to *widget*

Return Value

Returns the widget in which a button press occurs. If the window in which a button press occurs is not a widget, the function returns NULL.

XmUninstallImage—A pixmap caching function that removes an image from the image cache

AES Support Level

Full-use

Synopsis

#include <Xm/Xm.h>

Boolean XmUninstallImage (*image*)
    XImage   * *image*;

Description

XmUninstallImage removes an image from the image cache.

image   Points to the image structure given to the **XmInstallImage**() routine

Return Value

Returns True when successful; returns False if the *image* is NULL, or if it cannot be found to be uninstalled.

Related Information

XmInstallImage(3X), **XmGetPixmap(3X)**, and **XmDestroyPixmap(3X)**.

XmUpdateDisplay—A function that processes all pending exposure events immediately

AES Support Level

Full-use

Synopsis

void XmUpdateDisplay (*widget*)
    Widget   *widget*;

Description

XmUpdateDisplay provides the application with a mechanism for forcing all pending exposure events to be removed from the input queue and processed immediately.

When a user selects a button within a MenuPane, the MenuPanes are unposted and then any activation callbacks registered by the application are invoked. If one of the callbacks performs a time-consuming action, the portion of the application window that was covered by the MenuPanes is not redrawn; normal exposure processing does not occur until all of the callbacks have been invoked. If the application writer suspects that a callback will take a long time, then the callback may choose to invoke **XmUpdateDisplay** before starting its time-consuming operation.

This function is also useful any time a transient window, such as a dialog box, is unposted; callbacks are invoked before normal exposure processing can occur.

widget   Specifies any widget or gadget.

Index

D

M

X

OPEN SOFTWARE FOUNDATION™

INFORMATION REQUEST FORM

Please send me the following:

( ) OSF Membership Information

( ) OSF/Motif™ License Materials

( ) OSF/Motif™ Training Information

Contact Name ____

Company Name _____________________________________

Street Address ____________________________________

Mail Stop _______________________

City _____________ State _________ Zip ________

Phone ________________ FAX ______________

Electronic Mail __________________________________

MAIL TO:

Open Software Foundation
11 Cambridge Center
Cambridge, MA 02142

Attn: OSF/Motif™

For more information about OSF/Motif™ call **617 621 7300.**